THE CROSSWORD COMPANION

THE CROSSWORD COMPANION

Being a work compiled expressly for the assistance and amusement of those who enjoy composing or solving crossword puzzles

by

M.R.W∴

TIGER BOOKS INTERNATIONAL
LONDON

A Cresset Press Book

First published 1952
Reprinted 1962, 1968, 1972, 1974
New revised edition 1975
Reprinted 1976, 1977
This edition published 1992

Copyright © Herbert Jenkins Ltd 1952, 1968, 1972, 1975

ISBN 1–85501–257–X

Printed and bound in Great Britain

INTRODUCTION

CROSSWORD puzzle enthusiasts will be quick to appreciate the simplicity of this " Companion " which, ignoring meaning and derivation, concerns itself only with the number of letters any given word may contain. The general principle adopted has been to take all the two-letter words in common usage and group them together alphabetically under the one head, then to do similarly with the three-letter words, the four-letter words, the five-letter words and so on up to the twenty-letter words. Thus all words of the same length have been brought together in a form most likely to be of assistance to the solver or compiler of crossword puzzles.

It may be objected that some of the groups—those of five, six, and seven letters, in particular—comprise many hundreds of words and that to search systematically through them would involve a labour of some magnitude. In certain circumstances this may well be true, but the extent of the search will be greatly reduced in cases where one or more letters of the word are known, since these letters can be used as " keys." The value of the key letters will depend both on the letters themselves and on their position in the word. If the first letter is known, the required word must obviously lie within the limits of that letter in its appropriate group, and if both first and second letters are available the search will be narrowed infinitely.

Often when only one letter is known, commonsense will suggest the alternative letters which may precede it—or follow it. In the word " scholar," for instance, if the letter " c " were the only one known, a moment's thought would reveal that the preceding letter must be one of " a," " e," " i," " o," " s," " u " and " y," and a rapid glance down the list of seven-letter words beginning with any of these letters and having " c " as the second letter will quickly produce the desired result.

Finally, where a single letter only is known—say, the fourth— a very rapid inspection can be made by running the eye down the fourth letter of the appropriate column, pausing for closer inspection only where the known letter occurs. Using again the word " scholar " as an example, " o " would be the known letter and, in glancing quickly down the list, only those words having " o " as the fourth letter would require a second thought.

A few minutes' practice will show how useful and rapid this book can be in producing the required word.

CONTENTS

CONTINENTS AND COUNTRIES
OF THE WORLD

*Where names of countries have been changed both new and former names
appear in the appropriate columns*

4 letters	5 letters	6 letters	7 letters
ASIA	BURMA	AFRICA	ALBANIA
BALI	CHILE	ANGOLA	ALGERIA
CHAD	CHINA	AZORES	AMERICA
CUBA	CONGO	ARABIA	ANDORRA
EIRE	CRETE	BELIZE	ANTIGUA
FIJI	EGYPT	BHUTAN	ARMENIA
GAZA	GABON	BORNEO	AUSTRIA
GUAM	GHANA	BRAZIL	BAHAMAS
IRAN	HAITI	BRUNEI	BAHRAIN
IRAQ	INDIA	CANADA	BELGIUM
JAVA	ITALY	CEYLON	BERMUDA
LAOS	JAPAN	CYPRUS	BOLIVIA
MALI	KENYA	EUROPE	BRITAIN
OMAN	KHMER	FRANCE	BURUNDI
PERU	KOREA	GAMBIA	CORSICA
SIAM	LIBYA	GREECE	CURACAO
TOGO	MACAO	GUIANA	DAHOMEY
USSR	MALAY	GUINEA	DENMARK
	MALTA	GUYANA	ECUADOR
	NEPAL	HAWAII	ENGLAND
	NIGER	ISRAEL	ERITREA
	PAPUA	JORDAN	ESTONIA
	QATOR	KUWAIT	FINLAND
	SABAH	LATVIA	FORMOSA
	SAMOA	MALAWI	GERMANY
	SPAIN	MEXICO	GRENADA
	SUDAN	MONACO	HOLLAND
	SYRIA	NORWAY	HUNGARY
	TIBET	PANAMA	ICELAND
	TIMOR	PERSIA	IRELAND
	TONGA	POLAND	JAMAICA
	WALES	RUSSIA	LAPLAND
	YEMEN	RWANDA	LEBANON
	ZAIRE	SOMALI	LESOTHO
		SERBIA	LIBERIA
		SWEDEN	MADEIRA
		TAI WAN	MAJORCA
		TOBAGO	MOROCCO
		TURKEY	NIGERIA
		UGANDA	REUNION
		ZAMBIA	RUMANIA
			ST. KITTS
			SARAWAK
			SENEGAL
			SOMALIA
			SUMATRA
			SURINAM
			TANGIER
			TUNISIA
			URUGUAY
			VIETNAM

CONTINENTS AND COUNTRIES OF THE WORLD—continued

8 letters

ANTILLES
BARBADOS
BOTSWANA
BULGARIA
CAMBODIA
COLOMBIA
CAMEROON
DOMINICA
ETHIOPIA
HONDURAS
HONG KONG
MALAGASY
MALAYSIA
MONGOLIA
PAKISTAN
PARAGUAY
PORTUGAL
RHODESIA
ST. HELENA
SALVADOR
SCOTLAND
SRI LANKA
TANZANIA
TASMANIA
THAILAND
TRINIDAD
ZANZIBAR

9 letters

ABYSSINIA
ARGENTINA
AUSTRALIA
CALEDONIA
COSTA RICA
GIBRALTAR
GOLD COAST
GREENLAND
GUATEMALA
INDO-CHINA
INDONESIA
LITHUANIA
MANCHURIA
MAURITIUS
NICARAGUA
NYASALAND
POLYNESIA
SAN MARINO
SINGAPORE
SWAZILAND
VENEZUELA

10 letters

ANTARCTICA
BANGLADESH
GUADELOUPE
IVORY COAST
LUXEMBOURG
MADAGASCAR
MAURITANIA
MONTENEGRO
MONTSERRAT
MOZAMBIQUE
NEW ZEALAND
PUERTO RICO
SEYCHELLES
SOMALILAND
SOUTH YEMEN
TANGANYIKA
UPPER VOLTA
WEST INDIES
YUGOSLAVIA

11 letters

AFGHANISTAN
AUSTRALASIA
COOK ISLANDS
NAURU ISLAND
NETHERLANDS
NEW HEBRIDES
PHILIPPINES
SAUDI ARABIA
SIERRA LEONE
SOUTH AFRICA
SWITZERLAND

12 letters

COCOS ISLANDS
FAROE ISLANDS
LIECHENSTEIN
UNITED STATES

13 letters

CAYMAN ISLANDS
CENTRAL AFRICA
CANARY ISLANDS
COMORO ISLANDS
NORFOLK ISLAND
TRUCIAL STATES
UNITED KINGDOM
VIRGIN ISLANDS

14 letters

CAROLINE ISLAND
CZECHOSLOVAKIA
GILBERT ISLANDS
LEEWARD ISLAND
MALDIVE ISLANDS
MARIANA ISLANDS
SOCIETY ISLANDS
SOLOMON ISLANDS

15 letters

BALEARIC ISLANDS
FALKLAND ISLANDS
MARSHALL ISLANDS
WINDWARD ISLANDS

16 letters

CAPE VERDE ISLANDS
VATICAN CITY STATE

17 letters

CONGOLESE REPUBLIC
SANTA CRUZ ISLANDS

18 letters

UNITED ARAB EMIRATES
UNITED ARAB REPUBLIC
SYRIAN ARAB REPUBLIC

COUNTIES OF THE UNITED KINGDOM

Both new and former names appear in the appropriate columns

4 letters

AVON
BUTE
DOWN
FIFE
KENT
ROSS

5 letters

ANGUS
CLWYD
DYFED
ESSEX
GWENT
MORAY
NAIRN
POWYS
SALOP

6 letters

ANTRIM
ARMAGH
DURHAM
LONDON
ORKNEY
SURREY
SUSSEX
TYRONE

7 letters

CUMBRIA
GWYNEDD
KINROSS
NORFOLK
PEEBLES
RENFREW
SELKIRK
SUFFOLK
WIGTOWN
ZETLAND

8 letters

ABERDEEN
ANGLESEY
AYRSHIRE
CHESHIRE
CORNWALL
CROMARTY
ROXBURGH
STIRLING

9 letters

BERKSHIRE
CAITHNESS
CLEVELAND
FERMANAGH
HAMPSHIRE
MIDDLESEX
WILTSHIRE
YORKSHIRE

10 letters

BANFFSHIRE
CUMBERLAND
DERBYSHIRE
DEVONSHIRE
FLINTSHIRE
WEST SUSSEX
MERSEYSIDE
HUMBERSIDE
EAST SUSSEX
KINCARDINE
LANCASHIRE
MIDLOTHIAN
PERTHSHIRE
SHROPSHIRE
SUTHERLAND

11 letters

ARGYLLSHIRE
CLACKMANNAN
DORSETSHIRE
EAST LOTHIAN
LANARKSHIRE
LONDONDERRY
OXFORDSHIRE
RADNORSHIRE
TYNE AND WEAR
WEST LOTHIAN
WESTMORLAND

12 letters

BEDFORDSHIRE
BERWICKSHIRE
DENBIGHSHIRE
LINCOLNSHIRE
MID GLAMORGAN
WEST MIDLANDS
RUTLANDSHIRE
WARWICKSHIRE

13 letters

CARDIGANSHIRE
DUMFRIESSHIRE
HEREFORDSHIRE
HERTFORDSHIRE
KIRKCUDBRIGHT
MONMOUTHSHIRE
PEMBROKESHIRE
SOMERSETSHIRE
STAFFORDSHIRE
WEST GLAMORGAN
WEST YORKSHIRE

14 letters

BRECKNOCKSHIRE
CAMBRIDGESHIRE
DUMBARTONSHIRE
GLAMORGANSHIRE
INVERNESS-SHIRE
LEICESTERSHIRE
MERIONETHSHIRE
NORTHUMBERLAND
NORTH YORKSHIRE
SOUTH GLAMORGAN
SOUTH YORKSHIRE
WORCESTERSHIRE

15 letters

BUCKINGHAMSHIRE
CAERNARVONSHIRE
CARMARTHENSHIRE
GLOUCESTERSHIRE
HUNTINGDONSHIRE
MONTGOMERYSHIRE
NOTTINGHAMSHIRE
ROSS AND CROMARTY

16 letters

NORTHAMPTONSHIRE

17 letters

GREATER MANCHESTER

20 letters

HEREFORD AND
WORCESTER

THE STATES OF THE UNITED STATES OF AMERICA

4 letters

IOWA
OHIO
UTAH

5 letters

IDAHO
MAINE
TEXAS

6 letters

ALASKA
HAWAII
KANSAS
NEVADA
OREGON

7 letters

ALABAMA
ARIZONA
FLORIDA
GEORGIA
INDIANA
MONTANA
NEW YORK
VERMONT
WYOMING

8 letters

ARKANSAS
COLORADO
COLUMBIA
DELAWARE
ILLINOIS
KENTUCKY
MARYLAND
MICHIGAN
MISSOURI
NEBRASKA
OKLAHOMA
VIRGINIA

9 letters

LOUISIANA
MINNESOTA
NEW JERSEY
NEW MEXICO
TENNESSEE
WISCONSIN

10 letters

CALIFORNIA
WASHINGTON

11 letters

CONNECTICUT
MISSISSIPPI
NORTH DAKOTA
RHODE ISLAND
SOUTH DAKOTA

12 letters

NEW HAMPSHIRE
PENNSYLVANIA
WEST VIRGINIA

13 letters

MASSACHUSETTS
NORTH CAROLINA
SOUTH CAROLINA

SOME FLOWERING PLANTS

3 letters

HOP
IVY
RUE
TEA
YAM

4 letters

ALOE
ARUM
BALM
COCO
COLE
FLAG
IRIS
LILY
MUSK
PINK
ROSE
SAGE
VINE

5 letters

AGAVE
ASPIC
ASTER
DAISY
LOTUS
LUPIN
OXLIP
PANSY
PEONY
PHLOX
POPPY
TANSY
TULIP
VIOLA
YUCCA

6 letters

AZALEA
BORAGE
CACTUS
CATNIP
CISTUS
CLOVER
COSMOS
CROCUS
DAHLIA
MADDER
MALLOW
MIMOSA
ORCHID
ROCKET
SESAME
SORREL
THRIFT
VIOLET
ZINNIA

7 letters

ACONITE
ANEMONE
BUGLOSS
BEGONIA
CAMPION
CATMINT
CLARKIA
COWSLIP
DAY LILY
DITTANY
DOG-ROSE
FUCHSIA
GENTIAN
JACINTH
JASMINE
JONQUIL
LOBELIA
MAY-LILY
OPUNTIA
PETUNIA
SEA-PINK
SYRINGA
SPIRAEA
VANILLA
VERBENA
VERVAIN

8 letters

AMARANTH
ANGELICA
ASPHODEL
AURICULA
BIGNONIA
BLUEBELL
CAMELLIA
CAMOMILE
CATCHFLY
CLEMATIS
DAFFODIL
DROPWORT
FOXGLOVE
GERANIUM
GIRASOLE
GLOXINIA
HAREBELL
HYACINTH
LARKSPUR
MARIGOLD
MUSK-ROSE
POND-LILY
PRIMROSE
SCABIOUS
SNOWDROP
STAPELIA
SWEETPEA
TOAD-FLAX
VALERIAN
VERONICA
WISTERIA

9 letters

AMARYLLIS
BUTTERCUP
CAMPANULA
CANDYTUFT
CARNATION
CELANDINE
CHINA-ROSE
CINERARIA
CLOVE-PINK
COLUMBINE
DANDELION
DIGITALIS
EDELWEISS
EGLANTINE
GLADIOLUS
GOLDEN-ROD
HELLEBORE
HOLLYHOCK
NELUMBIUM
PIMPERNEL
PYRETHRUM
SAXIFRAGE
SPEEDWELL
SPIKENARD
SUNFLOWER
WATER-LILY

10 letters

CHINA-ASTER
CORNFLOWER
CRANE'S BILL
DAMASK-ROSE
DELPHINIUM
FRITILLARY
GELDER ROSE
GRANADILLA
HEARTSEASE
HELIOTROPE
NASTURTIUM
ORANGE-LILY
POLYANTHUS
RANUNCULUS
SNAPDRAGON
SWEET-BRIAR
WALLFLOWER

11 letters

ANTIRRHINUM
CABBAGE-ROSE
CALCEOLARIA
CONVOLVULUS
EVERLASTING
FORGET-ME-NOT
GILLYFLOWER
GLOBE-FLOWER
HONEYSUCKLE
RAGGED ROBIN

12 letters

CORN MARIGOLD
LADY'S SLIPPER
PASQUE-FLOWER
SWEET WILLIAM
VIRGIN'S BOWER

13 letters

CHRYSANTHEMUM
MARSH MARIGOLD
ODONTOGLOSSUM
PASSION FLOWER
TRUMPET FLOWER

14 letters

CANTERBURY
BELL

15 letters

MICHAELMAS
DAISY

SOME SHRUBS AND TREES

3 letters	4 letters	5 letters	6 letters	7 letters
ASH	ALOE	ABELE	ACACIA	AMBATCH
		ALDER	ALMOND	APRICOT
BEN	BASS	ALMUG	ANANAS	ARBUTUS
BAY		APPLE	AZALEA	
BOX	COLA	ARECA		BEBEERU
	CORK	ASPEN	BANANA	BLUE-GUM
ELM	CRAB		BANYAN	BOX-WOOD
		BEECH	BEOBAB	BUCK-EYE
FIG	GALE	BIRCH		
FIR	GEAN		CARAPA	CAJUPUT
		CAROB	CASHEW	CASSAVA
NUT	LIME	CEDAR	CHERRY	CHAMPAC
		CLOVE	CITRON	COWTREE
OAK	PALM	COCOA	COFFEE	CYPRESS
	PEAR	CYCAD	CORNEL	
SAL	PINE			DOG-WOOD
	PLUM	EBONY	DAMSON	DURMAST
YEW		ELDER	DAPHNE	
	ROSE		DEODAR	FAN-PALM
		GUAVA	DURIAN	
	SORB			GUM-TREE
		HAZEL	GOMUTI	
	TEAK	HENNA		HICKORY
		HOLLY	JAROOL	HOLM-OAK
	UPAS		JARRAH	
		LARCH	JUJUBE	JUNIPER
		LEMON		
		LIANA	LAUREL	LIVE-OAK
			LINDEN	
		MANGO		MAMMOTH
		MAPLE	MALLEE	
		MYRRH	MEDLAR	OIL-PALM
			MYRTLE	
		OLIVE		RED-PINE
		OSIER	NUTMEG	RED-WOOD
		PEACH	ORANGE	SEQUOIA
		PLANE		SYRINGA
			PLATAN	SPINDLE
		SUMAC	POPLAR	
				TAMARIX
		THORN	QUINCE	
				WYCH-ELM
		YUCCA	RATTAN	
			SALLOW	
			SPRUCE	
			STORAX	
			SUMACH	
			WALNUT	
			WATTLE	
			WILLOW	

SOME SHRUBS AND TREES—continued

8 letters	9 letters	10 letters	11 letters
AILANTUS	AZEDARACH	ALMOND-TREE	CABBAGE-PALM
			CAJUPUT-TREE
BAYBERRY	BEAR-BERRY	BIRD-CHERRY	CAMEL'S-THORN
BEAM-TREE	BLUEBERRY	BLACK-THORN	CAMPHOR-TREE
BERBERIS	BUCKTHORN	BOTTLE-TREE	COTTONEASTER
BERGAMOT	BUSSU-PALM	BRUSH-WOOD	COTTON-PLANT
BUDDLEIA	BUTTER-NUT	BUTTER-TREE	
		BUTTON-BUSH	GUELDER-ROSE
CARNAUBA	CASUARINA	BUTTON-WOOD	
CHESTNUT	CHERIMOYA		LAURUSTINUS
CINCHONA	CHINKAPIN	COTTON-TREE	
CINNAMON	CRAB-APPLE	COWRIE-PINE	PALMYRA-PALM
CLEMATIS	CRANBERRY		POMEGRANATE
COCCULUS	CROWBERRY	DRAGON-TREE	PRICKLY-PEAR
CRAB-TREE			
	GELSEMIUM	EUCALYPTUS	SERVICE-TREE
DATE-PALM			SHITTAH-TREE
DATE-TREE	HYDRANGEA	FIDDLE-WOOD	SPINDLE-TREE
DATE PLUM			
DIVI-DIVI	LANCE-WOOD	GOOSE-BERRY	VARNISH-TREE
		GREEN-HEART	
EUCALYPT			12 letters
	PERSIMMON	HACKMATACK	
GUAIACUM	PISTACHIO		CALABASH-TREE
	PITCH-PINE	JAPATI-PALM	CHRIST'S-THORN
HAWTHORN	PLANE-TREE		
HEMP-PALM		QUERCITRON	MONKEY-PUZZLE
HORN-BEAM	SAGE-BRUSH		
	SAPODILLA	SANDAL-WOOD	PLANTAIN-TREE
IRON-BARK	SATIN-WOOD	SUGAR-MAPLE	
	SCREW-PILE		RHODODENDRON
JACK-TREE	SILVER-FIR	TALLOW-TREE	
	SNOW-BERRY		SPURGE-LAUREL
LABURNUM	STONE-PINE	WHITE-THORN	
		WITCH-HAZEL	WELLINGTONIA
MAGNOLIA	TULIP-TREE		WHORTLE-BERRY
MAHOGANY			
MESQUITE	WAX-MYRTLE		13 letters
MULBERRY	WHITEBEAM		
MUSK-PEAR	WHITE-WOOD		BUTCHER'S-BROOM
MUSK-PLUM	WYCH-HAZEL		
			HORSE-CHESTNUT
OLEANDER			
			TRAVELLER'S-JOY
PINASTER			
PLANTAIN			14 letters
ROSE-WOOD			BREADFRUIT-TREE
SAGO-PALM			STRAWBERRY-TREE
SCRUB-OAK			
SHADDOCK			TRAVELLER'S-TREE
SWEET-BAY			
SYCAMINE			TURPENTINE-TREE
SYCAMORE			
			15 letters
TREE-FERN			
			TREMBLING-POPLAR
VIBURNUM			
WISTERIA			
WITCH-ELM			

MAMMALS

2 letters	3 letters	4 letters	5 letters	
OX	APE	BEAR	ADDAX	TABBY
	ASS	BOAR	ARNEE	TAPIR
		BUCK		TIGER
	BAT	BULL	BISON	
			BITCH	VIXEN
	CAT	CALF	BRUIN	
	COB	CAVY	BUNNY	WHALE
	COW	COLT		WHELP
	CUB		CAMEL	
	CUR	DEER	CIVET	ZEBRA
			COATI	ZIBET
	DAM	FAWN	CONEY	ZORIL
	DOE	FOAL	CUDDY	
	DOG			
		GAUR	DAMAN	
	ELK	GOAT	DHOLE	
	EMU		DINGO	
	EWE	HACK		
		HARE	ELAND	
	FOX	HART		
		HIND	FILLY	
	GNU		FITCH	
		IBEX		
	HOG		GAYAL	
		LAMB	GENET	
	KID	LION	GORAL	
		LOVO	GRICE	
	NAG	LYNX		
			HINNY	
	PIG	MARE	HORSE	
	PUG	MACE	HOUND	
		MINK	HYENA	
	RAT	MOLE	HYRAX	
	RAM	MULE		
		MUSK	LEMUR	
	TOD		LLAMA	
	TUP	NEAT	LORIS	
	YAK	ORYX	MANIS	
			MOOSE	
		PACA	MOUSE	
		PONY		
		PUMA	OTTER	
			OUNCE	
		SEAL		
		STAG	PANDA	
			PUNCH	
		TIKE	PUPPY	
		URUS	SABLE	
			SAIGA	
		VOLE	SASIN	
			SHEEP	
		WOLF	SHREW	
		WORM	SKUNK	
			SLOTH	
		ZEBU	STEER	
			STOAT	
			SWINE	

MAMMALS—continued

6 letters

AGOUTI
ALPACA
ARGALI
ASWAIL
AYE-AYE

BABOON
BADGER
BANDOG
BEAGLE
BEAVER

CASTOR
CATTLE
CHACMA
CHETAH
COCKER
CONGAR
COYOTE
COYPOU
CUSCUS

DESMAN
DONKEY

ERMINE

FARROW
FERRET
FOX-BAT

GALAGO
GIBBON
GOPHER

HACKEE

JACKAL
JAGUAR
JENNET
JERBOA

KITTEN
KOODOO

MARMOT
MARTEN
MARINO
MATACO
MUSK-OX

NILGAU

OCELOT
ONAGER

PALLAH
POODLE
PUG-DOG
PYGARG

QUAGGA

RABBIT
RACOON
RHESUS

SERVAL
SETTER

TARPAN
TENREE
TOM-CAT
TUSKER

URCHIN

VICUNA

WAIRUS
WALRUS
WAPITI
WEASEL
WETHER
WOMBAT

7 letters

ANT-BEAR
AUROCHS

BIGHORN
BLESBOK
BROCKET
BUFFALO
BULL-DOG
BULLOCK
BUSH-CAT

CARACAL
CARIBOO
CHAMOIS
CHEETAH
CHIKARA

DOLPHIN

EANLING
ECHIDNA
ECHINUS

FIN-BACK
FITCHET
FOUMART

GAZELLE
GEMSBOK
GIRAFFE
GLUTTON
GORILLA
GUANACO

HAMSTER
HARRIER

JACKASS

LEMMING
LEOPARD
LEVERET
LIONESS
LURCHER

MAMMOTH
MANATEE
MOUFLON
MUSK-RAT

NARWHAL

OPOSSUM

PANTHER
POLE-CAT

RACCOON
RED-DEER
ROE-BUCK
ROE-DEER
RORQUAL

SAPAJOU
SEA-BEAR
SEA-CALF
SEA-LION
SIAMANG
SPANIEL

TERRIER
TIGRESS

URODELE

VOENGRA

WALLABY
WART-HOG
WILD-ASS
WILD-CAT
WISTITI
WOLF-DOG

8 letters

AARDVARK
ANT-EATER
ANTELOPE

BULL-CALF

CACHELOT
CAPTBARA
CAPUCHIN
CARCAJOU
CARIACOU
CAVE-BEAR
CHIPMUNK
CIVET-CAT
COACH-DOG

DEMI-WOLF
DUCK-BILL
DUCK-MOLE

EARTH-HOG
ELEPHANT

FOX-HOUND

GALLOWAY

HEDGEHOG

KANGAROO
KINKAJOU
KIWI-KIWI

MACROPOD
MANDRILL
MARMOSET
MUSK-DEER

OUISTITI

PANGOLIN
PLATYPUS
PORPOISE

REINDEER
RIVER-HOG

SQUIRREL
STALLION
STEENBOK
TABBY-CAT
TIGER-CAT

WANDEROO
WATER-RAT
WILD-BOAR

MAMMALS—continued

9 letters

ARMADILLO

BABYRUSSA
BANDICOOT
BINTURONG
BUCK-HOUND

CANPAGNOL
CATAMOUNT

DACHSHUND
DEER-HOUND
DEER-MOUSE
DROMEDARY
DZIGGETAI

EARTH-WOLF

GREYHOUND
GROUND-HOG
GUINEA-PIG

ICHNEUMON

PADEMELON
PHALANGER
PIPISTREL
PORCUPINE

RAZOR-BACK
RETRIEVER

SHORT-HORN
SHREW-MOLE
SILVER-FOX
SPRING-BOK

WATER-MOLE
WATER-VOLE
WOLVERINE
WOODCHUCK

10 letters

BLOOD-HOUND
BOTTLE-NOSE

CAMELOPARD
CHIMPANZEE
CHINCHILLA

FIELD-MOUSE
FREE-MARTIN

PANTHERESS
PRAIRIE-DOG

RHINOCEROS
ROCK-RABBIT

SEA-LEOPARD
SEA-UNICORN
SPERM-WHALE

VAMPIRE-BAT

11 letters

BULL-TERRIER

FLYING LEMUR

GLOBIGERINA

HORNED-HORSE

MOUNTAIN-CAT

ORANG-OUTANG

SEA-ELEPHANT
SLEUTH-HOUND

12 letters

FLITTER-MOUSE

HARVEST-MOUSE
HIPPOPOTAMUS

SPIDER-MONKEY

OURANG-OUTANG

WATER-SPANIEL

14 letters

FLYING-SQUIRREL

GROUND-SQUIRREL

FISH AND AQUATIC ANIMALS

3 letters	4 letters	5 letters	6 letters
COD	BASS	BLEAK	ANGLER
DAB	CARP	BORER	
EEL	CHAR	BREAM	BARBEL
HAG	CHUB	BRILL	BLENNY
RAY	CLAM		BONITO
	CRAB	DORSE	BARBOT
	DACE	FLUKE	CAPLIN
	DORY		CHEVIN
	GOBY	GAPER	COCKLE
	HAKE	LOACH	CONGER
	KELT	LEECH	CUTTLE
	LING	MATTY	DOCTOR
	LUCE	MUREX	DUGONG
	PARR	PERCH	GURAMI
	PIKE	PRAWN	GRILSE
	RUDD	ROACH	GURNET
	SCAD	SHARK	KELTIE
	SHAD	SIREN	LIMPET
	SOLE	SKATE	MEDUSA
	TOPE	SMELT	MILTER
		SMOLT	MINNOW
		SNAIL	MUD-EEL
		SPRAT	MULLET
		SQUID	(red and grey)
		TENCH	MUSSEL
		TORSK	NEREID
		TROUT	OYSTER
		TUNNY	PHOLAS
		WHELK	PLAICE
			POLLAN
			REMORA
			SALMON
			SEACAT
			SEADOG
			SEA-EEL
			SEA-FOX
			SHANNY
			SHRIMP
			SUCKER
			TARPON
			TAUTOG
			TEREDO
			TURBOT
			WEEVER
			WRASSE

FISH AND AQUATIC ANIMALS—continued

7 letters

ALEWIFE
ANCHOVY

CATFISH
COD FISH
CODLING

DOG FISH
DOLPHIN

EEL-POUT

GARFISH
GRAMPUS
GUDGEON

HADDOCK
HALIBUT
HERRING

LAMPERN
LAMPREY
LOBSTER

MUDFISH
MURAENA

OCTOPOD
OCTOPUS

PIDDOCK
POLLACK

ROTIFER

SAND-EEL
SARDINE
SAW-FISH
SCALLOP
SCULPIN
SEA-COW
SEA-HARE
SEA-PIKE
SEA-SLUG
SEA-WOLF
SUNFISH

TORPEDO
TREPANG

WHITING

8 letters

ARGONAUT

BAND-FISH

CALAMARY
CHIMAERA
COAL-FISH
CRAYFISH

DEAL-FISH

EAR-SHELL

FILE-FISH
FLOUNDER
FOX-SHARK

GOLD-FISH
GRAYLING

JOHN DORY

KING-CRAB

LANCELET
LUMP-FISH

MACKEREL
MALARMAT
MENHADEN
MONKFISH

OCTOPEDE

PENNY-DOG
PICKEREL
PILCHARD
PIPE-FISH
PHYSALIA

RHIZOPOD

SEA-ACORN
SEA-DEVIL
SEA-LEMON
SEA-LOUSE
SEA-SNIPE
STARFISH
STING-RAY
STURGEON

TOAD-FISH

WOLF-FISH

ZOOPHYTE

9 letters

ANGEL-FISH

BARRACUDA
BLACK-FISH
BRANDLING
BULL-TROUT

CERATODUS

DEVIL-FISH
DIMYARIAN

FISH-LOUSE

GLOBE-FISH

HOUND-FISH

LAMP-SHELL

OSTRACIAN

PILOT-FISH

SEA-NEEDLE
SEA-NETTLE
SEA-SQUIRT
SEA-URCHIN
SURMULLET
SWORD-FISH

TIFFEN BAT
TRUNK-FISH

WHITE-BAIT

10 letters

ACORN-SHELL
ARCHER-FISH

BOTTLE-FISH

CANDLE-FISH
CUTTLE-FISH

FLYING-FISH

HAMMER-FISH
HERMIT-CRAB
HORSE-LEECH

PARROT-FISH
PERIWINKLE
PURPLE-FISH

RIBBON-FISH
RIBBON-WORM

SAND-HOPPER
SILVER-FISH

FISH AND AQUATIC ANIMALS—continued

11 letters

BELLOWS-FISH
BRINE-SHRIMP

CALLING-CRAB

FLYING-SQUID

HIPPO-CAMPUS
HOLOTHURIAN

PAPER-SAILOR
PEARL-MUSSEL
PEARL-OYSTER

SALMON-TROUT
SEA-CUCUMBER
SEA-HEDGEHOG
SERPENT-FISH
STICKLEBACK
SUCKING-FISH

TRUMPET-FISH

WHEEL-ANIMAL

12 letters

SEA-PORCUPINE

13 letters

HORSE-MACKEREL
PAPER-NAUTILUS

AMPHIBIANS AND REPTILES

3 letters

ASP

BOA

EFT

4 letters

FROG

NEWT

PAMA

TOAD

5 letters

ABOMA
ADDER
ASPIC

COBRA

GECKO

SKINK
SNAKE

VIPER

6 letters

CAYMAN

DRAGON

IGUANA

LIZARD

PYTHON

TRITON
TURTLE

7 letters

AXOLOTL

PADDOCK

SERPENT

TADPOLE

URODELA

8 letters

ANACONDA

BASILISK
BULL-FROG

TORTOISE
TERRAPIN
TREE-FROG

9 letters

ALLIGATOR

BLIND-WORM

CHAMELEON
CROCODILE

PUFF-ADDER

10 letters

FER-DE-LANCE

GLASS-SNAKE

SALAMANDER

WATER-SNAKE

11 letters

RATTLE-SNAKE

13 letters

ICHTHYOSAURUS

14 letters

BOA-CONSTRICTOR

COBRA-DE-CAPELLO

SNAPPING-TURTLE

INSECTS AND INVERTEBRATES

3 letters	4 letters	5 letters	6 letters	7 letters
ANT	CLEG	APHIS	BEETLE	ANT-LION
	FLEA	BRIZE	BOTFLY	ANNELID
BEE	GNAT	DRONE	CHAFER	BEAN-FLY
BUG	GRIG	EMMET	CHIGOE	BEE-MOTH
DOR	GRUB		CHINCH	BLOW-FLY
	LICE	FLUKE	CICADA	BOAT-FLY
FLY	MITE	LARVA	DAYFLY	CESTOID
NIT	MOTH	LOUSE	EARWIG	CRICKET
	SLUG	MIDGE	ELATOR	EPIZOON
	TICK	SNAIL	GADFLY	FIREFLY
	WASP		HORNET	FROG-FLY
	WORM		JIGGER	GALL-FLY
			LOCUST	HIVE-BEE
			MAGGOT	KATYDID
			MANTIS	LOBWORM
			MAYBUG	LUGWORM
			MAYFLY	MAWWORM
			SAW-FLY	MOLLUSC
			SCARAB	SAND-FLY
			SPIDER	TERMITE
			THRIPS	WOOD-ANT
			TSETSE	
			WEEVIL	

INSECTS AND INVERTEBRATES—continued

8 letters

BOOK-WORM

CASE-WORM
CRANE-FLY

EPHEMERA

FLATWORM
FLESH-FLY

GALL-GNAT
GLOW-WORM

HAIR-WORM
HONEY-BEE
HORSE-FLY
HOUSE-FLY

ITCH-MITE

LADY-BIRD

MILLIPED
MOSQUITO
MYRIAPOD

SCORPION
SHIP-WORM

TAPE-WORM

WATER-BUG
WHEAT-FLY
WHIRLWIG
WIRE-WORM

9 letters

BOOK-LOUSE
BREEZE-FLY
BUMBLE-BEE
BUTTER-FLY

CANKER-FLY
CENTIPEDE
CHEESE-FLY
CHRYSALIS
CLAVICORN
COCHINEAL
COCKROACH
COFFEE-BUG
COLEOPTER

DRAGON-FLY

EARTH-WORM

HUMBLE-BEE

TARANTULA
TURNIP-FLY

WATER-FLEA
WOOD-LOUSE

10 letters

ARTHROPODS

BIRD-SPIDER
BLISTER-FLY
BLUE-BOTTLE

CADDICE-FLY
CANKER-WORM
COCKCHAFER
CORN-BEETLE

DEATH'S-HEAD
DEATH-WATCH

FROG-HOPPER

HARVEST-BUG
HESSIAN-FLY

LEAF-INSECT

PALMER-WORM
PHYLLOXERA

RIBBON-WORM

SHEEP-LOUSE
STAG-BEETLE

WHEAT-MIDGE

11 letters

BLACK BEETLE
BLOOD-SUCKER

CABBAGE-MOTH
CATERPILLAR
CLOTHES-MOTH

GRASSHOPPER

SCOLOPENDRA
STICK-INSECT

TIGER-BEETLE

12 letters

BOOK-SCORPION
BUZZARD-CLOCK

SPRING-BEETLE

WALKING-STICK
WATER-BOATMAN

13 letters

BLISTER-BEETLE

CARPENTER'S-BEE

DADDY-LONG-LEGS

PRAYING-MANTIS

15 letters

SERRICORN-BEETLE

16 letters

CABBAGE-BUTTERFLY

BIRDS

3 letters	4 letters	5 letters	6 letters	
AUK	CHAT	AGAMI	ARGALA	SCOTER
	COOT		AVOCET	SEA-EEL
DAW	COCK	BOOBY		SEA-MEW
	CROW		BANTAM	SHRIKE
EMU		CAPON	BARBET	SISKIN
	DODO	CRAKE	BULBUL	
FOP	DOVE	CRANE		THRUSH
	DUCK		CANARY	TOMTIT
HEN	DUPE	DIVER	CHOUGH	TOUCAN
		DRAKE	CONDOR	TROGON
JAY	ERNE		CORBIE	TURKEY
	EYAS	EAGLE	CUCKOO	
MEW		EGRET	CULVER	WIGEON
	FOWL	EIDER	CURLEW	
MOA			CUSHAT	
(running	GULL	FINCH	CYGNET	
bird)				
	HAWK	GLEDE	DARTER	
OWL	HERN	GOOSE	DIPPER	
		GEESE	DUNLIN	
PIE	IBIS	GREBE		
			FALCON	
ROC	KAKA	HARPY		
	KITE	HERON	GANDER	
TIT	KIWI	HOBBY	GANNET	
	KNOT		GARROT	
		MACAW	GODWIT	
	LARK	MAVIS	GROUSE	
	LOON	MERLE		
	LORY		HAMMER	
		NODDY	HOOPER	
	MINA		HOOPOE	
		OUZEL	HOWLET	
	RAIL	OWLET		
	RHEA		JACANA	
	ROOK	PIPIT		
	RUFF		LANNER	
	RUNT	QUAIL	LINNET	
		RAVEN	MAGPIE	
	SHAG	REEVE	MARTIN	
	SKUA	ROBIN	MERLIN	
	SMEW			
	SWAN	SAKER	ORIOLE	
		SCAUP	OSPREY	
	TEAL	SNIPE		
	TERN	SQUAB	PARROT	
		STORK	PEEWIT	
	WREN	SWIFT	PETREL	
			PIGEON	
		WADER	PLOVER	
			POUTER	
			PUFFIN	
			PULLET	
			RACAMA	

BIRDS—continued

7 letters

BARN OWL
BITTERN
BLUECAP
BUNTING
BUSTARD
BUZZARD

CATBIRD
CHICKEN
COLIBRI
COURSER
CREEPER

DOR-HAWK

EGG-BIRD

FANTAIL
FERN-OWL

GADWALL
GOBBLER
GORCOCK
GOR-CROW
GOSHAWK
GOSLING
GRACKLE
GRAYLEG
GRAY-OWL
GRIFFIN

HAGGARD
HARRIER

JACKDAW

KESTREL
KINGLET

LAPWING

MALLARD
MANAKIN
MARTLET
MOORHEN

ORTOLAN
OSTRICH

PARTLET
PEACOCK
PEAFOWL
PELICAN
PENGUIN
PINTAIL
POCHARD
PUTTOCK

REDPOLL
REDWING
RUDDOCK

SEA-DUCK
SKYLARK
SPARROW
SUN-BIRD
SWALLOW

TANAGER
TIERCEL
TITLARK
TITLING
TUMBLER

VULTURE

WAGTAIL
WARBLER
WAXWING
WIDGEON
WRYNECK

8 letters

ADJUTANT
AMADAVAT

BARNACLE
BEE-EATER
BLACKCAP
BLUEBIRD
BOBOLINK

CARDINAL
COCKATOO
COCKEREL
CURASSOW

DABCHICK
DIDAPPER
DOTTEREL
DUCKLING

EAGLE-OWL

FLAMINGO

GAMECOCK

HAWFINCH
HERNSHAW

KIWI-KIWI

LANDRAIL
LOVEBIRD
LYRE-BIRD

MEGAPODE
MOOR-COCK
MOOR-FOWL
MUSK-DUCK

NIGHTJAR
NUTHATCH

PHEASANT
POPINJAY

REDSHANK
REDSTART
RICE-BIRD
RING-DOVE

SAGE-COCK
SEA-EAGLE
SHELDUCK
SKUA-GULL
SNOW-BIRD
STARLING

THROSTLE
TITMOUSE
TRAGOPAN

WATERHEN
WHEATEAR
WHIMBREL
WHINCHAT
WOODCOCK
WOODLARK

BIRDS—continued

9 letters

ALBATROSS

BALD-EAGLE
BEAN-GOOSE
BECCAFICO
BEEF-EATER
BLACKBIRD
BLACKCOCK
BLACK GAME
BOTTLE-TIT
BOWERBIRD
BRAMBLING
BULLFINCH

CAMPANERO
CASSOWARY
CHAFFINCH
CORMORANT
CORNCRAKE
CROSSBILL

FIELDFARE

GALLINULE
GER FALCON
GIER-EAGLE
GOLDCREST
GOLDENEYE
GOLDFINCH
GOOSANDER
GUILLEMOT

HEATH-COCK
HERON-SHAW

NIGHT-HAWK

PARRAKEET
PARTRIDGE
PASSERINE
PEREGRINE
PHALAROPE
PINE-FINCH
PTARMIGAN

RAZORBILL
REDBREAST
RINGOUZEL

SALANGANE
SANDPIPER
SEA-PARROT
SHELDRAKE
SNAKE-BIRD
SNOW-FLECK
SPOONBILL
STILT-BIRD
STOCKDOVE
STONECHAT

TRUMPETER
TURNSTONE

WATER-FOWL
WATERRAIL
WILD GOOSE
WINDHOVER

10 letters

ABERDEVINE

BRENT-GOOSE
BURROW-DUCK
BUSH-SHRIVE
BUTTER-BIRD

CANVAS BACK
COW-BUNTING

DEMOISELLE
DIDUNCULUS

FALLOW-CHAT
FLYCATCHER

GOATSUCKER
GREENFINCH
GREENSHANK
GUINEAFOWL

HARPY-EAGLE
HENHARRIER

KINGFISHER

NIGHT-HERON
NUTCRACKER

SAGE-GROUSE
SANDERLING
SAND-GROUSE
SANDMARTIN
SCREECH-OWL
SEA-SWALLOW
SHEARWATER
SOLAN-GOOSE
SONGTHRUSH
SUMMER-DUCK

TAILOR-BIRD
TROPIC-BIRD
TURTLE-DOVE

WATER-OUSEL
WEAVER-BIRD
WILLOW-WREN
WOOD-GROUSE
WOODPECKER
WOOD-PIGEON

11 letters

BARN-SWALLOW
BRUSH-TURKEY
BUTCHER-BIRD

COCHIN CHINA

FALLOW-FINCH
FRIGATE-BIRD

HUMMING-BIRD

KING-VULTURE

LAMMERGEIER

MOCKING-BIRD

NIGHTINGALE

REED-BUNTING
REED-SPARROW

SCISSOR-BILL
SNOW-BUNTING
SNOW ORTOLAN
SONG-SPARROW
SPARROW-HAWK
STILT-PLOVER

WHITETHROAT
WOODWARBLER

BIRDS—continued

12 letters

ADJUTANT-BIRD

BURROWING-OWL

CAPERCAILZIE
CARDINAL-BIRD

FALCON-GENTIL

HEDGE-SPARROW
HEDGE-WARBLER

MARSH-HARRIER
MISSEL-THRUSH

SEDGE-WARBLER
SERPENT-EATER
STONE-CHATTER
STUBBLE-GOOSE

WATTLE-TURKEY
WHIP-POOR-WILL

YELLOW HAMMER

13 letters

SECRETARY BIRD

{ TURKEY-BUZZARD
{ TURKEY-VULTURE

WILLOW-WARBLER

YELLOW-BUNTING

14 letters

BIRD-OF-PARADISE

SOME MYTHOLOGICAL NAMES

2 letters	4 letters (cont)	5 letters (cont)	7 letters
EA	LUNA	MAZDA	ARIADNE
RA	MAAT	MIDAS	BACCHUS
	MARS	PLUTO	BELLONA
	ODIN	THOTH	JUPITER
3 letters	PTAH	VENUS	MERCURY
	SIVA	WODEN	MINERVA
	THOR	WOTAN	MITHRAS
ANU	ZEUS		PERSEUS
HAP			PROTEUS
NOX			SERAPIS
NUT	**5 letters**	**6 letters**	ULYSSES
PAN			
SET			
SOL	AMMON	ADONIS	**8 letters**
TIW	ASHUR	ANUBIS	
TYR	ATLAS	APOLLO	
	CERES	ATHENA	HERCULES
	COMUS	AURORA	NEPHTHYS
4 letters	CUPID	BAALIM	
	DAGON	HATHOR	
	DIANA	HERMES	**9 letters**
AJAX	DURGA	ISHTAR	
APIS	ENLIL	MARDUK	
ATON	FLORA	MEDUSA	APHRODITE
BAST	FRIGU	MILCOM	ASHTAROTH
EROS	HORUS	MOLOCH	NARCISSUS
HAPI	HYMEN	OSIRIS	PYGMALION
HERA	INDRA	PSYCHE	
ISIS	JANUS	SATURN	
JUNO	JASON	SOMNUS	
LEDA		VISHNU	
LOKI		VULCAN	

CHEMICAL ELEMENTS, METALS, ALLOYS AND MANUFACTURED SUBSTANCES

2 letters	3 letters	4 letters	5 letters
MU	TIN	ALUM	ARGON
		COKE	BORAX
		GOLD	BORON
			BRASS
		IRON	ETHER
		LEAD	GLASS
		LIME	INVAR
		MOND (metal)	LYSOL
		SODA	MUNTZ
		ZINC	NITON
			NITRE
			NYLON
			OZONE
			RADON
			SALOL
			STEEL
			WOOTZ
			XENON

CHEMICAL ELEMENTS, METALS, ALLOYS AND
MANUFACTURED SUBSTANCES—continued

6 letters	7 letters	8 letters	9 letters
ALKALI	ALCOHOL	ACTINIUM	ACETYLENE
AMATOL	ALUMINA	ANTIMONY	ALUMINIUM
	AMALGAM	ASTATINE	
BARIUM	AMMONAL	ATROPINE	BERYLLIUM
BARYTA	AMMONIA		BLACKLEAD
BRONZE	ANILINE	BAKELITE	
	ARSENIC		CELLULOSE
CARBON	ASPIRIN	CAFFEINE	COLUMBIUM
CASEIN		CHARCOAL	
CERIUM	BENZENE	CHLORINE	DEUTERIUM
COBALT	BISMUTH	CHROMIUM	DIGITALIN
COPPER	BROMIDE	CINCHONA	DURALUMIN
CRESOL	BROMINE		
		DIDYMIUM	GERMANIUM
ERBIUM	CADMIUM		GUNCOTTON
	CALCIUM	EUROPIUM	GUNPOWDER
HELIUM	CALOMEL		
	CAMPHOR	FLUORINE	LANTHANUM
INDIUM	COCAINE	FORMALIN	
IODINE	CODEINE	FRANCIUM	MAGNESIUM
IONIUM	CYANIDE		MANGANESE
		GLUCINUM	
NICKEL	EBONITE	GRAPHITE	NEPTUNIUM
		GUNMETAL	
OSMIUM	FERMIUM		PALLADIUM
OXYGEN		HYDROGEN	PLUTONIUM
	GALLIUM		POTASSIUM
PEWTER	GELATIN	IODOFORM	
PHENOL	GLUCOSE		QUICKLIME
POTASH		LITHARGE	
	HAFNIUM	LUTECIUM	STRONTIUM
RADIUM	HOLMIUM		
		MANGANIN	VERDIGRIS
SILVER	IRIDIUM	MASURIUM	VULCANITE
SODIUM		MORPHINE	
SOLDER	KRYPTON		WHITE-LEAD
STARCH		NICHROME	
	LITHIUM	NICOTINE	YTTERBIUM
TANNIN		NITROGEN	
	MENTHOL		ZIRCONIUM
	MERCURY	PLATINUM	
		PLUMBAGO	
	NIOBIUM	POLONIUM	
	PERSPEX	RUBIDIUM	
	QUININE		
		SAMARIUM	
	RED-LEAD	SCANDIUM	
	RHENIUM	SELERIUM	
	RHODIUM		
		TANTALUM	
	SILICON	THALLIUM	
	SODA-ASH	TITANIUM	
	SULPHUR	TUNGSTEN	
	TERBIUM		
	THORIUM		
	TOLUESE		
	URANIUM		
	VERONAL		
	VITRIOL		
	YTTRIUM		

CHEMICAL ELEMENTS, METALS, ALLOYS AND MANUFACTURED SUBSTANCES—continued

10 letters

CAOUTCHOUC
CHLOROFORM
CONSTANTIN

DYSPROSIUM

GADOLINIUM

MOLYBDENUM

PHOSPHORUS
PROMETHIUM

11 letters

CARBORUNDUM

EINSTEINIUM

GLAUBER-SALT

IPECACUANHA

PARALDEHYDE

QUICK-SILVER

12 letters

PRAESODYMIUM

13 letters

PROTO-ACTINIUM

14 letters

BRITANNIA-METAL

PHOSPHOR-BRONZE

MINERAL ORES

4 letters	5 letters	6 letters	7 letters	8 letters
ALUM	AGATE	ALBITE	APATITE	ASBESTOS
	AMBER	AUGITE	ASPHALT	
CALX	ARGON		AZURITE	BLUE-JOHN
CAUK		CERITE		BORACITE
CLAY	BERYL		BARYTES	BRONZITE
COAL	BORAX	GALENA	BAUXITE	BROOKITE
		GARNET	BITUMEN	
GRIT	CHALK	GYPSUM	BORNITE	CALAMINE
	CHERT			CALCSPAR
LIAS		IOLITE	CALCITE	CHLORITE
	EMERY		CALICHE	CHROMITE
MAWL		JARGON		CINNABAR
MICA	FLINT	JASPER	DIAMOND	CORUNDUM
				CRYOLITE
ONYX	NITRE	KAOLIN	EMERALD	
OPAL			EPIDOTE	DIOPTASE
	PITCH	MARBLE		DOLOMITE
RUBY			FELSPAR	
	SILEX	POTASH		FLUORITE
SPAR		PYRITE	GRANITE	
				GRAPHITE
TALC		QUARTZ	KAINITE	
TUFA				HYACINTH
		SCHORL	LIQUITE	
WADD		SILICA		IDOCRASE
			OLIVINE	ILMENITE
		THORIA		
			PYRITES	LIMONITE
		ZIRCON		
			REALGAR	MAGNESIA
				MASSICOT
			SULPHUR	MELANITE
				MONAZITE
			TRIPOLI	
				ORPIMENT
			WOLFRAM	
			WURGITE	PYROXENE
			ZEOLITE	ROCK-SALT
				ROCK-SOAP
				ROCKWOOD
				SAPPHIRE
				SIDERITE
				STEATITE
				STIBNITE
				TINSTONE
				ZIRCONIA

MINERAL ORES—continued

9 letters

ALABASTER
AMIANTHUS
ANGLESITE
ANHYDRITE
ARAGONITE
ARGENTITE

BYSSOLITE

CASHOLONG
CAT-SILVER
COLUMBITE

EARTH-FLAX

FLUORSPAR

GREENSAND

IRON-STONE

LIMESTONE
LODESTONE

MAGNESITE
MAGNETITE
MALACHITE
MARCASITE
MISPICKEL

OZOCERITE

PETROLEUM

SALT PETRE
SCAPOLITE
STREAM-TIN

TRIDYMITE
TURQUOISE

10 letters

ACTINOLITE
ANTHRACITE
AQUAMARINE

CARNALLITE
CHALCEDONY
CHALYBEATE

HORNBLENDE

INFUSORIAL
  (EARTH)

KIESELGUHR

MEERSCHAUM

PYROLUSITE

SERPENTINE
SPHALERITE

TOURMALINE

11 letters

CASSITERITE
CHRYSOPRASE
CHALCEDONYX

ICELAND-SPAR

LAPIS-LAZULI

PITCH BLENDE

ROCK-CRYSTAL

12 letters

AEROSIDERATE

CHALCOPYRITE

FULLER'S-EARTH

MOUNTAIN-CORK

MOUNTAIN-FLAX

SILVER-GLANCE
STRONTIANITE

14 letters

BRITANNIA-METAL

TWO-LETTER WORDS

AH!	GO	MA	SI
AM		ME	SO
AN		MI	
AS		MY	
AT			
AX	HA!		
AY	HE		TO
	HI!		
	HO!	NO	
BE			UP
BO			US
BY	IF	OD	
	I'M	OF	
	IN	OH!	
	IS	ON	
	IT	OR	WE
DI		OX	WO!
DO			
	JO		YE
		PA	
EH!		PO	
EM			
	LA		
	LO!		
		RE	
FA			
FY!			

THREE-LETTER WORDS

A	BIB	DAN	FAG	HAG	JOB	MET	OWN
	BID	DAP	FAR	HAH!	JOE	MEW	
	BIG	DAW	FAT	HAM	JOG	MID	
ABB	BIN	DAY	FAY	HAP	JOT	MIX	**P**
ABY	BIS	DEE	FED	HAS	JOY	MOA	
ACE	BIT	DEN	FEE	HAT	JUG	MOB	PAD
ACT	BOA	DEW	FEN	HAW	JUT	MOO	PAH
ADD	BOB	DEY	FEU	HAY		MOP	PAL
ADO	BOG	DID	FEW	HEM		MOW	PAN
ADZ	BOO	DIE	FEY	HEN	**K**	MUD	PAP
AFT	BOT	DIG	FEZ	HER		MUG	PAR
AGA	BOW	DIM	FIB	HEW		MUM	PAS
AGE	BOX	DIN	FID	HEY!	KAW		PAT
AGO	BOY	DIP	FIE	HID	KAY		PAW
AHA!	BUD	DOE	FIG	HIE	KEG		PAX
AID	BUG	DOG	FIN	HIM	KEN	**N**	PAY
AIL	BUM	DON	FIR	HIN	KEX		PEA
AIM	BUN	DOR	FIT	HIP	KEY	NAB	PED
AIR	BUR	DOT	FIX	HIS	KID	NAG	PEE
AIT	BUS	DRY	FLU	HIT	KIN	NAY	PEG
ALB	BUT	DUB	FLY	HOB	KIP	NEB	PEN
ALE	BUY	DUD	FOB	HOD	KIT	NEE	PEP
ALL	BYE	DUE	FOE	HOE	KYE	NET	PER
ALP		DUG	FOG	HOG		NEW	PET
ALT		DUN	FOH	HOP		NIB	PEW
AND	**C**	DUO	FOP	HOT	**L**	NIL	PIE
ANT		DUX	FOR	HOW		NIP	PIG
ANY	CAB	DYE	FOX	HOY	LAC	NIT	PIN
APE	CAD		FOY	HUB	LAD	NOD	PIP
APT	CAM		FRO	HUE	LAG	NOG	PIT
ARC	CAN		FRY	HUG	LAP	NOR	PIX
ARE	CAP	**E**	FUN	HUH!	LAW	NOT	PLY
ARK	CAR		FUR	HUM	LAX	NOW	POD
ARM	CAT	EAR		HUN	LAY	NUN	POH
ART	CAW	EAT		HUT	LEA	NUT	POP
ASH	CAY	EAU	**G**		LED	NUX	POT
ASK	CIT	EBB			LEE		POX
ASP	COB	EEL	GAB	**I**	LEG		PRY
ASS	COD	E'EN	GAD		LEO		PUB
ATE	COG	E'ER	GAG		LET	**O**	PUG
AUK	COL	EFT	GAM	ICE	LID		PUN
AVE	CON	EGG	GAP	ICY	LIE	OAF	PUP
AWE	COO	EGO	GAR	ILK	LIP	OAK	PUR
AWL	COR	EKE	GAS	ILL	LIT	OAR	PUS
AWN	COT	ELD	GAT	IMP	LOB	OAT	PUT
AXE	COW	ELF	GAY	INK	LOG	OBI	PYX
AYE	COX	ELK	GEM	INN	LOO	ODD	
	COY	ELL	GET	IOU	LOP	ODE	
	COZ	ELM	GIG	IRE	LOT	O'ER	
B	CRY	EMU	GIN	IRK	LOW	OFF	**Q**
	CUB	END	GNU	IVY	LUG	OFT	
BAA	CUD	ENS	GOB		LYE	OHM	QUA
BAD	CUE	EON	GOD			OHO!	
BAG	CUP	ERA	GOT	**J**		OIL	
BAH!	CUR	ERE	GUM		**M**	OKE	**R**
BAN	CUT	ERG	GUN	JAB		OLD	
BAR		ERN	GUT	JAG	MAC	ONE	RAG
BAT		ERR	GUY	JAH	MAD	OPE	RAM
BAY		EVE	GYM	JAM	MAM	ORB	RAN
BED	**D**	EWE	GYP	JAR	MAN	ORE	RAP
BEE		EYE		JAW	MAP	ORT	RAT
BEG	DAB			JAY	MAR	OUR	RAW
BEN	DAD			JET	MAT	OUT	RAY
BET	DAG	**F**	**H**	JEW	MAW	OVA	RED
BEY	DAK			JIB	MAY	OWE	REP
	DAM	FAD	HAD	JIG	MEN	OWL	RET

34

RIB	SAD	SOD	TAP	TOP		WED	
RID	SAG	SOG	TAR	TOR	**V**	WEE	
RIG	SAL	SOL	TAW	TOT		WEN	**Y**
RIM	SAP	SON	TAX	TOW	VAN	WET	YAK
RIP	SAT	SOP	TAY	TOY	VAT	WEY	YAM
ROB	SAW	SOT	TEA	TRY	VEX	WHO	YAP
ROC	SAY	SOU	TED	TUB	VIA	WHY	YAW
ROD	SEA	SOW	TEE	TUG	VIE	WIG	YEA
ROE	SEE	SOY	TEN	TUM	VIM	WIN	YEN
ROI	SET	SPA	THE	TUN	VIS	WIT	YES
ROT	SEW	SPY	THO'	TUP	VOW	WOE	YET
ROW	SEX	STY	THY	TUT!		WON	YEW
RUB	SHE	SUB	TIC	TWO		WOO	YON
RUE	SHY	SUE	TIE		**W**	WOP	YOU
RUG	SIC	SUM	TIN			WOT	
RUM	SIN	SUN	TIP	**U**	WAD	WRY	
RUN	SIP	SUP	'TIS		WAG		
RUT	SIR		TIT	UGH!	WAN		**Z**
RYE	SIT		T.N.T.	URN	WAP		
	SIX	**T**	TOD	USE	WAR	**X**	ZAX
	SKI		TOE	UNA	WAS		ZOO
S	SKY	TAB	TOM		WAX	**—**	
	SLY	TAG	TON		WAY		
SAC	SOB	TAN	TOO		WEB		

FOUR-LETTER WORDS

A	APEX	BARK	BOER	BYRE	CITY	CRAN
	APSE	BARM	BOGY		CIVE	CRAW
	AQUA	BARN	BOIL		CLAD	CREW
ABBA	ARAB	BASE	BOLD	**C**	CLAM	CRIB
ABBE	ARCH	BASH	BOLE		CLAN	CROP
ABED	AREA	BASK	BOLL	CADE	CLAP	CROW
ABET	ARIA	BASS	BOLT	CADI	CLAW	CRUM
ABIB	ARID	BAST	BOMB	CAFE	CLAY	CRUT
ABLE	ARIL	BATE	BOND	CAGE	CLEF	CRUX
ABLY	ARMS	BATH	BONE	CAIN	CLEG	CUBE
ABUT	ARMY	BAWD	BONY	CAKE	CLEM	CUES
ACES	ARNI	BAWL	BOOB	CALF	CLEW	CUFF
ACHE	ARUM	BEAD	BOOK	CALK	CLIP	CULL
ACID	ASCI	BEAK	BOOM	CALL	CLOD	CULM
ACME	ASHY	BEAM	BOON	CALM	CLOG	CULT
ACNE	ASIA	BEAN	BOOR	CALP	CLOT	CURB
ACRE	ASPS	BEAR	BOOT	CALX	CLOY	CURD
ADAM	ATOM	BEAT	BORE	CAME	CLUB	CURE
ADAR	ATOP	BEAU	BORN	CAMP	CLUE	CURE
ADIT	AUNT	BECK	BORT	CANE	COAL	CURL
ADRY	AURA	BEEF	BOSH	CANT	COAT	CURT
ADZE	AUTO	BEEN	BOSK	CAN'T	COAX	CUSP
AEON	AVER	BEER	BOSS	CAPE	COCA	CUSS
AERO	AVID	BEET	BOTH	CARD	COCK	CUTE
AERY	AVIS	BELL	BOTT	CARE	COCO	CYMA
AFAR	AVON	BELT	BOUT	CARK	CODE	CYME
AFFY	AVOW	BEMA	BOWL	CARL	COIF	CYST
AGED	AWAY	BEND	BOZO	CARP	COIL	CZAR
AGES	AWED	BENT	BRAD	CART	COIN	
AGIO	AWRY	BERE	BRAE	CASE	COIR	
AGOG	AXES	BERG	BRAG	CASH	COKE	
AGUE	AXIL	BERM	BRAN	CASK	COLA	**D**
AHOY	AXIS	BEST	BRAT	CAST	COLD	
AIDE	AXLE	BEVY	BRAY	CATE	COLE	DACE
AIRY	AYAH	BIAS	BRED	CAUK	COLT	DADO
AJAR	AYES	BICE	BREW	CAUL	COMA	DAFF
AKEE	AZYM	BIDE	BRIG	CAVE	COMB	DAFT
AKIN		BIER	BRIM	CAVY	COME	DAGO
ALAR		BIFF	BRIO	CEDE	CONE	DAIS
ALAS	**B**	BIGG	BROW	CEIL	CONK	DALE
ALEE		BIKE	BUBO	CELL	CONY	DAME
ALFA	BAAL	BILE	BUCK	CELT	COOK	DAMN
ALLY	BABE	BILK	BUFF	CENT	COON	DAMP
ALMA	BABU	BILL	BUHL	CERE	COOP	DANE
ALMS	BABY	BIND	BULB	CESS	COOT	DANK
ALOE	BACH	BINE	BULK	CHAM	COPE	DARE
ALOW	BACK	BING	BULL	CHAP	COPT	DARK
ALPS	BADE	BIRD	BUMP	CHAR	COPY	DARN
ALSO	BAGS	BISE	BUND	CHAT	CORD	DART
ALTO	BAIL	BISK	BUNG	CHAW	CORE	DASH
ALUM	BAIT	BITE	BUNK	CHAY	CORF	DATA
AMAH	BAKE	BITT	BUNT	CHEF	CORK	DATE
AMBO	BALD	BLAB	BUOY	CHEW	CORM	DAUB
AMEN	BALE	BLAE	BURG	CHIC	CORN	DAUK
AMID	BALK	BLED	BURL	CHID	COSE	DAVY
AMIR	BALL	BLEW	BURN	CHIN	COST	DAWK
AMOK	BALM	BLOB	BURR	CHIP	COSY	DAWN
AMYL	BAND	BLOT	BURY	CHIT	COTE	DAZE
ANAL	BANE	BLOW	BUSH	CHOP	COUP	DEAD
ANEW	BANG	BLUE	BUSK	CHOW	COVE	DEAF
ANNA	BANK	BLUR	BUSS	CHUB	COWS	DEAL
ANON	BANT	BOAR	BUST	CHUM	COZY	DEAN
ANTE	BARB	BOAT	BUSY	CIEL	CRAB	DEAR
ANTI	BARD	BODE	BUTT	CIST	CRAG	DEBT
ANUS	BARE	BODY	BUZZ	CITE	CRAM	DECK

36

DEED	DOSS	EGIS	FEAT	FORD	GHEE	GYVE
DEEM	DOST	EIRE	FEED	FORE	GIBE	
DEEP	DOTE	ELAN	FEEL	FORK	GIFT	**H**
DEER	DOTH	ELMO	FEES	FORM	GILD	
DEFT	DOUR	ELMY	FEET	FORT	GILL	
DEFY	DOUT	ELSE	FELL	FOSS	GILT	HACK
DELF	DOVE	ELUL	FELT	FOUL	GIMP	HADE
DELL	DOWL	EMEU	FEND	FOUR	GINN	HADJ
DELT	DOWN	EMIR	FENT	FOWL	GIRD	HAFT
DEME	DOXY	EMIT	FEOD	FOXY	GIRL	HA'HA
DEMI	DOZE	ENDS	FERN	FRAY	GIRT	HAIL
DEMY	DOZY	ENEW	FETE	FREE	GIST	HAIR
DENE	DRAB	ENID	FEUD	FRET	GIVE	HAKE
DENT	DRAG	ENOW	FIAT	FRIT	GLAD	HALE
DENY	DRAM	ENVY	FIBS	FROG	GLEE	HALF
DERM	DRAT	EPHA	FICO	FROM	GLEN	HALL
DESK	DRAW	EPIC	FIEF	FUEL	GLIB	HALM
DEVA	DRAY	EPOS	FIFE	FULL	GLOW	HALO
DEWY	DREG	ERGO	FIGS	FUME	GLUE	HALT
DHAK	DREW	ERIN	FILE	FUMY	GLUM	HAME
DHAL	DRIP	ERNE	FILL	FUND	GLUT	HAND
DHOW	DROP	EROS	FILM	FUNK	GNAT	HANG
DIAL	DRUB	ERSE	FIND	FURL	GNAW	HANK
DIBS	DRUG	ERST	FINE	FURY	GNOO	HARD
DICE	DRUM	ESPY	FINN	FUSE	GOAD	HARE
DICK	DUAL	ETCH	FIRE	FUSS	GOAL	HARK
DIDO	DUAN	ETNA	FIRM	FUZE	GOAT	HARM
DIED	DUCK	ETUI	FISC	FUZZ	GOBY	HARP
DIEM	DUCT	EVEN	FISH	FYRD	GO BY	HART
DIES	DUDE	EVER	FISK		GOER	HASH
DIET	DUEL	EVIL	FIST		GOLD	HASP
DIKE	DUET	EWER	FITS	**G**	GOLF	HATE
DILL	DUKE	EWES	FIVE		GONE	HATH
DIME	DULL	EXAM	FIZZ	GABY	GONG	HAUL
DINE	DULY	EXIT	FLAG	GAEL	GOOD	HAUM
DING	DUMB	EXON	FLAK	GAFF	GORE	HAVE
DINT	DUMP	EYAS	FLAM	GAGE	GORY	HAWK
DIRE	DUNE	EYED	FLAN	GAIL	GOSH!	HAZE
DIRK	DUNG	EYES	FLAP	GAIN	GOTH	HAZY
DIRT	DUPE	EYOT	FLAT	GAIT	GOUR	HEAD
DISC	DUSK	EYRE	FLAW	GALA	GOUT	HEAL
DISH	DUST	EYRY	FLAX	GALE	GOWK	HEAP
DISK	DUTY		FLAY	GALL	GOWN	HEAR
DISS	DYAD		FLEA	GAME	GRAB	HEAT
DIVA	DYER	**F**	FLED	GAMP	GRAM	HEED
DIVE	DYKE		FLEE	GAMY	GRAY	HEEL
DIXY	DYNE	FACE	FLEW	GANG	GREW	HEFT
DOAB		FACT	FLEX	GOAL	GREY	HEIR
DOCK		FADE	FLIP	GAPE	GRID	HELD
DODO	**E**	FAIL	FLIT	GARB	GRIG	HELL
DOER		FAIN	FLOE	GASH	GRIM	HELM
DOES	EACH	FAIR	FLOG	GASP	GRIN	HELP
DOFF	EARL	FAKE	FLOP	GATE	GRIP	HEMP
DOGE	EARN	FALL	FLOW	GAUD	GRIT	HERB
DOIT	EARS	FAMA	FLUE	GAUL	GROG	HERD
DOLE	EASE	FAME	FLUX	GAUR	GROT	HERE
DOLL	EAST	FANE	FOAL	GAVE	GROW	HERN
DOLT	EASY	FANG	FOAM	GAWD	GRUB	HERO
DOME	EBON	FARE	FOCI	GAWK	GRUM	HERR
DONE	ECHO	FARL	FOES	GAZE	GULF	HERS
DON'T	EDDA	FARM	FOGY	GEAN	GULL	HEST
DOOL	EDDY	FARO	FOIL	GEAR	GULP	HEWN
DOOM	EDEN	FASH	FOIN	GEAT	GURU	HIDE
DOOR	EDGE	FAST	FOLD	GECK	GUSH	HIGH
DOPE	EDGY	FATE	FOLK	GELD	GUST	HILL
DORA	EDIT	FAUN	FOND	GENS	GUTS	HILT
DORP	EELS	FAUX	FONT	GENT	GYAL	HIND
DORR	EFTS	FAWN	FOOD	GERM	GYBE	HINT
DORY	EGAD!	FAYS	FOOL	GEST	GYRE	HIRE
DOSE	EGGS	FEAR	FOOT	GHAT	GYRI	HISS

HIST	IRON	KICK	LEER	LORE	MEAT	MUSK
HIVE	ISIS	KILL	LEES	LORN	MEED	MUST
HOAR	ISLE	KILN	LEFT	LORY	MEEK	MUTE
HOAX	ITCH	KILT	LEND	LOSE	MEET	MYTH
HOCK	ITEM	KIND	LENO	LOSS	MELT	
HOLD		KINE	LENS	LOST	MEND	
HOLE		KING	LENT	LOTE	MENU	**N**
HOLM	**J**	KINK	LESS	LOTH	MERE	
HOLP		KINO	LEST	LOTO	MERK	NAIF
HOLT	JACK	KIRK	LEVY	LOUD	MESH	NAIL
HOLY	JADE	KISS	LEWD	LOUT	MESS	NAME
HOME	JAIL	KITE	LIAR	LOTS	METE	NAPE
HONE	JAMB	KITH	LIAS	LOVE	MEWL	NARD
HOOD	JAPE	KIWI	LICE	LUCE	MEWS	NAVE
HOOF	JARL	KNAG	LICH	LUCK	MICA	NAVY
HOOK	JAWS	KNAP	LICK	LUFF	MICE	NEAP
HOOP	JAZZ	KNAR	LIDO	LULL	MIEN	NEAR
HOOT	JEAN	KNEE	LIED	LUMP	MIFF	NEAT
HOPE	JEER	KNEW	LIEF	LUNA	MILD	NECK
HOPS	JEHU	KNIT	LIEN	LUNE	MILE	NEED
HORN	JERK	KNOB	LIER	LUNG	MILK	NE'ER
HOSE	JESS	KNOP	LIES	LURE	MILL	NEON
HOST	JEST	KNOT	LIEU	LURK	MILT	NERO
HOUR	JIBE	KNOW	LIFE	LUSH	MIME	NESS
HOVE	JILT	KNUB	LIFT	LUST	MINA	NEST
HOWL	JINN	KOHL	LIKE	LUTE	MIND	NETT
HUED	JOBS	KOLA	LILT	LYNX	MINE	NEWS
HUFF	JOIN	KRIS	LILY	LYRE	MINK	NEWT
HUGE	JOKE		LIMB		MINT	NEXT
HULK	JOLE		LIME		MINX	NICE
HULL	JOLL	**L**	LIMN	**M**	MINY	NICK
HUMP	JOLT		LIMP		MIRE	NIGH
HUNG	JOSS	LACE	LIMY	MA'AM	MIRY	NINE
HUNK	JOVE	LACK	LINE	MACE	MISS	NISI
HUNT	JOWL	LACY	LING	MADE	MIST	NODE
HURL	JUBE	LADE	LINK	MAGE	MITE	NOEL
HURT	JUDY	LADY	LINN	MAGI	MITT	NOME
HUSH	JULY	LAIC	LINO	MAID	MITY	NONE
HUSK	JUMP	LAID	LINT	MAIL	MOAN	NOOK
HYMN	JUNE	LAIN	LIPS	MAIM	MOAT	NOON
	JUNK	LAIR	LION	MAIN	MOCK	NORE
	JUNO	LAKE	LIRA	MAKE	MODE	NORM
I	JURY	LAKH	LIRE	MALE	MOIL	NOSE
	JUST	LAKY	LISP	MALL	MOLD	NOTE
IAMB	JUTE	LAMA	LIST	MALM	MOLE	NOUN
IBEX		LAMB	LITH	MALT	MOLY	NOUS
IBIS		LAME	LIVE	MAMA	MONK	NUDE
ICED		LAMP	LOAD	MANE	MOOD	NULL
ICON	**K**	LAND	LOAF	MANX	MOON	NUMB
IDEA		LANE	LOAM	MANY	MOOR	NUTS
IDEM	KADI	LANK	LOAN	MARE	MOOT	
IDES	KAIL	LARD	LOTH	MARK	MOPE	
IDLE	KAKA	LARK	LOBE	MARL	MORE	**O**
IDLY	KALE	LASH	LOCH	MARS	MORN	
IDOL	KALI	LASS	LOCK	MART	MOSS	OAKS
IDYL	KATE	LAST	LOCI	MASH	MOST	OAKY
IKON	KAVA	LATE	LODE	MASK	MOTE	OARS
ILEX	KEEK	LATH	LOFT	MASS	MOTH	OARY
IMAM	KEEL	LAUD	LOIN	MAST	MOUE	OAST
IMAN	KEEN	LAVA	LOLL	MATE	MOVE	OATH
IMPI	KEEP	LAVE	LONE	MATE	MOYA	OATS
INCA	KELP	LAWN	LONG	MATH	MUCH	OBEY
INCH	KELT	LAZY	LOOK	MATT	MUCK	OBIT
INKY	KENT	LEAD	LOOM	MAUD	MUFF	OBOE
INLY	KEPT	LEAF	LOON	MAUL	MULE	ODDS
INTO	KERB	LEAK	LOOP	MAZE	MULL	ODIC
IONA	KERF	LEAL	LOOT	MAZY	MUMM	ODOR
IOTA	KERN	LEAN	LOPE	MEAD	MUMP	OGEE
IRAN	KEYS	LEAP	LOPS	MEAL	MURK	OGLE
IRIS	KIBE	LEEK	LORD	MEAN	MUSE	OGRE

OGPU	PAUL	POND	RAKE	ROOT	SECT	SLED
OILY	PAVE	PONY	RÂLE	ROPE	SEED	SLEW
OLIO	PAWL	POOH!	RAMP	ROPY	SEEK	SLEY
OLLA	PAWN	POOL	RAND	ROSE	SEEL	SLID
OMEN	PEAK	POOP	RANG	ROSY	SEEM	SLIM
OMIT	PEAL	POOR	RANK	ROTA	SEEN	SLIP
ONCE	PEAR	POPE	RANT	ROTE	SEEP	SLIP
ONER	PEAT	PORE	RAPE	ROUÉ	SEER	SLOE
ONLY	PECK	PORK	RAPT	ROUP	SEIN	SLOP
ONUS	PEEL	PORT	RARE	ROUT	SELF	SLOT
ONYX	PEEN	PORY	RASE	ROVE	SELL	SLOW
OOID	PEEP	POSE	RASH	RUBY	SEMI	SLUB
OOZE	PEER	POST	RASP	RUCK	SEND	SLUE
OOZY	PEKE	POSY	RATE	RUDD	SEPT	SLUG
OPAL	PELF	POUR	RATH	RUDE	SERB	SLUM
OPEN	PELL	POUT	RAVE	RUFF	SERE	SLUR
OPUS	PELT	PRAM	RAZE	RUGA	SERF	SLUT
ORAL	PEND	PRAY	READ	RUIN	SETA	SMEE
ORBY	PENT	PREY	REAL	RULE	SHAD	SMEW
ORGY	PEON	PRIG	REAM	RUMP	SHAG	SMIT
ORTS	PERI	PRIM	REAP	RUNE	SHAH	SMUG
ORYX	PERK	PROA	REAR	RUNG	SHAM	SMUT
OTTO	PERT	PROD	RECK	RUNT	SHAW	SNAG
OUCH	PESO	PROP	REED	RUSE	SHEA	SNAP
OUST	PEST	PROW	REEF	RUSH	SHED	SNIP
OVAL	PHEW!	PUCE	REEK	RUSK	SHEW	SNOB
OVEN	PHIZ	PUCK	REEL	RUSS	SHIN	SNOT
OVER	PICA	PUFF	REIN	RUST	SHIP	SNOW
OVUM	PICE	PUKE	RELY	RUTH	SHOD	SNUB
OWED	PICK	PULE	REND	RYOT	SHOE	SNUG
OWNS	PIED	PULL	RENO		SHOG	SOAK
OXEN	PIER	PULP	RENT		SHOP	SOAP
OYER	PIKE	PUMA	REPP	**S**	SHOT	SOAR
OYES!	PILE	PUMP	REST		SHOW	SOCK
OYEZ!	PILL	PUNK	RHEA	SACK	SHUN	SODA
	PIMP	PUNT	RICE	SAFE	SHUT	SOFA
	PINE	PUNY	RICH	SAGA	SICE	SOFT
P	PING	PUPA	RICK	SAGE	SICK	SOHO
	PINK	PURE	RIDE	SAGO	SIDE	SOIL
PACA	PINT	PURL	RIFE	SAID	SIFT	SOLD
PACE	PINY	PURR	RIFT	SAIL	SIGH	SOLE
PACK	PIPE	PUSH	RILL	SAKE	SIGN	SOLI
PACO	PIPY	PUSS	RIME	SALE	SIKH	SOLO
PACT	PISÉ	PUTT	RIMY	SALT	SILK	SOMA
PAGE	PISH!	PYRE	RIND	SAME	SILL	SOME
PAID	PISS		RING	SAMP	SILO	SONG
PAIL	PITH		RINK	SAND	SILT	SOON
PAIN	PITY	**Q**	RIOT	SANE	SINE	SOOT
PAIR	PIXY		RIPE	SANK	SING	SOPH
PALE	PLAN	QUAD	RIPT	SANS	SINK	SORB
PALI	PLAT	QUAG	RISE	SARD	SIRE	SORE
PALL	PLAY	QUAY	RISK	SARK	SIST	SORN
PALM	PLEA	QUID	RITE	SASH	SITE	SORT
PALP	PLIM	QUIP	RIVE	SATE	SIZE	SO-SO
PALT	PLOD	QUIT	ROAD	SAVE	SIZY	SOUL
PALY	PLOP	QUIZ	ROAM	SCAB	SKEW	SOUͰ
PANE	PLOT		ROAN	SCAD	SKID	SOUR
PANG	PLOW		ROAR	SCAN	SKIM	SOYA
PANT	PLUG	**R**	ROBE	SCAR	SKIN	SPAN
PAPA	PLUM		ROCK	SCAT	SKIP	SPAR
PARA	PLUS	RACE	RODE	SCOT	SKIT	SPAT
PARD	POCK	RACK	ROIL	SCOW	SKUA	SPAY
PARE	POEM	RACY	ROLE	SCUD	SKYE	SPEC
PARK	POET	RAFF	ROLL	SCUM	SLAB	SPED
PARR	POKE	RAFT	ROME	SCUT	SLAG	SPEW
PART	POLE	RAGE	ROMP	SCYE	SLAM	SPIN
PASS	POLL	RAHU	ROOD	SEAL	SLAP	SPIR
PAST	POLO	RAID	ROOF	SEAM	SLAT	SPIT
PATE	POME	RAIL	ROOK	SEAR	SLAV	SPOT
PATH	POMP	RAIN	ROOM	SEAT	SLAY	SPRY

SPUD	TALL	TINT	TUSH	VERB	WAXY	WOMB
SPUE	TAME	TINY	TUSK	VERT	WEAK	WON'T
SPUN	TAMP	TIRE	'TWAS	VERY	WEAL	WONT
SPUR	TANG	TIRO	TWIG	VEST	WEAN	WOOD
STAB	TANK	TOAD	TWIN	VETO	WEAR	WOOF
STAG	TAPE	TO-DO	TWIT	VIAL	WEED	WOOL
STAR	TARE	TOED	TYPE	VICE	WEEK	WORD
STAY	TARN	TOFT	TYRE	VIDE	WEEN	WORE
STEM	TARO	TOGA	TYRO	VIEW	WEEP	WORK
STEP	TART	TOIL	TZAR	VILE	WEFT	WORM
STET	TASK	TOLD		VILL	WEIR	WORN
STEW	TASS	TOLL		VINE	WELD	WORT
STIR	TA-TA	TOLU	**U**	VINY	WELL	WOVE
STOA	TAUT	TOMB		VIOL	WELT	WRAP
STOP	TAXI	TOME	UGLY	VISE	WEND	WREN
STOW	TEAK	TONE	ULAN	VISE	WENT	WRIT
STUB	TEAL	TONG	ULNA	VIVA	WEPT	WYCH
STUD	TEAM	TONY	UMBO	VLEI	WERE	
STUN	TEAR	TOOK	UNDO	VLEY	WERT	
STYE	TEAT	TOOL	UNIT	VOCE	WEST	**Y**
SUCH	TEEM	TOOT	UNTO	VOID	WHAT	
SUCK	TEEN	TOPE	UPAS	VOLE	WHEN	YARD
SUDS	TEIL	TORE	UPON	VOLT	WHET	YARE
SUER	TELL	TORN	URDU	VOTE	WHEW!	YARN
SUET	TEMS	TORT	UREA		WHEY	YAWL
SUEZ	TEND	TORI	URGE		WHIG	YAWN
SUIT	TENE	TORY	URIC	**W**	WHIM	YAWS
SULK	TENT	TOSS	URIM		WHIN	YEAN
SUMP	TERM	TOUR	URSA	WADD	WHIP	YEAR
SUNG	TERN	TOUT	URUS	WADE	WHIR	YELK
SUNK	TEST	TOWN	USED	WADI	WHIT	YELL
SUNN	TEXT	TRAM	USER	WADY	WHIZ	YELP
SURD	THAN	TRAP	UTAH	WAFT	WHOA!	YOKE
SURE	THAT	TRAY	UVEA	WAGE	WHOP	YOLK
SURF	THAW	TREE		WAIF	WHOM	YORE
SWAB	THEE	TREK		WAIL	WICK	YOUR
SWAG	THEM	TRET	**V**	WAIN	WIDE	YOWL
SWAM	THEN	TRIG		WAIT	WIFE	YULE
SWAN	THEW	TRIM	VAIL	WAKE	WILD	YO-YO
SWAP	THEY	TRIO	VAIN	WALE	WILE	Y-WIS
SWAY	THIN	TRIP	IVAN	WALK	WILL	
SWIG	THIS	TROD	VAIR	WALL	WILT	
SWIM	THOU	TROT	VALE	WAND	WILY	**Z**
SWOP	THRO'	TROW	VAMP	WANE	WIND	
SWUM	THUD	TROY	VANE	WANT	WINE	ZANY
	THUG	TRUE	VARY	WARD	WING	ZEAL
	THUS	TSAR	VASE	WARE	WINK	ZEBU
T	TIED	TUBA	VAST	WARM	WINY	ZEND
	TICK	TUBE	VEAL	WARN	WIPE	ZERO
TACH	TIDE	TUCK	VEDA	WARP	WIRE	ZEST
TACK	TIDY	TUFA	VEER	WART	WIRY	ZEUS
TACT	TIER	TUFF	VEGA	WARY	WISE	ZINC
TAEL	TIFF	TUFT	VEIL	WASH	WISH	ZION
TA'EN	TIKE	TUNA	VEIN	WASP	WISP	ZOEA
TAIL	TILE	TUNE	VELD	WAST	WITH	ZONE
TAKE	TILL	TURF	VELA	WATT	WIVE	ZOON
TALC	TILT	TURK	VENA	WAUL	WOAD	ZULU
TALE	TIME	TURN	VEND	WAVE	WOLD	
TALK	TINE	TUSH!	VENT	WAVY	WOLF	

FIVE-LETTER WORDS

A	AGAVE	AMISS	ARMOR	B	BEDEW
	AGENT	AMITY	ARNEE		BEDIM
	AGILE	AMMON	AROMA		BEECH
ABACA	AGIST	AMONG	AROSE	BABEL	BEEFY
ABACK	AGLET	AMORT	ARRAN	BABOO	BEERY
ABAOI	AGNEL	AMOUR	ARRAS	BACON	BEFAL
ABAFT	AGNUS	AMPLE	ARRAY	BADGE	BEFIT
ABASE	AGONY	AMPLY	ARRIS	BADLY	BEFOG
ABASH	AGORA	AMUCK	ARROW	BAGGY	BEGAN
ABATE	AGREE	AMUSE	ARSIS	BAIRN	BEGET
ABBEY	AGRIN	ANCLE	ARSON	BAIZE	BEGIN
ABBOT	AGUED	ANDES	ARYAN	BAKED	BEGUM
ABEAM	AHEAD	ANEAR	ASCUS	BAKER	BEGUN
ABELE	AHEAP	ANELE	ASHEN	BALAS	BEIGE
ABHOR	AIDER	ANENT	ASHES	BALER	BEING
ABIDE	AIRED	ANGEL	ASIAN	BALMY	BELAY
ABIES	AISLE	ANGER	ASIDE	BANAL	BELCH
ABODE	AITCH	ANGLE	ASKED	BANCO	BELIE
ABORT	ALACK!	ANGLO	ASKER	BANDY	BELLE
ABOUT	ALARM	ANGRY	ASKEW	BANJO	BELLY
ABOVE	ALATE	ANILE	ASPEN	BANKS	BELOW
ABUSE	ALBUM	ANIME	ASPIC	BANNS	BENCH
ABYSM	ALDER	ANISE	ASSAY	BARBS	BENNE
ABYSS	ALERT	ANKER	ASSES	BARED	BERME
ACERB	ALGAL	ANKLE	ASSET	BARGE	BERRY
ACHED	ALGID	ANNEX	ASTER	BARIC	BERTH
ACHOR	ALGUM	ANNOY	ASTIR	BARKY	BERYL
ACORN	ALIAS	ANNUL	ASTRA	BARMY	BESET
ACRED	ALIBI	ANODE	ATAXY	BARON	BESOM
ACRID	ALIEN	ANTIC	ATILT	BASAL	BESOT
ACTED	ALIGN	ANTRE	ATLAS	BASED	BETEL
ACTON	ALIKE	ANURA	ATOLL	BASEL	BETON
ACTOR	ALIVE	ANVIL	ATONE	BASES	BETLE
ACUTE	ALLAH	AORTA	ATONY	BASIC	BEVEL
ADAGE	ALLAY	APACE	ATRIP	BASIL	BEZEL
ADOPT	ALLEY	APART	ATTAR	BASIN	BHANG
ADAYS	ALLOT	APEAK	ATTIC	BASIS	BIBLE
ADDAX	ALLOW	APERY	AUDIT	BASON	BIDET
ADDED	ALLOY	APHIS	AUGER	BASSE	BIFID
ADDER	ALMUG	APING	AUGHT	BASSO	BIGHT
ADDLE	ALOES	APISH	AUGUR	BASTA	BIGLY
ADEPT	ALOFT	APPAL	AULIC	BASTE	BIGOT
ADIEU	ALONE	APPLE	AURAL	BATCH	BIJOU
ADMIT	ALONG	APPLY	AURIC	BATED	BILBO
ADMIX	ALOOF	APPUI	AVAIL	BATHE	BILGE
ADOBE	ALOUD	APRIL	AVAST	BATON	BINGE
ADOPT	ALPHA	APRON	AVENS	BATTA	BIPED
ADORE	ALTAR	APSIS	AVERT	BATTY	BIRCH
ADORN	ALTER	APTLY	AVION	BAULK	BIRTH
ADOWN	ALULA	ARACK	AVOID	BAVIN	BISON
ADSUM	ALWAY	ARBOR	AWAIT	BAWDY	BITCH
ADULT	AMAIN	AREAS	AWAKE	BAYED	BITER
ADUST	AMASS	ARECA	AWARD	BAZAR	BLACK
AEGIS	AMATE	ARENA	AWARE	BEACH	BLADE
AERIE	AMAZE	ARGIL	AWASH	BEADS	BLAIN
AESOP	AMBER	ARGOL	AWFUL	BEADY	BLAME
AFFIX	AMBIT	ARGON	AWNED	BE-ALL	BLAND
AFOOT	AMBLE	ARGOT	AWNER	BEAMY	BLANK
AFORE	AMBON	ARGUE	AXIAL	BEANO	BLARE
AFRIT	AMBRY	ARGUS	AXILE	BEARD	BLASE
AFTER	AMEER	ARIAN	AXIOM	BEAST	BLAST
AGAIN	AMEND	ARIEL	AXLED	BEAUS	BLAZE
AGAMI	AMENT	ARIES	AZOTE	BEAUX	BLEAK
AGAPE	AMICE	ARISE	AZURE	BEDAD!	BLEAR
AGATE	AMIDE	ARMED		BEDEL	BLEAT

BLEED	BOWEL	BULKY	CARGO	CHINK	COACT
BLEND	BOWER	BULLA	CARIB	CHIRK	COALY
BLESS	BOWIE	BULLY	CARLE	CHIRM	COAST
BLEST	BOXEN	BULSE	CAROB	CHIRP	COATI
BLIND	BOXER	BUNCH	CAROL	CHIVE	COBLE
BLINK	BOYAR	BUNNY	CAROM	CHODE	COBRA
BLISS	BRACE	BURGH	CARRY	CHOIR	COCOA
BLITE	BRACH	BURIN	CARSE	CHOKE	CODEX
BLITZ	BRACT	BURKE	CARTE	CHOKY	COIGN
BLOAT	BRAID	BURLY	CARUS	CHORD	COLIC
BLOBS	BRAIL	BURNT	CARVE	CHOSE	COLLY
BLOCK	BRAIN	BURRY	CASTE	CHUCK	COLON
BLOKE	BRAKE	BURSA	CATCH	CHUFF	COLOR
BLOND	BRAKY	BURSE	CATER	CHUMP	COLZA
BLOOD	BRAND	BURST	CATES	CHUNK	COMER
BLOOM	BRANK	BUSES	CATTY	CHURL	COMET
BLOWN	BRANT	BUSBY	CAULK	CHURN	COMIC
BLOWS	BRASH	BUSHY	CAUSE	CHUSE	COMMA
BLOWY	BRASS	BUSSU	CAVIL	CHUTE	CONCH
BLUES	BRAVE	BUTTE	CAVIN	CHYLE	CONEY
BLUFF	BRAVO	BUTTY	CEASE	CHYME	CONGE
BLUNT	BRAWL	BUXOM	CEDAR	CIBOL	CONIC
BLURS	BRAWN	BUYER	CELTS	CIDER	COOEE
BLURT	BRAXY	BY-END	CENSE	CIGAR	COOIE
BLUSH	BRAZE	BY-LAW	CENTO	CILIA	COOMB
BOARD	BREAD	BYSSI	CEORL	CINCH	CO-OPT
BOAST	BREAK	BY-WAY	CHACO	CIPPI	COPAL
BODLE	BREAM		CHAFE	CIRRI	COPED
BOGEY	BREED		CHAFF	CIVET	COPRA
BOGGY	BRENT	**C**	CHAIN	CIVIC	COPSE
BOGIE	BREVE		CHAIR	CIVIL	COPSY
BOGLE	BRIAR	CAABA	CHALK	CLACK	CORAL
BOGUS	BRIBE	CABAL	CHAMP	CLAIM	CORKY
BOHEA	BRICK	CABAS	CHANK	CLAMP	CORNY
BOIAR	BRIDE	CABBY	CHANT	CLANG	CORPS
BOLAR	BRIEF	CABER	CHAOS	CLANK	CORSE
BOLAS	BRIER	CABIN	CHAPE	CLARY	CORVE
BOLUS	BRILL	CABLE	CHAPT	CLASH	COSEN
BONED	BRINE	CABOB	CHARD	CLASP	COSEY
BONNE	BRING	CACAO	CHARE	CLASS	COUCH
BONNY	BRINK	CACHE	CHARM	CLAVE	COUGH
BONUS	BRINY	CACTI	CHARR	CLEAN	COULD
BONCE	BRISE	CADDY	CHART	CLEAR	COUNT
BOOBY	BRISK	CADET	CHARY	CLEAT	COUPE
BOOKS	BRIZE	CADGE	CHASE	CLEEK	COURT
BOOSE	BROAD	CADRE	CHASM	CLEFT	COVED
BOOSY	BROCK	CAECA	CHAYA	CLEPE	COVER
BOOTH	BROIL	CAIRN	CHEAP	CLERK	COVET
BOOTS	BROKE	CAIRO	CHEAT	CLICK	COVEY
BOOTY	BROME	CALID	CHECK	CLIFF	COVIN
BOOZE	BROOD	CALIF	CHEEK	CLIMB	COWER
BOOZY	BROOK	CALVE	CHEEP	CLIME	COWRY
BORAX	BROOM	CALYX	CHEER	CLING	COYLY
BORED	BROSE	CAMEL	CHELA	CLINK	COYPU
BORER	BROTH	CAMEO	CHERT	CLOAK	COZEN
BORIC	BROWN	CANAL	CHESS	CLOCK	CRACK
BORNE	BRUIN	CANDY	CHEST	CLOFF	CRAFT
BORON	BRUIT	CANNY	CHIAN	CLOKE	CRAKE
BOSKY	BRUNT	CANOE	CHICA	CLOMB	CRAMP
BOSOM	BRUSH	CANON	CHICH	CLOSE	CRANE
BOSSY	BRUTE	CANTO	CHICK	CLOTH	CRANK
BOTCH	BUDGE	CANTY	CHICO	CLOUD	CRAPE
BOTHY	BUFFO	CAPER	CHIDE	CLOUT	CRASH
BOUGH	BUFFY	CAPON	CHIEF	CLOVE	CRASS
BOUND	BUGGY	CAPOT	CHILD	CLOWN	CRATE
BOURG	BUGLE	CARAP	CHILL	CLUBS	CRAVE
BOURN	BUILD	CARAT	CHIMB	CLUCK	CRAWL
BOUSE	BUILT	CARED	CHIME	CLUMP	CRAZE
BOUTS	BULGE	CARET	CHINA	CLUNG	CRAZY
BOWED	BULGY	CAREX	CHINE	COACH	CREAK

CREAM		DIRTY	DRYAD	EMBAY	EXTRA
CREDO	**D**	DITCH	DRYER	EMBED	EXUDE
CREED		DITTO	DRYLY	EMBER	EXULT
CREEK	DADDY	DITTY	DUCAL	EMEND	EYRIE
CREEL	DAILY	DIVAN	DUCAT	EMERY	
CREEP	DAIRY	DIVER	DUCHY	EMMET	
CREPE	DAISY	DIXIE	DULLY	EMPTY	**F**
CREPT	DALLY	DIZEN	DULSE	ENACT	
CRESS	DAMAN	DIZZY	DUMMY	ENDER	FABLE
CREST	DAMAR	DOCKS	DUMPY	ENDOW	FACED
CRICK	DANCE	DODGE	DUNCE	ENDUE	FACER
CRIED	DANDY	DOGAL	DUPER	ENEMA	FACET
CRIER	DARIC	DOGGO	DUPLE	ENEMY	FADDY
CRIME	DARKY	DOGMA	DURRA	ENJOY	FADGE
CRIMP	DATUM	DOILY	DURST	ENNUI	FAERY
CRISP	DAUBY	DOING	DUSKY	ENROL	FAGOT
CROAK	DAUNT	DONNA	DUSTY	ENTIA	FAINT
CROCK	DAVIT	DONOR	DUTCH	ENSKY	FAIRY
CROFT	DAZED	DOOLY	DWALE	ENSUE	FAITH
CRONE	DEARY	DORIC	DWARF	ENTER	FAKIR
CRONY	DEATH	DORSE	DWELL	ENTRY	FALSE
CROOK	DEBAR	DOTAL	DYING	ENURE	FAMED
CROON	DEBIT	DOTER		ENVOY	FANCY
CRORE	DEBUT	DOTTY		EOLIC	FARAD
CROSS	DECAD	DOUBT	**E**	EPACT	FARCE
CROUP	DECAY	DOUGH		EPHAH	FARCY
CROWD	DECOY	DOUSE	EAGER	EPHOD	FATAL
CROWN	DECRY	DOWDY	EAGLE	EPHOR	FATED
CRUDE	DEDAL	DOWEL	EAGRE	EPOCH	FATLY
CRUEL	DEFER	DOWER	EARED	EPODE	FATTY
CRUET	DEIFY	DOWLE	EARLY	EPSOM	FAUGH
CRUMB	DEIGN	DOWNY	EARTH	EQUAL	FAULT
CRUMP	DEISM	DOWRY	EASEL	EQUIP	FAUNA
CRUSE	DEIST	DOWSE	EATER	ERASE	FAVOR
CRUSH	DEITY	DOZEN	EAVES	ERATO	FAVUS
CRUST	DELAY	DOZER	EBLIS	ERECT	FEAST
CRWTH	DELFT	DRAFF	EBONY	ERGOT	FEAZE
CRYER	DELTA	DRAFT	ECLAT	ERICA	FECAL
CRYPT	DELVE	DRAIN	EDEMA	ERODE	FECES
CUBEB	DEMED	DRAKE	EDGED	EROSE	FEIGN
CUBIC	DEMIT	DRAMA	EDICT	ERRED	FEINT
CUBIT	DEMON	DRANK	EDIFY	ERROR	FELLY
CUDDY	DEMOS	DRAPE	EDILE	ERUCT	FELON
CUISH	DEMUR	DRAVE	EDUCE	ERUPT	FEMUR
CULCH	DENSE	DRAWL	EDUCT	ESKAR	FENCE
CULLY	DEPOT	DRAWN	EERIE	ESKER	FENNY
CUMIN	DEPTH	DREAD	EGEST	ESSAY	FEOFF
CUPEL	DERBY	DREAM	EGGER	ESTOP	FERAE
CUPID	DERMA	DREAR	EGRET	ETERN	FERAL
CURDY	DETER	DREGS	EIDER	ETHER	FERNY
CURER	DEUCE	DRESS	EIGHT	ETHIC	FERRY
CURIA	DEVIL	DREST	EIKON	ETHOS	FESSE
CURIO	DHOLE	DRIER	EJECT	ETHYL	FETAL
CURLY	DIANA	DRIFT	ELAND	ETWEE	FETCH
CURRY	DAIRY	DRILL	ELATE	EUCRE	FETED
CURSE	DICED	DRILY	ELBOW	EVADE	FETID
CURST	DICER	DRINK	ELDER	EVENS	FETOR
CURVE	DICKY	DRIVE	ELECT	EVENT	FETUS
CUTCH	DICTA	DROIT	ELEGY	EVERY	FEVER
CUTIS	DIDST	DROLL	ELEMI	EVICT	FEWER
CYCAD	DIGHT	DRONE	ELFIN	EVOKE	FIBRE
CYCLE	DIGIT	DROOP	ELIDE	EXACT	FICHU
CYDER	DIGYN	DROPS	ELITE	EXALT	FIELD
CYMAR	DIKED	DROSS	ELMEN	EXCEL	FIEND
CYNIC	DILLY	DROVE	ELOGE	EXEAT	FIERY
CZECH	DIMLY	DROWN	ELOGY	EXERT	FIFER
	DINER	DRUID	ELOPE	EXILE	FIFTH
	DINGO	DRUNK	ELUDE	EXIST	FIFTY
	DINGY	DRUPE	ELVAN	EXPEL	FIGHT
	DIRGE	DRUSE	ELVES	EXTOL	FILCH

FILER	FORAY	GAMMA	GODLY	GUISE	HILAR
FILLY	FORCE	GAMUT	GOING	GULAR	HILLY
FILMY	FORDO	GAPER	GOODS	GULCH	HILUM
FILTH	FORGE	GARTH	GOODY	GULES	HINDU
FINAL	FORGO	GASSY	GOOSE	GULLY	HINGE
FINCH	FORKY	GATED	GORGE	GUMMY	HINNY
FINER	FORME	GAUDY	GORSE	GUNNY	HIRED
FINIS	FORTE	GAUGE	GORSY	GUSTO	HIRER
FINNY	FORTH	GAULT	GOUDA	GUSTY	HITCH
FIORD	FORTY	GAUNT	GOUGE	GUTTA	HIVES
FIRER	FORUM	GAUZE	GOURD	GYPSY	HOARD
FIRRY	FOSSA	GAUZY	GOUTY	GYRAL	HOARY
FIRST	FOSSE	GAWKY	GOWAN	GYRUS	HOBBY
FIRTH	FOUND	GAYAL	GRAAL		HOCUS
FISHY	FOUNT	GAYLY	GRACE		HODGE
FISTY	FRAIL	GAZEL	GRADE	**H**	HOIST
FITCH	FRAME	GAZER	GRAFF		HOLLA!
FITLY	FRANC	GECKO	GRAFT	HABIT	HOLLO!
FIVES	FRANK	GEESE	GRAIL	HADES	HOLLY
FIXED	FRANK	GELID	GRAIN	HAILY	HOMER
FJORD	FRAUD	GEMMA	GRAIP	HAIRY	HONEY
FLAIL	FREAK	GEMMY	GRAND	HAKIM	HONOR
FLAKE	FREED	GENET	GRANT	HALLO!	HOOFS
FLAKY	FREER	GENIE	GRAPE	HALMA	HOOKY
FLAME	FRESH	GENII	GRAPY	HALOS	HOPPY
FLAMY	FRIAR	GENRE	GRASP	HALVE	HORAL
FLANK	FRIED	GENUS	GRASS	HANCH	HORDE
FLARE	FRILL	GET-UP	GRATE	HANDY	HORNY
FLASH	FRISK	GHAUT	GRAVE	HAPLY	HORSE
FLASK	FRITH	GHOST	GRAVY	HAPPY	HORSY
FLAWY	FRIZZ	GHOUL	GRAZE	HARDS	HORUS
FLAXY	FROCK	GIANT	GREAT	HARDY	HOTEL
FLEAM	FROND	GIBER	GREBE	HAREM	HOTLY
FLECK	FRONT	GIBUS	GREED	HARPY	HOUGH
FLEER	FRORE	GIDDY	GREEK	HARRY	HOUND
FLEET	FROST	GIGOT	GREEN	HARSH	HOURI
FLESH	FROTH	GIPSY	GREET	HARUM	HOUSE
FLICK	FROWN	GIRTH	GRICE	HASTE	HOVEL
FLIER	FRUIT	GIVEN	GRIDE	HASTY	HOVER
FLIES	FRUMP	GIVER	GRIEF	HATCH	HOWEL
FLING	FRUSH	GLADE	GRILL	HATER	HUFFY
FLINT	FUDGE!	GLADY	GRIME	HATTI	HULKY
FLIRT	FUGAL	GLAIR	GRIMY	HAUGH	HULLO!
FLOAT	FUGUE	GLAND	GRIND	HAULM	HULLY
FLOCK	FULLY	GLARE	GRIPE	HAUNT	HUMAN
FLOOD	FUMID	GLASS	GRIST	HAVEN	HUMID
FLOOR	FUNGI	GLAVE	GROAN	HAWSE	HUMOR
FLORA	FUNNY	GLAZE	GROAT	HAZEL	HUMPH!
FLOSS	FUROR	GLEAM	GROIN	HEADY	HUMPY
FLOUR	FURRY	GLEAN	GROOM	HEALD	HUMUS
FLOUT	FURZE	GLEBE	GROPE	HEARD	HUNCH
FLOWN	FURZY	GLEBY	GROSS	HEART	HUNKS
FLUFF	FUSEE	GLEDE	GROUP	HEATH	HURLY
FLUID	FUSEL	GLEED	GROUT	HEAVE	HURRA!
FLUKE	FUSIL	GLEET	GROVE	HEAVY	HURRY
FLUME	FUSSY	GLIDE	GROWL	HEDGE	HURST
FLUNG	FUSTY	GLINT	GROWN	HEIGH!	HUSKY
FLUOR	FUZEE	GLOAT	GRUEL	HELIX	HUSSY
FLUSH	FUZZY	GLOBE	GRUFF	HELLO!	HUTCH
FLUTE		GLOOM	GRUME	HELOT	HUZZA!
FLUTY		GLORY	GRUNT	HELVE	HYADS
FLYER		GLOSS	GUANO	HEMAL	HYDRA
FOAMY	**G**	GLOVE	GUARD	HENCE	HYDRO
FOCAL		GLOZE	GUAVA	HENNA	HYENA
FOCUS	GABEL	GLUEY	GUESS	HERBY	HYMEN
FOGEY	GABLE	GLUME	GUEST	HERON	HYOID
FOGGY	GAILY	GNARL	GUIDE	HERSE	HYRAX
FOIST	GALEA	GNARR	GUILD	HEWER	HYSON
FOLIO	GALOP	GNASH	GUILE	HIDER	
FOLLY	GAMEY	GNOME	GUILT	HIGHT	
	GAMIN				

44

I

IAMBI
ICHOR
ICTUS
IDEAL
IDIOM
IDIOT
IDLER
IDOLA
ILEUM
ILIAC
ILIUM
IMAGE
IMAGO
IMAUM
IMBED
IMBUE
IMPEL
IMPLY
INANE
INAPT
INCOG
INCUR
INCUS
INDEX
INDIA
INDUE
INEPT
INERT
INFER
INFIX
INGOT
INKLE
INLAY
INLET
INNER
INSET
INTER
INURE
INURN
IODIC
IONIC
IRADE
IRATE
IRISH
IRONS
IRONY
ISLAM
ISLET
ISSUE
TCHY
IVIED
IVORY
IXTLE

J

JABOT
JAGGY
JALAP
JAPAN
JASEY
JAUNT
JAWED
JELLY
JEMMY
JENNY

JERID
JERKY
JESUS
JETTY
JEWEL
JEWRY
JIFFY
JIGOT
JINGO
JINKS
JOINT
JOIST
JOKER
JOLLY
JORUM
JOUST
JUDAS
JUDGE
JUICE
JUICY
JULEP
JUMPY
JUNTA
JUNTO
JUROR
JUTTY

K

KAABA
KAFIR
KALIF
KAROB
KAURI
KAYAK
KEDGE
KEEVE
KELPY
KERNE
KETCH
KEYED
KHAKI
KIOSK
KNACK
KNARL
KNAVE
KNEAD
KNEED
KNEEL
KNELL
KNELT
KNIFE
KNOCK
KNOLL
KNOUT
KNOWN
KNUBS
KNURL
KODAK
KORAN
KRAAL
KUDOS

L

LABEL
LABIA
LABOR

LADEN
LADLE
LAGER
LAIRD
LAITY
LAMED
LANCE
LANDE
LANKY
LAPEL
LAPSE
LARCH
LARDY
LARGE
LARGO
LARUM
LARVA
LASSO
LATCH
LATER
LATEX
LATHE
LATHY
LATIN
LAUGH
LAURA
LAVER
LAWNY
LAXLY
LAYER
LAZAR
LEACH
LEADY
LEAFY
LEAKY
LEARN
LEASE
LEASH
LEAST
LEAVE
LEAVY
LEDGE
LEDGY
LEECH
LEGAL
LEGGY
LEMAN
LEMMA
LEMON
LEMUR
LENTO
LEPER
LEPTA
LETCH
LETHE
LEVEE
LEVEL
LEVER
LEVIN
LEWIS
LIANA
LIBEL
LIBER
LIBRA
LICIT
LIEGE
LIEVE
LIGAN
LIGHT
LIKEN

LILAC
LIMBO
LIMIT
LINEN
LINER
LINGO
LINKS
LISLE
LISSE
LISTS
LITHE
LITRE
LIVED
LIVER
LIVES
LIVID
LIVRE
LLAMA
LOACH
LOAMY
LOATH
LOBAR
LOBBY
LOBED
LOCAL
LOCUS
LODGE
LOFTY
LOGAN
LOGIC
LOGOS
LOOBY
LOOFA
LOOSE
LORIS
LORRY
LOSER
LOTAS
LOTTO
LOTUS
LOUSE
LOUSY
LOVER
LOWED
LOWER
LOWLY
LOYAL
LUCID
LUCKY
LUCRE
LUMPY
LUNAR
LUNCH
LUNGE
LUPUS
LURCH
LURID
LUSTY
LYING
LYMPH
LYNCH
LYRIC

M

MACAW
MACER
MACLE
MADAM

MADIA
MADLY
MADRE
MAGIC
MAGMA
MAHDI
MAIZE
MAJOR
MAKER
MALAR
MALAY
MALIC
MAMMA
MANED
MANES
MANGE
MANGO
MANGY
MANIA
MANIS
MANLY
MANNA
MANOR
MANSE
MANUS
MAORI
MAPLE
MARCH
MARGE
MARLY
MARRY
MARSH
MASON
MASSY
MATCH
MATER
MATIN
MATTE
MATTY
MAUND
MAUVE
MAVIS
MAXIM
MAYOR
MAZER
MEALY
MEANS
MEANT
MEASE
MECCA
MEDAL
MEDIA
MEDOC
MÊLÉE
MELON
MERCY
MERGE
MERIT
MERLE
MERRY
MESHY
MESNE
METAL
METER
METRE
MEZZO
MIAUL
MIDGE
MIDST
MIGHT

MILAN
MILCH
MILKY
MIMIC
MINCE
MINER
MINIM
MINOR
MINUS
MIRTH
MISDO
MISER
MISTY
MITER
MITRE
MIXED
MIXEN
MIXER
MIZEN
MODAL
MODEL
MODUS
MOGUL
MOHUR
MOIRE
MOIST
MOLAR
MONAD
MONDE
MONEY
MONTE
MONTH
MOODY
MOONY
MOOSE
MOPER
MORAL
MOREL
MORSE
MOSSY
MOTET
MOTHY
MOTIF
MOTOR
MOTTO
MOULD
MOULT
MOUND
MOUNT
MOURN
MOUSE
MOUTH
MOVER
MOWER
MUCKY
MUCUS
MUDDY
MUFTI
MUGGY
MULCH
MULCT
MULSH
MUMMY
MUMPS
MUNCH
MUNGO
MURAL
MUREX
MURKY
MURRY

MUSER	NONES	ORNIS	PATIN	PLANK	PSHAW
MUSES	NOOSE	ORPIN	PATTY	PLANT	PSOAS
MUSIC	NORSE	ORRIS	PAUSE	PLASH	PSORA
MUSKY	NORTH	OSCAN	PAVER	PLATE	PUBES
MUSTY	NOSED	OSIER	PAVID	PLEAD	PUBIC
MUZZY	NOTCH	OTARY	PAWED	PLICA	PUDGY
MYOPE	NOTED	OTHER	PAYEE	PLUCK	PUFFY
MYOPS	NOVEL	OTTER	PAYER	PLUMB	PUKKA
MYOPY	NOWAY	OUGHT	PEACE	PLUME	PULPY
MYRRH	NOYAU	OUNCE	PEACH	PLUMP	PULSE
	NUDGE	OUSEL	PEAKY	PLUMY	PUNCH
	NURSE	OUTDO	PEARL	PLUSH	PUNIC
N	NUTTY	OUTER	PEASE	PLUTO	PUNKA
	NYLON	OUTGO	PEATY	PLYER	PUPAE
NABOB	NYMPH	OUTRE	PECAN	POACH	PUPAL
NACRE		OUZEL	PEDAL	POCKY	PUPIL
NADIR		OVARY	PEKOE	PODGY	PUPPY
NAIAD		OVATE	PENAL	POESY	PURGE
NAIVE	**O**	OVERT	PENCE	POINT	PURSE
NAKED		OVINE	PENIS	POISE	PURSY
NAMER	OAKEN	OVOID	PENNY	POKER	PUSSY
NANDU	OAKUM	OVOLO	PEONY	POLAR	PUTID
NAPPY	OARED	OVULE	PERCH	POLKA	PUTTY
NASAL	OASIS	OWING	PERDU	POLYP	PYGMY
NASTY	OASES	OWLET	PERIL	POPPY	PYLON
NATAL	OATEN	OWNER	PERKY	PORCH	
NATCH	OATHS	OX-EYE	PERRY	PORER	
NATTY	OBEAH	OXIDE	PETAL	PORES	
NAVAL	OBESE	OXLIP	PETIT	PORGY	**Q**
NAVEL	OCCUR	OZONE	PETTO	PORTE	
NAVEW	OCEAN		PETTY	POSER	QUACK
NAVVY	OCHER		PEWIT	POSIT	QUAFF
NAWAB	OCHRE		PHARO	POSSE	QUAIL
NEEDS	OCHRY	**P**	PHASE	POUCH	QUAKE
NEEDY	OCREA		PHIAL	POULT	QUAKY
NEESE	ODDLY	PACED	PHLOX	POUND	QUALM
NEGRO	ODEON	PACER	PHONE	POWER	QUART
NEGUS	ODEUM	PACHA	PHOTO	PRANK	QUASH
NEIGH	ODIUM	PADDY	PHYLA	PRASE	QUASI
NERVE	ODOUR	PADRE	PIANO	PRATE	QUEAN
NERVY	OFFAL	PAEAN	PICRA	PRAWN	QUEEN
NETTY	OFFER	PAGAN	PICUL	PREEN	QUEER
NEVER	OFTEN	PAINS	PIECE	PRESS	QUELL
NEWEL	OGHAM	PAINT	PIEND	PRICE	QUERN
NEWLY	OGLER	PALEA	PIETY	PRICK	QUERY
NEXUS	OILED	PALMY	PIGMY	PRIDE	QUEST
NICHE	OILER	PALPI	PIKED	PRIER	QUEUE
NIDOR	OLDEN	PALSY	PILAU	PRIMA	QUICK
NIDUS	OLEIC	PANDA	PILAW	PRIME	QUIET
NIECE	OLIVE	PANED	PILCH	PRINK	QUILL
NIGHT	OMBRE	PANEL	PILES	PRINT	QUILT
NINNY	OMEGA	PANIC	PILOT	PRIOR	QUINT
NINON	ONION	PANSY	PINCH	PRISE	QUIRE
NINTH	ONSET	PAPAL	PINEY	PRISM	QUIRK
NIOBE	OOZED	PAPAW	PINNA	PRIVY	QUITE
NISAN	OPERA	PAPER	PIOUS	PRIZE	QUITS
NITRE	OPINE	PAPPY	PIPED	PROBE	QUOIN
NITRY	OPIUM	PARCH	PIPER	PROEM	QUOIT
NIVAL	OPTIC	PARED	PIPIT	PRONE	QUOTA
NIZAM	ORACH	PARER	PIQUE	PRONG	QUOTE
NOBBY	ORANG	PARRY	PITCH	PROOF	QUOTH
NOBLE	ORATE	PARSE	PITHY	PROSE	
NOBLY	ORBED	PARTY	PIVOT	PROSY	
NODAL	ORBIT	PASHA	PIXIE	PROUD	
NODDY	ORDER	PASSE	PLACE	PROVE	**R**
NOILS	OREAD	PASTE	PLACK	PROWL	RABBI
NOISE	ORGAN	PASTY	PLAID	PROXY	RABID
NOISY	ORIEL	PATCH	PLAIN	PRUDE	RACED
NOMAD	ORION	PATED	PLAIT	PRUNE	RACER
NONCE	ORLOP	PATEN	PLANE	PSALM	RADAR
	ORMER	PATHS			RADII

RADIO	RETCH		SCOLD	SHARK	SIREN
RADIX	REVEL	**S**	SCOOP	SHARP	SIRUP
RAGED	REVET		SCOPE	SHAVE	SISAL
RAINY	RHEUM	SABER	SCORE	SHAWL	SITES
RAISE	RHOMB	SABLE	SCORN	SHAWM	SIVAN
RAJAH	RHUMB	SABOT	SCOTS	SHEAF	SIXTH
RAKED	RHYME	SABRE	SCOTT	SHEAL	SIXTY
RAKER	RIANT	SACRE	SCOUR	SHEAR	SIZAR
RALLY	RIDER	SADLY	SCOUT	SHEEN	SIZED
RAMEE	RIDGE	SAHIB	SCOWL	SHEEP	SIZER
RAMIE	RIDGY	SAIGA	SCRAG	SHEER	SIZES
RANCH	RIFLE	SAINT	SCRAM	SHEET	SKAIN
RANGE	RIGHT	SAJOU	SCRAP	SHEIK	SKALD
RAPHE	RIGID	SAKER	SCREW	SHELF	SKATE
RAPID	RIGOR	SAKIA	SCRIP	SHELL	SKEAN
RASPY	RILED	SALAD	SCRUB	SHERD	SKEIN
RATCH	RINSE	SALEP	SCRUM	SHEWN	SKIFF
RATED	RIPEN	SALES	SCUDO	SHIAH	SKILL
RATEL	RISEN	SALIC	SCUDI	SHIFT	SKINK
RATER	RISER	SALIX	SCULK	SHILY	SKIRT
RATHE	RISKY	SALLY	SCULL	SHINE	SKULK
RATIO	RIVAL	SALMI	SCURF	SHINY	SKULL
RATTY	RIVEL	SALON	SCUTE	SHIPS	SKUNK
RAVEL	RIVER	SALOP	SEALS	SHIRE	SKIES
RAVEN	RIVET	SALSE	SEAMY	SHIRK	SKYEY
RAVED	ROACH	SALTS	SEDAN	SHIRT	SLABS
RAVER	ROAST	SALTY	SEDGE	SHIVE	SLACK
RAVIN	ROBIN	SALVE	SEDGY	SHOAL	SLAIN
RAWLY	ROBOT	SALVO	SEEDY	SHOCK	SLAKE
RAYED	ROCKY	SAMBO	SEEMS	SHOES	SLANG
RAYON	RODEO	SANDY	SEINE	SHOON	SLANT
RAZOR	ROGER	SAPAN	SEIZE	SHOER	SLASH
REACH	ROGUE	SAPID	SEMEN	SHONE	SLATE
REACT	ROMAN	SAPOR	SENNA	SHOOK	SLATY
READY	ROMEO	SAPPY	SEÑOR	SHOOT	SLAVE
REALM	RONDO	SASIN	SENSE	SHORE	SLEEK
REAST	ROOKY	SATIN	SEPAL	SHORL	SLEEP
REAVE	ROOMY	SATYR	SEPIA	SHORN	SLEET
REBEC	ROOST	SAUCE	SEPIC	SHORT	SLICE
REBEL	ROOTY	SAUCY	SEPOY	SHOUT	SLIDE
REBUS	ROPER	SAVED	SEPTA	SHOVE	SLILY
REBUT	RORIC	SAVER	SERAI	SHOWN	SLIME
RECTO	ROSIN	SAVIN	SERGE	SHOWY	SLIMY
RECUR	ROTOR	SAVOR	SERIF	SHRED	SLING
REDAN	ROUGE	SAVOY	SERUM	SHREW	SLINK
REDLY	ROUGH	SAWER	SERVE	SHRUB	SLIPS
REEDY	ROUND	SAXON	SETAE	SHRUG	SLOID
REEFY	ROUSE	SAYER	SETON	SHUCK	SLOOP
REEKY	ROUST	SCALA	SET-TO	SHUNT	SLOPE
REEVE	ROUTE	SCALD	SEVEN	SHYLY	SLOPS
REFER	ROVER	SCALE	SEVER	SIBYL	SLOPY
REFIT	ROWAN	SCALL	SEWER	SIDED	SLOTH
REFIX	ROWDY	SCALP	SEXES	SIDER	SLOTS
REGAL	ROWEL	SCALY	SHACK	SIDES	SLOYD
REIGN	ROWER	SCAMP	SHADE	SIDLE	SLUMP
REINS	ROYAL	SCANT	SHADY	SIEGE	SLUNG
RELAX	RUBLE	SCAPA	SHAFT	SIEVE	SLUNK
RELAY	RUCHE	SCAPE	SHAKE	SIGHT	SLUSH
RELET	RUDDY	SCAPI	SHAKO	SILEX	SLYLY
RELIC	RUGAE	SCARE	SHAKY	SILKY	SMACK
RELIT	RULER	SCARP	SHALE	SILLY	SMALL
REMIT	RUMBA	SCART	SHALL	SILTY	SMALT
RENAL	RUMEN	SCATT	SHALM	SILVA	SMART
RENEW	RUMMY	SCAUP	SHALY	SIMAR	SMASH
RENTE	RUNIC	SCAUR	SHAME	SINCE	SMEAR
REPAY	RUPEE	SCENA	SHANK	SINEW	SMELL
REPEL	RURAL	SCENE	SHAN'T	SINGE	SMELT
REPLY	RUSHY	SCENT	SHAPE	SINKS	SMILE
RESET	RUSTY	SCION	SHARD	SINUS	SMIRK
RESIN	RUTTY	SCOFF	SHARE	SIOUX	SMITE

SMITH	SPEAK	STARK	SUGAR	TAKEN	THIEF
SMOCK	SPEAR	STARS	SUINT	TAKER	THIGH
SMOKE	SPECK	START	SUITE	TAKES	THILL
SMOKY	SPECS	STATE	SULCI	TALES	THINE
SMOLT	SPEED	STAVE	SULKS	TALLY	THING
SMOTE	SPELL	STAYS	SULKY	TALON	THINK
SNACK	SPELT	STEAD	SULLY	TALUS	THIRD
SNAIL	SPEND	STEAK	SUMAC	TAMED	THOLE
SNAKE	SPENT	STEAL	SUNNY	TAMER	THONG
SNAKY	SPERM	STEAM	SUPER	TAMIL	THORN
SNARE	SPICE	STEED	SURAH	TAMIS	THORP
SNARL	SPICK	STEEL	SURAL	TAMMY	THOSE
SNARY	SPICY	STEEP	SURFY	TANGO	THOWL
SNEAK	SPIES	STEER	SURGE	TANKS	THREE
SNEER	SPIKE	STELA	SURGY	TANSY	THREW
SNICK	SPIKY	STELE	SURLY	TAPER	THRID
SNIFF	SPILE	STEPS	SWAIN	TAPIR	THROB
SNIPE	SPILL	STERN	SWAMP	TAPIS	THROE
SNOOD	SPILT	STICH	SWANG	TARDY	THROW
SNOOP	SPINE	STICK	SWARD	TARES	THRUM
SNORE	SPINY	STIES	SWARE	TARGE	THUMB
SNORT	SPIRE	STIFF	SWARM	TARRY	THUMP
SNOUT	SPIRT	STILE	SWART	TARSI	THYME
SNOWY	SPIRY	STILL	SWASH	TASKS	THYMY
SNUFF	SPITE	STILT	SWATH	TASSE	TIARA
SOAKY	SPLAY	STING	SWEAR	TASTE	TIBIA
SOAPY	SPLIT	STINK	SWEAT	TASTY	TICKS
SOBER	SPODE	STINT	SWEDE	TAUNT	TIDAL
SOCKS	SPOIL	STIPE	SWEEP	TAWER	TIERS
SOCLE	SPOKE	STOAT	SWEET	TAWNY	TIGER
SODDY	SPOOK	STOCK	SWELL	TAXED	TIGHT
SOFAS	SPOOL	STOIC	SWEPT	TAXER	TILED
SOFTA	SPOON	STOKE	SWIFT	TAZZA	TILER
SOKEN	SPOOR	STOLE	SWILL	TEACH	TILES
SOLAN	SPORE	STOMA	SWINE	TEARS	TILTH
SOLAR	SPORT	STONE	SWING	TEASE	TIMED
SOLES	SPOTS	STONY	SWINK	TECHY	TIMES
SOL-FA	SPOUT	STOOD	SWIPE	TEENS	TIMID
SOLID	SPRAT	STOOK	SWIRL	TEETH	TINCT
SOLON	SPRAY	STOOL	SWISH	TEIND	TINED
SOLOS	SPREE	STOOP	SWISS	TELIC	TINGE
SOLUS	SPRIG	STORE	SWOLN	TEMPO	TINNY
SOLVE	SPRIT	STORK	SWOON	TEMPT	TIPSY
SONGS	SPUME	STORM	SWOOP	TEMSE	TIRES
SOOTH	SPUMY	STORY	SWORD	TENCH	TIROS
SOOTY	SPUNK	STOUP	SWORE	TENDS	TISAN
SOPPY	SPURN	STOUT	SWORN	TENET	TISRI
SORRY	SPURT	STOVE	SWUNG	TENON	TITAN
SORTS	SPUTA	STRAP	SYLPH	TENOR	TITHE
SORUS	SQUAB	STRAW	SYLVA	TENSE	TITLE
SOUGH	SQUAD	STRAY	SYNOD	TENTH	TIZRI
SOULS	SQUAT	STREW	SYRUP	TEPID	TOADY
SOUND	SQUAW	STRIA	SYTHE	TERCE	TOAST
SOUSE	SQUIB	STRIP		TERMS	TO-DAY
SOUTH	SQUID	STROP		TERRA	TODDY
SOWAR	STACK	STROW		TERSE	TOFFY
SOWER	STADE	STRUM	**T**	TESTY	TOILS
SPACE	STAFF	STRUT		THANE	TOISE
SPADE	STAGE	STUCK	TABBY	THANK	TOKAY
SPAIN	STAGY	STUBS	TABES	THAWS	TOKEN
SPAIT	STAID	STUDY	TABID	THECA	TOLLS
SPAKE	STAIN	STUFF	TABLE	THEFT	TOMAN
SPANK	STAIR	STUMP	TABOO	THEGN	TONAL
SPARE	STAKE	STUNG	TABOR	THEIR	TONED
SPARK	STALE	STUNK	TACHE	THEME	TONGA
SPASM	STALK	STUNT	TACKS	THERE	TONGS
SPATE	STALL	STUPE	TACIT	THERM	TONIC
SPATS	STAMP	STYLE	TAFIA	THESE	TONKA
SPAWL	STAND	SUAVE	TAILS	THEWS	TOOLS
SPAWN	STARE	SUETY	TAINT	THICK	TOOTH

TOPAZ	TRYST	UNMEW	VIRUS	WENCH	WORST
TOPER	TUBBY	UNPIN	VISIT	WHACK	WORTH
TOPIC	TUBER	UNSAY	VISOR	WHALE	WOULD
TOPSY	TUDOR	UNSET	VISTA	WHARF	WOUND
TOQUE	TUFTS	UNSEX	VITAL	WHEAL	WRACK
TORCH	TUFTY	UNTIE	VITTA	WHEAT	WRAPT
TORSK	TULIP	UNTIL	VIVID	WHEEL	WRATH
TORSO	TULLE	UNWED	VIXEN	WHELK	WREAK
TORUS	TUMID	UPPER	VIZOR	WHELM	WRECK
TOTAL	TUMOR	UPSET	VOCAL	WHELP	WREST
TOTEM	TUNED	URBAN	VODKA	WHERE	WRING
TOUCH	TUNER	URGES	VOGUE	WHICH	WRIST
TOUGH	TUNIC	URINE	VOICE	WHIFF	WRITE
TOUSE	TUNNY	USAGE	VOMER	WHILE	WRONG
TOWED	TURFS	USHER	VOMIT	WHIMS	WROTE
TOWEL	TURFY	USUAL	VOTER	WHINE	WROTH
TOWER	TURNS	USURP	VOUCH	WHIRL	WRUNG
TOXIC	TURPS	USURY	VOWEL	WHISK	WRYLY
TOXIN	TURVY	UTTER	VULVA	WHIST	
TOYER	TUSKS	UVULA	VYING	WHITE	
TRACE	TUSKY			WHIZZ	**X**
TRACK	TUTOR			WHOLE	
TRACT	TWAIN	**V**	**W**	WHOOP	XEBEC
TRADE	TWANG			WHORE	XYLEM
TRAIL	TWANK	VAGUE	WACKE	WHORL	
TRAIN	TWEAK	VALET	WADDY	WHORT	
TRAIT	TWEED	VALID	WADER	WHOSE	**Y**
TRAMP	TWICE	VALUE	WAFER	WHOSO	
TRAPE	TWILL	VALVE	WAFTS	WIDEN	YACCA
TRAPS	TWINE	VAPID	WAGER	WIDOW	YACHT
TRASH	TWINS	VAPOR	WAGES	WIDTH	YAGER
TRASS	TWIRL	VARIX	WAGON	WIELD	YAHOO
TRAVE	TWIST	VATIC	WAILS	WIGAN	YEARN
TRAWL	'TWIXT	VAULT	WAIST	WIGHT	YEARS
TREAD	TYPIC	VAUNT	WAITS	WILES	YEAST
TREAT	TYROS	VEDIC	WAIVE	WILLY	YEATS
TREND		VEINY	WAKED	WINCE	YIELD
TRESS		VELAR	WAKEN	WINCH	YODEL
TREWS	**U**	VELDT	WAKER	WINDY	YODLE
TRIAD		VELUM	WAKES	WINGS	YOGIN
TRIAL	UDDER	VENAL	WALTZ	WINZE	YOGIS
TRIAS	UHLAN	VENOM	WANLY	WIPED	YOICK
TRIBE	UKASE	VENUE	WARES	WIPER	YOKEL
TRICE	ULCER	VENUS	WARMS	WIRED	YOUNG
TRICK	ULNAR	VERGE	WARNS	WISER	YOURS
TRIED	ULTRA	VERSE	WARPS	WISPY	YOUTH
TRIER	UMBEL	VERSO	WARTY	WITAN	YUCCA
TRILL	UMBER	VERST	WASHY	WITCH	
TRINE	UMBRA	VERTU	WASTE	WITHE	
TRIPE	UNAPT	VERVE	WATCH	WITHY	**Z**
TRITE	UNBAR	VESTA	WATER	WITTY	
TROLL	UNBID	VETCH	WAVED	WIVES	ZAMBO
TROMP	UNCAP	VEXED	WAVER	WIZEN	ZAMIA
TROOP	UNCLE	VEXER	WAVES	WOFUL	ZEBEC
TROPE	UNCUT	VIAND	WAXED	WOMAN	ZEBRA
TROTH	UNDER	VICAR	WAXEN	WOMEN	ZIBET
TROUT	UNDUE	VIEWS	WEALD	WOODS	ZINCO
TRUCE	UNFIT	VIEWY	WEARY	WOODY	ZINKY
TRUCK	UNFIX	VIGIL	WEAVE	WOOER	ZONAL
TRULL	UNHAT	VIGOR	WEBBY	WOOTZ	ZONED
TRULY	UNIFY	VILLA	WEDGE	WORDY	ZOOID
TRUMP	UNION	VILLI	WEEDY	WORKS	ZORIL
TRUNK	UNITE	VIOLA	WEEDS	WORLD	ZYMIC
TRUSS	UNITS	VIPER	WEIGH	WORMY	
TRUST	UNITY	VIRGO	WEIRD	WORRY	
TRUTH	UNMAN	VIRTU	WELSH	WORSE	

SIX-LETTER WORDS

A	ADRIFT	ALGOUS	AORTIC	ASHAME
	ADROIT	ALIGHT	APACHE	ASHLAR
	ADVENE	ALIPED	APATHY	ASHLER
ABACUS	ADVENT	ALKALI	APEPSY	ASHORE
ABASER	ADVERB	ALLEGE	APERCU	ASKANT
ABATED	ADVERT	ALLIED	APEXES	ASLANT
ABATER	ADVICE	ALLIES	APIARY	ASLEEP
ABATIS	ADVISE	ALLUDE	APICAL	ASLOPE
ABBACY	ADYTUM	ALLURE	APICES	ASPECT
ABBESS	AEDILE	ALMOND	APIECE	ASPICK
ABBEYS	AERATE	ALMOST	APLOMB	ASPIRE
ABDUCE	AERIAL	ALPACA	APNOEA	ASSAIL
ABDUCT	AERIFY	ALPINE	APODAL	ASSENT
ABJECT	AEROSE	ALUMNI	APOGEE	ASSERT
ABJURE	AFFAIR	ALVEUS	APPALL	ASSESS
ABLAZE	AFFECT	ALVINE	APPEAL	ASSETS
ABLOOM	AFFEER	ALWAYS	APPEAR	ASSIGN
ABOARD	AFFIRM	AMADOU	APPEND	ASSIST
ABROAD	AFFLUX	AMAZON	APPOINT	ASSIZE
ABOUND	AFFORD	AMBLER	APTOTE	ASSOIL
ABRADE	AFFRAY	AMBLES	ARABIC	ASSORT
ABROAD	AFFUSE	AMBUSH	ARABLE	ASSUME
ABRUPT	AFGHAN	AMENDE	ARBOUR	ASSURE
ABSENT	AFIELD	AMENDS	ARCADE	ASTERN
ABSORB	AFLAME	AMENTA	ARCHED	ASTHMA
ABSURD	AFLOAT	AMERCE	ARCHER	ASTONY
ABUSER	AFRAID	AMIDST	ARCHIL	ASTRAL
ACACIA	AFRESH	AMNION	ARCHLY	ASTRAY
ACAJOU	AFREET	AMOEBA	ARCHON	ASTRUT
ACARUS	AGAMIC	AMORCE	ARCTIC	ASTUTE
ACCEDE	AGARIC	AMORET	ARDENT	ASWARM
ACCENT	AGENCY	AMOUNT	ARDOUR	ASYLUM
ACCEPT	AGENDA	AMPERE	AREOLA	ATAXIA
ACCESS	AGHAST	AMULET	ARGALA	ATOMIC
ACCORD	AGNAIL	AMUSER	ARGALI	ATONED
ACCOST	AGNATE	AMYLIC	ARGENT	ATONIC
ACCRUE	AGOING	ANANAS	ARGIVE	ATRIAL
ACCUSE	AGOUTA	ANARCH	ARGOSY	ATRIUM
ACETIC	AGOUTI	ANCHOR	ARGUER	ATTACH
ACHEAN	AGUISH	ANDEAN	ARGUTE	ATTACK
ACHENE	AIGLET	ANEMIA	ARIGHT	ATTAIN
ACHING	AIGRET	ANERGY	ARMADA	ATTEND
ACQUIT	AIR-BED	ANGINA	ARMFUL	ATTEST
ACROSS	AIR-GAS	ANGLED	ARMLET	ATTIRE
ACTING	AIR-GUN	ANGLER	ARMOUR	ATTORN
ACTION	AIRILY	ANGORA	ARMPIT	ATTUNE
ACTIVE	AIRING	ANIGHT	ARNICA	AUBADE
ACTUAL	AIR-SAC	ANIMAL	AROUND	AUBURN
ACUMEN	AIR-WAY	ANIMUS	AROUSE	AUGEAN
ADAGIO	AISLED	ANKLED	AROINT!	AUGITE
ADAMIC	AKIMBO	ANKLET	AROYNT!	AUGURY
ADDICT	ALALIA	ANNALS	ARRACK	AUGUST
ADDUCE	ALARUM	ANNEAL	ARRANT	AURATE
ADHERE	ALBATA	ANNUAL	ARREAR	AURIGA
ADIEUS	ALBEDO	ANOINT	ARRECT	AURIST
ADIEUX	ALBEIT	ANSWER	ARREST	AURORA
ADIPIC	ALBINO	ANTHEM	ARRIDE	AUTHOR
ADJOIN	ALBITE	ANTHER	ARRIVE	AUTUMN
ADJURE	ALBUGO	ANTIAR	ARROBA	AVANTI
ADJUST	ALCAIC	ANTLER	ARROWY	AVATAR
ADMIRE	ALCOVE	ANTLIA	ARTERY	AVAUNT
ADNATE	ALDERN	ANYHOW	ARTFUL	AVENGE
ADNOUN	ALDINE	ANYWAY	ARTIST	AVENUE
ADONIS	ALEGAR	AORIST	ASCEND	AVERSE
ADORER	ALGINE	AORTAL	ASCENT	AVIARY

AVOCET	BARYTA	BELIAL	BLAMER	BRAISE
AVOSET	BASALT	BELIEF	BLANCH	BRAIZE
AVOUCH	BASELY	BELIKE	BLAZER	BRANCH
AVOWAL	BASHAW	BELLED	BLAZON	BRANDY
AVOWER	BASKET	BELLOW	BLEACH	BRANKS
AWAKEN	BASNET	BELONG	BLENCH	BRANNY
AWAKES	BASQUE	BELTED	BLENDE	BRASSY
AWEARY	BASSET	BELUGA	BLENNY	BRAVOS
AWEIGH	BATEAU	BEMIRE	BLIGHT	BRAWNY
AWHILE	BATHER	BEMOAN	BLITHE	BRAYER
AWNING	BATHOS	BENIGN	BLONDE	BRAZEN
AXILLA	BATIST	BENUMB	BLOODY	BRAZIL
AYE-AYE	BATLET	BERATE	BLOOMY	BREACH
AZALEA	BATMAN	BERBER	BLOTCH	BREAST
AZOTIC	BATOON	BEREFT	BLOUSE	BREATH
	BATTEN	BERLIN	BLOWER	BREECH
	BATTER	BESEEM	BLOWZE	BREEKS
B	BATTLE	BESIDE	BLOWZY	BREEZE
	BATTUE	BESMUT	BLUFFY	BREEZY
BABBLE	BAUBLE	BESPOT	BLUISH	BRETON
BABISH	BAWBLE	BESTIR	BOBBIN	BREVET
BABOON	BAWDRY	BESTOW	BOB-WIG	BREWER
BABIES	BAYARD	BESTUD	BODICE	BRIARY
BACKER	BAY-RUM	BETAKE	BODIED	BRIBER
BADGER	BAZAAR	BETIDE	BODILY	BRIBES
BAFFLE	BEACON	BETONY	BODKIN	BRICKY
BAGMAN	BEADED	BETOOK	BOGGLE	BRIDAL
BAGNIO	BEADLE	BETRAY	BOILER	BRIDGE
BAG-WIG	BEAGLE	BETTER	BOLARY	BRIDLE
BAILIE	BEAKED	BETTOR	BOLDLY	BRIERY
BAKERY	BEAKER	BEWAIL	BOLERO	BRIGHT
BAKING	BEARER	BEWARE	BOLIDE	BRIONY
BALATA	BEATER	BEWEEP	BOLTER	BRITON
BALDLY	BEAUTY	BEWRAY	BON-BON	BROACH
BALEEN	BEAVER	BEYOND	BONDED	BROGUE
BALKAN	BECALM	BEZANT	BONDER	BROKEN
BALLAD	BECAME	BEZOAR	BONITO	BROKER
BALLET	BECKON	BIASED	BON-MOT	BROMIC
BALLOT	BECOME	BIASES	BONNET	BRONZE
BALSAM	BEDAUB	BIAXAL	BON-TON	BROOCH
BAMBOO	BEDECK	BIBBER	BOOTED	BROODY
BANANA	BEDELL	BICEPS	BOOTES	BROOMY
BANDED	BEDLAM	BICKER	BORAGE	BROWSE
BANDIT	BEDRID	BICORN	BORATE	BRUISE
BANDOG	BEDROP	BIDDER	BORDER	BRUMAL
BANGLE	BEECHY	BIDERY	BOREAL	BRUSHY
BANIAN	BEETLE	BIFFIN	BORROW	BRYONY
BANISH	BEEVES	BIFOLD	BOTANY	BUBBLE
BANKER	BEFALL	BIFORM	BOTCHY	BUBBLY
BANNER	BEFELL	BIGAMY	BOT-FLY	BUBOES
BANTAM	BEFOOL	BIGGIN	BOTHER	BUCCAL
BANTER	BEFORE	BIJOUX	BOTHIE	BUCKER
BANYAN	BEFOUL	BILLED	BOTTLE	BUCKLE
BAOBAB	BEGGAR	BILLET	BOTTOM	BUCKRA
BARBED	BEGIRD	BILLON	BOUGHT	BUDDLE
BARBEL	BEGONE	BILLOW	BOUGIE	BUDGET
BARBER	BEHALF	BIMANA	BOUNCE	BUDLET
BARBET	BEHAVE	BINARY	BOUNTY	BUFFER
BARDIC	BEHEAD	BINATE	BOURNE	BUFFET
BAREGE	BEHEST	BINDER	BOURSE	BUGLER
BARELY	BEHIND	BIOTIC	BOVINE	BULBED
BARGEE	BEHOLD	BIREME	BOWERY	BULBEL
BARIUM	BEHOOF	BISECT	BOWLER	BULBUL
BARLEY	BEHOVE	BISHOP	BOWMAN	BULIMY
BARONY	BEIRAM	BISQUE	BOWMEN	BULLET
BARQUE	BELACE	BISSON	BOW-SAW	BUMPER
BARREL	BELATE	BISTRE	BOWYER	BUNCHY
BARREN	BELAUD	BITING	BOXING	BUNDLE
BARROW	BELDAM	BITTER	BOYISH	BUNGLE
BARTER	BELFRY	BLADED	BRAINS	

BUNION	CALKIN	CASERN	CHANCE	CITRON
BUNKER	CALLER	CASHEW	CHANGE	CIVICS
BUNKUM	CALLET	CASING	CHAPEL	CIVISM
BUNYON	CALLOW	CASINO	CHAPPY	CLAMMY
BURBOT	CALLUS	CASKET	CHARGE	CLAMOR
BURDEN	CALMER	CASQUE	CHARRY	CLAQUE
BUREAU	CALMLY	CASSIA	CHASER	CLARET
BURGEE	CALMUC	CASTER	CHASTE	CLAUSE
BURGLE	CALQUE	CASTLE	CHATTY	CLAWED
BURGOO	CALXES	CASTOR	CHEERY	CLAYEY
BURIAL	CAMBER	CASUAL	CHEESE	CLEANS
BURIED	CAMERA	CATSUP	CHEESY	CLEAVE
BURLAP	CAMLET	CATENA	CHELAE	CLENCH
BURNER	CANAAN	CATGUT	CHEMIC	CLERGY
BURNET	CANARD	CATHAY	CHEQUE	CLERIC
BURROW	CANARY	CATKIN	CHERRY	CLEVER
BURSAR	CANCAN	CAT-LAP	CHERTY	CLICHE
BURTON	CANCEL	CATNIP	CHERUB	CLIENT
BUSHEL	CANCER	CATTLE	CHETAH	CLIFFY
BUSILY	CANDID	CAUCUS	CHEVIN	CLIMAX
BUSKIN	CANDLE	CAUDAL	CHIGOE	CLINCH
BUSSED	CANDOR	CAUDEX	CHIGRE	CLINGY
BUSTLE	CANINE	CAUDLE	CHILDE	CLINIC
BUTLER	CANING	CAUGHT	CHILLI	CLIQUE
BUTTER	CANKER	CAUKER	CHILLY	CLOACA
BUTTON	CANNON	CAULIS	CHINCH	CLODDY
BUZZER	CANNOT	CAUSAL	CHINED	CLOGGY
BY-BLOW	CANNIE	CAUSER	CHINKY	CLONIC
BY-GONE	CANOPY	CAUSEY	CHINTZ	CLOSER
BY-LANE	CANTAB	CAUTEL	CHIPPY	CLOSET
BY-NAME	CANTER	CAVASS	CHISEL	CLOTHE
BY-PATH	CANTHI	CAVEAT	CHITIN	CLOTTY
BY-PLAY	CANTLE	CAVERN	CHITON	CLOUDY
BY-ROAD	CANTOS	CAVIAR	CHOICE	CLOUGH
BYSSUS	CANTON	CAVITY	CHOLER	CLOVEN
BY-VIEW	CANTOR	CAWASS	CHOOSE	CLOVER
BY-WORD	CANUTE	CAYMAN	CHOPIN	CLUMPY
	CANVAS	CEDARA	CHOPPY	CLUMSY
	CANYON	CEDRAN	CHORAL	CLUTCH
	CAPFUL	CELERY	CHOREA	COAITA
C	CAPIAS	CELLAR	CHOREE	COARSE
	CAPLIN	CELLED	CHORIC	COATEE
CABALA	CAPOTE	CELTIC	CHORUS	COAXER
CABMAN	CAPPED	CEMENT	CHOUGH	CO-AXAL
CACHET	CAPRIC	CENSER	CHOUSE	COBALT
CACHOU	CAPTOR	CENSOR	CHOWRY	COBBLE
CACKLE	CARACK	CENSUS	CHRISM	COBURG
CACOON	CARAFE	CENTAL	CHRIST	COBWEB
CACTUS	CARBON	CENTER	CHROME	COCCYX
CADDIE	CARBOY	CENTOS	CHROMO	COCKED
CADDIS	CARDER	CENTRE	CHUBBY	COCKER
CADENT	CAREEN	CERATE	CHUFFY	COCKET
CADGER	CAREER	CEREAL	CHURCH	COCKLE
CAECAL	CARESS	CEREUS	CICADA	COCOON
CAECUM	CARIES	CERIPH	CICOLA	CODDED
CAESAR	CARINA	CERISE	CICELY	CODDLE
CAFFRE	CARMAN	CERITE	CICUTA	CODIFY
CAIMAN	CARMEN	CERIUM	CIERGE	CODLIN
CAIQUE	CARNAL	CEROON	CINDER	COERCE
CAIRUS	CARPAL	CERTES	CINQUE	COEVAL
CAJOLE	CARPEL	CERUSE	CIPHER	COFFEE
CALASH	CARPET	CESTUS	CIPPUS	COFFER
CALCAR	CARPUS	CESURA	CIRCLE	COFFIN
CALCES	CARROT	CHABUK	CIRCUS	COGENT
CALCIC	CARTEL	CHACMA	CIRQUE	COGNAC
CALEFY	CARTER	CHAFER	CIRRUS	COHEIR
CALVES	CARTON	CHAFFY	CISTUS	COHERE
CALICE	CARVEL	CHAISE	CITHER	COHORT
CALICO	CARVER	CHALET	CITRIC	COIFED
CALIPH	CASEIN	CHALKY		COILED
CALKER				

COINER	CORTEX	CROAKY	CYCLIC	DEBILE
COLDLY	CORVEE	CROCUS	CYCLOP	DEBLAI
COLLAR	CORYMB	CROPPY	CYGNET	DEBRIS
COLLET	CORYZA	CROSSE	CYMBAL	DEBTOR
COLLIE	COSHER	CROTCH	CYMOSE	DECADE
COLLOP	COSILY	CROTON	CYMOUS	DECAMP
COLONY	CO-SINE	CROUCH	CYMRIC	DECANT
COLOUR	COSMIC	CRUISE	CYPHER	DECEIT
COLTER	COSMOS	CRUIVE	CYPRUS	DECENT
COLUMN	COSSET	CRUMBY	CYSTIC	DECERN
COLURE	COSTAL	CRUMMY		DECIDE
COMBAT	COSTER	CRUNCH		DECKER
COMBED	COSTLY	CRURAL	**D**	DECOCT
COMBER	COTTAR	CRUSET		DECREE
COMEDO	COTTER	CRUSTS	DABBER	DEDUCE
COMEDY	COTTON	CRUSTY	DABBLE	DEDUCT
COMELY	COTYLE	CRUTCH	DACAPO	DEEPEN
COMFIT	COUGAR	CRYING	DACOIT	DEEPLY
COMFRY	COULEE	CUBAGE	DACTYL	DEFACE
COMING	COUNTS	CUBOID	DAEDAL	DEFAME
COMITY	COUNTY	CUCKOO	DAEMON	DEFEAT
COMMIT	COUPLE	CUDDLE	DAGGER	DEFECT
COMMIX	COUPON	CUDGEL	DAGGLE	DEFEND
COMMON	COURSE	CUISSE	DAGOBA	DEFIER
COMPEL	COUSIN	CULDEE	DAHLIA	DEFILE
COMPLY	COVERT	CULLER	DAIMIO	DEFINE
CONCUR	COVING	CULLET	DAINTY	DEFORM
CONDOR	COWARD	CULLIS	DAKOIT	DEFRAY
CONFAB	COW-BOY	CULMEN	DAMAGE	DEFTLY
CONFER	COWLED	CULTCH	DAMASK	DEFYER
CONGEE	COW-POX	CULTER	DAMMAR	DEGREE
CONGER	COYOTE	CULTUS	DAMNED	DEHORT
CONGOU	COYPOU	CULVER	DAMPEN	DEIFIC
CONICS	COZILY	CUMBER	DAMPER	DEJECT
CONOID	CRADLE	CUMMIN	DAMSEL	DELATE
CONSUL	CRAFTY	CUMULI	DAMSON	DELETE
CONVEX	CRAGGY	CUNEAL	DANCER	DELIAN
CONVEY	CRAMBO	CUPFUL	DANDLE	DELUDE
CONVOY	CRANCH	CUPOLA	DANGER	DELUGE
COOLER	CRANKY	CUPRIC	DANGLE	DELVER
COOLIE	CRANNY	CUPULA	DANISH	DEMAIN
COOLLY	CRASIS	CUPULE	DAPPER	DEMAND
COOPER	CRATER	CURACY	DAPPLE	DEMEAN
COPECK	CRAVAT	CURARE	DARING	DEMENT
COPIER	CRAVEN	CURARI	DARKEN	DEMISE
COPING	CRAVER	CURATE	DARKLE	DEMURE
COPPER	CRAYON	CURDLE	DARKLY	DENARY
COPTIC	CRAZED	CURFEW	DARNEL	DENGUE
COPULA	CREAKY	CURIOS	DARNER	DENIAL
COPYER	CREAMY	CURLED	DARTER	DENIER
COQUET	CREASE	CURLER	DARTRE	DENOTE
CORBEL	CREASY	CURLEW	DARWIN	DENTAL
CORBIE	CREATE	CURSED	DASHER	DENTIL
CORCLE	CRECHE	CURSER	DATIVE	DENUDE
CORDED	CREDIT	CURTAL	DAUBER	DEODAR
CORDON	CREEKY	CURTLY	DAWDLE	DEPART
CORIUM	CREEPY	CURTSY	DAY-BED	DEPEND
CORKED	CREESE	CURULE	DAYFLY	DEPICT
CORNEA	CREMOR	CURVED	DAZZLE	DEPLOY
CORNED	CREOLE	CURVET	DEACON	DEPONE
CORNEL	CRESSY	CUSCUS	DEADEN	DEPORT
CORNER	CRESTA	CUSHAT	DEADLY	DEPOSE
CORNET	CRETIN	CUSTOM	DEAFEN	DEPUTE
CORONA	CREWEL	CUSTOS	DEAFLY	DEPUTY
CORPSE	CRINAL	CUTLER	DEALER	DERIDE
CORPUS	CRINGE	CUTLET	DEARLY	DERIVE
CORRAL	CRISES	CUT-OFF	DEARTH	DERMAL
CORRIE	CRISIS	CUTTER	DEBARK	DERMIC
CORSET	CRISPY	CUTTLE	DEBASE	DERMIS
CORTES	CRITIC	CYANIC	DEBATE	DERVIS

DESCRY	DIVERS	DUFFEL	ELICIT	EPODIC
DESERT	DIVERT	DUGONG	ELIJAH	EPONYM
DESIGN	DIVEST	DULCET	ELISHA	EPOPEE
DESIRE	DIVIDE	DUMBLY	ELIXIR	EQUATE
DESIST	DIVINE	DUNDER	ELOHIM	EQUERY
DESMAN	DIVING	DUNLIN	ELTCHI	EQUINE
DESPOT	DJERID	DUNNER	ELVISH	EQUITY
DETACH	DOCILE	DUPERY	ELYTRA	ERASER
DETAIL	DOCKET	DUPLEX	EMBALM	ERBIUM
DETAIN	DOCTOR	DURBAR	EMBANK	EREBUS
DETECT	DODDER	DURESS	EMBARK	ERENOW
DETENT	DODGER	DURIAN	EMBLEM	ERINGO
DETEST	DOGATE	DURION	EMBODY	ERMINE
DETOUR	DOG-DAY	DURING	EMBOSS	EROTIC
DEUCED	DOGGED	DUSTER	EMBRUE	ERRAND
DEVEST	DOGGER	DYNAMO	EMBRYO	ERRANT
DEVICE	DOINGS	DYNAST	EMERGE	ERRATA
DEVISE	DOLENT	DYSURY	EMETIC	ERYNGO
DEVOID	DOLLAR		ÉMEUTE	ESCAPE
DEVOIR	DOLMAN		ÉMIGRÉ	ESCARP
DEVOTE	DOLMEN	**E**	EMPALE	ESCHAR
DEVOUR	DOLOUR		EMPERY	ESCHEW
DEVOUT	DOMAIN	EAGLET	EMPIRE	ESCORT
DEWLAP	DOMINO	EARING	EMPLOY	ESCUDO
DEXTER	DONATE	EARNER	ENABLE	ESKIMO
DHURRA	DONJON	EARTHY	ENAMEL	ESPIAL
DIADEM	DONKEY	EAR-WAX	ENCAGE	ESPIED
DIAPER	DOOMED	EARWIG	ENCAMP	ESPIER
DIATOM	DORIAN	EASILY	ENCAVE	ESPRIT
DIBBER	DORMER	EASTER	ENCORE	ESSENE
DIBBLE	DORSAL	EATAGE	ENCYST	ESTATE
DICAST	DOSAGE	EATING	ENDEAR	ESTEEM
DICING	DOSSIL	ECARTÉ	ENDING	ESTHER
DICKER	DOTAGE	ECHOES	ENDIVE	ESTRAY
DICKEY	DOTARD	ECLAIR	ENDURE	ETCHER
DICTUM	DOTING	ECTYPE	ENERGY	ETHICS
DIDDLE	DOUBLE	ECZEMA	ENFOLD	ETHNIC
DIETER	DOUBLY	EDDISH	ENGAGE	ETYMIC
DIFFER	DOUCHE	EDENIC	ENGINE	ETYMON
DIGEST	DOUGHY	EDGING	ENGIRD	ETYPIC
DIGGER	DOWLAS	EDIBLE	ENGORE	EUCHRE
DILATE	DRACHM	EDITOR	ENGULF	EUCLID
DILUTE	DRAFFY	EFFACE	ENIGMA	EULOGY
DIMITY	DRAGON	EFFECT	ENJOIN	EUNUCH
DIMPLE	DRAPER	EFFETE	ENLACE	EUREKA
DIMPLY	DRAWEE	EFFIGY	ENLIST	EUTAXY
DINGEY	DRAWER	EFFLUX	ENNUYÉ	EVENLY
DINGHY	DREAMT	EFFORT	ENOUGH	EVICTS
DINGLE	DREAMY	EFFUSE	ENRAGE	EVINCE
DINNER	DREARY	EFREET	ENRICH	EVOLVE
DIODON	DREDGE	EGENCE	ENROBE	EXARCH
DIPLEX	DREGGY	EGESTA	ENROLE	EXCAMB
DIPLOE	DRENCH	EGG-CUP	ENSIGN	EXCEED
DIPNOI	DRESSY	EGGLER	ENSILE	EXCEPT
DIPPER	DRIFTY	EGGERY	ENSURE	EXCESS
DIRECT	DRIVEL	EGG-NOG	ENTAIL	EXCISE
DISARM	DRIVER	EGOISM	ENTICE	EXCITE
DISBAR	DROPSY	EGOIST	ENTIRE	EXCUSE
DISBUD	DROSKY	EGRESS	ENTITY	EXEMPT
DISCAL	DROSSY	EIGHTH	ENTOMB	EXHALE
DISCUS	DROUTH	EIGHTY	ENTRAP	EXHORT
DISHES	DROVER	EITHER	ENTREE	EXHUME
DISMAL	DROWSE	ELAPSE	ENVIER	EXODUS
DISMAY	DROWSY	ELATED	ENWRAP	EXOGEN
DISOWN	DRUDGE	ELATER	EOCENE	EXOTIC
DISPEL	DRY-ROT	ELDEST	EOLIAN	EXPAND
DISTAL	DUCKER	ELECTS	EOZOIC	EXPECT
DISTIL	DUELLO	ELENCH	EPARCH	EXPEND
DISUSE	DUENNA	ELEVEN	EPAULE	EXPERT
DITONE	DUETTO	ELFISH	EPIZOA	EXPIRE

EXPIRY	FEEBLY	FISCAL	FOREGO	FYLFOT
EXPORT	FEEDER	FISHES	FOREST	
EXPOSE	FEELER	FISHER	FORGER	
EXPUGN	FELINE	FISTIC	FORGET	**G**
EXTANT	FELLAH	FITFUL	FORGOT	
EXTASY	FELLER	FITTER	FORKED	GABBLE
EXTEND	FELLOE	FIXITY	FORMAL	GABIES
EXTENT	FELLOW	FIZGIG	FORMER	GABION
EXTERN	FELONY	FIZZLE	FORMIC	GABLES
EXTORT	FEMALE	FLABBY	FORTED	GABLET
EXTRAS	FENCED	FLAGGY	FOSSAE	GADDER
EX-VOTO	FENCER	FLAGON	FOSSIL	GADFLY
EYELET	FENDER	FLAMEN	FOSTER	GADOID
EYELID	FENIAN	FLANGE	FOTHER	GAELIC
	FENNEC	FLASHY	FOUGHT	GAFFER
	FENNEL	FLATLY	FOULLY	GAGGLE
F	FEODAL	FLAUNT	FOURTH	GAIETY
	FERIAL	FLAVOR	FOWLER	GAINER
FABIAN	FERINE	FLAXEN	FOX-BAT	GAINLY
FABLED	FERITY	FLAYER	FRACAS	'GAINST
FABRIC	FERRET	FLÉCHE	FRAISE	GAITED
FACADE	FERRIC	FLEDGE	FRAMER	GAITER
FACETE	FERULE	FLEECE	FREELY	GALAXY
FACIAL	FERVID	FLEECY	FREEZE	GALENA
FACILE	FERVOR	FLENSE	FRENCH	GALIOT
FACING	FESCUE	FLESHY	FRENZY	GALLEY
FACTOR	FESTAL	FLEXOR	FRESCO	GALLIC
FACULA	FESTER	FLIGHT	FRETTY	GALLON
FADING	FETICH	FLIMSY	FRIDAY	GALLOP
FAECAL	FETISH	FLINCH	FRIEND	GALORE
FAECES	FETTER	FLINTY	FRIEZE	GALOSH
FAG-END	FETTLE	FLITCH	FRIGHT	GAMBIR
FAGGOT	FEUDAL	FLOCKY	FRIGID	GAMBIT
FAILLE	FIACRE	FLOPPY	FRINGE	GAMBLE
FAIRLY	FIANCÉ	FLORAL	FRINGY	GAMBOL
FAKEER	FIASCO	FLORET	FRISKY	GAMING
FALCON	FIBBER	FLORID	FRIZZY	GAMMER
FALLOW	FIBRIL	FLORIN	FROLIC	GAMMON
FALTER	FIBRIN	FLOSSY	FROSTY	GANDER
FAMILY	FIBULA	FLOURY	FROTHY	GANGER
FAMINE	FICKLE	FLOWER	FROUZY	GANGUE
FAMISH	FIDDLE	FLUENT	FROWZY	GANNET
FAMOUS	FIDGET	FLUFFY	FROZEN	GANOID
FANGED	FIERCE	FLUNKY	FRUGAL	GAOLER
FANNER	FIGURE	FLURRY	FRUITY	GARBLE
FANTOM	FILIAL	FLUTED	FRUSTA	GARDEN
FARDEL	FILING	FLYING	FRYING	GARGLE
FARINA	FILLER	FODDER	FUCOID	GARISH
FARMER	FILLET	FOEMAN	FUDDLE	GARLIC
FAR-OFF	FILLIP	FOEMEN	FULCRA	GARNER
FARROW	FILOSE	FOETAL	FULFIL	GARNET
FASCES	FILTER	FOETUS	FULGID	GARRET
FASCIA	FILTHY	FOGEYS	FULLER	GARROT
FASTEN	FINALE	FOGIES	FULMAR	GARTER
FASTER	FINDER	FOIBLE	FUMBLE	GASCON
FASTLY	FINELY	FOILER	FUNGAL	GASIFY
FATHER	FINERY	FOISON	FUNGUS	GAS-JET
FATHOM	FINGER	FOLDER	FUNNEL	GASKET
FATTEN	FINIAL	FOLIAR	FURFUR	GAS-TAR
FAUCES	FINING	FOLLOW	FURORE	GATHER
FAUCET	FINISH	FOMENT	FURRED	GAUCHO
FAULTY	FINITE	FONDLE	FURROW	GAUGER
FAUNAL	FINNED	FONDLY	FURIES	GAYETY
FAVOSE	FINNER	FONTAL	FUSILE	GAZING
FAVOUR	FIN-RAY	FOOTED	FUSION	GEMINI
FAWNER	FIORIN	FORAGE	FUSTED	GEMMAE
FEALTY	FIRING	FORBID	FUSTET	GENDER
FECULA	FIRKIN	FORCAT	FUSTIC	GENERA
FECUND	FIRMAN	FORCED	FUTILE	GENEVA
FEEBLE	FIRMLY	FORCER	FUTURE	GENIAL

GENIUS	GORGON	GYPSUM	HECKLE	HOOKER
GENTES	GOSPEL	GYRATE	HECTIC	HOOPER
GENTLE	GOSSIP	GYROSE	HECTOR	HOOPOE
GENTLY	GOTHIC		HEDDLE	HOOPOO
GENTRY	GOTTEN		HEDGER	HOOVES
GEORGE	GOVERN	**H**	HEGIRA	HOPPER
GERMAN	GRAINY		HEIFER	HOPPLE
GERMEN	GRAITH		HEIGHT	HORARY
GERUND	GRAKLE	HACKEE	HEJIRA	HORNED
GESTIC	GRAMME	HACKLE	HELMED	HORNER
GETTER	GRANGE	HADJEE	HELMET	HORNET
GEW-GAW	GRASSY	HAEMAL	HELPER	HORRID
GEYSER	GRATER	HAGBUT	HEMPEN	HORROR
GHETTO	GRATIS	HAGGED	HEPTAD	HORSEY
GIBBER	GRAVEL	HAGGIS	HERALD	HOSIER
GIBBET	GRAVER	HAGGLE	HERBAL	HOSTEL
GIBBON	GRAVES	HAIRED	HEREAT	HOT-BED
GIB-CAT	GRAVID	HALLOH!	HEREBY	HOUDAH
GIBLET	GRAYLY	HALLOO!	HEREIN	HOURLY
GIFTED	GRAZER	HALLOW	HEREOF	HOUSES
GIGGLE	GREASE	HALLUX	HEREON	HOUSEL
GIGLET	GREASY	HALTER	HERESY	HOWDAH
GIGLOT	GREAVE	HALVES	HERETO	HOWLER
GILDER	GREEDY	HAMATE	HERIOT	HOWLET
GILLIE	GREENY	HAMITE	HERMIT	HOYDEN
GIMLET	GRIEVE	HAMLET	HERNIA	HUBBUB
GINGER	GRILLE	HAMMER	HEROES	HUCKLE
GIRDER	GRILSE	HAMOSE	HEROIC	HUDDLE
GIRDLE	GRIMLY	HAMOUS	HERPES	HUGELY
GLACIS	GRIPPE	HAMPER	HERMAN	HUMANE
GLADLY	GRISLY	HANDED	HEYDAY	HUMBLE
GLAIVE	GRITTY	HANDLE	HIATUS	HUMBLY
GLANCE	GROATS	HANGER	HIBRID	HUMBUG
GLASSY	GROCER	HANKER	HICCUP	HUMERI
GLAZER	GROGGY	HANSOM	HICKUP	HUMMER
GLEAMY	GROOVE	HAPPEN	HIDDEN	HUMOUR
GLIBLY	GROPED	HARASS	HIDING	HUMOUS
GLOOMY	GROTTO	HARBOR	HIEMAL	HUMPED
GLORIA	GROUND	HARDEN	HIGGLE	HUNGER
GLOSSY	GROUSE	HARDLY	HIGHER	HUNGRY
GLOVED	GROVEL	HARKEN	HIGHLY	HUNTER
GLOVER	GROWER	HARLOT	HILTED	HURDLE
GLOWED	GROWTH	HARPER	HINDER	HURLER
GLUMLY	GROYNE	HARROW	HINDOO	HURRAH
GLUTEN	GRUDGE	HASTEN	HIPPED	HURTLE
GNARLY	GRUMPY	HATRED	HISPID	HUSKED
GNAWER	GUEBER	HATTED	HITHER	HUSSAR
GNEISS	GUEBRE	HATTER	HITTER	HUSSIF
GNOMIC	GUFFAW	HAULER	HOARSE	HUSTLE
GNOMON	GUGGLE	HAUNCH	HOBBLE	HYADES
GNOSIS	GUIDON	HAVANA	HOBNOB	HYAENA
GOBBET	GUILTY	HAVING	HOCKEY	HYBRID
GOBBLE	GUINEA	HAVOCK	HODMAN	HYEMAL
GOBLET	GUISER	HAWHAW	HOIDEN	HYETAL
GOBLIN	GUITAR	HAWKER	HOLDER	HYMNAL
GOBIES	GULDEN	HAWSER	HOLILY	HYMNIC
GO-CART	GULLET	HAZARD	HOLLOA!	HYPHEN
GODSON	GUM-LAC	HEADED	HOLLOW	HYSSOP
GODWIT	GUNNEL	HEADER	HOLPEN	
GOFFER	GUNNER	HEALER	HOMAGE	
GOGGLE	GUN-WAD	HEALTH	HOMELY	**I**
GOITER	GURGLE	HEARER	HOMILY	
GOITRE	GURNET	HEARSE	HOMING	IAMBIC
GOLDEN	GUSHER	HEARTH	HOMINY	IAMBUS
GOLFER	GUSSET	HEARTY	HONEST	IATRIC
GOLOSH	GUTTAE	HEATER	HONOUR	IBISES
GOMUTI	GUTTER	HEATHY	HOODED	ICE-SAW
GOODLY	GUTTLE	HEAVEN	HOOFED	ICICLE
GOPHER	GUZZLE	HEAVER	HOOKAH	IDIOCY
GORGET	GYMNIC	HEBREW	HOOKED	IDOLON

IGNITE	INKING	JARGON	KECKSY	LANCET
IGNORE	INKSAC	JAROOL	KEELED	LANDAU
IGUANA	INLAID	JARRAH	KEENLY	LANDED
ILLUDE	INLAND	JASPER	KEEPER	LANKLY
ILLUME	INMATE	JAUNTY	KELPIE	LANNER
IMBIBE	INMOST	JEERER	KELSON	LAPDOG
IMBODY	INNATE	JEJUNE	KELTIC	LAPPER
IMBRUE	INNING	JENNET	KENNEL	LAPPET
IMMESH	INROAD	JERBOA	KERMES	LAPSED
IMMUNE	INRUSH	JEREED	KERNEL	LARDER
IMMURE	INSANE	JERKED	KERSEY	LARIAT
IMPACT	INSECT	JERKIN	KETTLE	LARVAE
IMPAIR	INSERT	JERSEY	KIBBLE	LARVAL
IMPALE	INSIDE	JESSED	KIBLAH	LARYNX
IMPARK	INSIST	JESTER	KICKER	LASCAR
IMPART	INSPAN	JESUIT	KIDNAP	LASHER
IMPAWN	INSTEP	JETSAM	KIDNEY	LASTLY
IMPEDE	INSTIL	JETSON	KILLER	LATEEN
IMPEND	INSULT	JEWELS	KILTED	LATELY
IMPISH	INSURE	JEWESS	KIMONO	LATENT
IMPLEX	INTACT	JEWISH	KINCOB	LATHEN
IMPORT	INTAKE	JIGGER	KINDLE	LATHER
IMPOSE	INTEND	JINGAL	KINDLY	LATISH
IMPOST	INTENT	JINGLE	KINGLY	LATTEN
IMPUGN	INTERN	JINNEE	KIPPER	LATTER
IMPURE	INTONE	JOBBER	KIRTLE	LAUNCH
IMPUTE	INTUIT	JOCKEY	KISMET	LAUREL
INARCH	INVADE	JOCOSE	KIT-CAT	LAVISH
INBORN	INVENT	JOCUND	KITTEN	LAWFUL
INBRED	INVERT	JOGGER	KNAGGY	LAWYER
INCAGE	INVEST	JOGGLE	KNIVES	LAXITY
INCASE	INVITE	JOINER	KNIGHT	LAYMAN
INCEST	INVOKE	JOSEPH	KNOBBY	LAZILY
INCISE	INWALL	JOSTLE	KNOTTY	LAZULI
INCITE	INWARD	JOTTER	KNOWER	LEADED
INCOME	INWORN	JOVIAL	KOBOLD	LEADEN
INCUBI	INWRAP	JOYFUL	KOODOO	LEADER
INCULT	IODIDE	JOYOUS	KOSMOS	LEAFED
INCUSE	IODINE	JUBATE	KRAKEN	LEAGUE
INDEED	IODISM	JUDAIC	KRONER	LEANLY
INDENT	IODIZE	JUGATE	KUMISS	LEAN-TO
INDIAN	IOLITE	JUGGLE	KÜMMEL	LEAPER
INDICT	IONIAN	JUJUBE		LEASED
INDIGO	IREFUL	JULIAN		LEAVED
INDITE	IRIDAL	JUMBLE	**L**	LEAVEN
INDIUM	IRISES	JUMPER		LEAVES
INDOOR	IRISED	JUNGLE	LAAGER	LECHER
INDUCE	IRITIS	JUNGLY	LABIAL	LEDGER
INDUCT	IRONER	JUNIOR	LABIUM	LEEWAY
INFAMY	ISABEL	JUNKER	LABOUR	LEGACY
INFANT	ISLAND	JUNKET	LABRET	LEGATE
INFECT	ISOBAR	JURIST	LABRUM	LEGATO
INFELT	ISOPOD	JURIES	LACHES	LEGEND
INFEST	ISSUED	JUSTLE	LACING	LEGGED
INFIRM	ITALIC	JUSTLY	LACKER	LEGION
INFLOW	ITSELF		LACKEY	LEGIST
INFLUX			LACMUS	LEGUME
INFOLD		**K**	LACTIC	LENDER
INFORM	**J**		LACUNA	LENGTH
INFULA		KAFFIR	LADDER	LENITY
INFUSE	JABBER	KAFTAN	LADING	LENSES
INGEST	JACANA	KAISER	LADIES	LENTEN
INGULF	JACKAL	KALIUM	LAGOON	LENTIL
INHALE	JACKET	KALMUK	LAGUNE	LENTOR
INHERE	JADISH	KAMALA	LAMELY	L'ENVOI
INHUME	JAGGED	KAOLIN	LAMENT	L'ENVOY
INJECT	JAGUAR	KARROO	LAMINA	LESION
INJURE	JAILER	KAVASS	LAMMAS	LESSEE
INJURY	JAILOR	KAWASS	LANATE	LESSEN
INK-BAG	JANGLE	KEBLAH	LANCER	LESSER

LESSON	LOCKET	MAGNUM	MATRON	MIDWAY
LESSOR	LOCK-UP	MAGPIE	MATTED	MIGHTY
LETHAL	LOCULI	MAGYAR	MATTER	MIKADO
LETTER	LOCUST	MAHOUT	MATURE	MILDEN
LEVANT	LODGER	MAIDEN	MAUGRE	MILDEW
LEVIER	LOGGAT	MAIGRE	MAY-BUG	MILDLY
LEVITE	LOG-HUT	MAINLY	MAY-DAY	MILKER
LEVIES	LOGGIA	MAKE-UP	MAY-DEW	MILLED
LEVITY	LOGGIE	MAKING	MAY-FLY	MILLER
LEWDLY	LOITER	MALADY	MAYHAP	MILLET
LIABLE	LOMENT	MALAGA	MAYHEM	MILTER
LIBYAN	LONELY	MALICE	MAYING	MIMOSA
LICHEN	LOOKER	MALIGN	MAZARD	MINDED
LICTOR	LOOSEN	MALLEE	MAZILY	MINDER
LIDDED	LOPPER	MALLET	MEADOW	MINGLE
LIFTER	LORATE	MALLOW	MEAGRE	MINIFY
LIGHTS	LORCHA	MALTHA	MEANLY	MINIMA
LIGNUM	LORDLY	MAMMAE	MEASLY	MINING
LIGULA	LORICA	MAMMAL	MEATUS	MINION
LIGULE	LORRIE	MAMMEE	MEDDLE	MINISH
LIGURE	LOSING	MAMMON	MEDIAL	MINIUM
LIKELY	LOTION	MANAGE	MEDIAN	MINNOW
LIKING	LOUDLY	MANANA	MEDICA	MINTER
LILIES	LOUNGE	MANCHU	MEDICI	MINUET
LIMBED	LOUVRE	MANEGE	MEDIUM	MINUTE
LIMBER	LOVELY	MANFUL	MEDLAR	MIRAGE
LIMNER	LOVING	MANGER	MEDLEY	MIRROR
LIMOUS	LOWERY	MANGLE	MEDUSA	MISERY
LIMPET	LOWEST	MANIAC	MEEKLY	MISFIT
LIMPID	LOWING	MANILA	MEETLY	MISHAP
LINDEN	LUBBER	MANIOC	MEGILP	MISLAY
LINEAL	LUCENT	MANITO	MEGOHM	MISSAL
LINEAR	LUCERN	MANNER	MEGRIM	MISSEE
LINGAM	LUGGER	MANTEL	MELLAY	MISTER
LINGER	LUMBAR	MANTIS	MELLEY	MISUSE
LINHAY	LUMBER	MANTLE	MELLOW	MITRAL
LINING	LUMPER	MANTUA	MELODY	MITRED
LINNET	LUNACY	MANUAL	MELTER	MITTEN
LINTEL	LUNATE	MANURE	MEMBER	MIZZEN
LIONEL	LUNGED	MAORIS	MEMOIR	MIZZLE
LIONET	LUNULA	MARAUD	MEMORY	MOB-CAP
LIPLET	LUNULE	MARBLE	MENACE	MOBILE
LIPPED	LUPINE	MARBLY	MENAGE	MOB-LAW
LIQUID	LURDAN	MARCID	MENDER	MOCKER
LIQUOR	LURKER	MARGIN	MENHIR	MODERN
LISPER	LUSTRA	MARINE	MENIAL	MODEST
LISSOM	LUSTRE	MARISH	MENSES	MODIFY
LISTEN	LUTINE	MARKED	MENTAL	MODISH
LITANY	LUTIST	MARKEE	MENTOR	MODULE
LITHIA	LUXATE	MARKER	MERCER	MOHAIR
LITHIC	LUXURY	MARKET	MERELY	MOIETY
LITMUS	LYCEUM	MARMOT	MERINO	MOLDER
LITTER	LYDIAN	MAROON	MERLIN	MOLEST
LITTLE	LYRATE	MARQUE	MERLON	MOLLAH
LIVELY	LYRIST	MARROW	MERMAN	MOLOCH
LIVERY		MARSHY	MESIAL	MOLTEN
LIVING		MARTEN	METAGE	MOMENT
LIZARD	**M**	MARTIN	METEOR	MONDAY
LLANOS		MARTYR	METHOD	MONEYS
LLOYD'S	MACRON	MARVEL	METHYL	MONGER
LOADED	MACULA	MASCLE	METOPE	MONGOL
LOADER	MADCAP	MASCOT	METRIC	MONIED
LOAFER	MADDEN	MASHER	METTLE	MONISM
LOATHE	MADDER	MASKED	MIASMA	MONIST
LOAVES	MADMAN	MASKER	MICKLE	MONKEY
LOBATE	MAENAD	MASQUE	MID-AIR	MONODY
LOBULE	MAGGOT	MASTED	MID-DAY	MOORVA
LOCALE	MAGIAN	MASTER	MIDDEN	MOPISH
LOCATE	MAGILP	MASTIC	MIDDLE	MOPSEY
LOCKER	MAGNET	MATRIX	MID-LEG	MORALE

MORASS		NOTARY	OMENED	OVERDO
MORBID	**N**	NOTICE	ONAGER	OVISAC
MOREEN		NOTIFY	ONRUSH	OWLERY
MORGUE	NAEVUS	NOTION	ONWARD	OWLISH
MORION	NAILER	NOUGAT	OOIDAL	OXALIC
MORMON	NAMELY	NOUGHT	OOLITE	OX-EYED
MOROSE	NANKIN	NOUNAL	OOLOGY	OX-GALL
MORRIS	NAPERY	NOVICE	OOMIAK	OXGANG
MORROW	NAPKIN	NOWAYS	OPAQUE	OXYGEN
MORSEL	NARIAL	NOWISE	OPENED	OXYMEL
MORTAL	NARROW	NOZZLE	OPENER	OYSTER
MORTAR	NARWAL	NUANCE	OPENLY	
MORULA	NASEBY	NUBILE	OPHITE	
MOSAIC	NASUTE	NUCHAL	OPIATE	**P**
MOSLEM	NATANT	NUCLEI	OPPOSE	
MOSQUE	NATION	NUDELY	OPPUGN	PACIFY
MOSTLY	NATIVE	NUDGED	OPTICS	PACKER
MOTETT	NATRON	NUDITY	OPTION	PACKET
MOTHER	NATURE	NUGGET	ORACHE	PADDER
MOTILE	NAUGHT	NULLAH	ORACLE	PADDLE
MOTION	NAUSEA	NUMBER	ORALLY	PAGODA
MOTIVE	NEAPED	NUNCIO	ORANGE	PAIGLE
MOTLEY	NEARLY	NURSED	ORATOR	PALACE
MOTORY	NEATLY	NUTANT	ORCHID	PALATE
MOTTLE	NEBULA	NUTMEG	ORCHIS	PALEAE
MOTTOS	NECKED	NUTRIA	ORDAIN	PALELY
MOULDY	NECTAR	NUZZLE	ORDEAL	PALING
MOUSER	NEEDED	NYLGAU	ORDERS	PALISH
MOUTHS	NEEDLE		ORDURE	PALLAH
MOVING	NEEDLY		OREGON	PALLET
MOWING	NEPHEW	**O**	ORGASM	PALLID
MUCOSE	NEREID		ORGEAT	PALLIA
MUCOUS	NERVED	OAFISH	ORGIES	PALLOR
MUDDLE	NESTLE	OBELUS	ORIENT	PALMAR
MUFFIN	NETHER	OBEYER	ORIGIN	PALMED
MUFFLE	NETTED	OBJECT	ORIOLE	PALMER
MUFTEE	NETTLE	OBLATE	ORISON	PALPUS
MULISH	NEURAL	OBLIGE	ORMOLU	PALTER
MULLEN	NEUTER	OBLONG	ORNATE	PALTRY
MULLET	NEWARK	OBOIST	OROIDE	PAMPAS
MUMBLE	NEWISH	OBOLUS	ORPHAN	PAMPER
MUMMER	NIBBLE	OBSESS	ORPHIC	PANARY
MUMPER	NICELY	OBTAIN	ORRERY	PANDER
MURDER	NICENE	OBTEST	OSIERY	PANDIT
MURMUR	NICETY	OBTUSE	OSMIUM	PANTRY
MURREY	NICHED	OCCULT	OSMOSE	PAPACY
MUSCAT	NICKEL	OCCUPY	OSPRAY	PAPERY
MUSCLE	NIDIFY	OCELLI	OSPREY	PAPIST
MUSEUM	NIELLO	OCELOT	OSSEIN	PAPPUS
MUSING	NIGGER	OCHREA	OSSIFY	PAPULA
MUSKET	NILGAU	OCTANT	OSTLER	PAPYRI
MUSK-OX	NIMBLE	OCTAVE	OSWALD	PARADE
MUSLIM	NIMBLY	OCTAVO	OTALGY	PARAPH
MUSLIN	NIMBUS	OCTROI	OTIOSE	PARCEL
MUSSEL	NINETY	OCULAR	OTITIS	PARDON
MUSTER	NIPPER	ODDITY	OUSTER	PARENT
MUTELY	NIPPLE	ODIOUS	OUTBID	PARGET
MUTINY	NITRIC	OEDEMA	OUTCRY	PARIAH
MUTTER	NOBODY	OFF-DAY	OUTFIT	PARIAN
MUTTON	NODDLE	OFFEND	OUTING	PARING
MUTUAL	NODOSE	OFFICE	OUTLAW	PARISH
MUZZLE	NODULE	OFFING	OUTLAY	PARITY
MYOPIA	NOETIC	OFFSET	OUTLET	PARLEY
MYOSIS	NOGGIN	OGRESS	OUTPUT	PARLOR
MYOTIC	NOMADE	OIDIUM	OUTRUN	PARODY
MYRIAD	NONAGE	OILERY	OUTSET	PAROLE
MYRTLE	NON-EGO	OIL-GAS	OUTSIT	PARROT
MYSELF	NOODLE	OLDISH	OUTVIE	PARSEE
MYSTIC	NORMAL	OMASUM	OUTWIT	PARSON
MYTHIC	NORMAN	OMELET	OVALLY	PARTLY

PARVIS	PERUKE	PLAICE	PORTER	PUNCHY
PASSEE	PERUSE	PLAINT	PORTLY	PUNDIT
PASSER	PESETA	PLANET	POSSET	PUNISH
PASSIM	PESTER	PLAQUE	POSTAL	PUNKAH
PASTEL	PESTLE	PLASHY	POSTER	PUNTER
PASTIL	PETARD	PLASMA	POT-ALE	PUPPET
PASTOR	PETITE	PLATAN	POTASH	PURELY
PASTRY	PETREL	PLATEN	POTATO	PURFLE
PATCHY	PETROL	PLATER	POT-BOY	PURGER
PATENT	PEWTER	PLAYER	POTEEN	PURIFY
PATERA	PHAROS	PLEACH	POTENT	PURISM
PATHOS	PHASES	PLEASE	POTHER	PURIST
PATINA	PHASIS	PLEDGE	POTION	PURITY
PATOIS	PHLEGM	PLEIAD	POTTER	PURPLE
PATROL	PHLOEM	PLENTY	POTTLE	PURSER
PATRON	PHOLAS	PLENUM	POUNCE	PURSUE
PATTEN	PHONIC	PLEURA	POUTER	PURVEY
PATTER	PHRASE	PLEXUS	POWDER	PUTLOG
PAUNCH	PHYLUM	PLIANT	PRAISE	PUTRID
PAUPER	PHYSIC	PLIERS	PRANCE	PUTTER
PAVING	PIANOS	PLIGHT	PRATER	PUZZLE
PAVIOR	PIAZZA	PLINTH	PRAXIS	PYGARG
PAVISE	PICKED	PLOUGH	PRAYER	PYTHON
PAWNER	PICKER	PLOVER	PREACH	
PAX-WAX	PICKET	PLUCKY	PRECIS	
PAY-DAY	PICKLE	PLUMED	PREFER	**Q**
PAYNIM	PICNIC	PLUMPY	PREFIX	
PEACHY	PICRIC	PLUNGE	PREPAY	QUAGGA
PEAKED	PIDDLE	PLURAL	PRESTO	QUAGGY
PEA-NUT	PIECER	POACHY	PRETOR	QUAINT
PEARLY	PIERCE	POCKET	PRETTY	QUAKER
PEBBLE	PIGEON	PODDED	PRICED	QUARRY
PEBBLY	PIGGIN	PODIUM	PRIEST	QUARTE
PECKER	PIG-NUT	POETIC	PRIMAL	QUARTO
PECTEN	PIG-STY	POETRY	PRIMER	QUARTZ
PECTIC	PILEUS	POISER	PRIMLY	QUAVER
PEDANT	PILFER	POISON	PRIMUS	QUEASY
PEDATE	PILING	POLICE	PRINCE	QUENCH
PEDDLE	PILLAR	POLICY	PRIORY	QUINCE
PEDLAR	PILLAU	POLISH	PRISON	QUINOA
PEDLER	PILLAW	POLITE	PRIVET	QUINSY
PEELER	PILLOW	POLITY	PROFIT	QUIRKY
PEEPER	PILULE	POLLAN	PROLEG	QUITCH
PEEWIT	PIMPLE	POLLED	PROLIX	QUIVER
PEGGED	PIMPLY	POLLEN	PROMPT	QUORUM
PEG-TOP	PINEAL	POLLEX	PROPEL	QUOTER
PELAGE	PINERY	POLONY	PROPER	QUOTHA!
PELLET	PINION	POLYPE	PROSER	
PELTRY	PINKED	POLYPI	PROVEN	
PELVIC	PINNAE	POMACE	PROVER	**R**
PELVIS	PINTLE	POMADE	PRUNER	
PENCIL	PIPING	POMMEL	PRYING	RABBET
PENMAN	PIPKIN	PONCHO	PSEUDO	RABBIS
PENMEN	PIPPIN	PONDER	PSYCHE	RABBIN
PENNER	PIQUET	PONGEE	PUBLIC	RABBIT
PENNON	PIRACY	PONIES	PUCKER	RABBLE
PENULT	PIRATE	POODLE	PUDDLE	RABIES
PENURY	PISCES	POONAC	PUDDLY	RACEME
PEOPLE	PISGAH	POORLY	PUFFER	RACHIS
PEPLUS	PISTIL	POPERY	PUFFIN	RACIAL
PEPPER	PISTOL	POPGUN	PUG-DOG	RACILY
PEPSIN	PISTON	POLISH	PUISNE	RACING
PEPTIC	PITCHY	POPLAR	PULING	RACKER
PERDUE	PITIER	POPLIN	PULKHA	RACKET
PERIOD	PITMAN	POPPET	PULLET	RACOON
PERISH	PIT-SAW	PORGIE	PULLEY	RADDLE
PERMIT	PITTED	PORISM	PULPIT	RADIAL
PERRON	PLACER	PORKER	PUMICE	RADISH
PERSON	PLACID	POROUS	PUMMEL	RADIUM
PERTLY	PLAGUE	PORTAL	PUMPER	RADIUS

RAFFIA	RECANT	REMOVE	RIDDLE	RUMMER
RAFFLE	RECAST	RENAME	RIDING	RUMOUR
RAFTER	RECEDE	RENARD	RIFELY	RUMPLE
RAGGED	RECENT	RENDER	RIFLER	RUMPUS
RAGMAN	RECESS	RENNET	RIGGER	RUNLET
RAGOUT	RECIPE	RENOWN	RIGOUR	RUNNEL
RAIDER	RECITE	RENTAL	RILLET	RUNNER
RAILER	RECKON	RENTER	RIMPLE	RUNNET
RAISER	RECOIL	REOPEN	RINGED	RUNRIG
RAISIN	RECORD	REPAID	RINGER	RUSHES
RAKING	RECOUP	REPAIR	RINSER	RUSKIN
RAKISH	RECTOR	REPAND	RIOTER	RUSSET
RAMBLE	RECTUM	REPASS	RIPELY	RUSTIC
RAMIFY	REDACT	REPAST	RIPPLE	RUSTLE
RAMMER	REDCAR	REPEAL	RIPRAP	
RAMOSE	REDDEN	REPEAT	RISING	
RAMOUS	REDDLE	REPENT	RISKER	S
RAMROD	REDEEM	REPINE	RITUAL	
RAMSON	RED-HOT	REPORT	SAVAGE	SACHEM
RANCHE	REDOUT	REPOSE	RIVERY	SACHET
RANCHO	REDRAW	REPUTE	ROAMER	SACKER
RANCID	REDUCE	RESCUE	ROARER	SACQUE
RANDOM	RE-ECHO	RESEAT	ROBBER	SACRAL
RANGER	REECHY	RESECT	ROBUST	SACRED
RANKLE	REEDED	RESENT	ROCHET	SACRUM
RANKLY	REEFER	RESHIP	ROCKER	SADDEN
RANSOM	REFILL	RESIDE	ROCKET	SADDLE
RANTER	REFINE	RESIGN	ROCOCO	SAFELY
RAPIDS	REFLEX	RESILE	RODENT	SAFETY
RAPIER	REFLUX	RESINY	ROLLER	SAGELY
RAPINE	REFOLD	RESIST	ROMAIC	SAGGER
RAPPEE	REFORM	RESORE	ROMISH	SAILER
RAPPER	RE-FORM	RESORT	RONDEL	SAILOR
RAREFY	REFUGE	RESULT	RONION	SAKIEH
RARELY	REFUND	RESUME	RONYON	SALAAM
RARITY	REFUSE	RETAIL	ROOFER	SALAMI
RASCAL	REFUTE	RETAIN	ROOTED	SALARY
RASHER	REGAIN	RETAKE	ROPERY	SALIFY
RASHLY	REGALE	RETARD	ROPILY	SALINA
RASPER	REGARD	RETINA	ROSARY	SALINE
RASURE	REGENT	RETIRE	ROSERY	SALIVA
RATHER	REGIME	RETORT	ROSINY	SALLOW
RATIFY	REGINA	RETURN	ROSTER	SALMIS
RATING	REGION	RETUSE	ROSTRA	SALMON
RATION	REGIUS	REVAMP	ROTARY	SALOON
RATIOS	REGLET	REVEAL	ROTATE	SALOOP
RATITE	REGNAL	REVELS	ROTTEN	SALTER
RATLIN	REGRET	REVERE	ROTUND	SALTLY
RAT-PIT	REHASH	REVERT	ROUBLE	SALUTE
RATTAN	REHEAR	REVIEW	RUBBER	SALVER
RATTEN	REJECT	REVILE	RUBBLE	SALVOR
RATTER	REJOIN	REVISE	RUBIED	SAMARA
RATTLE	RELATE	REVIVE	RUBIES	SAMIAN
RAVAGE	RELENT	REVOKE	RUBIGO	SAMITE
RAVINE	RELICT	REVOLT	RUBINE	SAMLET
RAVING	RELIEF	REWARD	RUBRIC	SAMPAN
RAVISH	RELIER	REXINE	RUDDER	SAMPLE
RAWISH	RELISH	RHESUS	RUDDLE	SANDAL
RAZZIA	RELIVE	RHEUMY	RUDDOC	SANDIX
READER	RELUME	RHINAL	RUDELY	SANDYX
REALLY	REMAIN	RHYMER	RUEFUL	SANIES
REALTY	REMAKE	RHYTHM	RUFFLE	SANITY
REAPER	REMAND	RIALTO	RUFOUS	SANJAK
REASON	REMARK	RIANCY	RUGATE	SANTON
REAVER	RE-MARK	RIBALD	RUGGED	SAPPER
REBATE	REMEDY	RIBAND	RUGOSE	SARONG
REBECK	REMIND	RIBBED	RUGOUS	SASINE
REBUFF	REMISS	RIBBON	RUINER	SATEEN
REBUKE	REMORA	RICHES	RULING	SATINY
RECALL	REMOTE	RICHLY	RUMBLE	SATIRE

SATRAP	SEARED	SEXUAL	SIMILE	SMOOTH
SATURN	SEASON	SHABBY	SIMMER	SMUDGE
SAUCER	SEA-WAY	SHADOW	SIMONY	SMUGLY
SAVAGE	SECANT	SHAGGY	SIMOOM	SMUTCH
SAVANT	SECEDE	SHAKEN	SIMOUS	SMUTTY
SAVINE	SECERN	SHAKER	SIMPER	SNAGGY
SAVING	SECOND	SHALLI	SIMPLE	SNARER
SAVORY	SECRET	SHAMMY	SIMPLY	SNATCH
SAVOUR	SECTOR	SHAMOY	SINAIC	SNEAKY
SAW-FLY	SECUND	SHANNY	SINEWY	SNEEZE
SAW-PIT	SECURE	SHANTY	SINFUL	SNIVEL
SAWYER	SEDATE	SHAPER	SINGER	SNOBBY
SAYING	SEDUCE	SHARER	SINGLE	SNOOZE
SCABBY	SEEDED	SHAVER	SINGLY	SNORER
SCALED	SEEING	SHEAFY	SINKER	SNOUTY
SCALER	SEEKER	SHEARS	SINNER	SNUFFY
SCANTY	SEEMER	SHEATH	SINTER	SNUGLY
SCAPUS	SEEMLY	SHEAVE	SIPHON	SOAKED
SCARAB	SEE-SAW	SHEENY	SIPPET	SOAKER
SCARCE	SEETHE	SHEERS	SIRDAR	SOCAGE
SCARFS	SEGGAR	SHEKEL	SIRIUS	SOCIAL
SCARRY	SEINER	SHELFY	SIRRAH	SOCKET
SCATHE	SEIZER	SHELLY	SISKIN	SODDEN
SCENIC	SEIZIN	SHELVE	SISTER	SODIUM
SCHEIK	SEJANT	SHELVY	SITTER	SODOMY
SCHEME	SELDOM	SHERRY	SIZING	SOEVER
SCHISM	SELECT	SHEWED	SKATER	SOFFIT
SCHIST	SELLER	SHIELD	SKERRY	SOFTEN
SCHOOL	SELVES	SHIFTY	SKETCH	SOFTLY
SCONCE	SEMITE	SHINER	SKEWER	SOIREE
SCORCH	SEMOLA	SHINTY	SKINNY	SOLACE
SCORER	SENARY	SHIVER	SKIVER	SOLDER
SCORIA	SENATE	SHOALY	SKURRY	SOLELY
SCOTCH	SENDAL	SHODDY	SLABBY	SOLEMN
SCOTER	SENDER	SHOPPY	SLAGGY	SOLEUS
SCOTIA	SENECA	SHORED	SLANGY	SOLVER
SCRAPE	SENEGA	SHOULD	SLATED	SOMBRE
SCRAWL	SENILE	SHOVEL	SLATER	SOMITE
SCREAK	SENIOR	SHOWER	SLAVER	SONANT
SCREAM	SENNIT	SHREWD	SLAVIC	SONATA
SCREED	SENORA	SHRIEK	SLAYER	SONNET
SCREEN	SENTRY	SHRIFT	SLEAVE	SOOTHE
SCREES	SEPTET	SHRIKE	SLEAZY	SOPHIE
SCRIBE	SEPTIC	SHRILL	SLEDGE	SORDID
SCRIMP	SEPTUM	SHRIMP	SLEEKY	SORELY
SCRIPT	SEQUAL	SHRINE	SLEEPY	SORREL
SCROLL	SEQUIN	SHRINK	SLEETY	SORROW
SCUMMY	SERAPH	SHRIVE	SLEEVE	SORTER
SCURFY	SERENE	SHROUD	SLEAZY	SORTIE
SCURRY	SERIAL	SICKEN	SLEIGH	SOULED
SCURVY	SERIES	SICKLE	SLICER	SOURCE
SCUTCH	SERIPH	SICKLY	SLIDER	SOURLY
SCUTUM	SERMON	SIDING	SLIGHT	SOVRAN
SCYTHE	SEROON	SIENNA	SLIVER	SOWANS
SEA-CAT	SEROUS	SIERRA	SLOGAN	SOWENS
SEA-COW	SERVAL	SIESTA	SLOPPY	SPADIX
SEA-DOG	SERVER	SIFTER	SLOUCH	SPARRY
SEA-EAR	SESAME	SIGNAL	SLOUGH	SPARSE
SEA-EEL	SESTET	SIGNER	SLOVEN	SPARTA
SEA-EGG	SET-OFF	SIGNET	SLOWLY	SPATHE
SEA-FIR	SETOSE	SIGNOR	SLUDGE	SPAVIN
SEA-FOX	SETTEE	SILAGE	SLUDGY	SPECIE
SEA-GOD	SETTER	SILENT	SLUICE	SPEECH
SEALER	SETTLE	SILICA	SLUICY	SPEEDY
SEAMAN	SEVERE	SILKEN	SLUSHY	SPENCE
SEAMER	SEVERN	SILURE	SMILER	SPHERE
SEA-MEW	SEVRES	SILVAN	SMIRCH	SPHERY
SEANCE	SEWAGE	SILVER	SMITER	SPHINX
SEARCE	SEWING	SIMIAN	SMITHY	SPIDER
SEARCH	SEXTON	SIMION	SMOKER	SPIGOT

SPILTH	STEAMY	STYMIE		TEATED
SPINAL	STEELY	SUABLE	**T**	TEA-URN
SPINED	STEEPY	SUBDUE		TEDDER
SPINEL	STEEVE	SUBLET	TABARD	TEDIUM
SPINET	STELAE	SUBMIT	TABLET	TEEMER
SPINNY	STENCH	SUBORN	TABOUR	TEETHE
SPIRAL	STEPPE	SUBTLE	TABRET	TELLER
SPIRED	STEREO	SUBTLY	TABULA	TELSON
SPIRIT	STICKY	SUBURB	TACKLE	TEMPER
SPLASH	STIFLE	SUBWAY	TACTIC	TEMPLE
SPLEEN	STIGMA	SUCCOR	TAENIA	TENANT
SPLICE	STILLY	SUCKER	TAG-RAG	TENDER
SPLINT	STINGO	SUCKLE	TAILED	TENDON
SPOKEN	STINGY	SUDDEN	TAILOR	TENNIS
SPONGE	STIPES	SUFFER	TAKING	TENREC
SPONGY	STITCH	SUFFIX	TALCKY	TENSOR
SPOONY	STITHY	SUGARY	TALENT	TENTED
SPORAN	STIVER	SUITOR	TALION	TENTER
SPOTTY	STODGE	SULCUS	TALKER	TENURE
SPOUSE	STODGY	SULLEN	TALLOW	TEPEFY
SPRAIN	STOCKS	SULTAN	TALMUD	TERAPH
SPRANG	STOKER	SULTRY	TAMELY	TERCEL
SPRAWL	STOLEN	SUMACH	TAMINE	TEREDO
SPREAD	STOLID	SUMMER	TAMINY	TERETE
SPRING	STOLON	SUMMIT	TAMPER	TERGAL
SPRINT	STONER	SUMMON	TAM-TAM	TERMLY
SPRITE	STONES	SUN-BOW	TAN-BED	TERROR
SPROUT	STOOGE	SUNDAY	TANDEM	TESTER
SPRUCE	STORAX	SUNDER	TANGLE	TETCHY
SPRUNG	STORER	SUN-DEW	TANGLY	TETHER
SPUNGE	STOREY	SUNDRY	TANIST	TETRAD
SPURGE	STORMY	SUNKEN	TANNER	TETTER
SPUTUM	STRAIN	SUNLIT	TANNIC	TEUTON
SQUALL	STRAIT	SUNSET	TANNIN	THALER
SQUAMA	STRAKE	SUPERB	TAN-PIT	THANKS
SQUARE	STRAND	SUPINE	TANREC	THATCH
SQUASH	STRASS	SUPPER	TAN-VAT	THEBES
SQUAWK	STRATA	SUPPLE	TAPPET	THECAL
SQUEAK	STRATH	SUPPLY	TARGET	THEINE
SQUEAL	STRAWY	SURELY	TARGUM	THEISM
SQUILL	STREAK	SURETY	TARIFF	THEIST
SQUINT	STREAM	SURTAX	TARPAN	THENCE
SQUIRE	STREET	SURVEY	TARPON	THEORY
SQUIRM	STRESS	SUTILE	TARPUM	THESES
SQUIRT	STRIAE	SUTLER	TARSAL	THESIS
STABLE	STRICT	SUTTEE	TARSIA	THETIS
STABLY	STRIDE	SUTURE	TARSUS	THEWED
STACTE	STRIFE	SWAMPY	TARTAN	THIEVE
STAFFS	STRIKE	SWARDY	TARTAR	THINLY
STAGER	STRING	SWARTH	TARTER	THIRST
STAGEY	STRIPE	SWATHE	TARTLY	THIRTY
TSAITH	STRIVE	SWEATY	TASKER	THISBE
STALKY	STROKE	SWEEPY	TASSEL	THORAX
STAMEN	STROLL	SWERVE	TASTER	THORNY
STANCH	STRONG	SWINGE	TATTER	THORPE
STANZA	STROVE	SWIPES	TATTLE	THOUGH
STAPES	STRUCK	SWITCH	TATTOO	THOWEL
STAPLE	STRUMA	SWIVEL	TAURUS	THRALL
STARCH	STRUNG	SYLVAN	TAUTOG	THRASH
STARED	STUBBY	SYMBOL	TAVERN	THREAD
STARER	STUCCO	SYNDIC	TAWDRY	THREAT
STARRY	STUDIO	SYNTAX	TAWERY	THRENE
STARVE	STUFFY	SYPHON	T-CLOTH	THRESH
STATED	STUMPY	SYRIAC	TEA-CUP	THRICE
STATIC	STUPID	SYRIAN	TEA-POT	THRIFT
STATUE	STUPOR	SYRINX	TEAPOY	THRILL
STATUS	STURDY	SYRUPY	TEARER	THRIPS
STAVES	STYLAR	SYSTEM	TEASEL	THRIVE
STAYER	STYLET	SYZYGY	TEASER	THROAT
STEADY	STYLUS		TEA-SET	THRONE

THRONG	TONSOR	TRUANT	UNCIAL	UNTOLD
THROVE	TOOTER	TRUDGE	UNCOIL	UNTROD
THROWN	TOOTHY	TRUISM	UNCORD	UNTRUE
THRUSH	TOPPER	TRUMPS	UNCORK	UNTUNE
THRUST	TOPPLE	TRUSTY	UNCURL	UNUSED
THWACK	TORIES	TRYING	UNDINE	UNVEIL
THWART	TORPID	TSETSE	UNDOER	UNWARY
THYMOL	TORPOR	TUBFUL	UNDONE	UNWELL
THYMUS	TORQUE	TUBING	UNDULY	UNWEPT
THYRSE	TORRID	TUBULE	UNEASY	UNWIND
THYRSI	TOSSER	TUCKER	UNEVEN	UNWISE
TIBIAL	TOSS-UP	TUCKET	UNFAIR	UNWORN
TICKET	TOTHER	TUFTED	UNFELT	UNWRAP
TICKLE	TOTTER	TUGGER	UNFOLD	UNYOKE
TIDBIT	TOUCAN	TULWAR	UNFREE	UPBEAR
TIDILY	TOUCHY	TUMBLE	UNFURL	UPBIND
TIERCE	TOUPEE	TUMEFY	UNGIRD	UPCAST
TIE-ROD	TOUPET	TUMOUR	UNGLUE	UPCOIL
TIE-WIG	TOUSLE	TUMULT	UNGUAL	UPCURL
TIFFIN	TOUTER	TUNDRA	UNHAND	UPHILL
TIGHTS	TOWAGE	TUNING	UNHOLY	UPHOLD
TILERY	TOWARD	TUNNEL	UNHOOD	UPKEEP
TILING	TOWERY	TURBAN	UNHOOK	UPLAND
TILLER	TOYMAN	TURBID	UNHUNG	UPLIFT
TILTER	TRACER	TURBOT	UNHURT	UP-LINE
TIMBER	TRACES	TUREEN	UNHUSK	UPMOST
TIMBRE	TRADER	TURFEN	UNIPED	UPPISH
TIMELY	TRAGIC	TURGID	UNIQUE	UPREAR
TIMIST	TRANCE	TURKEY	UNISON	UPRISE
TIMOUS	TRAPAN	TURNER	UNITED	UPROAR
TINDER	TRAPES	TURNIP	UNITER	UPROOT
TINGES	TRASHY	TURRET	UNJUST	UPRUSH
TINGLE	TRAVEL	TURTLE	UNKIND	UPSHOT
TINKER	TRAVIS	TURVES	UNKNIT	UPSIDE
TINKLE	TREATY	TUSCAN	UNLACE	UPSOAR
TINMAN	TREBLE	TUSKED	UNLADE	UPWARD
TINNER	TREBLY	TUSKER	UNLESS	URANIC
TINSEL	TREMOR	TUSSLE	UNLIKE	URANUS
TIP-CAT	TRENCH	TUYERE	UNLINK	URBANE
TIPPET	TREPAN	TWELVE	UNLOAD	URCHIN
TIPPLE	TRESSY	TWENTY	UNLOCK	UREMIA
TIPTOE	TRIBAL	TWIGGY	UNMAKE	URETER
TIPTOP	TRICKY	TWINGE	UNMASK	URGENT
TIRADE	TRIFID	TWITCH	UNMEET	URINAL
TIRING	TRIFLE	TWO-PLY	UNMIXT	URSINE
TISSUE	TRIGON	TYMPAN	UNMOOR	USABLE
TITBIT	TRIGYN	TYPHUS	UNPACK	USANCE
TITHER	TRIMLY	TYPIFY	UNPAID	USEFUL
TITLED	TRINAL	TYPIST	UNREAD	USURER
TITTER	TRIPLE	TYRANT	UNREAL	UTERUS
TITTLE	TRIPLY	TYRIAN	UNREST	UTMOST
TMESIS	TRIPOD		UNRIPE	UTOPIA
TOCSIN	TRIPOS		UNROBE	UVULAR
TODDLE	TRITON		UNROLL	
TOFFEE	TRIUNE	**U**	UNROOF	
TOGGLE	TRIVET		UNROOT	**V**
TOILER	TRIUNE	UBIETY	UNRULY	
TOILET	TROCAR	UGLILY	UNSAFE	VACANT
TOLLER	TROCHE	ULLAGE	UNSAID	VACATE
TOMATO	TROGON	ULSTER	UNSEAL	VACUUM
TOMAUN	TROJAN	ULTIMO	UNSEAT	VAGARY
TOMBAC	TROLLY	UMBLES	UNSEEN	VAGINA
TOMBAK	TROOPS	UMLAUT	UNSENT	VAINLY
TOMBOY	TROPHI	UMPIRE	UNSHED	VALISE
TOM-CAT	TROPHY	UNABLE	UNSHIP	VALLAR
TOMTIT	TROPIC	UNBEND	UNSHOD	VALLEY
TOMTOM	TROUGH	UNBIAS	UNSOLD	VALOUR
TONGUE	TROUPE	UNBIND	UNSTOP	VALUER
TONITE	TROVER	UNBOLT	UNSUNG	VALVED
TONSIL	TROWEL	UNBORN	UNTIDY	VAMPER
		UNCASE		

64

VANDAL
VANISH
VANITY
VAPOUR
VARIED
VARLET
VASSAL
VASTLY
VATFUL
VAWARD
VEINED
VELLUM
VELVET
VENDEE
VENDER
VENDOR
VENDUE
VENEER
VENERY
VENIAL
VENOSE
VENOUS
VENTER
VERBAL
VERGER
VERIFY
VERILY
VERITY
VERMIN
VERNAL
VERSED
VERSUS
VERTEX
VESPER
VESSEL
VESTAL
VESTED
VESTRY
VETCHY
VIABLE
VIBRIO
VICTIM
VICTOR
VICUNA
VIELLE
VIEWER
VIGOUR
VIKING
VILELY
VILIFY
VINERY
VINOUS
VINOSE
VIOLAS
VIOLET
VIOLIN

VIRAGO
VIRGIN
VIRILE
VIROSE
VIRTUE
VISAGE
VISCID
VISCUM
VISIER
VISION
VISUAL
VITALS
VITRIC
VITTAE
VIVACE
VIVIFY
VIZIER
VOICED
VOIDER
VOLANT
VOLLEY
VOLUME
VOLUTE
VOODOO
VORTEX
VOTARY
VOTIVE
VOYAGE
VULCAN
VULGAR

W

WABBLE
WADDLE
WADMAL
WAFFLE
WAFTER
WAGGLE
WAGGON
WAITER
WAINER
WALKER
WALLER
WALLET
WALLOW
WALNUT
WALRUS
WAMPUM
WANDER
WANION
WANTER
WANTON
WAPITI
WARBLE

WAR-CRY
WARDEN
WARDER
WARILY
WARMER
WARMLY
WARMTH
WARNER
WARPED
WARPER
WARREN
WASHER
WASTER
WATERY
WATTLE
WAX-END
WAYLAY
WEAKEN
WEAKLY
WEALTH
WEAPON
WEARER
WEASEL
WEAVER
WEAZEN
WEBBED
WEB-EYE
WEDDED
WEEDER
WEEKLY
WEEPER
WEEVER
WEEVIL
WEIGHT
WELDER
WELKIN
WELTER
WETHER
WHALER
WHARFS
WHEEZE
WHEEZY
WHENCE
WHERRY
WHEYEY
WHILOM
WHILST
WHIMSY
WHINER
WHINNY
WHISKY
WHITEN
WHITES
WHOLLY
WHOOPS!
WICKED

WICKER
WICKET
WIDELY
WIELDY
WIFELY
WIGEON
WIGGED
WIGWAM
WILDER
WILDLY
WILFUL
WILILY
WILLOW
WIMBLE
WIMPLE
WINCER
WINCEY
WINDER
WINDOW
WIND-UP
WINGED
WINKER
WINKLE
WINNER
WINNOW
WINSEY
WINTER
WINTRY
WISDOM
WISELY
WISHER
WITHAL
WITHER
WITHIN
WITTED
WIVERN
WIZARD
WOBBLE
WOEFUL
WOLVES
WOMBAT
WONDER
WONTED
WOODED
WOODEN
WOOING
WOOLLY
WORKER
WORMED
WORRIT
WORSEN
WORSER
WORTHY
WRAITH
WREATH
WRENCH

WRESTS
WRETCH
WRIGHT
WRITER
WRITHE
WRONGS
WYVERN

X

XYLOID
XYSTUS

Y

YANKEE
YARROW
YCLEPT
YEARLY
YEASTY
YELLOW
YEOMAN
YEOMEN
YESTER
YIELDS!
YOICKS!
YONDER
YTTRIA

Z

ZAFFRE
ZANDER
ZAREBA
ZEALOT
ZEBECK
ZECHIN
ZENANA
ZENITH
ZEPHYR
ZEREBA
ZEUGMA
ZIGZAG
ZINCKY
ZIRCON
ZITHER
ZODIAC
ZONARY
ZONATE
ZONULE
ZOUAVE
ZOUNDS!
ZYGOMA

SEVEN-LETTER WORDS

A

AARONIC
ABALONE
ABANDON
ABATTIS
ABAXIAL
ABDOMEN
ABETTER
ABIDING
ABIETIC
ABIGAIL
ABILITY
ABLUENT
ABOLISH
ABREAST
ABRIDGE
ABROACH
ABSCESS
ABSCIND
ABSCOND
ABSENCE
ABSOLVE
ABSTAIN
ABUSIVE
ABYSMAL
ABYSSAL
ACADEMY
ACANTHA
ACCLAIM
ACCOMPT
ACCOUNT
ACCURSE
ACCUSED
ACCUSER
ACEROUS
ACETATE
ACETIFY
ACETOUS
ACHAEAN
ACHIEVE
ACICULA
ACIDIFY
ACIDITY
ACOLYTE
ACONITE
ACORNED
ACQUIRE
ACREAGE
ACROBAT
ACROGEN
ACTABLE
ACTINIA
ACTINIC
ACTRESS
ACTUARY
ACTUATE
ACUTELY
ADAGIAL
ADAMANT
ADAMITE
ADAPTER
ADDABLE
ADDIBLE

ADDRESS
ADDUCER
ADENOID
ADHERER
ADHIBIT
ADIPOSE
ADJOURN
ADJUDGE
ADJUNCT
ADJURER
ADMIRAL
ADMIRER
ADOPTER
ADULATE
ADVANCE
ADVERSE
ADVISED
ADVISER
AEOLIAN
AERATOR
AFFABLE
AFFABLY
AFFIXAL
AFFLICT
AFFRONT
AFRICAN
AGAINST
AGATINE
AGATIZE
AGGRESS
AGILELY
AGILITY
AGITATE
AGNOMEN
AGONIST
AGONIZE
AGRAFFE
AGROUND
AIDLESS
AILMENT
AIMLESS
AIR-BATH
AIR-CELL
AIRLESS
AIR-PUMP
AJUTAGE
ALAMODE
ALBUMEN
ALCALDE
ALCAZAR
ALCHEMY
ALCOHOL
ALCORAN
ALE-COST
ALEMBIC
ALE-WIFE
ALFALFA
ALGEBRA
ALIFORM
ALIMENT
ALIMONY
ALIQUOT
ALKANET
ALKORAN
ALLEGRO

ALL-HAIL
ALLOWER
ALMANAC
ALMONER
ALMONRY
ALMS-MAN
ALOETIC
ALREADY
ALUMINA
ALUMNUS
AMALGAM
AMATEUR
AMATIVE
AMATORY
AMAZING
AMBATCH
AMBIENT
AMENDER
AMENITY
AMENTIA
AMIABLE
AMIABLY
AMIANTH
AMMONIA
AMNESIA
AMNESTY
AMORINO
AMOROUS
AMPHORA
AMPLIFY
AMPULLA
AMUSING
AMUSIVE
AMYLENE
AMYLOID
ANAEMIA
ANAEMIC
ANAGOGE
ANAGRAM
ANALECT
ANALOGY
ANALYSE
ANALYST
ANALYZE
ANAPEST
ANARCHY
ANATOMY
ANBERRY
ANCHOVY
ANCIENT
ANDANTE
ANDIRON
ANEMONE
ANEROID
ANGELIC
ANGELUS
ANGEVIN
ANGLIFY
ANGLING
ANGRILY
ANGUISH
ANGULAR
ANILINE
ANIMATE
ANIMISM

ANIMIST
ANISEED
ANNATES
ANNATTO
ANNELID
ANNOTTO
ANNUENT
ANNUITY
ANNULAR
ANNULET
ANNULUS
ANODYNE
ANOMALY
ANOREXY
ANOSMIA
ANOTHER
ANTACID
ANT-BEAR
ANTENNA
ANT-HILL
ANTHINE
ANTHRAX
ANTIQUE
ANT-LION
ANTONYM
ANUROUS
ANXIETY
ANXIOUS
ANYBODY
ANYWISE
APANAGE
APATITE
APEPSIA
APHASIA
APHEMIA
APHESIS
APHETIC
APHONIA
APHTHAE
APISHLY
APOCOPE
APOLOGY
APOSTLE
APPAREL
APPEASE
APPLAUD
APPOINT
APPRISE
APPROVE
APPULSE
APRICOT
APRIORI
APROPOS
APSIDAL
APTERYX
APTNESS
AQUATIC
AQUEOUS
ARABIAN
ARACHIS
ARAMAIC
ARAMEAN
ARANEID
ARBITER
ARBLAST

ARBUTUS
ARCADED
ARCANUM
ARCHAIC
ARCHERY
ARCHIVE
ARCHWAY
ARCUATE
ARDENCY
ARDUOUS
AREOLAR
ARGYRIA
ARIETTA
ARIDITY
ARMHOLE
ARMIGER
ARMILLA
ARMORIC
ARMOURY
ARNOTTO
ARRAIGN
ARRANGE
ARRIVAL
ARSENAL
ARSENIC
ARTISAN
ARTISTE
ARTLESS
ARUSPEX
ASCETIC
ASCITES
ASCRIBE
ASEXUAL
ASHAMED
ASIATIC
ASININE
ASKANCE
ASPERSE
ASPHALT
ASPIRER
ASQUINT
ASSAGAI
ASSAULT
ASSAYER
ASSEGAI
ASSIZER
ASSUAGE
ASSUMER
ASSURED
ASSURER
ASTATIC
ASTERIA
ASTOUND
ASTRICT
ASTRIDE
ASUNDER
ATAVISM
ATELIER
ATHEISM
ATHEIST
ATHEOUS
ATHIRST
ATHLETE
ATHWART
ATOMISM

ATOMIST	BANDAGE	BEES-WAX	BISTORT	BOREDOM
ATOMIZE	BANDANA	BEGGARY	BITTERN	BOROUGH
ATROPAL	BANDBOX	BEGHARD	BITTERS	BOSCAGE
ATROPHY	BANDEAU	BEGONIA	BITUMEN	BOSKAGE
ATROPIN	BANDLET	BEGUILE	BIVALVE	BOTANIC
ATTACHE	BANDORE	BEGUINE	BIVOUAC	BOTARGO
ATTAINT	BANDROL	BELGIAN	BIZARRE	BOTCHER
ATTEMPT	BANDSAW	BELIEVE	BLABBER	BOTTINE
ATTRACT	BANEFUL	BELLIED	BLACKEN	BOUDOIR
AUCTION	BANKING	BELLITE	BLACKLY	BOUILLI
AUDIBLE	BANQUET	BELL-MAN	BLADDER	BOULDER
AUDIBLY	BANSHEE	BELLOWS	BLANKET	BOUNCER
AUDITOR	BAPTISM	BELOVED	BLANKLY	BOUNDED
AUGITIC	BAPTIST	BELTANE	BLARNEY	BOUNDEN
AUGMENT	BAPTIZE	BELTING	BLASTER	BOUQUET
AUGURAL	BARBULE	BEMUSED	BLATANT	BOURDON
AURATED	BARGAIN	BENCHER	BLEAKLY	BOW-HAND
AURELIA	BARILLA	BENEATH	BLEATER	BOWLINE
AUREOLA	BAR-IRON	BENEFIT	BLEMISH	BOWLING
AURICLE	BARK-BED	BENIGHT	BLES-BOK	BOWSHOT
AUROCHS	BARMAID	BENISON	BLESSED	BOX-TREE
AURORAL	BARN-OWL	BENZENE	BLEWITS	BOXWOOD
AUSPICE	BARONET	BENZOIN	BLINDED	BOYCOTT
AUSTERE	BAROQUE	BEQUEST	BLINDER	BOYHOOD
AUSTRAL	BARRACK	BEREAVE	BLINDLY	BRABBLE
AUTO-CAR	BARRAGE	BERRIED	BLINKER	BRACING
AVARICE	BARRIER	BESEECH	BLISTER	BRACKEN
AVENGER	BAR-SHOT	BESHREW	BLOATED	BRACKET
AVERAGE	BARWOOD	BESIEGE	BLOATER	BRAD-AWL
AVERTER	BARYTES	BESMEAR	BLOSSOM	BRAGGET
AVIATOR	BARYTIC	BESPEAK	BLOTCHY	BRAHMAN
AVIDITY	BASCULE	BESTEAD	BLOTTER	BRAIDED
AVOIDER	BASHFUL	BESTIAL	BLOUSED	BRAINED
AWARDER	BASILAR	BESTREW	BLOW-FLY	BRAMBLE
AWFULLY	BASSOON	BETHINK	BLOWZED	BRAMBLY
AWKWARD	BASTARD	BETIMES	BLUBBER	BRANCHY
AXIALLY	BASTION	BETOKEN	BLUCHER	BRANDED
AXILLAR	BATTERY	BETROTH	BLUE-CAP	BRANDER
AXOLOTL	BATTISH	BETWEEN	BLUE-GUM	BRANGLE
AZIMUTH	BAYONET	BETWIXT	BLUEING	BRAN-NEW
AZOTISE	BAY-SALT	BEWITCH	BLUNDER	BRASIER
AZURITE	BAY-WOOD	BEZETTA	BLUNTLY	BRATTLE
AZYGOUS	BEACHED	BEZIQUE	BLUSTER	BRAVADO
	BEAMING	BIBASIC	BOARDED	BRAVELY
	BEARDED	BICYCLE	BOARDER	BRAVERY
B	BEARING	BIDDING	BOARISH	BRAVURA
	BEARISH	BIFILAR	BOASTER	BRAWLER
BAALISM	BEASTLY	BIGGISH	BOAT-FLY	BRAZIER
BAALITE	BEATIFY	BIG-HORN	BOATMAN	BREADTH
BABBLER	BEATING	BIGNESS	BOBSTAY	BREAKER
BABYISH	BEAUISH	BIGOTED	BOB-TAIL	BREAK-UP
BABYISM	BEBEERU	BIGOTRY	BODEFUL	BREATHE
BACCATE	BECAUSE	BILIARY	BOGGLER	BRECCIA
BACCHIC	BECHARM	BILIOUS	BOILING	BREEDER
BACKING	BECLOUD	BILLION	BOLETUS	BREVIER
BADDISH	BEDDING	BILL-MAN	BOLLARD	BREVITY
BADNESS	BEDEGAR	BILLOWY	BOLSTER	BREWAGE
BAFFLER	BEDEVIL	BINACLE	BOMBARD	BREWERY
BAGASSE	BEDIGHT	BINDERY	BOMBAST	BREWING
BAGGAGE	BEDIZEN	BINDING	BONANZA	BRIBERY
BAGGING	BEDOUIN	BINOCLE	BONDAGE	BRICOLE
BAGPIPE	BED-POST	BIOGENY	BONDMAN	BRIDOON
BAILIFF	BEDROOM	BIOLOGY	BONE-BED	BRIEFLY
BALANCE	BED-TICK	BIOTAXY	BONE-ASH	BRIGATE
BALANUS	BEECHEN	BIPLANE	BONFIRE	BRIGAND
BALCONY	BEEF-TEA	BIPOLAR	BOOKISH	BRIMFUL
BALEFUL	BEE-HIVE	BIRCHEN	BOOKLET	BRIMMER
BALLADE	BEE-LINE	BIRETTA	BOOKMAN	BRINDED
BALLAST	BEE-MOTH	BISCUIT	BOORISH	BRINDLE
BALLOON	BEESTIE	BISMUTH	BORACIC	BRINGER

67

BRINISH
BRISKET
BRISKLY
BRISTLE
BRISTLY
BRITISH
BRITTLE
BROADEN
BROADLY
BROCADE
BROCAGE
BROCARD
BROCKET
BROIDER
BROILER
BROKAGE
BROKING
BROMATE
BROMIDE
BROMINE
BRONZED
BROTHEL
BROTHER
BROUGHT
BROWNIE
BRUISER
BRUSQUE
BRUTIFY
BRUTISH
BRYOZOA
BUCK-EYE
BUCKISH
BUCKLER
BUCKRAM
BUCOLIC
BUDDING
BUFFALO
BUFFOON
BUGBEAR
BUGLOSS
BUILDER
BULBOUS
BULIMIA
BULLACE
BULLATE
BULL-DOG
BULLION
BULLOCK
BULRUSH
BULWARK
BUM-BOAT
BUMPKIN
BUNGLER
BUNTING
BUOYAGE
BUOYANT
BURDOCK
BURGAGE
BURGEON
BURGESS
BURGHAL
BURGHER
BURGLAR
BURMESE
BURNING
BURNISH
BURROCK
BURSARY
BURTHEN
BUSH-CAT

BUSHMAN
BUSTARD
BUSTLER
BUTCHER
BUTMENT
BUTTERY
BUTTOCK
BUTYRIC
BUXOMLY
BUZZARD
BY-GONES
BYSSINE

C

CABARET
CABBAGE
CABBALA
CABINED
CABINET
CABOOSE
CACHEXY
CACIQUE
CACKLER
CACOLET
CADDICE
CADENCE
CADENZA
CADMEAN
CADMIUM
CAESIUM
CAESURA
CAISSON
CAITIFF
CAJOLER
CAJUPUT
CALAMUS
CALCIFY
CALCINE
CALCITE
CALCIUM
CALDRON
CALENDS
CALIBRE
CALIPEE
CALIVER
CALL-BOY
CALLING
CALLOUS
CALMUCK
CALOMEL
CALORIC
CALOTTE
CALOYER
CALTROP
CALUMBA
CALUMET
CALUMNY
CALVARY
CALYCLE
CAMAIEU
CAMBIST
CAMBIUM
CAMBRIC
CAMELRY
CAMPHOR
CAMPION
CAMWOOD
CANAKIN

CANDENT
CANDIED
CANDOUR
CANELLA
CANNERY
CANNULA
CANONRY
CANTATA
CANTEEN
CANTHUS
CANTING
CANTLET
CANVASS
CANZONE
CAPABLE
CAP-A-PIE
CAPERER
CAPITAL
CAPITOL
CAPRICE
CAPRINE
CAPSIZE
CAPSTAN
CAPSULE
CAPTAIN
CAPTION
CAPTIVE
CAPTURE
CARACAL
CARAMEL
CARAVAN
CARAVEL
CARAWAY
CARBIDE
CARBINE
CARCASS
CARDIAC
CARDOON
CAREFUL
CARIBOO
CARIOLE
CARIOUS
CARLINE
CARLIST
CARLOCK
CARMINE
CARNAGE
CARNIFY
CAROCHE
CAROLUS
CAROTID
CAROUSE
CARPING
CARRACK
CARRIER
CARRION
CARROTY
CARTAGE
CARTOON
CART-WAY
CARVING
CASCADE
CASEOUS
CASHIER
CASSADA
CASSAVA
CASSOCK
CASTING
CASTLED
CAST-OFF

CASUIST
CATALAN
CATARRH
CATAWBA
CATBIRD
CATCALL
CATCHER
CATCHUP
CATECHU
CATERAN
CATERER
CAT-FISH
CAT-HEAD
CATHODE
CATHOOD
CATLING
CATMINT
CAT'S-EYE
CAT'S-PAW
CAUDATE
CAULINE
CAUSTIC
CAUTERY
CAUTION
CAVALRY
CAVESON
CAVIARE
CAYENNE
CAZIQUE
CEDILLA
CEDRATE
CEILING
CELADON
CELLULE
CENSURE
CENTAGE
CENTAUR
CENTIME
CENTNER
CENTRAL
CENTRIC
CENTURY
CERAMIC
CEREOUS
CERTAIN
CERTIFY
CERUMEN
CERVINE
CESSION
CESTOID
CETACEA
CHABLIS
CHABOUK
CHAFFER
CHAGRIN
CHALDEE
CHALICE
CHAMADE
CHAMBER
CHAMFER
CHAMOIS
CHAMPAC
CHANCEL
CHANCRE
CHANGER
CHANNEL
CHANTER
CHANTRY
CHAOTIC
CHAPLET

CHAPMAN
CHAPPED
CHAPTER
CHARADE
CHARGER
CHARILY
CHARIOT
CHARITY
CHARMED
CHARMER
CHARNEL
CHARPIE
CHARPOY
CHARQUI
CHARTER
CHASMED
CHASSIS
CHASTEN
CHATEAU
CHATTEL
CHATTER
CHEAPEN
CHEAPLY
CHEATER
CHECKER
CHEDDAR
CHEERER
CHEERLY
CHEETAH
CHEMISE
CHEMIST
CHEQUER
CHERISH
CHEROOT
CHERVIL
CHESNUT
CHESSEL
CHESTED
CHEVIOT
CHEVRON
CHIASMA
CHICANE
CHICKEN
CHICORY
CHIEFLY
CHIGNON
CHIKARA
CHILIAD
CHIMERE
CHIMNEY
CHINESE
CHINNED
CHIPPER
CHIRPER
CHIRRUP
CHISLEU
CHLAMYS
CHLORAL
CHLORIC
CHOLERA
CHOOSER
CHOPINE
CHOPPER
CHORION
CHORIST
CHOROID
CHRISOM
CHROMIC
CHRONIC
CHUCKLE

CHUTNEY	COAL-BED	COMPLOT	CONVERT	COWHERD
CHYLIFY	COAL-GAS	COMPORT	CONVICT	COWHIDE
CHYLOUS	COAL-PIT	COMPOSE	CONVOKE	COW-ITCH
CHYMIFY	COAL-TAR	COMPOST	COOKERY	COWSLIP
CHYMOUS	COAMING	COMPUTE	COOLISH	COW-TREE
CILIARY	COASTER	COMRADE	COOPERY	COXCOMB
CIMBRIC	COATING	CONACRE	COPAIBA	COYNESS
CIMETER	CO-AXIAL	CONCAVE	COPYIST	COZENER
CINDERY	COBBLER	CONCEAL	COPIOUS	CRABBED
CIPOLIN	COCAINE	CONCEDE	COPPERY	CRAB-OIL
CIRCEAN	COCHLEA	CONCEIT	COPPICE	CRACKED
CIRCLED	COCKADE	CONCEPT	CORACLE	CRACKER
CIRCLER	COCKNEY	CONCERN	CORCULE	CRACKLE
CIRCLET	COCK-PIT	CONCERT	CORDAGE	CRAGGED
CIRCUIT	COCO-NUT	CONCISE	CORDATE	CRAMMER
CIRROSE	COCTILE	CONCOCT	CORDIAL	CRAMPED
CISSOID	COCTION	CONCORD	CORDITE	CRAMPON
CISTERN	CODICIL	CONCUSS	CORK-LEG	CRANAGE
CITABLE	CODILLA	CONDEMN	CORNICE	CRANIAL
CITADEL	CODLING	CONDIGN	CORNISH	CRANIUM
CITHARA	COEHORN	CONDOLE	COROLLA	CRANKLE
CITHERN	COELIAC	CONDONE	CORONAL	CRANNOG
CITIZEN	COEQUAL	CONDUCE	CORONER	CRAUNCH
CITRINE	COEXIST	CONDUCT	CORONET	CRAVING
CIVILLY	COGENCY	CONDUIT	CORRECT	CRAWLER
CLACHAN	COGNATE	CONDYLE	CORRODE	CRAZILY
CLACKER	COGNIZE	CONFECT	CORRUPT	CREATIN
CLAMANT	COHABIT	CONFESS	CORSAGE	CREATOR
CLAMBER	COHIBIT	CONFEST	CORSAIR	CREDENT
CLAMOUR	COINAGE	CONFIDE	CORSNED	CREEPER
CLAP-NET	COITION	CONFINE	CORTEGE	CREMATE
CLAPPER	COJUROR	CONFIRM	CORVINE	CREMONA
CLARION	COLDISH	CONFLUX	COSAQUE	CRENATE
CLARITY	COLIBRI	CONFORM	COSMISM	CRESSET
CLASPER	COLICKY	CONFUSE	COSSACK	CRESTED
CLASSIC	COLLATE	CONFUTE	COSTARD	CREVICE
CLATTER	COLLECT	CONGEAL	COSTATE	CRIBBLE
CLAVATE	COLLEGE	CONGEST	COSTIVE	CRICKET
CLAVIER	COLLIDE	CONICAL	COSTREL	CRICOID
CLAY-PIT	COLLIER	CONIFER	COSTUME	CRIMPER
CLEANER	COLLOID	CONJOIN	COTERIE	CRIMPLE
CLEANLY	COLLUDE	CONJURE	COTHURN	CRIMSON
CLEANSE	COLONEL	CONJURY	COTIDAL	CRINGER
CLEARER	COLOURY	CONNATE	COTTAGE	CRINGLE
CLEARLY	COLTISH	CONNECT	COTTIER	CRINITE
CLEAVER	COLUMBA	CONNING	COTTONY	CRINKLE
CLEMENT	COMBINE	CONNIVE	COUCHEE	CRINOID
CLERISY	COMBING	CONNOTE	COUCHER	CRIPPLE
CLERKLY	COMFORT	CONQUER	COUGHER	CRISPER
CLICKER	COMFREY	CONSENT	COULOMB	CRISPIN
CLIMATE	COMICAL	CONSIGN	COULTER	CRISPLY
CLIMBER	COMIQUE	CONSIST	COUNCIL	CRIZZEL
CLINGER	COMITIA	CONSOLE	COUNSEL	CROAKER
CLINKER	COMMAND	CONSOLS	COUNTER	CROCHET
CLIPPER	COMMEND	CONSORT	COUNTRY	CROCKET
CLIVERS	COMMENT	CONSULT	COUPLER	CROFTER
CLOACAL	COMMODE	CONSUME	COUPLET	CROOKED
CLOSELY	COMMOVE	CONTACT	COUPURE	CROPPER
CLOSING	COMMUNE	CONTAIN	COURAGE	CROQUET
CLOSURE	COMMUTE	CONTEMN	COURIER	CROSIER
CLOTHES	COMPACT	CONTEND	COURSER	CROSSED
CLOUDED	COMPANY	CONTENT	COURTER	CROSSLY
CLOUTED	COMPARE	CONTEST	COURTLY	CROWBAR
CLOVERY	COMPART	CONTEXT	COUVADE	CROWDED
CLOYING	COMPASS	CONTORT	COVERER	CROWNED
CLUB-LAW	COMPEER	CONTOUR	COVETER	CROZIER
CLUSTER	COMPEND	CONTROL	COW-BANE	CRUCIAL
CLUTTER	COMPETE	CONTUSE	COW-CALF	CRUCIFY
CLYSTER	COMPILE	CONVENE	COWHAGE	CRUDELY
COAGENT	COMPLEX	CONVENT	COW-HEEL	CRUDITY

CRUELLY	CZARINA	DEFACER	DEVELOP	DISCOUS
CRUELTY		DEFAMER	DEVIATE	DISCUSS
CRUISER		DEFAULT	DEVILRY	DISDAIN
CRUISIE	**D**	DEFENCE	DEVIOUS	DISEASE
CRUMBLE		DEFIANT	DEVISEE	DISGUST
CRUMBLY	DABBLER	DEFICIT	DEVISER	DISHING
CRUMPET	DACOITY	DEFILER	DEVISOR	DISJOIN
CRUMPLE	DAISIED	DEFINED	DEVOLVE	DISLIKE
CRUPPER	DAKOITY	DEFINER	DEVOTED	DISLINK
CRUSADE	DALLIER	DEFLECT	DEVOTEE	DISMASK
CRUSADO	DAMNIFY	DEFORCE	DEW-CLAW	DISMAST
CRUSHER	DAMNING	DEFRAUD	DEWDROP	DISMISS
CRYPTAL	DAMPISH	DEFUNCT	DEWFALL	DISOBEY
CRYPTIC	DANDIFY	DEGRADE	DEXTRAL	DISPARK
CRYSTAL	DANGLER	DEHISCE	DIABASE	DISPART
CTENOID	DAPPLED	DEICIDE	DIAGRAM	DISPLAY
CUBHOOD	DARKISH	DEICTIC	DIALECT	DISPONE
CUBICAL	DARLING	DEIFORM	DIALIST	DISPORT
CUBICLE	DASHING	DEISTIC	DIALYSE	DISPOSE
CUBITAL	DASH-POT	DELAINE	DIAMOND	DISPUTE
CUCKOLD	DASTARD	DELAYER	DIAPASM	DISROBE
CUDBEAR	DASYURE	DELIGHT	DIARCHY	DISROOT
CUDWEED	DAUNTER	DELIVER	DIARIAN	DISRUPT
CUIRASS	DAUPHIN	DELPHIC	DIARIST	DISSECT
CUISINE	DAWDLER	DELTAIC	DIBBLER	DISSENT
CULLION	DAWNING	DELTOID	DICE-BOX	DISTAFF
CULPRIT	DAY-BOOK	DELUDER	DICKENS	DISTAIN
CULTURE	DAY-LILY	DEMERIT	DICTATE	DISTANT
CULVERT	DAYLONG	DEMESNE	DICTION	DISTEND
CUMFREY	DAYSMAN	DEMI-GOD	DIETARY	DISTICH
CUMSHAW	DAY-STAR	DEMIREP	DIETIST	DISTORT
CUMULUS	DAYTIME	DEMONIC	DIFFORM	DISTURB
CUNEATE	DAYWORK	DEMOTIC	DIFFUSE	DISYOKE
CUNNING	DAZZLER	DENIZEN	DIGAMMA	DITCHER
CUPPING	DEAD-EYE	DENSELY	DIGGING	DITTANY
CUPROUS	DEAD-PAY	DENSITY	DIGITAL	DIURNAL
CUPRITE	DEAD-SET	DENTATE	DIGNIFY	DIVERGE
CURABLE	DEALING	DENTINE	DIGNITY	DIVERSE
CURACAO	DEANERY	DENTIST	DIGRAPH	DIVIDER
CURATOR	DEATHLY	DEODAND	DIGRESS	DIVINER
CURIOUS	DEBACLE	DEPLETE	DILATER	DIVISOR
CURLING	DEBASED	DEPLORE	DILATOR	DIVORCE
CURRANT	DEBASER	DEPLUME	DILEMMA	DIVULGE
CURRENT	DEBATER	DEPOSER	DILUENT	DIZZILY
CURRIER	DEBAUCH	DEPOSIT	DIMETER	DJEREED
CURRISH	DEBOUCH	DEPRAVE	DIMMISH	DOCKAGE
CURSING	DECADAL	DEPRESS	DIMNESS	DOESKIN
CURSIVE	DECAGON	DEPRIVE	DIMPLED	DOG-CART
CURSORY	DECAGYN	DERANGE	DIMYARY	DOGFISH
CURSTLY	DECANAL	DERIDER	DINETTE	DOGGISH
CURTAIL	DECAPOD	DERIVER	DIOCESE	DOG-HOLE
CURTAIN	DECEASE	DERMOID	DIORAMA	DOG-ROSE
CURVITY	DECEIVE	DERRICK	DIORITE	DOG'S-EAR
CUSHION	DECENCY	DERVISH	DIOXIDE	DOG-SICK
CUSTARD	DECIDED	DESCANT	DIPLOMA	DOGSKIN
CUSTODY	DECIDER	DESCEND	DIPLOPY	DOG-STAR
CUT-AWAY	DECIDUA	DESCENT	DIPOLAR	DOG-TROT
CUTICLE	DECIMAL	DESERVE	DIPTYCH	DOGWOOD
CUTLASS	DECLAIM	DESIRER	DIREFUL	DOLABRA
CUTLERY	DECLARE	DESPAIR	DIRT-BED	DOLEFUL
CUTTING	DECLINE	DESPISE	DIRTILY	DOLPHIN
CYANEAN	DECORUM	DESPOIL	DIRT-PYE	DOLTISH
CYANIDE	DECREER	DESPOND	DISABLE	DOMICAL
CYCLIST	DECREET	DESSERT	DISAVOW	DOMINIE
CYCLOID	DECRIAL	DESTINE	DISBAND	DONNISH
CYCLONE	DECRIER	DESTINY	DISCAGE	DOORWAY
CYCLOPS	DECUMAN	DESTROY	DISCARD	DOR-HAWK
CYNICAL	DECUPLE	DETERGE	DISCERN	DORMANT
CYPRESS	DEEDFUL	DETRACT	DISCOID	DOUBLET
CYPRIAN	DEEP-SEA	DETRUDE	DISCORD	DOUBTER

DOUCEUR
DOUGHTY
DOVE-COT
DOVELET
DOWAGER
DOWERED
DRACHMA
DRAGGLE
DRAG-NET
DRAGOON
DRAINER
DRAPERY
DRASTIC
DRAUGHT
DRAWING
DRAYAGE
DRAYMAN
DREAMER
DREDGER
DRESSER
DRIBBLE
DRIBLET
DRIFTER
DRINKER
DRIZZLE
DRIZZLY
DROMOND
DRONISH
DROPLET
DROPPER
DROUGHT
DROUTHY
DRUGGET
DRUIDIC
DRUMMER
DRUNKEN
DRYNESS
DRY-SHOD
DUALISM
DUALIST
DUALITY
DUBIETY
DUBIOUS
DUCALLY
DUCHESS
DUCTILE
DUDGEON
DUKEDOM
DULCIFY
DULLARD
DULLISH
DULNESS
DUMPISH
DUNCERY
DUNGEON
DUNNAGE
DUNNISH
DUPABLE
DURABLE
DURABLY
DURAMEN
DURANCE
DURMAST
DUSKILY
DUSKISH
DUST-MAN
DUTEOUS
DUTIFUL
DUUMVIR
DWELLER

DWINDLE
DYE-WOOD
DYE-WORK
DYINGLY
DYNAMIC
DYNASTY
DYSLOGY
DYSURIA
DYSURIC

E

EAGERLY
EANLING
EAR-ACHE
EAR-DROP
EAR-DRUM
EAR-HOLE
EARLDOM
EARLESS
EAR-MARK
EARNEST
EARNING
EAR-PICK
EAR-RING
EAR-SHOT
EARTHEN
EARTHLY
EASEFUL
EASTERN
EASTING
EATABLE
EBB-TIDE
EBONITE
EBONIZE
EBRIETY
ECBATIC
ECBOLIC
ECDYSIS
ECHELON
ECHIDNA
ECHINUS
ECLIPSE
ECLOGUE
ECONOMY
ECSTASY
ECTOPIA
ECTOZOA
ECTYPAL
EDACITY
EDICTAL
EDIFICE
EDITION
EDUCATE
EEL-BUCK
EEL-POUT
EFFABLE
EFFENDI
EFFULGE
EGG-BIRD
EGG-FLIP
EGOTISM
EGOTIST
EGOTIZE
EJECTOR
ELASTIC
ELATION
ELDERLY
ELECTOR

ELECTRO
ELEGANT
ELEGIAC
ELEGIST
ELEGIZE
ELEMENT
ELEVATE
ELF-BOLT
ELF-LAND
ELF-LOCK
ELISION
ELIXATE
ELLAGIC
ELLIPSE
ELOGIUM
ELOHIST
ELUSION
ELUSIVE
ELUSORY
ELYSIAN
ELYSIUM
ELYTRON
ELYTRUM
ELZEVIR
EMANANT
EMANATE
EMBARGO
EMBASSY
EMBLAZE
EMBOSOM
EMBOWEL
EMBOWER
EMBRACE
EMBROIL
EMBROWN
EMBRYOS
EMERALD
EMERODS
EMINENT
EMOTION
EMPEROR
EMPIRIC
EMPOWER
EMPRESS
EMPRISE
EMPTIER
EMPYEMA
EMULATE
EMULOUS
ENACTOR
ENAMOUR
ENCENIA
ENCHAIN
ENCHANT
ENCHASE
ENCLASP
ENCLAVE
ENCLOSE
ENCRUST
ENDEMIC
ENDLESS
ENDLONG
ENDOGEN
ENDORSE
ENDOWER
ENDWISE
ENERGIC
ENFEOFF
ENFORCE
ENGAGED

ENGLISH
ENGORGE
ENGRAFT
ENGRAIL
ENGRAIN
ENGRAVE
ENGROSS
ENHANCE
ENJOYER
ENLARGE
ENLIVEN
ENNOBLE
ENOUNCE
ENQUIRE
ENSLAVE
ENSNARE
ENTASIS
ENTENTE
ENTERIC
ENTHRAL
ENTICER
ENTITLE
ENTOMIC
ENTONIC
ENTRAIL
ENTRAIN
ENTRANT
ENTREAT
ENTRUST
ENTWINE
ENTWIST
ENVELOP
ENVIOUS
ENVENOM
ENVIRON
EPACRIS
EPARCHY
EPAULET
EPERGNE
EPICARP
EPICENE
EPICURE
EPIDERM
EPIDOTE
EPIGENE
EPIGRAM
EPISODE
EPISTLE
EPITAPH
EPITHET
EPITOME
EPIZOAN
EPIZOON
EPOCHAL
EQUABLE
EQUABLY
EQUALLY
EQUATOR
EQUERRY
EQUINOX
ERASION
ERASURE
ERECTER
ERECTOR
ERECTLY
ERELONG
EREMITE
ERGOTED
ERISTIC
ERMINED

ERODENT
EROSION
EROSIVE
ERRATIC
ERRATUM
ERRHINE
ERUDITE
ESCAPER
ESCHEAT
ESCUAGE
ESPARTO
ESPOUSE
ESQUIRE
ESSAYER
ESSENCE
ESTHETE
ESTIVAL
ESTRADE
ESTREAT
ESTUARY
ETAGERE
ETCHING
ETERNAL
ETESIAN
ETHICAL
ETHMOID
EUGENIC
EULOGIC
EUPEPSY
EUPHONY
EUPNOEA
EVANGEL
EVANISH
EVASION
EVASIVE
EVENING
EVICTOR
EVIDENT
EVOLVER
EXACTER
EXACTOR
EXALTER
EXAMINE
EXAMPLE
EXCERPT
EXCITER
EXCLAIM
EXCLAVE
EXCLUDE
EXCRETA
EXCRETE
EXCUSER
EXECUTE
EXEGETE
EXERGUE
EXHAUST
EXHIBIT
EXIGENT
EXOGAMY
EXPANSE
EXPENSE
EXPIATE
EXPLAIN
EXPLODE
EXPLOIT
EXPLORE
EXPOSED
EXPOSER
EXPOUND
EXPRESS

EXPUNGE
EXSCIND
EXTATIC
EXTINCT
EXTRACT
EXTREME
EXTRUDE
EXUVIAE
EXUVIAL
EYEBALL
EYEBROW
EYELASH
EYELESS
EYESHOT
EYESORE

F

FABLIAU
FACETTE
FACTION
FACTORY
FACULAR
FACULTY
FADDIST
FADDISH
FADEDLY
FAECULA
FAGOTTO
FAIENCE
FAILING
FAILURE
FAINTLY
FAIRILY
FAIRING
FAIRISH
FALCATE
FALLACY
FALSELY
FALSIFY
FALSISM
FALSITY
FAMULUS
FANATIC
FANCIED
FANCIER
FANCIES
FANFARE
FAN-PALM
FANTAIL
FANTASM
FARADIC
FARCEUR
FARCING
FARDAGE
FARMING
FARMOST
FARNESS
FARRAGO
FARRIER
FARTHER
FASCINE
FASHION
FAST-DAY
FATALLY
FATEFUL
FATIGUE
FATLING
FATNESS

FATUITY
FATUOUS
FAUNIST
FAUX-PAS
FEARFUL
FEASTER
FEATHER
FEATURE
FEBRILE
FEDERAL
FEEDING
FEELING
FEIGNED
FEIGNER
FELSITE
FELSPAR
FELTING
FELUCCA
FENCING
FEODARY
FEOFFEE
FEOFFER
FEOFFOR
FERMENT
FERNERY
FERN-OWL
FERRUGO
FERRULE
FERTILE
FERVENT
FERVOUR
FESTIVE
FESTOON
FETLOCK
FEUDARY
FEWNESS
FIANCÉE
FIASCOS
FIBSTER
FIBRINE
FIBROID
FIBROUS
FICTILE
FICTION
FICTIVE
FIDGETY
FIELDER
FIERILY
FIFTEEN
FIFTHLY
FIGHTER
FIGMENT
FIGURAL
FIGURED
FILBERT
FILCHER
FILEMOT
FILIATE
FILIBEG
FILICAL
FILINGS
FILLING
FINABLE
FINALLY
FINANCE
FINBACK
FINDING
FINESSE
FINICAL
FINIKIN

FINLESS
FINNISH
FIREARM
FIRE-BOX
FIRE-DOG
FIREFLY
FIREMAN
FIRE-NEW
FIRE-PAN
FIRE-POT
FIRSTLY
FISHERY
FISH-FAG
FISHING
FISSILE
FISSION
FISSURE
FISTULA
FITCHET
FITCHEW
FITNESS
FITTING
FIXABLE
FIXEDLY
FIXTURE
FLACCID
FLAMING
FLANEUR
FLANKER
FLANNEL
FLAPPER
FLARING
FLATTEN
FLATTER
FLAUNTY
FLAVOUR
FLEECED
FLEECER
FLEERER
FLEETLY
FLEMING
FLEMISH
FLESHED
FLESHER
FLESHLY
FLEURET
FLEXILE
FLEXION
FLEXURE
FLICKER
FLIGHTY
FLIPPER
FLITTER
FLOATER
FLOGGER
FLOORER
FLORIST
FLOTSAM
FLOUNCE
FLOUTER
FLOWAGE
FLOWERY
FLOWING
FLUENCY
FLUNKEY
FLUORIC
FLUSTER
FLUTINA
FLUTING
FLUTIST

FLUTTER
FLUVIAL
FLUXION
FOGGAGE
FOGYISM
FOGGILY
FOLIAGE
FOLIATE
FOLIOLE
FOOLERY
FOOLISH
FOOTING
FOOTMAN
FOOTPAD
FOOTWAY
FOPLING
FOPPERY
FOPPISH
FORAGER
FORAMEN
FORAYER
FORBADE
FORBEAR
FORBORE
FORCEPS
FORCING
FOREARM
FOREIGN
FORELEG
FOREMAN
FORERUN
FORESEE
FORETOP
FOREVER
FORFEIT
FORFEND
FORGAVE
FORGERY
FORGING
FORGIVE
FORGOER
FORLORN
FORMULA
FORSAKE
FORTIFY
FORTLET
FORTUNE
FORWARD
FOSSICK
FOULARD
FOUMART
FOUNDER
FOUNDRY
FOURGON
FOVEATE
FRAGILE
FRAILTY
FRAMING
FRANKLY
FRANTIC
FRAUGHT
FRECKLE
FRECKLY
FREEDOM
FREEMAN
FREIGHT
FRESHEN
FRESHET
FRESHLY
FRETFUL

FRETTED
FRIABLE
FRIBBLE
FRIEZED
FRIGATE
FRINGED
FRISIAN
FRISKET
FRITTER
FRIZZLE
FRIZZLY
FROCKED
FROGGED
FRONTAL
FRONTED
FROUNCE
FROWARD
FRUSTUM
FUCHSIA
FUDDLER
FUGUIST
FULCRUM
FULGENT
FULLING
FULMINE
FULNESS
FULSOME
FULVOUS
FUMBLER
FUMETTE
FUNERAL
FUNGOID
FUNGOUS
FUNICLE
FUNNILY
FURBISH
FURCATE
FURCULA
FURIOSO
FURIOUS
FURLONG
FURMITY
FURNACE
FURNISH
FURRIER
FURRING
FURROWY
FURTHER
FURTIVE
FUSCOUS
FUSIBLE
FUSSILY
FUSTIAN

G

GABBLER
GABELLE
GADWELL
GAINFUL
GAINING
GAINSAY
GAIRISH
GALANGA
GALEATE
GALENIC
GALILEE
GALIPOT
GALLANT

GALLEON	GIBBOSE	GOUACHE	GUANACO	HATCHER
GALLERY	GIBBOUS	GOURMET	GUARDED	HATCHET
GALLING	GIDDILY	GOUTILY	GUDGEON	HATEFUL
GALLIOT	GIGGLER	GRABBER	GUERDON	HAUBERK
GALLIUM	GILDING	GRACILE	GUESSER	HAUGHTY
GALLOON	GIMBALS	GRACKLE	GUILDER	HAULAGE
GALLOWS	GIMBLET	GRADATE	GUILDRY	HAUNTED
GALUMPH	GINGHAM	GRADUAL	GUIPURE	HAUNTER
GAMBIER	GINSENG	GRAFTER	GUMMING	HAUTBOY
GAMBLER	GIPSIES	GRAINED	GUMMOUS	HAUTEUR
GAMBOGE	GIRAFFE	GRAMARY	GUNNERY	HAWKING
GAMBREL	GIRLISH	GRAMMAR	GUNSHOT	HAZELLY
GANGWAY	GITTERN	GRAMPUS	GUNWALE	HEADILY
GANTLET	GIZZARD	GRANARY	GURNARD	HEADING
GARBAGE	GLACIAL	GRANDAM	GUSHING	HEADWAY
GARBLER	GLACIER	GRANDEE	GUTTATE	HEALING
GARBOIL	GLADDEN	GRANDLY	GUTTLER	HEALTHY
GARDANT	GLAMOUR	GRANGER	GUZZLER	HEARING
GARFISH	GLARING	GRANITE	GYMNAST	HEARKEN
GARGOIL	GLAZIER	GRANTEE		HEARSAY
GARLAND	GLEANER	GRANTER		HEARTED
GARMENT	GLEBOUS	GRANTOR	**H**	HEARTEN
GARNISH	GLEEFUL	GRANULE		HEATHEN
GAROTTE	GLEEMAN	GRAPERY	HABITAT	HEATHER
GARROTS	GLIMMER	GRAPHIC	HABITED	HEATING
GASEITY	GLIMPSE	GRAPNEL	HABITUÉ	HEAVILY
GASEOUS	GLISTEN	GRAPPLE	HACHURE	HEBRAIC
GASTRIC	GLISTER	GRASPER	HACKBUT	HECKLER
GATEWAY	GLITTER	GRATIFY	HACKING	HECTARE
GAUDILY	GLOBATE	GRATING	HACKLER	HEDGING
GAUFFER	GLOBOSE	GRAVELY	HACKNEY	HEDONIC
GAULISH	GLOBOUS	GRAVITY	HADDOCK	HEEDFUL
GAUNTLY	GLOBULE	GRAYISH	HAGGARD	HEINOUS
GAVOTTE	GLORIFY	GRAZIER	HAGGISH	HEIRDOM
GAYNESS	GLOSSER	GRAZING	HAGGLER	HEIRESS
GAZELLE	GLOSSIC	GREATLY	HALBERD	HELICAL
GAZETTE	GLOTTAL	GREAVES	HALCYON	HELICES
GEARING	GLOTTIC	GRECIAN	HALIBUT	HELLISH
GEHENNA	GLOTTIS	GREENLY	HALIDOM	HELOTRY
GELATIN	GLOWING	GREENTH	HALYARD	HELPFUL
GELDING	GLUCINA	GRENADE	HAMITIC	HEMLOCK
GELIDLY	GLUCOSE	GRIDDLE	HAMMOCK	HENBANE
GEMMATE	GLUTEAL	GRIFFIN	HAMSTER	HENNERY
GEMMULE	GLUTTON	GRIFFON	HANAPER	HENOTIC
GENERAL	GLYPHIC	GRIMACE .	HANDFUL	HEPATIC
GENERIC	GLYPTIC	GRIMILY	HANDILY	HERBAGE
GENESIS	GNARLED	GRINDER	HANDSEL	HERBOSE
GENETTE	GNATHIC	GRIPING	HANGING	HERETIC
GENETIC	GNOSTIC	GRIPPER	HANGMAN	HERNIAL
GENEVAN	GOATISH	GRISKIN	HAPLESS	HEROINE
GENIPAP	GOBBLER	GRISLED	HAPPILY	HEROISM
GENITAL	GODDESS	GRISTLE	HARBOUR	HEROIZE
GENITOR	GODHEAD	GRISTLY	HARDILY	HERONRY
GENTEEL	GODLESS	GRIZZLE	HARDISH	HERRING
GENTIAN	GODLIKE	GRIZZLY	HARELIP	HERSELF
GENTILE	GODLILY	GROCERY	HARICOT	HESSIAN
GENUINE	GODSEND	GROGRAM	HARMFUL	HETAERA
GENUSES	GODSHIP	GROGRAN	HARMONY	HETAIRA
GEODESY	GODWARD	GROINED	HARNESS	HEXAGON
GEOGENY	GOITRED	GROOVED	HARPIST	HEXAPLA
GEOGONY	GOLFING	GROSSLY	HARPOON	HEXAPOD
GEOLOGY	GONDOLA	GROTTOS	HARRIER	HICKORY
GEORGIC	GONIDIA	GROWLER	HARSHLY	HIDALGO
GERMANE	GOOSERY	GRUBBER	HARVEST	HIDEOUS
GESTURE	GORDIAN	GRUDGER	HASHISH	HIGGLER
GHASTLY	GORILLA	GRUFFLY	HASSOCK	HIGHWAY
GHERKIN	GORMAND	GRUMBLE	HASTATE	HILDING
GHOSTLY	GOSHAWK	GRUMOUS	HASTILY	HILLOCK
GIANTLY	GOSLING	GRUNTER	HATABLE	HILLTOP
GIANTRY	GOSSIPY	GRUYÉRE	HATCHEL	HIMSELF

HIPPISH	ICEFOOT	INDUSIA	IRIDIAN	KEELSON
HIRCINE	ICHNITE	INDWELL	IRIDIUM	KEEPING
HIRSUTE	ICINESS	INEPTLY	IRKSOME	KERAMIC
HISTORY	IDEALLY	INERTIA	ISCHIUM	KESTREL
HOARDER	IDENTIC	INERTLY	ISOLATE	KETCHUP
HOBNAIL	IDIOTCY	INEXACT	ISONOMY	KHALIFF
HOGGISH	IDIOTIC	INFANCY	ISTHMUS	KHANATE
HOLDING	IDOLIZE	INFANTA	ITALIAN	KHEDIVE
HOLIBUT	IDYLLIC	INFANTE	ITERATE	KILLING
HOLIDAY	IGNEOUS	INFEOFF		KINDRED
HOLLAND	IGNOBLE	INFIDEL		KINETIC
HOLSTER	IGNOBLY	INFLAME	**J**	KINGDOM
HOMERIC	ILLAPSE	INFLATE		KINGLET
HOMONYM	ILLEGAL	INFLECT	JACINTH	KINLESS
HONESTY	ILLICIT	INFLICT	JACKASS	KINSMAN
HOPEFUL	ILLNESS	INFULAE	JACKDAW	KINSMEN
HOPLITE	IMAGERY	INGESTA	JACOBIN	KIRTLED
HORIZON	IMAGINE	INGOING	JACOBUS	KITCHEN
HORNLET	IMBIBER	INGRAFT	JACONET	KNACKER
HORRENT	IMBOSOM	INGRAIL	JAGGERY	KNAGGED
HOSANNA	IMBOWEL	INGRAIN	JAGHIRE	KNARRED
HOSEMAN	IMBOWER	INGRATE	JANITOR	KNARLED
HOSIERY	IMBROWN	INGRESS	JANUARY	KNAVERY
HOSPICE	IMITANT	INHABIT	JARGOON	KNAVISH
HOSTAGE	IMITATE	INHALER	JASMINE	KNEELER
HOSTESS	IMMENSE	INHERIT	JASPERY	KNITTER
HOSTILE	IMMERGE	INHIBIT	JAVELIN	KNOBBED
HOSTLER	IMMERSE	INHUMAN	JEALOUS	KNOCKER
HOTNESS	IMMORAL	INITIAL	JEHOVAH	KNOTTED
HOTSPUR	IMPANEL	INJURER	JEJUNUM	KNOWING
HOUSING	IMPASTE	INKHORN	JELLIES	KNUCKLE
HOWBEIT	IMPASTO	INKLING	JEMADAR	KOUMISS
HOWEVER	IMPEACH	INLAYER	JEMIDAR	KREUZER
HOWLING	IMPEARL	INNERVE	JEOPARD	KURSAAL
HUELESS	IMPERIL	INQUEST	JETTIES	KYANIZE
HUFFISH	IMPETUS	INQUIRE	JEWELRY	
HULKING	IMPIETY	INQUIRY	JOBBERY	
HUMANLY	IMPINGE	INSHORE	JOCULAR	**L**
HUMDRUM	IMPIOUS	INSIGHT	JOINERY	
HUMERAL	IMPLANT	INSIPID	JOINING	LABIATE
HUMERUS	IMPLEAD	INSNARE	JOINTED	LACONIC
HUMIDLY	IMPLORE	INSPECT	JOINTLY	LACQUER
HUMMOCK	IMPOUND	INSPIRE	JOLLILY	LACTEAL
HUMORAL	IMPRESS	INSTALL	JOLLITY	LACTINE
HUNDRED	IMPRINT	INSTANT	JONQUIL	LACTOSE
HUNTING	IMPROVE	INSTATE	JOTTING	LACUNAE
HURRIED	IMPULSE	INSTEAD	JOURNAL	LACUNAR
HURTFUL	IMPUTER	INSULAR	JOURNEY	LADANUM
HUSBAND	INANITY	INSURER	JOUSTER	LAGGARD
HUSKILY	INBOARD	INTEGER	JOYLESS	LAICIZE
HUSSITE	INBREAK	INTENSE	JUBILEE	LAKELET
HUSWIFE	INBREED	INTERIM	JUDAISM	LAMBENT
HYALINE	INCENSE	INTITLE	JUDAIZE	LAMBKIN
HYALITE	INCISOR	INTRANT	JUDASES	LAMELLA
HYALOID	INCIVIL	INTROIT	JUGATED	LAMINAE
HYDATID	INCLINE	INTRUDE	JUGGLER	LAMINAR
HYDRANT	INCLOSE	INTRUST	JUGULAR	LAMPION
HYDRATE	INCLUDE	INTWINE	JUNIPER	LAMPOON
HYDRIDE	INCOMER	INTWIST	JUPITER	LAMPREY
HYDROUS	INCRUST	INVADER	JURYMAN	LANDING
HYGEIAN	INCUBUS	INVALID	JUSSIVE	LANGUID
HYGIENE	INCURVE	INVEIGH	JUSTICE	LANGUOR
HYMNODY	INDEXES	INVERSE	JUSTIFY	LANIARY
	INDEXER	INVITER		LANTERN
	INDICES	INVOICE		LANYARD
	INDITER	INVOLVE	**K**	LAPELLE
	INDOORS	INWARDS		LAPILLI
I	INDORSE	INWEAVE	KAINITE	LAPWING
IAMBIZE	INDUCER	IRANIAN	KALMUCK	LARCENY
IBERIAN	INDULGE	IRICISM	KATYDID	LARGELY
ICEBERG				

LARGESS
LASHING
LASTING
LATCHET
LATENCY
LATERAL
LATHING
LATRINE
LATTICE
LAUGHER
LAUNDRY
LAWLESS
LAWSUIT
LAXNESS
LAZARET
LEADING
LEAFAGE
LEAFLET
LEAGUED
LEAGUER
LEAKAGE
LEARNED
LEARNER
LEASING
LEATHER
LECHERY
LECTERN
LECTION
LECTURE
LEEWARD
LEGALLY
LEGATEE
LEGGING
LEGHORN
LEGIBLE
LEGIBLY
LEGITIM
LEGLESS
LEISTER
LEISURE
LEMMING
LENGTHY
LENIENT
LENTOID
LENTIGO
LEONINE
LEOPARD
LEPROSE
LEPROSY
LEPROUS
LETHEAN
LETTUCE
LEUCOMA
LEVATOR
LEVELLY
LEVERET
LEVITIC
LEXICAL
LEXICON
LIAISON
LIASSIC
LIBERAL
LIBERTY
LIBRARY
LIBRATE
LICENCE
LICENSE
LICITLY
LIDLESS
LIGHTEN

LIGHTER
LIGHTLY
LIGNIFY
LIGNINE
LIGNITE
LIMITED
LIMITER
LIMOSIS
LINEAGE
LINEATE
LINGUAL
LINGULA
LINNEAN
LINSEED
LIONESS
LIONISM
LIONIZE
LIQUATE
LIQUEFY
LIQUEUR
LISSOME
LITERAL
LITHIUM
LITHOID
LITOTES
LITUATE
LITURGY
LIVERED
LOADING
LOATHER
LOATHLY
LOBATED
LOBELET
LOBELIA
LOBIPED
LOBSTER
LOBULAR
LOBWORM
LOCALLY
LOCKAGE
LODGING
LOFTILY
LOGICAL
LOGWOOD
LOLLARD
LOMBARD
LONGING
LONGISH
LOOSELY
LOPPING
LORGNON
LOTTERY
LOUNGER
LOUTISH
LOVABLE
LOWLAND
LOWNESS
LOYALLY
LOYALTY
LOZENGE
LUCARNE
LUCENCY
LUCERNE
LUCIDLY
LUCIFER
LUCKILY
LUGGAGE
LUGWORM
LULLABY
LUMBAGO

LUMPING
LUMPISH
LUNATED
LUNATIC
LUNETTE
LUNULAR
LUNULET
LUPULIN
LURCHER
LURDANE
LUSTFUL
LUSTILY
LUSTRAL
LUSTRUM
LYCOPOD
LYINGLY
LYRATED
LYRICAL

M

MACHETE
MACHINE
MACULAE
MADDING
MADEIRA
MADNESS
MADONNA
MAESTRO
MAGENTA
MAGGOTY
MAGICAL
MAGNATE
MAGNIFY
MAHATMA
MAJESTY
MALAISE
MALARIA
MALAYAN
MALEFIC
MALISON
MALLARD
MALLEUS
MALMSEY
MALTESE
MALTING
MALTMAN
MAMELON
MAMMARY
MAMMOTH
MANACLE
MANAGER
MANAKIN
MANATEE
MANCHET
MANCHOO
MANDATE
MANDREL
MANDRIL
MANGLER
MANHOLE
MANHOOD
MANIHOT
MANIKIN
MANILLA
MANIPLE
MANITOU
MANKIND
MANLIKE

MANNISH
MANNITE
MANSION
MANTLET
MANUMIT
MARABOU
MARINER
MARITAL
MARLINE
MARPLOT
MARQUEE
MARQUIS
MARRIED
MARROWY
MARSALA
MARSHAL
MARTIAL
MARTLET
MASONIC
MASONRY
MASSAGE
MASSIVE
MASTERY
MASTICH
MASTIFF
MASTOID
MATADOR
MATINÉE
MATRASS
MATTERY
MATTING
MATTOCK
MAUDLIN
MAUNDER
MAWKISH
MAWWORM
MAXILLA
MAXIMAL
MAXIMUM
MAYORAL
MAZURKA
MAZZARD
MEADOWY
MEALIES
MEANDER
MEANING
MEASLED
MEASLES
MEASURE
MECHLIN
MECONIC
MEDALET
MEDDLER
MEDIATE
MEDICAL
MEDIUMS
MEDULLA
MEDUSAE
MEETING
MEIOSIS
MÉLANGE
MELANIC
MELILOT
MELODIC
MELTING
MEMENTO
MENISCI
MENTHOL
MENTION
MERCERY

MERCIES
MERCURY
MERMAID
MERRILY
MERSION
MESEEMS
MESSAGE
MESSIAH
MESTIZO
METAYER
METTLED
MIASMAL
MICROBE
MICROHM
MIDLAND
MIDLENT
MIDMOST
MIDNOON
MIDRIFF
MIDSHIP
MIDWIFE
MIGRANT
MIGRATE
MILEAGE
MILFOIL
MILIARY
MILITIA
MILKMAN
MILKSOP
MILLING
MILLION
MILREIS
MIMETIC
MIMICRY
MINARET
MINCING
MINDFUL
MINERAL
MINIATE
MINIKIN
MINIMUM
MINIVER
MINSTER
MINTAGE
MINUEND
MIOCENE
MIRACLE
MIRIFIC
MISCALL
MISDATE
MISDEED
MISDEEM
MISDOER
MISERLY
MISGIVE
MISLEAD
MISLIKE
MISNAME
MISRULE
MISSILE
MISSING
MISSION
MISSIVE
MISTAKE
MISTILY
MISTIME
MIXABLE
MIXEDLY
MIXTURE
MOANFUL

75

MOBBISH	MULLION	NEPTUNE	OBLIGOR	ORATION
MOCKERY	MULTURE	NERVOUS	OBLIQUE	ORATORY
MODALLY	MUMBLER	NERVURE	OBLOQUY	ORBITAL
MODESTY	MUMMERY	NETTING	OBOVATE	ORCHARD
MODICUM	MUMMIFY	NEUTRAL	OBSCENE	ORDERER
MODISTE	MUMPISH	NEWNESS	OBSCURE	ORDERLY
MODULAR	MUNCHER	NEWSMAN	OBSERVE	ORDINAL
MODULUS	MUNDANE	NIBBLER	OBTRUDE	ORGANIC
MOIDORE	MURAENA	NIBLICK	OBVERSE	ORGANON
MOISTEN	MURICES	NICTATE	OBVIATE	ORGANUM
MOLLIFY	MURIATE	NIGGARD	OBVIOUS	ORIFICE
MOLLUSC	MURKILY	NIGHTLY	OCARINA	ORLEANS
MOLLUSK	MURRAIN	NILOTIC	OCCIPUT	OROGENY
MOMENTA	MURTHER	NINTHLY	OCCLUDE	OROLOGY
MONADIC	MUSCLED	NIOBIUM	OCEANIC	OROTUND
MONARCH	MUSCOID	NIPPERS	OCELLUS	ORPHEAN
MONEYED	MUSICAL	NITRATE	OCREATE	ORTOLAN
MONEYER	MUSROLE	NITRIFY	OCTAGON	OSCULUM
MONGREL	MUSTANG	NITROUS	OCTAVOS	OSIERED
MONITOR	MUSTARD	NIVEOUS	OCTOBER	OSMANLI
MONKEYS	MUSTILY	NOCTURN	OCTOPOD	OSMOTIC
MONKISH	MUTABLE	NODATED	OCTOPUS	OSSEINE
MONOCLE	MUTABLY	NODDING	OCTUPLE	OSSELET
MONODIC	MYALGIA	NODULAR	OCULATE	OSSEOUS
MONOGYN	MYCELIA	NOISILY	OCULIST	OSSICLE
MONSOON	MYELOID	NOISOME	ODALISK	OSSIFIC
MONSTER	MYLODON	NOMADIC	ODDMENT	OSSUARY
MONTERO	MYOLOGY	NOMARCH	ODDNESS	OSTIOLE
MONTHLY	MYOTOMY	NOMINAL	ODOROUS	OSTITIS
MOONISH	MYRRHIC	NOMINEE	OESTRUS	OSTRICH
MOORAGE	MYSTERY	NONAGON	OFFENCE	OTALGIA
MOORING	MYSTIFY	NONPLUS	OFFENSE	OTARIES
MOORISH		NONSUIT	OFFERER	OTOCYST
MORAINE		NOOLOGY	OFFICER	OTOLITE
MORALLY	**N**	NOONDAY	OGREISH	OTOLITH
MORASSY		NOONING	OLDNESS	OTOLOGY
MORCEAU	NAILERY	NOSEGAY	OLITORY	OTTOMAN
MORDANT	NAIVELY	NOSTRIL	OLIVINE	OURSELF
MORISCO	NAIVETE	NOSTRUM	OLYMPIC	OUTCAST
MORNING	NAKEDLY	NOTABLE	OMENTUM	OUTCOME
MOROCCO	NAMABLE	NOTABLY	OMENTAL	OUTCROP
MORPHIA	NANKEEN	NOTHING	OMINOUS	OUTDARE
MORRICE	NAPHTHA	NOURISH	OMNIBUS	OUTDOOR
MORTICE	NAPLESS	NOVELTY	ONENESS	OUTFACE
MORTIFY	NARDINE	NOWHERE	ONERARY	OUTFALL
MORTISE	NARRATE	NOXIOUS	ONEROUS	OUTFLOW
MOSELLE	NARTHEX	NUCLEUS	ONESELF	OUTGROW
MOTHERY	NARWHAL	NULLIFY	ONGOING	OUTLAST
MOTTLED	NASALLY	NULLITY	ONICOLO	OUTLIER
MOTTOES	NASCENT	NUMBLES	ONWARDS	OUTLINE
MOUFLON	NASTILY	NUMERAL	OOLITIC	OUTLIVE
MOULDER	NATTILY	NUMMARY	OOTHECA	OUTLOOK
MOUNTED	NATURAL	NUNNERY	OPACITY	OUTMOST
MOURNER	NAUGHTY	NUNNISH	OPACOUS	OUTPOST
MOUSING	NAVVIES	NUPTIAL	OPALINE	OUTPOUR
MOUTHED	NEBULAE	NURSERY	OPALIZE	OUTRAGE
MOUTHER	NEBULAR	NURTURE	OPENING	OUTRIDE
MOVABLE	NECKLET		OPERANT	OUTROOT
MOVABLY	NECTARY		OPERATE	OUTRUSH
MOWBURN	NEEDFUL	**O**	OPEROSE	OUTSAIL
MUCIFIC	NEEDILY		OPINION	OUTSIDE
MUDDILY	NEGLECT	OAKLING	OPOSSUM	OUTSPAN
MUEZZIN	NEGRESS	OARSMAN	OPPIDAN	OUTSTAY
MUEDDIN	NEGROES	OBCONIC	OPPOSED	OUTSTEP
MUFFLED	NEGROID	OBELISK	OPPOSER	OUTTALK
MUFFLER	NEITHER	OBELIZE	OPPRESS	OUTVOTE
MUGGISH	NELUMBO	OBESITY	OPTICAL	OUTWALK
MUGWORT	NEMESIS	OBLIGED	OPULENT	OUTWARD
MULATTO	NEMORAL	OBLIGEE	OPUNTIA	OUTWEAR
MULLEIN	NEOLOGY	OBLIGER	OPUSCLE	OUTWORK

OVARIAN	PANTHER	PEDDLER	PHAETON	PISTOLE
OVARIAL	PANTILE	PEDICEL	PHALANX	PITCHER
OVATION	PANTLER	PEDLARY	PHALLIC	PITEOUS
OVERACT	PAPALLY	PEDLERY	PHALLUS	PITFALL
OVERAWE	PAPILLA	PEERAGE	PHANTOM	PITHILY
OVERBID	PAPULAE	PEERESS	PHARYNX	PITIFUL
OVERDUE	PAPULAR	PEEVISH	PHILTER	PIVOTAL
OVEREAT	PAPYRUS	PELAGIC	PHILTRE	PIVOTED
OVERJOY	PARABLE	PELECAN	PHLOEUM	PLACARD
OVERLAP	PARADOX	PELICAN	PHOEBUS	PLACATE
OVERLAY	PARAGON	PELISSE	PHOENIX	PLACKET
OVERLIE	PARAPET	PELORIA	PHONICS	PLACOID
OVERPAY	PARASOL	PELORIC	PHRENIC	PLAGUER
OVERRUN	PARBOIL	PELTATE	PHYSICS	PLAIDED
OVERSEA	PAREIRA	PENALLY	PHYTOID	PLAINLY
OVERSEE	PARESIS	PENALTY	PIANINO	PLAITED
OVERSET	PARETIC	PENANCE	PIANIST	PLAITER
OVERTAX	PARLOUR	PENATES	PIASTER	PLANISH
OVERTLY	PARODIC	PENDANT	PIASTRE	PLANNER
OVERTOP	PARONYM	PENDENT	PIBROCH	PLANTAR
OVIDUCT	PAROTID	PENDING	PICADOR	PLANTER
OVIFORM	PARQUET	PENFOLD	PICCOLO	PLASMIC
OVOIDAL	PARSLEY	PENGUIN	PICEOUS	PLASTER
OXIDATE	PARSNIP	PENNANT	PICKAXE	PLASTIC
OXIDIZE	PARTAKE	PENNIES	PICKING	PLATANE
OXONIAN	PARTIAL	PENSILE	PICOTEE	PLATEAU
OXYTONE	PARTING	PENSION	PICQUET	PLATINA
OZONIZE	PARTLET	PENSIVE	PICTURE	PLATING
	PARTNER	PENTILE	PIDDOCK	PLATOON
	PARTOOK	PEONAGE	PIEBALD	PLATTER
P	PARTIES	PEONISM	PIERAGE	PLAUDIT
	PARVENU	PEPPERY	PIERCER	PLAYFUL
	PARVISE	PEPSINE	PIETISM	PLEADER
PABULAR	PASCHAL	PEPTICS	PIETIST	PLEASER
PABULUM	PASQUIL	PERCHER	PIGGERY	PLEDGEE
PACABLE	PASQUIN	PERCUSS	PIGGISH	PLEDGER
PACIFIC	PASSAGE	PERDURE	PIGMENT	PLEDGET
PACKAGE	PASSANT	PERFECT	PIKEMAN	PLEIADS
PACKING	PASSING	PERFIDY	PILEATE	PLENARY
PACTION	PASSION	PERFORM	PILGRIM	PLENISH
PADDING	PASSIVE	PERFUME	PILLAGE	PLEURAE
PADDLER	PASTERN	PERHAPS	PILLION	PLEURAL
PADDOCK	PASTIME	PERIAPT	PILLORY	PLIABLE
PADELLA	PASTURE	PERIGEE	PILLOWY	PLIABLY
PADLOCK	PATCHER	PERIWIG	PILULAR	PLIANCY
PAGEANT	PATELLA	PERJURE	PIMENTO	PLICATE
PAILFUL	PATERAE	PERJURY	PIMENTA	PLODDER
PAINFUL	PATHWAY	PERMIAN	PIMPLED	PLOTTER
PAINTER	PATIENT	PERMUTE	PINCASE	PLUCKER
PAKTONG	PATRIAL	PERPEND	PINCERS	PLUGGER
PALADIN	PATRIOT	PERPLEX	PINCHER	PLUMAGE
PALATAL	PATRIST	PERSIAN	PINETUM	PLUMBER
PALAVER	PATTERN	PERSIST	PINFOLD	PLUMBIC
PALETOT	PATTIES	PERTAIN	PINHOLE	PLUMERY
PALETTE	PAUCITY	PERTURB	PINNACE	PLUMMET
PALFREY	PAULINE	PERTUSE	PINNATE	PLUMOSE
PALLIAL	PAUNCHY	PERUSAL	PINNERS	PLUMOUS
PALLIUM	PAVIOUR	PERUSER	PINNULA	PLUMPER
PALMARY	PAYABLE	PERVADE	PINNULE	PLUMPLY
PALMATE	PAYMENT	PERVERT	PINTAIL	PLUMULE
PALUDAL	PEACOCK	PESSARY	PIONEER	PLUNDER
PAMPEAN	PEARLED	PETALED	PIOUSLY	PLUNGER
PANACEA	PEASANT	PETIOLE	PIPETTE	PLUVIAL
PANCAKE	PEASCOD	PETRIFY	PIQUANT	POACHER
PANDEAN	PEBBLED	PETRINE	PIRAGUA	POCHARD
PANDECT	PECCANT	PETROUS	PIRATIC	PODAGRA
PANDORE	PECCARY	PETTILY	PIROGUE	POETESS
PANICLE	PECCAVI	PETTISH	PISCINA	POETICS
PANNIER	PECKISH	PETUNIA	PISCINE	POETIZE
PANOPLY	PECTOSE	PEWTERY	PISMIRE	POINTED
PANSIES				

POINTER	PRELECT	PROTEIN		RATTEEN
POITREL	PRELUDE	PROTEND	**Q**	RAUCOUS
POLACCA	PREMIER	PROTEST		RAVAGER
POLEMIC	PREMISE	PROUDLY	QUADRAT	RAVELIN
POLENTA	PREMISS	PROVERB	QUESTER	RAWNESS
POLITIC	PREMIUM	PROVIDE	QUAFFER	RAYLESS
POLLACK	PREPAID	PROVISO	QUALIFY	REACHER
POLLARD	PREPARE	PROVOKE	QUALITY	READILY
POLLUTE	PREPUCE	PROVOST	QUANTUM	READING
POLYGON	PRESAGE	PROWESS	QUARREL	READMIT
POLYGYN	PRESENT	PROWLER	QUARTAN	REAGENT
POLYPUS	PRESIDE	PROXIMO	QUARTER	REALGAR
POLYZOA	PRESUME	PRUDENT	QUARTET	REALISM
POMATUM	PRETEND	PRUDERY	QUARTZY	REALIST
POMPION	PRETENT	PRUDISH	QUASSIA	REALITY
POMPOUS	PRETEXT	PRURIGO	QUAYAGE	REALIZE
PONIARD	PREVAIL	PSALTER	QUEENLY	REANNEX
PONTAGE	PREVENT	PSYCHIC	QUEERLY	REARGUE
PONTIFF	PREVISE	PTARMIC	QUELLER	REBOUND
PONTOON	PRICKER	PUBERTY	QUERIST	REBUILD
POPEDOM	PRICKET	PUBLISH	QUERIES	REBUKER
POPPIED	PRICKLE	PUCKERY	QUESTOR	RECEIPT
POPULAR	PRICKLY	PUDDING	QUIBBLE	RECEIVE
PORCINE	PRIDIAN	PUDDLER	QUICKEN	RECENCY
PORIFER	PRIMACY	PUDENCY	QUICKLY	RECENSE
PORRIGO	PRIMAGE	PUDENDA	QUIETEN	RECITAL
PORTAGE	PRIMARY	PUERILE	QUIETLY	RECITER
PORTEND	PRIMATE	PUFFERY	QUIETUS	RECLAIM
PORTENT	PRIMELY	PULLEYS	QUILLED	RECLINE
PORTICO	PRIMING	PULSATE	QUINARY	RECLUSE
PORTION	PRINTER	PUMPION	QUININE	RECOUNT
PORTRAY	PRITHEE	PUMPKIN	QUINTAL	RECOVER
POSSESS	PRIVACY	PUNCHER	QUINTAN	RECRUIT
POSTAGE	PRIVATE	PUNGENT	QUINTET	RECTIFY
POSTBOY	PRIVILY	PUNNING	QUONDÀM	RECTORY
POSTERN	PRIVITY	PUNSTER		RECURVE
POSTFIX	PROBANG	PUPPIES		REDCOAT
POSTMAN	PROBATE	PURGING	**R**	REDDISH
POSTURE	PROBITY	PURITAN		REDNESS
POTABLE	PROBLEM	PURLIEU	RABIDLY	REDOUBT
POTASSA	PROCEED	PURLOIN	RACCOON	REDOUND
POTENCY	PROCESS	PURPLES	RADIANT	REDPOLL
POTTAGE	PROCTOR	PURPORT	RADIATE	REDRAFT
POTTERY	PROCURE	PURPOSE	RADICAL	REDRESS
POUCHED	PRODIGY	PURPURA	RADICLE	REDSKIN
POULTRY	PRODUCE	PURSUER	RAFFISH	REDTAIL
POUNCED	PRODUCT	PURSUIT	RAGWORT	REDUCER
POUNDER	PROFANE	PURVIEW	RAILING	REDWING
POVERTY	PROFESS	PUSHING	RAILWAY	REDWOOD
POWDERY	PROFFER	PUSTULE	RAIMENT	REFEREE
PRAETOR	PROFILE	PUTREFY	RAINBOW	REFINED
PRAIRIE	PROFUSE	PUTTOCK	RAMADAN	REFINER
PRAISER	PROGENY	PUZZLER	RAMBLER	REFLECT
PRANCER	PROJECT	PYAEMIA	RAMMISH	REFORGE
PRATING	PROLATE	PYAEMIC	RAMPAGE	REFOUND
PRATTLE	PROLONG	PYGMEAN	RAMPANT	REFRACT
PRAVITY	PROMISE	PYGMIES	RAMPART	REFRAIN
PRAYING	PROMOTE	PYLORUS	RAMPION	REFRESH
PREBEND	PRONELY	PYLORIC	RAMSONS	REFUGEE
PRECEDE	PRONGED	PYRAMID	RANCOUR	REFUSAL
PRECEPT	PRONOUN	PYRETIC	RANSACK	REFUSER
PRECISE	PROPHET	PYREXIA	RAPIDLY	REFUTER
PREDATE	PROPOSE	PYRITES	RAPTURE	REGALER
PREDIAL	PROSAIC	PYRITIC	RAREBIT	REGALIA
PREDICT	PROSODY	PYRRHIC	RASORES	REGALLY
PREDOOM	PROSPER	PYTHIAN	RATABLE	REGATTA
PREFACE	PROTEAN		RATABLY	REGENCY
PREFECT	PROTECT		RATAFIA	REGIMEN
PRELACY	PROTÉGÉ		RATCHET	REGNANT
PRELATE	PROTEID		RATLINE	REGORGE

REGRANT	RESTORE	ROMPISH	SAILING	SCARFED
REGRATE	RETIARY	RONDEAU	SAINTED	SCARIFY
REGREET	RETINAL	ROOFING	SAINTLY	SCARLET
REGRESS	RETINUE	ROOKERY	SALABLE	SCARPED
REGULAR	RETIRAL	ROOMFUL	SALICIN	SCATTER
REGULUS	RETIRED	ROOMILY	SALIENT	SCENERY
REINTER	RETOUCH	ROOSTER	SALIQUE	SCEPTER
REISSUE	RETRACE	ROOTLET	SALLIES	SCEPTIC
REJOICE	RETRACT	RORQUAL	SALMIAC	SCEPTRE
REJUDGE	RETREAT	ROSEATE	SALSIFY	SCHEMER
RELAPSE	REUNION	ROSEOLA	SALTANT	SCHERZO
RELATED	REUNITE	ROSETTE	SALTERN	SCHNAPS
RELATER	REVELRY	ROSOLIO	SALTIER	SCHOLAR
RELATOR	REVENGE	ROSTRAL	SALTIRE	SCHOLIA
RELEASE	REVENUE	ROSTRUM	SALTISH	SCHORLY
RELIANT	REVERER	ROTATOR	SALUTER	SCIATIC
RELIEVE	REVERIE	ROTIFER	SALVAGE	SCIENCE
RELIEVO	REVERSE	ROTUNDA	SAMOVAR	SCISSEL
RELIGHT	REVILER	ROUGHEN	SAMPLER	SCISSIL
REMARRY	REVISAL	ROUGHLY	SANABLE	SCOFFER
REMNANT	REVISER	ROULADE	SANCTUM	SCOLDER
REMODEL	REVISIT	ROULEAU	SANCTUS	SCOLLOP
REMORSE	REVIVAL	ROUNDEL	SANICLE	SCOOPER
REMOULD	REVIVER	ROUNDER	SANIOUS	SCORIAE
REMOUNT	REVOLVE	ROUNDLY	SAPAJOU	SCORIFY
REMOVAL	REWRITE	ROUSING	SAPIENT	SCORNER
REMOVED	REYNARD	ROUTINE	SAPLESS	SCORPIO
REMOVER	RHENISH	ROWLOCK	SAPLING	SCOURER
RENEWAL	RHIZOID	ROYALLY	SAPPHIC	SCOURGE
RENEWER	RHIZOMA	ROYALTY	SARACEN	SCRAGGY
RENTIER	RHIZOME	RUBASSE	SARCASM	SCRAPER
RENUENT	RHODIUM	RUBBING	SARCODE	SCRAPPY
REPAINT	RHOMBIC	RUBBISH	SARCOID	SCRATCH
REPINER	RHOMBUS	RUBELLA	SARCOMA	SCREECH
REPLACE	RHUBARB	RUBEOLA	SARCOUS	SCREWER
REPLANT	RIBBING	RUBIFIC	SARDINE	SCRIBAL
REPLETE	RICKETS	RUCKING	SARDIUS	SCROTAL
REPLEVY	RICKETY	RUDDILY	SATANIC	SCROTUM
REPLICA	RIGGING	RUDDOCK	SATCHEL	SCRUBBY
REPLIER	RIGHTER	RUFFIAN	SATIATE	SCRUNCH
REPOSAL	RIGHTLY	RUFFLED	SATIETY	SCRUPLE
REPOSER	RIGIDLY	RUFFLER	SATINET	SCUDDER
REPOSIT	RILIEVO	RUINATE	SATIRIC	SCUFFLE
REPRESS	RINGENT	RUINOUS	SATISFY	SCULLER
REPRINT	RINGLET	RULABLE	SATRAPY	SCULPIN
REPROOF	RIOTOUS	RUMMAGE	SATYRIC	SCUMBLE
REPROVE	RIPOSTE	RUNAWAY	SAUCILY	SCUMMER
REPTANT	RISIBLE	RUNDLET	SAUNTER	SCUPPER
REPTILE	RISIBLY	RUNNING	SAURIAN	SCUTAGE
REPULSE	RISSOLE	RUPTURE	SAUROID	SCUTATE
REQUEST	RIVALRY	RURALLY	SAUSAGE	SCUTTLE
REQUIEM	RIVETED	RUSSIAN	SAVABLE	SCYTHED
REQUIRE	RIVETER	RUSTILY	SAVANNA	SEALING
REQUITE	RIVULET	RUTHFUL	SAVELOY	SEAWARD
REREDOS	ROADWAY	RUTTISH	SAVIOUR	SEBACIC
RESCIND	ROARING		SAVOURY	SECEDER
RESCUER	ROASTER		SAWDUST	SECLUDE
RESEIZE	ROBBERY	**S**	SCABBED	SECRECY
RESERVE	ROCKERY		SCABIES	SECRETE
RESIDUE	ROEBUCK	SABAOTH	SCABRID	SECTARY
RESOLVE	ROGUERY	SABBATH	SCALDIC	SECTILE
RESOUND	ROGUISH	SACCULE	SCALENE	SECTION
RESPECT	ROISTER	SACKAGE	SCALLED	SECTIVE
RESPELL	ROLLICK	SACKBUT	SCALLOP	SECULAR
RESPIRE	ROLLING	SACKING	SCALPEL	SECURER
RESPITE	ROLLOCK	SACRING	SCAMPER	SEDILIA
RESPOND	ROMANCE	SACRIST	SCANDAL	SEDUCER
RESTFUL	ROMANIC	SADDLER	SCANTLY	SEEDILY
RESTIFF	ROMMANY	SADNESS	SCAPULA	SEEMING
RESTIVE	ROMAUNT	SAFFRON	SCARVES	SEGMENT

SEISMAL	SHERIFF	SIXFOLD	SOAKAGE	SPHERIC
SEISMIC	SHIFTER	SIXTEEN	SOAKING	SPICATE
SEIZURE	SKIMMER	SIXTHLY	SOBERLY	SPICERY
SEJEANT	SHINESS	SIZABLE	SOCCAGE	SPICILY
SELENIC	SHINGLE	SKEPTIC	SOCIETY	SPICULA
SELFISH	SHINGLY	SKETCHY	SOFTISH	SPICULE
SELVAGE	SHINING	SKILFUL	SOJOURN	SPILLER
SEMINAL	SHIPPER	SKILLED	SOLDIER	SPINACH
SEMITIC	SHIPPON	SKILLET	SOLICIT	SPINAGE
SENATOR	SHIPPER	SKIMMER	SOLIDLY	SPINDLE
SENATUS	SHIRKER	SKINFUL	SOLIPED	SPINNER
SENSORY	SHIVERY	SKINNER	SOLOIST	SPINNEY
SENSUAL	SHOOTER	SKIPPER	SOLUBLE	SPINOSE
SEQUELA	SHOPMAN	SKIRRET	SOLVENT	SPINOUS
SEQUENT	SHORTEN	SKULKER	SOMATIC	SPIRAEA
SEQUOIA	SHORTLY	SKULPIN	SOMEHOW	SPIRANT
SERAPHS	SHOTTEN	SKYLARK	SONANCE	SPITTER
SERFDOM	SHOUTER	SKYWARD	SONLESS	SPITTLE
SERIATE	SHOWERY	SLABBER	SONSHIP	SPLASHY
SERIOUS	SHOWILY	SLACKEN	SOOTHER	SPLEENY
SERPENT	SHOWING	SLACKLY	SOPHISM	SPLENIC
SERPIGO	SHOWMAN	SLANDER	SOPHIST	SPLOTCH
SERRATE	SHREDDY	SLANGEY	SOPRANI	SPOILER
SERRIED	SHRILLY	SLANTLY	SOPRANO	SPONDEE
SERVANT	SHRIVEL	SLASHED	SORCERY	SPONGER
SERVICE	SHRUBBY	SLATING	SORGHUM	SPONSOR
SERVILE	SHUDDER	SLAVERY	SORORAL	SPOONEY
SESSILE	SHUFFLE	SLAVISH	SOROSIS	SPORRAN
SESSION	SHUTTER	SLEEKLY	SORRILY	SPORULE
SETTING	SHUTTLE	SLEEPER	SOTTISH	SPOTTED
SETTLED	SHYNESS	SLEEVED	SOUFFLE	SPOUSAL
SETTLER	SIAMANG	SLEIGHT	SOUNDLY	SPOUTER
SEVENTH	SIAMESE	SLENDER	SOURISH	SPRAYEY
SEVENTY	SICCATE	SLIDING	SOUTANE	SPRIGGY
SEVERAL	SICCITY	SLINESS	SPACIAL	SPRIGHT
SEXTAIN	SICKISH	SLINGER	SPANGLE	SPRINGE
SEXTANT	SIGHTED	SLIPPER	SPANGLY	SPRINGY
SHACKLE	SIGHTLY	SLITTER	SPANIEL	SPURNER
SHADILY	SIGMOID	SLOBBER	SPANISH	SPURRED
SHADING	SIGNIFY	SLOUGHY	SPANKER	SPURNER
SHADOOF	SIGNIOR	SLUBBER	SPANNER	SPURNEY
SHADOWY	SIGNORA	SLUMBER	SPARELY	SPUTTER
SHAFTED	SILENCE	SLYNESS	SPARING	SQUABBY
SHALLOP	SILICIC	SMARTEN	SPARKLE	SQUALID
SHALLOT	SILICLE	SMARTLY	SPARRER	SQUALLY
SHALLOW	SILICON	SMASHER	SPARROW	SQUALOR
SHAMBLE	SILIQUA	SMATTER	SPARTAN	SQUAMAE
SHAMMER	SILIQUE	SMELLER	SPASTIC	SQUASHY
SHAMPOO	SILLERY	SMELTER	SPATHAL	SQUEEZE
SHANDRY	SILLILY	SMILING	SPATHED	SQUELCH
SHANKED	SILURUS	SMITTEN	SPATHIC	SQUINCH
SHAPELY	SILVERN	SMOKILY	SPATIAL	STABBER
SHARDED	SILVERY	SMOKING	SPATTER	STABLER
SHARPEN	SILIMAR	SMOLDER	SPATTLE	STADDLE
SHARPER	SIMIOUS	SMOTHER	SPATULA	STADIUM
SHARPLY	SIMITAR	SMUGGLE	SPAWNER	STAGGER
SHASTER	SINCERE	SNAFFLE	SPEAKER	STAGING
SHASTRA	SINEWED	SNAKISH	SPECIAL	STAIDLY
SHATTER	SINKING	SNAPPER	SPECIES	STAINER
SHAVING	SINLESS	SNARLER	SPECIFY	STALKED
SHEAVES	SINOPLE	SNEERER	SPECKLE	STALKER
SHEARER	SINUATE	SNIGGER	SPECTER	STAMINA
SHEATHY	SINUOUS	SNIPPER	SPECTRE	STAMMER
SHEBEEN	SIRENIA	SNIPPET	SPECTRA	STAMPER
SHEDDER	SIRLOIN	SNORTER	SPECULA	STANDER
SHELLAC	SIRNAME	SNOUTED	SPELLER	STANIEL
SHELLED	SIROCCO	SNOWISH	SPELTER	STANNIC
SHELTER	SISTRUM	SNUFFER	SPENCER	STANZAS
SHELVES	SITTING	SNUFFLE	SPENDER	STAPLER
SHERBET	SITUATE	SNUGGLE	SPHERAL	STARCHY

STARING	STRETCH	SULPHUR	TENABLE
STARKLY	STRIATE	SULTANA	TENANCY
STARLIT	STRIGIL	SUMLESS	**T**
STARRED	STRIKER	SUMMARY	TABARET	TENDRIL
STARTER	STRINGY	SUMMONS	TABBIES	TENFOLD
STARTLE	STRIPED	SUMPTER	TABETIC	TENIOID
STATELY	STRIVER	SUNBEAM	TABINET	TENSELY
STATICS	STROKER	SUNDOWN	TABLEAU	TENSILE
STATION	STROPHE	SUNFISH	TABORER	TENSION
STATIST	STRUMAE	SUNLESS	TABORET	TENSITY
STATUED	STUBBED	SUNRISE	TABULAE	TENTHLY
STATURE	STUBBLE	SUNWARD	TABULAR	TENUITY
STATUTE	STUBBLY	SUPPORT	TACITLY	TENUOUS
STAUNCH	STUDDED	SUPPOSE	TACTICS	TERBIUM
STEALER	STUDENT	SUPREME	TACTILE	TERMINI
STEALTH	STUDIED	SURBASE	TACTION	TERMITE
STEAMER	STUDIER	SURCOAT	TACTUAL	TERNARY
STEARIC	STUDIES	SURFACE	TADPOLE	TERNATE
STEARIN	STUFFER	SURFEIT	TAFFETA	TERRACE
STEEPEN	STUMBLE	SURGEON	TAFFETY	TERRENE
STEEPER	STUMPER	SURGERY	TALCOSE	TERRIER
STEEPLE	STUNNER	SURLILY	TALCOUS	TERRIFY
STEEPLY	STUNTED	SURLOIN	TALIPED	TERSELY
STEERER	STUPEFY	SURMISE	TALIPES	TERTIAN
STELLAR	STUTTER	SURNAME	TALIPOT	TESSERA
STENCIL	STYGIAN	SURPASS	TALKING	TESTACY
STEPPER	STYLISH	SURPLUS	TALLAGE	TESTATE
STEPSON	STYLIST	SURTOUT	TALLIER	TESTIFY
STERILE	STYLITE	SURVIVE	TALLOWY	TESTILY
STERLET	STYLOID	SUSPECT	TALLIES	TETANIC
STERNAL	STYPTIC	SUSPEND	TAMABLE	TETANUS
STERNED	SUASION	SUSTAIN	TAMBOUR	TEXTILE
STERNLY	SUASIVE	SUTLING	TAMPION	TEXTUAL
STERNUM	SUAVELY	SUTURAL	TANAGER	TEXTURE
STEWARD	SUAVITY	SUTURED	TANGENT	THALAMI
STHENIC	SUBACID	SWABBER	TANGHIN	THALLUS
STIBIAL	SUBDEAN	SWADDLE	TANKARD	THANAGE
STICHIC	SUBDUAL	SWAGGER	TANLING	THEATER
STICKER	SUBDUCE	SWALLOW	TANNAGE	THEATRE
STICKLE	SUBDUCT	SWARTHY	TANNERY	THEORBO
STIFFEN	SUBDUED	SWEARER	TANNING	THEOREM
STIFFLY	SUBDUER	SWEATER	TANTIVY	THEREAT
STIGMAS	SUBERIC	SWEDISH	TANTRUM	THEREBY
STILLER	SUBJECT	SWEEPER	TAPIOCA	THEREIN
STILTED	SUBJOIN	SWEETEN	TAPPING	THEREOF
STILTON	SUBLIME	SWEETLY	TAPSTER	THEREON
STIMULI	SUBSIDE	SWELTER	TARDILY	THERETO
STINTER	SUBSIDY	SWELTRY	TARNISH	THERMAE
STIPEND	SUBSIST	SWIFTLY	TARTISH	THERMAL
STIPPLE	SUBSOIL	SWILLER	TASTILY	THERMIC
STIPULE	SUBSUME	SWIMMER	TATTING	THEURGY
STIRRER	SUBTEND	SWINDLE	TATTLER	THICKEN
STIRRUP	SUBTILE	SWINGLE	TAUNTER	THICKET
STOICAL	SUBVENE	SWINISH	TAURINE	THICKLY
STOMACH	SUBVERT	SWITZER	TAXABLE	THIEVES
STOMATA	SUCCEED	SWOLLEN	TAXICAB	THILLER
STONILY	SUCCESS	SYCOSIS	TEACHER	THIMBLE
STOPPER	SUCCORY	SYENITE	TEARFUL	THINKER
STOPPLE	SUCCOUR	SYLPHID	TEASING	THIRDLY
STORAGE	SUCCUMB	SYNCOPE	TECHILY	THIRSTY
STORIED	SUCKING	SYNODAL	TECHNIC	THISTLE
STORIES	SUCROSE	SYNODIC	TEDIOUS	THISTLY
STOUTLY	SUCTION	SYNONYM	TEEMING	THITHER
STOWAGE	SUFFICE	SYNOVIA	TEGULAR	THORIUM
STRANGE	SUFFUSE	SYRINGA	TELLING	THOUGHT
STRATUM	SUGGEST	SYRINGE	TEMPERA	THREADY
STRATUS	SUICIDE	SYSTOLE	TEMPEST	THRIFTY
STRAYER	SULCATE		TEMPLAR	THRIVER
STREAKY	SULKILY		TEMPLET	THROATY
STREAMY	SULLENS		TEMPTER	THROUGH
				THROWER

THRUMMY	TORTIVE	TRINGLE	TWIBILL	UNIFORM
THUGGEE	TORTURE	TRINITY	TWIDDLE	UNITARY
THUMBED	TORYISM	TRINKET	TWINING	UNITIVE
THUMMIN	TOTALLY	TRIOLET	TWINKLE	UNITIES
THUMPER	TOTEMIC	TRIPANG	TWINNED	UNKEMPT
THUNDER	TOTTERY	TRIPERY	TWISTER	UNKNOWN
THYROID	TOUCHER	TRIPLET	TWITTER	UNLATCH
THYRSUS	TOUGHEN	TRIPOLI	TYMPANA	UNLEARN
THYSELF	TOUGHLY	TRIPPER	TYPHOID	UNLEASH
TIARAED	TOURIST	TRIREME	TYPHOON	UNLOOSE
TICKING	TOURNEY	TRISECT	TYPHOUS	UNLUCKY
TICKLER	TOWARDS	TRISMUS	TYPICAL	UNMANLY
TIDINGS	TOWERED	TRITELY	TYRANNY	UNMIXED
TIERCEL	TOXICAL	TRIUMPH	TZARINA	UNMOVED
TIFFANY	TOYSHOP	TRIVIAL		UNNAMED
TIGHTEN	TRACERY	TROCHAR		UNNERVE
TIGHTLY	TRACHEA	TROCHEE	**U**	UNNOTED
TIGRESS	TRACING	TRODDEN		UNOWNED
TIGRINE	TRACKER	TROLLER	ULCERED	UNPAVED
TIGRISH	TRADING	TROLLEY	ULULATE	UNQUIET
TILLAGE	TRADUCE	TROLLOP	UMBILIC	UNRAVEL
TIMBREL	TRAFFIC	TROOPER	UMBRAGE	UNREADY
TIMEOUS	TRAGEDY	TROPIST	UNACTED	UNSCREW
TIMIDLY	TRAILER	TROTTER	UNAIDED	UNSHORN
TINDERY	TRAINED	TROUBLE	UNARMED	UNSIZED
TINNING	TRAINER	TROUNCE	UNASKED	UNSLING
TINTING	TRAIPSE	TRUANCY	UNAWARE	UNSOUND
TINWARE	TRAITOR	TRUCKER	UNBEGOT	UNSPENT
TIPPLER	TRAMMEL	TRUCKLE	UNBLEST	UNSWEPT
TIPSILY	TRAMPER	TRUFFLE	UNBOSOM	UNSWORN
TITANIC	TRAMPLE	TRUMPET	UNBOUND	UNTAMED
TITHING	TRAMWAY	TRUNDLE	UNBRACE	UNTAXED
TITLARK	TRANSIT	TRUNKED	UNBURNT	UNTEACH
TITLING	TRANSOM	TRUSSED	UNCANNY	UNTRIED
TITMICE	TRAPEZE	TRUSTEE	UNCARED	UNTRULY
TITRATE	TRAPPER	TRUSTER	UNCHAIN	UNTRUTH
TITULAR	TRAVAIL	TRIABLE	UNCIVIL	UNTWINE
TOADIES	TRAWLER	TRYABLE	UNCLASP	UNTWIST
TOASTER	TREACLE	TUBBING	UNCLEAN	UNUSUAL
TOBACCO	TREADER	TUBBISH	UNCLOAK	UNWEAVE
TOBOGAN	TREADLE	TUBULAR	UNCLOSE	UNWOOED
TODDLER	TREASON	TUESDAY	UNCOUTH	UNWRUNG
TOGATED	TREATER	TUITION	UNCOVER	UPBRAID
TOILFUL	TREDDLE	TUMBLER	UNCROWN	UPBREAK
TOLLAGE	TREFOIL	TUMBREL	UNCTION	UPHEAVE
TOMBOLA	TRELLIS	TUMBRIL	UNDATED	UPRAISE
TOMFOOL	TREMBLE	TUMIDLY	UNDERDO	UPRIGHT
TOMPION	TREMOLO	TUMULAR	UNDERGO	UPROUSE
TONGUED	TRENAIL	TUMULUS	UNDOING	UPSTART
TONNAGE	TRENTAL	TUNABLE	UNDRESS	UPTHROW
TONSILE	TREPANG	TUNABLY	UNDYING	UPWARDS
TONSURE	TRESSED	TUNEFUL	UNEARTH	URAEMIA
TONTINE	TRESSEL	TUNNAGE	UNEQUAL	URANIUM
TOOLING	TRESTLE	TUNNIES	UNFITLY	URETHRA
TOOTHED	TRIABLE	TURBINE	UNFROCK	URGENCY
TOPIARY	TRIADIC	TURGENT	UNGLOVE	URINARY
TOPICAL	TRIBUNE	TURKISH	UNGODLY	URINATE
TOPLESS	TRIBUTE	TURKOIS	UNGUENT	URODELA
TOPMAST	TRICKER	TURMOIL	UNHANDY	URODELE
TOPMOST	TRICKLE	TURNERY	UNHAPPY	USELESS
TOPPING	TRICKSY	TURNING	UNHARDY	USUALLY
TORMENT	TRIDENT	TURNKEY	UNHEARD	USURPER
TORMINA	TRIFLER	TURNSOL	UNHINGE	UTENSIL
TORNADO	TRIFORM	TUSSOCK	UNHITCH	UTERINE
TORPEDO	TRIGAMY	TUTELAR	UNHOPED	UTILITY
TORPIFY	TRIGGER	TWADDLE	UNHORSE	UTILIZE
TORREFY	TRIGRAM	TWADDLY	UNHOUSE	UTOPIAN
TORRENT	TRILITH	TWANGLE	UNIAXIAL	UTRICLE
TORSION	TRILOGY	TWATTLE	UNICORN	UTTERER
TORTILE	TRIMMER	TWELFTH	UNIDEAL	UTTERLY

UXORIAL

V

VACANCY
VACCINE
VACUITY
VACUOLE
VACUOUS
VACUUMS
VAGINAE
VAGINAL
VAGRANT
VAGUELY
VALANCE
VALENCE
VALENCY
VALIANT
VALIDLY
VALLARY
VALLEYS
VALONIA
VALVATE
VALVULE
VAMPIRE
VANILLA
VANTAGE
VAPIDLY
VAPOURY
VARIANT
VARIETY
VARIOLA
VARIOUS
VARICES
VARNISH
VASCULA
VATICAN
VAULTED
VAULTER
VAUNTER
VAVASOR
VEDETTE
VEERING
VEGETAL
VEHICLE
VEINING
VEINLET
VELARIA
VELVETY
VENDACE
VENISON
VENTAGE
VENTRAL
VENTURE
VERANDA
VERBENA
VERBOSE
VERDANT
VERDICT
VERDURE
VERMEIL
VERNIER
VERSANT
VERSIFY
VERSION
VERTIGO
VERVAIN
VESICAL
VESICLE

VESTIGE
VESTURE
VETERAN
VEXILLA
VIADUCT
VIBRANT
VIBRATE
VIBRIOS
VICEROY
VICIOUS
VICTORY
VICTUAL
VICUGNA
VIDETTE
VIDIMUS
VIDUITY
VILLAGE
VILLAIN
VILLEIN
VILLOUS
VILLOSE
VINCULA
VINEGAR
VINTAGE
VINTNER
VIOLATE
VIOLENT
VIOLIST
VIRELAY
VIRGATE
VIRTUAL
VISAGED
VISCERA
VISCOUS
VISIBLE
VISIBLY
VISITER
VISITOR
VISORED
VITALLY
VITIATE
VITRIFY
VITRIOL
VIVARIA
VIVIDLY
VIVIFIC
VIXENLY
VOCABLE
VOCALIC
VOCALLY
VOLAPUK
VOLCANO
VOLLEYS
VOLTAIC
VOLUBLE
VOLUBLY
VOLUMED
VOLUTED
VOUCHER
VOYAGER
VULGATE
VULPINE
VULTURE

W

WADDING
WADDLER
WADDLES

WADMOLL
WAFTAGE
WAGERER
WAGGERY
WAGGISH
WAGONER
WAGTAIL
WAILING
WAKEFUL
WAKENER
WALKING
WALLABY
WALLING
WALLOON
WALTZER
WANNESS
WANNISH
WARBLER
WARFARE
WARLIKE
WARNING
WARRANT
WARRING
WARRIOR
WASHING
WASPISH
WASSAIL
WASTAGE
WASTING
WATCHER
WATERED
WATTLED
WAVELET
WAVERER
WAYSIDE
WAYWARD
WAYWORN
WEALDEN
WEALTHY
WEARILY
WEARING
WEASAND
WEAZAND
WEATHER
WEAVING
WEBBING
WEDDING
WEDLOCK
WEEPING
WEEVILY
WEIGHER
WEIGHTY
WELCOME
WELFARE
WENCHER
WERGILD
WERWOLF
WESTERN
WESTING
WETNESS
WETTISH
WHALING
WHARVES
WHEATEN
WHEEDLE
WHEELED
WHEELER
WHENE'ER
WHEREAS
WHEREAT

WHEREBY
WHEREIN
WHEREOF
WHEREON
WHERETO
WHERE'ER
WHETHER
WHETTER
WHIFFLE
WHIMPER
WHIMSEY
WHIPPER
WHIRLER
WHISKER
WHISKEY
WHISPER
WHISTLE
WHITHER
WHITING
WHITISH
WHITLOW
WHITSUN
WHITTLE
WHOEVER
WHOPPER
WHORISH
WHORLED
WIDGEON
WIDOWER
WIELDER
WIGGERY
WIGGING
WIGLESS
WILDING
WILDISH
WILEFUL
WILLING
WILLOWY
WINDAGE
WINDING
WINDROW
WINGLET
WINNING
WINSOME
WINTERY
WISHFUL
WISTFUL
WISTITI
WITHERS
WITHOUT
WITHIES
WITLESS
WITLING
WITNESS
WITTILY
WIZENED
WOFULLY
WOLFISH
WOLFKIN
WOLFRAM
WOMANLY
WOODMAN
WOOLLEN
WOORALI
WORDILY
WORDING
WORKING
WORKMAN
WORLDLY
WORRIER

WORSHIP
WORSTED
WOUNDER
WOURALI
WRANGLE
WRAPPER
WREATHE
WREATHY
WRECKER
WRESTER
WRESTLE
WRIGGLE
WRINGER
WRINKLE
WRINKLY
WRITING
WRITTEN
WRONGER
WRONGLY
WROUGHT
WRYNECK
WRYNESS

X

XANTHIC
XANTHIN
XERASIA
XEROTES
XIPHOID

Y

YACHTER
YCLEPED
YELLING
YIELDER
YOUNGLY
YOUNKER
YTTRIUM

Z

ZANYISM
ZEALOUS
ZEBRINE
ZEDOARY
ZEOLITE
ZETETIC
ZINCODE
ZINCOID
ZINCOUS
ZITHERN
ZONULAR
ZONULET
ZOOGAMY
ZOOGONY
ZOOGENY
ZOOLITE
ZOOLOGY
ZOONOMY
ZOOTOMY
ZYMOGEN
ZYMOSIS
ZYMOTIC
ZYMURGY

EIGHT-LETTER WORDS

A

AARDVARK
AARDWOLF
ABATTOIR
ABBATIAL
ABDICANT
ABDICATE
ABDUCENT
ABDUCTOR
ABERRANT
ABETMENT
ABEYANCE
ABHORRER
ABJECTLY
ABLATION
ABLATIVE
ABLEPSIA
ABLUTION
ABNEGATE
ABOMASUS
ABORTION
ABORTIVE
ABRADANT
ABRASION
ABROGATE
ABRUPTLY
ABSCISSA
ABSENTEE
ABSENTLY
ABSINTHE
ABSOLUTE
ABSOLVER
ABSONANT
ABSTERGE
ABSTRACT
ABSTRUSE
ABSURDLY
ABUNDANT
ABUTMENT
ACADEMIC
ACANTHUS
ACARIDAN
ACARPOUS
ACAULOUS
ACAULINE
ACCADIAN
ACCENTOR
ACCEPTER
ACCIDENT
ACCOLADE
ACCOUTRE
ACCREDIT
ACCRESCE
ACCURACY
ACCURATE
ACCURSED
ACCUSTOM
ACENTRIC
ACERBITY
ACERVATE
ACESCENT
ACHIEVER
ACICULAR

ACIDIFIC
ACIERAGE
ACONITIC
ACONITIN
ACORN-CUP
ACOSMISM
ACOUSTIC
ACQUAINT
ACQUIRER
ACREABLE
ACRIDITY
ACRIMONY
ACRITUDE
ACROLITH
ACROMION
ACROSTIC
ACROTISM
ACTINISM
ACTIVELY
ACTIVITY
ACTUALLY
ACULEATE
ADAMITIC
ADDENDUM
ADDITION
ADDITIVE
ADDUCENT
ADDUCTOR
ADENITIS
ADEQUACY
ADEQUATE
ADHERENT
ADHESION
ADHESIVE
ADIANTUM
ADJACENT
ADJUSTER
ADJUTANT
ADMONISH
ADOPTION
ADOPTIVE
ADORABLE
ADORABLY
ADROITLY
ADSCRIPT
ADULATOR
ADULTERY
ADUNCOUS
ADVANCER
ADVISORY
ADVOCACY
ADVOCATE
ADVOWSON
AERATION
AERIALLY
AERIFORM
AEROCYST
AEROLITE
AEROLOGY
AERONAUT
AEROSTAT
AESTHETE
AESTIVAL
AFFECTED
AFFERENT

AFFIANCE
AFFINITY
AFFIRMER
AFFLATUS
AFFLUENT
AFFOREST
AFFRIGHT
AFFUSION
AGAR-AGAR
AGASTRIC
AGGRIEVE
AGIOTAGE
AGITATED
AGITATOR
AGNOSTIC
AGNUS DEI
AGRAPHIA
AGRARIAN
AGRESTIC
AGRIMONY
AGRONOMY
AGUE-CAKE
AIGUILLE
AILANTUS
AIR-BORNE
AIR-BRAKE
AIR-BUILT
AIR-DRAIN
AIRINESS
AIR-PLANT
AIR-SHAFT
AIR-TIGHT
ALACRITY
ALARM-GUN
ALARMING
ALARMIST
ALBACORE
ALBINISM
ALBURNUM
ALCHEMIC
ALDEHYDE
ALDERMAN
ALEATORY
ALE-BERRY
ALE-HOUSE
ALGERIAN
ALGIDITY
ALGUAZIL
ALIENAGE
ALIENATE
ALIENISM
ALIENIST
ALKALIFY
ALKALIZE
ALKALINE
ALKALOID
ALKARSIN
ALLEGORY
ALL-FOURS
ALLIANCE
ALLOCATE
ALLODIAL
ALLODIUM
ALLOPATH
ALLOYAGE

ALLSPICE
ALLURING
ALLUSION
ALLUSIVE
ALLUVIAL
ALLUVION
ALLUVIUM
ALMIGHTY
ALMS-DEED
ALOPECIA
ALPHABET
ALPINERY
ALQUIFOU
ALSATIAN
ALTARAGE
ALTERANT
ALTHOUGH
ALTITUDE
ALTRUISM
ALUMINUM
ALUM-ROOT
ALVEOLAR
ALVEOLUS
AMADAVAT
AMARANTH
AMAZEDLY
AMBITION
AMBLOTIC
AMBLYGON
AMBROSIA
AMBULANT
AMENABLE
AMENABLY
AMERICAN
AMETHYST
AMICABLE
AMICABLY
AMMONIAC
AMMONITE
AMMONIUM
AMOEBEAN
AMORETTI
AMORTIZE
AMPHIBIA
AMPHIPOD
AMPHORAL
AMPUTATE
ANABASIS
ANACONDA
ANAGLYPH
ANALOGUE
ANALYSIS
ANALYTIC
ANARCHIC
ANASARCA
ANATHEMA
ANCESTOR
ANCESTRY
ANCHORET
ANECDOTE
ANEURISM
ANGELICA
ANGLICAN
ANIMATED
ANISETTE

ANKYLOSE	ARCHAISM	ATHLETIC	BALE-FIRE
ANNALIST	ARCHDUKE	ATLANTES	BALL-COCK
ANNOTATE	ARCHNESS	ATLANTIC	BALLISTA
ANNOUNCE	ARCHWISE	ATMOLOGY	BALSAMIC
ANNUALLY	ARCTURUS	ATOMIZER	BALUSTER
ANNULATA	ARDENTLY	ATONABLE	BANDELET
ANNULATE	ARGENTAL	ATROCITY	BAND-FISH
ANNULOSE	ARGONAUT	ATTACKER	BANISHER
ANOINTER	ARGUABLE	ATTEMPER	BANISTER
ANSERINE	ARGUMENT	ATTENDER	BANK-NOTE
ANSWERER	ARHIZOUS	ATTESTER	BANKRUPT
ANTALGIC	ARIANISM	ATTICISM	BANNERED
ANT-EATER	ARMAMENT	ATTITUDE	BANNERET
ANTECEDE	ARMATURE	ATTORNEY	BANTERER
ANTEDATE	ARMENIAN	AUCIPIAL	BANTLING
ANTELOPE	ARMINIAN	AUDACITY	BANXRING
ANTEPAST	ARMORIAL	AUDIENCE	BAPTIZER
ANTERIOR	ARMOURER	AUDITORY	BARBACAN
ANTEROOM	ARMY-LIST	AUGURIAL	BARBARIC
ANTIDOTE	ARMY-WORM	AUGUSTAN	BARBECUE
ANTILOGY	AROMATIC	AUGUSTLY	BARBERRY
ANTIMASK	ARPEGGIO	AURICULA	BARBETTE
ANTIMONY	ARQUEBUS	AURIFORM	BARBICAN
ANTIPHON	ARRANGER	AUSTRIAN	BARDLING
ANTIPODE	ARRESTER	AUTOCRAT	BAREFOOT
ANTIPOPE	ARROGANT	AUTO-DA-FE	BARENESS
ANTITYPE	ARROGATE	AUTO-DE-FE	BARGEMAN
ANTLERED	ARTERIAL	AUTONOMY	BARITONE
ANYTHING	ARTESIAN	AUTOPSIA	BARNACLE
ANYWHERE	ARTFULLY	AUTOTYPE	BARN-YARD
AORISTIC	ARTIFICE	AUTUMNAL	BARONAGE
APERIENT	ARTISTIC	AVE-MARIA	BARONESS
APERTURE	ARUSPICY	AVERMENT	BARONIAL
APHELION	ASBESTOS	AVERSION	BAROUCHE
APHORISM	ASCIDIAN	AVIATION	BARRATOR
APIARIST	ASCIDIUM	AVIFAUNA	BARRATRY
APODOSIS	ASPERITY	AVOUCHER	BARRETOR
APOLOGUE	ASPHODEL	AVOWABLE	BARTERER
APOPLEXY	ASPHYXIA	AVOWEDLY	BARTIZAN
APOSTASY	ASPIRANT	AVULSION	BARYTONE
APOSTATE	ASPIRATE	AWEATHER	BASALTIC
APOSTEME	ASPIRING		BASANITE
APOTHEGM	ASPOROUS		BASCINET
APPANAGE	ASSAILER		BASE-BALL
APPARENT	ASSASSIN	**B**	BASE-BORN
APPENDIX	ASSAYING		BASELESS
APPETENT	ASSEMBLE	BABYHOOD	BASE-LINE
APPETITE	ASSEMBLY	BACCARAT	BASEMENT
APPETIZE	ASSENTER	BACCHANT	BASENESS
APPLAUSE	ASSERTOR	BACHELOR	BASICITY
APPLE-PIE	ASSESSOR	BACILLAR	BASILICA
APPOSITE	ASSIGNEE	BACILLUS	BASILISK
APPRAISE	ASSIGNER	BACKBITE	BASS-CLEF
APPROACH	ASSONANT	BACKBONE	BASSINET
APPROVAL	ASSORTED	BACK-DOOR	BASS-VIOL
APPROVER	ASSUAGER	BACKHAND	BASTARDY
APTEROUS	ASSUMING	BACKMOST	BATAVIAN
APTITUDE	ASSYRIAN	BACKSIDE	BAT-HORSE
APYRETIC	ASTERISK	BACK-STAY	BAYADERE
AQUARIUM	ASTERISM	BACKWARD	BAYBERRY
AQUARIUS	ASTEROID	BACONIAN	BDELLIUM
AQUATINT	ASTHENIA	BACULITE	BEACONED
AQUEDUCT	ASTHENIC	BADIGEON	BEAD-ROLL
AQUIFORM	ASTONISH	BADINAGE	BEADS-MAN
AQUILINE	ASTRAGAL	BAILABLE	BEAM-ENDS
ARBALIST	ASTUCITY	BAILMENT	BEAMLESS
ARBORIST	ASTUTELY	BAKSHISH	BEAM-TREE
ARBOURED	ATHELING	BALANCER	BEAN-KING
ARCADIAN	ATHENIAN	BALD-ERNE	BEARABLE
ARCHAEAN	ATHEROMA	BALDNESS	BEARABLY
		BALDRICK	

BEARSKIN	BILANDER	BLUNTISH	BRAND-NEW
BEARWARD	BILBERRY	BLUSHING	BRATTICE
BEATIFIC	BILL-HOOK	BOARDING	BRAWLING
BEAUTIFY	BILLY-BOY	BOASTFUL	BRAZENLY
BEAVERED	BILOBATE	BOAT-BILL	BREAD-NUT
BECHAMEL	BIMANOUS	BOAT-HOOK	BREAKAGE
BECHANCE	BIMENSAL	BOBBINET	BREASTED
BECOMING	BIND-WEED	BOBOLINK	BREATHER
BEDABBLE	BINNACLE	BOCK-BEER	BREECHED
BEDESMAN	BINOMIAL	BODEMENT	BREECHES
BEDRENCH	BIOLOGIC	BODILESS	BREEDING
BEDSTEAD	BIOMETRY	BOG-EARTH	BRETHREN
BEDSTRAW	BIOPLASM	BOGGLING	BRETTICE
BEEF-WOOD	BIPAROUS	BOHEMIAN	BREVIARY
BEES'-WING	BIRAMOUS	BOLDNESS	BREVIATE
BEETLING	BIRD-BOLT	BOLT-HEAD	BREVIPED
BEET-ROOT	BIRD-CALL	BOLT-ROPE	BREWSTER
BEFRIEND	BIRD-LIME	BOMBAZET	BRIBABLE
BEGETTER	BIRD'S-EYE	BONA FIDE	BRICKBAT
BEGGARLY	BIRTHDAY	BONDMAID	BRICK-TEA
BEGINNER	BISERIAL	BONE-DUST	BRIGHTEN
BEGRUDGE	BISEXUAL	BONE-LACE	BRIGHTLY
BEGUILER	BISTOURY	BONE-MILL	BRIMLESS
BEHEMOTH	BITHEISM	BONIFACE	BRIMMING
BEHOLDEN	BITING-IN	BONNETED	BRINDLED
BEHOLDER	BITINGLY	BOOBYISH	BRINE-PAN
BELABOUR	BITNOBEN	BOOK-DEBT	BRINE-PIT
BELIEVER	BITTACLE	BOOK-OATH	BRISTLED
BELITTLE	BITTERLY	BOOK-POST	BRITZSKA
BELL-PULL	BIWEEKLY	BOOK-WORM	BROACHER
BELL-ROPE	BLACK-CAP	BOOKWORM	BROCADED
BELLYFUL	BLACKING	BOOT-HOOK	BROCATEL
BELLY-GOD	BLACKISH	BOOT-HOSE	BROCCOLI
BEMOANER	BLACK-LEG	BOOT-JACK	BROCHURE
BENDABLE	BLACK-TIN	BOOT-LACE	BROIDERY
BENEDICK	BLACK-WAD	BOOTLESS	BROKENLY
BENEFICE	BLADDERY	BOOT-RACK	BROMELIA
BENGALEE	BLAMABLE	BOOT-TREE	BRONCHIA
BENIGNLY	BLAMABLY	BOOT-LAST	BRONCHUS
BENJAMIN	BLAMEFUL	BORACHIO	BRONZITE
BEPRAISE	BLANDISH	BORACITE	BROOKLET
BEQUEATH	BLASTULA	BORDERER	BROUGHAM
BERGAMOT	BLAZONER	BORECOLE	BROWBEAT
BERGMEHL	BLAZONRY	BORROWER	BROWNING
BERTHAGE	BLEACHER	BOSTANGI	BROWNISH
BESIEGER	BLEEDING	BOTANIST	BRUNETTE
BESLAVER	BLENHEIM	BOTANIZE	BRUTALLY
BESOTTED	BLESSING	BOTCHERY	BRYOLOGY
BESPREAD	BLINDAGE	BOTHERER	BUCK-SHOT
BESPRENT	BLINDING	BOTRYOID	BUCKSKIN
BESTIARY	BLINKARD	BOTTOMED	BUDDHISM
BESTOWAL	BLISSFUL	BOTTOMRY	BUDDHIST
BESTOWER	BLISTERY	BOUNCING	BUFONITE
BESTRIDE	BLITHELY	BOUNDARY	BUILDING
BETEL-NUT	BLIZZARD	BOURGEON	BUKSHISH
BETRAYAL	BLOCKADE	BOW-DRILL	BULK-HEAD
BETRAYER	BLOCKISH	BOWSPRIT	BULL-CALF
BEVERAGE	BLOCK-TIN	BOYISHLY	BULLETIN
BEWAILER	BLOODILY	BRACELET	BULL-FROG
BEWILDER	BLOOMERY	BRACHIAL	BULL-HEAD
BEZONIAN	BLOOMING	BRACKISH	BULL'S-EYE
BIBLICAL	BLOSSOMY	BRADYPOD	BULRUSHY
BIBULOUS	BLOW-HOLE	BRAGGART	BUNCOMBE
BICONVEX	BLOWPIPE	BRAIDING	BUNGALOW
BICUSPID	BLUDGEON	BRAINISH	BUNG-HOLE
BIDDABLE	BLUEBELL	BRAKEMAN	BUNGLING
BIDENTAL	BLUE-BIRD	BRAKE-VAN	BUNTLINE
BIENNIAL	BLUE-BOOK	BRANCHED	BUOYANCY
BIGAMIST	BLUENESS	BRANDIED	BURGAMOT
BIGNONIA	BLUE-PILL	BRANDISH	BURGANET

BURGEOIS
BURGLARY
BURGRAVE
BURGUNDY
BURLETTA
BURNABLE
BURNOOSE
BURNT-EAR
BURROWER
BUSINESS
BUSKINED
BUSY-BODY
BUTCHERY
BUTTRESS
BY-CORNER
BY-STREET

C

CABALLER
CABIN-BOY
CABRIOLE
CACHALOT
CACHUCHA
CACODYLE
CACOLOGY
CADASTRE
CADUCEAN
CADUCEUS
CADUCOUS
CAESURAL
CAFFEINE
CAGELING
CAIMACAM
CAJOLERY
CALABASH
CALAMARY
CALAMINE
CALAMINT
CALAMITE
CALAMITY
CALCINER
CALC-SPAR
CALC-TUFF
CALCULAR
CALCULUS
CALENDAR
CALENDER
CALF-LOVE
CALIFATE
CALIPASH
CALIPERS
CALISAYA
CALL-BIRD
CALL-NOTE
CALMNESS
CALOTYPE
CALYCINE
CALYCOID
CALYPTRA
CAMBRIAN
CAMELEON
CAMELINE
CAMELLIA
CAMISADE
CAMISOLE
CAMOMILE
CAMPAIGN
CAMPHINE

CANADIAN
CANAILLE
CANALIZE
CANASTER
CANCELLI
CANCROID
CANDIDLY
CANE-MILL
CANISTER
CANNIBAL
CANNIKIN
CANOEIST
CANONESS
CANONIST
CANONIZE
CANOPIED
CANOROUS
CANTICLE
CANTONAL
CANZONET
CAPACITY
CAPELINE
CAPITATE
CAPRIOLE
CAPSICUM
CAPSIZAL
CAPSULAR
CAPTIOUS
CAPUCHIN
CAPYBARA
CARABINE
CARACARA
CARACOLE
CARAPACE
CARAP-OIL
CARBOLIC
CARBONIC
CARBURET
CARCAJOU
CARCANET
CARDAMOM
CARD-CASE
CARDIGAN
CARDINAL
CARDITIS
CARELESS
CARE-WORN
CARIACOU
CARIATID
CARILLON
CARINATE
CARNALLY
CARNAUBA
CARNEOUS
CARNIVAL
CAROLINE
CAROUSAL
CAROUSEL
CARRIAGE
CARRIOLE
CARROCHE
CART-LOAD
CARTOUCH
CARUCATE
CARUNCLE
CARYATID
CASCABEL
CASEMATE
CASEMENT

CASE-SHOT
CASE-WORM
CASH-BOOK
CASHMERE
CASTANET
CASTAWAY
CAST-IRON
CASTLING
CASTRATE
CASUALLY
CASUALTY
CATACOMB
CATAPULT
CATARACT
CATCHFLY
CATCHING
CATEGORY
CATENARY
CATERESS
CATHEDRA
CATHETER
CATONIAN
CAT'S-TAIL
CAUDICLE
CAULDRON
CAULICLE
CAUSABLE
CAUSALLY
CAUSEWAY
CAUTIOUS
CAVALIER
CAVATINA
CAVE-BEAR
CAVERNED
CAVICORN
CAVILLER
CELERITY
CELIBACY
CELIBATE
CELLARER
CELLARET
CELLULAR
CEMETERY
CENOBITE
CENOTAPH
CENTURY
CENTOIST
CENTUPLE
CEPHALIC
CERASTES
CERATOSE
CERBERUS
CEREBRAL
CEREBRIN
CEREBRUM
CEREMONY
CERULEAN
CERULEIN
CERUSITE
CERVICAL
CESAREAN
CESSPOOL
CETACEAN
CETOLOGY
CHAIRMAN
CHALDAIC
CHALDRON
CHAMFRON
CHAMPION
CHANCERY

CHANDLER
CHANTAGE
CHAP-BOOK
CHAPERON
CHAPITER
CHAPLAIN
CHAPTREL
CHARCOAL
CHARLOCK
CHARMING
CHARTISM
CHARTIST
CHASE-GUN
CHASSEUR
CHASTELY
CHASTISE
CHASTITY
CHASUBLE
CHAUFFER
CHEATERY
CHEATING
CHEERFUL
CHEERILY
CHEERING
CHEMICAL
CHENILLE
CHERUBIC
CHESS-MAN
CHESTNUT
CHETVERT
CHICANER
CHICK-PEA
CHIEFDOM
CHIEFERY
CHIEFESS
CHILDBED
CHILDING
CHILDISH
CHILDREN
CHILIASM
CHILLING
CHIMAERA
CHINA-INK
CHINAMAN
CHINLESS
CHIPMUNK
CHIPPING
CHIRAGRA
CHIT-CHAT
CHIVALRY
CHLOASMA
CHLORIDE
CHLORINE
CHLORITE
CHOICELY
CHOLERIC
CHOPPING
CHORAGUS
CHORALLY
CHOULTRY
CHOW-CHOW
CHRISMAL
CHRISTEN
CHROMATE
CHROMIUM
CHROMITE
CHUFFILY
CHURLISH
CHYLURIA
CHYMICAL

CIBORIUM	CLUB-FOOT	COMMENCE	CONVOLVE
CICATRIX	CLUB-MOSS	COMMERCE	CONVULSE
CICERONE	CLUB-ROOM	COMMONER	CONY-WOOL
CIDERKIN	CLUMSILY	COMMONLY	COOLNESS
CI-DEVANT	CLYPEATE	COMMUNAL	COPPERAS
CILIATED	COACH-BOX	COMPILER	COPULATE
CIMOLITE	COACH-DOG	COMPLAIN	COPY-BOOK
CINCHONA	COACHMAN	COMPLECT	COPYHOLD
CINCTURE	COACTIVE	COMPLETE	COQUETRY
CINERARY	COAGENCY	COMPLICE	COQUETTE
CINNABAR	COAGULUM	COMPLIER	CORACOID
CINNAMON	COALESCE	COMPLINE	CORAL-RAG
CIRCULAR	COAL-FISH	COMPOSED	CORBEILE
CIRRIPED	COAL-MINE	COMPOSER	CORDOVAN
CISELURE	COAL-WORK	COMPOUND	CORDUROY
CISTELLA	COARSELY	COMPRESS	CORDWAIN
CITATION	COASTING	COMPRISE	COREGENT
CITATORY	COBALTIC	COMPUTER	CORELESS
CIVET-CAT	CO-BISHOP	CONCEDER	CORMOGEN
CIVILIAN	COBWEBBY	CONCEIVE	CORNEOUS
CIVILIST	COCCULUS	CONCERTO	CORNERED
CIVILITY	COCKADED	CONCHOID	CORNETCY
CIVILIZE	COCKATOO	CONCLAVE	CORN-FLAG
CLAIMANT	COCK-BOAT	CONCLUDE	CORN-LAWS
CLAMANCY	COCK-CROW	CONCRETE	CORN-MILL
CLANGOUR	COCKEREL	CONDENSE	CORN-PIPE
CLANNISH	COCK-LOFT	CONFEREE	CORN-ROSE
CLANSHIP	COCKSURE	CONFERVA	CORN-RENT
CLANSMAN	COCKTAIL	CONFLATE	CORNUTED
CLAP-SILL	CODIFIER	CONFLICT	CORONACH
CLAPTRAP	COERCION	CONFOUND	CORONARY
CLAQUEUR	COERCIVE	CONFRERE	CORONOID
CLARENCE	COEXTEND	CONFRONT	CORPORAL
CLASSIFY	COFFERED	CONFUSED	CORRIDOR
CLAVECIN	COGENTLY	CONGENER	CORRIVAL
CLAVICLE	COGITATE	CONGLOBE	CORSELET
CLAWBACK	COGNOMEN	CONGRESS	CORTICAL
CLAY-COLD	COG-WHEEL	CONGREVE	CORUNDUM
CLAY-MARL	COHERENT	CONICITY	CORVETTE
CLAY-MILL	COHESION	CONIFORM	CORYBANT
CLAYMORE	COHESIVE	CONJOINT	CORYPHEE
CLEANSER	COHOBATE	CONJUGAL	CO-SECANT
CLEARING	COIFFURE	CONJUNCT	COSENAGE
CLEAVAGE	COINCIDE	CONJURER	COSMETIC
CLEAVERS	CO-INHERE	CONNIVER	COST-FREE
CLEMATIS	COLANDER	CONQUEST	COSTLESS
CLEMENCY	COLDNESS	CONSERVE	COSTMARY
CLENCHER	COLE-SEED	CONSIDER	COSTUMED
CLERICAL	COLEWORT	CONSOLER	CO-SURETY
CLEVERLY	COLICKED	CONSPIRE	CO-TENANT
CLEW-LINE	COLLAPSE	CONSTANT	COTQUEAN
CLIENTAL	COLLARET	CONSTRUE	COTTAGER
CLIMATIC	COLLATOR	CONSULAR	COTYLOID
CLIMBING	COLLIERY	CONSUMER	COUCHANT
CLINCHER	COLLOQUY	CONSUMPT	COULISSE
CLINICAL	COLONIAL	CONTANGO	COUNTESS
CLIPPING	COLONIST	CONTEMPT	COUPLING
CLIQUISH	COLONIZE	CONTINUE	COURSING
CLIQUISM	COLOPHON	CONTRACT	COURT-DAY
CLOAK-BAG	COLOSSAL	CONTRARY	COURTESY
CLODDISH	COLOSSUS	CONTRAST	COURTIER
CLODPOLL	COLOURED	CONTRITE	COUSINLY
CLOISTER	COLUMNAR	CONTRIVE	COVENANT
CLOTHIER	COLUMNED	CONVENER	COVERING
CLOTHING	COMATOSE	CONVERGE	COVERLET
CLOUDILY	COMBINED	CONVERSE	COVERLID
CLOUDLET	COMBINER	CONVEXLY	COVERTLY
CLOVERED	COMEDIAN	CONVEYAL	COVETOUS
CLOWNISH	COMETARY	CONVEYER	COVINOUS
CLUBBIST	COMITIAL	CONVINCE	COWARDLY

COW-BERRY	CUCUMBER	DANSEUSE	DEFERENT
COWORKER	CUCURBIT	DARINGLY	DEFERRER
COXSWAIN	CUL-DE-SAC	DARKLING	DEFIANCE
COZENAGE	CULINARY	DARKNESS	DEFILADE
CRAB-WOOD	CULPABLE	DARKSOME	DEFINITE
CRAB-TREE	CULPABLY	DASTARDY	DEFLOWER
CRACKNEL	CULTRATE	DATELESS	DEFLUENT
CRAFTILY	CULTURAL	DATE-PALM	DEFORMED
CRAGSMEN	CULTURED	DATE-TREE	DEFORMER
CRANE-FLY	CULVERIN	DATE-PLUM	DEFRAYAL
CRANKILY	CUMBRIAN	DATURINE	DEFRAYER
CRANNIED	CUMBROUS	DAUGHTER	DEFTNESS
CRAWFISH	CUMULATE	DAVY-LAMP	DEGRADED
CRAYFISH	CUPBOARD	DAYBREAK	DEJECTED
CREAMERY	CUPIDITY	DAY-DREAM	DEJEUNER
CREASOTE	CUPREOUS	DAYLIGHT	DELATION
CREATION	CURASSOU	DAZZLING	DELEGATE
CREATIVE	CURATIVE	DEAD-BEAT	DELETION
CREATURE	CURATRIX	DEAD-BORN	DELICACY
CREDENCE	CURBABLE	DEAD-FALL	DELICATE
CREDIBLE	CURB-ROOF	DEADHEAD	DELIRIUM
CREDIBLY	CURCULIO	DEAD-HEAT	DELIVERY
CREDITOR	CURELESS	DEAD-LOCK	DELPHIAN
CREMATOR	CURRENCY	DEAD-MEAT	DELUSION
CRENELLE	CURRICLE	DEADNESS	DELUSIVE
CREOSOTE	CURSEDLY	DEAD-WORK	DELUSORY
CRESCENT	CURSORES	DEAF-MUTE	DEMANDER
CRETONNE	CURTAL-AX	DEAFNESS	DEMENTED
CREUTZER	CURTNESS	DEAL-FISH	DEMENTIA
CREVASSE	CUSHIONY	DEANSHIP	DEMIJOHN
CRIBBAGE	CUSPIDOR	DEARNESS	DEMI-LUNE
CRIBRATE	CUSTOMER	DEATH-BED	DEMIURGE
CRIMEFUL	CUTPURSE	DEATHFUL	DEMI-VOLT
CRIMINAL	CUTWATER	DEBASING	DEMI-WOLF
CRIMPING	CYANOGEN	DEBILITY	DEMOCRAT
CRISPATE	CYANOSIS	DEBONAIR	DEMOLISH
CRISTATE	CYCLAMEN	DEBUTANT	DEMONIAC
CRITICAL	CYCLONIC	DECADENT	DEMONISM
CRITIQUE	CYCLOPIC	DECAGRAM	DEMONIST
CROAKING	CYCLOPES	DECANTER	DEMONIZE
CROCKERY	CYLINDER	DECEASED	DEMURELY
CROMLECH	CYNANCHE	DECEIVER	DEMURRER
CROMORNE	CYNICISM	DECEMBER	DENARIUS
CROP-FULL	CYNOSURE	DECEMVIR	DENDRITE
CROP-SICK	CYRENAIC	DECENTLY	DENDROID
CROSSBOW	CYRILLIC	DECIMATE	DENIABLE
CROSSCUT	CYSTITIS	DECIPHER	DENOUNCE
CROSS-EYE	CZAREVNA	DECISION	DENTICLE
CROSSING		DECISIVE	DEPARTED
CROSSLET		DECK-LOAD	DEPENDER
CROSSWAY	**D**	DECK-HAND	DEPILATE
CROTCHED		DECLARED	DEPLORER
CROTCHET	DABCHICK	DECLARER	DEPONENT
CROUPIER	DACRYOMA	DECLINAL	DEPRAVED
CROW-FOOT	DACTYLIC	DECOLOUR	DEPRAVER
CROWNING	DAFFODIL	DECORATE	DEPRIVER
CROWNLET	DAHABIEH	DECOROUS	DEPURATE
CROWN-SAW	DAINTILY	DECREASE	DERANGED
CRUCIBLE	DAIRYING	DECREPIT	DERELICT
CRUCIFER	DAIRYMAN	DECRETAL	DERISION
CRUCIFIX	DALESMAN	DECURION	DERISIVE
CRUMPLED	DALMATIC	DEDICATE	DERMATIC
CRUSADER	DAL SEGNO	DEEDLESS	DEROGATE
CRUSH-HAT	DAMASSIN	DEEMSTER	DESCRIBE
CRUSHING	DAMNABLE	DEEP-LAID	DESCRIER
CRUSTILY	DAMNABLY	DEEPNESS	DESERTER
CRUTCHED	DAMPNESS	DEER-HAIR	DESERVER
CRYOLITE	DANDRUFF	DEFECATE	DESIGNER
CUBATURE	DANDYISH	DEFENDEE	DESIROUS
CUBIFORM	DANDYISM	DEFENDER	DESOLATE

DESPATCH	DILUVIAN	DIVIDEND	DRAUGHTY
DESPISER	DILUVION	DIVI-DIVI	DRAWABLE
DESPOTIC	DILUVIUM	DIVIDUAL	DRAWBACK
DETACHED	DIMEROUS	DIVINELY	DRAW-WELL
DETAILED	DIMINISH	DIVINITY	DREADFUL
DETAILER	DINGDONG	DIVISION	DREAMILY
DETAINER	DINORNIS	DIVISIVE	DREARILY
DETECTOR	DINOSAUR	DIVORCEE	DRESSING
DETESTER	DIOCESAN	DIVORCER	DRIFT-NET
DETHRONE	DIOECIAN	DOCILITY	DRILLING
DETONATE	DIOPSIDE	DOCIMASY	DRIPPING
DETONIZE	DIOPTASE	DOCKYARD	DROLLERY
DETRITAL	DIOPTRIC	DOCTORAL	DROPPING
DETRITUS	DIORAMIC	DOCTRINE	DROPSIED
DEUCEDLY	DIPLOMAT	DOCUMENT	DROPWORT
DEVILISH	DIPLOPIA	DODDERED	DROUGHTY
DEVONIAN	DIPTERAL	DOG-CHEAP	DROWSILY
DEVOTION	DIRECTLY	DOG-EARED	DRUBBING
DEVOUTLY	DIRECTOR	DOGGEDLY	DRUDGERY
DEW-BERRY	DISABUSE	DOGGEREL	DRUGGIST
DEWINESS	DISAGREE	DOG-GRASS	DRUIDISM
DEW-POINT	DISANNEX	DOG-LATIN	DRUMHEAD
DEXTRINE	DISANNUL	DOGMATIC	DRUNKARD
DEXTROSE	DISARRAY	DOG'S-BANE	DRY-NURSE
DIABETES	DISASTER	DOG-SLEEP	DRY-POINT
DIABETIC	DISBURSE	DOG-TOOTH	DUBITATE
DIABOLIC	DISCIPLE	DOG-WATCH	DUCATOON
DIACONAL	DISCLAIM	DOLDRUMS	DUCK-BILL
DIADELPH	DISCLOSE	DOLERITE	DUCKLING
DIADEMED	DISCOUNT	DOLOMITE	DUCK-MOLE
DIAGLYPH	DISCOVER	DOLOROUS	DUCK-WEED
DIAGNOSE	DISCREET	DOMAINAL	DUELLING
DIAGONAL	DISCRETE	DOMESTIC	DUELLIST
DIALLAGE	DISCROWN	DOMICILE	DULCIMER
DIALLING	DISEASED	DOMINANT	DULLNESS
DIALOGUE	DISENDOW	DOMINATE	DUMB-BELL
DIALYSER	DISGORGE	DOMINEER	DUMBNESS
DIALYSIS	DISGRACE	DOMINION	DUMPLING
DIAMETER	DISGUISE	DOMINOES	DUNG-FORK
DIAPASON	DISHEVEL	DONATION	DUNGHILL
DIASTASE	DISHORSE	DONATIVE	DUODENUM
DIASTEMA	DISINTER	DOOMSDAY	DUOLOGUE
DIASTOLE	DISJOINT	DOOMSMAN	DURATION
DIATOMIC	DISJUNCT	DOOR-NAIL	DUST-BALL
DIATONIC	DISLODGE	DOOR-POST	DUST-CART
DIATRIBE	DISLOYAL	DOOR-STEP	DUTIABLE
DICHROIC	DISMALLY	DORMANCY	DWARFISH
DICLINIC	DISMOUNT	DORMOUSE	DWELLING
DICTATOR	DISORDER	DOTATION	DYE-HOUSE
DIDACTIC	DISPATCH	DOTINGLY	DYE-STUFF
DIDAPPER	DISPEACE	DOTTEREL	DYNAMICS
DIDYMIUM	DISSEVER	DOUBLING	DYNAMITE
DIDYMOUS	DISSOLVE	DOUBLOON	DYNASTIC
DIERESIS	DISSUADE	DOUBTFUL	DYSPNOEA
DIETETIC	DISTALLY	DOUGH-NUT	
DIFFRACT	DISTANCE	DOVETAIL	
DIFFUSER	DISTASTE	DOWNCAST	
DIGESTER	DISTINCT	DOWN-COME	**E**
DIGGABLE	DISTRACT	DOWNFALL	
DIGITATE	DISTRAIN	DOWNHILL	EAGLE-OWL
DIGYNIAN	DISTRAIT	DOWN-LINE	EAR-SHELL
DIGYNOUS	DISTRESS	DOWNPOUR	EARTH-HOG
DIHEDRAL	DISTRICT	DOWNWARD	EARTH-PIG
DIHEDRON	DISTRUST	DOXOLOGY	EARTH-NUT
DILATION	DISUNION	DRACONIC	EASEMENT
DILATIVE	DISUNITE	DRAGOMAN	EASINESS
DILATORY	DISUSAGE	DRAGONET	EASTERLY
DILIGENT	DITHEISM	DRAINAGE	EASTWARD
DILUTION	DITHEIST	DRAMATIC	EAU DE VIE
DILUVIAL	DIURETIC	DRAM-SHOP	EBURNEAN
			EBURNINE

ECAUDATE	EMACIATE	ENSAMPLE	ERRORIST
ECHINATE	EMBALMER	ENSCONCE	ERUCTATE
ECHINITE	EMBATTLE	ENSEMBLE	ERUPTION
ECHINOLD	EMBEZZLE	ENSHRINE	ERUPTIVE
ECLECTIC	EMBITTER	ENSIFORM	ERYTHEMA
ECLIPTIC	EMBLAZON	ENSILAGE	ESCALADE
ECONOMIC	EMBOLDEN	ENSLAVER	ESCALLOP
ECOSTATE	EMBOLISM	ENTAILER	ESCAPADE
ECRASEUR	EMBRASOR	ENTANGLE	ESCHALOT
ECSTATIC	EMERGENT	ENTELLUS	ESCULENT
ECUMENIC	EMERITUS	ENTHRALL	ESOTERIC
EDACIOUS	EMERSION	ENTHRONE	ESPALIER
EDENTATA	EMIGRANT	ENTICING	ESPECIAL
EDENTATE	EMIGRATE	ENTIRELY	ESPOUSAL
EDGE-BONE	EMINENCE	ENTIRETY	ESPOUSER
EDGELESS	EMISSARY	ENTOMOID	ESSAYIST
EDGE-TOOL	EMISSION	ENTOZOAL	ESQUIMAU
EDGEWAYS	EMISSIVE	ENTOZOIC	ESTHETIC
EDGEWISE	EMISSORY	ENTOZOON	ESTIMATE
EDIFYING	EMPANNEL	ENTR'ACTE	ESTOPPEL
EDITRESS	EMPHASIS	ENTRANCE	ESTOVERS
EDUCABLE	EMPHATIC	ENTREATY	ESTRANGE
EDUCATOR	EMPLOYEE	ENTRENCH	ESURIENT
EDUCIBLE	EMPLOYER	ENTREPOT	ETERNITY
EEL-SPEAR	EMPOISON	ENTRESOL	ETERNIZE
EERINESS	EMPORIUM	ENURESIS	ETHELING
EFFECTER	EMPURPLE	ENVELOPE	ETHEREAL
EFFECTOR	EMPYREAL	ENVIABLE	ETHERIFY
EFFERENT	EMPYREAN	ENVIABLY	ETHERISM
EFFICACY	EMULATOR	ENVIRONS	ETHERIZE
EFFLUENT	EMULGENT	ENVISAGE	ETHICIST
EFFUSION	EMULSION	ENZOOTIC	ETHIOPIC
EFFUSIVE	EMULSIVE	EOLIPILE	ETHNICAL
EGESTION	ENACTIVE	EPHEMERA	ETHOLOGY
EGG-APPLE	ENALLAGE	EPHESIAN	ETHYLENE
EGG-GLASS	ENCEINTE	EPICALYX	ETIOLATE
EGG-PLANT	ENCHORIC	EPICYCLE	ETIOLOGY
EGG-SHELL	ENCIRCLE	EPIDEMIC	ETRUSCAN
EGG-SLICE	ENCLITIC	EPIGEOUS	ETYPICAL
EGG-SPOON	ENCOMIUM	EPIGRAPH	EUCALYPT
EGOISTIC	ENCRINAL	EPILEPSY	EUGENICS
EGRESSOR	ENCRINIC	EPILOGIC	EULOGIST
EGYPTIAN	ENCROACH	EPILOGUE	EULOGIUM
EIGHT-DAY	ENCUMBER	EPINASTY	EULOGIZE
EIGHTEEN	ENCYCLIC	EPIPHANY	EUPEPSIA
EIGHTHLY	ENDAMAGE	EPIPHYTE	EUPEPTIC
EJECTION	ENDANGER	EPIPLOIC	EUPHONIC
ELAPSION	ENDERMIC	EPIPLOON	EUPHRASY
ELATEDLY	ENDOCARP	EPISODIC	EUPHUISM
EL DORADO	ENDOGAMY	EPISPERM	EUPHUIST
ELECTION	ENDORSER	EPISTLER	EURASIAN
ELECTIVE	ENDURING	EPONYMIC	EUROPEAN
ELECTRIC	ENERGIZE	EPULOTIC	EVACUANT
ELECTRON	ENERVATE	EPYORNIS	EVACUATE
ELEGANCE	ENFEEBLE	EQUALITY	EVADABLE
ELEGANCY	ENFILADE	EQUALIZE	EVADIBLE
ELEGIAST	ENFOREST	EQUATION	EVALUATE
ELENCHUS	ENGENDER	EQUIPAGE	EVANESCE
ELEPHANT	ENGINEER	EQUITANT	EVENNESS
ELEVATOR	ENGORGED	EQUIVOKE	EVENTFUL
ELEVENTH	ENGRAVER	ERASTIAN	EVENTIDE
ELF-ARROW	ENHANCER	ERECTILE	EVENTUAL
ELIGIBLE	ENKINDLE	ERECTION	EVERMORE
ELIGIBLY	ENLARGED	ERECTIVE	EVERSION
ELLIPSIS	ENLARGER	EREMITIC	EVERYDAY
ELLIPTIC	ENNEAGON	ERETHISM	EVERYONE
ELONGATE	ENORMITY	ERGOTINE	EVICTION
ELOQUENT	ENORMOUS	ERGOTISM	EVIDENCE
ELUDIBLE	ENROLLER	EROTETIC	EVILDOER
ELVISHLY		ERRANTRY	EVILNESS

EVULSION	FACE-ACHE	FERN-SEED	FLAMBEAU
EXACTING	FACETIAE	FEROCITY	FLAMINGO
EXACTION	FACIALLY	FERREOUS	FLASHILY
EXAMINEE	FACILITY	FERRETER	FLATTING
EXAMINER	FACTIOUS	FERRIAGE	FLATLONG
EXCAVATE	FACTOTUM	FERRYMAN	FLATNESS
EXCHANGE	FADELESS	FERVENCY	FLATTERY
EXCISION	FADINGLY	FERVIDLY	FLATTING
EXCITANT	FAIRNESS	FESTALLY	FLATWISE
EXCITING	FAITHFUL	FESTIVAL	FLAUNTER
EXCURSUS	FALCATED	FETATION	FLAUTIST
EXECRATE	FALCHION	FETICIDE	FLAWLESS
EXECUTOR	FALCONER	FEUDALLY	FLEABITE
EXEGESIS	FALCONET	FEVERFEW	FLECTION
EXEGETIC	FALCONRY	FEVERISH	FLEETING
EXEMPLAR	FALLIBLE	FIBRILLA	FLESHPOT
EXEQUIAL	FALLIBLY	FIBROSIS	FLEXIBLE
EXEQUIES	FALL-TRAP	FIDELITY	FLEXIBLY
EXERCISE	FALSETTO	FIDUCIAL	FLEXUOSE
EXERTION	FAMELESS	FIELD-DAY	FLEXUOUS
EXHALANT	FAMILIAR	FIELD-GUN	FLIMSILY
EXHALENT	FAMOUSLY	FIENDISH	FLIPPANT
EXHORTER	FANCIFUL	FIERCELY	FLOATAGE
EXIGENCE	FANDANGO	FIFTIETH	FLOATING
EXIGENCY	FANFARON	FIGHTING	FLOCCOSE
EXIGIBLE	FAN-LIGHT	FIGULINE	FLOGGING
EXIGUOUS	FANTASIA	FIGURANT	FLOODING
EXIGUITY	FARCICAL	FIGURATE	FLOORING
EXISTENT	FARCY-BUD	FIGURINE	FLORALLY
EXORABLE	FAREWELL	FIGURING	FLORIDLY
EXORCISE	FARMABLE	FILAMENT	FLOSCULE
EXORCISM	FARMYARD	FILATORY	FLOTILLA
EXORCIST	FARRIERY	FILATURE	FLOUNDER
EXORCIZE	FARTHEST	FILE-FISH	FLOURISH
EXORDIAL	FARTHING	FILIALLY	FLOWERED
EXORDIUM	FASCIATE	FILICOID	FLOWERET
EXOSMOSE	FASCICLE	FILIFORM	FLUENTLY
EXOTERIC	FASHIOUS	FILIGREE	FLUIDITY
EXPECTER	FASTENER	FILLIBEG	FLUMMERY
EXPEDITE	FASTNESS	FILTHILY	FLUORITE
EXPELLER	FATALISM	FILTRATE	FLUXIBLE
EXPERTLY	FATALIST	FINALITY	FOCALIZE
EXPIABLE	FATALITY	FINEDRAW	FOGEYISM
EXPIATOR	FATHERLY	FINENESS	FOLIATED
EXPLICIT	FATTENER	FINESPUN	FOLLICLE
EXPLORER	FAULTILY	FINGERED	FOLLOWER
EXPONENT	FAUTEUIL	FINISHER	FOMENTER
EXPORTER	FAVONIAN	FINITELY	FONDLING
EXPOSURE	FAVOURED	FINITUDE	FONDNESS
EXSERTED	FAVOURER	FIREBALL	FONTANEL
EXTENDER	FEARLESS	FIRE-CLAY	FOODLESS
EXTENSOR	FEASIBLE	FIRE-DAMP	FOOLSCAP
EXTERIOR	FEASIBLY	FIRELOCK	FOOTBALL
EXTERNAL	FEATHERY	FIRE-PLUG	FOOTFALL
EXTOLLER	FEATURED	FIRE-SHIP	FOOTGEAR
EXTRADOS	FEBRUARY	FIRESIDE	FOOTHOLD
EXTRORSE	FECULENT	FIREWOOD	FOOTMARK
EXULTANT	FEDERATE	FIRMNESS	FOOTPATH
EXUVIATE	FEED-PIPE	FISH-HOOK	FOOTSTEP
EYE-GLASS	FEED-PUMP	FISHWIFE	FORAMINA
EYE-PIECE	FELDSPAR	FISTULAR	FORBORNE
EYESIGHT	FELICITY	FITFULLY	FORCEDLY
EYE-TOOTH	FELLNESS	FIVEFOLD	FORCEFUL
EYE-WATER	FELO-DE-SE	FIXATION	FORCIBLE
	FELSTONE	FIXATIVE	FORCIBLY
	FEME-SOLE	FLABBILY	FORCLOSE
	FENCIBLE	FLABELLA	FORDABLE
F	FERACITY	FLAGELLA	FOREBODE
	FERETORY	FLAGGING	FORECAST
FABULIST	FERINGEE	FLAGRANT	FOREDATE
FABULOUS			

FOREDOOM	FRIBBLER	GALVANIC	GLAUCOMA
FOREFEND	FRICTION	GAMENESS	GLAUCOUS
FOREGOER	FRIENDLY	GAMESOME	GLEESOME
FOREGONE	FRIGHTEN	GAMESTER	GLIBNESS
FOREHAND	FRIGIDLY	GANGLIAC	GLISSADE
FOREHEAD	FRILLING	GANGLION	GLOAMING
FOREKNOW	FRIPPERY	GANGRENE	GLOBATED
FORELAND	FRISKILY	GANISTER	GLOBULAR
FORELOCK	FRONTAGE	GANTLOPE	GLOBULET
FOREMAST	FRONTIER	GARDENER	GLOBULIN
FOREMOST	FRONTLET	GARDENIA	GLOOMILY
FORENOON	FROSTILY	GARGOYLE	GLORIOLE
FORENSIC	FROSTING	GARISHLY	GLORIOUS
FOREPART	FROTHILY	GARLICKY	GLOSSARY
FOREPEAK	FRUCTIFY	GAROTTER	GLOSSILY
FORESAID	FRUCTOSE	GARRISON	GLOWWORM
FORESAIL	FRUGALLY	GARROTTE	GLOXINIA
FORESHEW	FRUITAGE	GASALIER	GLUCINUM
FORESHOW	FRUITERY	GASELIER	GLUMNESS
FORESIDE	FRUITFUL	GASOGENE	GLUTTONY
FORESKIN	FRUITION	GASTRULA	GLYPTICS
FORESTAL	FRUMENTY	GATHERER	GNATLING
FORESTER	FRUMPISH	GAUNTLET	GNOMICAL
FORESTRY	FRUSTULE	GAZOGENE	GNOMONIC
FORETELL	FRUSTUMS	GELATINE	GOATHERD
FOREWARN	FUGACITY	GELIDITY	GODCHILD
FOREWARD	FUGITIVE	GEMINATE	GODWARDS
FORMALIN	FUGLEMAN	GEMINOUS	GOITERED
FORMALLY	FULCRATE	GEMMEOUS	GOITROUS
FORMERLY	FULCRUMS	GENDARME	GOLGOTHA
FORMLESS	FULGENCY	GENERANT	GONFALON
FORMULAE	FULLNESS	GENERATE	GONFANON
FORSAKER	FULMINIC	GENEROUS	GONIDIUM
FORSOOTH	FUMAROLE	GENEVESE	GOODNESS
FORSWEAR	FUMELESS	GENIALLY	GORGEOUS
FORTIETH	FUMIGATE	GENITALS	GOSSAMER
FORTRESS	FUMITORY	GENITIVE	GOSSIPRY
FORTUITY	FUNCTION	GENIUSES	GOURMAND
FORWARDS	FUNDABLE	GEODESIC	GOUTWORT
FOSTERER	FUNEREAL	GEODETIC	GOUTWEED
FOULNESS	FUNGUSES	GEOGNOSY	GOVERNOR
FOUNDERY	FURBELOW	GEOLATRY	GOWNSMAN
FOUNTAIN	FURCATED	GEOMANCY	GRAAFIAN
FOURFOLD	FURLOUGH	GEOMETER	GRACEFUL
FOURTEEN	FURMENTY	GEOMETRY	GRACIOUS
FOURTHLY	FURRIERY	GEOPONIC	GRADIENT
FOXGLOVE	FURTHEST	GEORGIAN	GRADUATE
FRACTION	FUSAROLE	GERANIUM	GRAFFITI
FRACTURE	FUSIFORM	GERMANIC	GRAFFITO
FRAGMENT	FUSILEER	GERMINAL	GRAINING
FRAGRANT	FUTILELY	GESTURAL	GRALLOCK
FRAMPOLD	FUTILITY	GIANTESS	GRANDEUR
FRANKISH	FUTURITY	GIBINGLY	GRANDSON
FRANKLIN		GIGANTIC	GRANITIC
FRAUDFUL		GIGGLING	GRANULAR
FREAKISH	**G**	GIMCRACK	GRAPHITE
FRECKLED		GINGERLY	GRASPING
FREEBORN	GABIONED	GIRASOLE	GRATEFUL
FREEDMAN	GADABOUT	GIRLHOOD	GRATUITY
FREEHAND	GADHELIC	GLABROUS	GRAVAMEN
FREEHOLD	GAINLESS	GLACIATE	GRAVELLY
FREENESS	GALACTIC	GLADIATE	GRAYLING
FREEZING	GALANGAL	GLADIOLI	GRAYNESS
FRENETIC	GALBANUM	GLADNESS	GREASILY
FRENZIED	GALEATED	GLADSOME	GREEDILY
FREQUENT	GALLIARD	GLANDERS	GREENERY
FRESCOES	GALLICAN	GLANDULE	GREENING
FRESCOED	GALLIPOT	GLAREOUS	GREENISH
FRESHMAN	GALLOPER	GLASSFUL	GREETING
FRETWORK	GALLOWAY	GLASSILY	GREWSOME

GRIDIRON
GRIEVOUS
GRILLADE
GRIMNESS
GRINDING
GRISETTE
GRIZZLED
GROINING
GROSBEAK
GROSCHEN
GROTTOES
GROUPING
GROWLING
GRUDGING
GRUESOME
GRUMBLER
GRUMPILY
GRUMPISH
GRUNTING
GUAIACUM
GUARDIAN
GUERNSEY
GUERILLA
GUICOWAR
GUIDABLE
GUIDANCE
GUILEFUL
GUILTILY
GULLIBLE
GUMPTION
GUNSMITH
GURGOYLE
GUTTURAL
GYMNASIA
GYMNOGEN
GYMNOTUS
GYNANDER
GYNARCHY
GYPSEOUS
GYRATION
GYRATORY
GYROIDAL
GYROSTAT

H

HABITANT
HABITUAL
HABITUDE
HACIENDA
HAEMATIC
HAEMATIN
HAIRLESS
HALENESS
HALLIARD
HAMIFORM
HANDBILL
HANDBOOK
HANDCUFF
HANDGRIP
HANDICAP
HANDLINE
HANDMAID
HANDRAIL
HANDSOME
HANGNAIL
HARANGUE
HARDENED
HARDNESS

HARDSHIP
HARDWARE
HAREBELL
HARLOTRY
HARMLESS
HARMONIC
HARRIDAN
HARUSPEX
HASTENER
HATCHWAY
HAUTBOIS
HAVANNAH
HAVILDAR
HAWTHORN
HAYMAKER
HAZINESS
HEADACHE
HEADACHY
HEADLAND
HEADLESS
HEADLONG
HEADMOST
HEADSHIP
HEADSMAN
HEALABLE
HEARTILY
HEAVENLY
HEBETATE
HEBETUDE
HEBRAISM
HEBRAIST
HEBRAIZE
HECATOMB
HEDGEHOG
HEDGEROW
HEDONISM
HEDONIST
HEEDLESS
HEELBALL
HEGELIAN
HEGEMONY
HEIGHTEN
HEIRLOOM
HEIRSHIP
HELIACAL
HELICOID
HELLENIC
HELMETED
HELMSMAN
HELOTISM
HELPLESS
HELPMATE
HELVETIC
HEMATINE
HEMATITE
HEMIPTER
HENCHMAN
HENEQUEN
HEPATITE
HEPATIZE
HEPTAGON
HERALDIC
HERALDRY
HERBARIA
HERDSMAN
HEREDITY
HEREUNTO
HEREUPON
HEREWITH
HERITAGE

HERMETIC
HERNSHAW
HEROSHIP
HERPETIC
HESITANT
HESITATE
HETARISM
HIATUSES
HIBERNAL
HICCOUGH
HIDDENLY
HIERARCH
HIERATIC
HIGHLAND
HIGHNESS
HIGHROAD
HILARITY
HINDERER
HINDMOST
HINDUISM
HIRELING
HISTORIC
HITHERTO
HOARDING
HOARSELY
HOGSHEAD
HOLDFAST
HOLINESS
HOLLANDS
HOLLOWLY
HOMEBORN
HOMEFELT
HOMELESS
HOMESPUN
HOMEWARD
HOMICIDE
HOMILIST
HOMILIES
HOMODONT
HOMOLOGY
HOMONYMY
HOMOPTER
HOMOTYPE
HONESTLY
HONORARY
HONOURER
HOODWINK
HOPELESS
HORATIAN
HORNBEAM
HORNBILL
HORNPIPE
HORNWORK
HOROLOGE
HOROLOGY
HORRIBLE
HORRIBLY
HORRIDLY
HORRIFIC
HORSEMAN
HOSEPIPE
HOSPITAL
HOSTELRY
HOTCHPOT
HOWITZER
HUCKSTER
HUGENESS
HUGUENOT
HUMANELY
HUMANISM

HUMANIST
HUMANITY
HUMANIZE
HUMBLING
HUMIDITY
HUMILITY
HUMORIST
HUMOROUS
HUMPBACK
HUNGERER
HUNGRILY
HUNTRESS
HUNTSMAN
HURTLESS
HUSTINGS
HYACINTH
HYDROGEN
HYDROMEL
HYDROPIC
HYDROZOA
HYGIENIC
HYMENEAL
HYMENEAN
HYMENIUM
HYPNOSIS
HYPNOTIC
HYSTERIA
HYSTERIC

I

IAMBUSES
IATRICAL
ICHOROUS
IDEALESS
IDEALISM
IDEALIST
IDEALITY
IDEALIZE
IDEATION
IDENTIFY
IDENTITY
IDEOGRAM
IDEOLOGY
IDIOTISM
IDLENESS
IDOCRASE
IDOLATER
IDOLATRY
IDOLIZER
IGNITION
IGNOMINY
IGNORANT
ILLATION
ILLATIVE
ILLUMINE
ILLUSION
ILLUSIVE
ILLUSORY
IMBECILE
IMBITTER
IMBLAZON
IMBOLDEN
IMBORDER
IMBUTION
IMITABLE
IMITANCY
IMITATOR
IMMANATE

IMMANENT	INFERNAL	INTRORSE	JOKINGLY
IMMANUEL	INFILTER	INTRUDER	JOLTHEAD
IMMATURE	INFINITE	INUNDATE	JOVIALLY
IMMINENT	INFINITY	INVASION	JOYFULLY
IMMINGLE	INFIRMLY	INVASIVE	JOYOUSLY
IMMOBILE	INFLATED	INVEIGLE	JUBILANT
IMMODEST	INFLATUS	INVENTOR	JUBILATE
IMMOLATE	INFLEXED	INVERTED	JUDAICAL
IMMORTAL	INFLUENT	INVESTOR	JUDGMENT
IMMUNITY	INFORMAL	INVITING	JUDICIAL
IMPANATE	INFORMER	INVOCATE	JUGGLERY
IMPARITY	INFRINGE	INVOLUTE	JULIENNE
IMPERIAL	INFUSION	INWARDLY	JUNCTION
IMPETIGO	INFUSIVE	IODOFORM	JUNCTURE
IMPLICIT	INFUSORY	IREFULLY	JURASSIC
IMPOISON	INGUINAL	IRISATED	JURISTIC
IMPOLICY	INHALANT	IRISCOPE	JUSTNESS
IMPOLITE	INHALENT	IRISHISM	JUVENILE
IMPORTER	INHERENT	IRIDITIS	
IMPOSING	INHESION	IRONBARK	
IMPOSTOR	INIMICAL	IRONICAL	**K**
IMPOTENT	INIQUITY	IRONSIDE	
IMPRIMIS	INITIATE	IRONWARE	KAKEMONO
IMPRISON	INJECTOR	IRRIGATE	KAKODYLE
IMPROPER	INKINESS	IRRISION	KALENDER
IMPROVER	INKSTAND	IRRITANT	KANGAROO
IMPUDENT	INLANDER	IRRITATE	KEELHAUL
IMPUGNER	INLAYING	ISABELLA	KEENNESS
IMPUNITY	INNATELY	ISAGOGIC	KEEPSAKE
IMPURELY	INNOCENT	ISCHURIA	KERCHIEF
IMPURITY	INNOVATE	ISLAMISH	KERNELLY
IMPURPLE	INNUENDO	ISLAMITE	KEROSENE
INACTION	INQUIRER	ISLANDER	KEYSTONE
INACTIVE	INSANELY	ISOCHEIM	KICKSHAW
INASMUCH	INSANITY	ISOCRYME	KILOGRAM
INCEPTOR	INSCRIBE	ISOGONIC	KILOWATT
INCHOATE	INSECURE	ISOLATED	KINDLING
INCIDENT	INSERTED	ISOMERIC	KINDNESS
INCISION	INSIGNIA	ISOTHERM	KINETICS
INCISIVE	INSOLATE	ISSUABLE	KINGLIKE
INCISORY	INSOLENT	ITERANCE	KINGLING
INCISURE	INSOMNIA		KINGSHIP
INCLINED	INSOMUCH		KINKAJOU
INCOMING	INSPIRED		KINSFOLK
INCREASE	INSPIRER	**J**	KNAPSACK
INCUBATE	INSPIRIT		KNICKERS
INDAGATE	INSTANCE	JACKETED	KNIGHTLY
INDEBTED	INSTINCT	JACOBEAN	KNITTING
INDECENT	INSTRUCT	JACOBITE	KNOTLESS
INDENTED	INSULATE	JAILBIRD	KNOWABLE
INDEVOUT	INTAGLIO	JALOUSIE	KREASOTE
INDIAMAN	INTEGRAL	JANIZARY	KREOSOTE
INDICANT	INTENDED	JAPANNER	KREUTZER
INDICATE	INTENTLY	JAPHETIC	KRYOLITE
INDIGENE	INTERACT	JAUNDICE	
INDIGENT	INTEREST	JAUNTILY	
INDIRECT	INTERIOR	JEALOUSY	**L**
INDOCILE	INTERMIT	JEHOVIST	
INDOLENT	INTERMIX	JEJUNELY	LABIALLY
INDURATE	INTERNAL	JEOPARDY	LABOURED
INDUSIUM	INTERVAL	JEREMIAD	LABOURER
INDUSIAL	INTHRALL	JEROBOAM	LABURNUM
INDUSTRY	INTIMACY	JESUITIC	LACERATE
INEDITED	INTIMATE	JESUITRY	LACONISM
INEQUITY	INTONATE	JETTISON	LACROSSE
INEXPERT	INTRADOR	JEWELLER	LACRYMAL
INFAMOUS	INTRENCH	JEWISHLY	LACUNOUS
INFANTRY	INTREPID	JOCOSELY	LADYHOOD
INFECUND	INTRIGUE	JOCOSITY	LADYLIKE
INFERIOR	INTROMIT	JOCUNDLY	LADYSHIP
		JOINTURE	

LAICALLY
LAMASERY
LAMBLIKE
LAMBLING
LAMBSKIN
LAMELLAE
LAMELLAR
LAMENESS
LAMINARY
LAMINATE
LANCELET
LANDFALL
LANDLADY
LANDLESS
LANDLORD
LANDMARK
LANDSLIP
LANDSMAN
LANDSMEN
LANDWARD
LANDWEHR
LANGSYNE
LANGUAGE
LANGUISH
LANKNESS
LANNERET
LANOLINE
LANTHORN
LAPELLED
LAPIDARY
LAPIDATE
LAPIDIFY
LAPPETED
LAPSABLE
LARBOARD
LARCENER
LARKSPUR
LARYNGES
LARYNXES
LATENESS
LATENTLY
LATINISM
LATINIST
LATINITY
LATINIZE
LATITUDE
LATTERLY
LAUDABLE
LAUDABLY
LAUDANUM
LAUGHTER
LAUREATE
LAVATORY
LAVENDER
LAVISHLY
LAWFULLY
LAWGIVER
LAXATIVE
LAZINESS
LEADLESS
LEAFLESS
LEANNESS
LEARNING
LEATHERN
LEATHERY
LEAVINGS
LECTURER
LEGALISM
LEGALITY
LEGALIZE

LEGATINE
LEGATION
LEISURED
LEMONADE
LENGTHEN
LENIENCE
LENIENCY
LENITIVE
LEPORINE
LETHARGY
LETTERED
LEUCOSIS
LEVANTER
LEVELLER
LEVERAGE
LEVIABLE
LEVIGATE
LEVIRATE
LEVITATE
LEWDNESS
LEWISSON
LIBATION
LIBATORY
LIBELLER
LIBERATE
LIBRETTO
LICENSEE
LICENSER
LICHENED
LICHENIC
LICORICE
LIEGEMAN
LIENTERY
LIFELESS
LIFELIKE
LIFELONG
LIFETIME
LIGAMENT
LIGATION
LIGATURE
LIGNEOUS
LIGNITIC
LIGULATE
LIKEABLE
LIKENESS
LIKEWISE
LIMITARY
LIMONITE
LINCTURE
LINEALLY
LINEARLY
LINEATED
LINGERER
LINGUIST
LINIMENT
LINNAEAN
LINOLEUM
LINSTOCK
LIPOGRAM
LIQUIDLY
LISTENER
LISTLESS
LITERARY
LITERATE
LITERATO
LITERATI
LITHARGE
LITIGANT
LITIGATE
LITTORAL

LITURGIC
LIVELILY
LIVELONG
LIVERIED
LIVIDITY
LIXIVIAL
LIXIVIUM
LOADSTAR
LOANABLE
LOATHFUL
LOATHING
LOCALISM
LOCALITY
LOCALIZE
LOCATION
LOCATIVE
LOCUTION
LODESTAR
LODGMENT
LOGICIAN
LOGISTIC
LOGOGRAM
LOGOTYPE
LOITERER
LOLLARDY
LOLLIPOP
LOMENTUM
LONESOME
LONGEVAL
LONGHAND
LONGSOME
LONGWAYS
LONGWISE
LOOPHOLE
LORDLING
LORDSHIP
LORICATE
LORIKEET
LOTHARIO
LOUDNESS
LOVELESS
LOVINGLY
LOWERING
LOYALIST
LUBBERLY
LUCERNAL
LUCIDITY
LUCKLESS
LUCULENT
LUKEWARM
LUMBERER
LUMINARY
LUMINOUS
LUMPFISH
LUNATION
LUNCHEON
LUNGWORT
LUNULATE
LUPULINE
LUSCIOUS
LUSTRATE
LUSTRING
LUSTROUS
LUSTRUMS
LUTANIST
LUTENIST
LUTHERAN
LUXATION
LYCOPODE
LYMPHOID

M

MACARONI
MACAROON
MACERATE
MACKEREL
MACROPOD
MACRURAL
MACULATE
MADRIGAL
MAESTOSO
MAGAZINE
MAGDALEN
MAGICIAN
MAGNESIA
MAGNETIC
MAGNIFIC
MAGNOLIA
MAHARANI
MAHOGANY
MAIDENLY
MAIEUTIC
MAINLAND
MAINTAIN
MAJESTIC
MAJOLICA
MAJORATE
MAJORITY
MALAPERT
MALARIAL
MALARIAN
MALIGNLY
MALINGER
MALODOUR
MALSTICK
MALTSTER
MALTREAT
MALTWORM
MAMMALIA
MAMMIFER
MAMMILLA
MANCIPLE
MANDAMUS
MANDARIN
MANDIBLE
MANDOLIN
MANDRAKE
MANDRILL
MANELESS
MANEQUIN
MANFULLY
MANGANIC
MANGONEL
MANGROVE
MANIACAL
MANICHEE
MANICURE
MANIFEST
MANIFOLD
MANIFORM
MANNERED
MANNERLY
MANORIAL
MANSUETE
MANTELET
MANTILLA
MANUALLY
MANURIAL
MARABOUT

MARABOUT	MELASSES	MINUSCLE	MONOLITH
MARASMUS	MELIBEAN	MINUTELY	MONOPOLY
MARAUDER	MELINITE	MINUTIAE	MONOTONE
MARAVEDI	MELODEON	MIRINESS	MONOTONY
MARBLING	MELODICS	MIRTHFUL	MONSIEUR
MARGINAL	MELODIST	MISAPPLY	MONTICLE
MARGINED	MELODIZE	MISCARRY	MONUMENT
MARGRAVE	MEMBERED	MISCHIEF	MOONBEAM
MARIGOLD	MEMBRANE	MISCIBLE	MOONLESS
MARINADE	MEMORIAL	MISCOUNT	MOONSHEE
MARITIME	MEMORIZE	MISDOUBT	MOORLAND
MARJORAM	MENHADEN	MISGUIDE	MOOTABLE
MARKEDLY	MENINGES	MISJUDGE	MORALIST
MARKSMAN	MENISCUS	MISNOMER	MORALITY
MARMOSET	MENOLOGY	MISOGAMY	MORALIZE
MARONITE	MENSTRUA	MISOGYMY	MORAVIAN
MARQUESS	MENTAGRA	MISPLACE	MORBIDLY
MARQUISE	MENTALLY	MISPRINT	MORBIFIC
MARRIAGE	MEPHITIC	MISPRISE	MORCEAUX
MARRYING	MEPHITIS	MISPRIZE	MOREOVER
MARTAGON	MERCHANT	MISQUOTE	MORESQUE
MARTINET	MERCIFUL	MISSHAPE	MORIBUND
MASCOTTE	MERCURIC	MISSPEAK	MOROSELY
MASSACRE	MERIDIAN	MISSPELL	MORPHINE
MASSEUSE	MEROSOME	MISSPEND	MORTALLY
MASSETER	MESMERIC	MISSPENT	MORTGAGE
MASSICOT	MESOZOIC	MISSTATE	MORTMAIN
MASTERLY	MESQUITE	MISTAKEN	MORTUARY
MASTICOT	MESSMATE	MISTITLE	MOSAICAL
MASTITIS	MESSUAGE	MISTRESS	MOSQUITO
MASTLESS	MESTIZOS	MISTRUST	MOTHERLY
MASTODON	METALLED	MITIGANT	MOTILITY
MATELESS	METALLIC	MITIGATE	MOTIVITY
MATERIAL	METAMERE	MITTIMUS	MOTORIAL
MATERNAL	METAPHOR	MNEMONIC	MOUFFLON
MATRICES	METEORIC	MOBILITY	MOULDING
MATRONAL	METEWAND	MOBILIZE	MOUNTAIN
MATRONLY	METEYARD	MOCCASIN	MOUNTING
MATTRESS	METHINKS	MODALITY	MOURNFUL
MATURELY	METHODIC	MODELLER	MOURNING
MATURITY	METHYLIC	MODERATE	MOUTHFUL
MAXILLAE	METONYMY	MODESTLY	MOVELESS
MAXILLAR	METRICAL	MODIFIER	MOVEMENT
MAXIMIST	MEZEREON	MODISHLY	MOVINGLY
MAXIMIZE	MIASMATA	MODULATE	MUCHNESS
MAYORESS	MICROBIC	MOISTURE	MUCIFORM
MAZARINE	MICROZOA	MOLASSES	MUCILAGE
MAZINESS	MIDDLING	MOLECULE	MUCOSITY
MAZOURKA	MIDNIGHT	MOLESKIN	MULBERRY
MEAGRELY	MIGHTILY	MOLOSSUS	MULETEER
MEANNESS	MILDNESS	MOLYBDIC	MULISHLY
MEANTIME	MILESIAN	MOMENTLY	MULTIFID
MEASURED	MILITANT	MOMENTUM	MULTIPED
MECHANIC	MILITARY	MONACHAL	MULTIPLE
MEDALLIC	MILITATE	MONANDER	MULTIPLY
MEDALIST	MILKMAID	MONANDRY	MUMBLING
MEDDLING	MILLEPED	MONARCHY	MUNGOOSE
MEDIATOR	MILLIPED	MONASTIC	MUNIMENT
MEDICATE	MILLIARD	MONETARY	MUNITION
MEDICINE	MILLINER	MONETIZE	MURDERER
MEDIEVAL	MIMICKER	MONGOOSE	MURIATIC
MEDIOCRE	MINATORY	MONISTIC	MURICATE
MEDITATE	MINDLESS	MONITION	MURIFORM
MEDULLAR	MINIMIZE	MONITORY	MURMURER
MEEKNESS	MINIMUMS	MONITRIX	MURRHINE
MEETNESS	MINISTER	MONOCARP	MUSCADEL
MEGAPODE	MINISTRY	MONOCRAT	MUSCATEL
MEIOCENE	MINORITE	MONODIST	MUSCULAR
MELANISM	MINORITY	MONOGAMY	MUSHROOM
MELANITE	MINSTREL	MONOGRAM	MUSICIAN

MUS	N	O	OUT
MUSINGLY	NEMATODE		OPOPANAX
MUSLINET	NEMATOID		OPPONENT
MUSQUASH	NEOLOGIC	**O**	OPPOSITE
MUSQUITO	NEOPHYTE		OPTATIVE
MUSTACHE	NEOTERIC	OBDURACY	OPTICIAN
MUTATION	NEPENTHE	OBDURATE	OPTIMISM
MUTCHKIN	NEPHRITE	OBEDIENT	OPTIMIST
MUTENESS	NEPOTISM	OBITUARY	OPTIMIZE
MUTILATE	NEPOTIST	OBJECTOR	OPTIONAL
MUTINEER	NESTLING	OBLATION	OPULENCE
MUTINOUS	NEURITIS	OBLIGANT	OPUSCULE
MUTTERER	NEUROSIS	OBLIGATE	ORACULAR
MUTUALLY	NEUROTIC	OBLIGATO	ORAGIOUS
MYCELIUM	NICENESS	OBLIGING	ORANGERY
MYCOLOGY	NICKELIC	OBLIVION	ORATORIC
MYELITIS	NICKNAME	OBSCURER	ORBITARY
MYRIAPOD	NICOTIAN	OBSERVER	ORCADIAN
MYRMIDON	NICOTINE	OBSIDIAN	ORCHELLA
MYSTICAL	NIHILISM	OBSOLETE	ORDAINER
MYTHICAL	NIHILIST	OBSTACLE	ORDINAND
	NIHILITY	OBSTRUCT	ORDINANT
	NINEPINS	OBTAINER	ORDINARY
N	NINETEEN	OBTRUDER	ORDINATE
	NITROGEN	OBTURATE	ORDNANCE
NACREOUS	NOACHIAN	OBTUSELY	ORDUROUS
NAINSOOK	NOBILITY	OBVOLUTE	ORGANISM
NAMEABLE	NOBLEMAN	OCCASION	ORGANIST
NAMELESS	NOBLESSE	OCCIDENT	ORGANIZE
NAMESAKE	NOCTURNE	OCCULTLY	ORICHALC
NAPIFORM	NODOSITY	OCCUPANT	ORIENTAL
NAPOLEON	NOETICAL	OCCUPIER	ORIGINAL
NARCOSIS	NOMADISH	OCCELATE	ORNAMENT
NARCOTIC	NOMARCHY	OCHREOUS	ORNATELY
NARGHILE	NOMINATE	OCTOPEDE	ORNITHIC
NARGILEH	NOMOLOGY	OCTOROON	ORPIMENT
NARRATOR	NONESUCH	OCULARLY	ORTHODOX
NARROWLY	NONSENSE	OCULATED	ORTHOEPY
NASALIZE	NOONTIDE	ODIOUSLY	ORTHOGON
NASCENCY	NORMALLY	ODOMETER	OSCITANT
NASICORN	NORSEMAN	ODONTOID	OSCULANT
NASIFORM	NORTHERN	OENOLOGY	OSCULATE
NATATION	NOSELESS	OFFENDER	OSMANLIS
NATATORY	NOSOLOGY	OFFERING	OSNABURG
NATIONAL	NOTARIAL	OFFICIAL	OTIOSITY
NATIVELY	NOTATION	OFFSHOOT	OTOSCOPE
NATIVITY	NOTCHING	OFTTIMES	OUISTITI
NAUMACHY	NOTELESS	OILINESS	OUTARGUE
NAUSEATE	NOTIONAL	OINTMENT	OUTBRAVE
NAUSEOUS	NOVELIST	OLEANDER	OUTBREAK
NAUTICAL	NOVEMBER	OLIBANUM	OUTBURST
NAUTILUS	NOVERCAL	OLIGARCH	OUTDOORS
NAVIGATE	NOWADAYS	OLYMPIAD	OUTFLANK
NAZAREAN	NUCIFORM	OLYMPIAN	OUTGOING
NAZARENE	NUCLEATE	OMISSION	OUTLAWRY
NAZARITE	NUCLEOLI	OMISSIVE	OUTLYING
NEARCTIC	NUDENESS	OMNIFORM	OUTMARCH
NEARNESS	NUGATORY	OMOHYOID	OUTRANCE
NEATHERD	NUISANCE	OMOPLATE	OUTREACH
NEATNESS	NUMBERER	OMPHALIC	OUTRIDER
NEBULOSE	NUMBNESS	ONCOMING	OUTRIGHT
NEBULOUS	NUMERARY	ONCOTOMY	OUTSHINE
NECKLACE	NUMERATE	ONLOOKER	OUTSIDER
NECROSIS	NUMEROUS	ONTOGENY	OUTSKIRT
NECROSED	NUMMULAR	ONTOLOGY	OUTSPEAK
NECTARED	NUMSKULL	OOLOGIST	OUTSTARE
NEEDFIRE	NUPTIALS	OPAQUELY	OUTSTRIP
NEEDLESS	NURSLING	OPENNESS	OUTSWEAR
NEGATION	NUTATION	OPERATIC	OUTVALUE
NEGATIVE	NUTRIENT	OPERATOR	OUTWARDS
NEIGHBOR	NYMPHEAN	OPERETTA	OUTWATCH
		OPHIDIAN	

OUTWEIGH	PALATINE	PARTIZAN	PERIGEAN
OVERALLS	PALENESS	PASHALIC	PERILOUS
OVERARCH	PALESTRA	PASSABLE	PERINEUM
OVERBEAR	PALINODE	PASSABLY	PERINEAL
OVERBOLD	PALISADE	PASSERES	PERIODIC
OVERBRIM	PALLIATE	PASSIBLE	PERIPLUS
OVERCAST	PALLMALL	PASSOVER	PERJURER
OVERCOAT	PALMATED	PASSPORT	PERMEATE
OVERCOME	PALMETTE	PASTILLE	PERONEAL
OVERDATE	PALMETTO	PASTORAL	PERORATE
OVERDOSE	PALMIPED	PATAGIUM	PEROXIDE
OVERDRAW	PALMITIC	PATCHERY	PERRUQUE
OVERFLOW	PALPABLE	PATENTEE	PERSIMON
OVERGROW	PALPABLY	PATERNAL	PERSONAL
OVERHAND	PALSTAFF	PATHETIC	PERSPIRE
OVERHANG	PALSTAVE	PATHLESS	PERSUADE
OVERHAUL	PALTERER	PATIENCE	PERTNESS
OVERHEAD	PALUDINE	PATULOUS	PERTUSED
OVERHEAR	PALUDISM	PAULDRON	PERUVIAN
OVERHEAT	PALUDOSE	PAVEMENT	PERVERSE
OVERHUNG	PAMPERER	PAVILION	PERVIOUS
OVERLAND	PAMPHLET	PAVONINE	PESTERER
OVERLEAP	PANCREAS	PAWNSHOP	PETALINE
OVERLIVE	PANDANUS	PEACEFUL	PETALOID
OVERLOAD	PANDEMIC	PEARLASH	PETIOLAR
OVERLOOK	PANGOLIN	PEASECOD	PETIOLED
OVERLORD	PANICLED	PECCABLE	PETITION
OVERMUCH	PANNIKIN	PECCANCY	PETITORY
OVERNICE	PANORAMA	PECTINAL	PETRIFIC
OVERPASS	PANTHEON	PECTORAL	PETRONEL
OVERPLUS	PAPALIST	PECULATE	PETROSAL
OVERRATE	PAPALIZE	PECULIAR	PETTIFOG
OVERRIDE	PAPILLAE	PEDAGOGY	PETULANT
OVERRIPE	PAPISTIC	PEDANTIC	PEWTERER
OVERRULE	PAPISTRY	PEDANTRY	PHALANGE
OVERSEAS	PAPULOSE	PEDESTAL	PHANTASM
OVERSEER	PAPULOUS	PEDICURE	PHANTASY
OVERSHOE	PARABOLA	PEDIGREE	PHARISEE
OVERSMAN	PARADIGM	PEDIMANE	PHARMACY
OVERSTAY	PARADISE	PEDIMENT	PHEASANT
OVERSTEP	PARAFFIN	PEDUNCLE	PHENOGAM
OVERTAKE	PARAGOGE	PEERLESS	PHILABEG
OVERTASK	PARAGRAM	PELAGIAN	PHILIBEG
OVERTIME	PARAKEET	PELASGIC	PHILOMEL
OVERTONE	PARALLAX	PELERINE	PHOLADES
OVERTURE	PARALLEL	PELLAGRA	PHONETIC
OVERTURN	PARALYSE	PELLICLE	PHORMINX
OVERWEEN	PARALYZE	PELLUCID	PHORMIUM
OVERWIND	PARAMERE	PELTATED	PHTHISIC
OVERWISE	PARAMOUR	PEMMICAN	PHTHISIS
OVERWORK	PARASANG	PENCHANT	PHYLARCH
OVERWORN	PARASITE	PENDENCY	PHYLETIC
OXIDIZER	PARCENER	PENDULUM	PHYLLOID
OXYMORON	PARDONER	PENITENT	PHYSALIA
	PARENTAL	PENKNIFE	PHYSICAL
	PARERGON	PENOLOGY	PHYSIQUE
P	PARHELIC	PENSTOCK	PIACULAR
	PARHELIA	PENTACLE	PIANETTE
PACIFIER	PARIETAL	PENTAGON	PIASSAVA
PACKFONG	PARISIAN	PENTAGYN	PICAROON
PADISHAH	PARLANCE	PENUMBRA	PICIFORM
PADUASOY	PARMESAN	PEPERINE	PICKEREL
PAGANISH	PARODIST	PEPERINO	PICKLOCK
PAGANISM	PARONYMY	PERCEIVE	PIERCING
PAGANIZE	PAROXYSM	PERFORCE	PIGEONRY
PAGINATE	PARTAKER	PERFUMER	PILASTER
PAINLESS	PARTERRE	PERIAGUA	PILCHARD
PAINTING	PARTHIAN	PERIANTH	PILEATED
PAIRWISE	PARTIBLE	PERICARP	PILEWORT
PALATIAL	PARTISAN	PERIDERM	PILFERER

PILIFORM
PILLAGER
PILLARED
PILLOWED
PILLWORM
PILOTAGE
PINAFORE
PINASTER
PINDARIC
PINNACLE
PINNATED
PINNIPED
PINWHEEL
PIQUANCY
PISCATOR
PISIFORM
PISOLITE
PITHLESS
PITIABLE
PITIABLY
PITILESS
PITTANCE
PITYROID
PLACABLE
PLACEMAN
PLACENTA
PLACIDLY
PLAGIARY
PLAGUILY
PLANCHET
PLANGENT
PLANLESS
PLANTAIN
PLANTLET
PLASTERY
PLASTRON
PLATEAUS
PLATEAUX
PLATFORM
PLATINUM
PLATONIC
PLATTING
PLATYPUS
PLAUSIVE
PLAYBILL
PLAYGOER
PLAYMATE
PLEADING
PLEASANT
PLEASING
PLEASURE
PLEBEIAN
PLECTRUM
PLEIADES
PLEONASM
PLETHORA
PLEURISY
PLIANTLY
PLICATED
PLIGHTER
PLIOCENE
PLODDING
PLOUGHER
PLUCKILY
PLUMBAGO
PLUMBEAN
PLUMBERY
PLUMBING
PLUMBERY
PLUMELET

PLUMIPED
PLURALLY
PLUTONIC
PLUVIOUS
PODAGRAL
PODAGRIC
PODALGIA
POETICAL
POIGNANT
POISONER
POLARITY
POLARIZE
POLEMICS
POLICIES
POLISHED
POLISHER
POLITELY
POLITICS
POLLUTER
POLTROON
POLYGAMY
POLYGLOT
POLYGRAM
POLYGYNY
POLYPARY
POLYPITE
POLYPODY
POLYPOUS
POLYZOON
POMANDER
POMOLOGY
POORNESS
POPINJAY
POPISHLY
POPULACE
POPULATE
POPULOUS
PORIFORM
PORISTIC
POROSITY
POROUSLY
PORPHYRY
PORPOISE
PORRIDGE
PORT-WINE
PORTABLE
PORT-FIRE
PORT-HOLE
PORTICOS
PORTRAIT
PORTRESS
POSITION
POSITIVE
POSSIBLY
POST-CARD
POST-DATE
POST-HORN
POST-MARK
POST-OBIT
POST-PAID
POSTPONE
POST-TOWN
POSTURER
POTASSIC
POTATION
POTATOES
POTATORY
POTENTLY
POT-HOUSE
POTSHERD

POULTICE
POUNDAGE
POWDERED
POWERFUL
PRACTICE
PRACTISE
PRANDIAL
PRANKISH
PRATTLER
PREACHER
PREAMBLE
PRECINCT
PRECIOUS
PRECLUDE
PRE-EXIST
PREGNANT
PREJUDGE
PRELATIC
PREMOLAR
PREMORSE
PRENTICE
PREPARER
PREPENSE
PRESCIND
PRESENCE
PRESERVE
PRESSING
PRESSMAN
PRESSURE
PRESTIGE
PRETENCE
PRETENSE
PRETERIT
PRETTILY
PREVIOUS
PRICKING
PRIDEFUL
PRIE-DIEU
PRIESTLY
PRIGGISH
PRIMEVAL
PRIMNESS
PRIMROSE
PRINCELY
PRINCESS
PRINTING
PRIORATE
PRIORESS
PRIORITY
PRIORIES
PRISMOID
PRISONER
PRISTINE
PROBABLE
PROBABLY
PROCEEDS
PROCLAIM
PROCUROR
PRODIGAL
PRODUCER
PROEMIAL
PROFANER
PROFOUND
PROGRESS
PROHIBIT
PROLAPSE
PROLIFIC
PROLOGUE
PROMISER
PROMOTER

PROMPTER
PROMPTLY
PROPENSE
PROPERLY
PROPERTY
PROPHECY
PROPHESY
PROPLASM
PROPOLIS
PROPOSAL
PROPOSER
PROPOUND
PROPYLON
PROROGUE
PROSODIC
PROSPECT
PROSTATE
PROSTYLE
PROTASIS
PROTOCOL
PROTOZOA
PROTRACT
PROTRUDE
PROVABLE
PROVABLY
PROVIDED
PROVIDER
PROVINCE
PROXIMAL
PRUDENCE
PRUNELLA
PRURIENT
PRUSSIAN
PSALMIST
PSALMODY
PSALTERY
PSYCHIST
PTEROPOD
PTOMAINE
PTYALISM
PUBLICAN
PUBLICLY
PUDDLING
PUFF-BALL
PUGILISM
PUGILIST
PUISSANT
PULINGLY
PULMONIC
PUMPROOM
PUNCHEON
PUNCTATE
PUNCTUAL
PUNCTURE
PUNGENCY
PUNINESS
PUNISHER
PUNITIVE
PUNITORY
PUPARIAL
PUPILAGE
PUPILARY
PUPPYISH
PUPPYISM
PURBLIND
PURCHASE
PURENESS
PURIFIER
PURPLISH
PURSEFUL

PURSENET
PURSLANE
PURSUANT
PURULENT
PURVEYOR
PUSTULAR
PUTATIVE
PYOGENIC
PYRIFORM
PYROLOGY
PYROXENE
PYTHONIC
PYXIDIUM

Q

QUADRANT
QUADRATE
QUADRIGA
QUADROON
QUAESTOR
QUAGMIRE
QUAINTLY
QUALMISH
QUANDARY
QUANTITY
QUARRIER
QUARTERN
QUATRAIN
QUEASILY
QUEERISH
QUENCHER
QUESTION
QUIBBLER
QUICKSET
QUIDDITY
QUIDNUNC
QUIETISM
QUIETIST
QUIETUDE
QUILLING
QUILTING
QUINCUNX
QUIRKISH
QUITRENT
QUIVERED
QUIXOTIC
QUOTABLE
QUOTIENT

R

RABBINIC
RACEMOSE
RACHITIC
RACHITIS
RACINESS
RACK-RENT
RADIALLY
RADIANCE
RADIATOR
RADICATE
RAGGEDLY
RAG-STONE
RAILLERY
RAILROAD
RAINBAND
RAINFALL

RAINLESS
RAISABLE
RAISONNE
RAKEHELL
RAKISHLY
RAMBLING
RAMPANCY
RANCHERO
RANCIDLY
RANKNESS
RANSOMER
RAPACITY
RAPE-CAKE
RAPIDITY
RAPTORES
RAPTURED
RARENESS
RASCALLY
RASHNESS
RASORIAL
RATIONAL
RATSBANE
RAVENOUS
RAVINGLY
RAVISHER
RE-ABSORB
REACTION
REACTIVE
READABLE
READABLY
READJUST
REAFFIRM
REALISER
REALNESS
REAPPEAR
REARMOST
REARWARD
REASONER
REASSERT
REASSIGN
REASSUME
REASSURE
REATTACH
REBUTTAL
REBUTTER
RECANTER
RECEIVER
RECENTLY
RECESSED
RECKLESS
RECKONER
RECOMMIT
RECONVEY
RECORDER
RECOURSE
RECOVERY
RECREANT
RECREATE
RECUSANT
REDACTOR
REDARGUE
REDEEMER
REDOLENT
REDOUBLE
REDSHANK
REDSTART
REED-BAND
REED-MACE
REED-PIPE
RE-ENGAGE

RE-ENLIST
RE-EXPORT
RE-FASTEN
REFERRER
REFINERY
REFLEXED
REFLEXLY
REFLUENT
REFOREST
REFORMED
REFORMER
REFUNDER
REGALITY
REGARDER
REGATHER
REGICIDE
REGIMENT
REGIONAL
REGISTER
REGISTRY
REGRATER
REGROWTH
REGULATE
REHEARSE
REIMPORT
REIMPOSE
REINLESS
REINSERT
REINSURE
REINVEST
REJECTER
REJOICER
REKINDLE
RELATIVE
RELEASER
RELEGATE
RELEVANT
RELIABLE
RELIABLY
RELIANCE
RELIEVER
RELIGION
RELISTEN
REMANENT
REMARKER
REMARQUE
REMEDIAL
REMEMBER
REMINDER
REMISSLY
REMITTAL
REMITTEE
REMITTER
REMOTELY
RENDERER
RENDIBLE
RENEGADE
RENIFORM
RENNETED
RENOUNCE
RENOVATE
RENOWNED
RENTABLE
REOCCUPY
REOMETER
REORDAIN
REPAIRER
REPARTEE
REPEALER
REPEATER

REPELLER
REPENTER
REPEOPLE
REPERUSE
REPETEND
REPLEVIN
REPORTER
REPOUSSE
REPRIEVE
REPRISAL
REPROACH
REPROVAL
REPROVER
REPTILIA
REPUBLIC
REQUITAL
REQUITER
REREWARD
RESCRIPT
RESEARCH
RESEMBLE
RESENTER
RESERVED
RESERVER
RESETTER
RESIDENT
RESIDUAL
RESIDUUM
RESIGNED
RESIGNER
RESINOUS
RESISTER
RESOLUTE
RESOLVED
RESOLVER
RESONANT
RESORTER
RESOURCE
RESPONSE
RESTLESS
RESTORER
RESTRAIN
RESTRICT
RESUPINE
RETAILER
RETAINER
RETARDER
RETICENT
RETICULE
RETIFORM
RETIRING
RETRENCH
RETRIEVE
RETROACT
RETRORSE
RETURNER
REVEALER
REVEILLE
REVELLER
REVENGER
REVEREND
REVERENT
REVERSAL
REVIEWAL
REVIEWER
REVISION
REVIVIFY
REVOLTER
REVOLUTE
REVOLVER

REWARDER	ROTATORY	SAMAROID	SCHEMING
RHAPSODE	ROTIFORM	SAMENESS	SCHEMIST
RHAPSODY	ROTTENLY	SAMPHIRE	SCHIEDAM
RHEOSTAT	ROULETTE	SANATIVE	SCHNAPPS
RHEOTOME	ROWDYISM	SANATORY	SCHOLIUM
RHETORIC	ROYALISM	SANCTIFY	SCHOONER
RHIZANTH	ROYALIST	SANCTION	SCIATICA
RHIZOGEN	RUBICUND	SANCTITY	SCILICET
RHIZOPOD	RUBIDIUM	SAND-BANK	SCIMITAR
RHOMBOID	RUBRICAL	SAND-BATH	SCIOLISM
RHONCHUS	RUDENESS	SAND-FLEA	SCIOLIST
RHYTHMIC	RUDIMENT	SAND-HILL	SCIOLOUS
RIBALDRY	RUEFULLY	SANDIVER	SCIOPTIC
RICHNESS	RUFFLING	SAND-MOLE	SCIRRHUS
RICOCHET	RUGGEDLY	SANDWICH	SCISSION
RIDDANCE	RUGOSITY	SANENESS	SCISSORS
RIDICULE	RUINABLE	SANGAREE	SCIURINE
RIFENESS	RULELESS	SANGUINE	SCLEROMA
RIFFRAFF	RUMINANT	SANITARY	SCOLDING
RIFLEMAN	RUMINATE	SANSKRIT	SCOOP-NET
RIGADOON	RUMMAGER	SAP-GREEN	SCORNFUL
RIGHTFUL	RUM-SHRUB	SAPIDITY	SCORPION
RIGIDITY	RUNAGATE	SAPIENCE	SCOT-FREE
RIGOROUS	RUNOLOGY	SAPONIFY	SCOTSMAN
RING-BOLT	RURALISM	SAPPHIRE	SCOTTICE
RING-BONE	RURALISE	SARABAND	SCOTTISH
RING-DOVE	RUTABAGA	SARCENET	SCOURGER
RINGWORM	RUTHLESS	SARDONIC	SCOWLING
RIPARIAL	RYE-GRASS	SARDONYX	SCRABBLE
RIPENESS		SARGASSO	SCRAGGED
RITUALLY		SARMENTA	SCRAMBLE
RIVERINE	**S**	SARSENET	SCRANNEL
RIVETING		SATIABLE	SCRAPING
ROAD-BOOK	SABBATIC	SATIRIST	SCRAWLER
ROADSTER	SABULOUS	SATIRIZE	SCREAMER
ROBORANT	SACCULAR	SATURATE	SCREECHY
ROBURITE	SACREDLY	SATURDAY	SCREW-KEY
ROCK-CORK	SACRISTY	SAUCE-BOX	SCRIBBLE
ROCK-ROSE	SADDLERY	SAUCE-PAN	SCROFULA
ROCK-RUBY	SADDUCEE	SAVAGELY	SCROLLED
ROCK-SALT	SAFENESS	SAVAGERY	SCRUBBER
ROCK-SOAP	SAGACITY	SAVAGISM	SCRUB-OAK
ROCK-WOOD	SAGAMORE	SAVANNAH	SCRUPLER
ROCK-WORK	SAGE-COCK	SAVINGLY	SCRUTINY
RODENTIA	SAGENESS	SAVOYARD	SCUFFLER
ROLL-CALL	SAILLESS	SAW-FRAME	SCULLERY
ROLY-POLY	SAIL-LOFT	SAXATILE	SCULLION
ROMANCER	SAINFOIN	SAXONISM	SCULPTOR
ROMANISM	SALAD-OIL	SAXONIST	SCURRILE
ROMANIST	SALARIED	SCABBARD	SCURVILY
ROMANIZE	SALARIES	SCABIOUS	SCUTCHER
ROMANTIC	SALEABLE	SCABROUS	SCUTELLA
ROOD-BEAM	SALEABLY	SCAFFOLD	SCYTHIAN
ROOD-LOFT	SALESMAN	SCALABLE	SEA-ACORN
ROOFLESS	SALICINE	SCALLION	SEA-BOARD
ROOF-TREE	SALIENCE	SCAMMONY	SEA-COAST
ROOT-CROP	SALIVANT	SCAMPISH	SEA-DEVIL
ROOTEDLY	SALIVARY	SCANDENT	SEA-EAGLE
ROPE-WALK	SALIVATE	SCANSION	SEAFARER
ROPINESS	SALMONET	SCANTILY	SEAFIGHT
ROSARIAN	SALT-BUSH	SCAPHOID	SEA-GOING
ROSEMARY	SALT-JUNK	SCAPULAR	SEA-GRASS
ROSE-PINK	SALTLESS	SCARCELY	SEA-GREEN
ROSEWOOD	SALT-LICK	SCARCITY	SEA-HORSE
ROSINESS	SALT-MINE	SCATHING	SEA-LEMON
ROSOGLIO	SALTNESS	SCENARIO	SEA-LEVEL
ROSTELLA	SALT-WORK	SCENICAL	SEA-LOUSE
ROSTRATE	SALTWORT	SCENTFUL	SEAL-SKIN
ROTATION	SALUTARY	SCEPTRAD	SEAMLESS
ROTATIVE	SALVABLE	SCHEDULE	SEA-ONION

SEARCHER	SERIALLY	SIBILATE	SKITTISH
SEA-ROVER	SERIATIM	SICK-LIST	SKITTLES
SEA-SCAPE	SERJEANT	SICKNESS	SKUA-GULL
SEA-SHORE	SEROSITY	SICK-ROOM	SKULLESS
SEA-SNAKE	SERRATED	SIDE-ARMS	SKY-LIGHT
SEASONAL	SERVITOR	SIDE-DISH	SLAP-DASH
SEASONER	SESAMOID	SIDELONG	SLASHING
SEA-WRACK	SESS-POOL	SIDEREAL	SLATTERN
SECLUDED	SESTERCE	SIDERITE	SLAVERER
SECONDER	SESTETTE	SIDESMAN	SLAVONIC
SECONDLY	SETIFORM	SIDE-WALK	SLEEPILY
SECRETLY	SETTLING	SIDEWAYS	SLEEPING
SECTORAL	SEVERELY	SIDE-WIND	SLIGHTLY
SECURELY	SEVERITY	SIDEWISE	SLIME-PIT
SECURITY	SEWERAGE	SIGMATIC	SLIMNESS
SEDATELY	SEXANGLE	SIGNABLE	SLIP-DOCK
SEDATIVE	SEXTUPLE	SIGNALLY	SLIPPERY
SEDERUNT	SEXUALLY	SIGNETED	SLIP-SHOD
SEDIMENT	SHABBILY	SIGN-POST	SLIPSLOP
SEDITION	SHABRACK	SILENTLY	SLOBBERY
SEDULITY	SHADDOCK	SILICATE	SLOP-SHOP
SEDULOUS	SHAFTING	SILICIFY	SLOTHFUL
SEED-CAKE	SHAGREEN	SILICULA	SLOVENLY
SEED-CORN	SHALLOON	SILICULE	SLOWNESS
SEEDLING	SHAMANIC	SILICIUM	SLOW-WORM
SEEDSMAN	SHAMBLES	SILIQUAE	SLUGGARD
SEERSHIP	SHAMEFUL	SILK-MILL	SLUGGISH
SEIGNIOR	SHAMROCK	SILK-WORM	SLUTTERY
SEIGNORY	SHANTIES	SILLABUB	SLUTTISH
SEIZABLE	SHAPABLE	SILURIAN	SMACKING
SELECTOR	SHARP-CUT	SILVERLY	SMALLAGE
SELENITE	SHARP-SET	SIMONIAC	SMELLING
SELENIUM	SHATTERY	SIMPERER	SMELTERY
SELF-HELP	SHEALING	SIMPLIFY	SMITHERY
SELF-LOVE	SHEARING	SIMULATE	SMOKE-BOX
SELF-MADE	SHEATHED	SINAITIC	SMOOTHEN
SELF-SAME	SHEEP-DOG	SINAPISM	SMOOTHLY
SELF-WILL	SHEEPISH	SINCIPUT	SMOTHERY
SELVEDGE	SHEEP-RUN	SINECURE	SMOULDER
SEMESTER	SHEETING	SINFULLY	SMUGGLER
SEMI-DOME	SHEILING	SING-SONG	SMUGNESS
SEMI-MUTE	SHELVING	SINGULAR	SMUT-BALL
SEMINARY	SHEMITIC	SINISTER	SMUTTILY
SEMITONE	SHEPHERD	SINOLOGY	SNAPPISH
SEMOLINA	SHILLING	SIPHONAL	SNAP-SHOT
SENILITY	SHIN-BONE	SIPHONIC	SNARLING
SENORITA	SHINGLED	SIRENIAN	SNATCHER
SENSIBLE	SHINGLES	SISTERLY	SNEAKING
SENSIBLY	SHIPMATE	SITOLOGY	SNEEZING
SENSIFIC	SHIPMENT	SITUATED	SNIVELLY
SENSUOUS	SHIPPING	SITZ-BATH	SNOBBERY
SENTENCE	SHIP-WORM	SIXPENCE	SNOBBISH
SENTIENT	SHIP-YARD	SIXPENNY	SNOBBISM
SENTINEL	SHIRTING	SIXTIETH	SNOW-BALL
SENTRIES	SHOCKING	SIZEABLE	SNOW-BIRD
SEPALINE	SHOE-HORN	SKEAN-DHU	SNOW-BOOT
SEPALOID	SHOELESS	SKELETAL	SNOW-DROP
SEPALOUS	SHOOTING	SKELETON	SNOW-LINE
SEPARATE	SHORTAGE	SKERRIES	SNOW-SHOE
SEPTETTE	SHORT-RIB	SKETCHER	SNOW-SLIP
SEPTICLE	SHOT-BELT	SKEW-BALD	SNUB-NOSE
SEQUELAE	SHOULDER	SKILLESS	SNUFF-BOX
SEQUENCE	SHOW-ROOM	SKIMMING	SNUFFLER
SERAGLIO	SHRAPNEL	SKIN-DEEP	SNUGGERY
SERAPHIM	SHREWDLY	SKINLESS	SNUGNESS
SERAPHIC	SHREWISH	SKIN-WOOL	SOBRIETY
SERENADE	SHRIMPER	SKIP-JACK	SOCIABLE
SERENELY	SHRUNKEN	SKIPPING	SOCIABLY
SERENITY	SHUFFLER	SKIRMISH	SOCIALLY
SERGEANT	SIBILANT	SKIRRHUS	SOCINIAN

SOCRATIC	SPECIMEN	STAGNANT	STRAIGHT
SODOMITE	SPECIOUS	STAGNATE	STRAINED
SOFTENER	SPECKLED	STAIR-ROD	STRAINER
SOFTNESS	SPECTRAL	STAKE-NET	STRAITEN
SOIL-PIPE	SPECTRUM	STALKING	STRAITLY
SOLATIUM	SPECULAR	STALLAGE	STRANGER
SOLDERER	SPECULUM	STALLION	STRANGLE
SOLDIERY	SPEEDILY	STALWART	STRAPPER
SOLECISM	SPELAEAN	STAMENED	STRATEGY
SOLECIST	SPELLING	STAMINAL	STRATIFY
SOLECIZE	SPERM-OIL	STAMP-ACT	STREAMER
SOLEMNLY	SPHAGNUM	STAMPEDE	STRENGTH
SOLENESS	SPHENOID	STAMPING	STRIATED
SOLIDIFY	SPHERICS	STANCHER	STRICKEN
SOLIDITY	SPHEROID	STANCHLY	STRICKLE
SOLITARY	SPHERULE	STANDARD	STRICTLY
SOLITUDE	SPHYGMIC	STANDING	STRIDENT
SOLSTICE	SPICULAR	STANDISH	STRIKING
SOLUTION	SPIKELET	STANHOPE	STRINGED
SOLVABLE	SPIKE-OIL	STANNARY	STRINGER
SOLVENCY	SPINELLE	STANZAIC	STRIPPER
SOMATIST	SPINIFEX	STAPELLA	STROBILE
SOMBRELY	SPINSTER	STARCHED	STRONGLY
SOMBRERO	SPIRICLE	STARCHER	STRONTIA
SOMBROUS	SPIRALLY	STARFISH	STROPHIC
SOMEBODY	SPIRILLA	STARLESS	STRUGGLE
SOMERSET	SPIRITED	STARLIKE	STRUMOSE
SOME-SUCH	SPITEFUL	STARLING	STRUMOUS
SOMETIME	SPITFIRE	STATEDLY	STRUMPET
SOMEWHAT	SPITTOON	STATICAL	STRUTTER
SOMNIFIC	SPLENDID	STATUARY	STUBBLED
SONG-BIRD	SPLENDOR	STEADILY	STUBBORN
SONGLESS	SPLINTER	STEALING	STUD-BOOK
SONGSTER	SPLITTER	STEALTHY	STUDIOUS
SON-IN-LAW	SPLOTCHY	STEAM-TUG	STUFFING
SONORITY	SPLUTTER	STEARINE	STULTIFY
SONOROUS	SPOLIATE	STEATITE	STUMBLER
SOOTHING	SPONDAIC	STEDFAST	STUNNING
SOPRANOS	SPONSION	STEELING	STUPIDLY
SORCERER	SPONTOON	STEENBOK	STUPRATE
SORDIDLY	SPOOKISH	STEEPLED	STURDILY
SORENESS	SPOONFUL	STEERAGE	STURGEON
SORTABLE	SPORADIC	STELLARY	SUBACRID
SORTMENT	SPORIDIA	STELLATE	SUBACUTE
SOUCHONG	SPORTFUL	STEM-LEAF	SUBCLASS
SOULLESS	SPORTING	STEMLESS	SUBEROSE
SOUNDING	SPORTIVE	STERLING	SUBEROUS
SOURNESS	SPOTLESS	STIBNITE	SUB-GENUS
SOUTHERN	SPRIGGED	STICKLER	SUB-LEASE
SOUTHING	SPRINGER	STILETTO	SUBLUNAR
SOUVENIR	SPRINKLE	STIMULUS	SUBMERGE
SOW-BREAD	SPRUCELY	STINGILY	SUBMERSE
SPACIOUS	SPURGALL	STINGING	SUBORDER
SPADEFUL	SPUR-GEAR	STING-RAY	SUBORNER
SPALPEEN	SPURIOUS	STINK-POT	SUBOVATE
SPANDREL	SQUABBLE	STIPULAR	SUBPOENA
SPANGLED	SQUADRON	STIRLESS	SUB-POLAR
SPANIARD	SQUAMATE	STIRRING	SUBSERVE
SPANKING	SQUAMOUS	STOCKADE	SUBTLETY
SPAN-ROOF	SQUANDER	STOCK-POT	SUB-TONIC
SPARABLE	SQUARELY	STOICISM	SUBTRACT
SPAR-DECK	SQUATTER	STOMATIC	SUBULATE
SPARERIB	SQUEAKER	STOOPING	SUBURBAN
SPARKISH	SQUEEZER	STOP-COCK	SUCCINCT
SPARSELY	SQUIRREL	STOPPAGE	SUCCINIC
SPATHOSE	STABLE-BOY	STOPPING	SUCHWISE
SPAVINED	STABLE-MAN	STORMFUL	SUCKLING
SPEAKING	STABLING	STOWAWAY	SUDATORY
SPEARMAN	STABLISH	STRADDLE	SUDDENLY
SPECIFIC	STACCATO	STRAGGLE	SUFFERER

SUFFRAGE
SUICIDAL
SUITABLE
SUITABLY
SULCATED
SULLENLY
SULPHATE
SULPHOID
SULPHITE
SULPHURY
SULTANIC
SUMMONER
SUN-BURNT
SUNLIGHT
SUN-SHADE
SUNSHINE
SUNSHINY
SUPERADD
SUPERBLY
SUPERIOR
SUPINELY
SUPPLANT
SUPPLIER
SUPPOSER
SUPPRESS
SURCEASE
SURGICAL
SURMISER
SURMOUNT
SURPLICE
SURROUND
SURVEYOR
SURVIVAL
SURVIVOR
SUSPENSE
SUTTLING
SUZERAIN
SWANNERY
SWANSKIN
SWASHING
SWEEPING
SWEET-BAY
SWEETING
SWEETISH
SWEET-PEA
SWEET-SOP
SWELLING
SWIMMING
SWINDLER
SWORD-ARM
SYBARITE
SYCAMINE
SYCAMORE
SYLLABIC
SYLLABLE
SYLLABUS
SYMBOLIC
SYMMETRY
SYMPATHY
SYMPHONY
SYMPOSIA
SYNOPSIS
SYNOPTIC
SYNOVIAL
SYPHILIS
SYSTEMIC
SYSTOLIC
SYZYGIES

T

TABBINET
TABBY-CAT
TABLEAUX
TABOURET
TABULATE
TACITURN
TACKLING
TACKSMAN
TACTICAL
TACTLESS
TAENIOID
TAFFERAL
TAFFEREL
TAILLESS
TAIL-RACE
TAKINGLY
TALISMAN
TALLIAGE
TALLNESS
TALLOWER
TALLYMAN
TALMUDIC
TAMEABLE
TAMANDUA
TARAMACK
TAMARIND
TAMARISK
TAMELESS
TAMENESS
TAMPERER
TAN-BALLS
TANGENCY
TANGIBLE
TANGIBLY
TANISTRY
TANNABLE
TANTALUM
TAPE-LINE
TAPESTRY
TAPE-WORM
TAP-HOUSE
TARA-FERN
TARBOOSH
TARGETED
TARLATAN
TARTARIC
TARTNESS
TARTRATE
TASK-WORK
TASTABLE
TASTEFUL
TATTERED
TATTLING
TATTOOER
TAUNTING
TAVERNER
TAWDRILY
TAXATION
TAXOLOGY
TAXONOMY
TEA-CADDY
TEA-CHEST
TEACHING
TEAMSTER
TEAR-DROP
TEARLESS
TEASELER

TECHNICS
TECTONIC
TEETHING
TEETOTAL
TEE-TOTUM
TEGUMENT
TELEGRAM
TELLABLE
TELL-TALE
TELLURAL
TELLURIC
TEMERITY
TEMPERED
TEMPORAL
TEMPTING
TEMULENT
TENACITY
TENANTRY
TENDANCE
TENDENCY
TENDERLY
TENEMENT
TENESMIC
TENESMUS
TENON-SAW
TENT-WINE
TENTACLE
TERMINAL
TERMINUS
TERMLESS
TERRAPIN
TERRIBLE
TERRIBLY
TERRIFIC
TERTIARY
TESSERAE
TESTATOR
TESTICLE
TETANOID
TETRAGON
TETRAPOD
TETRARCH
TEUTONIC
TEXT-BOOK
TEXT-HAND
THALAMUS
THALLINE
THALLIUM
THANEDOM
THANKFUL
THATCHER
THEARCHY
THEATRIC
THEISTIC
THEMATIC
THEOCRAT
THEODICY
THEOGONY
THEOLOGY
THEORIST
THEORIZE
THEORIES
THEREFOR
THEREOUT
THESPIAN
THEURGIC
THICKISH
THICKSET
THIEVERY
THIEVISH

THINKING
THINNESS
THINNISH
THIRSTER
THIRTEEN
THOLE-PIN
THORACIC
THORINUM
THOROUGH
THOUSAND
THRALDOM
THRASHER
THREATEN
THRENODY
THRIVING
THROMBUS
THROSTIC
THROTTLE
THRUMMER
THUMPING
THUNDERY
THURIBLE
THURIFER
THURSDAY
THWARTER
THWARTLY
TICKLING
TICKLISH
TIDE-GATE
TIDELESS
TIDE-MILL
TIDE-WAVE
TIDINESS
TIGERISH
TILLABLE
TIMBERED
TIME-BALL
TIME-BILL
TIME-FUSE
TIMELESS
TIME-WORN
TIMIDITY
TIMOROUS
TINCTURE
TINKLING
TINPLATE
TINSMITH
TINTLESS
TIP-STAFF
TIRESOME
TITANIAN
TITANIUM
TITHABLE
TITHE-PIG
TITMOUSE
TITULARY
TOAD-FISH
TOAD-FLAX
TOAD-SPIT
TOADYISM
TO-AND-FRO
TOBOGGAN
TOGETHER
TOILLESS
TOILSOME
TOIL-WORN
TOLBOOTH
TOLERANT
TOLERATE
TOLLABLE

TOLL-GATE
TOLL-MAN
TOMAHAWK
TOMATOES
TOMBLESS
TOMENTUM
TOM-NODDY
TOMORROW
TONALITY
TONELESS
TONICITY
TONSILAR
TONSURED
TOOTHFUL
TOP-BOOTS
TOP-DRESS
TOP-HEAVY
TOPONOMY
TOREADOR
TOREUTIC
TORTIOUS
TORTOISE
TORTUOSE
TORTUOUS
TORTURER
TOTALITY
TOTEMISM
TOTTERER
TOUCHILY
TOUCHING
TOUGHISH
TOURNURE
TOWARDLY
TOWERING
TOWN-HALL
TOWNSHIP
TOWNSMAN
TOWN-TALK
TOWNWARD
TOXICANT
TRACHEAL
TRACHYTE
TRACKAGE
TRACTATE
TRACTION
TRACTIVE
TRADUCER
TRAGICAL
TRAGOPAN
TRAIL-NET
TRAINING
TRAIN-OIL
TRAMPLER
TRAM-ROAD
TRANQUIL
TRANSACT
TRANSEPT
TRANSFER
TRANSFIX
TRANSHIP
TRANSMIT
TRANSUDE
TRAP-BALL
TRAP-DOOR
TRAPEZIA
TRAPPEAN
TRAPPING
TRAPPIST
TRAP-TUFA
TRASHILY

TRAVELED
TRAVELER
TRAVERSE
TRAVESTY
TRAWLING
TRAWL-NET
TREASURE
TREASURY
TREATING
TREATISE
TREELESS
TREENAIL
TREMBLER
TRENCHER
TREPHINE
TRESPASS
TRIANDER
TRIANGLE
TRIARCHY
TRIASSIC
TRIBRACH
TRIBUNAL
TRICHINA
TRICHOMA
TRICHORD
TRICKERY
TRICKING
TRICKISH
TRICYCLE
TRIFLING
TRIGLYPH
TRIGONAL
TRIGRAPH
TRILLION
TRIMETER
TRIMMING
TRIMNESS
TRIPPING
TRIPTOTE
TRIPTYCH
TRIUMVIR
TRIVALVE
TROCHAIC
TROCHOEA
TROCHOID
TROLLING
TROMBONE
TROOPIAL
TROPHIED
TROPHIES
TROPICAL
TROUBLER
TROUSERS
TROUTLET
TROUVERE
TRUCKAGE
TRUCKLER
TRUEBLUE
TRUEBORN
TRUEBRED
TRUELOVE
TRUENESS
TRUFFLED
TRUMPERY
TRUNCATE
TRUNNION
TRUSSING
TRUSTFUL
TRUSTILY
TRUTHFUL

TUBERCLE
TUBEROSE
TUBEROUS
TUBEWELL
TUBIFORN
TUBULOSE
TUBULOUS
TUMBLING
TUMIDITY
TUNELESS
TUNGSTEN
TUNGSTIC
TUNICATE
TURANIAN
TURBANED
TURGIDLY
TURMERIC
TURN-COAT
TURN-COCK
TRUNPIKE
TURNSOLE
TURNSPIT
TURRETED
TUTELAGE
TUTELARY
TUTORAGE
TUTORESS
TUTORIAL
TWADDLER
TWEAZERS
TWILIGHT
TWIN-BORN
TWINLING
TWITCHER
TWO-EDGED
TWO-FACED
TWOPENCE
TWOPENNY
TYMPAMIC
TYMPANUM
TYPIFIER
TYPOLOGY
TYRANNIC
TYROLESE

U

UBIQUITY
UDOMETER
UGLINESS
ULCERATE
ULCEROUS
ULTERIOR
ULTIMATE
ULTRAISM
ULTRAIST
UMBONATE
UMBRELLA
UMPIRAGE
UNABATED
UNALLIED
UNATONED
UNAVOWED
UNAWARES
UNBELIEF
UNBIASED
UNBIDDEN
UNBOLTED
UNBOUGHT

UNBROKEN
UNBUCKLE
UNBURDEN
UNBURIED
UNBURNED
UNBUTTON
UNCALLED
UNCANDID
UNCHASED
UNCHURCH
UNCIFORM
UNCINATE
UNCLOTHE
UNCOMELY
UNCOMMON
UNCOUPLE
UNCTUOUS
UNDECKED
UNDERBID
UNDERBUY
UNDERLAY
UNDERLIE
UNDERPIN
UNDULATE
UNEARNED
UNEASILY
UNENDING
UNENVIED
UNERRING
UNEVENLY
UNFADING
UNFAIRLY
UNFASTEN
UNFETTER
UNFILIAL
UNFORGOT
UNFORMED
UNFUNDED
UNGAINLY
UNGENTLE
UNGENTLY
UNGLAZED
UNGULATE
UNHANGED
UNHARMED
UNHEEDED
UNHOLILY
UNIAXIAL
UNIFILAR
UNIONISM
UNIONIST
UNIPOLAR
UNIQUELY
UNITEDLY
UNIVALVE
UNIVERSE
UNIVOCAL
UNJUSTLY
UNKENNEL
UNKINDLY
UNLAWFUL
UNLIKELY
UNLIMBER
UNLOVELY
UNMEETLY
UNMUFFLE
UNMUZZLE
UNPATHED
UNPEOPLE
UNPITIED

UNPOETIC
UNPOLITE
UNPROVED
UNREASON
UNREPAID
UNRIDDLE
UNSADDLE
UNSAFELY
UNSEALED
UNSEEMLY
UNSETTLE
UNSHAKEN
UNSHAPEN
UNSHROUD
UNSIFTED
UNSLAKED
UNSOCIAL
UNSOILED
UNSOUGHT
UNSOURED
UNSPOKEN
UNSTABLE
UNSTEADY
UNSTRING
UNSTRUNG
UNSUITED
UNSWATHE
UNTASTED
UNTHREAD
UNTHRIFT
UNTIDILY
UNTIMELY
UNTINGED
UNTIRING
UNTITLED
UNTOWARD
UNVALUED
UNVARIED
UNVERSED
UNVOICED
UNWARILY
UNWARPED
UNWASHED
UNWASHEN
UNWIELDY
UNWISDOM
UNWISELY
UNWISHED
UNWANTED
UNWORTHY
UPGROWTH
UPHEAVAL
UPHOLDER
UPLANDER
UPRISING
UPSPRING
UP-STROKE
URBANITY
URETHRAL
URGENTLY
UROSCOPY
URSULINE
URTICATE
USEFULLY
USUFRUCT
USURIOUS
UXORIOUS

V

VACATION
VAGABOND
VAGINATE
VAGRANCY
VAINNESS
VALERIAN
VALIDATE
VALIDITY
VALOROUS
VALUABLE
VALUATOR
VALVULAR
VANADIUM
VANDALIC
VANGUARD
VANQUISH
VAPORIZE
VAPOROSE
VAPOROUS
VAPOURER
VARIABLE
VARIABLY
VARIANCE
VARICOSE
VARIETAL
VARIFORM
VARIOLAR
VARIORUM
VARLETRY
VASCULAR
VASCULUM
VASELINE
VASIFORM
VASSALRY
VASTNESS
VAULTING
VEGETATE
VEHEMENT
VEILLESS
VEINLESS
VELARIUM
VELLEITY
VELOCITY
VENALITY
VENATION
VENDETTA
VENDIBLE
VENDIBLY
VENERATE
VENEREAL
VENETIAN
VENGEFUL
VENIALLY
VENOMOUS
VENOSITY
VENTURER
VERACITY
VERANDAH
VERATRIN
VERBALLY
VERBATIM
VERBIAGE
VERDANCY
VERDERER
VERDITER
VERDURED
VERIFIER

VERJUICE
VERONICA
VERSICLE
VERTEXES
VERTICES
VERTICLE
VERTICAL
VESICANT
VESICATE
VESPIARY
VESTMENT
VESTURED
VESUVIAN
VEXATION
VEXILLAR
VEXILLUM
VIATICUM
VIBRATOR
VICARAGE
VICARIAL
VICENARY
VICINAGE
VICINITY
VICTORIA
VICTRESS
VIENNESE
VIEWLESS
VIGILANT
VIGNERON
VIGNETTE
VIGOROUS
VILENESS
VILIFIER
VILIPEND
VILLAGER
VILLAINY
VINCIBLE
VINCULUM
VINE-CLAD
VINEYARD
VINOSITY
VINTAGER
VINTNERY
VIOLABLE
VIOLATOR
VIOLENCE
VIPERINE
VIPERISH
VIPEROUS
VIRGINAL
VIRIDITY
VIRILITY
VIRTUOSO
VIRTUOUS
VIRULENT
VISCERAL
VISCOUNT
VISIGOTH
VISIONAL
VISITANT
VISITING
VITALISM
VITALIST
VITALITY
VITALIZE
VITELLUS
VITIATOR
VITREOUS
VITULINE
VIVACITY

VIVARIUM
VIVAVOCE
VIXENISH
VOCALIST
VOCALITY
VOCALIZE
VOCATION
VOCATIVE
VOICEFUL
VOIDABLE
VOIDANCE
VOIDNESS
VOLATILE
VOLCANIC
VOLITION
VOLITIVE
VOLTAISM
VOMITING
VOMITORY
VORACITY
VORTICES
VORTICLE
VOTARESS
VOTARIST
VOTARIES
VOTIVELY
VOUSSOIR
VOWELISM
VOWELLED
VOYAGEUR
VOLCANIC
VULGARLY

W

WAGONAGE
WAINSCOT
WAITRESS
WALL-EYED
WALLOWER
WALL-TREE
WANDERER
WANDEROO
WANTONLY
WAR-DANCE
WARDENRY
WARDROBE
WARD-ROOM
WARDSHIP
WAR-HORSE
WARINESS
WARMNESS
WAR-PAINT
WARRANTY
WARRENER
WAR-WHOOP
WASHABLE
WASTEFUL
WATCH-DOG
WATCHFUL
WATCHMAN
WATER-DOG
WATER-GAS
WATER-HEN
WATERING
WATERMAN
WATER-POT
WATER-POX
WATER-RAM

WATER-RAT
WATTLING
WAVELESS
WAVE-WORN
WAX-CLOTH
WAXED-END
WAXINESS
WAX-LIGHT
WAYFARER
WEAKLING
WEAKNESS
WEANLING
WEAPONED
WEARABLE
WEEKLIES
WEEVILED
WELCOMER
WELDABLE
WELLADAY
WELL-BORN
WELL-BRED
WELL-KNIT
WELL-READ
WELL-ROOM
WELL-TO-DO
WELL-WORN
WEREWOLF
WESLEYAN
WESTERLY
WESTMOST
WESTWARD
WET-NURSE
WHARFAGE
WHATEVER
WHEATEAR
WHEAT-EEL
WHEAT-FLY
WHEEDLER
WHEELMAN
WHENEVER
WHEREVER
WHERRIES
WHEY-FACE
WHIFFLER
WHIGGERY
WHIGGISH
WHIMBREL
WHIMSIES

WHIN-CHAT
WHIP-CORD
WHIP-HAND
WHIP-LASH
WHIPPING
WHIPSTER
WHIRLWIG
WHIRRING
WHISTLER
WHITEBOY
WHITE-LEG
WHITENER
WHOREDOM
WHORESON
WICKEDLY
WICKERED
WIDENESS
WIFEHOOD
WIFELIKE
WIG-BLOCK
WILD-BOAR
WILDFIRE
WILD-FOWL
WILDNESS
WILD-WOOD
WILFULLY
WILINESS
WINDFALL
WINDGALL
WINDLASS
WINDLESS
WIND-MILL
WINDOWED
WINDPIPE
WINDROSE
WIND-SAIL
WINDWARD
WING-CASE
WINGLESS
WINNOWER
WINTERLY
WIRE-DRAW
WIRE-ROPE
WIRE-WORM
WIRE-WOVE
WIRINESS
WISEACRE
WISENESS

WISH-BONE
WISTERIA
WITCH-ELM
WITCHERY
WITCHING
WITHDRAW
WITHHOLD
WOEFULLY
WOLF-FISH
WOMANISH
WONDERER
WONDROUS
WOODBINE
WOOD-COAL
WOODCOCK
WOODENLY
WOODLAND
WOOD-LARK
WOODRUFF
WOOD-WORK
WOOINGLY
WOOL-DYED
WOOL-MILL
WOOLPACK
WOOLSACK
WOOLWARD
WORD-BOOK
WORKABLE
WORKADAY
WORKSHOP
WORM-CAST
WORMLING
WORMWOOD
WORRYING
WORTHILY
WRANGLER
WRAPPAGE
WRAPPING
WRATHFUL
WRECKAGE
WRESTLER
WRETCHED
WRIGGLER
WRINKLED
WRISTLET
WRONGFUL
WRONGOUS

X

XANTHOMA
XANTHOUS
XENOGAMY
XYLOCARP

Y

YACHTING
YATAGHAN
YEANLING
YEAR-BOOK
YEARLING
YEARNING
YEOMANLY
YEOMANRY
YIELDING
YOKE-MATE
YOUNGISH
YOURSELF
YOUTHFUL
YULE-TIDE

Z

ZAMINDAR
ZEALOTRY
ZEMINDAR
ZENITHAL
ZEOLITIC
ZIGZAGGY
ZODIACAL
ZOETROPE
ZOOLATRY
ZOOPHILE
ZOOPHILY
ZOOPHYTE
ZOOSPERM
ZOOSPORE
ZOOTOMIC
ZYMOLOGY

NINE-LETTER WORDS

A

ABANDONED
ABANDONER
ABASHMENT
ABATEMENT
ABBOTSHIP
ABDOMINAL
ABDUCTION
ABERRANCE
ABHORRENT
ABHORRING
ABIDINGLY
ABJECTION
ABNEGATOR
ABOLISHER
ABOLITION
ABOMINATE
ABORIGINE
ABRAHAMIC
ABSCONDER
ABSINTHIC
ABSORBENT
ABSTAINER
ABSTINENT
ABSURDITY
ABUNDANCE
ABUSIVELY
ACALEPHAE
ACCENTUAL
ACCESSARY
ACCESSION
ACCESSORY
ACCIDENCE
ACCIPITER
ACCLIMATE
ACCLIVITY
ACCLIVOUS
ACCOMPANY
ACCORDANT
ACCORDING
ACCORDION
ACCRETION
ACCRETIVE
ACCUMBENT
ACCUSABLE
ACESCENCE
ACETIFIER
ACETYLENE
ACIDIFIER
ACIDULATE
ACIDULENT
ACIDULOUS
ACINIFORM
ACOUSTICS
ACQUIESCE
ACQUITTAL
ACROBATIC
ACROPOLIS
ACROSPIRE
ACTUALIST
ACTUALITY
ACUMINATE
ACUTENESS

ADAPTABLE
ADDICTION
ADDRESSED
ADDRESSEE
ADDRESSER
ADDUCIBLE
ADDUCTION
ADENOTOMY
ADHERENCE
ADIPOCERE
ADJACENCE
ADJECTIVE
ADJOINING
ADJUTANCY
ADMEASURE
ADMINICLE
ADMIRABLE
ADMIRABLY
ADMIRALTY
ADMISSION
ADMIXTION
ADMIXTURE
ADMONITOR
ADOPTABLE
ADORATION
ADORINGLY
ADORNMENT
ADULATION
ADULTERER
ADULTNESS
ADUMBRANT
ADUMBRATE
ADVANTAGE
ADVENTUAL
ADVENTURE
ADVERBIAL
ADVERSARY
ADVERSELY
ADVERTENT
ADVERTISE
ADVISABLE
ADVISABLY
ADVISEDLY
ADVOCATOR
AEGOPHONY
AEPYORNIS
AEROMETER
AEROMETRY
AEROPHYTE
AEROPLANE
AESTHETIC
AETIOLOGY
AFFECTING
AFFECTION
AFFIANCED
AFFIDAVIT
AFFILIATE
AFFIRMANT
AFFLICTER
AFOREHAND
AFORESAID
AFORETIME
AFTER-CROP
AFTER-DAMP
AFTER-GLOW

AFTER-LIFE
AFTERMATH
AFTERMOST
AFTERNOON
AFTERWARD
AGGRAVATE
AGGREGATE
AGGRESSOR
AGITATION
AGONISTIC
AGONIZING
AGREEABLE
AGREEABLY
AGREEMENT
AIMLESSLY
AIR-ENGINE
AIR-JACKET
AITCHBONE
AITIOLOGY
ALABASTER
ALACK-A-DAY
ALARM-BELL
ALBATROSS
ALBESCENT
ALBUGINEA
ALBURNOUS
ALCHEMIST
ALCOHOLIC
ALE-CONNER
ALERTNESS
ALGEBRAIC
ALIENABLE
ALIENATOR
ALIGNMENT
ALIMENTAL
ALIZARINE
ALLANTOIS
ALLAYMENT
ALLEGORIC
ALLELUIAH
ALLEVIATE
ALL-HALLOW
ALLIGATOR
ALLOGRAPH
ALLOPATHY
ALLOTMENT
ALLOTROPY
ALLOWABLE
ALLOWABLY
ALLOWANCE
ALMA MATER
ALMANDINE
ALMOND-OIL
ALMS-GIVER
ALMS-HOUSE
ALOES-WOOD
ALONGSIDE
ALPENHORN
ALTAR-TOMB
ALTERABLE
ALTERCATE
ALTERNATE
ALTISCOPE
ALUMINIUM
ALUMINOUS

AMARYLLIS
AMASSMENT
AMAUROSIS
AMAUROTIC
AMAZEMENT
AMAZINGLY
AMAZONIAN
AMBERGRIS
AMBIGUITY
AMBIGUOUS
AMBITIOUS
AMBLYOPIA
AMBROSIAL
AMBULACRA
AMBULANCE
AMBUSCADE
AMENDABLE
AMENDMENT
AMIANTHUS
AMIDSHIPS
AMOROUSLY
AMORPHOUS
AMPERSAND
AMPHIBIAN
AMPHIBOLE
AMPHIGORY
AMPHIOXUS
AMPLENESS
AMPLIFIER
AMPLITUDE
AMUSEMENT
AMUSINGLY
AMUSIVELY
ANALECTIC
ANALGESIA
ANALOGIST
ANALOGIZE
ANALOGOUS
ANALYTICS
ANANDROUS
ANAPESTIC
ANAPLASTY
ANARCHIST
ANASTATIC
ANATOMISM
ANATOMIST
ANATOMIZE
ANATROPAL
ANCESTRAL
ANCHORAGE
ANCHORITE
ANCHYLOSE
ANCIENTLY
ANCILLARY
ANECDOTAL
ANGLE-IRON
ANGLICISM
ANGLICIZE
ANGULARLY
ANGULATED
ANHYBRITE
ANHYDROUS
ANIMALISM
ANIMALITY
ANIMALIZE

ANIMATING
ANIMATION
ANIMISTIC
ANIMOSITY
ANKYLOSIS
ANNOTATOR
ANNOUNCER
ANNOYANCE
ANNUITANT
ANNULARLY
ANNULMENT
ANOMALOUS
ANONYMITY
ANONYMOUS
ANTALKALI
ANTARCTIC
ANTE-CHOIR
ANTELUCAN
ANTEMETIC
ANTENATAL
ANTHELION
ANTHEMION
ANTHEROID
ANTHODIUM
ANTHOLOGY
ANTHOZOON
ANTHROPIC
ANTICHLOR
ANTIDOTAL
ANTIPAPAL
ANTIPATHY
ANTIPHONY
ANTIPODAL
ANTIPODES
ANTIPYRIN
ANTIQUARY
ANTIQUITY
ANTI-TRADE
ANXIOUSLY
APARTMENT
APATHETIC
APERITIVE
APETALOUS
APHERESIS
APHYLLOUS
APISHNESS
APLANATIC
APOCOPATE
APOCRYPHA
APOLOGIST
APOLOGIZE
APOPHYSIS
APOSTOLIC
APOTHECIA
APPALLING
APPARATUS
APPARITOR
APPELLANT
APPELLATE
APPENDAGE
APPENDANT
APPERTAIN
APPETENCE
APPETIZER
APPLE-JOHN
APPLIANCE
APPLICANT
APPOINTED
APPORTION
APPRAISER

APPREHEND
APPROBATE
ARABESQUE
ARACHNIDA
ARACHNOID
ARAUCARIA
ARBITRAGE
ARBITRARY
ARBITRATE
ARBOREOUS
ARBORETUM
ARCHANGEL
ARCHDUCAL
ARCHDUCHY
ARCHETYPE
ARCHITECT
ARCHIVIST
ARCHSTONE
ARCTOGEAL
ARCUATION
ARDUOUSLY
AREOMETER
AREOPAGUS
ARGENTINE
ARMADILLO
ARMILLARY
ARMISTICE
ARMY-CORPS
AROMATIZE
ARRAIGNER
ARRHIZOUS
ARRISWISE
ARROGANCE
ARROWROOT
ARSENICAL
ARSENIOUS
ARTHRITIC
ARTHRITIS
ARTICHOKE
ARTICULAR
ARTIFICER
ARTILLERY
ARTLESSLY
ASAFETIDA
ASBESTINE
ASCENDANT
ASCENSION
ASCERTAIN
ASPARAGUS
ASPERMOUS
ASPERSION
ASPERSIVE
ASPHALTIC
ASPHALTUM
ASPLENIUM
ASSAILANT
ASSERTION
ASSERTIVE
ASSIDUITY
ASSIDUOUS
ASSISTANT
ASSOCIATE
ASSONANCE
ASSUASIVE
ASSURABLE
ASSURANCE
ASSUREDLY
ASTHMATIC
ASTRADDLE
ASTRAKHAN

ASTROLABE
ASTROLOGY
ASTRONOMY
ASTUCIOUS
ASYMMETRY
ASYMPTOTE
ASYNDETIC
ASYNDETON
ATHANASIA
ATHEISTIC
ATHENAEUM
ATHLETICS
ATMOLYSIS
ATMOMETER
ATONEMENT
ATROCIOUS
ATTAINDER
ATTENDANT
ATTENTION
ATTENTIVE
ATTENUANT
ATTENUATE
ATTOLLENT
ATTRACTER
ATTRIBUTE
ATTRITION
AUDACIOUS
AUDIPHONE
AUGMENTER
AUGURSHIP
AURICULAR
AURISCOPE
AUSTERELY
AUSTERITY
AUTHENTIC
AUTHORESS
AUTHORIAL
AUTHORITY
AUTHORIZE
AUTOCRACY
AUTOGRAPH
AUTOMATIC
AUTOMATON
AUXILIARY
AVAILABLE
AVALANCHE
AVOCATION
AVOIDABLE
AVOIDANCE
AVUNCULAR
AWAKENING
AWE-STRUCK
AWFULNESS
AWKWARDLY
AXIOMATIC
AZEDARACH
AZIMUTHAL

B

BABIRUSSA
BACCHANAL
BACCHANTE
BACCIFORM
BACKBITER
BACKBOARD
BACKSHISH
BACKSLIDE
BACKSTAIR

BACKSWORD
BACKWOODS
BACTERIUM
BADMINTON
BAGATELLE
BAILIWICK
BAKEHOUSE
BALCONIED
BALDACHIN
BALD-EAGLE
BALD-FACED
BALEFULLY
BALLADIST
BALLISTIC
BALLOT-BOX
BAMBOOZLE
BANDEROLE
BANDICOOT
BANDOLEER
BANDOLINE
BANEFULLY
BANK-AGENT
BANK-STOCK
BANQUETER
BANQUETTE
BAPTISMAL
BARBARIAN
BARBARISM
BARBARITY
BARBARIZE
BARBAROUS
BAREFACED
BARGAINER
BARNACLES
BAROGRAPH
BAROMETER
BARONETCY
BAROSCOPE
BARRELLED
BARRICADE
BARRISTER
BASHFULLY
BASILICON
BAS-RELIEF
BASTINADO
BASTIONED
BATH-BRICK
BATH-CHAIR
BATRACHIA
BATTALION
BATTLE-AXE
BAWDINESS
BAY-WINDOW
BEACONAGE
BEAN-FEAST
BEAN-GOOSE
BEAR-BERRY
BEARDLESS
BEATITUDE
BEAU-IDEAL
BEAUMONDE
BEAUTEOUS
BEAUTIFUL
BERBERINE
BECCAFICO
BEDLAMITE
BEDRAGGLE
BEDRIDDEN
BEECH-MAST
BEEF-EATER

BEER-HOUSE	BISHOPRIC	BOOT-MAKER	BRUTISHLY
BEER-MONEY	BISMUTHAL	BOTTLE-TIT	BUCCANEER
BEESTINGS	BISULCATE	BOULEVARD	BUCENTAUR
BEFITTING	BITTERISH	BOUNDLESS	BUCKETFUL
BEGINNING	BLACK-BALL	BOUNTEOUS	BUCK-HOUND
BEHAVIOUR	BLACK-BAND	BOUNTIFUL	BUCKSHISH
BELEAGUER	BLACKBIRD	BOURGEOIS	BUCKTHORN
BELEMNITE	BLACKCOCK	BOWER-BIRD	BUCK-TOOTH
BELIEVING	BLACK-FISH	BOW-LEGGED	BUCKWHEAT
BELL-GLASS	BLACK-GAME	BOW-STRING	BUFF-STICK
BELLICOSE	BLACK-IRON	BOW-WINDOW	BUFF-WHEEL
BELL-METAL	BLACK-JACK	BOXING-DAY	BUGLE-HORN
BELL-PUNCH	BLACK-LEAD	BOX-KEEPER	BUHRSTONE
BELL-TOWER	BLACK-LIST	BOYCOTTER	BULGARIAN
BELLY-BAND	BLACK-MAIL	BRACHYURA	BULKINESS
BELONGING	BLACKNESS	BRACTEATE	BULL-FIGHT
BELVEDERE	BLADDERED	BRAHMANIC	BULL-TROUT
BENCH-MARK	BLADE-BONE	BRAINLESS	BUMBAILIF
BENEFICED	BLAEBERRY	BRAIN-SICK	BUMBLE-BEE
BENIGNANT	BLAMELESS	BRAMBLING	BUMBLEDOM
BENIGNITY	BLANDNESS	BRANCHIAE	BUMPTIOUS
BERGAMASK	BLANKNESS	BRANCHIAL	BUOYANTLY
BERSERKER	BLASPHEME	BRANCHLET	BURLESQUE
BERYLLINE	BLASPHEMY	BRAND-IRON	BURLINESS
BESEECHER	BLAST-PIPE	BRANDLING	BURNISHER
BESEEMING	BLEACHERY	BRASS-BAND	BURSIFORM
BESETTING	BLEAKNESS	BRAVENESS	BUSHINESS
BESPANGLE	BLEAR-EYED	BRAZIL-NUT	BUSH-METAL
BESPATTER	BLESSEDLY	BREAD-CORN	BUSSU-PALM
BESPECKLE	BLINDFOLD	BREAKABLE	BUTTER-BUR
BESTIALLY	BLINDNESS	BREAK-DOWN	BUTTERCUP
BETROTHAL	BLIND-WORM	BREAKFAST	BUTTERFLY
BEVEL-GEAR	BLOCKADER	BREAK-NECK	BUTTERINE
BEWITCHER	BLOCKHEAD	BREAST-PIN	BUTTER-NUT
BIANGULAR	BLOND-LACE	BREATHING	BY-PRODUCT
BIBACIOUS	BLONDNESS	BREECHING	BYSSOLITE
BIBLICIST	BLOOD-HEAT	BREEZE-FLY	BY-STANDER
BICAMERAL	BLOODLESS	BRESSOMER	BYZANTINE
BICIPITAL	BLOOD-SHOT	BRIAR-ROOT	
BICONCAVE	BLOSSOMED	BRIC-A-BRAC	
BICYCLIST	BLUE-GRASS	BRICK-CLAY	**C**
BIESTINGS	BLUE-STONE	BRICK-KILN	
BIFARIOUS	BLUFFNESS	BRICKWORK	CABALLINE
BIFOLIATE	BLUNDERER	BRIDE-CAKE	CABBALISM
BIFURCATE	BLUNTNESS	BRIDESMAN	CABBALIST
BIGOTEDLY	BLUSTERER	BRIDEWELL	CABLEGRAM
BILABIATE	BOATSWAIN	BRIEFLESS	CABRIOLET
BILATERAL	BODY-GUARD	BRIEFNESS	CACHAEMIA
BILINGUAL	BOG-BUTTER	BRIER-ROOT	CACHOLONG
BILITERAL	BOLD-FACED	BRIGADIER	CACODEMON
BILLIARDS	BOLTSPRIT	BRILLIANT	CACOETHES
BILOCULAR	BOMBARDON	BRIMSTONE	CACOPHONY
BIMONTHLY	BOMBASTIC	BRIQUETTE	CADASTRAL
BINDINGLY	BOMBAZINE	BRISKNESS	CADAVERIE
BINERVATE	BOMB-KETCH	BRITANNIC	CADETSHIP
BINOCULAR	BOMB-PROOF	BROAD-BRIM	CAESAREAN
BINOMINAL	BOMB-SHELL	BROADCAST	CAESARISM
BINTURONG	BOND-SLAVE	BROADNESS	CAINOZOIC
BIOGRAPHY	BONE-BLACK	BROADSIDE	CAIRNGORM
BIOLOGIST	BONE-BROWN	BROIDERER	CALAMANCO
BIPARTITE	BONE-EARTH	BROKERAGE	CALCANEUM
BIPENNATE	BON-VIVANT	BRONCHIAL	CALCEDONY
BIRCH-WINE	BOOKISHLY	BROOM-CORN	CALCULARY
BIRD-ORGAN	BOOK-LOUSE	BROOM-RAPE	CALCULATE
BIRD'S-FOOT	BOOK-MAKER	BROTHERLY	CALCULOUS
BIRD'S-NEST	BOOK-PLATE	BROWNNESS	CALENDRER
BIRTH-MARK	BOOK-STALL	BRUSHWOOD	CALENTURE
BIRTH-ROOT	BOOMERANG	BRUSQUELY	CALIBERED
BISECTION	BOORISHLY	BRUTALITY	CALIBRATE
BISEGMENT		BRUTALIZE	CALIPHATE

CALLIPERS	CARPENTER	CELANDINE	CHEAPNESS
CALLOSITY	CARPENTRY	CELEBRANT	CHEATABLE
CALLOUSLY	CARPET-BAG	CELEBRATE	CHECKMATE
CALMATIVE	CARPETING	CELEBRITY	CHEEK-BONE
CALORIFIC	CARPET-ROD	CELESTIAL	CHEERLESS
CALVINISM	CARPINGLY	CELESTINE	CHEESE-FLY
CALVINIST	CARPOLOGY	CELLARAGE	CHELONIAN
CALVITIES	CARRAGEEN	CELLARMAN	CHEMISTRY
CAMARILLA	CARRONADE	CELLULOID	CHEMITYPE
CAMBISTRY	CARRON-OIL	CELLULOSE	CHEQUERED
CAMERATED	CARROUSEL	CELTICISM	CHERIMOYA
CAMPAGNOL	CARTESIAN	CENOBITIC	CHERISHER
CAMPANERO	CART-HORSE	CENSORIAL	CHERRY-PIT
CAMPANILE	CARTILAGE	CENTENARY	CHEVALIER
CAMPANULA	CARTRIDGE	CENTERING	CHEVELURE
CAMPHORIC	CARTULARY	CENTIPEDE	CHEVRONED
CAMP-STOOL	CASE-KNIFE	CENTRALLY	CHIBOUQUE
CANAANITE	CASEMATED	CENTRE-BIT	CHICKLING
CANCEROUS	CASHEW-NUT	CENTURIAL	CHICKWEED
CANDIDATE	CASSAREEP	CENTURION	CHIDINGLY
CANDLE-NUT	CASSATION	CEPHALATE	CHIEFTAIN
CANDLEMAS	CASSEROLE	CEPHALOID	CHILBLAIN
CANDYTUFT	CASSIMERE	CERACEOUS	CHILDHOOD
CANE-BRAKE	CASSOCKED	CERATITIS	CHILDLESS
CANE-CHAIR	CASSONADE	CERATODUS	CHILDLIKE
CANESCENT	CASSOWARY	CERAUNITE	CHILIARCH
CANE-SUGAR	CASTALIAN	CERBEREAN	CHILLNESS
CANKER-FLY	CASTELIAN	CERCARIAN	CHINAWARE
CANKEROUS	CASTIGATE	CERECLOTH	CHINA-CLAY
CANNELURE	CASTILIAN	CEROGRAPH	CHINA-ROOT
CANNONADE	CASTOR-OIL	CERTAINLY	CHINA-ROSE
CANNONEER	CAST-STEEL	CERTAINTY	CHINA-SHOP
CANONICAL	CASUALISM	CERTIFIER	CHINCAPIN
CANTICLES.	CASUALIST	CERTITUDE	CHINCHONA
CANVASSER	CASUARINA	CESPITOSE	CHINCOUGH
CAPACIOUS	CASUISTIC	CESSATION	CHINKAPIN
CAPARISON	CASUISTRY	CETACEOUS	CHIROLOGY
CAPILLARY	CATACLYSM	CEVADILLA	CHISELLED
CAPILLOSE	CATALEPSY	CHAFFERER	CHIVALRIC
CAPITALLY	CATALOGUE	CHAFFINCH	CHLOROSIS
CAPITULAR	CATAMARAN	CHAIN-GANG	CHLOROTIC
CAPITULUM	CATAMENIA	CHAIN-PIER	CHOCK-FULL
CAPONIERE	CATAMOUNT	CHAIN-PUMP	CHOCOLATE
CAPRICCIO	CATAPLASM	CHAIN-SHOT	CHOKE-BORE
CAPRICORN	CATARRHAL	CHALLENGE	CHOKE-DAMP
CAPRIFORM	CATCHMENT	CHALYBITE	CHOKE-FULL
CAPSICINE	CATCH-POLL	CHAMBERED	CHOLAEMIA
CAPSULATE	CATCH-WORD	CHAMBERER	CHOLERAIC
CAPTAINCY	CATECHISM	CHAMELEON	CHONDRIFY
CAPTIVATE	CATECHIST	CHAMOMILE	CHOP-HOUSE
CAPTIVITY	CATECHIZE	CHAMPAGNE	CHORISTER
CARAMBOLA	CATERWAUL	CHAMPAIGN	CHRISTIAN
CARAMBOLE	CATHARIST	CHANCEFUL	CHRISTMAS
CARBONADO	CATHARTIC	CHANDLERY	CHROMATIC
CARBONATE	CATHEDRAL	CHANGEFUL	CHRONICLE
CARBONIZE	CATOPTRIC	CHARACTER	CHRYSALID
CARBUNCLE	CAT-SILVER	CHARINESS	CHRYSALIS
CARCINOMA	CATTLE-PEN	CHARIOTED	CHTHONIAN
CARDBOARD	CAUCASIAN	CHARIVARI	CHUBB LOCK
CAREENAGE	CAUSALITY	CHARLATAN	CHUB-FACED
CAREFULLY	CAUSATION	CHARTERED	CHURCHING
CARE-TAKER	CAUSATIVE	CHARTERER	CHURCHISM
CARMELITE	CAUSELESS	CHAR-WOMAN	CHURCHMAN
CARNALIST	CAUTELOUS	CHASTENER	CICATRIZE
CARNALITY	CAUTERIZE	CHASTISER	CIGARETTE
CARNALIZE	CAUTIONER	CHATOYANT	CILIOFORM
CARNATION	CAVALCADE	CHATTERER	CIMMERIAN
CARNELIAN	CAVERNOUS	CHAUFFEUR	CINCHONIC
CARNIVORA	CEASELESS	CHAW-BACON	CINCHONIN
CARNIVORE	CEBADILLA	CHEAP-JACK	CINCTURED

CINERARIA
CINEREOUS
CINGALESE
CIRCINATE
CIRCULATE
CIRRHOSIS
CISALPINE
CIVILIZED
CIVILIZER
CLACK-DISH
CLAIMABLE
CLAMOROUS
CLAMOURER
CLAPBOARD
CLARET-CUP
CLARET-JUG
CLARIFIER
CLARIONET
CLASSABLE
CLASSICAL
CLASS-MATE
CLAUSTRAL
CLAUSALAR
CLAVICORN
CLAY-SLATE
CLAY-STONE
CLEANNESS
CLEARANCE
CLEARNESS
CLEAVABLE
CLEMENTLY
CLEPSYDRA
CLERGYMAN
CLERICISM
CLERKSHIP
CLEVERISH
CLIENTAGE
CLIENTELE
CLIMATIZE
CLIMBABLE
CLOAK-ROOM
CLOCK-WORK
CLOG-DANCE
CLOISTRAL
CLOSENESS
CLOSE-TIME
CLOTH-HALL
CLOTH-YARD
CLOUDLESS
CLOVE-PINK
CLUBBABLE
CLUB-HOUSE
COACH-HIRE
COADJUTOR
COADUNATE
COAGULANT
COAGULATE
COAL-BLACK
COAL-BRASS
COAL-FIELD
COALITION
COAL-PLANT
COAST-LINE
COASTWISE
COAXINGLY
COCCOLITE
COCCOLITH
COCCYGEAL
COCHINEAL
COCHLEATE

COCK-A-HOOP
COCK-FIGHT
COCKLE-HAT
COCKNEYFY
COCKROACH
COCK'S-COMB
COCKSWAIN
COCOONERY
COEMPTION
COENOBITE
COENOSARE
COEQUALLY
COERCIBLE
COETERNAL
COFFEE-BUG
COFFEE-POT
COFFER-DAM
COFOUNDER
COGITABLE
COGNATION
COGNITION
COGNITIVE
COGNIZANT
COHEIRESS
COHERENCE
COLCHICUM
COLCOTHAR
COLD-BLAST
COLD-CREAM
COLEOPTER
COLLATION
COLLATIVE
COLLEAGUE
COLLECTOR
COLLEGIAL
COLLEGIAN
COLLIGATE
COLLIMATE
COLLINEAR
COLLISION
COLLOCATE
COLLODION
COLLOIDAL
COLLUSION
COLLUSIVE
COLLYRIUM
COLOCYNTH
COLONELCY
COLONIZER
COLONNADE
COLOPHONY
COLORIFIC
COLOSSEUM
COLOSTRUM
COLOURING
COLOURIST
COLOURMAN
COLTISHLY
COLT'S-FOOT
COLUBRINE
COLUMBARY
COLUMBINE
COLUMBIUM
COLUMBITE
COLUMELLA
COMBATANT
COMBATIVE
COMICALLY
COMMANDER
COMMENDAM

COMMENDER
COMMENSAL
COMMENTER
COMMINGLE
COMMINUTE
COMMITTAL
COMMITTEE
COMMITTER
COMMODITY
COMMODORE
COMMONAGE
COMMOTION
COMMUNION
COMMUNISM
COMMUNIST
COMMUNITY
COMPACTLY
COMPANION
COMPELLER
COMPETENT
COMPLAINT
COMPLEXLY
COMPLEXUS
COMPLIANT
COMPONENT
COMPOSITE
COMPOSURE
COMRADERY
CONCAVELY
CONCAVITY
CONCEALER
CONCEITED
CONCENTRE
CONCERNED
CONCERTED
CONCILIAR
CONCISELY
CONCISION
CONCOCTER
CONCORDAT
CONCOURSE
CONCREATE
CONCUBINE
CONDEMNER
CONDENSER
CONDIMENT
CONDITION
CONDUCIVE
CONDUCTOR
CONFERRER
CONFESSED
CONFESSOR
CONFIDANT
CONFIDENT
CONFIDING
CONFIGURE
CONFIRMED
CONFIRMEE
CONFIRMER
CONFLUENT
CONFORMER
CONFUCIAN
CONFUSION
CONGENIAL
CONGERIES
CONGESTED
CONGRUENT
CONGRUITY
CONGRUOUS
CONICALLY

CONJUGATE
CONNATURE
CONNECTOR
CONNEXION
CONNUBIAL
CONQUEROR
CONSCIOUS
CONSCRIPT
CONSENSUS
CONSERVER
CONSIGNEE
CONSIGNER
CONSONANT
CONSPIRER
CONSTABLE
CONSTANCY
CONSTRAIN
CONSTRICT
CONSTRUCT
CONSULATE
CONSULTER
CONSUMING
CONTAGION
CONTAGIUM
CONTAINER
CONTEMNER
CONTENDER
CONTENTED
CONTICENT
CONTINENT
CONTINUAL
CONTINUED
CONTINUER
CONTORTED
CONTRALTO
CONTRIVER
CONTUMACY
CONTUMELY
CONTUSION
CONUNDRUM
CONVERTER
CONVEXITY
CONVIVIAL
CONVOCATE
CONVOLUTE
COOPERAGE
CO-OPERANT
CO-OPERATE
COPARTNER
COPE-STONE
COPIOUSLY
COPPERING
COPPERISH
COPROLITE
COPROLOGY
COPSE-WOOD
COPYRIGHT
CORALLINE
CORALLITE
CORALLOID
CORAL-REEF
CORAL-TREE
CORAL-WOOD
CORDATELY
CORDELIER
CORDIALLY
CORDIFORM
CORIANDER
CORKSCREW
CORMORANT

CORN-CRAKE	CRASSNESS	CULTIVATE	DEAD-MARCH
CORNELIAN	CRAVATTED	CUMBRANCE	DEAFENING
CORNETIST	CRAVINGLY	CUNEIFORM	DEATH-BELL
CORN-FLOUR	CRAZINESS	CUNNINGLY	DEATH-BLOW
CORNOPEAN	CREAM-CAKE	CUP-BEARER	DEATH-FIRE
CORN-POPPY	CREAM-LAID	CURB-STONE	DEATHLESS
COROLLARY	CREAM-WOVE	CURDINESS	DEATHLIKE
COROLLINE	CREATABLE	CURIOSITY	DEATH-RATE
CORONETED	CREATRESS	CURIOUSLY	DEATH'S-MAN
COROZO-NUT	CREDENDUM	CURLINESS	DEBARMENT
CORPORATE	CREDULITY	CURRENTLY	DEBATABLE
CORPOREAL	CREDULOUS	CURRY-COMB	DEBAUCHED
CORPOSANT	CREEPHOLE	CURSORIAL	DEBAUCHEE
CORPULENT	CREMATION	CURSORILY	DEBAUCHER
CORPUSCLE	CREMATORY	CURSTNESS	DEBENTURE
CORRECTLY	CRENATION	CURTAILER	DEBUTANTE
CORRECTOR	CRENATURE	CURVATURE	DECACHORD
CORRELATE	CRENELATE	CUSHIONED	DECADENCE
CORRODENT	CREPITANT	CUSPIDATE	DECAGONAL
CORROSION	CREPITATE	CUSTODIAL	DECALCIFY
CORROSIVE	CRESCENDO	CUSTODIAN	DECALITRE
CORRUGATE	CRESTLESS	CUSTODIER	DECALOGUE
CORRUPTED	CRETINISM	CUSTOMARY	DECAMETRE
CORRUPTER	CRICKETER	CUTANEOUS	DECAPODAL
CORRUPTLY	CRIMELESS	CUT-THROAT	DECASTYLE
CORTICATE	CRIMINATE	CUTTINGLY	DECEITFUL
CORTICOSE	CRIMINOUS	CYCLOIDAL	DECEPTION
CORUSCANT	CRINOLINE	CYCLOPEAN	DECEPTIVE
CORUSCATE	CRISPNESS	CYLINDRIC	DECIDABLE
CORYMBOSE	CRITERION	CYMBALIST	DECIDEDLY
COSMOGONY	CRITICISM	CYMOPHANE	DECIDUATE
COSMOLOGY	CRITICIZE	CYNEGITIC	DECIDUOUS
COSMORAMA	CROCODILE	CYNICALLY	DECILITRE
COSTIVELY	CROOKEDLY	CYSTIFORM	DECILLION
COSTUMIER	CROP-EARED	CYSTOTOMY	DECIMALLY
CO-TANGENT	CROSIERED	CYTHEREAN	DECIMATOR
COTHURNUS	CROSSBILL	CYTOBLAST	DECIMETRE
COTILLION	CROSS-BRED		DECK-CARGO
CO-TRUSTEE	CROSS-FIRE		DECLAIMER
COTTONADE	CROSS-HEAD	**D**	DECLINATE
COTTON-GIN	CROSSNESS		DECLINOUS
COTYLEDON	CROSS-ROAD	DACHSHUND	DECLINING
COUMARINE	CROSSWISE	DAIRY-FARM	DECLIVITY
COUNTABLE	CROTCHETY	DAIRY-MAID	DECLIVOUS
COUNTLESS	CROW-BERRY	DALLIANCE	DECOCTION
COUNTSHIP	CROWNLESS	DAMASCENE	DECOLLATE
COURTEOUS	CROWN-WORK	DAMASKEEN	DECOMPLEX
COURTESAN	CROW-QUILL	DAMNATION	DECOMPOSE
COURTHAND	CROW'S-BILL	DAMNATORY	DECORATED
COURTLING	CROW'S-FEET	DAMPISHLY	DECORATOR
COURT-ROLL	CROW'S-FOOT	DANDELION	DECOY-DUCK
COURTSHIP	CROW'S-NEST	DANDIPRAT	DECREMENT
COURT-YARD	CRUCIFIER	DANGEROUS	DECRETIST
COVERTURE	CRUCIFORM	DAPPLE-BAY	DECRETIVE
COVERT-WAY	CRUDENESS	DARE-DEVIL	DECRETORY
COVETABLE	CRUSH-ROOM	DARWINIAN	DECUMBENT
COWARDICE	CRUSTACEA	DARWINISM	DECURRENT
COWFEEDER	CRYPTOGAM	DASH-BOARD	DECUSSATE
COXCOMBRY	CRYPTONYM	DASH-WHEEL	DEDICATEE
CRAB-APPLE	CUBICALLY	DASTARDLY	DEDICATOR
CRABBEDLY	CUBICULAR	DASYMETER	DEDUCIBLE
CRAB-STICK	CUCKOLDLY	DATE-SUGAR	DEDUCTION
CRACKLING	CUCKOLDOM	DAUNTLESS	DEDUCTIVE
CRAFTLESS	CUCKOLDRY	DAY-LABOUR	DEER-HOUND
CRAFTSMAN	CUCULLATE	DAY-SCHOOL	DEER-MOUSE
CRAMP-IRON	CUDGELLER	DAYSPRING	DEFALCATE
CRANBERRY	CULULAWAN	DEACONESS	DEFAULTER
CRANKNESS	CULLENDER	DEAD-DRUNK	DEFECTION
CRAPULENT	CULMINATE	DEAD-HOUSE	DEFECTIVE
CRAPULOUS	CULPATORY	DEAD-LIGHT	DEFENDANT

DEFENSIVE
DEFENSORY
DEFERENCE
DEFERMENT
DEFIANTLY
DEFICIENT
DEFINABLE
DEFINABLY
DEFLECTED
DEFLECTOR
DEFLORATE
DEFLUXION
DEFOLIATE
DEFORMITY
DEFRAUDER
DEGRADING
DEHISCENT
DEINORNIS
DEIPAROUS
DEJECTION
DELICIOUS
DELIGHTED
DELINEATE
DELIQUIUM
DELIRIANT
DELIRIOUS
DELIVERER
DELUDABLE
DEMAGOGIC
DEMAGOGUE
DEMANDANT
DEMEANOUR
DEMI-DEVIL
DEMI-LANCE
DEMI-MONDE
DEMISABLE
DEMISSION
DEMIURGIC
DEMOCRACY
DEMULCENT
DEMURRAGE
DENDRITIC
DENOTABLE
DENOUNCER
DENSENESS
DENTATELY
DENTIFORM
DENTISTRY
DENTITION
DENYINGLY
DEODORANT
DEODORIZE
DEOXIDATE
DEOXIDIZE
DEPARTURE
DEPASTURE
DEPENDANT
DEPENDENT
DEPICTURE
DEPLETION
DEPLETIVE
DEPLETORY
DEPOSABLE
DEPOSITOR
DEPRAVITY
DEPRECATE
DEPREDATE
DEPRESSED
DEPRESSOR
DEPURATOR

DERIVABLE
DERIVABLY
DERMATOID
DERRINGER
DESCANTER
DESCENDER
DESCRIBER
DESECRATE
DESERTION
DESERVING
DESSICANT
DESSICATE
DESIGNATE
DESIGNING
DESIRABLE
DESIRABLY
DESMOLOGY
DESOLATER
DESOLATOR
DESPAIRER
DESPERADO
DESPERATE
DESPOILER
DESPONDER
DESPOTISM
DESTINATE
DESTINIST
DESTITUTE
DESTROYER
DESUETUDE
DESULTORY
DETECTION
DETECTIVE
DETENTION
DETERGENT
DETERMENT
DETERMINE
DETERRENT
DETERSION
DETERSIVE
DETHRONER
DETONATOR
DETRACTER
DETRACTOR
DETRIMENT
DETRITION
DETRUSION
DEVASTATE
DEVELOPER
DEVIATION
DEVIL-FISH
DEVILMENT
DEVIL'S-BIT
DEVILSHIP
DEVIOUSLY
DEVISABLE
DEVITRIFY
DEVONPORT
DEVOTEDLY
DEWLAPPED
DEXTERITY
DEXTEROUS
DEXTRORSE
DIABLERIE
DIABOLISM
DIABROSIS
DIACHYLON
DIACHYLUM
DIACONATE
DIACRITIC

DIATRINIC
DIAERESIS
DIAGNOSIS
DIALECTAL
DIALECTIC
DIALOGISM
DIALOGIST
DIALOGIZE
DIAL-PLATE
DIAMETRIC
DIAMETRAL
DIAMONDED
DIANDROUS
DIANOETIC
DIAPHRAGM
DIARRHOEA
DIASTOLIC
DIATHESIS
DIATHETIC
DIATOMITE
DICASTERY
DICHOGAMY
DICHOTOMY
DICHROISM
DICKY-BIRD
DECLINOUS
DICOELOUS
DICTATION
DICTATURE
DICTATORY
DICTATRIX
DIDACTICS
DIDACTILE
DIDELPHIA
DIDELPHIC
DIE-SINKER
DIETARIAN
DIETETICS
DIETETIST
DIFFERENT
DIFFICULT
DIFFIDENT
DIFFLUENT
DIFFUSION
DIFFUSIVE
DIGENESIS
DIGESTION
DIGESTIVE
DIGITALIN
DIGITALIS
DIGITATED
DIGNIFIED
DIGNITARY
DILATABLE
DILIGENCE
DIMENSION
DIMIDIATE
DIMISSORY
DIMYARIAN
DINGINESS
DINOCERAS
DINOTHERE
DIOECIOUS
DIONYSIAC
DIONYSIAN
DIOPTRICS
DIPHTHONG
DIPHYCERC
DIPLOMACY
DIPTEROUS

DIRECTION
DIRECTIVE
DIRECTORY
DIRECTRIX
DIREFULLY
DIRIGIBLE
DIRTINESS
DISAFFECT
DISAFFIRM
DISAPPEAR
DISAVOUCH
DISAVOWAL
DISAVOWER
DISBELIEF
DISBURDEN
DISBURSER
DISCERNER
DISCHARGE
DISCHURCH
DISCOIDAL
DISCOLOUR
DISCOMFIT
DISCOMMON
DISCOURSE
DISCOVERY
DISCREDIT
DISCUSSER
DISEMBARK
DISEMBODY
DISENABLE
DISENGAGE
DISENROLL
DISENTAIL
DISENTOMB
DISESTEEM
DISFAVOUR
DISFIGURE
DISFOREST
DISGORGER
DISGRACER
DISGUISER
DISH-CLOTH
DISH-CLOUT
DISHONEST
DISHONOUR
DISINFECT
DISINHUME
DISLOCATE
DISMANTLE
DISMEMBER
DISMISSAL
DISNATURE
DISOBLIGE
DISPARAGE
DISPARATE
DISPARITY
DISPAUPER
DISPELLER
DISPENSER
DISPEOPLE
DISPERSAL
DISPERSER
DISPLAYER
DISPLEASE
DISPONDEE
DISPOSURE
DISPRAISE
DISPROVAL
DISPUTANT
DISREGARD

DISRELISH
DISREPAIR
DISREPUTE
DISSECTOR
DISSEIZOR
DISSEMBLE
DISSENTER
DISSIDENT
DISSIPATE
DISSOLUTE
DISSOLVER
DISSONANT
DISTANTLY
DISTILLER
DISTEMPER
DISTORTED
DISTRAINT
DISTURBER
DITHYRAMB
DIURNALLY
DIVERGENT
DIVERSELY
DIVERSIFY
DIVERSION
DIVERSITY
DIVERTING
DIVIDABLE
DIVISIBLE
DIVISIBLY
DIVORCIVE
DIVULSION
DIVULSIVE
DIZZINESS
DOCTORATE
DOCTORESS
DOCTRINAL
DODECAGON
DOGMATICS
DOGMATISM
DOGMATIST
DOGMATIZE
DOLEFULLY
DOMINATOR
DOMINICAL
DOMINICAN
DOOR-PLATE
DORMITIVE
DORMITORY
DOUBTABLE
DOUBTLESS
DOUGHTILY
DOWERLESS
DOWNINESS
DOWNRIGHT
DOWNTHROW
DOWN-TRAIN
DOWNWARDS
DRAFTSMAN
DRAGONISH
DRAGON-FLY
DRAINABLE
DRAIN-TILE
DRAIN-TRAP
DRAMATIST
DRAMATIZE
DRAPERIED
DRAVIDIAN
DRAY-HORSE
DREADLESS
DREAMLAND

DREAMLESS
DRESS-COAT
DRIFTLESS
DRIFT-WEED
DRIFT-WOOD
DRINKABLE
DRIVELLER
DROMEDARY
DROP-PRESS
DROP-SCENE
DROPSICAL
DRUIDICAL
DRUM-MAJOR
DRUM-STICK
DRYSALTER
DUALISTIC
DUBIOUSLY
DUCTILELY
DUCTILITY
DULCAMARA
DUMBFOUND
DUODECIMO
DUODENARY
DUPLICATE
DUPLICITY
DURA-MATER
DUSKINESS
DUST-BRAND
DUTEOUSLY
DUTIFULLY
DYER'S-WEED
DYNAMICAL
DYNAMITER
DYSCRASIA
DYSENTERY
DYSPEPSIA
DYSPEPTIC
DZIGGETAI

E

EAGERNESS
EAGLE-EYED
EAGLE-WOOD
EALDORMAN
EAR-COCKLE
EARLINESS
EARNESTLY
EARTH-BORN
EARTH-FLAX
EARTHLING
EARTHWARD
EARTH-WOLF
EARTHWORK
EARTHWORM
EASY-CHAIR
EAVESDROP
EBULLIENT
ECCENTRIC
ECHINATED
ECLAMPSIA
ECONOMICS
ECONOMIST
ECONOMIZE
ECSTASIED
ECTOBLAST
ECTOPLASM
EDELWEISS
EDIBILITY

EDIFICIAL
EDITORIAL
EDUCATION
EDUCATIVE
EEL-BASKET
EFFECTIVE
EFFECTUAL
EFFICIENT
EFFLUENCE
EFFLUVIAL
EFFLUVIUM
EFFLUXION
EFFODIENT
EFFULGENT
EGLANTINE
EGOTHEISM
EGOTISTIC
EGREGIOUS
EGRESSION
EIDER-DUCK
EIDER-DOWN
EIDOGRAPH
EIGHTFOLD
EIGHTIETH
EIRENICON
EJACULATE
EJECTMENT
ELABORATE
ELATERIUM
ELBOW-ROOM
ELDERSHIP
ELDER-WINE
ELECTORAL
ELECTRIFY
ELECTUARY
ELEGANTLY
ELEMENTAL
ELEVATION
ELEVATORY
ELIMINATE
ELLIPSOID
ELMO'S-FIRE
ELOCUTION
ELOHISTIC
ELOPEMENT
ELOQUENCE
ELSEWHERE
ELUCIDATE
ELUTRIATE
EMACIATED
EMANATION
EMBARRASS
EMBATTLED
EMBAY-MENT
EMBELLISH
EMBER-DAYS
EMBER-TIDE
EMBER-WEEK
EMBEZZLER
EMBLEMENT
EMBRACEOR
EMBRACERY
EMBRASURE
EMBROCATE
EMBROIDER
EMBRYONAL
EMBRYONIC
EMBRYOTIC
EMENDATOR
EMERGENCE

EMERGENCY
EMINENTLY
EMMENSITE
EMOLLIENT
EMOLUMENT
EMOTIONAL
EMPHASIZE
EMPHYSEMA
EMPIRICAL
EMPTINESS
EMPYREUMA
EMULATION
EMULATIVE
EMULATORY
EMULOUSLY
EMUNCTORY
ENACTMENT
ENAMELIST
ENCAUSTIC
ENCHANTED
ENCHANTER
ENCHORIAL
ENCLOSURE
ENCOMIAST
ENCOMPASS
ENCOUNTER
ENCOURAGE
ENCRIMSON
ENCRINATE
ENDEARING
ENDEAVOUR
ENDECAGON
ENDEICTIC
ENDEMICAL
ENDLESSLY
ENDOLYMPH
ENDOMORPH
ENDOPLASM
ENDOPLAST
ENDOMOSE
ENDOSPERM
ENDOSTEUM
ENDOSTOME
ENDOWMENT
ENDURABLE
ENDURABLY
ENDURANCE
ENERGETIC
ENERGICAL
ENFEEBLER
ENGINEMAN
ENGISCOPE
ENGLISHRY
ENGRAILED
ENGRAINER
ENGRAVING
ENGROSSER
ENGYSCOPE
ENHYDROUS
ENIGMATIC
ENJOYABLE
ENJOYMENT
ENLIGHTEN
ENLIVENER
ENNEANDER
ENRAPTURE
ENROLMENT
ENTELECHY
ENTERALGY
ENTERITIS

ENTERTAIN
ENTHYMEME
ENTOMICAL
ENTOPHYTE
ENTREATER
ENTREMETS
ENTROCHAL
ENTROPIUM
ENUCLEATE
ENUMERATE
ENUNCIATE
ENVIOUSLY
ENVOYSHIP
EPAULETTE
EPHEMERAL
EPHEMERIS
EPHEMERON
EPICLINAL
EPICUREAN
EPICURISM
EPIDERMAL
EPIDERMIC
EPIDERMIS
EPIDICTIC
EPIGAEOUS
EPIGENOUS
EPIGRAPHY
EPIGYNOUS
EPILEPTIC
EPILOGIZE
EPIPHRAGM
EPIPHYSIS
EPIPHYTIC
EPIPHYTAL
EPISCOPAL
EPISODIAL
EPISTOLIC
EPITAPHIC
EPITOMIST
EPITOMIZE
EPIZOOTIC
EPONYMOUS
EPSOM SALT
EQUALNESS
EQUIPMENT
EQUIPOISE
EQUISETUM
EQUITABLE
EQUITABLY
EQUIVALVE
EQUIVOCAL
EQUIVOQUE
ERADICATE
ERASEMENT
ERECTNESS
EREMITISM
ERIOMETER
ERISTICAL
ERRONEOUS
ERSTWHILE
ERUDITELY
ERUDITION
ERUGINOUS
ERYTHRITE
ESCAPABLE
ESCHEATOR
ESCLANDRE
ESOTERISM
ESPIONAGE
ESPLANADE

ESSENTIAL
ESTAFETTE
ESTAMINET
ESTIMABLE
ESTIMABLY
ESTUARIAN
ESTUARINE
ESURIENCE
ESURIENCY
ET CAETERA
ETERNALLY
ETHICALLY
ETHIOPIAN
ETHMOIDAL
ETHNICISM
ETHNOLOGY
ETIQUETTE
ETYMOLOGY
EUCHARIST
EUCHOLOGY
EULOGICAL
EUPHEMISM
EUPHEMIZE
EUPHONIUM
EUPHORBIA
EVAGINATE
EVANGELIC
EVAPORATE
EVASIVELY
EVENTUATE
EVERGREEN
EVERYBODY
EVIDENTLY
EVOCATION
EVOLUTION
EVOLUTIVE
EXACTNESS
EXAMINANT
EXAMINING
EXANTHEMA
EXARCHATE
EXCAVATOR
EXCEEDING
EXCELLENT
EXCENTRIC
EXCEPTING
EXCEPTION
EXCESSIVE
EXCHANGER
EXCHEQUER
EXCIPIENT
EXCISABLE
EXCISEMAN
EXCITABLE
EXCLAIMER
EXCLUSION
EXCLUSIVE
EXCORIATE
EXCREMENT
EXCRETION
EXCRETIVE
EXCRETORY
EXCULPATE
EXCURRENT
EXCURSION
EXCURSIVE
EXCUSABLE
EXCUSABLY
EXECRABLE
EXECRABLY

EXECUTANT
EXECUTION
EXECUTIVE
EXECUTORY
EXECUTRIX
EXEGETIST
EXEGETICS
EXEMPLARY
EXEMPLIFY
EXEMPTION
EXEQUATUR
EXERCISER
EXFOLIATE
EXHALABLE
EXHAUSTED
EXHIBITER
EXHIBITOR
EXISTENCE
EXOGAMOUS
EXOGENOUS
EXONERATE
EXORCISER
EXOSMOSIS
EXOSMOTIC
EXPANSILE
EXPANSION
EXPANSIVE
EXPECTANT
EXPEDIENT
EXPENSIVE
EXPIATION
EXPIATORY
EXPIRABLE
EXPISCATE
EXPLAINER
EXPLETIVE
EXPLETORY
EXPLICATE
EXPLOITER
EXPLOSION
EXPLOSIVE
EXPOSITOR
EXPOUNDER
EXPRESSLY
EXPULSION
EXPULSIVE
EXPURGATE
EXQUISITE
EXSERTILE
EXSICCATE
EXSICCANT
EXTEMPORE
EXTENSILE
EXTENSION
EXTENSITY
EXTENSIVE
EXTENUATE
EXTERNALS
EXTIRPATE
EXTORTION
EXTRACTOR
EXTRADITE
EXTREMELY
EXTREMIST
EXTREMITY
EXTRICATE
EXTRINSIC
EXTRORSAL
EXTRUSION
EXUBERANT

EXUDATION
EYE-BRIGHT

F

FABACEOUS
FABRICATE
FACETIOUS
FACSIMILE
FACTITIVE
FACTORAGE
FACTORIAL
FAGOT-VOTE
FAINTNESS
FAIRY-LAND
FAITH-CURE
FAITHLESS
FALCATION
FALCONINE
FALDSTOOL
FALLOPIAN
FALSEHOOD
FALSENESS
FALSIFIER
FALTERING
FANATICAL
FANCILESS
FANCY-BALL
FANCY-FAIR
FANCY-FREE
FANCY-WORK
FANTASTIC
FARMHOUSE
FARMSTEAD
FAR-SOUGHT
FASCIATED
FASCICLED
FASCICULE
FASCINATE
FASHIONER
FASTENING
FATEFULLY
FATTINESS
FAULTLESS
FAVEOLATE
FAVOURITE
FEARFULLY
FEATHERED
FEBRICULA
FEBRIFUGE
FECULENCE
FECUNDATE
FECUNDITY
FEELINGLY
FEIGNEDLY
FELLOW-MAN
FELONIOUS
FEMME-SOLE
FENESTRAL
FENIANISM
FENUGREEK
FEOFFMENT
FERACIOUS
FEROCIOUS
FERROTYPE
FERRY-BOAT
FERTILELY
FERTILITY
FERTILIZE

FERVENTLY	FLABELLUM	FORGATHER	FUNNELLED
FERVIDITY	FLACCIDLY	FORGETFUL	FURBISHER
FESTINATE	FLAGELLUM	FORGIVING	FURCATION
FESTIVELY	FLAGEOLET	FORGOTTEN	FURFUROUS
FESTIVITY	FLAGRANCY	FORLORNLY	FURIOUSLY
FETICIDAL	FLAKINESS	FORMALISM	FURNISHED
FOETICIDE	FLAP-EARED	FORMALIST	FURNISHER
FETIDNESS	FLATTERER	FORMALITY	FURNITURE
FETICHISM	FLATULENT	FORMATION	FURTHERER
FETISHISM	FLAUNTING	FORMATIVE	FURTIVELY
FETLOCKED	FLAVOROUS	FORMICARY	FUSILLADE
FEUDALISM	FLAVOURED	FORMULARY	FUSSINESS
FEUDALIST	FLAYFLINT	FORMULATE	FUSTIGATE
FEUDALITY	FLECKLESS	FORMULIZE	FUSTINESS
FEUDALIZE	FLEETNESS	FORNICATE	
FEUDATORY	FLESH-HOOK	FORTHWITH	
FEU-DE-JOIE	FLESHINGS	FORTIFIER	
FIBRIFORM	FLESHLESS	FORTITUDE	**G**
FIBRINOUS	FLESH-MEAT	FORTNIGHT	
FICTIONAL	FLIGHTILY	FORTUNATE	GABARDINE
FIDDLE-BOW	FLINT-LOCK	FOSSILIZE	GABIONAGE
FIDUCIARY	FLIPPANCY	FOSTERSON	GAINSAYER
FIELD-BOOK	FLOOD-GATE	FOUNDLING	GALANTINE
FIELDFARE	FLOOD-MARK	FOUNDRESS	GALENICAL
FIELD-WORK	FLOOD-TIDE	FOUNDRIES	GALINGALE
FIERINESS	FLOREATED	FOURPENCE	GALLANTLY
FIFE-MAJOR	FLORIDITY	FOURSCORE	GALLANTRY
FIFTEENTH	FLOSCULAR	FOVEOLATE	GALLERIES
FIGURABLE	FLOSS-SILK	FOXHUNTER	GALLICISM
FIGURANTE	FLOTATION	FRACTIONS	GALLINULE
FILACEOUS	FLOWERING	FRAGRANCE	GALLIVANT
FILIATION	FLOWER-POT	FRAGRANCY	GALLOONED
FILIGREED	FLUCTUANT	FRANCHISE	GALLOPADE
FILLETING	FLUCTUATE	FRANCOLIN	GALLOWSES
FILLISTER	FLUOR-SPAR	FRANGIBLE	GALVANISM
FILMINESS	FLUXIONAL	FRANKNESS	GALVANIST
FILOPLUME	FLYBITTEN	FRATERNAL	GALVANIZE
FIMBRIATE	FLY-FISHER	FRAUDLESS	GAMBADOES
FINANCIAL	FLYING-FOX	FREEMASON	GANGLIONS
FINANCIER	FOGGINESS	FREESTONE	GANNISTER
FINEDRAWN	FOG-SIGNAL	FREEZIBLE	GARDENING
FIN-FOOTED	FOLIATION	FREIGHTER	GARGARISM
FINGERING	FOLLOWING	FRENCHMAN	GARMENTED
FINICALLY	FOOLHARDY	FREQUENCY	GARNISHER
FINICKING	FOOLISHLY	FRESHNESS	GARNITURE
FIRE-ALARM	FOOT-BOARD	FRETFULLY	GARRETEER
FIRE-BRAND	FOOT-CLOTH	FRICASSEE	GARROTTER
FIRE-BRICK	FOOT-POUND	FRICATIVE	GARRULITY
FIRE-EATER	FOOTPRINT	FRIGHTFUL	GARRULOUS
FIRE-GUARD	FOOT-STALK	FRIGIDITY	GASCONADE
FIRE-IRONS	FOOTSTOOL	FRIVOLITY	GASHOLDER
FIREPLACE	FOPPISHLY	FRIVOLOUS	GASOMETER
FIRE-PROOF	FORASMUCH	FRONTLESS	GASOMETRY
FIRMAMENT	FORBEARER	FROSTBITE	GASPINGLY
FIRST-BORN	FROBIDDEN	FROSTWORK	GASTROPOD
FIRST-HAND	FORCELESS	FROWARDLY	GASTRALGY
FIRSTLING	FORCEMEAT	FRUGALITY	GASTRITIS
FIRST-RATE	FORECLOSE	FRUITERER	GATHERING
FISHERMAN	FOREFRONT	FRUITLESS	GAUCHERIE
FISHINESS	FOREGOING	FRUTICOSE	GAUDEAMUS
FISH-JOINT	FOREIGNER	FRUTICOUS	GAUDINESS
FISH-LOUSE	FOREJUDGE	FUGACIOUS	GAUGEABLE
FISH-PLATE	FORENAMED	FULGURITE	GAVELKIND
FISH-SLICE	FORESTALL	FULGUROUS	GAZETTEER
FISH-SPEAR	FORESTINE	FULMINATE	GELSEMIUM
FISHWOMAN	FORETASTE	FULSOMELY	GEMMATION
FISTULOSE	FORETOKEN	FUNDAMENT	GENEALOGY
FISTULOUS	FORETOOTH	FUNGIFORM	GENERABLE
FITTINGLY	FOREWOMAN	FUNGOLOGY	GENERALLY
FIXEDNESS	FORFEITER	FUNICULAR	GENERATOR
			GENERICAL

GENETICAL
GENIALITY
GENITIVAL
GENTEELLY
GENTILITY
GENTLEMAN
GENTLEMEN
GENUFLECT
GENUINELY
GEODESIST
GEOGRAPHY
GEOLOGIST
GEOLOGIAN
GEOMANCER
GEOMANTIC
GEOMETRIC
GEOPONICS
GERFALCON
GERMANDER
GERMANIUM
GERMICIDE
GERMINANT
GERMINATE
GERUNDIAL
GERUNDIVE
GIANTSHIP
GIBBERISH
GIBBOSITY
GIBBOUSLY
GIDDINESS
GINGLYMUS
GIPSOLOGY
GIRANDOLE
GLADIATOR
GLANDERED
GLANDULAR
GLASSWORT
GLAUCOSIS
GLOBOSITY
GLOBULOSE
GLOMERATE
GLOWINGLY
GLUEYNESS
GLUTINATE
GLUTINOUS
GLYCERINE
GLYPTODON
GNATHONIC
GNOMONICS
GNOMONIST
GODFATHER
GODLESSLY
GODLINESS
GODMOTHER
GOFFERING
GOLDFINCH
GOLDSMITH
GONOPHORE
GOOSANDER
GORGONEAN
GORGONIZE
GOSPELLER
GOSSAMERY
GOSSIPPED
GOTHICISM
GOUTINESS
GOVERNESS
GRACELESS
GRACILITY
GRADATION

GRADATORY
GRADUALLY
GRADUATOR
GRAMINEAL
GRAMMATIC
GRANDIOSE
GRANDNESS
GRANDSIRE
GRANITOID
GRANTABLE
GRANULATE
GRANULITE
GRANULOUS
GRANULOSE
GRASPABLE
GRATIFIER
GRATITUDE
GRATULATE
GRAUWACKE
GRAVELESS
GRAVENESS
GRAVITATE
GRAYHOUND
GRAYWACKE
GREATCOAT
GREATNESS
GREENBACK
GREENHORN
GREENNESS
GREGORIAN
GRENADIER
GRENADINE
GREYHOUND
GRIEVANCE
GRIMALKIN
GRIMINESS
GRIPINGLY
GRISAILLE
GROCERIES
GROOMSMAN
GROPINGLY
GROSSBEAK
GROSSNESS
GROTESQUE
GROUNDSEL
GROVELLER
GRUFFNESS
GUARANTEE
GUARANTOR
GUARDABLE
GUARDEDLY
GUARDSMAN
GUERRILLA
GUIDELESS
GUILDHALL
GUILELESS
GUILLEMOT
GUILTLESS
GUMMINESS
GUNPOWDER
GUSHINGLY
GUSTATORY
GYMNASIAL
GYMNASIUM
GYMNASTIC
GYNOECIUM
GYNOPHORE
GYRFALCON
GYROSCOPE

H

HABERGEON
HABITABLE
HABITUATE
HACKBERRY
HACKNEYED
HAEMATOID
HAGGARDLY
HAGIOLOGY
HAILSTONE
HAIRINESS
HALFPENNY
HALFPENCE
HALLOWMAS
HALOPHYTE
HALOSCOPE
HAMADRYAD
HAMMERMAN
HAMSTRING
HANDINESS
HANDIWORK
HANDSPIKE
HARANGUER
HARBOURER
HARDIHOOD
HARDINESS
HARLEQUIN
HARMFULLY
HARMONICA
HARMONICS
HARMONIST
HARMONIUM
HARMONIZE
HARMOTOME
HARNESSER
HARPOONER
HARSHNESS
HARVESTER
HASTINESS
HATCHMENT
HATEFULLY
HAUGHTILY
HAVERSACK
HAYMAKING
HAZARDOUS
HEADINESS
HEALTHFUL
HEALTHILY
HEARTACHE
HEARTBURN
HEARTFELT
HEARTLESS
HEARTSOME
HEATHENRY
HEAVINESS
HEBRAICAL
HEBRIDIAN
HEEDFULLY
HEGEMONIC
HEINOUSLY
HELIOSTAT
HELIOTYPE
HELLEBORE
HELLENISM
HELLENIST
HELLENIZE
HELLISHLY
HEMATOSIS

HEMICYCLE
HEMIPLEGY
HEMISTICH
HENDIADYS
HEPATICAL
HEPTAGLOT
HEPTARCHY
HERBALIST
HERBARIUM
HERBIVORE
HERCULEAN
HEREABOUT
HEREAFTER
HERETICAL
HERITABLE
HERITABLY
HERMITAGE
HERMITARY
HERONSHAW
HESITANCY
HESITATOR
HESPERIAN
HETAIRISM
HETERODOX
HETERONYM
HETEROPOD
HEURISTIC
HEXACHORD
HEXAGONAL
HEXAMETER
HEXASTYLE
HEXATEUCH
HIBERNATE
HIBERNIAN
HIDEOUSLY
HIEMATION
HIERARCHY
HIEROGRAM
HIEROLOGY
HILARIOUS
HILLINESS
HINDRANCE
HINDOOISM
HIPPIATRY
HIPPOCRAS
HIRUNDINE
HISPIDITY
HISTOGENY
HISTOLOGY
HISTORIAN
HOARHOUND
HOARINESS
HOBGOBLIN
HOBNAILED
HODIERNAL
HODOMETER
HOIDENISH
HOLLYHOCK
HOLOCAUST
HOLOGRAPH
HOMESTEAD
HOMEWARDS
HOMICIDAL
HOMILETIC
HOMOGRAPH
HOMOLOGUE
HOMOPHONE
HOMUNCULE
HONORABIC
HONORABLE

HOPEFULLY	ICHNOLOGY	IMPROBITY	INELASTIC
HOREHOUND	ICHTHYOID	IMPROMPTU	INELEGANT
HOROLOGER	ICONOLOGY	IMPROVING	INEQUABLE
HOROMETRY	IDEALIZER	IMPROVISE	INERTNESS
HOROSCOPE	IDENTICAL	IMPRUDENT	INFANTILE
HOROSCOPY	IDEOGRAPH	IMPUDENCE	INFANTINE
HORSEBACK	IDIOGRAPH	IMPULSION	INFATUATE
HORSEWHIP	IDIOMATIC	IMPULSIVE	INFECTION
HORTATION	IDIOPATHY	IMPUTABLE	INFECTIVE
HORTATIVE	IDIOTICAL	INABILITY	INFERABLE
HORTATORY	IGNITABLE	INAMORATO	INFERENCE
HOSTILELY	IGNORAMUS	INAMORATA	INFERTILE
HOSTILITY	IGNORANCE	INANIMATE	INFIRMARY
HOTTENTOT	IGUANODON	INANITION	INFIRMITY
HOUNDFISH	ILLEGALLY	INAUDIBLE	INFLATION
HOUSEHOLD	ILLEGIBLE	INAUGURAL	INFLEXION
HOUSELESS	ILLEGIBLY	INBREATHE	INFLUENCE
HOUSEMAID	ILLIBERAL	INCAPABLE	INFLUENZA
HOUSEROOM	ILLICITLY	INCARNATE	INFLUXION
HOUSEWIFE	ILLOGICAL	INCAUTION	INFORMANT
HOWSOEVER	IMAGINARY	INCENTIVE	INFURIATE
HUCKABACK	IMBRICATE	INCEPTION	INFUSIBLE
HUFFINESS	IMBROGLIO	INCEPTIVE	INFUSORIA
HUMANNESS	IMBUEMENT	INCESSANT	INGENIOUS
HUMECTATE	IMITATION	INCIDENCE	INGENUITY
HUMILIATE	IMITATIVE	INCIPIENT	INGENUOUS
HUMOURIST	IMMANENCE	INCLEMENT	INGLUVIES
HUNCHBACK	IMMANENCY	INCLOSURE	INHABITER
HUNDREDTH	IMMEDIACY	INCLUSIVE	INHERENCE
HUNGARIAN	IMMEDIATE	INCOGNITO	INHERENCY
HURRICANE	IMMENSELY	INCOGNITA	INHERITOR
HURRIEDLY	IMMENSITY	INCOMMODE	INHUMANLY
HURTFULLY	IMMERSION	INCORRECT	INJECTION
HUSBANDLY	IMMIGRANT	INCORRUPT	INJURIOUS
HUSBANDRY	IMMIGRATE	INCREMATE	INJUSTICE
HUSKINESS	IMMINENCE	INCREMENT	INNERMOST
HYBRIDISM	IMMODESTY	INCUBATOR	INNERVATE
HYBRIDITY	IMMOLATOR	INCUBUSES	INNKEEPER
HYBRIDIZE	IMMORALLY	INCULCATE	INNOCENCE
HYDRANGEA	IMMOVABLE	INCULPATE	INNOCENCY
HYDRAULIC	IMMOVABLY	INCUMBENT	INNOCUOUS
HYDROLOGY	IMMUTABLE	INCURABLY	INNOVATOR
HYDROPULT	IMMUTABLY	INCURVATE	INNUENDOS
HYDROSOMA	IMPARTIAL	INDECORUM	INOCULATE
HYDROZOON	IMPASSION	INDELIBLE	INODOROUS
HYETOLOGY	IMPASSIVE	INDELIBLY	INORGANIC
HYGIENISM	IMPATIENT	INDEMNIFY	INQUILINE
HYLOZOISM	IMPEACHER	INDEMNITY	INQUIRING
HYMNOLOGY	IMPEDANCE	INDENTURE	INQUIRIES
HYPALLAGE	IMPELLENT	INDEXICAL	INSATIATE
HYPERBOLA	IMPENDENT	INDICATOR	INSENSATE
HYPERBOLE	IMPERFECT	INDICTION	INSERTION
HYPETHRAL	IMPERIOUS	INDIGENCE	INSIDIOUS
HYPNOTISM	IMPETRATE	INDIGNANT	INSINCERE
HYPNOTIZE	IMPETUOUS	INDIGNITY	INSINUATE
HYPOCAUST	IMPINGENT	INDISPOSE	INSOLENCE
HYPOCRISY	IMPIOUSLY	INDOLENCE	INSOLUBLE
HYPOCRITE	IMPLEADER	INDUCIBLE	INSOLVENT
HYPOGAEON	IMPLEMENT	INDUCTILE	INSPECTOR
HYPONASTY	IMPLICATE	INDUCTION	INSTANTLY
HYPOSTYLE	IMPLIEDLY	INDUCTIVE	INSTIGATE
HYSTERICS	IMPOLITIC	INDUEMENT	INSTITUTE
	IMPORTANT	INDULGENT	INSULARLY
	IMPORTUNE	INDWELLER	INSULATOR
	IMPOSABLE	INEBRIANT	INSULTING
I	IMPOSTURE	INEBRIATE	INSURABLE
	IMPOTENCE	INEBRIETY	INSURANCE
ICELANDER	IMPOTENCY	INEBRIOUS	INSURGENT
ICELANDIC	IMPOUNDER	INEFFABLE	INTEGRANT
ICHNEUMON	IMPRECATE	INEFFABLY	INTEGRATE
ICHNOLITE			

INTEGRITY
INTELLECT
INTENDANT
INTENSELY
INTENSIFY
INTENSION
INTENSITY
INTENSIVE
INTENTION
INTERMENT
INTERCEDE
INTERCEPT
INTERDICT
INTERFACE
INTERFERE
INTERFUSE
INTERJECT
INTERLACE
INTERLARD
INTERLINE
INTERLOCK
INTERLOPE
INTERLUDE
INTERMENT
INTERNODE
INTERPOSE
INTERPRET
INTERRUPT
INTERSECT
INTERVENE
INTERVIEW
INTESTACY
INTESTATE
INTESTINE
INTORTION
INTRICACY
INTRICATE
INTRIGUER
INTRINSIC
INTRODUCE
INTROVERT
INTRUSION
INTRUSIVE
INTUITION
INTUITIVE
INTUMESCE
INUREMENT
INUTILITY
INVECTIVE
INVENTION
INVENTIVE
INVENTORY
INVERSELY
INVERSION
INVIDIOUS
INVIOLATE
INVISIBLE
INVISIBLY
INVOLUTED
INWREATHE
INWROUGHT
IRASCIBLE
IRASCIBLY
IRKSOMELY
IRONSMITH
IRRADIANT
IRRADIATE
IRREGULAR
IRRIGUOUS
IRRITABLE

IRRITABLY
IRRUPTION
IRRUPTIVE
ISINGLASS
ISOCLINAL
ISOCLINIC
ISOLATION
ISOMERISM
ISOMETRIC
ISOSCELES
ISRAELITE
ISSUELESS
ITCHINESS
ITERATIVE
ITERATION
ITINERANT
ITINERARY
ITINERATE

J

JABORANDI
JACOBINIC
JACOBITIC
JANSENIST
JANSENISM
JEALOUSLY
JEERINGLY
JENNETING
JEREMIADE
JERFALCON
JESSAMINE
JESUITISM
JETTINESS
JEWELLERY
JOCUNDITY
JOCULARLY
JOLLINESS
JOURNEYER
JOVIALITY
JOYLESSLY
JUDGESHIP
JUDICIARY
JUDICIOUS
JUICELESS
JUICINESS
JUNIORITY
JURIDICAL
JUSTIFIER
JUXTAPOSE

K

KAINOZOIC
KENTLEDGE
KERATITIS
KERNELLED
KIDNAPPER
KILOMETRE
KILLINGLY
KINEMATIC
KINGCRAFT
KINSWOMAN
KITCHENER
KITTENISH
KITTIWAKE
KNAVISHLY
KNIGHTAGE

KNOWINGLY
KNOWLEDGE
KRUMMHORN

L

LABIALIZE
LABORIOUS
LABOURING
LABYRINTH
LACERABLE
LACERATED
LACERTINE
LACHRYMAL
LACINIATE
LACONICAL
LACTATION
LACTIFUGE
LACUNARIA
LACUSTRAL
LAEVIGATE
LAMINATED
LARGENESS
LARGHETTO
LARVIFORM
LARYNGEAL
LARYNGEAN
LASSITUDE
LASTINGLY
LATERALLY
LAUDATORY
LAUGHABLE
LAUGHABLY
LAUNDRESS
LAURELLED
LAWGIVING
LAWLESSLY
LAZARETTO
LEAFINESS
LEAKINESS
LEARNEDLY
LEASEHOLD
LECHEROUS
LEGENDARY
LEGIONARY
LEGISLATE
LEISURELY
LENGTHILY
LENIENTLY
LENTIFORM
LEPROUSLY
LEPROSITY
LETHARGIC
LETTERING
LEVANTINE
LEVELLING
LEVELNESS
LEVIATHAN
LEVIGABLE
LEVITICAL
LEXICALLY
LIABILITY
LIBELLOUS
LIBERALLY
LIBERATOR
LIBRARIAN
LIBRATION
LIBRATORY
LICHENOUS

LICKERISH
LIENTERIC
LIGATURED
LIGHTNESS
LIGHTNING
LIGHTSOME
LIGNIFORM
LIGULATED
LIMACEOUS
LIMESTONE
LIMITABLE
LIMITEDLY
LIMITLESS
LIMPIDITY
LIMPINGLY
LINEAMENT
LINEOLATE
LINGERING
LINGULATE
LIPPITUDE
LIQUATION
LIQUEFIER
LIQUIDATE
LIQUIDITY
LIQUORICE
LISTERISM
LITERALLY
LITHENESS
LITHESOME
LITHOIDAL
LITHOLOGY
LITHOTOMY
LITHOTYPY
LITIGABLE
LITIGATOR
LITURGIES
LITURGIST
LIVERWORT
LIVERYMAN
LIVIDNESS
LIXIVIATE
LIXIVIOUS
LODESTONE
LOATHSOME
LOCKSMITH
LOCOMOTOR
LOFTINESS
LOGARITHM
LOGICALLY
LOGOMACHY
LOGOMANIA
LONGEVITY
LONGEVOUS
LONGICORN
LONGINGLY
LONGITUDE
LOOPHOLED
LOOSENESS
LOQUACITY
LORGNETTE
LORICATED
LOTOPHAGI
LOUSINESS
LOWERMOST
LOWLANDER
LOWLINESS
LUBRICATE
LUBRICITY
LUCIDNESS
LUCIFUGAL

LUCKINESS	MARCASITE	MENISCOID	MISDIRECT
LUCRATIVE	MARCHPANE	MENSTRUAL	MISEMPLOY
LUCIDNESS	MARGARINE	MENSTRUUM	MISERABLE
LUCUBRATE	MARKETING	MENTATION	MISERABLY
LUDICROUS	MARMALADE	MERCENARY	MISGIVING
LUMPISHLY	MARMOREAL	MERCILESS	MISGOVERN
LUNULATED	MARQUETRY	MERCURIAL	MISINFORM
LUSTFULLY	MARSUPIAL	MERCUROUS	MISMANAGE
LUSTINESS	MARSUPIUM	MERGANSER	MISREPORT
LUXURIANT	MARTIALLY	MERRIMENT	MISSELTOE
LUXURIATE	MARTINMAS	MESENTERY	MISSHAPEN
LUXURIOUS	MARTYRDOM	MESMERISM	MISTINESS
LYMPHATIC	MARTYRIZE	MESMERIST	MISTLETOE
	MASCULINE	MESMERIZE	MITRIFORM
	MASSAGIST	MESSENGER	MNEMONICS
	MASSINESS	MESSIANIC	MOBOCRACY
	MASSIVELY	MESSIEURS	MOCKINGLY
M	MASTERFUL	METALLINE	MODELLING
	MASTICATE	METALLIST	MODERATOR
MACARONIS	MATCHABLE	METALLIZE	MODERNISM
MACARONIC	MATCHLESS	METALLOID	MODERNIST
MACHINATE	MATCHLOCK	METEORITE	MODERNIZE
MACHINERY	MATERNITY	METHEGLIN	MODILLION
MACHINIST	MATRICIDE	METHODISM	MODULATOR
MACINTOSH	MATRIMONY	METHODIST	MOISTNESS
MACROCOSM	MATRONAGE	METHODIZE	MOLECULAR
MACRUROUS	MATRONIZE	METHOUGHT	MOLLIFIER
MADREPORE	MATUTINAL	METHYSTIC	MOMENTARY
MAGDALENE	MAUNDERER	METONYMIC	MOMENTOUS
MAGICALLY	MAUSOLEAN	METROLOGY	MONACHISM
MAGNALIUM	MAUSOLEUM	METRONOME	MONADICAL
MAGNESIAN	MAWKISHLY	MEZZANINE	MONADELPH
MAGNESIUM	MAXILLARY	MEZZOTINT	MONARCHAL
MAGNETISM	MAYONAISE	MIASMATIC	MONARCHIC
MAGNETIZE	MAYORALTY	MICACEOUS	MONASTERY
MAGNIFIER	MEALINESS	MICROBIAL	MONATOMIC
MAGNITUDE	MEANINGLY	MICROBIAN	MONEYLESS
MAHARAJAH	MEANWHILE	MICROCOSM	MONGOLIAN
MAHARANEE	MEATINESS	MICROCYTE	MONITRESS
MAHOMEDAN	MECHANICS	MICROLOGY	MONKEYISM
MAHOMETAN	MECHANISM	MICROPYLE	MONOCHORD
MAJORSHIP	MECHANIST	MICROTOME	MONODRAMA
MAJUSCULE	MECHANIZE	MICROZOON	MONOGRAPH
MALACHITE	MEDALLION	MICROZYME	MONOLOGUE
MALADROIT	MEDALLIST	MICTURATE	MONOMANIA
MALARIOUS	MEDIAEVAL	MIDDLEMAN	MONOPLANE
MALICIOUS	MEDIATELY	MIDSUMMER	MONOPTOTE
MALIGNANT	MEDIATIVE	MIDWIFERY	MONOSPERM
MALIGNITY	MEDIATIZE	MIDWINTER	MONSIGNOR
MALLEABLE	MEDICABLE	MIGRATION	MONSTROUS
MALLEOLUS	MEDICALLY	MIGRATORY	MONTICULE
MAMMALIAN	MEDICINAL	MILESTONE	MOODINESS
MAMMALOGY	MEDULLARY	MILITANCY	MOONLIGHT
MAMMONISM	MEGAFARAD	MILKINESS	MOONSHINE
MAMMONIST	MELANOSIS	MILLIPORE	MOONSHINY
MAMMONITE	MELAPHYRE	MILLINERY	MOONSTONE
MANDATARY	MELIBOEAN	MILLIONTH	MORALIZER
MANDATORY	MELIORATE	MILLSTONE	MORBIDITY
MANDOLINE	MELODIOUS	MIMETICAL	MORDACITY
MANDUCATE	MELODRAMA	MINDFULLY	MORMONISM
MANGANESE	MELODRAME	MINEINGLY	MORMONITE
MANGANITE	MELTINGLY	MINIATURE	MORMONIST
MANICHEAN	MEMOIRIST	MINORSHIP	MORTALITY
MANIFESTO	MEMORABLE	MIRIFICAL	MORTGAGEE
MANIPULAR	MEMORANDA	MIRTHLESS	MORTGAGER
MANLINESS	MEMORIZER	MISBEHAVE	MOSAICIST
MANNERISM	MENAGERIE	MISBELIEF	MOSSINESS
MANNERIST	MENDACITY	MISCHANCE	MOULDABLE
MANOEUVRE	MENDICANT	MISCREANT	MOUSTACHE
MANOMETER	MENDICITY	MISDEMEAN	MUCRONATE

MUDDINESS
MUFFETTEE
MULTIFOIL
MULLIONED
MULTIFORM
MULTIPLEX
MULTITUDE
MUMPISHLY
MUNDANELY
MUNICIPAL
MURDERESS
MURDEROUS
MURICATED
MURMURING
MUSCADINE
MUSCOLOGY
MUSCOVADO
MUSCOVITE
MUSICALLY
MUSKETTER
MUSKETOON
MUSKETRY
MUSSULMAN
MUSTINESS
MUTILATOR
MUTTERING
MYOGRAPHY
MYONICITY
MYRIORAMA
MYROBALAN
MYSTERIES
MYSTICISM
MYTHOLOGY

N

NAILERESS
NAKEDNESS
NAPPINESS
NARCISSUS
NARCOTISM
NARCOTIZE
NARRATION
NARRATIVE
NASEBERRY
NASTINESS
NATROLITE
NATTINESS
NATURALLY
NAUGHTILY
NAUTILOID
NAVIGABLE
NAVIGABLY
NAVIGATOR
NECESSARY
NECESSITY
NECKCLOTH
NECROLOGY
NECTAREAL
NECTAREAN
NECTARINE
NECTAROUS
NEEDFULLY
NEEDINESS
NEFARIOUS
NEGLIGENT
NEGOCIATE
NEGOTIATE
NEIGHBOUR

NEOLITHIC
NEOLOGIAN
NEOLOGISM
NEOLOGIST
NEOLOGIZE
NEOTERISM
NEOTERIZE
NEPENTHES
NEPHALISM
NEPHALIST
NEPHELOID
NEPHRITIC
NEPHRITIS
NEPTUNIAN
NERVATION
NERVELESS
NERVOUSLY
NESCIENCE
NESTORIAN
NEURALGIA
NEURALGIC
NEURILITY
NEUROLOGY
NEUROPTER
NEUROTOMY
NEUTRALLY
NEVERMORE
NEWSPAPER
NEWTONIAN
NICTATION
NICTITATE
NIGGARDLY
NIGHTFALL
NIGHTLESS
NIGHTMARE
NIGHTWARD
NIGRITUDE
NINETIETH
NOBLENESS
NOCTURNAL
NOISELESS
NOISINESS
NOISOMELY
NOMINALLY
NOMINATOR
NONENTITY
NONPAREIL
NORMALIZE
NORTHERLY
NORTHWARD
NORWEGIAN
NOSTALGIA
NOTOCHORD
NOTORIETY
NOTORIOUS
NOURISHER
NOVELTIES
NOVENNIAL
NOVITIATE
NOWHITHER
NOXIOUSLY
NUCLEOLUS
NULLIFIER
NUMERABLE
NUMERALLY
NUMERATOR
NUMERICAL
NUMMULARY
NUMMULITE
NUNNERIES

NUTRIMENT
NUTRITION
NUTRITIVE
NYSTAGMUS

O

OASTHOUSE
OBBLIGATO
OBCONICAL
OBCORDATE
OBEDIENCE
OBEISANCE
OBESENESS
OBFUSCATE
OBJECTIFY
OBJECTION
OBJECTIVE
OBJURGATE
OBLIQUELY
OBLIQUITY
OBLIVIOUS
OBNOXIOUS
OBSCENELY
OBSCENITY
OBSCURANT
OBSCURELY
OBSCURITY
OBSECRATE
OBSEQUIES
OBSERVANT
OBSERVING
OBSESSION
OBSTETRIC
OBSTINACY
OBSTINATE
OBSTRUENT
OBTRUSION
OBTRUSIVE
OBTURATOR
OBVIOUSLY
OBVOLUTED
OCCIPITAL
OCCLUSION
OCCULTISM
OCCUPANCY
OCELLATED
OCTAGONAL
OCTASTYLE
OCTENNIAL
OCTOPUSES
OCULIFORM
ODALISQUE
ODDFELLOW
ODONTALGY
ODOROUSLY
ODOURLESS
OENANTHIC
OFFENSIVE
OFFERTORY
OFFICIATE
OFFICINAL
OFFICIOUS
OFFSPRING
OLECRANON
OLEOGRAPH
OLFACTORY
OLIGARCHY
OMINOUSLY

OMISSIBLE
ONEROUSLY
ONSLAUGHT
OPERATION
OPERATIVE
OPERCULAR
OPERCULUM
OPEROSELY
OPEROSITY
OPHIOLOGY
OPINIONED
OPODELDOC
OPPORTUNE
OPPOSABLE
OPPRESSOR
OPPUGNANT
OPTICALLY
OPTIMATES
OPTIMETER
OPTOMETER
OPULENTLY
ORANGEADE
ORANGEMAN
ORANGEISM
ORBICULAR
ORCHESTRA
ORDERLESS
ORDINANCE
ORGANICAL
ORGANIZED
ORGANIZER
ORGANZINE
ORGIASTIC
ORIENTATE
ORIFLAMME
ORIGINATE
OROGRAPHY
ORPHANAGE
ORTHODOXY
ORTHOEPIC
ORTHOGAMY
ORTHOPTER
OSCILLATE
OSCITANCY
OSSIFRAGE
OSTENSIVE
OSTEOLOGY
OSTEOTOMY
OSTIOLATE
OSTRACEAN
OSTRACION
OSTRACISM
OSTRACIZE
OSTROGOTH
OTHERNESS
OTHERWISE
OTOLOGIST
OTORRHOEA
OUBLIETTE
OURSELVES
OUTERMOST
OUTFITTER
OUTGROWTH
OUTNUMBER
OUTRIGGER
OUTSPOKEN
OUTSPREAD
OUTWARDLY
OVERBOARD
OVERBUILD

OVERCLOUD	PANTHEIST	PECULATOR	PETARDIER
OVERCROWD	PANTOMIME	PECUNIARY	PETECHIAE
OVERDRESS	PAPILLARY	PEDAGOGIC	PETECHIAL
OVERDRIVE	PAPILLATE	PEDAGOGUE	PETIOLARY
OVERGORGE	PAPILLOSE	PEDICULAR	PETIOLATE
OVERISSUE	PARABASIS	PEDOMETER	PETROLOGY
OVERMATCH	PARABOLIC	PEEVISHLY	PETROLEUM
OVERNIGHT	PARACHUTE	PERIASTIC	PETTICOAT
OVERPOWER	PARACLETE	PELASGIAN	PETTINESS
OVERREACH	PARAGRAPH	PELLITORY	PETTISHLY
OVERSHOOT	PARALYSIS	PENCILLED	PETTITOES
OVERSIGHT	PARALYTIC	PENDENTLY	PETULANCE
OVERSLEEP	PARAMATTA	PENDULATE	PETULANCY
OVERSTATE	PARAMOUNT	PENDULOUS	PHAENOGAM
OVERSTOCK	PARANYMPH	PENETRANT	PHALANGER
OVERTHROW	PARAPETED	PENETRATE	PHALANGES
OVERTRADE	PARAPODIA	PENINSULA	PHALANXES
OVERVALUE	PARATAXIS	PENITENCE	PHALAROPE
OVERWEIGH	PARBUCKLE	PENNILESS	PHARISAIC
OVERWHELM	PARCHMENT	PENNONCEL	PHAROLOGY
OVIFEROUS	PAREGORIC	PENSIONER	PHENICIAN
OVIGEROUS	PARENESIS	PENSIVELY	PHILATELY
OVIPAROUS	PARENETIC	PENTAGLOT	PHILIPPIC
OVULATION	PARENTAGE	PENTAGRAM	PHILOGYNY
OWNERSHIP	PARGETING	PENTANDER	PHILOLOGY
OXIDATION	PARHELION	PENTARCHY	PHILOMATH
OXYGENATE	PAROCHIAL	PENTECOST	PHILOMELA
OXYGENIZE	PARODICAL	PENTHOUSE	PHLEBITIS
OXYGENOUS	PAROTITIS	PENULTIMA	PHOCACEAN
OZOCERITE	PARQUETRY	PENURIOUS	PHONATION
OZOKERITE	PARRAKEET	PERCEIVER	PHONETICS
	PARRICIDE	PERCHANCE	PHONOGRAM
	PARSEEISM	PERCOLATE	PHONOLOGY
P	PARSIMONY	PERDITION	PHONOTYPE
	PARSONAGE	PERENNIAL	PHONOTYPY
PACHYDERM	PARTIALLY	PERFECTER	PHOSPHATE
PACKSHEET	PARTITION	PERFECTLY	PHOSPHIDE
PADEMELON	PARTITIVE	PERFERVID	PHOTOLOGY
PAEDAGOGY	PARTRIDGE	PERFORATE	PHOTOTYPE
PAGEANTRY	PASSENGER	PERFORMER	PHOTOTYPY
PAILLASSE	PASSERINE	PERFUMERY	PHRENETIC
PAINFULLY	PASSIONAL	PERIMETER	PHRENITIS
PALAESTRA	PASSIVELY	PERIPETIA	PHYCOLOGY
PALANKEEN	PASSIVITY	PERIPHERY	PHYLLOPOD
PALATABLE	PASTICCIO	PERISPERM	PHYSICIAN
PALATABLY	PASTORATE	PERISPORE	PHYSICISM
PALEOLOGY	PASTURAGE	PERISTOME	PHYSICIST
PALESTRAL	PATCHOULI	PERISTYLE	PHYTOGENY
PALESTRIC	PATCHOULY	PERMANENT	PHYTOTOMY
PALFREYED	PATCHWORK	PERMEABLE	PICANINNY
PALLADIUM	PATERNITY	PERMEABLY	PICKABACK
PALMARIAN	PATHOLOGY	PERMITTEE	PICKTHANK
PALMATELY	PATIENTLY	PERMITTER	PICTORIAL
PALMISTER	PATRIARCH	PERPETUAL	PEACEMEAL
PALMISTRY	PATRICIAN	PERSECUTE	PIETISTIC
PALPATION	PATRIMONY	PERSIMMON	PIGMENTAL
PALPEBRAL	PATRIOTIC	PERSONAGE	PIKESTAFF
PALPIFORM	PATRISTIC	PERSONATE	PILLORIED
PALPITATE	PATRONAGE	PERSONIFY	PIMPERNEL
PALSGRAVE	PATRONESS	PERSONNEL	PINCHBECK
PALUSTRAL	PATRONIZE	PERSUADER	PINNATELY
PANDERESS	PAUPERISM	PERTINENT	PIPISTREL
PANDERISM	PAUPERIZE	PERTURBER	PIQUANTLY
PANDURATE	PAYMASTER	PERTUSION	PIRATICAL
PANEGYRIC	PEACEABLE	PERVASIVE	PIROUETTE
PANELLING	PEACEABLY	PERVERTER	PISCIFORM
PANOPLIED	PEASANTRY	PESSIMISM	PISOLITIC
PANTALETS	PECCANTLY	PESSIMIST	PISTACHIO
PANTALOON	PECCARIES	PESSIMIZE	PITCHFORK
PANTHEISM	PECTINATE	PESTILENT	PITCHPIPE

PITEOUSLY	POLLARCHY	PRELATIST	PROLUSION
PITHECOID	POLLENIZE	PRELATURE	PROMENADE
PITHINESS	POLLINATE	PRELECTOR	PROMINENT
PITIFULLY	POLLUTION	PRELUSIVE	PROMISING
PITUITARY	POLONAISE	PREMATURE	PROMOTION
PITUITOUS	POLYANDRY	PREMONISH	PROMOTIVE
PITYINGLY	POLYARCHY	PREOCCUPY	PRONATION
PIZZICATO	POLYGONAL	PREORDAIN	PRONENESS
PLACELESS	POLYGRAPH	PREPOTENT	PRONOUNCE
PLACENTAL	POLYPHONY	PREPUTIAL	PROOEMIUM
PLACIDITY	POLYPIDOM	PRESBYTER	PROPAGATE
PLAINNESS	POLYSCOPE	PRESCIENT	PROPELLER
PLAINTIFF	POLYSTYLE	PRESCRIBE	PROPHETIC
PLAINTIVE	POLYZONAL	PRESCRIPT	PROROGATE
PLANETARY	POMACEOUS	PRESENTEE	PROSCRIBE
PLANETOID	POMPHOLYX	PRESENTLY	PROSECTOR
PLANTLESS	POMPOSITY	PRESERVER	PROSELUTE
PLAQUETTE	POMPOUSLY	PRESIDENT	PROSELYTE
PLASMATIC	PONDEROUS	PRESUMING	PROSINESS
PLASTERER	PONTONIER	PRETENDED	PROSODIAL
PLATINIZE	POORHOUSE	PRETENDER	PROSODIAN
PLATINOID	POPLITEAL	PRETERITE	PROSODIST
PLATINOUS	POPULARLY	PRETERMIT	PROSTRATE
PLATITUDE	PORBEAGLE	PRETTYISH	PROTECTOR
PLATONISM	PORCELAIN	PREVALENT	PROTESTER
PLATONIST	PORCUPINE	PREVENTER	PROTHORAX
PLAUSIBLE	PORTERAGE	PREVISION	PROTOTYPE
PLAUSIBLY	PORTICOES	PRICELESS	PROTOZOAL
PLAYFULLY	PORTICOED	PRIESTESS	PROTOZOON
PLAYHOUSE	PORTIONER	PRIMARILY	PROUDNESS
PLAYTHING	PORTRAYER	PRIMATIAL	PROVENCAL
PLEASANCE	POSSESSOR	PRIMITIVE	PROVENDER
PLENARILY	POSTILION	PRINCEDOM	PROVIDENT
PLENITUDE	POSTULANT	PRINCIPAL	PROVISION
PLENTEOUS	POSTULATE	PRINCIPIA	PROVISORY
PLENTIFUL	POSTURIST	PRINCIPLE	PROVOKING
PLEURITIS	POTASSIUM	PRIORSHIP	PROXIMATE
PLEURITIC	POTENTATE	PRISMATIC	PROXIMITY
PLICATION	POTENTIAL	PRIVATEER	PRUDENTLY
PLICATURE	POTENTITE	PRIVATELY	PRUDISHLY
PLOUGHBOY	POULTERER	PRIVATION	PRURIENCE
PLOUGHMAN	POUSSETTE	PRIVATIVE	PRURIENCY
PLUMBEOUS	POWERLESS	PRIVILEGE	PSALMODIC
PLUMELESS	PRACTICAL	PROBATION	PSEUDONYM
PLUMPNESS	PRACTISED	PROBATIVE	PSORIASIS
PLUNDERER	PRACTISER	PROBATORY	PSYCHICAL
PLURALISM	PRAGMATIC	PROBOSCIS	PSYCHOSIS
PLURALIST	PRAYERFUL	PROCEDURE	PTARMIGAN
PLURALITY	PREACHIFY	PROCLITIC	PTERYGOID
PLURALIZE	PREACHING	PROCOELUS	PTOLEMAIC
PLUTOCRAT	PREBENDAL	PROCONSUL	PUBESCENT
PLUTONIAN	PRECEDENT	PROCREANT	PUBLICIST
PLUTONIST	PRECENTOR	PROCREATE	PUBLICITY
PNEUMATIC	PRECEPTOR	PROCURACY	PUBLISHER
PNEUMONIA	PRECIPICE	PRODIGIES	PUERILELY
PNEUMONIC	PRECISELY	PROFANELY	PUERILITY
POCKETFUL	PRECISION	PROFANITY	PUERPERAL
POENOLOGY	PRECOCITY	PROFESSED	PUFFINESS
POETASTER	PRECURSOR	PROFESSOR	PUGNACITY
POETICULE	PREDATORY	PROFFERER	PUISSANCE
POIGNANCY	PREDICANT	PROFILIST	PULMONARY
POINTEDLY	PREDICATE	PROFUSELY	PULPINESS
POINTLESS	PREDICTOR	PROFUSION	PULPITEER
POINTSMAN	PREFATORY	PROGNOSIS	PULSATILE
POISONOUS	PREFERRER	PROGRAMME	PULSATION
POLARIZER	PREFIGURE	PROJECTOR	PULSATIVE
POLEMICAL	PREFIXION	PROLEPSIS	PULSATORY
POLICEMAN	PREGNABLE	PROLEPTIC	PULSELESS
POLITICAL	PREGNANCY	PROLETARY	PULVERIZE
POLITICLY	PREJUDICE	PROLIXITY	PULVEROUS

PULVINATE	QUOTATION	RECOVERER	RELIGIOUS
PUMICEOUS	QUOTIDIAN	RECREANCY	RELIQUARY
PUNCTILIO		RECREMENT	REMAINDER
PUNCTUATE		RECRUITER	REMIGRATE
PUNGENTLY	**R**	RECTANGLE	REMINDFUL
PURCHASER		RECTIFIER	REMISSION
PURGATION	RABIDNESS	RECTITUDE	REMISSIVE
PURGATIVE	RACKAROCK	RECTORIAL	REMISSORY
PURGATORY	RADIANTLY	RECTORATE	REMITTENT
PURITANIC	RADIATELY	RECUMBENT	REMOVABLE
PURLOINER	RADIATION	RECURRING	RENASCENT
PURPOSELY	RADICALLY	RECURVATE	RENDITION
PURPOSIVE	RAILINGLY	RECUSANCY	RENEWABLE
PURPUREAL	RAININESS	RECUSANCE	RENITENCE
PURSINESS	RAJAHSHIP	REDACTION	RENITENCY
PURSUANCE	RAMPANTLY	REDBREAST	RENOUNCER
PURULENCE	RANCHERIA	REDDITION	RENOVATOR
PURULENCY	RANCIDITY	REDELIVER	REPARABLE
PUSHINGLY	RANCOROUS	REDOLENCE	REPARABLY
PUSTULATE	RANTIFOLE	REDOLENCY	REPAYABLE
PUSTULOUS	RAPACIOUS	REDOUBTED	REPAYMENT
PUTRIDITY	RAPIDNESS	REDUCIBLE	REPEATING
PUZZOLANA	RAPTORIAL	REDUCTION	REPELLENT
PYRAMIDAL	RAPTUROUS	REDUNDANT	REPENTANT
PYRAMIDIC	RAREESHOW	REFECTION	REPERCUSS
PYRETHRUM	RASCALDOM	REFECTORY	REPERTORY
PYRITICAL	RASCALISM	REFERABLE	REPERUSAL
PYROGENIC	RASCALITY	REFERENCE	REPLENISH
PYROLATER	RASPBERRY	REFERMENT	REPLETION
PYROMETER	RATIONALE	REFINEDLY	REPLETORY
PYROXYLIC	RAVISHING	REFITMENT	REPLICANT
PYRRHONIC	REACHABLE	REFLECTOR	REPORTING
PYTHONESS	REACHLESS	REFLEXION	REPOSEFUL
PYTHONISM	READDRESS	REFLEXIVE	REPOSSESS
PYTHONIST	READINESS	REFORMING	REPREHEND
	READJOURN	REFORTIFY	REPRESENT
	REALISTIC	REFRACTOR	REPRESSER
Q	REALITIES	REFRESHER	REPRIMAND
	REANIMATE	REFULGENT	REPROBATE
QUADRATIC	REAPPOINT	REFURBISH	REPRODUCE
QUADRIFID	REARRANGE	REFURNISH	REPTATORY
QUADRILLE	REASONING	REFUSABLE	REPTILIAN
QUADRUPED	REATTEMPT	REFUTABLE	REPUBLISH
QUADRUPLE	REBAPTISM	REGARDANT	REPUDIATE
QUAKERESS	REBAPTIZE	REGARDFUL	REPUGNANT
QUAKERISH	REBELLION	REGARDING	REPULSION
QUAKERISM	REBUILDER	REGENESIS	REPULSIVE
QUALIFIED	REBUKEFUL	REGICIDAL	REPUTABLE
QUALITIES	RECAPTURE	REGIMINAL	REPUTEDLY
QUARRYMAN	RECEIPTOR	REGISTRAR	REQUISITE
QUARTERLY	RECEIVING	REGRETFUL	RESCUABLE
QUARTETTE	RECENSION	REGULARLY	RESECTION
QUARTZITE	RECEPTION	REGULATOR	RESENTFUL
QUARTZOSE	RECEPTIVE	REHEARSAL	RESERVOIR
QUEENHOOD	RECESSION	REHEARSER	RESIDENCE
QUEERNESS	RECESSIVE	REIMBURSE	RESIDENCY
QUERULOUS	RECHAUFFE	REIMPLANT	RESIDUARY
QUICKENER	RECHERCHE	REIMPRINT	RESILIENT
QUICKLIME	RECIPIENT	REINFORCE	RESISTANT
QUICKNESS	RECKONING	REINSPECT	RESISTENT
QUICKSAND	RECLINATE	REINSPIRE	RESOLVENT
QUIESCENT	RECLUSELY	REINSTALL	RESONANCY
QUIETNESS	RECLUSIVE	REINSURER	RESONATOR
QUINTETTE	RECOGNISE	REITERATE	RESPECTER
QUINTUPLE	RECOLLECT	REJECTION	RESTFULLY
QUITCLAIM	RECOMMEND	REJOICING	RESTIFORM
QUITTANCE	RECONCILE	REJOINDER	RESTIVELY
QUIXOTISM	RECONDITE	RELEVANCE	RESTRAINT
QUIZZICAL	RECONDUCT	RELEVANCY	RESULTANT
QUODLIBET	RECONQUER	RELIEVING	RESUMABLE

RESURGENT	RUSTICITY	SCALINESS	SECONDARY
RETAINING	RUSTINESS	SCALLOPED	SECRETARY
RETALIATE	RUTHENIUM	SCANSORES	SECRETION
RETENTION		SCANTNESS	SECRETIVE
RETENTIVE		SCANTLING	SECRETORY
RETICENCE	**S**	SCAPEMENT	SECTARIAN
RETICULUM		SCAPIFORM	SECTIONAL
RETINITIS	SABADILLA	SCAPOLITE	SECTORIAL
RETIREDLY	SABRETASH	SCAPULARY	SECULARLY
RETRACTOR	SACCHARIC	SCARECROW	SECUNDINE
RETRIEVAL	SACCHARIN	SCARIFIER	SECURABLE
RETRIEVER	SACCIFORM	SCARPINES	SEDENTARY
RETROCEDE	SACKCLOTH	SCATHEFUL	SEDITIOUS
RETROUSSE	SACRAMENT	SCATTERED	SEDUCIBLE
REVERENCE	SACRIFICE	SCATTERER	SEDUCTION
REVERSELY	SACRILEGE	SCAVENGER	SEDUCTIVE
REVERSION	SACRISTAN	SCENTLESS	SEEDINESS
REVERSIVE	SADDUCEAN	SCEPTICAL	SEEMINGLY
REVETMENT	SAFEGUARD	SCHEMATIC	SEGMENTAL
REVIVABLE	SAFFLOWER	SCHEMEFUL	SEGREGATE
REVOCABLE	SAGACIOUS	SCHISTOSE	SEIGNIORY
REVOLTING	SAGITTATE	SCHISTOUS	SELACHIAN
REVULSION	SAILBORNE	SCHOLARLY	SELECTION
REVULSIVE	SAINTFOIN	SCHOLIAST	SELECTIVE
RHACHITIS	SAINTHOOD	SCHOLIUMS	SELENIOUS
RHAPSODIC	SAINTSHIP	SCHOOLING	SELFISHLY
RHEOMETER	SALACIOUS	SCHOOLMAN	SELVEDGED
RHEUMATIC	SALANGANE	SCHORLOUS	SEMAPHORE
RHINOLITH	SALERATUS	SCIATICAL	SEMBLANCE
RHIZODONT	SALICYLIC	SCIENTIAL	SEMIBREVE
RHYMELESS	SALIENTLY	SCIENTIST	SEMICOLON
RHYTHMICS	SALIMETER	SCINTILLA	SEMIOLOGY
RIBBONISM	SALMONOID	SCIOMACHY	SEMITONIC
RIBBONMAN	SALTATION	SCIOMANCY	SENESCENT
RIDDLINGS	SALTATORY	SCIOPTRIC	SENESCHAL
RIGHTNESS	SALTPETRE	SCIRRHOID	SENIORITY
RIGIDNESS	SALUBRITY	SCIRRHOUS	SENSATION
RIGMAROLE	SALVATION	SCISSIBLE	SENSELESS
RINGLETED	SAMARITAN	SCLEROSIS	SENSITIVE
RIOTOUSLY	SANCTUARY	SCLEROTIC	SENSITIZE
RITUALISM	SANDALLED	SCORBUTIC	SENSORIAL
RITUALIST	SANDARACH	SCORCHING	SENSORIUM
RIVALSHIP	SANDINESS	SCORPIOID	SENSUALLY
ROADSTEAD	SANDPIPER	SCOTCHMAN	SENTENCER
ROCAMBOLE	SANDSTONE	SCOUNDREL	SENTIMENT
ROCKINESS	SANJAKATE	SCRAGGILY	SEPARABLE
ROGUISHLY	SAPIDNESS	SCRAMBLER	SEPARABLY
ROISTERER	SAPIENTLY	SCRATCHER	SEPARATOR
ROKAMBOLE	SAPODILLA	SCREAMING	SEPTEMBER
ROMANCIST	SAPPINESS	SCRIBBLER	SEPTENARY
ROMANIZER	SARCASTIC	SCRIMMAGE	SEPULCHRE
ROMPISHLY	SARCOCARP	SCRIPTORY	SEPULTURE
ROOMINESS	SARGASSUM	SCRIPTURE	SEQUESTER
ROSACEOUS	SARMENTUM	SCRIVENER	SERASKIER
ROSTELLUM	SARTORIAL	SCRUTOIRE	SERENADER
ROSTRATED	SARTORIUS	SCULPTURE	SERGEANCY
ROTUNDITY	SASSAFRAS	SCUMBLING	SERGEANTY
ROUGHNESS	SASSENACH	SCUMMINGS	SERIALITY
ROUNDELAY	SATANICAL	SCUTCHEON	SERICEOUS
ROUNDHEAD	SATELLITE	SCUTELLUM	SERIOUSLY
ROUNDNESS	SATIATION	SCUTIFORM	SERMONIZE
RUBESCENT	SATURABLE	SCYTHEMAN	SERRATION
RUDDINESS	SATURNIAN	SEAFARING	SERRATURE
RUFFIANLY	SATURNINE	SEARCHING	SERRICORN
RUINATION	SAUCINESS	SEASONING	SERVIETTE
RUINOUSLY	SAUNTERER	SEBACEOUS	SERVILELY
RUMINATOR	SAVOURILY	SECERNENT	SERVILITY
RUNCINATE	SAXIFRAGE	SECESSION	SERVITUDE
RUNECRAFT	SAXOPHONE	SECLUSION	SESSIONAL
RUSTICATE	SCAGLIOLA	SECLUSIVE	SETACEOUS

SEVENFOLD	SINCERITY	SOPHISTER	SPRINKLER
SEVENTEEN	SINEWLESS	SOPHISTIC	SPUMINESS
SEVENTHLY	SINISTRAL	SOPHISTRY	SPUTTERER
SEVERABLE	SINLESSLY	SOPHOMORE	SQUALIDLY
SEVERALLY	SINOLOGUE	SOPORIFIC	SQUARROSE
SEVERALTY	SINUATION	SOPRANIST	SQUEAMISH
SEVERANCE	SINUOSITY	SORCERESS	STABILITY
SEXENNIAL	SINUOUSLY	SORRINESS	STAGNANCY
SEXUALITY	SIPHONAGE	SORROWFUL	STAIDNESS
SEXUALIZE	SIPHUNCLE	SORTILEGE	STAINLESS
SFORZANDO	SITUATION	SOTTISHLY	STAIRCASE
SHADINESS	SIXTEENMO	SOUBRETTE	STALACTIC
SHAKINESS	SIXTEENTH	SOUNDABLE	STALENESS
SHALLOWLY	SIZARSHIP	SOUNDINGS	STALKLESS
SHAMANISM	SKETCHILY	SOUNDLESS	STALWORTH
SHAMBLING	SKILFULLY	SOUNDNESS	STAMINATE
SHAMELESS	SKINFLINT	SOUTHERLY	STAMMERER
SHAPEABLE	SLACKNESS	SOUTHMOST	STANCHION
SHAPELESS	SLAKENESS	SOUTHWARD	STARBOARD
SHARPNESS	SLANDERER	SOVEREIGN	STARCHILY
SHAVELING	SLANTWISE	SPARENESS	STARINGLY
SHEARLING	SLATINESS	SPARINGLY	STARLIGHT
SHEATHING	SLAUGHTER	SPARKLING	STARTLING
SHEBEENER	SLAVONIAN	SPARTERIE	STATEMENT
SHEEPFOLD	SLAVISHLY	SPASMODIC	STATESMAN
SHEEPHOOK	SLEEKNESS	SPATIALLY	STATIONAL
SHELDRAKE	SLEEPLESS	SPATULATE	STATIONER
SHIFTLESS	SLENDERLY	SPEAKABLE	STATISTIC
SHILLELAH	SLIMINESS	SPEARMINT	STATUETTE
SHINGLING	SLIPPERED	SPECIALLY	STATUTORY
SHIPBOARD	SLOUCHING	SPECIALTY	STAYMAKER
SHIPWRECK	SLUMBERER	SPECTACLE	STEADFAST
SHOEBLACK	SLUMBROUS	SPECTATOR	STEELYARD
SHOEMAKER	SMALLNESS	SPECULATE	STEEPNESS
SHORELESS	SMARTNESS	SPECULUMS	STEERSMAN
SHORTHAND	SMATTERER	SPEECHIFY	STELLATED
SHORTNESS	SMILINGLY	SPEEDWELL	STELLULAR
SHOVELFUL	SMOKELESS	SPERMATIC	STEPCHILD
SHOVELLER	SMOKINESS	SPHACELUS	STERILITY
SHOWINESS	SMUGGLING	SPHERICAL	STERILIZE
SHRINKAGE	SNIVELLER	SPHINCTER	STERNMOST
SHRUBBERY	SOBERNESS	SPICINESS	STERNNESS
SHUFFLING	SOBRIQUET	SPICULATE	STEVEDORE
SIBILANCE	SOCIALISM	SPIKENARD	STEWARTRY
SIBILANCY	SOCIALIST	SPILLIKIN	STIFFENER
SIBYLLINE	SOCIALITY	SPINDRIFT	STIFFNESS
SICCATION	SOCIALIZE	SPININESS	STIGMATIC
SICCATIVE	SOCIETIES	SPINNAKER	STILLNESS
SICKENING	SOCIOLOGY	SPINNERET	STIMULANT
SICKLEMAN	SOFTENING	SPINOSITY	STIMULATE
SIDEBOARD	SOJOURNER	SPIRILLUM	STINTLESS
SIGHINGLY	SOLDERING	SPIRITUAL	STIPITATE
SIGHTLESS	SOLDIERLY	SPLEENFUL	STIPULATE
SIGMOIDAL	SOLEMNESS	SPLEENISH	STITCHING
SIGNALIZE	SOLEMNITY	SPLENDENT	STOCKDOVE
SIGNATORY	SOLEMNIZE	SPLENDOUR	STOICALLY
SIGNATURE	SOLFATARA	SPLENETIC	STOLIDITY
SIGNITARY	SOLFEGGIO	SPLENITIS	STOMACHAL
SIGNORINA	SOLICITOR	SPLINTERY	STOMACHER
SILICEOUS	SOLIDNESS	SPOKESMAN	STOMACHIC
SILIQUOSE	SOLILOQUY	SPOLIATOR	STONINESS
SILKINESS	SOLITAIRE	SPONGIOLE	STOUTNESS
SILLINESS	SOMETHING	SPORANGIA	STRAGGLER
SILVERING	SOMETIMES	SPORIDIUM	STRANGELY
SILVERIZE	SOMEWHERE	SPOROCYST	STRANGLES
SIMILARLY	SOMNOLENT	SPORTSMAN	STRANGURY
SIMPERING	SONNETEER	SPOUTLESS	STRAPPING
SIMPLETON	SONNETIZE	SPRIGHTLY	STRATAGEM
SIMULATOR	SONOMETER	SPRINGING	STRATEGIC
SINCERELY	SOOTINESS	SPRINGLET	STREAMLET

STRENUOUS	SULTANATE	SYMPOSIAC	TELLURIAN
STRETCHER	SUMMARILY	SYMPOSIUM	TEMPERATE
STRIATION	SUMMARIST	SYNAGOGUE	TEMPERING
STRICTURE	SUMMARIZE	SYNCHRONY	TEMPORARY
STRINGENT	SUMMARIES	SYNCLINAL	TEMPORIZE
STRIPLING	SUMMATION	SYNCOPATE	TEMPTABLE
STROBILUS	SUMMERSET	SYNCOPIZE	TEMPTRESS
STRONTIUM	SUMMONSES	SYNDICATE	TEMULENCE
STRUCTURE	SUMPTUARY	SYNERESIS	TENACIOUS
STRUGGLER	SUMPTUOUS	SYNIZESIS	TENDINOUS
STRYCHNIA	SUNFLOWER	SYNODICAL	TENEBROUS
STUDIEDLY	SUNNINESS	SYNONYMIC	TENSENESS
STUPEFIER	SUNRISING	SYNTACTIC	TENSILITY
STUPIDITY	SUNSTROKE	SYNTHESIS	TENTACLED
STUTTERER	SUPERABLE	SYNTHETIC	TENTATIVE
STYLISHLY	SUPERFINE	SYPHILIZE	TEPIDNESS
STYLISTIC	SUPERHEAT	SYSTEMIZE	TEREBINTH
STYLOBATE	SUPERPOSE		TERMAGANT
SUABILITY	SUPERSEDE		TERMINATE
SUASIVELY	SUPERVENE	**T**	TERMITARY
SUBAERIAL	SUPERVISE		TERRITORY
SUBALPINE	SUPPLIANT	TABASHEER	TERRORISM
SUBALTERN	SUPPORTER	TABULARLY	TERRORIST
SUBARCTIC	SUPPURATE	TACAMAHAC	TERRORIZE
SUBCOSTAL	SUPREMACY	TACTICIAN	TERSENESS
SUBDEACON	SUPREMELY	TAILORESS	TESSELLAR
SUBDIVIDE	SURCHARGE	TAILORING	TESTACEAN
SUBDUABLE	SURCINGLE	TAINTLESS	TESTAMENT
SUBEREOUS	SURGEONCY	TALEGALLA	TESTATRIX
SUBFAMILY	SURLINESS	TALKATIVE	TESTIFIER
SUBGENERA	SURMISING	TALMUDIST	TESTIMONY
SUBJACENT	SURMULLET	TANTALIZE	TESTINESS
SUBJUGATE	SURPLICED	TARANTISM	TETRALOGY
SUBLESSEE	SURPRISAL	TARANTULA	TETRARCHY
SUBLIMATE	SURPRISED	TARAXACUM	TEXTORIAL
SUBLIMELY	SURRENDER	TARBOUCHE	TEXTUALLY
SUBLIMITY	SURROGATE	TARDINESS	THALLOGEN
SUBLUNARY	SURVEYING	TARENTULA	THANATOID
SUBMARINE	SUSPENDER	TARGETEER	THANEHOOD
SUBMERSED	SUSPENSOR	TARGETIER	THANESHIP
SUBREGION	SUSPICION	TARNISHER	THANKLESS
SUBSCRIBE	SUSTAINER	TARPAULIN	THATCHING
SUBSCRIPT	SWAGGERER	TARTAREAN	THEANDRIC
SUBSIDIZE	SWALLOWER	TARTARIZE	THEMATIST
SUBSIDIES	SWANSDOWN	TARTAROUS	THEOCRACY
SUBSTANCE	SWARTHILY	TASIMETER	THEOCRASY
SUBSULTUS	SWEEPINGS	TASMANIAN	THEOGONIC
SUBTENANT	SWEETENER	TASSELLED	THEOLOGIC
SUBTILELY	SWEETMEAT	TASTELESS	THEOMACHY
SUBTILIZE	SWEETNESS	TATTOOING	THEOMANCY
SUBTORRID	SWIFTNESS	TAURIFORM	THEOPHANY
SUBVERTER	SWIMMERET	TAUTOLOGY	THEOREMIC
SUCCEEDER	SWINDLING	TAWNINESS	THEORETIC
SUCCESSOR	SWINEHERD	TAXIDERMY	THEORIZER
SUCCOURER	SWINGEING	TAXONOMIC	THEOSOPHY
SUCCULENT	SWINISHLY	TEACHABLE	THEREAWAY
SUCCURSAL	SWORDSMAN	TECHINESS	THEREFORE
SUCTORIAL	SYBARITIC	TECHNICAL	THEREFROM
SUDORIFIC	SYCOPHANT	TECTONICS	THEREINTO
SUFFERING	SYLLABIFY	TEDIOUSLY	THEREUPON
SUFFIXION	SYLLOGISM	TEGULATED	THEREWITH
SUFFOCATE	SYLLOGIZE	TELEGRAPH	THERMALLY
SUFFRAGAN	SYMBIOSIS	TELEMETER	THESAURUS
SUFFUSION	SYMBIOTIC	TELEMETRY	THEURGIST
SUGGESTER	SYMBOLISM	TETEOLOGY	THICKNESS
SULCATION	SYMBOLIST	TELEPATHY	THINKABLE
SULKINESS	SYMBOLIZE	TELEPHONE	THIRSTILY
SULPHURET	SYMBOLOGY	TELEPHONY	THIRTIETH
SULPHURIC	SYMPHONIC	TELESCOPE	THRASHING
SULTANESS	SYMPHYSIS	TELESCOPY	THRESHING

THREEFOLD	TRANSFORM	TRUCELESS	UNDERNBRED
THRENETIC	TRANSFUSE	TRUCULENT	UNDERGRID
THRESHOLD	TRANSIENT	TRUEPENNY	UNDERHAND
THRIFTILY	TRANSLATE	TRUMPETER	UNDERHUNG
THRILLING	TRANSMUTE	TRUNCATED	UNDERLINE
THROBLESS	TRANSPIRE	TRUNCHEON	UNDERLING
THROTTLER	TRANSPORT	TRUSTLESS	UNDERMINE
THROWSTER	TRANSPOSE	TRUTHLESS	UNDERMOST
THUMBLESS	TRAPEZIUM	TUBERCLED	UNDERPLOT
THUNDERER	TRAPEZOID	TUBICOLAR	UNDERPROP
THYLACINE	TRAPPINGS	TUBULATED	UNDERRATE
TIERCELET	TRAUMATIC	TUFACEOUS	UNDERSELL
TIGHTNESS	TRAVELLED	TUMIDNESS	UNDERSHOT
TIMBERING	TRAVELLER	TUNEFULLY	UNDERSIGN
TIMIDNESS	TRAVERSER	TUNICATED	UNDERTAKE
TIPSINESS	TRAVERTIN	TURBIDITY	UNDERWEAR
TIREDNESS	TREACHERY	TURBINATE	UNDERWOOD
TITILLATE	TREADMILL	TURBULENT	UNDESIRED
TITRATION	TREASURER	TURFINESS	UNDILUTED
TITTLEBAT	TREATMENT	TURGIDITY	UNDIVIDED
TITULARLY	TREMATODE	TURNSTILE	UNDOUBTED
TOLERABLE	TREMATOID	TURNSTONE	UNDREAMED
TOLERABLY	TREMBLING	TURPITUDE	UNDRESSED
TOLERANCE	TREMULOUS	TURQUOISE	UNDULATED
TOLERATOR	TRENCHANT	TUSSILAGO	UNDUTIFUL
TOLLBOOTH	TRIATOMIC	TUTORSHIP	UNEARTHLY
TOMENTOSE	TRIBALISM	TWENTIETH	UNEATABLE
TOMENTOUS	TRIBESMAN	TWINKLING	UNENDOWED
TONGUELET	TRIBUNATE	TYPICALLY	UNENGAGED
TONSILLAR	TRIBUTARY	TYRANNIZE	UNENGLISH
TONSORIAL	TRICKSOME	TYRANNOUS	UNEQUABLE
TOOTHACHE	TRICKSTER		UNEQUALLY
TOOTHLESS	TRICLINIC		UNEXPIRED
TOOTHPICK	TRICOLOUR	**U**	UNEXPOSED
TOOTHSOME	TRICUSPID		UNFEELING
TOPIARIAN	TRIENNIAL	ULIGINOUS	UNFEIGNED
TOPICALLY	TRIFACIAL	ULTIMATUM	UNFITNESS
TORMENTER	TRIFLORAL	UMBELLATE	UNFITTING
TORMENTIL	TRIFORIUM	UMBILICAL	UNFLEDGED
TORMENTOR	TRIGAMIST	UMBILICUS	UNFOUNDED
TORNADOES	TRIGONOUS	UMBONATED	UNGALLANT
TORPEDOES	TRIGYNIAN	UNABASHED	UNGENTEEL
TORPIDITY	TRIGYNOUS	UNADORNED	UNGUARDED
TORQUATED	TRIHEDRAL	UNADVISED	UNGUIFORM
TORRIDITY	TRIHEDRON	UNALLOYED	UNHANDILY
TORSIONAL	TRILINEAR	UNAMIABLE	UNHAPPILY
TORTILITY	TRILITHON	UNANIMITY	UNHARNESS
TOTALNESS	TRILITHIC	UNANIMOUS	UNHEALTHY
TOUCHABLE	TRILOBATE	UNASSURED	UNHEEDFUL
TOUCHWOOD	TRILOBITE	UNAVENGED	UNHEEDING
TOUGHNESS	TRILOGIES	UNBENDING	UNHOPEFUL
TOURMALIN	TRIMEROUS	UNBIASSED	UNIFACIAL
TOWELLING	TRIMESTER	UNBLESSED	UNIFORMLY
TOWNSFOLK	TRINERVED	UNBOUNDED	UNIGENOUS
TOWNWARDS	TRINKETER	UNBRIDLED	UNINJURED
TRABECULA	TRINKETRY	UNBURTHEN	UNINVITED
TRACEABLE	TRINOMIAL	UNCEASING	UNIPAROUS
TRACEABLY	TRISERIAL	UNCERTAIN	UNISERIAL
TRACHEARY	TRITENESS	UNCIVILLY	UNISEXUAL
TRACHYTIC	TRITHEISM	UNCLEANLY	UNISONANT
TRACKLESS	TRITURATE	UNCLOUDED	UNISONOUS
TRACTABLE	TRIUMPHAL	UNCONCERN	UNITARIAN
TRACTABLY	TRIUMPHER	UNCORRUPT	UNIVALENT
TRADESMAN	TRIVIALLY	UNCOURTLY	UNIVALVED
TRADITION	TROCHLEAR	UNCOUTHLY	UNIVERSAL
TRADITIVE	TROPOLOGY	UNCROSSED	UNJOINTED
TRAGEDIAN	TROUBLOUS	UNCROWNED	UNKNOWING
TRAINABLE	TROUSERED	UNDAUNTED	UNLEARNED
TRAITRESS	TROUSSEAU	UNDECEIVE	UNLIMITED
TRANSCEND	TROUTLING	UNDEFINED	UNLUCKILY

UNMATCHED	UPPERMOST	VERITABLY	VOLUMETER
UNMEANING	UPRIGHTLY	VERMICIDE	VOLUNTARY
UNMERITED	URCEOLATE	VERMIFORM	VOLUNTEER
UNMINDFUL	URTICARIA	VERMIFUGE	VOODOOISM
UNMIXEDLY	USELESSLY	VERMINATE	VORACIOUS
UNMORTISE	USHERSHIP	VERMINOUS	VORTICOSE
UNMUSICAL	UTILITIES	VERNATION	VOUCHSAFE
UNNATURAL	UTRICULAR	VERRUCOSE	VULCANISM
UNNOTICED	UTTERABLE	VERRUCOUS	VULCANIAN
UNOPPOSED	UTTERANCE	VERSATILE	VULCANITE
UNPITYING	UTTERMOST	VERSIFIER	VULCANIZE
UNPLUMBED		VERTEBRAE	VULGARIAN
UNPOPULAR		VERTEBRAL	VULGARISM
UNQUIETLY	**V**	VESICULAR	VULGARITY
UNREALITY		VESTIBULE	VULGARIZE
UNREFINED	VACANCIES	VESTIGIAL	VULNERARY
UNRELATED	VACCINATE	VETCHLING	VULPICIDE
UNRESTING	VACILLATE	VEXATIOUS	VULPINITE
UNRUFFLED	VAGINATED	VEXILLARY	VULTURINE
UNSAVOURY	VAGUENESS	VIABILITY	VULTURISH
UNSCATHED	VAINGLORY	VIBRACULA	VULTUROUS
UNSELFISH	VALENTINE	VIBRATILE	
UNSETTLED	VALIANTLY	VIBRATION	
UNSHACKLE	VALUATION	VIBRATORY	**W**
UNSHAPELY	VALUELESS	VIBRISSAE	
UNSHEATHE	VAMPIRISM	VICARIATE	WAGGISHLY
UNSIGHTLY	VANDALISM	VICARIOUS	WAGONETTE
UNSKILFUL	VAPIDNESS	VICARSHIP	WAILINGLY
UNSKILLED	VAPORABLE	VICENNIAL	WAISTBAND
UNSOUNDLY	VAPORIFIC	VICIOUSLY	WAISTCOAT
UNSPARING	VAPOURISH	VICTIMIZE	WAKEFULLY
UNSPOTTED	VARIATION	VICTORESS	WALDENSES
UNSTAINED	VARICELLA	VICTORINE	WALLABIES
UNSTAMPED	VARIEGATE	VICTORIES	WANDERING
UNSTINTED	VARIETIES	VIDELICET	WAPENSHAW
UNSTUDIED	VARIOLOUS	VIGESIMAL	WAPENTAKE
UNSUBDUED	VARIOLOID	VIGILANCE	WAREHOUSE
UNSULLIED	VARIOUSLY	VILLIFORM	WARNINGLY
UNTAINTED	VARNISHER	VILLOSITY	WARRANTER
UNTAMABLE	VASCULOSE	VINACEOUS	WARRANTOR
UNTENABLE	VASOMOTOR	VINDICATE	WASHINESS
UNTHANKED	VASSALAGE	VIOLATION	WASPISHLY
UNTHOUGHT	VEERINGLY	VIOLENTLY	WASSAILER
UNTHRIFTY	VEGETABLE	VIOLINIST	WASTENESS
UNTIMEOUS	VEHEMENCE	VIRESCENT	WATCHWORD
UNTOUCHED	VEHEMENCY	VIRGILIAN	WATERFALL
UNTRACKED	VEHICULAR	VIRGINITY	WATERLESS
UNTRAINED	VELLICATE	VIRTUALLY	WATERSHED
UNTRODDEN	VELVETEEN	VIRTUOSOS	WAYFARING
UNTUNABLE	VELVETING	VIRULENCE	WAYWARDLY
UNTUTORED	VENEERING	VISCERATE	WEALTHILY
UNUSUALLY	VENERABLE	VISCIDITY	WEARINESS
UNVARYING	VENERABLY	VISCOUNTY	WEARISOME
UNVISITED	VENERATOR	VISIONARY	WEATHERED
UNWARLIKE	VENGEANCE	VISUALITY	WEATHERLY
UNWATCHED	VENIALITY	VITELLINE	WEDNESDAY
UNWATERED	VENTILATE	VITIATION	WEEPINGLY
UNWEARIED	VENTRICLE	VITRIFIED	WEIGHABLE
UNWEIGHED	VENTUROUS	VITRIFORM	WEEVILLED
UNWELCOME	VERACIOUS	VITRIOLIC	WEIGHTILY
UNWILLING	VERATRINE	VITRUVIAN	WEIRDNESS
UNWINKING	VERBALISM	VIVACIOUS	WESTERING
UNWITTING	VERBALIST	VIVIDNESS	WESTWARDS
UNWOMANLY	VERBALIZE	VIZIERATE	WHALEBONE
UNWORLDLY	VERBOSELY	VIZIERIAL	WHEEDLING
UNWOUNDED	VERBOSITY	VOCALNESS	WHEREFORE
UNWREATHE	VERDANTLY	VOICELESS	WHEREINTO
UNWRITTEN	VERDIGRIS	VOLCANISM	WHERENESS
UNWROUGHT	VERIDICAL	VOLCANIST	WHEREUNTO
UPHOLSTER	VERITABLE	VOLCANOES	WHEREUPON

WHEREWITH
WHERRYMAN
WHETSTONE
WHICHEVER
WHIMPERER
WHIMSICAL
WHININGLY
WHINSTONE
WHIRLIGIG
WHIRLPOOL
WHIRLWIND
WHISKERED
WHISPERER
WHITENESS
WHITEWASH
WHOLENESS
WHOLESALE
WHOLESOME
WHOSOEVER
WIDOWHOOD
WIELDABLE
WILLINGLY
WINDINESS

WINDINGLY
WINNINGLY
WINGFULLY
WISTFULLY
WITHERING
WITHSTAND
WITLESSLY
WITNESSER
WITTICISM
WITTINESS
WITTINGLY
WOEBEGONE
WOFULNESS
WOLFISHLY
WOLVERENE
WOMANHOOD
WOMANKIND
WOMANLIKE
WONDERFUL
WOODCRAFT
WOODINESS
WORDINESS
WORKHOUSE

WORKMANLY
WORKWOMAN
WORLDLING
WORRIMENT
WORSHIPER
WORTHLESS
WOUNDABLE
WRISTBAND
WRONGNESS
WRYNECKED

X

XERODERMA
XYLOGRAPH
XYLOPHONE

Y

YACHTSMAN
YANKEEISM

YELLOWISH
YESTERDAY
YESTEREVE
YOUNGLING
YOUNGNESS
YOUNGSTER
YTTERBIUM

Z

ZEALOUSLY
ZEMINDARY
ZEUGLODON
ZEUGMATIC
ZIRCONIUM
ZOOGRAPHY
ZOOLOGIST
ZOOPHYTIC
ZOOTOMIST
ZUMBOORUK
ZYGOMATIC
ZYMOMETER

TEN-LETTER WORDS

A

ABBREVIATE
ABDICATION
ABDOMINOUS
ABERDEVINE
ABERRATION
ABHORRENCE
ABIOGENIST
ABJECTNESS
ABJURATION
ABJURATORY
ABLE-BODIED
ABNEGATION
ABNORMALLY
ABOMINABLE
ABOMINABLY
ABORIGINAL
ABORIGINES
ABORTIVELY
ABOVE-BOARD
ABRIDGMENT
ABROGATION
ABROGATIVE
ABRUPTNESS
ABSCISSION
ABSENTMENT
ABSINTHIAN
ABSOLUTELY
ABSOLUTION
ABSOLUTISM
ABSOLUTORY
ABSORBABLE
ABSORBEDLY
ABSORPTION
ABSORPTIVE
ABSTEMIOUS
ABSTENTION
ABSTERGENT
ABSTERSION
ABSTINENCE
ABSTRACTED
ABSTRACTLY
ABSTRUSELY
ABSURDNESS
ABUNDANTLY
ABYSSINIAN
ACADEMICAL
ACCELERATE
ACCENTUATE
ACCEPTABLE
ACCEPTABLY
ACCEPTANCE
ACCEPTANCY
ACCESSIBLE
ACCESSIBLY
ACCIDENTAL
ACCIPITRAL
ACCOMPLICE
ACCOMPLISH
ACCORDANCE
ACCOUCHEUR
ACCOUNTANT
ACCRESCENT

ACCUBATION
ACCUMBENCY
ACCUMULATE
ACCURATELY
ACCUSATION
ACCUSATIVE
ACCUSATORY
ACCUSTOMED
ACEPHALOUS
ACETABULUM
ACETARIOUS
ACETIMETER
ACETOPATHY
ACHIEVANCE
ACHROMATIC
ACIDIMETER
ACINACEOUS
ACORN-SHELL
ACOTYLEDON
ACQUAINTED
ACQUIRABLE
ACROAMATIC
ACROGENOL'S
ACRONYCHAL
ACROTERIUM
ACTINOLITE
ACTINOZOON
ACTIONABLE
ACTIVENESS
ADAMANTINE
ADAM'S-APPLE
ADAPTATION
ADDER-STONE
ADDER'S-WORT
ADDITIONAL
ADEQUATELY
ADHERENTLY
ADHESIVELY
ADHIBITION
ADIACTINIC
ADJACENTLY
ADJECTIVAL
ADJUDGMENT
ADJUDICATE
ADJUNCTION
ADJUNCTIVE
ADJURATION
ADJURATORY
ADJUSTABLE
ADJUSTMENT
ADMEASURER
ADMINISTER
ADMIRATION
ADMIRINGLY
ADMISSIBLE
ADMITTABLE
ADMITTANCE
ADMITTATUR
ADMITTEDLY
ADMONISHER
ADMONITION
ADMONITIVE
ADMONITORY
ADOLESCENT
ADROITNESS

ADULTERANT
ADULTERATE
ADULTERESS
ADULTERINE
ADULTEROUS
ADVENTURER
ADVERTENCE
ADVERTISER
AERIFEROUS
AEROLOGIST
AERONAUTIC
AEROSTATIC
AERUGINOUS
AESTHETICS
AFFABILITY
AFFECTEDLY
AFFILIABLE
AFFIRMABLE
AFFLICTING
AFFLICTION
AFFLICTIVE
AFFRONTING
AFORENAMED
AFRICANDER
AFTER-BIRTH
AFTER-GRASS
AFTER-IMAGE
AFTER-PAINS
AFTER-PIECE
AFTER-STATE
AFTER-TASTE
AFTERWARDS
AGALLOCHUM
AGGRANDIZE
AGGRESSION
AGGRESSIVE
AGRYPNOTIC
AIDE-DE-CAMP
AIR-BLADDER
AIR-CUSHION
ALARMINGLY
ALBESCENCE
ALBUMINOID
ALBUMINOUS
ALCOHOLISM
ALCOHOLIZE
ALDERMANCY
ALDERMANIC
ALDERMANLY
ALEXANDERS
ALGEBRAIST
ALIENATION
ALIMENTARY
ALINEATION
ALLEGATION
ALLEGIANCE
ALLEGORIST
ALLEGORIZE
ALLEGRETTO
ALLEVIATOR
ALLIACEOUS
ALLIGATION
ALLITERATE
ALLOCATION
ALLOCUTION

ALLOPATHIC
ALLUREMENT
ALLURINGLY
ALLUSIVELY
ALMOND-CAKE
ALMOND-TREE
ALMS-GIVING
ALONGSHORE
ALPENSTOCK
ALPHABETIC
ALTAR-BREAD
ALTAR-CLOTH
ALTAR-PIECE
ALTAZIMUTH
ALTERATION
ALTERATIVE
ALTOGETHER
ALTRUISTIC
ALUM-SCHIST
AMALGAMATE
AMANUENSIS
AMATEURISH
AMAZEDNESS
AMBASSADOR
AMBIDEXTER
AMBULACRUM
AMBULATION
AMBULATORY
AMBUSHMENT
AMELIORATE
AMENDATORY
AMERCEABLE
AMERCEMENT
AMIABILITY
AMMUNITION
AMPHIBIOUS
AMPHIBRACH
AMPHIMACER
AMPUTATION
AMYGDALATE
AMYGDALINE
AMYGDALOID
AMYLACEOUS
ANABAPTISM
ANABAPTIST
ANACAMPTIC
ANACLASTIC
ANADROMOUS
ANAGOGICAL
ANALOGICAL
ANALYSABLE
ANAMNIOTIC
ANAPLASTIC
ANARTHROUS
ANASTOMOSE
ANATOMICAL
ANCESTRESS
ANCHORETIC
ANCHOR-HOLD
ANDROECIUM
ANDROGYNAL
ANDROPHAGI
ANECDOTIST
ANELECTRIC
ANEMOGRAPH
ANEMOMETER
ANEMOMETRY
ANEMOSCOPE
ANEURISMAL
ANGIOSPERM

ANGLO-IRISH
ANGLOMANIA
ANGLO-SAXON
ANGORA-WOOL
ANGULARITY
ANHUNGERED
ANIMADVERT
ANIMALCULE
ANISOMERIC
ANNEXATION
ANNIHILATE
ANNOTATION
ANNUNCIATE
ANOINTMENT
ANSWERABLE
ANSWERABLY
ANSWERLESS
ANTAGONISM
ANTAGONIST
ANTECEDENT
ANTE-CHAPEL
ANTEPENULT
ANTERIORLY
ANTHRACENE
ANTHROPOID
ANTICHRIST
ANTICIPATE
ANTI-CLIMAX
ANTICLINAL
ANTIEMETIC
ANTILITHIC
ANTIMONIAL
ANTINOMIAN
ANTIPHONAL
ANTIQUATED
ANTISEPTIC
ANTITHESIS
ANTITHETIC
APHAERESIS
APHORISTIC
APICULTURE
APLACENTAL
APOCALYPSE
APOCARPOUS
APOCRYPHAL
APODEICTIC
APOLOGETIC
APOLOGIZER
APOPHTHEGM
APOPLECTIC
APOSTATIZE
APOSTOLATE
APOSTROPHE
APOTHECARY
APOTHECIUM
APOTHEOSIS
APPARENTLY
APPARITION
APPEALABLE
APPEARANCE
APPEASABLE
APPETITIVE
APPLAUSIVE
APPLICABLE
APPLICANCY
APPOSITELY
APPOSITION
APPOSITIVE
APPRECIATE
APPRENTICE

APPROACHER
APPROVABLE
AQUAMARINE
AQUIFEROUS
ARACHNIDAN
ARBITRATOR
ARBOR-VITAE
ARCHBISHOP
ARCHDEACON
ARCHER-FISH
ARCHETYPAL
ARCHITRAVE
AREFACTION
ARENACEOUS
AREOLATION
AREOPAGITE
ARGUMENTAL
ARISTOCRAT
ARITHMETIC
ARMIPOTENT
ARRESTMENT
ARROGANTLY
ARROGATION
ARTFULNESS
ARTHROPODA
ARTICULATE
ARTIFICIAL
ASCENDABLE
ASCENDANCY
ASCETICISM
ASCRIBABLE
ASCRIPTION
ASPHYXIATE
ASPIRATION
ASPIRINGLY
ASSAILABLE
ASSEMBLAGE
ASSENTIENT
ASSESSABLE
ASSESSMENT
ASSEVERATE
ASSIBILATE
ASSIGNABLE
ASSIGNMENT
ASSIMILATE
ASSISTANCE
ASSOCIABLE
ASSORTMENT
ASSUMPTION
ASSUMPTIVE
ASTEROIDAL
ASTOMATOUS
ASTONISHED
ASTOUNDING
ASTRINGENT
ASTROLATRY
ASTROLOGER
ASTROMETER
ASTRONOMER
ASTRONOMIC
ASTUTENESS
ATHANASIAN
ATMOSPHERE
ATRABILIAR
ATRAMENTAL
ATTACHABLE
ATTACHMENT
ATTACKABLE
ATTAINABLE
ATTAINMENT

ATTENDANCE
ATTRACTION
ATTRACTIVE
AUCTIONEER
AUDIBILITY
AUDIOMETER
AUDITORIUM
AUGUSTNESS
AURICULATE
AURIFEROUS
AURIGATION
AUSPICIOUS
AUSTRALIAN
AUTHORSHIP
AUTOCHTHON
AUTOCRATIC
AUTOGENOUS
AUTOGRAPHY
AUTOMOBILE
AUTONOMOUS
AUTOPTICAL
AVANT-GUARD
AVANTURINE
AVARICIOUS
AVENTURINE
AVERSENESS
AVICULTURE
AVOUCHMENT
AWAKENMENT

B

BABBLEMENT
BABIROUSSA
BABY-FARMER
BABYLONIAN
BACKGAMMON
BACKGROUND
BACKSLIDER
BACKWARDLY
BAFFLINGLY
BALDERDASH
BALNEOLOGY
BALUSTRADE
BANISHMENT
BANKRUPTCY
BAPTISTERY
BARCAROLLE
BAREBACKED
BAREHEADED
BARGE-BOARD
BARKENTINE
BARLEY-CORN
BAROMETRIC
BARREL-BULK
BARRENNESS
BASE-MINDED
BASKET-HILT
BASSET-HORN
BASSOONIST
BASS-RELIEF
BASTARDIZE
BASTIONARY
BAT-FOWLING
BATHING-BOX
BATHOMETER
BATHYMETRY
BATRACHIAN
BATTLEDORE

BATTLEMENT
BATTLE-SHIP
BEADLESHIP
BEARD-GRASS
BEAR-GARDEN
BEAUTIFIER
BEAUTY-SPOT
BECHE-DE-MER
BECOMINGLY
BEDCHAMBER
BEER-ENGINE
BEFOREHAND
BEHINDHAND
BELIEVABLE
BELLADONNA
BELL-FLOWER
BELL-HANGER
BELL-RINGER
BELL-TURRET
BELL-WETHER
BENEDICITE
BENEDICTUS
BENEFACTOR
BENEFICENT
BENEFICIAL
BENEVOLENT
BENUMBMENT
BEQUEATHER
BESOTTEDLY
BESPRINKLE
BESTIALITY
BESTIALIZE
BESTIARIAN
BETTERMENT
BETTERMOST
BETTERNESS
BEVEL-WHEEL
BEWITCHERY
BEWITCHING
BIBLICALLY
BIBLIOLOGY
BIBLIOPEGY
BICHROMATE
BICORPORAL
BIENNIALLY
BIJOUTERIE
BILGE-WATER
BILINGUIST
BILL-BROKER
BILLET-DOUX
BIMACULATE
BIMETALLIC
BIOGENESIS
BIOGRAPHER
BIOPLASMIC
BIRD-CHERRY
BIRD-SPIDER
BIROSTRATE
BIRTHNIGHT
BIRTHPLACE
BIRTHRIGHT
BISHOP-WEED
BISMUTHITE
BISSEXTILE
BISULPHATE
BISULPHITE
BITTERNESS
BITUMINIZE
BITUMINOUS
BLACKAMOOR

BLACKBERRY
BLACK-BOARD
BLACK-CHALK
BLACK-FRIAR
BLACKGUARD
BLACK-SHEEP
BLACKSMITH
BLACKTHORN
BLAMEFULLY
BLANC-MANGE
BLANDISHER
BLANKETING
BLANK-VERSE
BLASPHEMER
BLASTODERM
BLAZONMENT
BLISSFULLY
BLITHENESS
BLITHESOME
BLOCK-HOUSE
BLOOD-HORSE
BLOOD-HOUND
BLOODINESS
BLOOD-MONEY
BLOOD-STONE
BLOODY-FLUX
BLOOMINGLY
BLUBBER-LIP
BLUE-BOTTLE
BLUE-JACKET
BLUISHNESS
BLUSHINGLY
BLUSTERING
BLUSTEROUS
BOARD-WAGES
BOASTFULLY
BOASTINGLY
BODY-COLOUR
BOG-TROTTER
BOISTEROUS
BOMBARDIER
BOMB-VESSEL
BOND-HOLDER
BONDS-WOMAN
BONE-SETTER
BONE-SPAVIN
BOOK-HUNTER
BOOK-KEEPER
BOOK-MUSLIN
BOOKSELLER
BOOTLESSLY
BORDER-LAND
BOTTLE-FISH
BOTTLE-NOSE
BOTTLE-TREE
BOTTOMLESS
BOUTS-RIMES
BOWDLERIZE
BOWIE-KNIFE
BOYISHNESS
BRACHIOPOD
BRACHYLOGY
BRACHYURAL
BRACKETING
BRACTEATED
BRAGGINGLY
BRAHMANISM
BRAIN-FEVER
BRANCHIATE
BRANCHLESS

BRANT-GOOSE
BRAWLINGLY
BRAWNINESS
BRAZENNESS
BRAZIL-WOOD
BRAZILETTO
BREADSTUFF
BREAKWATER
BREAST-BONE
BREAST-DEEP
BREAST-KNOT
BREAST-WALL
BREAST-WORK
BREATHABLE
BREATHLESS
BRENT-GOOSE
BRICK-FILLED
BRICKLAYER
BRIDEGROOM
BRIDESMAID
BRIDGE-DECK
BRIDLE-HAND
BRIDLE-PATH
BRIDLE-ROAD
BRIDLE-REIN
BRIGANDAGE
BRIGANDISM
BRIGANTINE
BRIGHTNESS
BRIGHTSOME
BRILLIANCE
BROAD-CLOTH
BROADSWORD
BROKEN-DOWN
BROKENNESS
BROKEN-WIND
BROME-GRASS
BRONCHITIS
BROOMSTICK
BROOMSTAFF
BROWBEATER
BROWN-STUDY
BRUSQUERIE
BUBONOCELE
BUCCINATOR
BUCK-BASKET
BUCK-JUMPER
BUDDHISTIC
BUFFOONERY
BUFFOONISH
BULLIONIST
BUNGLINGLY
BURDENSOME
BUREAUCRAT
BURROW-DUCK
BUSH-HARROW
BUSH-RANGER
BUSH-SHRIKE
BUTLERSHIP
BUTTER-BIRD
BUTTER-BOAT
BUTTERMILK
BUTTER-TREE
BUTTERWORT
BUTTERY-BAR
BUTTON-PUSH
BUTTON-HOLE
BUTTON-HOOK
BUTTON-WOOD

C

CACOGRAPHY
CADAVEROUS
CADDICE-FLY
CAESPITOSE
CALAMITOUS
CALCAREOUS
CALCINABLE
CALC-SINTER
CALCULABLE
CALCULATED
CALCULATOR
CALEDONIAN
CALIGINOUS
CALIGRAPHY
CALUMNIATE
CALUMNIOUS
CALYCIFORM
CALYPTRATE
CAMELOPARD
CAMERONIAN
CAMPAIGNER
CAMPESTRAL
CAMPHORATE
CAMPHOR-OIL
CANARY-WOOD
CANCELLATE
CANCELLOUS
CANDESCENT
CANDIDNESS
CANDLE-COAL
CANDLE-FISH
CANDLEWICK
CANDY-SUGAR
CANEPHORUS
CANKER-WORM
CANNEL-COAL
CANNON-BALL
CANNON-SHOT
CANONICALS
CANONICITY
CANTATRICE
CANTERBURY
CANTILEVER
CANTONMENT
CANVAS-BACK
CAOUTCHOUC
CAPABILITY
CAPACITATE
CAPILLAIRE
CAPITALIZE
CAPITATION
CAPITULATE
CAPNOMANCY
CAPRICIOUS
CAPTIOUSLY
CARABINEER
CARAVANEER
CARBAZOTIC
CARBONATED
CARBUNCLED
CARDIALGIA
CARELESSLY
CARICATURE
CARNALLITE
CARPELLARY
CARTHUSIAN
CARTWRIGHT

CASCARILLA
CASE-BOTTLE
CASE-HARDEN
CASEMENTED
CASSIA-BARK
CASSIA-BUDS
CASSIOPEIA
CASSOLETTE
CASTIGATOR
CASTRATION
CATAFALQUE
CATALECTIC
CATALEPTIC
CATAMENIAL
CATAPHRACT
CATARRHINE
CATCH-PENNY
CATECHETIC
CATECHUMEN
CATENARIAN
CATENATION
CATHOLICON
CATOPTRICS
CATTLE-SHOW
CAULESCENT
CAUSTICITY
CAUTIONARY
CAUTIOUSLY
CAVALIERLY
CELEBRATED
CELEBRATER
CELLULATED
CENOBITISM
CENSORIOUS
CENSORSHIP
CENSURABLE
CENSURABLY
CENTAURIAN
CENTENNIAL
CENTESIMAL
CENTIGRADE
CENTIMETRE
CENTIPEDAL
CENTRALISM
CENTRALITY
CENTRALIZE
CENTRICITY
CENTRIFUGE
CEPHALITIS
CEPHALOPOD
CEREBELLAR
CEREBELLUM
CEREBRITIS
CEREMONIAL
CEREGRAPHY
CERTIORARI
CERUMINOUS
CESSIONARY
CESTIODEAN
CESTRACION
CHAIN-CABLE
CHALCEDONY
CHALKINESS
CHALLENGER
CHALYBEATE
CHAMAELEON
CHAMBER-POT
CHAMBERTIN
CHAMPIGNON

CHANCELLOR	CHROMATICS	COASTWARDS
CHANDELIER	CHRONICLER	COAT-ARMOUR
CHANGEABLE	CHRONOGRAM	COCKATRICE
CHANGEABLY	CHRONOLOGY	COCKCHAFER
CHANGELESS	CHRYSOLITE	COCKNEYDOM
CHANGELING	CHUBBINESS	COCKNEYISH
CHANNELLED	CHURCH-GOER	COCKNEYISM
CHAPEL-CART	CHURCHLESS	COEQUALITY
CHAPLAINCY	CHURCH-RATE	COERCIVELY
CHARGEABLE	CHURCHYARD	COETANEOUS
CHARIOTEER	CHURLISHLY	COETERNITY
CHARITABLE	CICERONIAN	COEXECUTOR
CHARITABLY	CINCHONISM	COEXISTENT
CHARMINGLY	CINENCHYMA	COFFEE-MILL
CHARTREUSE	CINQUE-FOIL	COFFEE-ROOM
CHARTULARY	CINQUE-PACE	COGITATION
CHASTENESS	CIRCENSIAN	COGITATIVE
CHATELAINE	CIRCUITOUS	COGNIZABLE
CHATTER-BOX	CIRCULABLE	COGNIZABLY
CHAUCERIAN	CIRCULARLY	COGNIZANCE
CHAUVINISM	CIRCULATOR	COGNOMINAL
CHAUVINIST	CIRCUMCISE	COHERENTLY
CHEEK-POUCH	CIRCUMFLEX	COHESIVELY
CHEEK-TOOTH	CIRCUMFUSE	COINCIDENT
CHEERFULLY	CIRCUMMURE	COLD-CHISEL
CHEERINESS	CIRCUMVENT	COLEORHIZA
CHEERINGLY	CISMONTANE	COLLAR-BEAM
CHEESE-CAKE	CISTERCIAN	COLLARLESS
CHEESINESS	CITIZENIZE	COLLATABLE
CHEIROPTER	CLACK-VALVE	COLLATERAL
CHEMICALLY	CLAMMINESS	COLLECTION
CHEMISETTE	CLANGOROUS	COLLECTIVE
CHEQUE-BOOK	CLANNISHLY	COLLEGIATE
CHERSONESE	CLARENCEUX	COLLIMATOR
CHERUBIMIC	CLASP-KNIFE	COLLINGUAL
CHESS-BOARD	CLASSICISM	COLLIQUATE
CHICKEN-POX	CLASSICIST	COLLOCUTOR
CHIFFONIER	CLAVICHORD	COLLOQUIAL
CHILDBIRTH	CLAVICULAR	COLLOQUIST
CHILDISHLY	CLAW-HAMMER	COLLOQUIZE
CHILIASTIC	CLAY-GROUND	COLORATION
CHILLINESS	CLEANSABLE	COLOURABLE
CHILLINGLY	CLEAR-STORY	COLOURABLY
CHIMERICAL	CLERESTORY	COLOURLESS
CHIMNEY-CAN	CLERGIABLE	COLPORTEUR
CHIMNEY-TOP	CLEVERNESS	COMBATABLE
CHIMPANZEE	CLIENTSHIP	COMBINABLE
CHINA-ASTER	CLINGSTONE	COMBINEDLY
CHINCHILLA	CLINICALLY	COMBUSTION
CHIP-BONNET	CLINK-STONE	COMEDIETTA
CHIROGNOMY	CLINOMETER	COMELINESS
CHIROGRAPH	CLODHOPPER	COMESTIBLE
CHIROMANCY	CLOISTERER	COMFORTING
CHIRURGEON	CLOSE-STOOL	COMICALITY
CHISELLING	CLOUDBERRY	COMMANDANT
CHIVALROUS	CLOUD-BUILT	COMMANDEER
CHLORALISM	CLOUD-BURST	COMMENTARY
CHLORIDIZE	CLOUDINESS	COMMERCIAL
CHLORIDATE	CLOWNISHLY	COMMISSARY
CHLORODYNE	CLUB-FOOTED	COMMISSION
CHLOROFORM	CLUMSINESS	COMMISSURE
CHOICELESS	COACH-STAND	COMMITMENT
CHOLAGOGUE	COADJUTRIX	COMMIXTURE
CHOLIAMBUS	COAGULABLE	COMMODIOUS
CHOP-FALLEN	COAGULATOR	COMMONABLE
CHOPSTICKS	COALESCENT	COMMONALTY
CHORIAMBUS	COAL-HEAVER	COMMONNESS
CHRISTHOOD	COAL-MASTER	COMMONWEAL
CHRISTLESS	COARSENESS	COMMUTABLE
	COAST-GUARD	COMPARABLE

COMPARABLY
COMPARISON
COMPASSION
COMPASS-SAW
COMPATIBLE
COMPATIBLY
COMPATRIOT
COMPENDIUM
COMPENSATE
COMPETENCE
COMPETITOR
COMPLACENT
COMPLAINER
COMPLEMENT
COMPLETELY
COMPLETION
COMPLETIVE
COMPLETORY
COMPLEXION
COMPLEXITY
COMPLIANCE
COMPLICACY
COMPLICATE
COMPLICITY
COMPLIMENT
COMPOSEDLY
COMPOSITOR
COMPOUNDER
COMPREHEND
COMPRESSED
COMPRESSOR
COMPROMISE
COMPULSION
COMPULSIVE
COMPULSORY
COMPUTABLE
CONCENTRIC
CONCEPTION
CONCEPTUAL
CONCERNING
CONCERTINA
CONCESSION
CONCESSIVE
CONCHOIDAL
CONCHOLOGY
CONCILIATE
CONCINNITY
CONCLAVIST
CONCLUDING
CONCLUSION
CONCLUSIVE
CONCOCTION
CONCORDANT
CONCRETELY
CONCRETION
CONCUBINAL
CONCURRENT
CONCUSSION
CONCUSSIVE
CONDESCEND
CONDOLENCE
CONDUCTION
CONDUCTIVE
CONFECTION
CONFERENCE
CONFERVOID
CONFESSION
CONFIDANTE
CONFIDENCE
CONFINABLE

CONFISCATE
CONFLUENCE
CONFORMIST
CONFORMITY
CONFOUNDED
CONFOUNDER
CONFUSEDLY
CONFUTABLE
CONGENERIC
CONGENITAL
CONGESTION
CONGESTIVE
CONGLOBATE
CONGREGATE
CONGRUENCE
CONIFEROUS
CONJECTURE
CONJOINTLY
CONJUGALLY
CONJUNCTLY
CONNASCENT
CONNATURAL
CONNECTION
CONNECTIVE
CONNIVANCE
CONNIVENCE
CONQUERING
CONSCIENCE
CONSECRATE
CONSENSUAL
CONSEQUENT
CONSISTENT
CONSISTORY
CONSOCIATE
CONSOLABLE
CONSONANCE
CONSPECTUS
CONSPIRACY
CONSTANTLY
CONSTIPATE
CONSTITUTE
CONSTRAINT
CONSTRINGE
CONSUBSIST
CONSUETUDE
CONSULSHIP
CONSULTING
CONSULTIVE
CONSUMABLE
CONSUMEDLY
CONSUMMATE
CONTACTUAL
CONTAGIOUS
CONTAINANT
CONTENTION
CONTESTANT
CONTEXTUAL
CONTEXTURE
CONTIGUITY
CONTIGUOUS
CONTINENCE
CONTINGENT
CONTINUITY
CONTINUOUS
CONTORTION
CONTRABAND
CONTRACTED
CONTRACTOR
CONTRADICT
CONTRARILY

CONTRAVENE
CONTRIBUTE
CONTRITELY
CONTRITION
CONTROLLER
CONTROVERT
CONVALESCE
CONVECTION
CONVECTIVE
CONVENABLE
CONVENANCE
CONVENIENT
CONVENTION
CONVENTUAL
CONVERGENT
CONVERSANT
CONVERSELY
CONVERSION
CONVEXNESS
CONVEYABLE
CONVEYANCE
CONVICTION
CONVINCING
CONVULSION
CONVULSIVE
COOL-HEADED
CO-OPERATOR
CO-ORDINATE
COPARCENER
COPERNICAN
COPPER-HEAD
COPROLITIC
COPULATION
COPULATIVE
COPULATORY
COPYHOLDER
COQUETTISH
CO-RADICATE
CORDIALITY
CORDILLERA
CORDWAINER
CORELATIVE
CORIACEOUS
CORINTHIAN
CORK-CUTTER
CORKING-PIN
CORK-JACKET
CORN-BEETLE
CORN-COCKLE
CORNERWISE
CORN-FACTOR
CORN-FLOWER
CORNUCOPIA
CORONATION
CORONIFORM
CORPORALLY
CORPOREITY
CORPSE-GATE
CORPULENCE
CORRECTION
CORRECTIVE
CORRECTORY
CORRESPOND
CORRIGENDA
CORRIGIBLE
CORRODIBLE
CORRUGATED
CORRUGATOR
CORRUPTION
CORRUPTIVE

CORSELETED
CORYPHAEUS
COSMICALLY
COSMOGONAL
COSMORAMIC
COSTLINESS
COTHURNATE
COTTIERISM
COTTON-SEED
COTTON-TREE
COTTON-WOOD
COTTON-WOOL
COTYLIFORM
COUCH-GRASS
COUNCILLOR
COUNCIL-MAN
COUNSELLOR
COUNTERACT
COUNTRYMAN
COURAGEOUS
COURT-BARON
COURT-DRESS
COURTHOUSE
COURT-SWORD
COUSINHOOD
COUSINSHIP
COVENANTEE
COVENANTER
COVENANTOR
COVERED-WAY
COVETINGLY
COVETOUSLY
COW-BUNTING
COW-CATCHER
COW-CHERVIL
COW-PARSLEY
COWDIE-PINE
COW-PARSNIP
COWRIE-PINE
CRAFTINESS
CRAGGINESS
CRANE'S-BILL
CRANIOLOGY
CRAPULENCE
CRASSAMENT
CRASSITUDE
CRAWLINGLY
CREAM-FACED
CREAMINESS
CREATIONAL
CREDENTIAL
CREDITABLE
CREDITABLY
CRENELLATE
CRESCENTED
CRESCENTIC
CRETACEOUS
CRIBRIFORM
CRIMINALLY
CRINGELING
CRIO-SPHINX
CRISPATION
CRISS-CROSS
CRITICALLY
CRITICIZER
CROSS-BONES
CROSS-BREED
CROSS-STAFF
CROSS-STONE
CROSS-TREES

CROTCHETED
CROW-FLOWER
CROWN-GRASS
CROWN-WHEEL
CRUET-STAND
CRUMB-BRUSH
CRUMB-CLOTH
CRUSTACEAN
CRUSTATION
CRUSTINESS
CRYOPHORUS
CRYPTOGAMY
CRYPTOGRAM
CRYPTOLOGY
CTENOPHORA
CUCKOO-SPIT
CUCURBITAL
CUIRASSIER
CULTIVABLE
CULTIVATOR
CULTURABLE
CULVERTAIL
CUMBERLESS
CUMBERSOME
CUMBROUSLY
CUMMER-BUND
CUMULATION
CUMULATIVE
CURABILITY
CURATESHIP
CURMUDGEON
CURRICULUM
CURSEDNESS
CUSTOMABLE
CUTTLE-FISH
CUTTLE-BONE
CYATHIFORM
CYCLOMETER
CYLINDROID
CZAREVITCH

D

DAGGLE-TAIL
DAINTINESS
DAMAGEABLE
DAMASK-PLUM
DAMASK-ROSE
DAPPLE-GREY
DARK-BROWED
DAUGHTERLY
DAUPHINESS
DAY-DREAMER
DAZZLINGLY
DEACONHOOD
DEACONSHIP
DEAD-LETTER
DEADLINESS
DEAD-NETTLE
DEAD-WEIGHT
DEAR-BOUGHT
DEASPIRATE
DEATH-AGONY
DEATH'S-DOOR
DEATH'S-HEAD
DEATH-TOKEN
DEATH-WATCH
DEBASEMENT
DEBAUCHERY

DEBENTURED
DEBILITATE
DEBONAIRLY
DEBOUCHURE
DECAGYNIAN
DECAGYNOUS
DECAHEDRAL
DECALOGIST
DECAMPMENT
DECANDRIAN
DECANDROUS
DECANGULAR
DECAPITATE
DECAPODOUS
DECEIVABLE
DECEMBERLY
DECEMVIRAL
DECIGRAMME
DECIMALIZE
DECIMATION
DECIPHERER
DECISIVELY
DECLAIMANT
DECLARABLE
DECLARATOR
DECLAREDLY
DECLENSION
DECLINABLE
DECLINATOR
DECOLORANT
DECOLORATE
DECOLORIZE
DECOMPOUND
DECORATION
DECORATIVE
DECOROUSLY
DECREEABLE
DECRESCENT
DECUMBENCE
DECUMBENCY
DECURRENCY
DEDICATION
DEDICATORY
DEFACEMENT
DEFALCATOR
DEFAMATION
DEFEASANCE
DEFEASIBLE
DEFECATION
DEFENDABLE
DEFENSIBLE
DEFICIENCE
DEFICIENCY
DEFILEMENT
DEFINITELY
DEFINITION
DEFINITIVE
DEFLAGRATE
DEFLECTION
DEFLOWERER
DEFORMEDLY
DEFRAYMENT
DEGENERACY
DEGENERATE
DEHISCENCE
DEHUMANIZE
DEJECTEDLY
DEL CREDERE
DELECTABLE
DELECTABLY

DELEGATION
DELIBERATE
DELICATELY
DELIGHTFUL
DELINEATOR
DELINQUENT
DELIQUESCE
DELUSIVELY
DEMAGOGISM
DEMANDABLE
DEMI-QUAVER
DEMOBILISE
DEMOCRATIC
DEMOGORGON
DEMOGRAPHY
DEMOISELLE
DEMOLISHER
DEMOLITION
DEMONETIZE
DEMONOLOGY
DEMORALIZE
DEMURENESS
DEMURRABLE
DENDRIFORM
DENDROLITE
DENDROLOGY
DENIZATION
DENOMINATE
DENOTATION
DENOTATIVE
DENOUEMENT
DENSIMETER
DENTIFRICE
DENUDATION
DENUNCIATE
DEOBSTRUCT
DEODORIZER
DEONTOLOGY
DEPARTMENT
DEPENDABLE
DEPENDANCE
DEPENDENCE
DEPENDENCY
DEPILATION
DEPILATORY
DEPLORABLE
DEPLORABLY
DEPLOYMENT
DEPOLARIZE
DEPOPULATE
DEPORTMENT
DEPOSITARY
DEPOSITION
DEPRAVEDLY
DEPRECATOR
DEPRECIATE
DEPREDATOR
DEPRESSION
DEPRESSIVE
DEPURATION
DEPURATORY
DEPUTATION
DERACINATE
DERIDINGLY
DERISIVELY
DERIVATION
DERIVATIVE
DEROGATION
DEROGATORY
DESCENDANT

DESCENDENT
DESCENDING
DESCENSION
DESECRATER
DESERVEDLY
DESHABILLE
DESICCATOR
DESIDERATE
DESIGNATOR
DESIGNEDLY
DESOLATELY
DESOLATION
DESPAIRING
DESPATCHER
DESPICABLE
DESPICABLY
DESPISABLE
DESPITEFUL
DESPONDENT
DESQUAMATE
DESUDATION
DETACHMENT
DETAINMENT
DETECTABLE
DETERGENCE
DETERGENCY
DETERMINED
DETESTABLE
DETESTABLY
DETONATING
DETONATION
DETRACTION
DETRACTIVE
DETRACTORY
DETRUNCATE
DEUTOPLASM
DEVASTATOR
DEVILISHLY
DEVIL'S-DUST
DEVITALIZE
DEVOLUTION
DEVOTEMENT
DEVOTIONAL
DEVOURABLE
DIABETICAL
DIABOLICAL
DIACAUSTIC
DIACOUSTIC
DIAGLYPHIC
DIAGNOSTIC
DIAGONALLY
DIALECTICS
DIALOGICAL
DIAPEDESIS
DIAPHANOUS
DIAPHONICS
DIASKEUAST
DIATHERMAL
DIATHERMIC
DIATRIBIST
DICTATRESS
DICTIONARY
DIDACTICAL
DIDELPHIAN
DIDUNCULUS
DIDYNAMOUS
DIELECTRIC
DIE-SINKING
DIETETICAL
DIFFERENCE

DIFFICULTY
DIFFIDENCE
DIFFORMITY
DIFFUSIBLE
DIGESTIBLE
DIGITATELY
DIGITATION
DIGITIFORM
DIGITORIUM
DIGRESSION
DIGRESSIVE
DEJUDICATE
DILACERATE
DILAPIDATE
DILATATION
DILATORILY
DILETTANTE
DILIGENTLY
DILLY-DALLY
DILUCIDATE
DIMINISHER
DIMINUENDO
DIMINUTION
DIMINUTIVE
DIMORPHISM
DIMORPHOUS
DINING-ROOM
DINNER-HOUR
DINNERLESS
DINNER-TIME
DIOPTRICAL
DIPETALOUS
DIPHTHERIA
DIPHYLLOUS
DIPHYODONT
DIPLOMATIC
DIPROTODON
DIPSOMANIA
DIRECTNESS
DIRECTRESS
DISABILITY
DISANIMATE
DISAPPAREL
DISAPPOINT
DISAPPROVE
DISARRANGE
DISASTROUS
DISBELIEVE
DISBURTHEN
DISCERNING
DISCHARGER
DISCIPLINE
DISCLAIMER
DISCLOSURE
DISCOMFORT
DISCOMMEND
DISCOMPOSE
DISCONCERT
DISCONNECT
DISCONTENT
DISCOPHORA
DISCORDANT
DISCOUNTER
DISCOURAGE
DISCOURSER
DISCOVERER
DISCREETLY
DISCREPANT
DISCRETION
DISCRETIVE

DISCURSIVE
DISCUSSION
DISCUSSIVE
DISCUTIENT
DISDAINFUL
DISEMBOGUE
DISEMBOSOM
DISEMBOWEL
DISEMBROIL
DISENCHANT
DISENGAGED
DISENNOBLE
DISENSLAVE
DISENTITLE
DISFEATURE
DISFIGURER
DISFURNISH
DISGUSTFUL
DISGUSTING
DISHABILLE
DISHEARTEN
DISHONESTY
DISINCLINE
DISINHERIT
DISJOINTED
DISLOYALLY
DISLOYALTY
DISMALNESS
DISMISSION
DISMISSORY
DISOMATOUS
DISORDERED
DISORDERLY
DISOWNMENT
DISPARAGER
DISPASSION
DISPENSARY
DISPENSING
DISPEOPLER
DISPERMOUS
DISPERSION
DISPERSIVE
DISPIRITED
DISPLEASED
DISPLEASER
DISPOSABLE
DISPOSSESS
DISPUTABLE
DISQUALIFY
DISRESPECT
DISRUPTION
DISSATISFY
DISSECTING
DISSECTION
DISSEMBLER
DISSENSION
DISSENTING
DISSERVICE
DISSIDENCE
DISSILIENT
DISSIMILAR
DISSIPATED
DISSOCIATE
DISSOLUBLE
DISSOLVENT
DISSONANCE
DISSUASION
DISSUASIVE
DISSYMETRY
DISTENSIVE

DISTENTION
DISTICHOUS
DISTILLATE
DISTINCTLY
DISTORTION
DISTORTIVE
DISTRACTED
DISTRAINER
DISTRAINOR
DISTRAUGHT
DISTRESSED
DISTRIBUTE
DITHEISTIC
DIVAGATION
DIVARICATE
DIVERGENCE
DIVERGENCY
DIVINATION
DIVINENESS
DIVING-BELL
DIVISIONAL
DOCIMASTIC
DOCTORSHIP
DOCUMENTAL
DOGGEDNESS
DOGMATIZER
DOG-PARSLEY
DOLOROUSLY
DOMINATION
DOOR-KEEPER
DOUBLE-BASS
DOUBLE-DYED
DOUBLE-LOCK
DOUBLENESS
DOUBLE-STAR
DOUBTFULLY
DOWNLOOKED
DOWN-STAIRS
DRAGON-TREE
DRAMATICAL
DRAMATURGY
DRAUGHT-BAR
DRAWBRIDGE
DRAWLINGLY
DREADFULLY
DREAMINESS
DREARINESS
DRESSMAKER
DROOPINGLY
DROP-HAMMER
DROSOMETER
DROSSINESS
DROWSINESS
DRUDGINGLY
DRUPACEOUS
DRYSALTERY
DUBITATION
DUCK-BILLED
DULL-WITTED
DUMB-WAITER
DUNIWASSAL
DUODECIMAL
DUPABILITY
DURABILITY
DUUMVIRATE
DWARFISHLY
DYNAMITARD
DYSENTERIC

E

EARTH-BOUND
EARTHINESS
EARTH-PLATE
EARTHQUAKE
EARTH-SHINE
EAR-TRUMPET
EAR-WITNESS
EASTERLING
EASTERTIDE
EBOULEMENT
EBRACTEATE
EBULLIENCE
EBULLIENCY
EBULLITION
ECCHYMOSIS
ECCLESIAST
ECCOPROTIC
ECHINODERM
ECONOMICAL
ECTHLIPSIS
ECUMENICAL
ECZEMATOUS
EDACIOUSLY
EDENTULOUS
EDIBLENESS
EDIFYINGLY
EDITORSHIP
EDULCORATE
EFFACEABLE
EFFACEMENT
EFFECTIBLE
EFFECTLESS
EFFECTUATE
EFFEMINACY
EFFEMINATE
EFFERVESCE
EFFICIENCY
EFFLORESCE
EFFORTLESS
EFFRONTERY
EFFULGENCE
EFFUSIVELY
EGYPTOLOGY
EIGHTEENMO
EIGHTEENTH
EISTEDDFOD
ELABORATOR
ELASTICITY
ELBOW-CHAIR
ELDER-BERRY
ELECAMPANE
ELECTORATE
ELECTRICAL
ELEMENTARY
ELENCHICAL
ELEUSINIAN
ELIMINABLE
ELIQUATION
ELLIPTICAL
ELONGATION
ELOQUENTLY
ELUCIDATOR
EMACIATION
EMANCIPATE
EMARGINATE
EMASCULATE
EMBANKMENT
EMBASSADOR

EMBER-GOOSE
EMBLAZONER
EMBLEMATIC
EMBODIMENT
EMBOLISMAL
EMBOLISMIC
EMBONPOINT
EMBOSSMENT
EMBOUCHURE
EMBROIDERY
EMBRYOGENY
EMBRYOLOGY
EMBRYONARY
EMBRYOTOMY
EMENDATION
EMENDATORY
EMERGENTLY
EMETICALLY
EMIGRATION
EMMETROPIA
EMPHATICAL
EMPIRICISM
EMPLOYABLE
EMPLOYMENT
ENAMELLIST
ENANTIOSIS
ENCAMPMENT
ENCEPHALIC
ENCEPHALON
ENCHANTING
ENCLITICAL
ENCOURAGER
ENCRINITAL
ENCRINITIC
ENCROACHER
ENCYCLICAL
ENCYSTMENT
ENDEARMENT
ENDEMICITY
ENDERMATIC
ENDOGAMOUS
ENDOGENOUS
ENDOPLEURA
ENDORHIZAL
ENDORSABLE
ENDOSMOSIS
ENDOSMOTIC
ENDOSTITIS
ENDURINGLY
ENERVATION
ENFORCIBLE
ENGAGEMENT
ENGAGINGLY
ENGLISHMAN
ENHARMONIC
ENIGMATIST
ENJOINMENT
ENLACEMENT
ENLISTMENT
ENORMOUSLY
ENRICHMENT
ENROCKMENT
ENSANGUINE
ENSIGNSHIP
ENTAILMENT
ENTERALGIA
ENTEROCELE
ENTEROLITE
ENTEROLITH
ENTEROTOMY

ENTERPRISE
ENTHRONIZE
ENTHUSIASM
ENTHUSIAST
ENTICEABLE
ENTICEMENT
ENTICINGLY
ENTIRENESS
ENTOMBMENT
ENTOMOLOGY
ENTOPHYTIC
ENTROCHITE
ENTRY-MONEY
ENUMERATOR
ENUNCIABLE
ENUNCIATOR
EPAULEMENT
EPAULETTED
EPENTHESIS
EPENTHETIC
EPEXEGESIS
EPHEMERIST
EPICYCLOID
EPIDEICTIC
EPIDEMICAL
EPIGASTRIC
EPIGENESIS
EPIGENETIC
EPIGLOTTIC
EPIGLOTTIS
EPIGRAPHIC
EPILEPTOID
EPILOGICAL
EPILOGUIZE
EPIPHLOEUM
EPIRHIZOUS
EPISCOPACY
EPISCOPATE
EPISODICAL
EPISPASTIC
EPISTOLIST
EPISTOLIZE
EPITAPHIAN
EPITAPHIST
EPITHELIAL
EPITHELIUM
EPITOMIZER
EPITOMATOR
EPROUVETTE
EQUABILITY
EQUANIMITY
EQUANIMOUS
EQUATORIAL
EQUESTRIAN
EQUITATION
EQUIVALENT
EQUIVOCATE
ERADICABLE
ERADICATOR
ERECTILITY
EREMITICAL
ERETHISTIC
ERICACEOUS
EROTOMANIA
ERPETOLOGY
ERUBESCENT
ERUCTATION
ERUPTIONAL
ERYSIPELAS
ESCAPEMENT

ESCARPMENT
ESCHAROTIC
ESCRITOIRE
ESCULAPIAN
ESCUTCHEON
ESOPHAGOUS
ESPECIALLY
ESSAYISTIC
ESTEEMABLE
ESTIMATION
ESTIVATION
ESURIENTLY
ETERNALIST
ETERNALIZE
ETHEREALLY
ETHERIFORM
ETHNICALLY
ETHNOLOGIC
ETIOLATION
ETYMOLOGIC
EUCALYPTOL
EUCALYPTUS
EUDEMONISM
EUDEMONIST
EUDIOMETER
EUDIOMETRY
EUHEMERISM
EULOGISTIC
EUPHONIOUS
EUPHORBIUM
EUPHUISTIC
EUSTACHIAN
EUTHANASIA
EVACUATION
EVALUATION
EVANESCENT
EVANGELIST
EVANGELIZE
EVAPORABLE
EVEN-HANDED
EVENTUALLY
EVERLIVING
EVERYWHERE
EVIDENTIAL
EVISCERATE
EVOLVEMENT
EXACERBATE
EXACTITUDE
EXAGGERATE
EXALTATION
EXAMINABLE
EXAMINATOR
EXASPERATE
EX-CATHEDRA
EXCAVATION
EXCELLENCE
EXCELLENCY
EXCERPTION
EXCITATION
EXCITATIVE
EXCITATORY
EXCITEMENT
EXCOGITATE
EXCRESCENT
EXCRUCIATE
EXCUSATORY
EXCUSELESS
EXECRATION
EXECRATIVE
EXECRATORY

EXECUTABLE
EXEGITICAL
EXHALATION
EXHALEMENT
EXHAUSTING
EXHAUSTION
EXHAUSTIVE
EXHIBITION
EXHIBITIVE
EXHIBITORY
EXHILARANT
EXHILARATE
EXHUMATION
EXORBITANT
EXOTERICAL
EXPANSIBLE
EXPATIATOR
EXPATRIATE
EXPECTANCE
EXPECTANCY
EXPEDIENCY
EXPEDITION
EXPELLABLE
EXPERIENCE
EXPERIMENT
EXPERTNESS
EXPIRATORY
EXPLICABLE
EXPLOITAGE
EXPLICITLY
EXPLORABLE
EXPORTABLE
EXPOSITION
EXPOSITIVE
EXPOSITORY
EXPRESSION
EXPRESSIVE
EXPURGATOR
EXSICCATOR
EXTENDIBLE
EXTENSIBLE
EXTENUATOR
EXTERIORLY
EXTERNALLY
EXTINCTEUR
EXTINCTION
EXTINGUISH
EXTIRPABLE
EXTIRPATOR
EXTRACTION
EXTRACTIVE
EXTRAMURAL
EXTRANEOUS
EXTRICABLE
EXUBERANCE
EXUBERANCY
EXULCERATE
EXULTATION
EXUVIATION
EYELET-HOLE
EYE-SERVANT
EYE-SERVICE
EYE-WITNESS

F

FABRICATOR
FABULOUSLY
FABULOSITY

FACILENESS
FACILITATE
FACTIONARY
FACTIONIST
FACTIOUSLY
FACTITIOUS
FACTORSHIP
FAGOT-VOTER
FAHRENHEIT
FAIR-MINDED
FAIR-SPOKEN
FAITHFULLY
FALLACIOUS
FALLOW-CHAT
FALLOW-DEER
FAMILIARLY
FAMISHMENT
FANATICISM
FANATICIZE
FANCIFULLY
FANTOCCINI
FAN-TRACERY
FARCICALLY
FAR-FETCHED
FARMERSHIP
FAR-SIGHTED
FASCIATION
FASCICULAR
FASCICULUS
FASTIDIOUS
FASTIGIATE
FAT-BRAINED
FATALISTIC
FATHERHOOD
FATHERLAND
FATHERLESS
FATHERSHIP
FATHOMABLE
FATHOMLESS
FAULTINESS
FAVOURABLE
FAVOURABLY
FEARLESSLY
FEATHERING
FEBRIFUGAL
FEDERALISM
FEDERALIST
FEDERALIZE
FEDERATION
FEDERATIVE
FEEBLENESS
FELICITATE
FELICITOUS
FELLMONGER
FELLOW-HEIR
FELLOWSHIP
FELSPATHIC
FEME-COVERT
FEMININELY
FEMININITY
FENESTRATE
FER-DE-LANCE
FERTILIZER
FERVIDNESS
FETTERLESS
FETTERLOCK
FEUILLETON
FEVERISHLY
FIBRILLOUS
FICTIONIST

FICTITIOUS
FIDDLE-WOOD
FIELD-GLASS
FIELD-MOUSE
FIELD-SPORT
FIELD-TRAIN
FIERCENESS
FIGURATION
FIGURATIVE
FIGURE-HEAD
FILE-CUTTER
FILIBUSTER
FILTHINESS
FILTRATION
FIMBRIATED
FINE-SPOKEN
FINGER-POST
FINICALITY
FINITENESS
FIRE-BUCKET
FIRE-ENGINE
FIRE-SCREEN
FIRST-FRUIT
FIRST-WATER
FISH-CARVER
FISHING-ROD
FISHMONGER
FISTICUFFS
FITFULNESS
FLABBINESS
FLABELLATE
FLACCIDITY
FLAGELLANT
FLAGELLATE
FLAGGINESS
FLAGITIOUS
FLAGRANTLY
FLAMBOYANT
FLATTERING
FLATULENCE
FLATULENCY
FLAVESCENT
FLAVOUROUS
FLEABITTEN
FLECTIONAL
FLEDGELING
FLESHINESS
FLINTINESS
FLIPPANTLY
FLIRTATION
FLOATATION
FLOCCULENT
FLORENTINE
FLORIDNESS
FLOSCULOUS
FLUNKEYISM
FLUVIATILE
FLUXIONARY
FOLIACEOUS
FOOTBRIDGE
FOOTLIGHTS
FORAMINULE
FORAMINOUS
FORBEARANT
FORBEARING
FORBIDDING
FORCEFULLY
FORCIPATED
FORCLOSURE
FORECASTLE

FORECHOSEN
FOREFATHER
FOREGROUND
FOREHANDED
FOREORDAIN
FORERUNNER
FORESHADOW
FORETELLER
FORFEITURE
FORGIVABLE
FORMIDABLE
FORMIDABLY
FORNICATOR
FORTHGOING
FORTUITOUS
FOSTERLING
FOUNDATION
FOURCHETTE
FOURSQUARE
FOURTEENTH
FRACTIONAL
FRAGMENTAL
FRAGRANTLY
FRAMBOESIA
FRANCISCAN
FRATERNISE
FRATRICIDE
FRAUDFULLY
FRAUDULENT
FREAKISHLY
FREEBOOTER
FREEHANDED
FREEHOLDER
FREEMARTIN
FREIGHTAGE
FRENETICAL
FRENZIEDLY
FREQUENTER
FRICANDEAU
FRICTIONAL
FRIENDLESS
FRIENDSHIP
FRIGORIFIC
FRISKINESS
FRITILLARY
FROLICSOME
FROSTINESS
FROTHINESS
FROWNINGLY
FRUITERESS
FRUITFULLY
FRUSTRABLE
FRUTESCENT
FUCIVOROUS
FUGITIVELY
FULFILMENT
FUMIGATION
FUNCTIONAL
FUNEREALLY
FUNGACEOUS
FURBELOWED

G

GABIONNADE
GALIMATIAS
GALLOWGLAS
GALVANIZER
GAMEKEEPER

GANGLIONIC
GANGRENOUS
GARISHNESS
GARNISHING
GASTEROPOD
GASTRALGIA
GASTRONOME
GASTRONOMY
GELATINATE
GELATINIZE
GELATINOID
GELATINOUS
GEMINATION
GEMMACEOUS
GENERALITY
GENERALIZE
GENERATION
GENERATIVE
GENERATRIX
GENEROSITY
GENEROUSLY
GENETHLIAC
GENIALNESS
GENICULATE
GENTLEFOLK
GENTLENESS
GEOCENTRIC
GEOGNOSTIC
GEOGRAPHER
GEOLOGICAL
GEOPHAGISM
GEOPONICAL
GEOSELENIC
GEOTROPISM
GINGERBEER
GLACIALIST
GLACIATION
GLANCINGLY
GLANDIFORM
GLANDULOUS
GLASSINESS
GLIMMERING
GLOBULARLY
GLORIOUSLY
GLOSSARIAL
GLOSSARIST
GLOSSINESS
GLOSSOLOGY
GLOTTOLOGY
GLUCOSURIA
GLUMACEOUS
GLUTTONIZE
GNOSTICISM
GONIOMETER
GOODLINESS
GOOSEBERRY
GORGEOUSLY
GORGONEION
GORGONZOLA
GORMANDIZE
GRACEFULLY
GRACIOUSLY
GRAMOPHONE
GRANADILLA
GRANDCHILD
GRANDNIECE
GRANDUNCLE
GRANGERISM
GRAPHOLOGY
GRAPHOTYPE

GRAPTOLITE
GRASSINESS
GRATEFULLY
GRATIFYING
GRATUITOUS
GRAVEOLENT
GRAVIGRADE
GRAVIMETER
GREASINESS
GREGARIOUS
GRESSORIAL
GRIEVOUSLY
GRITTINESS
GROGGINESS
GROUNDLESS
GROUNDSILL
GROUNDWORK
GROVELLING
GRUDGINGLY
GUILLOTINE
GUILTINESS
GUTTURALLY
GYMNASIUMS
GYMNASTICS
GYMNOSPERM
GYNANDROUS
GYRATIONAL

H

HABILIMENT
HABILITATE
HABITUALLY
HACKMATACK
HAEMATOSIS
HAEMATOZOA
HAEMATURIA
HAGIOCRACY
HALBERDIER
HALLELUIAH
HANDICRAFT
HANDMAIDEN
HARASSMENT
HARBOURAGE
HARMLESSLY
HARMONIOUS
HARQUEBUSE
HAUSTELLUM
HEADSTRONG
HEARTINESS
HEAVENWARD
HEBDOMADAL
HECTICALLY
HEEDLESSLY
HELICOIDAL
HELIOGRAPH
HELIOTROPE
HELMINTHIC
HEMIPTERAN
HEMIHEDRAL
HEMIHEDRON
HEMORRHAGE
HENCEFORTH
HENOTHEISM
HENTACHORD
HEPTAGONAL
HEPTARCHIC
HEPTATEUCH
HERBESCENT

HEREABOUTS
HEREDITARY
HERESIARCH
HERMETICAL
HERPETICAL
HESITATION
HETERODOXY
HETEROTOPY
HEXAGYNIAN
HEXAHEDRAL
HEXAHEDRON
HEXAMETRIC
HEXANDRIAN
HIDDENNESS
HIERARCHAL
HIEROPHANT
HIGHWAYMAN
HINDERANCE
HINDUSTANI
HIPPOGRYPH
HIPPOPHILE
HIPPOPHAGY
HITHERMOST
HITHERWARD
HOARSENESS
HOLLOWNESS
HOLOPHOTAL
HOMELINESS
HOMEOPATHY
HOMILETICS
HOMOTONOUS
HONORARIUM
HONOURABLE
HOPELESSLY
HORIZONTAL
HOROGRAPHY
HOROLOGIST
HOROSCOPIC
HOSPITABLE
HOSPITABLY
HOUSEWIVES
HULLABALOO
HUMBLENESS
HUMORALISM
HUMORALIST
HUMORISTIC
HUMOROUSLY
HUMOURSOME
HUMPBACKED
HUSBANDMAN
HYDRAULICS
HYDROMANCY
HYDROMANIA
HYDROPATHY
HYDROPHANE
HYDROPHYTE
HYGROMETER
HYLOTHEISM
HYMENOPTER
HYMENOTOMY
HYPAETHRAL
HYPERBOLIC
HYPERDULIA
HYPERMETER
HYPNOTIZER
HYPODERMAL
HYPOGYNOUS
HYPOTENUSE
HYPSOMETER
HYPSOMETRY

HYSTERICAL

I

ICONOCLASM
ICONOCLAST
ICONOLATRY
IDEOGRAPHY
IDEOLOGIST
IDIOPATHIC
IDOLATROUS
IDOLOCLAST
IGNIPOTENT
IGNORANTLY
ILLATIVELY
ILLEGALITY
ILLITERACY
ILLITERATE
ILLUMINANT
ILLUMINATE
ILLUMINATI
ILLUSTRATE
IMAGINABLE
IMAGINABLY
IMMACULATE
IMMANATION
IMMATERIAL
IMMATURELY
IMMATURITY
IMMEMORIAL
IMMERSIBLE
IMMOBILITY
IMMODERATE
IMMODESTLY
IMMOLATION
IMMORALITY
IMMORTELLE
IMPALPABLY
IMPANATION
IMPASSABLE
IMPASSIBLE
IMPATIENCE
IMPECCABLE
IMPEDIMENT
IMPENITENT
IMPERATIVE
IMPERIALLY
IMPERSONAL
IMPLACABLE
IMPLACABLY
IMPLICITLY
IMPORTABLE
IMPORTANCE
IMPOSINGLY
IMPOSITION
IMPOSSIBLE
IMPOSSIBLY
IMPOSTHUME
IMPOTENTLY
IMPOUNDAGE
IMPOVERISH
IMPREGNATE
IMPRESARIO
IMPRESSION
IMPRIMULAR
IMPROBABLE
IMPROBABLY
IMPROPERLY

IMPRUDENCE
IMPUDENTLY
IMPUGNABLE
IMPUTATION
IMPUTATIVE
INACCURACY
INACCURATE
INACTIVELY
INACTIVITY
INADEQUATE
INAPTITUDE
INAUGURATE
INCAPACITY
INCASEMENT
INCENDIARY
INCESTUOUS
INCHOATELY
INCHOATIVE
INCIDENTAL
INCINERATE
INCLINABLE
INCLUDIBLE
INCOMPLETE
INCONSTANT
INCREDIBLE
INCREDIBLY
INCRESCENT
INCUBATION
INCUBATIVE
INCUMBENCY
INDAGATION
INDECENTLY
INDECISIVE
INDECOROUS
INDEFINITE
INDELICATE
INDICATION
INDICATIVE
INDICTABLE
INDICTMENT
INDIGENOUS
INDIRECTLY
INDISCREET
INDISTINCT
INDITEMENT
INDIVIDUAL
INDOCILITY
INDUCEMENT
INDULGENCE
INDURATION
INDUSTRIAL
INELEGANCE
INELIGIBLE
INELOQUENT
INEQUALITY
INEVITABLE
INEXPIABLE
INFALLIBLE
INFALLIBLY
INFAMOUSLY
INFATUATED
INFECTIOUS
INFEFTMENT
INFELICITY
INFERIORLY
INFERRIBLE
INFIDELITY
INFILTRATE
INFINITELY
INFINITIVE

INFINITUDE
INFLECTION
INFLECTIVE
INFLEXIBLE
INFLICTION
INFLICTIVE
INFORMALLY
INFRACTION
INFREQUENT
INFUSORIAL
INFUSORIAN
INGLORIOUS
INGREDIENT
INGULFMENT
INHABITANT
INHALATION
INHERENTLY
INHERITRIX
INHIBITION
INHIBITORY
INHUMANITY
INHUMATION
INIMICALLY
INIMITABLE
INIQUITOUS
INITIATION
INITIATIVE
INITIATORY
INJUDICIAL
INNATENESS
INNOCENTLY
INNOMINATE
INNOVATION
INNUENDOES
INOCULABLE
INOCULATOR
INOFFICIAL
INOSCULATE
INQUIETUDE
INQUISITOR
INSALUTARY
INSANENESS
INSATIABLE
INSECURELY
INSECURITY
INSENSIBLE
INSENSIBLY
INSINUATOR
INSIPIDITY
INSOBRIETY
INSOLATION
INSOLENTLY
INSOLVABLE
INSOLVENCY
INSOUCIANT
INSPECTION
INSPIRABLE
INSPISSATE
INSTALMENT
INSTIGATOR
INSTILMENT
INSTITUTOR
INSTRUCTOR
INSTRUMENT
INSULARITY
INSULATION
INTANGIBLE
INTANGIBLY
INTEGUMENT
INTENDANCY

INTERBREED
INTERCROSS
INTERESTED
INTERLOPER
INTERLUNAR
INTERMARRY
INTERMEZZO
INTERMURAL
INTERNALLY
INTERSPACE
INTERWEAVE
INTESTABLE
INTESTINAL
INTIMATELY
INTIMATION
INTIMIDATE
INTONATION
INTOXICATE
INTRAMURAL
INTREPIDLY
INTRODUCER
INTROSPECT
INUNDATION
INVAGINATE
INVALIDATE
INVALUABLE
INVARIABLE
INVARIABLY
INVENTIBLE
INVENTRESS
INVESTMENT
INVETERATE
INVIGORATE
INVIOLABLE
INVITATION
INVITATORY
INVITINGLY
INVOCATION
INVOCATORY
INVOLUCRAL
INVOLUCRUM
INVOLUTION
INWARDNESS
IRIDESCENT
IRIDOSMIUM
IRONMONGER
IRRADIANCE
IRRADIANCY
IRRATIONAL
IRRELEVANT
IRRELIGION
IRREMEABLE
IRRESOLUTE
IRREVERENT
IRRIGATION
IRRITATING
IRRITATION
ISAGOGICAL
ISHMAELITE
ISOCHRONAL
ISODYNAMIC
ISOMERICAL
ISRAELITIC

J

JACKANAPES
JAGGEDNESS
JANIZARIES

JARDINIERE
JARGONELLE
JEOPARDIZE
JEOPARDOUS
JESUITICAL
JINRIKISHA
JOCULARITY
JOLTERHEAD
JOURNEYMAN
JOVIALNESS
JOYFULNESS
JOYOUSNESS
JUBILATION
JUDAICALLY
JUDICIALLY
JUGGERNAUT
JUNCACEOUS
JUVENILITY
JUXTAPOSIT

K

KERCHIEFED
KERSEYMERE
KHITMUTGAR
KINDLINESS
KILOGRAMME
KINEMATICS
KINGFISHER
KINGLINESS
KNIGHTHOOD
KNOBKERRIE
KNOTTINESS
KRIEGSPIEL

L

LABORATORY
LACERATION
LACHRYMOSE
LACKADAISY
LACONICISM
LACTOMETER
LACTOSCOPE
LACUSTRINE
LAMBDACISM
LAMBDOIDAL
LAMENTABLE
LAMENTABLY
LAMINATION
LANCEOLATE
LANDHOLDER
LANDLOCKED
LANDLUBBER
LANDSPRING
LANGUOROUS
LANIFEROUS
LANIGEROUS
LANSQUENET
LARDACEOUS
LARYNGITIS
LASCIVIOUS
LAUGHINGLY
LAUREATION
LAWFULNESS
LEADERETTE
LEADERSHIP
LEGATESHIP

LEGISLATOR
LEGITIMACY
LEGITIMATE
LEGITIMIZE
LEGUMINOUS
LENTICULAR
LETHARGIZE
LEUCOPATHY
LEVIGATION
LEVITATION
LEVOGYRATE
LEXICOLOGY
LIBERALISM
LIBERALITY
LIBERALIZE
LIBERATION
LIBERATORY
LIBIDINIST
LIBRETTIST
LICENTIATE
LICENTIOUS
LIEUTENANT
LIFELESSLY
LIGAMENTAL
LIGHTHOUSE
LIKELIHOOD
LIKELINESS
LIMBERNESS
LIMITATION
LINGUIFORM
LINGUISTIC
LIQUESCENT
LITERALISM
LITERALIST
LITERALITY
LITERALIZE
LITERATURE
LITHOGRAPH
LITHOLOGIC
LITHOPHYTE
LITHOTRITY
LITIGATION
LITTLENESS
LITURGICAL
LIVELIHOOD
LIVELINESS
LOCOMOTION
LOCOMOTIVE
LOCULAMENT
LOGGERHEAD
LOGISTICAL
LOGOGRAPHY
LOLLARDISM
LONELINESS
LONESOMELY
LONGHEADED
LOQUACIOUS
LORDLINESS
LORICATION
LOVELINESS
LOWERINGLY
LOXODROMIC
LUBRICATOR
LUCIFUGOUS
LUCKLESSLY
LUCULENTLY
LUGUBRIOUS
LUMINOSITY
LUMINOUSLY
LUMPSUCKER

LUSCIOUSLY
LUSTRATION
LUSTRELESS
LUXURIANCE
LUTESTRING

M

MACADAMIZE
MACERATION
MACHINATOR
MACULATION
MAGISTRACY
MAGISTRATE
MAGNETIZER
MAGNIFICAL
MAIDENHAIR
MAIDENHEAD
MAIDENHOOD
MAINTAINER
MALACOLOGY
MALAPROPOS
MALCONTENT
MALEFACTOR
MALEVOLENT
MALIGNANCE
MALINGERER
MALODOROUS
MALPIGHIAN
MALVACEOUS
MAMMILLATE
MANAGEABLE
MANAGEMENT
MANCHINEEL
MANDIBULAR
MANFULNESS
MANGOSTEEN
MANIACALLY
MANIFESTLY
MANIFOLDLY
MANIPULATE
MANOEUVRER
MANUSCRIPT
MARASCHINO
MARCESCENT
MARGINALLY
MARGRAVINE
MARIOLATRY
MARIONETTE
MARKETABLE
MARLACEOUS
MARMORATED
MARQUISATE
MARROWLESS
MARSHALLER
MARSHINESS
MARTINGALE
MARVELLOUS
MASQUERADE
MASSASAUGA
MASTERLESS
MASTERSHIP
MASTICABLE
MASTICATOR
MASTODYNIA
MATCHMAKER
MATERIALLY
MATERNALLY
MATHEMATIC

MATRIARCHY
MATRONHOOD
MATURATION
MATURATIVE
MATURENESS
MAXILLIPED
MAYONNAISE
MEAGRENESS
MEASURABLE
MEASURABLY
MECHANICAL
MEDALLURGY
MEDDLESOME
MEDICAMENT
MEDICATION
MEDIOCRITY
MEDITATION
MEDITATIVE
MEERSCHAUM
MEGALITHIC
MEGALOSAUR
MEGAPODIUS
MELANÆMIA
MELANCHOLY
MEMBERSHIP
MEMBRANOUS
MEMORANDUM
MENACINGLY
MENDACIOUS
MENDICANCY
MENSTRUATE
MENSTRUUMS
MENSURABLE
MEPHITICAL
MERCANTILE
MERCHANTRY
MERCIFULLY
MESENTERIC
MESMERIZER
MESOTHORAX
METABOLISM
METACARPUS
METACARPAL
METACENTRE
METAPHORIC
METAPHRASE
METAPHRAST
METAPHYSIC
METASTASIS
METATARSUS
METATARSAL
METATHESIS
METATHORAX
METHODICAL
METHYLATED
METICULOUS
METRICALLY
METROGRAPH
METRONYMIC
METROPOLIS
METTLESOME
MICHAELMAS
MICROFARAD
MICROMETER
MICROMETRY
MICROPHONE
MICROPHYTE
MICROSCOPE
MICROSCOPY
MICROSEISM

MIDSHIPMAN
MIGHTINESS
MIGNONETTE
MILITARISM
MILITARIST
MILITIAMAN
MILLENNIAL
MILLENNIUM
MILLESIMAL
MINERALIZE
MINERALOGY
MINISTRANT
MINORITIES
MINSTRELSY
MINUTENESS
MIRACULOUS
MIRTHFULLY
MISADVISED
MISARRANGE
MISBELIEVE
MISCELLANY
MISCONDUCT
MISFORTUNE
MISMEASURE
MISOGAMIST
MISOGYNIST
MISPRISION
MISSIONARY
MISTAKABLE
MISTAKENLY
MNEMONICAL
MODERATION
MODERATELY
MODERATISM
MODERNIZER
MODERNNESS
MODIFIABLE
MODISHNESS
MODULATION
MOHAMMEDAN
MOLYBDENUM
MONARCHISM
MONARCHIST
MONASTICON
MONILIFORM
MONITORIAL
MONOCHROME
MONOCHROMY
MONOCULOUS
MONOECIOUS
MONOGAMIST
MONOGAMOUS
MONOLITHIC
MONOLOGIST
MONOMANIAC
MONOPOLIZE
MONOTHEISM
MONOTHEIST
MONOTONOUS
MONSIGNORE
MONUMENTAL
MOPISHNESS
MORATORIUM
MORBIDNESS
MORDACIOUS
MORGANATIC
MOROSENESS
MORPHOLOGY
MORTIFYING
MOSAICALLY

MOTHERHOOD
MOTHERLESS
MOTIONLESS
MOULDINESS
MOUNTEBANK
MOURNFULLY
MOVABILITY
MUCEDINOUS
MUCOUSNESS
MULATTRESS
MULISHNESS
MULTIPLIER
MULTIVALVE
MUMBLINGLY
MUSSULMANS
MUTABILITY
MUTILATION
MUTINOUSLY
MYCOLOGIST
MYSTAGOGUE
MYSTERIOUS
MYTHICALLY
MYTHOLOGIC

N

NAMELESSLY
NAPHTHALIC
NATATORIAL
NATIVENESS
NATTERJACK
NATURALISM
NATURALIST
NATURALIZE
NAUTICALLY
NAVIGATION
NEBULOSITY
NECROLATRY
NECROMANCY
NECROPOLIS
NEGATIVELY
NEGLECTFUL
NEGLIGIBLE
NEGOTIABLE
NEGOTIATOR
NEOLOGICAL
NEOTERICAL
NEPHROTOMY
NETHERMOST
NEUROPATHY
NEUROTONIC
NEUTRALITY
NEUTRALIZE
NEWSMONGER
NIDAMENTAL
NIDIFICATE
NIGHTSHADE
NIGRESCENT
NIHILISTIC
NIMBLENESS
NINCOMPOOP
NINETEENTH
NOBLEWOMAN
NOMINALISM
NOMINATELY
NOMINATION
NOMINATIVE
NONCHALANT
NORTHERNER

NORTHWARDS
NOSOLOGIST
NOTABILITY
NOTARIALLY
NOTEWORTHY
NOTICEABLE
NOTICEABLY
NOURISHING
NOVICESHIP
NUBIFEROUS
NUCIFEROUS
NUMERATION
NUMEROUSLY
NUMISMATIC
NURSERYMAN
NUTRITIOUS
NYCTALOPIA
NYMPHOLEPT

O

OBDURATELY
OBEDIENTLY
OBJECTLESS
OBJURATION
OBLATENESS
OBLIGATION
OBLIGATORY
OBLIGEMENT
OBLIGINGLY
OBLITERATE
OBSEQUIOUS
OBSERVABLE
OBSERVABLY
OBSERVANCE
OBSIDIONAL
OBSOLETELY
OBSTRETRICS
OBSTRUCTOR
OBTAINABLE
OBTAINMENT
OBTURATION
OBTUSENESS
OCCULTNESS
OCCUPATION
OCHLOCRACY
OCHRACEOUS
OCTAHEDRAL
OCTAHEDRON
OCTANDRIAN
OCTANGULAR
OCTOGENARY
OCTOHEDRON
ODIOUSNESS
ODONTALGIC
ODONTOLOGY
OESOPHAGUS
OFFICIALLY
OFFICIATOR
OFTENTIMES
OLEAGINOUS
OLERACEOUS
OLIGARCHIC
OLIGOCLASE
OLIVACEOUS
OMNIFEROUS
OMNIGENOUS
OMNIPOTENT
OMNISCIENT

OMNIVOROUS
ONEIROLOGY
ONTOLOGIST
OPALESCENT
OPERAMETER
OPHTHALMIA
OPHTHALMIC
OPPOSITELY
OPPOSITION
OPPRESSION
OPPRESSIVE
OPPROBRIUM
OPPUGNANCY
OPSIOMETER
OPTATIVELY
OPTIMISTIC
OPTIONALLY
ORACULARLY
ORATORICAL
ORCHESTRAL
ORCHIDEOUS
ORDAINABLE
ORDAINMENT
ORDINATION
OREOGRAPHY
ORGANOGENY
ORGANOLOGY
ORIGINALLY
ORIGINATED
ORIGINATOR
ORNAMENTAL
ORNAMENTER
OROLOGICAL
ORPHANHOOD
ORTHOCERAS
ORTHOCLASE
ORTHODOXLY
ORTHOEPIST
ORTHOPRAXY
OSCILLANCY
OSCULATION
OSCULATORY
OSSIFEROUS
OSSIVOROUS
OSTENSIBLE
OSTEOBLAST
OSTEOCOLIA
OSTEOLOGIC
OTHERWHERE
OUTLANDISH
OUTRAGEOUS
OUTSTRETCH
OVARIOTOMY
OVERBRIDGE
OVERBURDEN
OVERCANOPY
OVERCHARGE
OVERGROWTH
OVERMASTED
OVERSTRAIN
OVERTURNER
OVERWISELY
OVIPOSITOR
OXIDIZABLE
OZONOSCOPE

P

PACHYMETER

PACIFIABLE
PAGINATION
PAIDEUTICS
PAINSTAKER
PALAEOZOIC
PALATALIZE
PALATINATE
PALIMPSEST
PALINDROME
PALINODIST
PALLIATION
PALLIATIVE
PALLIDNESS
PALMACEOUS
PALPITATED
PALTRINESS
PALUDINOUS
PANCRATIUM
PANCREATIC
PANEGYRIST
PANEGYRIZE
PANGENESIS
PANICULATE
PANSLAVISM
PAPISTICAL
PARALLELLY
PARALOGISM
PARAPHRASE
PARAPLEGIA
PARAPODIUM
PARASELENE
PARASITISM
PARDONABLE
PARDONABLY
PARENCHYMA
PARENTLESS
PARISIENNE
PARLIAMENT
PARNASSIAN
PARONOMASY
PARONYMOUS
PAROXYSMAL
PAROXYSMIC
PAROXYTONE
PARTIALITY
PARTICIPLE
PARTICULAR
PARTURIENT
PASIGRAPHY
PASQUINADE
PASSIONARY
PASSIONATE
PASTEBOARD
PATENTABLE
PATRIARCHY
PATRICIATE
PATRIOTISM
PATRISTICS
PATRONIZER
PATRONYMIC
PAWNBROKER
PEACEFULLY
PECCADILLO
PECULATION
PECULIARLY
PEDANTICAL
PEDESTRIAN
PEDUNCULAR
PEERLESSLY
PEIRAMETER

PEJORATIVE
PELLICULAR
PENANNULAR
PENDENTIVE
PENETRABLE
PENETRALIA
PENETRATOR
PENGUINERY
PENNYROYAL
PENNYWORTH
PENSIONARY
PENTACHORD
PENTAGONAL
PENTAMETER
PENTASTYLE
PENTATEUCH
PEPPERMINT
PERCENTAGE
PERCEPTIVE
PERCHLORIC
PERCIPIENT
PERCOLATOR
PERCURRENT
PERCUSSION
PERCUSSIVE
PERCUTIENT
PERDURABLE
PERDURABLY
PERFIDIOUS
PERFORATOR
PERFORMING
PERIHELION
PERILOUSLY
PERIODICAL
PERIOSTEAL
PERIOSTEUM
PERIPHRASE
PERIPTERAL
PERISHABLE
PERITONEAL
PERITONEUM
PERIWINKLE
PERLACEOUS
PERMANENCE
PERMEATION
PERMISSION
PERMISSIVE
PERNICIOUS
PERPETRATE
PERPETUATE
PERPETUITY
PERPLEXING
PERPLEXITY
PERQUISITE
PERRUQUIER
PERSIFLAGE
PERSISTENT
PERSISTIVE
PERSONABLE
PERSONALLY
PERSONALLY
PERSONATOR
PERSTRINGE
PERSUASION
PERSUASIVE
PERTINENCE
PERVERSION
PERVERSITY
PERVERSIVE
PESTILENCE

PETITIONER
PETTICHAPS
PETTYCHAPS
PETULANTLY
PHAGEDAENA
PHALANGEAL
PHANEROGAM
PHANTASMAL
PHARISAISM
PHARYNGEAL
PHEASANTRY
PHENOMENAL
PHILOSOPHE
PHILOSOPHY
PHLEBOTOMY
PHLEGMASIA
PHLEGMATIC
PHLOGISTIC
PHLOGISTON
PHLYCTAENA
PHOENICIAN
PHONETICAL
PHONOMETER
PHOSPHORIC
PHOSPHORUS
PHOTOGRAPH
PHOTOMETER
PHOTOMETRY
PHOTOPHONE
PHRENOLOGY
PHYLLOXERA
PHYSICALLY
PHYTOPHAGY
PICKANINNY
PICKPOCKET
PIERCEABLE
PIERCINGLY
PIEZOMETER
PILGRIMAGE
PILIFEROUS
PINNATIFID
PISTILLARY
PISTILLATE
PITCHINESS
PITILESSLY
PITYRIASIS
PLAGIARISM
PLAGIARIST
PLAGIARIZE
PLANIMETER
PLANIMETRY
PLANOMETER
PLASTERING
PLACTICITY
PLATELAYER
PLATYRHINE
PLAUDITORY
PLAYGROUND
PLAYWRIGHT
PLEADINGLY
PLEASANTLY
PLEBISCITE
PLEONASTIC
PLEXIMETER
PLEXOMETER
PLODDINGLY
PLOUGHABLE
PLUMASSIER
PLUPERFECT
PNEUMATICS

POACHINESS
POCULIFORM
POEPHAGOUS
POETICALLY
POIGNANTLY
POLITENESS
POLITICIAN
POLLUTEDLY
POLYANTHUS
POLYCARPIC
POLYCHROME
POLYCHROMY
POLYGAMIST
POLYGAMOUS
POLYGENOUS
POLYGRAPHY
POLYHEDRAL
POLYHEDRON
POLYMERISM
POLYNOMIAL
POLYPOROUS
POLYTHEISM
POLYTHEIST
POMIFEROUS
POMOLOGIST
PONDERABLE
PONTIFICAL
POPULARITY
POPULARIZE
POPULATION
POPULOUSLY
POROUSNESS
PORPHYRITE
PORRACEOUS
PORTCULLIS
PORTENTOUS
PORTLINESS
PORTUGUESE
POSITIVELY
POSITIVISM
POSITIVIST
POSSESSION
POSSESSIVE
POSSESSORY
POSTMASTER
POSTCRIPT
POURPARLER
POWERFULLY
PRACTISING
PRAEMUNIRE
PRAETORIUM
PRAYERLESS
PREADAMITE
PREBENDARY
PRECARIOUS
PRECAUTION
PRECEDENCE
PRECEDENCY
PRECESSION
PRECIOUSLY
PRECLUSION
PRECLUSIVE
PRECOCIOUS
PRECONCERT
PRECURSORY
PREDACEOUS
PREDECEASE
PREDESTINE
PREDICABLE
PREDICTION

PREDICTIVE
PREFECTURE
PREFERABLE
PREFERABLY
PREFERENCE
PREFERMENT
PREHENSILE
PRELATICAL
PREMONITOR
PREPAYMENT
PRESBYOBIA
PRESBYTERY
PRESCIENCE
PRESENTIVE
PRESIDENCY
PRESIGNIFY
PRESSINGLY
PRESUMABLE
PRESUMABLY
PRESUPPOSE
PRETENSION
PREVAILING
PREVALENCE
PRIESTHOOD
PRIESTLIKE
PRIMEVALLY
PRIMORDIAL
PRINCIPLED
PROCEEDING
PROCLIVITY
PROCLIVOUS
PROCOELIAN
PROCREATOR
PROCTORIAL
PROCUMBENT
PROCURABLE
PROCURATOR
PRODUCIBLE
PRODUCTILE
PRODUCTION
PRODUCTIVE
PROFESSION
PROFITABLE
PROFITABLY
PROFLIGACY
PROFLIGATE
PROGENITOR
PROGNATHIC
PROJECTILE
PROJECTION
PROLOCUTOR
PROMINENCE
PROMISSORY
PROMONTORY
PROMPTNESS
PROMULGATE
PRONOMINAL
PROPAGANDA
PROPAGATOR
PROPERNESS
PROPERTIED
PROPITIOUS
PROPORTION
PROPULSION
PROPULSIVE
PROSCENIUM
PROSCRIBER
PROSECUTOR
PROSPECTUS
PROSPERITY

PROSPEROUS
PROSTITUTE
PROTECTION
PROTECTIVE
PROTECTRIX
PROTESTANT
PROTHALLUS
PROTOPHYTE
PROTOPLASM
PROTOPLAST
PROTRACTOR
PROTRUSIVE
PROTRUSION
PROVENANCE
PROVERBIAL
PROVIDENCE
PROVINCIAL
PRUDENTIAL
PSALMODIST
PSALMODIZE
PSITTACINE
PUBESCENCE
PUBLICNESS
PUGILISTIC
PUGNACIOUS
PUISSANTLY
PULSOMETER
PULVERIZER
PUNCTUALLY
PUPILARITY
PUPIPAROUS
PUPIVOROUS
PURBLINDLY
PURITANISM
PURULENTLY
PUTRESCENT
PUZZLEMENT
PYRAMIDION
PYROMETRIC
PYROTECHNY
PYRRHONISM
PYRRHONIST
PYTHOGENIC

Q

QUADRANTAL
QUADRATURE
QUADRICORN
QUADRIVIAL
QUADRUMANA
QUANDARIES
QUARANTINE
QUARRIABLE
QUARTERING
QUATERFOIL
QUATERNARY
QUATERNION
QUEASINESS
QUENCHABLE
QUENCHLESS
QUERCITRON
QUESTIONER
QUIESCENCE

R

RABBINICAL

RABBLEMENT
RADICALISM
RADIOMETER
RAGAMUFFIN
RAMBLINGLY
RANCIDNESS
RANGERSHIP
RANSOMABLE
RANSOMLESS
RATABILITY
RATTLEWORT
RAVENOUSLY
RAVISHMENT
REACTIVELY
READERSHIP
REAFFOREST
REALIZABLE
REAPPROACH
REASSEMBLE
REBELLIOUS
REBUKINGLY
RECALLABLE
RECEIVABLE
RECENTNESS
RECEPTACLE
RECIPIENCY
RECIPROCAL
RECITATION
RECKLESSLY
RECOMMENCE
RECOMPENSE
RECONCILER
RECONQUEST
RECONSIDER
RECOUPMENT
RECREANTLY
RECREATION
RECREATIVE
RECRUDESCE
RECTORSHIP
RECUMBENCY
RECUPERATE
RECURRENCE
REDEEMABLE
REDELIVERY
REDISCOVER
REDRESSIVE
REDUNDANCY
REDUNDANCE
REFERRIBLE
REFINEMENT
REFLECTING
REFLECTION
REFLECTIVE
REFLEXIBLE
REFORMABLE
REFRACTION
REFRACTING
REFRACTIVE
REFRAGABLE
REFRESHING
REFRINGENT
REFULGENCE
REFULGENCY
REFUTATION
REFUTATORY
REGALEMENT
REGARDLESS
REGELATION
REGENERATE

REGENERACY
REGENTSHIP
REGIMENTAL
REGISTERED
REGRESSION
REGRESSIVE
REGULATION
REGULATIVE
REJUVENATE
RELATIONAL
RELATIVELY
RELAXATION
RELAXATIVE
RELEASABLE
RELEGATION
RELENTLESS
RELIEVABLE
RELINQUISH
RELISHABLE
RELUCTANCE
RELUCTANCY
REMARKABLE
REMARKABLY
REMARRIAGE
REMEDIALLY
REMEDILESS
REMEMBERER
REMISSIBLE
REMISSNESS
REMITTANCE
REMONETIZE
REMORSEFUL
REMOTENESS
REMUNERATE
RENASCENCE
RENASCENCY
RENCOUNTER
RENDERABLE
RENDEZVOUS
RENOWNEDLY
REPAIRABLE
REPARATION
REPARATIVE
REPATRIATE
REPEALABLE
REPEATABLE
REPEATEDLY
REPELLENCE
REPELLENCY
REPENTANCE
REPERTOIRE
REPETITION
REPETITIVE
REPININGLY
REPLEVISOR
REPORTABLE
REPOSITION
REPOSITORY
REPRESSION
REPRESSIVE
REPROACHER
REPROBATER
REPRODUCER
REPROVABLE
REPROVABLY
REPUBLICAN
REPUDIATOR
REPUGNANCE
REPURCHASE
REPUTATION

REQUITABLE
RESCISSION
RESEARCHER
RESENTMENT
RESERVEDLY
RESHIPMENT
RESIDENTER
RESILIENCE
RESILIENCY
RESISTANCE
RESONANTLY
RESPECTFUL
RESPECTING
RESPIRABLE
RESPONDENT
RESPONSIVE
RESPONSORY
RESTAURANT
RESTHARROW
RESTLESSLY
RESTORABLE
RESTRAINER
RESULTLESS
RESUMPTION
RESUMPTIVE
RETAINABLE
RETARDMENT
RETICULATE
RETRACTILE
RETRACTION
RETRACTIVE
RETROCHOIR
RETROGRADE
RETROSPECT
RETURNABLE
REVEALABLE
REVELATION
REVENGEFUL
REVERENCER
REVERSIBLE
REVERTIBLE
REVIEWABLE
REVIVALISM
REVOCATION
REVOLUTION
REWARDABLE
RHABDOIDAL
RHAPSODIST
RHAPSODIZE
RHAPSODIST
RHETORICAL
RHEUMATISM
RHINOCEROS
RHINOSCOPE
RHOMBOIDAL
RIDICULOUS
RIGHTFULLY
RIGOROUSLY
RINDERPEST
RINGLEADER
RISIBILITY
ROBUSTNESS
ROMANESQUE
ROOTEDNESS
ROQUELAURE
ROSANILINE
ROTATIONAL
ROTTENNESS
ROUNDABOUT
RUBIGINOUS

RUBBISHING
RUBRICATOR
RUDIMENTAL
RUEFULNESS
RUFFIANISH
RUFFIANISM
RUGGEDNESS
RUMINATION
RUNOLOGIST
RUTHLESSLY

S

SACCHARIFY
SACCHARINE
SACERDOTAL
SACREDNESS
SACRIFICER
SALAMANDER
SALINENESS
SALIVATION
SALLOWNESS
SALMAGUNDI
SALMAGUNDY
SALUBRIOUS
SALUTARILY
SALUTATION
SALUTATORY
SANATORIUM
SANCTIFIED
SANCTIFIER
SANCTIMONY
SANDERLING
SANGUINARY
SANGUINELY
SANITARIAN
SANITATION
SAPPHIRINE
SARCOLEMMA
SARCOPHAGI
SARCOPHILE
SATURATION
SATISFYING
SATURNALIA
SATYRIASIS
SAUROPSIDA
SAVAGENESS
SAVOURLESS
SAXICAVOUS
SAXICOLOUS
SCABBINESS
SCANDALIZE
SCANDALOUS
SCANTINESS
SCARAMOUCH
SCARCENESS
SCARLATINA
SCATHELESS
SCEPTICISM
SCEPTICIZE
SCHEMATIZE
SCHEMINGLY
SCHISMATIC
SCHOLASTIC
SCIAGRAPHY
SCIENTIFIC
SCIOGRAPHY
SCIOLISTIC
SCIRROSITY

SCIRRHOSIS
SCOFFINGLY
SCORNFULLY
SCORZONERA
SCOTOGRAPH
SCOTTICISM
SCOWLINGLY
SCRAMBLING
SCREENINGS
SCRIMPNESS
SCRIPTURAL
SCROFULOUS
SCRUPULOUS
SCRUTINEER
SCRUTINIZE
SCRUTINOUS
SCULLIONLY
SCULPTURAL
SCULPTURED
SCURRILITY
SCURRILOUS
SCURVINESS
SEARCHABLE
SEARCHLESS
SEAREDNESS
SEASONABLE
SEASONABLY
SEASONLESS
SEBIFEROUS
SECRETNESS
SECULARIST
SECULARIZE
SECURENESS
SEDATENESS
SEDUCEMENT
SEDULOUSLY
SEEMLINESS
SEGUIDILLA
SELECTNESS
SEMEIOLOGY
SEMEIOTICS
SEMICIRCLE
SEMPSTRESS
SENATORIAL
SENSUALIST
SENSUALIZE
SEPARATELY
SEPARATION
SEPARATISM
SEPARATIST
SEPTENNIAL
SEPTICIDAL
SEPTILLION
SEQUACIOUS
SERENENESS
SEVENTIETH
SEXAGENARY
SEXTILLION
SHADOWLESS
SHAGGINESS
SHAMEFACED
SHAMPOOING
SHANDYGAFF
SHIBBOLETH
SHIELDLESS
SHIPWRIGHT
SHOCKINGLY
SHOEMAKING
SHOPKEEPER
SHREWDNESS

SHREWISHLY	SPACIOUSLY	STENTORIAN
SHRIEVALTY	SPADICEOUS	STEPFATHER
SHRILLNESS	SPARSENESS	STEPMOTHER
SHUDDERING	SPECIALISM	STERCORATE
SIALAGOGUE	SPECIALITY	STEREOTYPE
SIALOGOGUE	SPECIALIZE	STERILIZER
SIBILATORY	SPECIOUSLY	STERTOROUS
SICKLINESS	SPECTACLED	STEWARDESS
SIDEROSTAT	SPECTRALLY	STICKINESS
SIGILLARIA	SPECULATOR	STIFFENING
SILENTNESS	SPEECHLESS	STIGMATIST
SILHOUETTE	SPERMACETI	STIGMATIZE
SIMILARITY	SPHENOGRAM	STIPULATOR
SIMILITUDE	SPHENOIDAL	STOLIDNESS
SIMONIACAL	SPHERICITY	STOMATITIS
SIMPLICITY	SPHEROIDAL	STOOPINGLY
SIMULACRUM	SPHRIGOSIS	STOREHOUSE
SIMULATION	SPINESCENT	STRABISMUS
SIMULATORY	SPIRITEDLY	STRABOTOMY
SINECURIST	SPIRITLESS	STRAIGHTEN
SINFULNESS	SPIRITUOUS	STRAMONIUM
SINGULARLY	SPIROMETER	STRATEGIST
SINISTERLY	SPISSITUDE	STRATHSPEY
SINISTROUS	SPLANCHNIC	STRATIFORM
SINOLOGIST	SPLEENWORT	STRENGTHEN
SISTERHOOD	SPLENDIDLY	STRICTNESS
SISTERLESS	SPLENOLOGY	STRIDULOUS
SKITTISHLY	SPOLIATION	STRINGENCY
SKULKINGLY	SPONDAICAL	STRONGHOLD
SLANDEROUS	SPONGINESS	STRUCTURAL
SLANTINGLY	SPONSORIAL	STRUCTURED
SLEETINESS	SPOTLESSLY	STRYCHNINE
SLEEVELESS	SPRINKLING	STUBBORNLY
SLIGHTNESS	SPRUCENESS	STUDIOUSLY
SLIPPERILY	SPUMESCENT	STUFFINESS
SLOPPINESS	SPURIOUSLY	STULTIFIER
SLOTHFULLY	SQUADRONED	STUPENDOUS
SLUGGISHLY	SQUALIDITY	STUPIDNESS
SLUMBEROUS	SQUARENESS	STURDINESS
SLUTTISHLY	SQUEEZABLE	SUBAQUATIC
SMATTERING	SQUIREHOOD	SUBAQUEOUS
SMUTTINESS	SQUIRESHIP	SUBCLAVIAN
SNAPPISHLY	STABLENESS	SUBDUCTION
SNEAKINGLY	STAGNANTLY	SUBJECTION
SNEERINGLY	STAGNATION	SUBJECTIVE
SNIVELLING	STALACTITE	SUBJOINDER
SNOBBISHLY	STALAGMITE	SUBJUGATOR
SOCIOLOGIC	STAMINATED	SUBKINGDOM
SOCRATICAL	STAMINEOUS	SUBLIMABLE
SOLACEMENT	STAMMERING	SUBLINGUAL
SOLDIERING	STANCHLESS	SUBMERSION
SOLECISTIC	STANCHNESS	SUBMISSION
SOLEMNIZER	STAPHYLOMA	SUBMISSIVE
SOLICITANT	STARRINESS	SUBPREFECT
SOLICITOUS	STARVATION	SUBSCRIBER
SOLICITUDE	STARVELING	SUBSECTION
SOLIDARITY	STATICALLY	SUBSEQUENT
SOLITARILY	STATIONARY	SUBSIDENCE
SOLSTITIAL	STATIONERY	SUBSIDIARY
SOLUBILITY	STATISTICS	SUBSISTENT
SOMATOLOGY	STATUESQUE	SUBSPECIES
SOMBRENESS	STATUTABLE	SUBSTITUTE
SOMERSAULT	STATUTABLY	SUBSTRATUM
SOMNOLENCE	STAUROLITE	SUBTANGENT
SONOROUSLY	STEADINESS	SUBTERFUGE
SOOTHINGLY	STEALTHILY	SUBTLENESS
SOOTHSAYER	STEAMINESS	SUBTLETIES
SORDIDNESS	STELLIFORM	SUBTRACTER
SORORICIDE	STENCILLER	SUBTRAHEND
SOUTHERNER	STENOGRAPH	SUBVENTION

SUBVERSION	SYMBOLICAL	THEODICEAN
SUBVERSIVE	SYMMETRIZE	THEODOLITE
SUCCEDANEA	SYNCARPOUS	THEOGONIST
SUCCEEDING	SYNCHRONAL	THEOLOGIAN
SUCCESSFUL	SYNCRETISM	THEOLOGIZE
SUCCESSION	SYNECDOCHE	THEOPHANIC
SUCCESSIVE	SYNGENETIC	THEORETICS
SUCCINCTLY	SYNONYMIST	THEOSOPHIC
SUCCULENCE	SYPHILITIC	THEOSOPHER
SUCCULENCY	SYSTEMATIC	THEREABOUT
SUCCUSSION	SYSTEMLESS	THEREAFTER
SUCCUSSIVE		THEREUNDER
SUDATORIUM		THERIOTOMY
SUDDENNESS	**T**	THERMOSTAT
SUFFERABLE		THERMOTICS
SUFFERANCE		THICKENING
SUFFERABLY	TABERNACLE	THIEVISHLY
SUFFICIENT	TABULARIZE	THIMBLEFUL
SUFFRAGIST	TABULATION	THINKINGLY
SUGARINESS	TACHOMETER	THIRTEENTH
SUGGESTION	TACITURNLY	THOROUGHLY
SUGGESTIVE	TACTICALLY	THOUGHTFUL
SUICIDALLY	TALISMANIC	THOUSANDTH
SULLENNESS	TALMUDICAL	THREADBARE
SULPHURATE	TAMBOURINE	THREATENER
SULTANSHIP	TANGENTIAL	THREEPENCE
SULTRINESS	TANTAMOUNT	THREEPENNY
SUNSETTING	TARDIGRADE	THREESCORE
SUPERCARGO	TARPAULING	THRIFTLESS
SUPERHUMAN	TARTAREOUS	THRIVINGLY
SUPERLUNAR	TASTEFULLY	THROMBOSIS
SUPERTONIC	TAUNTINGLY	THRONELESS
SUPERVISAL	TAUTOLOGIC	THROUGHOUT
SUPERVISOR	TAWDRINESS	THUNDERING
SUPINATION	TAXABILITY	TICKLISHLY
SUPPERLESS	TAXIDERMIC	TIMELINESS
SUPPLANTER	TETCHINESS	TIMOROUSLY
SUPPLEMENT	TECHNOLOGY	TINCTORIAL
SUPPLENESS	TEETOTALER	TIRESOMELY
SUPPLETORY	TELEGRAPHY	TITULARITY
SUPPLIANCE	TELEOSTEAN	TOILSOMELY
SUPPLICATE	TELEPATHIC	TOLERANTLY
SUPPOSABLE	TELESCOPIC	TOLERATION
SUPPRESSOR	TELLERSHIP	TOMFOOLERY
SUPRARENAL	TELPHERAGE	TONGUELESS
SURETYSHIP	TEMPERABLE	TOPAZOLITE
SURFACEMAN	TEMPERANCE	TOPOGRAPHY
SURGICALLY	TEMPORIZER	TORMENTING
SURPASSING	TEMPTATION	TORPIDNESS
SURPLUSAGE	TEMPTINGLY	TORRENTIAL
SURPRISING	TENABILITY	TORRENTINE
SUSCEPTIVE	TENANTABLE	TORRIDNESS
SUSCIPIENT	TENANTLESS	TORTUOUSLY
SUSPENSION	TENDERNESS	TORTURABLE
SUSPENSIVE	TENDRILLED	TOUCHINESS
SUSPENSORY	TENEBRIFIC	TOUCHINGLY
SUSPICIOUS	TENEMENTAL	TOUCHSTONE
SUSTENANCE	TENTACULAR	TOURMALINE
SUZERAINTY	TERATOLOGY	TOURNAMENT
SWAGGERING	TESSELLATE	TOURNIQUET
SWEATINESS	TESTICULAR	TOXICOLOGY
SWEEPINGLY	TETRACHORD	TRABECULAR
SWEEPSTAKE	TETRAGONAL	TRACHEITIS
SWEETBREAD	TETRAMETER	TRACTARIAN
SWEETENING	TETRASTICH	TRADESFOLK
SWEETHEART	TETRASTYLE	TRAFFICKER
SWIMMINGLY	TEXTUALIST	TRAGACANTH
SYBARITISM	THANKFULLY	TRAGICALLY
SYCOPHANCY	THEATRICAL	TRAITOROUS
SYLLABICAL	THEMSELVES	TRAJECTORY

TRAMMELLED
TRAMMELLER
TRAMONTANE
TRANQUILLY
TRANSACTOR
TRANSCRIBE
TRANSFEREE
TRANSGRESS
TRANSIENCE
TRANSIENCY
TRANSITION
TRANSITIVE
TRANSITORY
TRANSLATOR
TRANSLUCID
TRANSLUNAR
TRANSPIRES
TRANSPLANT
TRANSPOSAL
TRANSPOSER
TRANSVERSE
TRASHINESS
TRAUMATISM
TRAVAILING
TRAVELLING
TREADWHEEL
TREASURIES
TREMENDOUS
TREPANNING
TRESPASSER
TRIANGULAR
TRICENNIAL
TRICHOTOMY
TRICKINESS
TRICLINIUM
TRICOSTATE
TRIDENTATE
TRIDENTINE
TRIFARIOUS
TRIFLINGLY
TRIFOLIATE
TRIFURCATE
TRIGEMINAL
TRILATERAL
TRILINGUAL
TRILITERAL
TRILOCULAR
TRIMEMBRAL
TRIMESTRAL
TRIMMINGLY
TRIMORPHIC
TRINERVATE
TRINOCTIAL
TRIPARTITE
TRIPHTHONG
TRIPINNATE
TRIPLICATE
TRIPPINGLY
TRIRADIATE
TRISECTION
TRISULCATE
TRITERNATE
TRITURABLE
TRIUMPHANT
TRIVIALITY
TROCHANTER
TROGLODYTE
TROPAEOLUM
TROPICALLY
TROUBADOUR

TROUSERING
TRUCULENCE
TRUCULENCY
TRUNNIONED
TRUSTFULLY
TRUSTINESS
TRUSTINGLY
TRUTHFULLY
TUBERCULAR
TUBEROSITY
TUBULIFORM
TUITIONARY
TUMBLERFUL
TUMULTANCY
TUMULTUOUS
TUNGSTENIC
TURBULENCE
TURBULENCY
TURBIDNESS
TURGESCENT
TURGIDNESS
TURPENTINE
TWITTERING
TWITTINGLY
TYMPANITIC
TYMPANITIS
TYPOGRAPHY
TYRANNICAL

U

UBIQUITOUS
ULCERATION
ULTIMATELY
ULTRONEOUS
UMBELLIFER
UMBRAGEOUS
UNAFFECTED
UNASPIRING
UNASSISTED
UNATTACHED
UNATTENDED
UNATTESTED
UNAVAILING
UNBALANCED
UNBEARABLE
UNBLUSHING
UNCHANGING
UNCHASTITY
UNCLERICAL
UNCOLOURED
UNCOMMONLY
UNCONFINED
UNCRITICAL
UNCTUOSITY
UNDECAYING
UNDEFENDED
UNDENIABLY
UNDERBRACE
UNDERBRUSH
UNDERDRAIN
UNDERSHRUB
UNDERSTATE
UNDERTAKER
UNDERVALUE
UNDERWORLD
UNDERWRITE
UNDETERRED
UNDISMAYED

UNDISPOSED
UNDISPUTED
UNDULATING
UNDULATION
UNDULATORY
UNEASINESS
UNEDIFYING
UNEDUCATED
UNEMPLOYED
UNENVIABLE
UNERRINGLY
UNEVENNESS
UNEXAMINED
UNEXECUTED
UNEXPECTED
UNEXPLORED
UNFAIRNESS
UNFAITHFUL
UNFAMILIAR
UNFATHERED
UNFATHERLY
UNFEMININE
UNFETTERED
UNFINISHED
UNFLAGGING
UNFORESEEN
UNFORGIVEN
UNGENEROUS
UNGOVERNED
UNGRACEFUL
UNGRACIOUS
UNGRATEFUL
UNGROUNDED
UNGRUDGING
UNHALLOWED
UNHAMPERED
UNHANDSOME
UNHISTORIC
UNHOLINESS
UNHONOURED
UNICOSTATE
UNIFLOROUS
UNIFORMITY
UNILATERAL
UNILOCULAR
UNIMAGINED
UNIMPAIRED
UNIMPOSING
UNIMPROVED
UNINCLOSED
UNINSPIRED
UNINVITING
UNISONANCE
UNIVERSITY
UNIVOCALLY
UNKINDNESS
UNLAMENTED
UNLEAVENED
UNLETTERED
UNLICENSED
UNMANNERLY
UNMEASURED
UNMERCIFUL
UNMOLESTED
UNMOTHERLY
UNNAMEABLE
UNNUMBERED
UNOBSERVED
UNOFFICIAL
UNPLEASANT

UNPLEASING
UNPOETICAL
UNPOLISHED
UNPOLLUTED
UNPREPARED
UNPROVIDED
UNPROVOKED
UNPUNCTUAL
UNPUNISHED
UNREADABLE
UNRECORDED
UNREDEEMED
UNREFORMED
UNREGARDED
UNRELIABLE
UNRELIEVED
UNREPEALED
UNREPENTED
UNREQUITED
UNRESERVED
UNRESISTED
UNRESOLVED
UNRESTORED
UNREVENGED
UNREWARDED
UNRIVALLED
UNROMANTIC
UNRULINESS
UNSALEABLE
UNSCHOOLED
UNSEASONED
UNSECONDED
UNSISTERLY
UNSMIRCHED
UNSOCIABLE
UNSOCIABLY
UNSTEADILY
UNSTRAINED
UNSUITABLE
UNSUITABLY
UNSWERVING
UNTAMEABLE
UNTEMPERED
UNTENANTED
UNTHANKFUL
UNTHINKING
UNTIDINESS
UNTILLABLE
UNTOWARDLY
UNTROUBLED
UNTRUTHFUL
UNWARINESS
UNWAVERING
UNWEARABLE
UNWEIGHING
UNWIELDILY
UNWONTEDLY
UNWORTHILY
UNYIELDING
UPBRAIDING
UPBRINGING
UPHOLSTERY
UPPISHNESS
UPROARIOUS
URINOSCOPY
URTICATION
USEFULNESS
USURPATION
UTRICULATE
UXORIOUSLY

V

VALOROUSLY
VANQUISHED
VANQUISHER
VARICOSITY
VARIEGATED
VARIOLITIC
VATICANISM
VATICINATE
VAUDEVILLE
VAUNTINGLY
VEGETALITY
VEGETARIAN
VEGETATION
VEGETATIVE
VEHEMENTLY
VEHICULARY
VELOCIPEDE
VELOCITIES
VELUTINOUS
VENERATION
VENGEFULLY
VENIALNESS
VENOMOUSLY
VENTILATOR
VENTRICOUS
VENTRICOSE
VERIFIABLE
VERMICELLI
VERMICULAR
VERNACULAR
VERTEBRATA
VERTEBRATE
VERTICALLY
VESICATION
VESICATORY
VESICULATE
VESICULOSE
VESICULOUS
VESPERTINE
VESTIBULAR
VETERINARY
VIBRACULUM
VICEREGENT
VICTORIOUS
VICTUALLER
VIGILANTLY
VIGOROUSLY
VILLAINOUS
VILLEINAGE
VINAIGROUS
VINDICATOR
VINDICTIVE
VIOLACEOUS
VIRTUELESS
VIRTUOUSLY
VIRULENTLY
VISITATION
VITRESCENT
VITRIOLATE
VITRIOLIZE
VITUPERATE
VIVANDIERE
VIVIPARITY
VIVISECTOR
VOCABULARY
VOCATIONAL
VOCIFERATE

VOCIFEROUS
VOLATILITY
VOLATILIZE
VOLITIONAL
VOLTAMETER
VOLUBILITY
VOLUMETRIC
VOLUMINOUS
VOLUPTUARY
VOLUPTUOUS
VOMITORIES
VORTIGINAL
VOYAGEABLE
VULNERABLE

W

WAPINSCHAW
WARDENSHIP
WASTEFULLY
WATCHFULLY
WATERINESS
WATERPROOF
WAVERINGLY
WEATHERING
WELLINGTON
WESTWARDLY
WHARFINGER
WHATSOEVER
WHENSOEVER
WHEREABOUT
WHIMPERING
WHISPERING
WHITSUNDAY
WHIZZINGLY
WICKEDNESS
WILDEREDLY
WILDERNESS
WILDERMENT
WILFULNESS
WITCHCRAFT
WITHDRAWAL
WITHHOLDER
WOEFULNESS
WOMANISHLY
WONDERMENT
WONDROUSLY
WOODPECKER
WORRYINGLY
WORSHIPFUL
WORSHIPPER
WORTHINESS
WRATHFULLY
WRETCHEDLY
WRITERSHIP
WRONGFULLY

X

XYLOGRAPHY

Y

YEARNINGLY
YEASTINESS
YESTEREVEN

YESTERMORN
YOURSELVES
YOUTHFULLY

Z
ZINCOGRAPH

ZOOMORPHIC
ZOOPHAGOUS
ZOOTOMICAL

ELEVEN-LETTER WORDS

A

AARON'S-BEARD
ABANDONMENT
ABBREVIATOR
ABECEDARIAN
ABHORRENTLY
ABIOGENESIS
ABLACTATION
ABNORMALITY
ABOLISHABLE
ABOMINATION
ABOVE-GROUND
ABRACADABRA
ABRANCHIATE
ABSENTATION
ABSENTEEISM
ABSOLVATORY
ABSTINENTLY
ABSTRACTION
ABSTRACTIVE
ABUSIVENESS
ACADEMICIAN
ACATALECTIC
ACCELERATOR
ACCEPTATION
ACCESSIONAL
ACCESSORIAL
ACCESSORILY
ACCIPITRINE
ACCLAMATION
ACCLAMATORY
ACCLIMATIZE
ACCOMMODATE
ACCOMPANIER
ACCOMPANIST
ACCORDANTLY
ACCORDINGLY
ACCOUCHEUSE
ACCOUNTABLE
ACCOUNTABLY
ACCUMULATOR
ACHIEVEMENT
ACIDIFIABLE
ACINACIFORM
ACKNOWLEDGE
ACOUSTICIAN
ACQUIESCENT
ACQUIREMENT
ACQUISITION
ACQUISITIVE
ACQUITTANCE
ACRIMONIOUS
ACTINOMETER
ACUMINATION
ACUPRESSURE
ACUPUNCTURE
ADAM'S-NEEDLE
ADDLE-HEADED
ADIAPHOROUS
ADIATHERMIC
ADJECTIVELY
ADJOURNMENT
ADJUDICATOR

ADMINICULAR
ADMIRALSHIP
ADOLESCENCE
ADOLESCENCY
ADSTRICTION
ADUMBRATION
ADUMBRATIVE
ADVANCEMENT
ADVENTURESS
ADVENTUROUS
ADVERBIALLY
ADVERSATIVE
ADVERSENESS
ADVERTISING
ADVISEDNESS
AEROLOGICAL
AERONAUTICS
AEROSTATICS
AEROSTATION
AESCULAPIAN
AESTIVATION
AFFECTATION
AFFECTINGLY
AFFECTIONED
AFFILIATION
AFFIRMATION
AFFIRMATIVE
AFFRANCHISE
AFTER-GROWTH
AGATIFEROUS
AGGLOMERATE
AGGLUTINANT
AGGLUTINATE
AGGRANDIZER
AGGRAVATING
AGGRAVATION
AGGREGATELY
AGGREGATION
AGNOSTICISM
AGNUS-CASTUS
AGONIZINGLY
AGRARIANISM
AGRICULTURE
AGUARDIENTE
AIMLESSNESS
ALBUMINURIA
ALCHEMISTIC
ALEXANDRIAN
ALEXANDRINE
ALKALESCENT
ALKALIMETER
ALKALIMETRY
ALLEVIATION
ALLEVIATE
ALL-FOOLS' DAY
ALLOPHYLIAN
ALL-SOULS' DAY
ALTERCATION
ALTERNATELY
ALTERNATION
ALTERNATIVE
ALTO-RILIEVO
AMALGAMATOR
AMARANTHINE
AMATIVENESS

AMBIGUOUSLY
AMBITIOUSLY
AMBROSIALLY
AMELANCHIER
AMELIORATOR
AMENORRHOEA
AMENTACEOUS
AMERICANISM
AMERICANIZE
AMETHYSTINE
AMIABLENESS
AMOENOMANIA
AMONTILLADO
AMOROUSNESS
AMPHIBOLOGY
AMPHISBAENA
AMPLEXICAUL
ANACANTHOUS
ANACHRONISM
ANACOLUTHON
ANACREONTIC
ANAESTHESIA
ANAESTHETIC
ANALLANTOIC
ANALOGOUSLY
ANAPLEROTIC
ANASTOMOSIS
ANASTOMOTIC
ANCHORITESS
ANCHOVY-PEAR
ANCIENTNESS
ANDROSPHINX
ANECDOTICAL
ANFRACTUOUS
ANGELICALLY
ANGELOLATRY
ANGELOPHANY
ANGLICANISM
ANGLO-INDIAN
ANGLOPHOBIA
ANIMALCULAR
ANIMATINGLY
ANNIHILABLE
ANNIHILATOR
ANNIVERSARY
ANNUNCIATOR
ANOMALISTIC
ANONYMOUSLY
ANTECEDENCE
ANTE-CHAMBER
ANTEMUNDANE
ANTENUPTIAL
ANTEPASCHAL
ANTEPENDIUM
ANTERIORITY
ANTHRACITIC
ANTIBILIOUS
ANTICARDIUM
ANTICYCLONE
ANTIFEBRILE
ANTIFEDERAL
ANTIPHRASIS
ANTIPYRETIC
ANTIQUARIAN
ANTIQUENESS

ANTIRRHINUM
ANTISPASTIC
ANTISTROPHE
ANTITYPICAL
ANTONOMASIA
ANXIOUSNESS
APHRODISIAC
APOCALYPTIC
APOLOGETICS
APONEUROSIS
APOPETALOUS
APOSIOPESIS
APOSTERIORI
APOSTLESHIP
APOSTROPHIC
APPALLINGLY
APPELLATION
APPELLATIVE
APPLE-BLIGHT
APPLICATION
APPLICATIVE
APPLICATORY
APPOINTMENT
APPORTIONER
APPRECIABLE
APPRECIABLY
APPREHENDER
APPROBATION
APPROPRIATE
APPROVINGLY
APPROXIMATE
APPURTENANT
ARBITRAMENT
ARBITRARILY
ARBITRATION
ARBITRAMENT
ARBORESCENT
ARCHAEOLOGY
ARCHANGELIC
ARCHDUCHESS
ARCHEGONIUM
ARCHIMEDEAN
ARCHIPELAGO
ARDUOUSNESS
ARISTOCRACY
ARMINIANISM
ARMOUR-PLATE
ARQUEBUSIER
ARRAIGNMENT
ARRANGEMENT
ARROW-HEADED
ARTERIALIZE
ARTERIOTOMY
ARTILLERIST
ARTLESSNESS
ASCENSIONAL
ASCERTAINER
ASCITITIOUS
ASPORTATION
ASSAFOETIDA
ASSASSINATE
ASSESTATION
ASSENTINGLY
ASSERTIVELY
ASSESSORIAL
ASSIDUOUSLY
ASSIGNATION
ASSOCIATION
ASSOCIATIVE
ASSUAGEMENT

ASSUREDNESS
ASSYRIOLOGY
ASTIGMATISM
ASTONISHING
ASTRINGENCY
ATHERMANOUS
ATHLETICISM
ATMIDOMETER
ATMOSPHERIC
ATOMIZATION
ATRABILIOUS
ATROCIOUSLY
ATTEMPTABLE
ATTENTIVELY
ATTENUATION
ATTESTATION
ATTITUDINAL
ATTRACTABLE
ATTRIBUTION
ATTRIBUTIVE
AUDACIOUSLY
AUDIBLENESS
AUDITORSHIP
AURICULARLY
AUSCULTATOR
AUSTERENESS
AUTOGRAPHIC
AVOIRDUPOIS
AWKWARDNESS

B

BACCHANALIA
BACCIFEROUS
BACCIVOROUS
BACILLICIDE
BALEFULNESS
BANDY-LEGGED
BARBAROUSLY
BAREFACEDLY
BARLEY-SUGAR
BARLEY-WATER
BARN-SWALLOW
BARQUENTINE
BARREL-ORGAN
BARYCENTRIC
BASHFULNESS
BASTARD-WING
BEAM-COMPASS
BEAR-BAITING
BEARING-REIN
BEAR'S-GREASE
BEASTLINESS
BEAUTEOUSLY
BEAUTIFULLY
BEDIZENMENT
BEGUILEMENT
BELIEVINGLY
BELL-FOUNDER
BELLIGERENT
BELLOWS-FISH
BENEDICTINE
BENEDICTION
BENEDICTIVE
BENEFACTION
BENEFICENCE
BENEFICIARY
BENEVOLENCE
BENGAL-LIGHT

BENIGNANTLY
BEREAVEMENT
BESEEMINGLY
BEWITCHMENT
BIBLIOLATER
BIBLIOLATRY
BIBLIOMANCY
BIBLIOMANIA
BIBLIOPHILE
BIBLIOTHECA
BICARBONATE
BICENTENARY
BIFURCATION
BILIOUSNESS
BILL-STICKER
BILOPHODONT
BIMETALLISM
BIMETALLIST
BIODYNAMICS
BIOGENESIST
BIPARTITION
BIQUADRATIC
BITTER-SWEET
BITUMINATED
BLACK-BEETLE
BLACK-LETTER
BLACK-MONDAY
BLADDER-FERN
BLADDERWORT
BLAMELESSLY
BLAMEWORTHY
BLASPHEMOUS
BLEACHFIELD
BLEPHARITIS
BLESSEDNESS
BLOCK-SYSTEM
BLOOD-BOUGHT
BLOOD-GUILTY
BLOODLESSLY
BLOOD-SUCKER
BLOOD-VESSEL
BLUE-COAT-BOY
BLUNDERBUSS
BOARD-SCHOOL
BODY-SERVANT
BOHEMIANISM
BOLTING-MILL
BOLT-UPRIGHT
BOMBARDMENT
BONAPARTIST
BONNET-ROUGE
BOOKBINDING
BOOKISHNESS
BOOK-KEEPING
BOOK-LEARNED
BOOK-SELLING
BOORISHNESS
BORBORYGMUS
BOTANICALLY
BOTHERATION
BOTTLE-CHART
BOTTLE-GLASS
BOTTLE-GREEN
BOTTLE-NOSED
BOULDER-CLAY
BOUNDLESSLY
BOUNTEOUSLY
BOUNTIFULLY
BOURGEOISIE
BOXING-GLOVE

BOXING-MATCH
BRABBLEMENT
BRACHIOPODA
BRAGGADOCIO
BRANCHIOPOD
BRAZEN-FACED
BREADTHWAYS
BREAD-WINNER
BREAST-PLATE
BREAST-WHEEL
BREECH-BLOCK
BRICKLAYING
BRILLIANTLY
BRINE-SHRIMP
BRISTLINESS
BRITTLENESS
BRONCHOCELE
BRONCHOTOMY
BRONZE-STEEL
BROTHERHOOD
BROTHERLESS
BRUSH-TURKEY
BRUSQUENESS
BRUTISHNESS
BUCKET-WHEEL
BUFFALO-ROBE
BULL-BAITING
BULLET-MOULD
BULLET-PROOF
BULL-FIGHTER
BULL-TERRIER
BUNCH-BACKED
BUREAUCRACY
BURGESS-SHIP
BURGLARIOUS
BURGOMASTER
BURNT-SIENNA
BUSYBODYISM
BUTCHER-BIRD
BUTTER-KNIFE
BUTTER-MOULD
BUTTER-PRINT
BUTYRACEOUS
BYSSIFEROUS

C

CABBAGE-MOTH
CABBAGE-PALM
CABBAGE-TREE
CABBAGE-ROSE
CABBAGE-WORM
CABBALISTIC
CACOGASTRIC
CACOPHONOUS
CALCEOLARIA
CALCIFEROUS
CALCINATION
CALCOGRAPHY
CALCULATING
CALCULATION
CALCULATIVE
CALEFACIENT
CALEFACTION
CALEFACTORY
CALIBRATION
CALLIGRAPHY
CALLING-CRAB
CALLOUSNESS

CALORIMETER
CALORIMETRY
CALUMNIATOR
CALVINISTIC
CAMARADERIE
CAMEL'S-THORN
CAMPANOLOGY
CAMPANULATE
CAMPHOR-TREE
CAMP-MEETING
CANARY-GRASS
CANCERATION
CANDELABRUM
CANDESCENCE
CANDIDATURE
CANDLE-BERRY
CANDLELIGHT
CANDLE-POWER
CANDLESTICK
CANNIBALISM
CANONICALLY
CANTHARIDES
CAPACIOUSLY
CAPILLAMENT
CAPILLARITY
CAPILLIFORM
CAPITULATOR
CAPTAINSHIP
CAPTIVATING
CARAVANSARY
CARBON-POINT
CARBUNCULAR
CARBURETTED
CARCINOLOGY
CARDINALATE
CARDIOGRAPH
CARD-SHARPER
CAREFULNESS
CARESSINGLY
CARMINATIVE
CARNATIONED
CARNIVOROUS
CAROLINGIAN
CARRIAGE-WAY
CARRION-CROW
CARTOGRAPHY
CARUNCULATE
CARVEL-BUILT
CASSITERITE
CASTELLATED
CASTIGATION
CASTIGATORY
CASTILE-SOAP
CASTING-VOTE
CATACAUSTIC
CATACHRESIS
CATACLYSMAL
CATACLYSMIC
CATAPHONICS
CATASTROPHE
CATECHETICS
CATEGORICAL
CATER-COUSIN
CATERPILLAR
CATHEDRATIC
CATHOLICISM
CATHOLICITY
CATHOLICIZE
CAULIFLOWER
CAUSATIVELY

CAUSATIVITY
CAUSELESSLY
CAUSTICALLY
CAVE-DWELLER
CAVERNULOUS
CAVO-RILIEVO
CEASELESSLY
CELEBRATION
CELESTIALLY
CELLIFEROUS
CEMENTATION
CENTENARIAN
CENTRE-BOARD
CENTRE-PIECE
CENTRICALLY
CENTRIFUGAL
CENTRIPETAL
CENTROBARIC
CEPHALALGIC
CEPHALASPIS
CEPHALOTOMY
CEREBRALISM
CEREBRATION
CEREBRIFORM
CEREMONIOUS
CEROPLASTIC
CERTAINNESS
CERTIFICATE
CESAREWITCH
CHAFING-DISH
CHAIN-BRIDGE
CHAIN-STITCH
CHALCEDONIC
CHALCEDONYX
CHALK-STONES
CHAMBERLAIN
CHAMBER-MAID
CHAMPIONESS
CHANGEFULLY
CHANTERELLE
CHANTICLEER
CHAOTICALLY
CHAPERONAGE
CHARLATANIC
CHARLATANRY
CHARTACEOUS
CHASTISABLE
CHECK-STRING
CHEERLESSLY
CHEESE-PRESS
CHEF-D'OEUVRE
CHEQUER-WORK
CHERRY-STONE
CHESS-PLAYER
CHEVAL-GLASS
CHIAROSCURO
CHIEFTAINCY
CHIEFTAINRY
CHILOGNATHA
CHIROGRAPHY
CHIROMANCER
CHIROMANTIC
CHIROPODIST
CHIRURGICAL
CHISEL-TOOTH
CHITTERLING
CHLOROMETER
CHLOROPHYLL
CHOIR-SCREEN
CHONDROLOGY

CHOROGRAPHY
CHRISMATORY
CHRISTENDOM
CHRISTENING
CHRISTOLOGY
CHROMATROPE
CHRONOGRAPH
CHRONOLOGER
CHRONOLOGIC
CHRONOMETER
CHRONOMETRY
CHRONOSCOPE
CHRYSOBERYL
CHRYSOCOLLA
CHRYSOPHYLL
CHRYSOPRASE
CHURCH-COURT
CHURCH-GOING
CHURCHWOMAN
CICATRICULE
CINERACEOUS
CINERITIOUS
CINNABARINE
CINQUE-PORTS
CIRCULARITY
CIRCULATING
CIRCULATION
CIRCULATIVE
CIRCULATORY
CIRCUMPOLAR
CIRCUMSPECT
CIRCUMVOLVE
CITIZENSHIP
CLAIRVOYANT
CLAMOROUSLY
CLANDESTINE
CLASS-FELLOW
CLASSICALLY
CLEAN-HANDED
CLEAN-LIMBED
CLEANLINESS
CLEAR-HEADED
CLEARING-NUT
CLEAR-STARCH
CLEFT-PALATE
CLEPTOMANIA
CLERICALISM
CLIMACTERIC
CLIMATOLOGY
CLINOMETRIC
CLOG-ALMANAC
CLOSE-FISTED
CLOSE-HANDED
CLOSE-HAULED
CLOTHES-MOTH
CLOUD-CAPPED
CLOVER-GRASS
COACH-OFFICE
COAGULATION
COAGULATIVE
COALESCENCE
COAL-TRIMMER
COAL-WHIPPER
COBBLE-STONE
COCHIN-CHINA
COCK-AND-BULL
CODICILLARY
COD-LIVER-OIL
COEFFICIENT
COESSENTIAL

COETERNALLY
COEXISTENCE
COEXTENSIVE
COFFEE-BERRY
COFFEE-HOUSE
COGNOSCIBLE
COINCIDENCE
COLD-BLOODED
COLD-HEARTED
COLLABORATE
COLLAPSIBLE
COLLECTANEA
COLLECTEDLY
COLLIMATION
COLLOCATION
COLLUSIVELY
COLONIALISM
COLORIMETER
COLUMBARIUM
COLUMNARITY
COMBINATION
COMBUSTIBLE
COMET-FINDER
COMFORTABLE
COMFORTABLY
COMFORTLESS
COMMANDMENT
COMMEMORATE
COMMENDABLE
COMMENDABLY
COMMENDATOR
COMMENTATOR
COMMINATION
COMMINATORY
COMMINUTION
COMMISERATE
COMMISSURAL
COMMONPLACE
COMMUNALISM
COMMUNALIST
COMMUNICANT
COMMUNICATE
COMMUNISTIC
COMMUTATION
COMMUTATIVE
COMPACTNESS
COMPARATIVE
COMPARTMENT
COMPASSABLE
COMPASS-CARD
COMPELLABLE
COMPENDIOUS
COMPENSATOR
COMPETENTLY
COMPETITION
COMPETITIVE
COMPILATION
COMPLACENCE
COMPLACENCY
COMPLAINANT
COMPLAISANT
COMPLIANTLY
COMPLICATED
COMPORTMENT
COMPOSITELY
COMPOSITION
COMPOSSIBLE
COMPRESSION
COMPRESSIVE
COMPRESSURE

COMPROMISER
COMPTROLLER
COMPUNCTION
COMPURGATOR
COMPUTATION
COMRADESHIP
CONCATENATE
CONCEALABLE
CONCEALMENT
CONCEITEDLY
CONCEIVABLE
CONCEIVABLY
CONCENTRATE
CONCEPTACLE
CONCERNMENT
CONCILIABLE
CONCILIATOR
CONCISENESS
CONCOMITANT
CONCORDANCE
CONCUBINAGE
CONCUBINARY
CONCURRENCE
CONDEMNABLE
CONDENSABLE
CONDITIONAL
CONDITIONED
CONDOLATORY
CONDOLEMENT
CONDONATION
CONDUCTIBLE
CONDUCTRESS
CONFABULATE
CONFEDERACY
CONFEDERATE
CONFERRABLE
CONFESSEDLY
CONFIDENTLY
CONFIDINGLY
CONFINEMENT
CONFIRMABLE
CONFISCABLE
CONFISCATOR
CONFLAGRATE
CONFLICTING
CONFLICTION
CONFORMABLE
CONFORMABLY
CONFUTATION
CONGEALABLE
CONGELATION
CONGRUOUSLY
CONIROSTRAL
CONJECTURAL
CONJUGALITY
CONJUGATION
CONJUNCTION
CONJUNCTIVE
CONJUNCTURE
CONJURATION
CONNECTEDLY
CONNOISSEUR
CONNOTATION
CONNOTATIVE
CONNUBIALLY
CONQUERABLE
CONSCIOUSLY
CONSECRATOR
CONSECUTION
CONSECUTIVE

CONSENTIENT
CONSEQUENCE
CONSERVABLE
CONSERVANCY
CONSERVATOR
CONSIDERATE
CONSIDERING
CONSIGNMENT
CONSILIENCE
CONSISTENCE
CONSOLATION
CONSOLATORY
CONSOLIDANT
CONSOLIDATE
CONSONANTAL
CONSORTSHIP
CONSPICUOUS
CONSPIRATOR
CONSTELLATE
CONSTERNATE
CONSTITUENT
CONSTITUTER
CONSTRAINED
CONSTRAINER
CONSTRICTOR
CONSTRUCTER
CONSTRUCTOR
CONSUMPTION
CONSUMPTIVE
CONTAINABLE
CONTAMINATE
CONTEMPLATE
CONTENTEDLY
CONTENTIOUS
CONTESTABLE
CONTINENTAL
CONTINENTLY
CONTINGENCE
CONTINGENCY
CONTINUABLE
CONTINUALLY
CONTINUANCE
CONTINUATOR
CONTINUEDLY
CONTRABASSO
CONTRACTILE
CONTRACTION
CONTRAJERVA
CONTRARIANT
CONTRARIETY
CONTRARIOUS
CONTRA-TENOR
CONTRAVENER
CONTRAYERVA
CONTRE-TEMPS
CONTRIBUTOR
CONTRIVANCE
CONTROLMENT
CONTROVERSY
CONVENIENCE
CONVENIENCY
CONVENTICLE
CONVERGENCE
CONVERSABLE
CONVERSABLY
CONVERTIBLE
CONVERTIBLY
CONVEYANCER
CONVINCIBLE

CONVIVIALLY
CONVOCATION
CONVOLUTION
CONVOLVULUS
CONVULSIBLE
COOL-TANKARD
CO-OPERATION
CO-OPERATIVE
COPARCENARY
COPIOUSNESS
COPPERPLATE
COPPERSMITH
COQUILLA-NUT
CORALLIFORM
CORBEL-TABLE
CORNER-STONE
CORNICULATE
CORNIGEROUS
CORPORALITY
CORPORATELY
CORPORATION
CORPOREALLY
CORPULENTLY
CORPUSCULAR
CORRECTABLE
CORRECTNESS
CORRELATION
CORRELATIVE
CORROBORANT
CORROBORATE
CORROSIVELY
CORRUGATION
CORRUPTIBLE
CORRUPTIBLY
CORRUPTLESS
CORRUPTNESS
CORUSCATION
CO-SIGNATORY
COSMOGONIST
COSMOGRAPHY
COSMOLOGIST
COSTIVENESS
COTERMINOUS
COTTON-GRASS
COTTON-PLANT
COTTON-PRESS
COTYLEDONAL
COUNTENANCE
COUNTERFEIT
COUNTERFOIL
COUNTERFORT
COUNTERMAND
COUNTERMARK
COUNTERMINE
COUNTER-MOVE
COUNTERPANE
COUNTERPART
COUNTERPLOT
COUNTERSEAL
COUNTERSIGN
COUNTERSINK
COUNTERVAIL
COUNTERWORK
COUNTRIFIED
COUNTRY-SIDE
COURTEOUSLY
COURTLINESS
COXCOMBICAL
CRABBEDNESS
CRACOVIENNE

CRANIOMETER
CRANIOMETRY
CRANIOSCOPY
CRATERIFORM
CREAM-CHEESE
CREATORSHIP
CREDIBILITY
CREDULOUSLY
CREMATORIUM
CREOPHAGOUS
CREPITATION
CREPUSCULAR
CRESTFALLEN
CRIMINALIST
CRIMINALITY
CRIMINATION
CRIMINATIVE
CRITICASTER
CROCIDOLITE
CROCODILIAN
CROOK-BACKED
CROOKEDNESS
CROSS-ACTION
CROSS-LEGGED
CROTCHETEER
CROWN-PRINCE
CRUCIFEROUS
CRUCIFIXION
CRUCIGEROUS
CRUSTACEOUS
CRYPTOGAMIC
CRYPTOGRAPH
CRYSTALLINE
CRYSTALLIZE
CRYSTALLOID
CUBICALNESS
CUIR-BOUILLI
CULMIFEROUS
CULMINATION
CULPABILITY
CULTIVATION
CUPELLATION
CUPRIFEROUS
CURATORSHIP
CURLY-HEADED
CURRANT-WINE
CURRY-POWDER
CURSORINESS
CURTAILMENT
CURVILINEAR
CURVILINEAL
CUSTOMARILY
CUSTOM-HOUSE
CYCADACEOUS
CYCLOPAEDIA
CYCLOPAEDIC
CYNOPHILIST
CYPERACEOUS
CYTOGENESIS

D

DACTYLOLOGY
DAMPISHNESS
DANCING-GIRL
DANGEROUSLY
DAUNTLESSLY
DAY-LABOURER
DEATH-RATTLE

DEATH-STROKE
DEBARKATION
DEBAUCHMENT
DECARBONIZE
DECEITFULLY
DECEMVIRATE
DECEPTIVELY
DECLAMATION
DECLAMATORY
DECLARATION
DECLARATIVE
DECLARATORY
DECLINATION
DECLINATORY
DECLINATURE
DECOLLATION
DECOMPOSITE
DECORTICATE
DECREPITATE
DECREPITUDE
DECRESCENDO
DECUMBENTLY
DECURRENTLY
DECUSSATELY
DECUSSATION
DEDUCTIVELY
DEEP-MOUTHED
DEER-STALKER
DEFALCATION
DEFECTIVELY
DEFENCELESS
DEFENSIVELY
DEFERENTIAL
DEFIANTNESS
DEFIBRINIZE
DEFIBRINATE
DEFICIENTLY
DEFLAGRATOR
DEFLORATION
DEFOLIATION
DEFORCEMENT
DEFORMATION
DEGLUTITION
DEGLUTITORY
DEGRADATION
DEGRADINGLY
DEHORTATION
DEHORTATIVE
DEHORTATORY
DEHYDRATION
DEICTICALLY
DEIFICATION
DEISTICALLY
DELECTATION
DELETERIOUS
DELICIOUSLY
DELIGHTEDLY
DELIGHTLESS
DELIGHTSOME
DELINEATION
DELINQUENCY
DELIRIOUSLY
DELITESCENT
DELIVERABLE
DELIVERANCE
DEMAGNETIZE
DEMARCATION
DEMESMERIZE
DEMI-BASTION
DEMI-CADENCE

DEMOCRATIZE
DEMOGRAPHIC
DEMONIACISM
DEMONOLATRY
DEMONOLOGIC
DEMONSTRATE
DENIZENSHIP
DENOMINABLE
DENOMINATOR
DENTICULATE
DENTIGEROUS
DENUNCIATOR
DEOBSTRUENT
DEOXIDATION
DEPAUPERATE
DEPAUPERIZE
DEPENDENTLY
DEPHLEGMATE
DEPOPULATOR
DEPORTATION
DEPRAVATION
DEPRECATION
DEPRECATORY
DEPRECATIVE
DEPREDATION
DEPREDATORY
DEPRIVATION
DEPRIVEMENT
DERANGEMENT
DERELICTION
DERMATOLOGY
DESCENDABLE
DESCENDIBLE
DESCRIBABLE
DESCRIPTION
DESCRIPTIVE
DESECRATION
DESERVINGLY
DESICCATION
DESIDERATUM
DESIGNATION
DESIGNATIVE
DESPERATELY
DESPERATION
DESPISINGLY
DESPONDENCE
DESPONDENCY
DESTINATION
DESTITUTION
DESTROYABLE
DESTRUCTION
DESTRUCTIVE
DESULTORILY
DETERIORATE
DETERMINANT
DETERMINATE
DETERMINISM
DETERMINIST
DETESTATION
DETRIMENTAL
DEUTEROGAMY
DEUTERONOMY
DEVASTATION
DEVELOPABLE
DEVELOPMENT
DEVIOUSNESS
DEVOLVEMENT
DEVOTEDNESS
DEXTEROUSLY
DIACRITICAL

DIAGNOSTICS
DIALECTICAL
DIALOGISTIC
DIAMAGNETIC
DIAMETRICAL
DIAPHANCITY
DIAPHORESIS
DIAPHORETIC
DIARTHROSIS
DIATHERMOUS
DICEPHALOUS
DICHOGAMOUS
DICHOTOMOUS
DICHROMATIC
DICHROSCOPE
DICOTYLEDON
DICTATORIAL
DIDACTYLOUS
DIFFERENTIA
DIFFERENTLY
DIFFICULTLY
DIFFIDENTLY
DIFFRACTION
DIFFRACTIVE
DIFFUSENESS
DIFFUSIVELY
DIGITIGRADE
DILAPIDATED
DILAPIDATOR
DILUVIALIST
DIMENSIONAL
DIMENSIONED
DINNER-TABLE
DINOSAURIAN
DINOTHERIUM
DIPHTHONGAL
DIPHYCERCAL
DIPLOMATICS
DIPLOMATIST
DIPLOMATIZE
DIPRISMATIC
DIPSOMANIAC
DIRECTORATE
DIRECTORIAL
DIREFULNESS
DISACCUSTOM
DISAFFECTED
DISAFFOREST
DISAPPROVAL
DISARMAMENT
DISBANDMENT
DISBELIEVER
DISCERNIBLE
DISCERNIBLY
DISCERNMENT
DISCONTINUE
DISCORDANCE
DISCORDANCY
DISCOURAGER
DISCOURTESY
DISCREPANCE
DISCREPANCY
DISCUSSABLE
DISEMBITTER
DISENCUMBER
DISENTANGLE
DISENTHRALL
DISENTHRONE
DISENTRANCE
DISGRACEFUL

DISGUISEDLY
DISHONESTLY
DISINTHRALL
DISJUNCTION
DISJUNCTIVE
DISLOCATION
DISMASTMENT
DISOBEDIENT
DISOBLIGING
DISORGANIZE
DISPENSABLE
DISPERSEDLY
DISPIRITING
DISPLEASING
DISPLEASURE
DISPOSITION
DISPUTATION
DISPUTATIVE
DISQUIETING
DISQUIETUDE
DISSECTIBLE
DISSENTIENT
DISSEPIMENT
DISSERTATOR
DISSILIENCE
DISSIMULATE
DISSIPATION
DISSOLUTELY
DISSOLUTION
DISSOLVABLE
DISSYLLABIC
DISSYLLABLE
DISTASTEFUL
DISTEMPERED
DISTENSIBLE
DISTILLABLE
DISTINCTION
DISTINCTIVE
DISTINGUISH
DISTRACTING
DISTRACTION
DISTRESSFUL
DISTRESSING
DISTRIBUTOR
DISTRUSTFUL
DISTURBANCE
DITHYRAMBIC
DITHYRAMBUS
DIVERSIFIED
DIVERTINGLY
DIVING-DRESS
DIVINING-ROD
DIVORCEABLE
DIVORCEMENT
DOCK-WARRANT
DOCTRINAIRE
DOCTRINALLY
DOCUMENTARY
DOLABRIFORM
DOLEFULNESS
DOMESTICATE
DOMESTICITY
DOMICILIARY
DOMICILIATE
DOMINEERING
DOUBLE-EDGED
DOUBLE-ENTRY
DOUBLE-FACED
DOUBLE-FIRST
DOUBLE-QUICK

DOUBTLESSLY
DOUGHTINESS
DOWNTRODDEN
DOXOLOGICAL
DRAMATURGIC
DRAUGHTSMAN
DREADNOUGHT
DREAMLESSLY
DRUNKENNESS
DUBIOUSNESS
DUCTILENESS
DUPLICATION
DUPLICATIVE
DUPLICATURE
DUTIFULNESS
DYNAMICALLY
DYSLOGISTIC

E

EARNESTNESS
EARTHENWARE
EARTHLINESS
ECCENTRICAL
ECLECTICISM
EDIFICATION
EDITOR'ALLY
EDUCATIONAL
EFFECTIVELY
EFFICACIOUS·
EFFICIENTLY
EFFOLIATION
EFFULGENTLY
EGLANDULOSE
EGLANDULOUS
EGREGIOUSLY
EIDOLOCLAST
EJACULATION
ELABORATELY
ELABORATIVE
ELABORATION
ELASTICALLY
ELECTIONEER
ELECTORSHIP
ELECTRICIAN
ELECTROCUTE
ELECTROGILD
ELECTROLYSE
ELECTROLYTE
ELECTROTYPE
ELEMENTALLY
ELEPHANTINE
ELEPHANTOID
ELIGIBILITY
ELIZABETHAN
ELLIPSOIDAL
ELLIPTICITY
ELUCIDATION
ELUCIDATIVE
ELUSORINESS
ELUTRIATION
EMANCIPATOR
EMBARKATION
EMBARRASSED
EMBLEMATIST
EMBLEMATIZE
EMBOWELMENT
EMBRACEMENT
EMBROCATION

EMBROILMENT
EMBRYOLOGIC
EMMENAGOGUE
EMMENAGOGIC
EMPIRICALLY
EMULATIVELY
EMULSIONIZE
ENARTHROSIS
ENCEPHALOID
ENCEPHALOUS
ENCHAINMENT
ENCHANTMENT
ENCHANTRESS
ENCOMIASTIC
ENCOURAGING
ENCUMBRANCE
ENCYSTATION
ENDOCARDIAC
ENDEMICALLY
ENDLESSNESS
ENDOCARDIUM
ENDORHIZOUS
ENDORSEMENT
ENDOSMOSMIC
ENDOSPERMIC
ENERGETICAL
ENFEOFFMENT
ENFORCEABLE
ENFORCEMENT
ENFRANCHISE
ENGINEERING
ENGORGEMENT
ENGRAILMENT
ENGROSSMENT
ENHANCEMENT
ENIGMATICAL
ENLARGEMENT
ENLIGHTENED
ENLIVENMENT
ENNEAGYNOUS
ENNEAHEDRAL
ENNEAHEDRON
ENNOBLEMENT
ENOUNCEMENT
ENSLAVEMENT
ENTABLATURE
ENTEROPATHY
ENTERTAINER
ENTHRALMENT
ENTOMOLOGIC
ENTOZOOLOGY
ENTREATABLE
ENTWINEMENT
ENUCLEATION
ENUMERATION
ENUNCIATION
ENUNCIATIVE
ENUNCIATORY
ENVELOPMENT
ENVIRONMENT
EPIDICTACAL
EPIGASTRIUM
EPIGRAPHICS
EPILOGISTIC
EPIPETALOUS
EPIPHYLLOUS
EPIPHYTICAL
EPISCOPALLY
EPISTOLICAL
EPITHALAMIC

EPITHELIOMA
EPITHETICAL
EQUABLENESS
EQUIANGULAR
EQUIDISTANT
EQUILATERAL
EQUILIBRATE
EQUILIBRIST
EQUILIBRIUM
EQUINOCTIAL
EQUIPOLLENT
EQUIVALENCE
EQUIVALENCY
EQUIVOCALLY
EQUIVOCATOR
ERADICATION
ERADICATIVE
ERASTIANISM
EREMACAUSIS
ERRATICALLY
ERRONEOUSLY
ERUBESCENCE
ERYTHEMATIC
ESCHATOLOGY
ESCHEATABLE
ESOTERICISM
ESSENTIALLY
ESTABLISHED
ESTABLISHER
ETHEREALITY
ETHEREALIZE
ETHNOGRAPHY
ETHNOLOGIST
ETYMOLOGIST
ETYMOLOGIZE
EUCHARISTIC
EUDAEMONISM
EUDAEMONIST
EUPHEMISTIC
EUROPEANIZE
EVANESCENCE
EVANGELICAL
EVAPORATION
EVAPORATIVE
EVENTUALITY
EVENTUATION
EVERLASTING
EVOLUTIONAL
EXAGGERATOR
EXAMINATION
EXCEEDINGLY
EXCELLENTLY
EXCEPTIONAL
EXCESSIVELY
EXCLAMATION
EXCLAMATORY
EXCLUSIVELY
EXCLUSIVISM
EXCORIATION
EXCORTICATE
EXCRESCENCE
EXCULPATION
EXCULPATORY
EXCURSIVELY
EXECUTIONER
EXECUTORIAL
EXEMPLARILY
EXEMPLIFIER
EXFOLIATION
EXHAUSTIBLE

EXHAUSTLESS
EXHORTATION
EXHORTATIVE
EXHORTATORY
EXISTENTIAL
EXONERATION
EXONERATIVE
EXORBITANCE
EXORBITANCY
EXOSKELETON
EXOSKELETAL
EXOTERICISM
EXPANSIVELY
EXPATIATION
EXPATIATORY
EXPECTATION
EXPECTATIVE
EXPECTORANT
EXPECTORATE
EXPEDIENTLY
EXPEDITIOUS
EXPENDITURE
EXPENSIVELY
EXPERIENCED
EXPISCATION
EXPLANATION
EXPLANATORY
EXPLICATION
EXPLICATIVE
EXPLICATORY
EXPLOITABLE
EXPLORATION
EXPLORATORY
EXPLOSIVELY
EXPONENTIAL
EXPORTATION
EXPOSEDNESS
EXPOSTULATE
EXPRESSIBLE
EXPROPRIATE
EXPURGATION
EXPURGATORY
EXQUISITELY
EXTEMPORARY
EXTEMPORIZE
EXTENSIVELY
EXTENUATION
EXTENUATORY
EXTERIORITY
EXTERMINATE
EXTERNALISM
EXTERNALITY
EXTERNALIZE
EXTIRPATION
EXTIRPATORY
EXTORTIONER
EXTRACTIBLE
EXTRADITION
EXTRAVAGANT
EXTRAVASATE
EXTRICATION
EXTRINSICAL
EXUBERANTLY

F

FABRICATION
FACETIOUSLY

FACSIMILIST
FACULTATIVE
FADDISHNESS
FAITHLESSLY
FALLIBILITY
FALTERINGLY
FAMILIARITY
FAMILIARIZE
FANATICALLY
FANFARONADE
FANTASTICAL
FARTHERMORE
FARTHERMOST
FARTHINGALE
FASCINATING
FASCINATION
FASHIONABLE
FASTIGIATED
FAULTLESSLY
FAUSSEBRAYE
FAVOURITISM
FEARFULNESS
FEASIBILITY
FEATHERLESS
FEATURELESS
FEBRICULOSE
FEBRIFEROUS
FECUNDATION
FELONIOUSLY
FELSPATHOSE
FERMENTABLE
FEROCIOUSLY
FERRIFEROUS
FERRUGINOUS
FERULACEOUS
FIDGETINESS
FILAMENTARY
FILAMENTOSE
FILAMENTOUS
FILAMENTOID
FILLIBUSTER
FIMETARIOUS
FINANCIALLY
FINICALNESS
FIRMAMENTAL
FISSIPAROUS
FLABBERGAST
FLACCIDNESS
FLATULENTLY
FLAVOURLESS
FLESHINESS
FLEXIBILITY
FLIGHTINESS
FLOCCULENCE
FLORESCENCE
FLORILEGIUM
FLOURISHING
FLOWERINESS
FLUCTUATING
FLUCTUATION
FLUORESCENT
FOMENTATION
FOOLISHNESS
FOPPISHNESS
FORAMINATED
FORAMINIFER
FORBEARANCE
FORCIPATION
FORECLOSURE
FOREIGNNESS

FOREPAYMENT
FORESHORTEN
FORESTALLER
FORETHOUGHT
FORFEITABLE
FORGIVENESS
FORMICATION
FORMULARIZE
FORMULATION
FORNICATION
FORTHCOMING
FORTIFIABLE
FORTNIGHTLY
FORTUNATELY
FORWARDNESS
FRACTIONIZE
FRACTIONATE
FRACTIOUSLY
FRAGILENESS
FRAGMENTARY
FRANGIPANNI
FRANTICALLY
FRATERNALLY
FRATRICIDAL
FRAUDLESSLY
FRAUDULENCE
FREEBOOTING
FREEMASONRY
FRETFULNESS
FRIGHTFULLY
FRIVOLOUSLY
FROWARDNESS
FRUGIFEROUS
FRUGIVOROUS
FRUITLESSLY
FRUSTRATION
FULGURATION
FULMINATING
FULMINATION
FULSOMENESS
FUNAMBULIST
FUNCTIONATE
FUNCTIONARY
FUNDAMENTAL
FUNGIVOROUS
FURIOUSNESS
FURTHERANCE
FURTHERMORE
FURTHERMOST

G

GAINFULNESS
GALLIMAUFRY
GALLOWGLASS
GAMOGENESIS
GARNISHMENT
GARRULOUSLY
GASTRONOMER
GEMMIPAROUS
GENDARMERIE
GENEALOGIST
GENERALSHIP
GENERICALLY
GENETICALLY
GENICULATED
GENTEELNESS
GENTLEMANLY
GENTLEWOMAN

GENTLEWOMEN
GENUFLEXION
GENUINENESS
GEOMETRICAL
GERMINATION
GERMINATIVE
GERRYMANDER
GESTICULATE
GHASTLINESS
GHOSTLINESS
GIGANTESQUE
GILLYFLOWER
GINGERBREAD
GIRLISHNESS
GLAUCESCENT
GLOBIGERINA
GLOBULARITY
GLOMERATION
GLUMIFEROUS
GLYPTOTHECA
GOATISHNESS
GODDAUGHTER
GODLESSNESS
GONFALONIER
GORMANDIZER
GOURMANDIZE
GRACELESSLY
GRADATIONAL
GRAMMATICAL
GRANDFATHER
GRANDIOSITY
GRANDMOTHER
GRANDNEPHEW
GRANIFEROUS
GRANITIFORM
GRANIVOROUS
GRANULATION
GRAPHICALLY
GRATULATION
GRATULATORY
GRAVIMETRIC
GRAVITATION
GRAVITATIVE
GREENGROCER
GRISTLINESS
GROTESQUELY
GROTESQUERY
GUANIFEROUS
GUARDEDNESS
GUILELESSLY
GUILTLESSLY
GULLIBILITY
GUMMIFEROUS
GUTTIFEROUS
GUTTURALIZE
GYNECOCRACY
GYNAECOLOGY
GYNAEOLATRY

H

HABERDASHER
HABITUATION
HAEMOGLOBIN
HAEMOPHILIA
HAEMOPTYSIS
HAEMORRHAGE
HAGIOGRAPHY
HAGIOLOGIST

HANDBREADTH
HANDICAPPER
HANDWRITING
HARBOURLESS
HARMFULNESS
HARPSICHORD
HATEFULNESS
HAUGHTINESS
HAUSTELLATE
HAZARDOUSLY
HEALTHFULLY
HEALTHINESS
HEARTHSTONE
HEARTLESSLY
HEAVENWARDS
HEBDOMADARY
HEEDFULNESS
HEINOUSNESS
HELIOCHROMY
HELIOGRAPHY
HELLENISTIC
HELLISHNESS
HELMINTHOID
HELPFULNESS
HEMATOXYLIN
HEMERALOPIA
HEMIHEDRISM
HEMIPTEROUS
HEMISPHERIC
HEMITROPOUS
HEMORRHAGIC
HEMORRHOIDS
HEPTAGYNOUS
HEPTAGYNIAN
HEPTAHEDRON
HEPTAHEDRAL
HEPTAMEROUS
HEPTANDROUS
HEPTANGULAR
HERBIVOROUS
HEREDITABLE
HEREINAFTER
HERESIOLOGY
HERETICALLY
HERMENEUTIC
HERPETOLOGY
HESPERORNIS
HETEROCLITE
HETEROPHEMY
HEXAGONALLY
HIBERNATION
HIBERNICISM
HIDEOUSNESS
HIERARCHISM
HIPPOCAMPUS
HISTORIETTE
HISTRIONISM
HOBBLEDEHOY
HOLOGRAPHIC
HOLOTHURIAN
HOMILETICAL
HOMOEOPATHY
HOMOGENEITY
HOMOGENEOUS
HOMOGENESIS
HOMOGENETTE
HOMOIOUSIAN
HOMOMORPHIC
HOMOPLASTIC
HONEYSUCKLE

HONOURABLES
HOPEFULNESS
HOROLOGICAL
HOROSCOPIST
HOSPITALITY
HOSPITALLER
HOUSEHOLDER
HOUSEKEEPER
HOUSEWIFELY
HOUSEWIFERY
HUCKLEBERRY
HUCKSTERAGE
HUMECTATION
HUMILIATING
HUMILIATION
HUMORSOMELY
HUNCHBACKED
HURTFULNESS
HYACINTHINE
HYALOGRAPHY
HYDROCARBON
HYDROCYANIC
HYDROGENOUS
HYDROGRAPHY
HYDROMETRIC
HYDROPATHIC
HYDROPHOBIA
HYDROPHOBIC
HYDROSTATIC
HYDROTHORAX
HYETOGRAPHY
HYGROMETRIC
HYGROSCOPIC
HYMNOGRAPHY
HYMNOLOGIST
HYPERBOLISM
HYPERBOLIZE
HYPERBOREAN
HYPERCRITIC
HYPERSTHENE
HYPERTROPHY
HYPOGASTRIC
HYPOGLOSSAL
HYPOSTATIZE
HYPOSTASIZE
HYPOTHECATE
HYPOTHENUSE
HYPOTHESIZE
HYSTEROTOMY

I

ICHTHYOLITE
ICHTHYOLOGY
ICHTHYORNIS
ICONOGRAPHY
ICOSAHEDRAL
IDENTICALLY
IDEOGRAPHIC
IDIOMATICAL
IDIOMORPHIC
IDIOTICALLY
IGNOBLENESS
IGNOMINIOUS
IGNORAMUSES
ILLIBERALLY
ILLIMITABLE
ILLOGICALLY
ILLUMINATOR

ILLUSIONIST
ILLUSTRATOR
ILLUSTRIOUS
IMAGINATION
IMAGINATIVE
IMBRICATION
IMITABILITY
IMITATIVELY
IMMEDIATELY
IMMENSENESS
IMMIGRATION
IMMORTALITY
IMMORTALIZE
IMPANELMENT
IMPARTATION
IMPARTIALLY
IMPASSIONED
IMPASSIVELY
IMPATIENTLY
IMPEACHABLE
IMPEACHMENT
IMPECUNIOUS
IMPENITENCE
IMPERFECTLY
IMPERFORATE
IMPERIALISM
IMPERIALIST
IMPERIALIZE
IMPERIOUSLY
IMPERMEABLE
IMPERMEABLY
IMPERSONATE
IMPERTINENT
IMPETUOSITY
IMPETUOUSLY
IMPIOUSNESS
IMPLACENTAL
IMPLEMENTAL
IMPLICATION
IMPLICATIVE
IMPLORATION
IMPLORATORY
IMPORTANTLY
IMPORTATION
IMPORTUNATE
IMPORTUNITY
IMPRECATION
IMPRECATORY
IMPREGNABLE
IMPREGNABLY
IMPRESSIBLE
IMPRESSIBLY
IMPRESSMENT
IMPROPRIATE
IMPROPRIETY
IMPROVEMENT
IMPRUDENTLY
IMPULSIVELY
INADVERTENT
INALIENABLE
INALIENABLY
INALTERABLE
INALTERABLY
INATTENTION
INATTENTIVE
INAUGURATOR
INCANTATION
INCANTATORY
INCARCERATE
INCARNADINE

INCARNATION
INCEPTIVELY
INCERTITUDE
INCESSANTLY
INCLEMENTLY
INCLINATION
INCLUSIVELY
INCOGITABLE
INCOHERENCE
INCOHERENCY
INCOMPETENT
INCONGRUENT
INCONGRUOUS
INCONSONANT
INCONSTANCY
INCONTINENT
INCORPORATE
INCORPOREAL
INCORRECTLY
INCREASABLE
INCREDULITY
INCREDULOUS
INCREMATION
INCRIMINATE
INCULCATION
INCULPATION
INCULPATORY
INCUMBRANCE
INCURIOUSLY
INCURVATION
INCURVATURE
INDECIDUATE
INDEFINABLE
INDENTATION
INDEPENDENT
INDEXTERITY
INDIFFERENT
INDIGESTION
INDIGNANTLY
INDIGNATION
INDIVIDUATE
INDIVISIBLE
INDIVISIBLY
INDOMITABLE
INDOMITABLY
INDORSEMENT
INDUBITABLE
INDUBITABLY
INDUCTIONAL
INDUCTIVELY
INDULGENTLY
INDUPLICATE
INDUSTRIOUS
INEBRIATION
INEFFECTIVE
INEFFECTUAL
INEFFICIENT
INELEGANTLY
INEQUITABLE
INESCAPABLE
INESSENTIAL
INESTIMABLE
INESTIMABLY
INEXCUSABLE
INEXCUSABLY
INEXPEDIENT
INEXPENSIVE
INEXPLOSIVE
INFANTICIDE
INFATUATION

INFECUNDITY
INFERENTIAL
INFERIORITY
INFERTILELY
INFERTILITY
INFESTATION
INFEUDATION
INFINITIVAL
INFLAMMABLE
INFLAMMABLY
INFLUENTIAL
INFORMALITY
INFORMATION
INFRACOSTAL
INFRANGIBLE
INFREQUENCY
INGATHERING
INGENIOUSLY
INGENUOUSLY
INGRATITUDE
INGURGITATE
INHABITABLE
INHERITABLE
INHERITABLY
INHERITANCE
INJUDICIOUS
INJURIOUSLY
INNAVIGABLE
INNERVATION
INNOCUOUSLY
INNOXIOUSLY
INNUMERABLE
INNUMERABLY
INNUTRITION
INOBSERVANT
INOBTRUSIVE
INOCULATION
INOFFENSIVE
INOPERATIVE
INOPPORTUNE
INORGANIZED
INQUISITION
INQUISITIVE
INSALUBRITY
INSATIATELY
INSCRIPTION
INSCRIPTIVE
INSCRUTABLE
INSCRUTABLY
INSECTICIDE
INSECTIVORE
INSENSITIVE
INSEPARABLE
INSEPARABLY
INSESSORIAL
INSIDIOUSLY
INSINCERELY
INSINCERITY
INSINUATING
INSINUATION
INSINUATIVE
INSOUCIANCE
INSPIRATION
INSPIRATORY
INSTABILITY
INSTIGATION
INSTINCTIVE
INSTITUTION
INSTRUCTION
INSTITUTIVE

INSTRUCTIVE
INSULTINGLY
INSUPERABLY
INTEGRATION
INTELLIGENT
INTEMPERANT
INTEMPERATE
INTENSENESS
INTENSIVELY
INTENTIONAL
INTENTIONED
INTERACTION
INTERCALARY
INTERCALATE
INTERCESSOR
INTERCHANGE
INTERCOSTAL
INTERCOURSE
INTERESTING
INTERFLUENT
INTERFUSION
INTERIORITY
INTERJACENT
INTERLINEAR
INTERLINEAL
INTERMEDDLE
INTERMEDIAL
INTERMEDIUM
INTERMINATE
INTERMINGLE
INTERNALITY
INTERNECINE
INTERNUNCIO
INTEROCULAR
INTERPOLATE
INTERPRETER
INTERREGNUM
INTERROGATE
INTERRUPTED
INTERSPERSE
INTERVIEWER
INTOLERABLE
INTOLERABLY
INTOLERANCE
INTRACTABLE
INTRACTABLY
INTREPIDITY
INTRICATELY
INTRINSICAL
INTRUSIVELY
INTUITIONAL
INTUITIVELY
INTUMESCENT
INVECTIVELY
INVENTIVELY
INVENTORIAL
INVESTIGATE
INVESTITURE
INVIDIOUSLY
INVIOLATELY
INVOLUNTARY
INVOLVEMENT
IPECACUANHA
IRIDESCENCE
IRKSOMENESS
IRONMONGERY
IRRADIATION
IRREDUCIBLE
IRREDUCIBLY
IRREFUTABLE

IRREFUTABLY
IRREGULARLY
IRRELEVANCE
IRRELEVANCY
IRRELIGIOUS
IRREMOVABLE
IRREMOVABLY
IRREPARABLE
IRREPARABLY
IRREVERENCE
IRREVOCABLE
IRREVOCABLY
ISOCHRONOUS
ISOCHRONISM
ISOMETRICAL
ISOMORPHISM
ISOMORPHOUS
ISRAELITISH
ITHYPHALLIC

J

JACOBITICAL
JACTITATION
JOYLESSNESS
JUDICIOUSLY
JURIDICALLY
JUSTICESHIP
JUSTIFIABLY
JUVENESCENT

K

KAMPTULICON
KINEMATICAL
KLEPTOMANIA
KNAVISHNESS

L

LABEFACTION
LABORIOUSLY
LABRADORITE
LACONICALLY
LACRYMATORY
LACTESCENCE
LACTIFEROUS
LAMELLICORN
LAMELLIFORM
LAMENTATION
LAMMERGEIER
LANCEOLATED
LANCINATING
LANCINATION
LANGUIDNESS
LANGUISHING
LAPIDESCENT
LARVIPAROUS
LARYNGOTOMY
LATIFOLIATE
LATIFOLIOUS
LATITUDINAL
LAURUSTINUS
LAWLESSNESS
LEASEHOLDER
LECHEROUSLY

LECTURESHIP
LEGERDEMAIN
LEGISLATION
LEGISLATIVE
LEGISLATURE
LENGTHINESS
LENTIGINOUS
LEPIDOSIREN
LETHARGICAL
LEUCORRHOEA
LIBELLOUSLY
LIBERTARIAN
LIBERTICIDE
LIBERTINISM
LICHENOLOGY
LICKERISHLY
LICKSPITTLE
LIEUTENANCY
LIGAMENTOUS
LIGHTKEEPER
LILLIPUTIAN
LINGERINGLY
LINGUISTICS
LIQUEFIABLE
LIQUESCENCY
LIQUIDAMBAR
LIQUIDATION
LISSOMENESS
LITERALNESS
LITHOGRAPHY
LITHOTOMIST
LITHOTRIPSY
LITHOTRITOR
LITIGIOUSLY
LITTERATEUR
LOATHLINESS
LOATHSOMELY
LOGARITHMIC
LOGICALNESS
LOGOMACHIST
LUBRICATION
LUDICROUSLY
LUMPISHNESS
LUSTFULNESS
LUTHERANISM
LUXURIANTLY
LUXURIOUSLY
LYCANTHROPE
LYCANTHROPY

M

MACHINATION
MACROBIOTIC
MAGISTERIAL
MAGISTRATIC
MAGNANIMITY
MAGNETICIAN
MAGNIFIABLE
MAGNIFICENT
MAGNIFICOES
MAINTENANCE
MALEDICTION
MALEFICENCE
MALEVOLENCE
MALFEASANCE
MALICIOUSLY
MALIGNANTLY
MALPOSITION

MALPRACTICE
MAMMIFEROUS
MANDARINATE
MANDIBULATE
MANDUCATION
MANDUCATORY
MANGANESIAN
MANIPULATOR
MANUFACTORY
MANUFACTURE
MANUMISSION
MARCHIONESS
MARMORATION
MARSHALLING
MARSHALSHIP
MARTYROLOGY
MASCULINITY
MASQUERADER
MASTICATION
MASTICATORY
MATCHLESSLY
MATERIALISM
MATERIALIST
MATERIALIZE
MATHEMATICS
MATRIARCHAL
MATRICULATE
MATRIMONIAL
MAWKISHNESS
MEANINGLESS
MEASURELESS
MEASUREMENT
MECHANICIAN
MECHANOLOGY
MEDIASTINUM
MEDIATENESS
MEDIATORIAL
MEDICINALLY
MEDIEVALISM
MEDIEVALIST
MEGALOMANIA
MEGATHERIUM
MELANCHOLIA
MELIORATION
MELLIFEROUS
MELLIFLUENT
MELLIFLUOUS
MELLIVOROUS
MELODIOUSLY
MEMORABILIA
MEMORANDUMS
MEMORIALIST
MEMORIALIZE
MENORRHAGIA
MENSURATION
MENTIONABLE
MERCENARILY
MERCHANDISE
MERCHANTMAN
MERCILESSLY
MERCURIALLY
MERITORIOUS
MESALLIANCE
MESOPHLOEUM
MESSIAHSHIP
METAGENESIS
METAMORPHIC
METAPHYSICS
METEOROLITE
METEOROLOGY

METHODISTIC
METHODOLOGY
METONYMICAL
MICROCOCCUS
MICROGRAPHY
MICROLITHIC
MICROMETRIC
MICROSCOPIC
MICTURITION
MILLENARIAN
MILLIGRAMME
MILLIONAIRE
MINDFULNESS
MINERALIZER
MINERALOGIC
MINIATURIST
MINISTERIAL
MINISTERING
MINNESINGER
MISALLIANCE
MISANTHROPE
MISANTHROPY
MISBECOMING
MISBEGOTTEN
MISBELIEVER
MISCARRIAGE
MISCHIEVOUS
MISCONCEIVE
MISCONSTRUE
MISFEASANCE
MISSPELLING
MISTRUSTFUL
MITIGATIONS
MIXTILINEAL
MIXTILINEAR
MOLESTATION
MOMENTARILY
MOMENTOUSLY
MONARCHICAL
MONASTICISM
MONODELPHIA
MONOGENESIS
MONOGRAPHER
MONOGRAPHIC
MONOMORPHIC
MONOPHTHONG
MONOPHYSITE
MONOPOLIZER
MONOTREMATA
MONSTROSITY
MONSTROUSLY
MOONLIGHTER
MORAVIANISM
MORPHOLOGIC
MOUNTAINEER
MOUNTAINOUS
MOVABLENESS
MULTANGULAR
MULTANIMOUS
MULTILINEAL
MULTIPOTENT
MULTISERIAL
MULTISONOUS
MUMPISHNESS
MUNIFICENCE
MURDEROUSLY
MURMURINGLY
MUSCULARITY
MUTABLENESS
MYCOLOGICAL

MYTHOLOGIST
MYTHOLOGIAN
MYTHOLOGIZE
MYTHOPOETIC

N

NARRATIVELY
NATIONALISE
NATIONALISM
NATIONALIST
NATIONALITY
NATURALNESS
NAUGHTINESS
NECESSARILY
NECESSITATE
NECESSITOUS
NECKERCHIEF
NECROBIOSIS
NECROLOGIST
NECROMANCER
NECROMANTIC
NEEDFULNESS
NEFARIOUSLY
NEGLIGENTLY
NEGOTIATION
NEGOTIATORY
NEIGHBOURLY
NEOTROPICAL
NEPHRITICAL
NEUTRALIZER
NICTITATION
NIGHTINGALE
NIMBIFEROUS
NITROGENIZE
NITROGENOUS
NOCTILUCOUS
NOCTIVAGANT
NOCTURNALLY
NOISELESSLY
NOISOMENESS
NOMENCLATOR
NOMINATIVAL
NONCHALANCE
NONDESCRIPT
NONSENSICAL
NORTHWARDLY
NOSOLOGICAL
NOTABLENESS
NOTHINGNESS
NOTORIOUSLY
NOURISHABLE
NOURISHMENT
NOXIOUSNESS
NUMERICALLY
NUMISMATICS
NUMISMATIST
NUNCUPATIVE
NUNCUPATORY
NUTRIMENTAL
NUTRITIVELY
NYCTITROPIC
NYMPHOLEPSY
NYMPHOMANIA

O

OBEDIENTIAL

OBFUSCATION
OBJECTIVELY
OBJECTIVITY
OBJURGATION
OBJURGATORY
OBLIQUENESS
OBLIVIOUSLY
OBNOXIOUSLY
OBSCENENESS
OBSCURATION
OBSCUREMENT
OBSCURENESS
OBSECRATION
OBSECRATORY
OBSERVANTLY
OBSERVATION
OBSERVATIVE
OBSERVATORY
OBSOLESCENT
OBSTETRICAL
OBSTINATELY
OBSTIPATION
OBSTRUCTION
OBSTRUCTIVE
OBTESTATION
OBTRUSIVELY
OBVIOUSNESS
OCCULTATION
OCHLOCRATIC
ODONTOPHORE
ODORIFEROUS
OENOPHILIST
OESOPHAGEAL
OFFENSIVELY
OFFICIALISM
OFFICIOUSLY
OFFSCOURING
OMINOUSNESS
OMNIFARIOUS
OMNIPOTENCE
OMNIPRESENT
OMNISCIENCE
OMNISCIENCY
OMPHALOTOMY
ONEIROMANCY
ONIROCRITIC
ONOMASTICON
ONOMATOLOGY
ONTOGENESIS
ONTOLOGICAL
OPALESCENCE
OPEIDOSCOPE
OPERATIVELY
OPEROSENESS
OPINIONABLE
OPINIONATED
OPPORTUNELY
OPPORTUNISM
OPPORTUNIST
OPPORTUNITY
OPPROBRIOUS
ORBICULARLY
ORBICULATED
ORCHESTRION
ORCHIDOLOGY
ORDERLINESS
ORGANICALLY
ORGANIZABLE
ORIENTALISM
ORIENTALIST

ORIENTALIZE
ORIGINALITY
ORIGINATION
ORIGINATIVE
ORNAMENTIST
ORNITHOLITE
ORNITHOLOGY
ORTHOGRAPHY
ORTHOPAEDIA
ORTHOPAEDIC
ORTHOPEDIST
ORTHOTROPAL
OSCILLATING
OSCILLATION
OSCILLATORY
OSTENTATION
OSTEOGRAPHY
OSTEOLOGIST
OSTEOPLASTY
OSTREACEOUS
OUTDISTANCE
OUTSTANDING
OVERBALANCE
OVERBEARING
OVERFLOWING
OVERWEENING
OVERWROUGHT
OXYGENATION
OXYHYDROGEN

P

PACIFICALLY
PACIFICATOR
PAEDAGOGICS
PAINFULNESS
PAINSTAKING
PALAEARCTIC
PALEOGRAPHY
PALMIFEROUS
PALPABILITY
PALPITATION
PALPIGEROUS
PALSGRAVINE
PAMPHLETEER
PAMPINIFORM
PANDEMONIUM
PANDURIFORM
PANEGYRICAL
PANHELLENIC
PANTHEISTIC
PAPYRACEOUS
PAPYROGRAPH
PARABOLICAL
PARACENTRIC
PARADOXICAL
PARAGOGICAL
PARAGRAPHIC
PARALLACTIC
PARALLELISM
PARASITICAL
PARCHEDNESS
PARENTHESIS
PARENTHESES
PARENTHETIC
PARENTICIDE
PARIPINNATE
PARISHIONER
PAROCHIALLY

PARONOMASIA
PARTIBILITY
PARTICIPATE
PARTICIPIAL
PARTICULATE
PARTITIVELY
PARTNERSHIP
PARTURITION
PARVANIMITY
PASSIBILITY
PASSIONLESS
PASSIVENESS
PASTURELESS
PATERNOSTER
PATHOLOGIST
PATRIARCHIC
PATRIMONIAL
PATRONIZING
PEARLACEOUS
PECCABILITY
PECTINATION
PECULIARITY
PECUNIARILY
PEDAGOGICAL
PEDICELLATE
PEDOBAPTISM
PEDOBAPTIST
PEDUNCULATE
PEEVISHNESS
PELAGIANISM
PELARGONIUM
PELLUCIDITY
PENETRATING
PENETRATION
PENETRATIVE
PENINSULATE
PENITENTIAL
PENNONCELLE
PENNYWEIGHT
PENSIVENESS
PENTAGYNIAN
PENTAGYNOUS
PENTAHEDRAL
PENTAHEDRON
PENTANDROUS
PENTANGULAR
PENTECOSTAL
PENULTIMATE
PENURIOUSLY
PERAMBULATE
PERCEIVABLE
PERCEIVABLY
PERCEPTIBLE
PERCEPTIBLY
PERCIPIENCE
PERCIPIENCY
PERCOLATION
PEREGRINATE
PERENNIALLY
PERFECTIBLE
PERFECTNESS
PERFORATION
PERFORATIVE
PERFORMABLE
PERFORMANCE
PERFUMATORY
PERFUNCTORY
PERICARDIAL
PERICARDIAC
PERICARDIUM

PERICARPIAL
PERICRANIUM
PERIGASTRIC
PERIODICITY
PERIOSTEOUS
PERIPATETIC
PERIPHRASIS
PERIPHRASES
PERISTALTIC
PERITONAEAL
PERITONAEUM
PERITONITIS
PERMANENTLY
PERMISSIBLE
PERMISSIBLY
PERMUTATION
PERPETRATOR
PERPETUABLE
PERPETUALLY
PERSECUTION
PERSECUTRIX
PERSEVERING
PERSISTENCE
PERSISTENCY
PERSONALISM
PERSONALITY
PERSONALIZE
PERSONATION
PERSPECTIVE
PERSPICUITY
PERSPICUOUS
PERSPIRABLE
PERSUADABLE
PERSUASIBLE
PERTINACITY
PERTINENTLY
PERTURBABLE
PERTURBANCE
PERVERTIBLE
PESSIMISTIC
PESTIFEROUS
PESTILENTLY
PETITIONARY
PETRIFIABLE
PETROGRAPHY
PETROLOGIST
PETTIFOGGER
PHAGEDAENIC
PHANTOMATIC
PHARISAICAL
PHARYNGITIS
PHENOMENISM
PHENOMENIST
PHILATELIST
PHILHELLENE
PHILOLOGIST
PHILOLOGIAN
PHILOMATHIC
PHILOSOPHER
PHILOSOPHIC
PHOSPHORATE
PHOSPHORIZE
PHOSPHOROUS
PHOTOCHROMY
PHOTOGLYPHY
PHOTOGRAPHY
PHOTOMETRIC
PHOTOSPHERE
PHRASEOLOGY
PHTHIRIASIS

PHYLACTERIC
PHYLLOTAXIS
PHYSIOGNOMY
PHYSIOLATRY
PHYSIOLOGIC
PHYTOGRAPHY
PHYTOLOGIST
PICROTOXINE
PICTORIALLY
PICTURESQUE
PIETISTICAL
PINNATISECT
PIPERACEOUS
PIPISTRELLE
PIRATICALLY
PISCATORIAL
PISCIVOROUS
PITEOUSNESS
PITIFULNESS
PLACABILITY
PLAGIOSTOME
PLAINTIVELY
PLANETARIUM
PLANETOIDAL
PLANISPHERE
PLANTIGRADE
PLATINOTYPE
PLAYFULNESS
PLEASURABLE
PLEASURABLY
PLEBEIANISM
PLEBEIANIZE
PLEISTOCENE
PLENARINESS
PLENIPOTENT
PLENTEOUSLY
PLENTIFULLY
PLETHORICAL
PLEURITICAL
PLIABLENESS
PLOUGHSHARE
PLURIPAROUS
PLUTOCRATIC
PLUVIOMETER
PNEUMOMETER
PNEUMONITIS
POCOCURANTE
PODOPHYLLIN
POINTEDNESS
POISONOUSLY
POLARIMETER
POLARISCOPE
POLARIZABLE
POLEMICALLY
POLITICALLY
POLTROONERY
POLYCARPOUS
POLYCHROMIC
POLYGASTRIC
POLYGENESIS
POLYMORPHIC
POLYONYMOUS
POLYPHONISM
POLYPHONIST
POLYPLASTIC
POLYRHIZOUS
POLYSPOROUS
POLYTECHNIC
POMEGRANATE
POMPELMOOSE

POMPOUSNESS
PONDEROSITY
PONDEROUSLY
PONTIFICATE
PORNOGRAPHY
PORPHYRITIC
PORTABILITY
PORTMANTEAU
PORTRAITURE
POSSIBILITY
POSTERIORLY
POSTULATORY
POTENTIALLY
POWERLESSLY
PRACTICABLE
PRACTICABLY
PRACTICALLY
PRAGMATICAL
PRAYERFULLY
PREAUDIENCE
PRECEPTRESS
PRECIPITANT
PRECIPITATE
PRECIPITOUS
PRECISENESS
PRECOGNOSCE
PRECONCEIVE
PRECONTRACT
PREDECESSOR
PREDICAMENT
PREDICATION
PREDICATIVE
PREDICATORY
PREDOMINANT
PREDOMINATE
PREHENSILE
PREHISTORIC
PREJUDGMENT
PREJUDICATE
PREJUDICIAL
PRELATESHIP
PRELIBATION
PRELIMINARY
PREMATURELY
PREMATURITY
PREMEDITATE
PREMIERSHIP
PREMONITION
PREMONITORY
PREOCCUPIED
PREPARATION
PREPARATIVE
PREPARATORY
PREPOSITION
PREPOSITIVE
PREROGATIVE
PRESAGEMENT
PRESENTABLE
PRESENTNESS
PRESERVABLE
PRESUMPTION
PRESUMPTIVE
PRETENDEDLY
PRETENTIOUS
PRETERITION
PRETERITIVE
PREVALENTLY
PREVENTABLE
PRICKLINESS
PRIESTCRAFT

PRIMATESHIP
PRIMIGENIAL
PRIMITIVELY
PRINCIPALLY
PRISMATICAL
PRIVATIVELY
PROBABILITY
PROBATIONER
PROBLEMATIC
PROBOSCIDES
PROCONSULAR
PROCREATION
PROCTORSHIP
PROCURATION
PROCUREMENT
PRODIGALITY
PROFANATION
PROFANENESS
PROFICIENCY
PROFUSENESS
PROGNATHISM
PROGNATHOUS
PROGRESSION
PROGRESSIVE
PROHIBITION
PROHIBITIVE
PROHIBITORY
PROLEGOMENA
PROLEPTICAL
PROLETARIAN
PROMINENTLY
PROMISCUOUS
PROMISINGLY
PROMPTITUDE
PROMULGATOR
PRONOUNCING
PROPAGATION
PROPAGATIVE
PROPHETICAL
PROPINQUITY
PROPITIABLE
PROPITIATOR
PROPOSITION
PROPRIETARY
PROPRIETRIX
PROPRIETIES
PROROGATION
PROSAICALLY
PROSECUTION
PROSECUTRIX
PROSELYTISM
PROSELYTIZE
PROSENCHYMA
PROSOPOPEIA
PROSPECTION
PROSPECTIVE
PROSTITUTOR
PROSTRATION
PROTECTORAL
PROTECTRESS
PROTOMARTYR
PROTONOTARY
PROTRACTILE
PROTRACTION
PROTRACTIVE
PROTRUSIBLE
PROTUBERANT
PROTUBERATE
PROVIDENTLY
PROVOCATION

PROVOCATIVE
PROVOKINGLY
PROVOSTSHIP
PROXIMATELY
PRUDISHNESS
PRURIGINOUS
PSALMODICAL
PSEUDOPODIA
PSITTACEOUS
PSYCHOLOGIC
PTERIDOLOGY
PTERODACTYL
PUBLICATION
PUBLISHABLE
PUERILITIES
PULVERULENT
PULVINIFORM
PUNCTILIOUS
PUNCTUALITY
PUNCTUATION
PURCHASABLE
PURGATIVELY
PURGATORIAL
PURGATORIAN
PURITANICAL
PURPOSELESS
PUTRIDINOUS
PUTRIFIABLE
PUTRESCENCE
PUTRESCIBLE
PYRAMIDACLE
PYRAMIDALLY
PYROTECHNIC
PYTHAGORISM
PYTHAGORISM

Q

QUACKSALVER
QUADRENNIAL
QUADRILLION
QUALITATIVE
QUARRELSOME
QUERULOUSLY
QUESTIONARY
QUIBBLINGLY
QUICKSILVER
QUIESCENTLY
QUINCUNCIAL
QUINTILLION
QUIVERINGLY

R

RALLENTANDO
RAPACIOUSLY
RAPSCALLION
RAPTUROUSLY
RAREFACTION
RATIOCINATE
RATIONALISM
RATIONALIST
RATIONALITY
RAVISHINGLY
REACTIONARY
REACTIONIST
READABILITY
READMISSION

REALIZATION
REANIMATION
REASSERTION
REASSURANCE
RECANTATION
RECELEBRATE
RECEPTIVITY
RECIPROCATE
RECIPROCITY
RECLAIMABLE
RECLAMATION
RECLINATION
RECOMMENDER
RECONNOITRE
RECONSTRUCT
RECOVERABLE
RECREMENTAL
RECRIMINATE
RECRUITMENT
RECTANGULAR
RECTIFIABLE
RECTILINEAL
RECTILINEAR
RECTISERIAL
RECUMBENTLY
REDDISHNESS
REDISCOVERY
REDOUBTABLE
REDRESSIBLE
REDUPLICATE
REDUNDANTLY
REFERENTIAL
REFLECTIBLE
REFLEXIVELY
REFORMATION
REFORMATIVE
REFORMATORY
REFRACTABLE
REFRAINMENT
REFRANGIBLE
REFRESHMENT
REFRIGERANT
REFRIGERATE
REFULGENTLY
REGARDFULLY
REGIMENTALS
REGRETFULLY
REGRETTABLE
REGURGITATE
REINSERTION
REINTRODUCE
REITERATION
REITERATIVE
RELIABILITY
RELIGIONISM
RELIGIONIST
RELIGIOUSLY
RELUCTANTLY
REMEMBRANCE
REMIGRATION
REMINISCENT
REMONSTRANT
REMONSTRATE
REMORSELESS
REMUNERABLE
RENAISSANCE
REPENTANTLY
REPLACEMENT
REPLENISHER
REPLEVIABLE

REPLICATION
REPORTORIAL
REPREHENDER
REPRESENTER
REPRESSIBLE
REPRESSIBLY
REPROACHFUL
REPROBATION
REPROVINGLY
REPUDIATION
REPUGNANTLY
REPULSIVELY
REQUIREMENT
REQUISITION
RESCINDMENT
RESEMBLANCE
RESENTFULLY
RESERVATION
RESIDENTIAL
RESIGNATION
RESPECTABLE
RESPECTABLY
RESPIRATION
RESPIRATORY
RESPLENDENT
RESPONDENCE
RESPONDENCY
RESPONSIBLE
RESPONSIBLY
RESPONSIONS
RESTITUTION
RESTIVENESS
RESTORATION
RESTORATIVE
RESTRICTION
RESTRICTIVE
RESUSCITATE
RETALIATION
RETALIATIVE
RETALIATORY
RETARDATION
RETARDATIVE
RETENTIVELY
RETICULARLY
RETICULATED
RETIREDNESS
RETRACTABLE
RETRANSLATE
RETRIBUTION
RETRIBUTIVE
RETRIBUTORY
RETRIEVABLE
RETRIEVABLY
RETROACTIVE
REVERBERANT
REVERBERATE
REVERENTIAL
REVERSELESS
REVERSIONER
REVOLTINGLY
RHABDOMANCY
RHAPSODICAL
RHETORICIAN
RHINOCERIAL
RIFACIMENTO
RIGHTEOUSLY
RIOTOUSNESS
RISIBLENESS
RITUALISTIC
RODOMONTADE

ROMANTICISM
ROMANTICIST
ROMPISHNESS
ROSICRUCIAN
RUBEFACIENT
RUDIMENTARY
RURIDECANAL
RUSTICATION

S

SABBATARIAN
SACRAMENTAL
SACRIFICIAL
SADDUCEEISM
SAGACIOUSLY
SALINOMETER
SALVABILITY
SANSKRITIST
SAPONACEOUS
SARACENICAL
SARCASTICAL
SARCOMATOUS
SARCOPHAGUS
SATIRICALLY
SATURNALIAN
SAVOURINESS
SAXIFRAGOUS
SCAFFOLDING
SCALPRIFORM
SCANDINAVIA
SCAPULARIES
SCENOGRAPHY
SCEPTICALLY
SCHOLARSHIP
SCHOLIASTIC
SCHOTTISCHE
SCIATICALLY
SCINTILLANT
SCINTILLATE
SCIRRHOSITY
SCLEROBASIC
SCLEROMETER
SCLEROTITIS
SCOLOPENDRA
SCOPIFEROUS
SCOUNDRELLY
SCRAGGINESS
SCRUTINIZER
SEARCHINGLY
SECONDARILY
SECONDARIES
SECRETARIAL
SECTIONALLY
SECULARNESS
SEDENTARILY
SEDIMENTARY
SEDITIONARY
SEDITIOUSLY
SEDUCTIVELY
SEGREGATION
SEIGNIORAGE
SEIGNIORIAL
SEISMOGRAPH
SEISMOMETER
SIESMOSCOPE
SIESMOMETRY
SELFISHNESS
SEMIOGRAPHY

SEMPITERNAL
SENSATIONAL
SENSELESSLY
SENSIBILITY
SENSIFEROUS
SENSITIVELY
SENSITIVITY
SENTENTIOUS
SENTIMENTAL
SENTINELLED
SEPTICAEMIA
SEPTIFEROUS
SEQUESTERED
SEQUESTRATE
SERICULTURE
SERIOUSNESS
SERVICEABLE
SERVICEABLY
SESQUIPEDAL
SEVENTEENTH
SEXAGESIMAL
SEXENNIALLY
SHADOWINESS
SHALLOWNESS
SHAMELESSLY
SHAPELINESS
SHAREHOLDER
SHELTERLESS
SHEPHERDESS
SHERIFFALTY
SHERIFFSHIP
SHIFTLESSLY
SHIVERINGLY
SHOPKEEPING
SHORTCOMING
SHOWERINESS
SHRINKINGLY
SHRUBBINESS
SHUFFLINGLY
SIDEROSCOPE
SIGHTLINESS
SIGNIFICANT
SILVERSMITH
SIMPERINGLY
SINGULARITY
SINISTRALLY
SINISTRORSE
SINLESSNESS
SKETCHINESS
SKILFULNESS
SLAUGHTERER
SLEEPLESSLY
SLENDERNESS
SLIGHTINGLY
SLUMBERLESS
SOCIABILITY
SOCINIANISM
SOJOURNMENT
SOLANACEOUS
SOLDATESQUE
SOLDIERSHIP
SOLEMNITIES
SOLILOQUIES
SOLILOQUIZE
SOLMIZATION
SOLUBLENESS
SOLVABILITY
SOMEWHITHER
SOMNAMBULIC
SOOTHSAYING

SOPHISTICAL
SORROWFULLY
SOTERIOLOGY
SOTTISHNESS
SOVEREIGNTY
SPARKLINGLY
SPATHACEOUS
SPECTACULAR
SPECTATRESS
SPECTROLOGY
SPECULATION
SPECULATIVE
SPENDTHRIFT
SPHERICALLY
SPHEROMETER
SPICIFEROUS
SPINIFEROUS
SPONSORSHIP
SPONTANEITY
SPONTANEOUS
SPRINGINESS
SPUMIFEROUS
SQUALIDNESS
SQUEAMISHLY
SQUIREARCHY
STALACTICAL
STALACTITIC
STAPHYLOSIS
STARCHINESS
STATELINESS
STATISTICAL
STEADFASTLY
STEEPLEJACK
STENOGRAPHY
STEPBROTHER
STEREOSCOPE
STEREOTROPE
STEREOTYPED
STEREOTYPER
STEREOTYPIC
STETHOMETER
STETHOSCOPE
STETHOSCOPY
STEWARDSHIP
STICHOMANCY
STICHOMETRY
STICKLEBACK
STIGMATICAL
STIMULATING
STIMULATION
STIMULATIVE
STINTEDNESS
STIPENDIARY
STIPULATION
STOCKBROKER
STOCKHOLDER
STRAIGHTWAY
STRAMINEOUS
STRANGENESS
STRANGULATE
STRATEGETIC
STRATEGICAL
STRENUOUSLY
STRINGENTLY
STRINGINESS
STUDENTSHIP
STUNTEDNESS
STYLISHNESS
STYLOGRAPHY
SUBAXILLARY

SUBCONTRACT
SUBCONTRARY
SUBDEACONRY
SUBDIVISION
SUBDOMINANT
SUBGLOBULAR
SUBJUGATION
SUBJUNCTIVE
SUBLIMATION
SUBLIMATORY
SUBLIMENESS
SUBMERGENCE
SUBMETALLIC
SUBMULTIPLE
SUBORDINACY
SUBORDINATE
SUBORNATION
SUBSCAPULAR
SUBSENSIBLE
SUBSEQUENCE
SUBSERVIENT
SUBSISTENCE
SUBSTANTIAL
SUBSTANTIVE
SUBTILENESS
SUBTRACTION
SUBTROPICAL
SUCCEDANEUM
SUCCOURLESS
SUFFICIENCY
SUFFOCATING
SUFFOCATION
SUFFOCATIVE
SUFFRAGETTE
SUFFUMIGATE
SUGGESTIBLE
SUITABILITY
SULPHURATOR
SULPHUREOUS
SUMMERSAULT
SUMPTUOUSLY
SUPERABOUND
SUPERFETATE
SUPERFICIAL
SUPERFICIES
SUPERFLUITY
SUPERFLUOUS
SUPERIMPOSE
SUPERINDUCE
SUPERINTEND
SUPERIORESS
SUPERIORITY
SUPERJACENT
SUPERLATIVE
SUPERLUNARY
SUPERNATANT
SUPERSCRIBE
SUPERSUBTLE
SUPERVISION
SUPERVISORY
SUPPLIANTLY
SUPPORTABLE
SUPPORTABLY
SUPPOSITION
SUPPRESSION
SUPPRESSIVE
SUPPURATION
SUPPURATIVE
SUPRACOSTAL
SUPRAORBITS

SUPRASPINAL
SURGEONSHIP
SURREBUTTER
SURROUNDING
SUSCEPTIBLE
SUSCEPTIBLY
SWARTHINESS
SWEEPSTAKES
SWINISHNESS
SYCOPHANTIC
SYLLABARIUM
SYLLABICATE
SYLLOGISTIC
SYMMETRICAL
SYMPATHETIC
SYMPATHIZER
SYMPHONIOUS
SYMPOSIARCH
SYMPTOMATIC
SYNCHRONISM
SYNCHRONIZE
SYNCHRONOUS
SYNCOPATION
SYNODICALLY
SYNTACTICAL
SYSTEMATIZE

T

TABEFACTION
TACHYGRAPHY
TACITURNITY
TALKATIVELY
TANGIBILITY
TASTELESSLY
TAUTOLOGIST
TAUTOLOGIZE
TAXABLENESS
TEARFULNESS
TEDIOUSNESS
TEETOTALLER
TEETOTALISM
TEGUMENTARY
TELEGRAMMIC
TELEGRAPHIC
TELESCOPIST
TEMERARIOUS
TEMPERATELY
TEMPERATURE
TEMPESTUOUS
TEMPORALITY
TEMPORARILY
TEMPORIZING
TENABLENESS
TENEBROSITY
TENEMENTARY
TENTATIVELY
TEPEFACTION
TEREBRATULA
TERMINATION
TERMINATIVE
TERMINOLOGY
TERRAQUEOUS
TERRESTRIAL
TERRICOLOUS
TERRIGENOUS
TERRITORIAL
TESSELLATED
TESTAMENTAL

TESTICULATE
TETRAGYNOUS
TETRAHEDRAL
TETRAHEDRON
TETRAMEROUS
TETRANDROUS
THALLOPHYTE
THANATOLOGY
THANKLESSLY
THANKSGIVER
THAUMATROPE
THAUMATURGE
THAUMATURGY
THEATRICALS
THENCEFORTH
THEODOLITIC
THEOLOGIZER
THEOPNEUSTY
THEOREMATIC
THEORETICAL
THEOSOPHIST
THEOTECHNIC
THEREABOUTS
THEREWITHAL
THERMOMETER
THERMOSCOPE
THITHERWARD
THOUGHTLESS
THRASONICAL
THREADINESS
THREATENING
THRIFTINESS
THRILLINGLY
THUNDERBOLT
TITILLATION
TITILLATIVE
TOBACCONIST
TONSILLITIS
TOPOGRAPHER
TOPOGRAPHIC
TORMENTILLA
TORPESCENCE
TORTURINGLY
TOTIPALMATE
TOTTERINGLY
TOXOPHILITE
TRACHEOTOME
TRACHEOTOMY
TRACKLESSLY
TRADITIONAL
TRADUCEMENT
TRAFFICLESS
TRAGEDIENNE
TRANSACTION
TRANSALPINE
TRANSCRIBER
TRANSFERRER
TRANSFIXION
TRANSFLUENT
TRANSFUSION
TRANSFUSIVE
TRANSIENTLY
TRANSLATION
TRANSLATORY
TRANSLUCENT
TRANSMARINE
TRANSMITTAL
TRANSMITTER
TRANSPARENT
TRANSPORTED

TRANSPORTER
TRANSVERSAL
TRAPEZIFORM
TRAPEZOIDAL
TREACHEROUS
TREASONABLE
TREASONABLY
TREMBLINGLY
TREMULOUSLY
TREPIDATION
TRIANGULATE
TRIBULATION
TRIBUNICIAN
TRIBUNITIAL
TRIBUTARILY
TRIBUTARIES
TRICAPSULAR
TRICKSINESS
TRICOLOURED
TRICUSPIDAL
TRIENNIALLY
TRIFOLIATED
TRIGEMINOUS
TRIMESTRIAL
TRINITARIAN
TRIPERSONAL
TRIPETALOUS
TRIPHYLLOUS
TRIQUETROUS
TRISEPALOUS
TRISTICHOUS
TRISYLLABLE
TRITURATION
TRITURATURE
TRIUMVIRATE
TRIVIALNESS
TROCHOIDALS
TROGLODYTIC
TROUBLESOME
TRUCULENTLY
TRUEHEARTED
TRUNCHEONED
TRUNCHEONER
TRUSTEESHIP
TRUSTWORTHY
TUBERCULATE
TUBERCULINE
TUBERCULIZE
TUBERCULOSE
TUBERCULOUS
TUMEFACTION
TUNABLENESS
TURBULENTLY
TURGESCENCE
TYPOGRAPHER
TYPOGRAPHIC
TYRANNICIDE
TYRANNOUSLY

U

ULTRAMARINE
UNABOLISHED
UNADVISABLE
UNADVISABLY
UNADVISEDLY
UNALTERABLE
UNAMBIGUOUS
UNAMBITIOUS

175

UNAPOSTOLIC
UNASPIRATED
UNBEFITTING
UNBLEMISHED
UNCANONICAL
UNCEASINGLY
UNCERTAINTY
UNCHRISTIAN
UNCIVILIZED
UNCOMMITTED
UNCONCEALED
UNCONCERNED
UNCONDEMNED
UNCONFIRMED
UNCONNECTED
UNCONSCIOUS
UNCONTESTED
UNCONVERTED
UNCORRECTED
UNCOURTEOUS
UNCOUTHNESS
UNDAUNTEDLY
UNDEFINABLY
UNDERCHARGE
UNDERGROUND
UNDERGROWTH
UNDERSTROKE
UNDERTAKING
UNDESERVING
UNDESIRABLE
UNDEVIATING
UNDIGNIFIED
UNDISGUISED
UNDISTURBED
UNDOUBTEDLY
UNDUTIFULLY
UNEMOTIONAL
UNENDURABLE
UNENLIVENED
UNESSENTIAL
UNEXERCISED
UNEXHAUSTED
UNFAILINGLY
UNFALTERING
UNFEELINGLY
UNFEIGNEDLY
UNFERMENTED
UNFLINCHING
UNFORGIVING
UNFORGOTTEN
UNFORTUNATE
UNFULFILLED
UNFURNISHED
UNGALLANTLY
UNGENTEELLY
UNGODLINESS
UNGUARDEDLY
UNGUICULATE
UNHARBOURED
UNHEALTHFUL
UNHEALTHILY
UNHEEDFULLY
UNHUMANISED
UNICELLULAR
UNIFICATION
UNIFORMNESS
UNIMPORTANT
UNINHABITED
UNIPERSONAL
UNIPETALOUS

UNIVALVULAR
UNIVERSALLY
UNKNOWINGLY
UNLUCKINESS
UNMANLINESS
UNMEANINGLY
UNMELODIOUS
UNMINDFULLY
UNMITIGABLE
UNMITIGATED
UNMURMURING
UNMUTILATED
UNNATURALLY
UNNECESSARY
UNOBSERVANT
UNOBSERVING
UNOBTRUSIVE
UNOFFENDING
UNORGANISED
UNPALATABLE
UNPARAGONED
UNPATRIOTIC
UNPERFORMED
UNPERVERTED
UNPOPULARLY
UNPRACTICAL
UNPRACTISED
UNPRESUMING
UMPROMISING
UNPROTECTED
UNPUBLISHED
UNQUALIFIED
UNREADINESS
UNREASONING
UNRECLAIMED
UNREDRESSED
UNRELENTING
UNREMITTING
UNREPENTANT
UNRESISTING
UNRIGHTEOUS
UNSATISFIED
UNSEAWORTHY
UNSECTARIAN
UNSENTENCED
UNSHRINKING
UNSMIRCHING
UNSOLICITED
UNSOUNDNESS
UNSPEAKABLE
UNSPEAKABLY
UNSPECIFIED
UNSPIRITUAL
UNSUPPORTED
UNSURPASSED
UNSUSPECTED
UNTARNISHED
UNTEACHABLE
UNTHINKABLE
UNTHRIFTILY
UNTINCTURED
UNTRACTABLE
UNTRAVELLED
UNUTTERABLE
UNUTTERABLY
UNVARNISHED
UNVERACIOUS
UNWARRANTED
UNWEDGEABLE
UNWHOLESOME

UNWILLINGLY
UNWITNESSED
UNWITTINGLY
UPHOLSTERER
URANOGRAPHY
URTICACEOUS
USELESSNESS
UTILITARIAN

V

VACCINATION
VACILLATING
VACILLATION
VAGABONDAGE
VAGABONDISM
VALEDICTION
VALEDICTORY
VARIABILITY
VARIEGATION
VARSOVIENNE
VASCULARITY
VATICINATOR
VELLICATION
VENDIBILITY
VENESECTION
VENTILATION
VENTRICULAR
VENTRILOQUY
VENTURESOME
VENTUROUSLY
VERACIOUSLY
VERBOSENESS
VERISIMILAR
VERMICULATE
VERMICULOUS
VERMIVOROUS
VERSATILELY
VERSATILITY
VERSICOLOUR
VERTEBRATED
VERTIGINOUS
VEXATIOUSLY
VICARIOUSLY
VICEREGENCY
VICEROYALTY
VICEROYSHIP
VICIOUSNESS
VICISSITUDE
VINAIGRETTE
VINCIBILITY
VINDICATION
VINDICATIVE
VINDICATORY
VINEGARETTE
VIOLONCELLO
VISCOUNTESS
VISIBLENESS
VISIONARIES
VITICULTURE
VITRESCENCE
VITRIFIABLE
VITUPERABLE
VITUPERATOR
VIVACIOUSLY
VIVISECTION
VOLCANICITY
VOLUBLENESS
VOLUNTARILY

VOLUNTARIES
VORACIOUSLY
VULCANICITY

W

WAGGISHNESS
WAKEFULNESS
WANDERINGLY
WARRANTABLY
WASHERWOMAN
WASPISHNESS
WAYWARDNESS
WEALTHINESS
WEARISOMELY
WEATHERMOST
WEIGHTINESS
WESLEYANISM
WESTERNMOST
WHEREABOUTS
WHERESOEVER
WHEREWITHAL
WHICHSOEVER
WHIMSICALLY

WHISKEYFIED
WHITSUNTIDE
WHOLESOMELY
WHOREMONGER
WILLINGNESS
WINDLESTRAW
WINSOMENESS
WISHFULNESS
WITENAGEMOT
WITHERINGLY
WITHSTANDER
WITLESSNESS
WOMANLINESS
WONDERFULLY
WONDERINGLY
WORKMANLIKE
WORKMANSHIP
WORLDLINESS
WORTHLESSLY

X

XANTHOPHYLL
XYLOGRAPHER

XYLOGRAPHIC
XYLOPHAGOUS
XYLOPHYLOUS

Y

YESTERNIGHT

Z

ZEALOUSNESS
ZINCIFEROUS
ZINCOGRAPHY
ZOANTHARIAN
ZOOMORPHISM
ZOROASTRIAN
ZYGODACTYLE
ZYMOTICALLY

TWELVE-LETTER WORDS

A

ABBREVIATION
ABBREVIATORY
ABOLITIONIST
ABORTIVENESS
ABSOLUTENESS
ABSORPTIVITY
ABSTEMIOUSLY
ABSTRACTEDLY
ABSTRACTEDNESS
ABSTRUSENESS
ACADEMICALLY
ACANTHACEOUS
ACCELERATION
ACCELERATIVE
ACCELERATORY
ACCENTUATION
ACCIDENTALLY
ACCOMMODATOR
ACCOMPLISHER
ACCOUCHEMENT
ACCUMULATION
ACCUMULATIVE
ACCURATENESS
ACHLAMYDEOUS
ACKNOWLEDGER
ACOUSTICALLY
ACQUAINTANCE
ACQUIESCENCE
ACROCEPHALIC
ACROSTICALLY
ADAPTABILITY
ADDER'S-TONGUE
ADDICTEDNESS
ADDITIONALLY
ADHESIVENESS
ADJUDICATION
ADJUNCTIVELY
ADMONITORIAL
ADORABLENESS
ADSCITITIOUS
ADULTERATION
ADULTEROUSLY
ADVANTAGEOUS
ADVENTITIOUS
ADVENTUREFUL
ADVOCATESHIP
AERODYNAMICS
AEROSIDERITE
AESTHETICISM
AETIOLOGICAL
AFFECTEDNESS
AFFECTIONATE
AFFLICTINGLY
AFTER-THOUGHT
AGALMATOLITE
AGAMOGENESIS
AGRICULTURAL
ALCOHOLMETER
ALEXIPHARMIC
ALIENABILITY
ALIMENTATION
ALKALESCENCE

ALLITERATION
ALLITERATIVE
ALLOMORPHISM
ALL-SAINTS' DAY
ALLUSIVENESS
ALMIGHTINESS
ALTERABILITY
AMALGAMATION
AMBASSADRESS
AMBIDEXTROUS
AMELIORATION
AMELIORATIVE
AMENABLENESS
AMICABLENESS
AMMONIAPHONE
AMORTIZATION
AMORTIZEMENT
AMPHICOELOUS
AMPHISTOMOUS
AMPHITHEATRE
AMYGDALOIDAL
ANABAPTISTIC
ANAESTHETIZE
ANALOGICALLY
ANALYTICALLY
ANAMORPHOSIS
ANAPODEICTIC
ANARTHROPODA
ANATHEMATIZE
ANATOMICALLY
ANEMOPHILOUS
ANGIOCARPOUS
ANGUILLIFORM
ANIMALCULINE
ANITROGENOUS
ANNIHILATION
ANNOMINATION
ANNOUNCEMENT
ANNUNCIATION
ANNUNCIATORY
ANOTHER-GUESS
ANTAGONISTIC
ANTARTHRITIC
ANTASTHMATIC
ANTEBRACHIAL
ANTECEDENTLY
ANTEDILUVIAN
ANTEMERIDIAN
ANTEPILEPTIC
ANTEPRANDIAL
ANTHELMINTIC
ANTHOCARPOUS
ANTHOLOGICAL
ANTHROPOGENY
ANTHROPOLOGY
ANTHROPOTOMY
ANTICIPATION
ANTICIPATIVE
ANTICIPATORY
ANTIDEMOCRAT
ANTIFRICTION
ANTIHYPNOTIC
ANTILEGOMENA
ANTI-MACASSAR
ANTIMONIATED

ANTIPATHETIC
ANTIPHRASTIC
ANTISTROPHIC
ANTITHEISTIC
ANTIVENEREAL
APHORISMATIC
APOSTROPHIZE
APPARITIONAL
APPENDICITIS
APPENDICULAR
APPERCEPTION
APPOGGIATURA
APPOSITIONAL
APPRAISEMENT
APPRECIATION
APPRECIATORY
APPREHENSION
APPREHENSIVE
APPROACHABLE
APPROPRIABLE
APPROPRIATOR
APPURTENANCE
ARBORESCENCE
ARBORIZATION
ARCHDEACONRY
ARCHIPELAGIC
ARCHITECTURE
ARGILLACEOUS
ARISTOCRATIC
ARISTOTELIAN
ARITHMETICAL
ARITHMOMETER
ARMOUR-BEARER
ARMOUR-PLATED
ARTICULATELY
ARTICULATION
ARTIFICIALLY
ARTIODACTYLE
ARTISTICALLY
ASH-WEDNESDAY
ASPHYXIATION
ASSASSINATOR
ASSEVERATION
ASSIMILATION
ASSIMILATIVE
ASTONISHMENT
ASTRINGENTLY
ASTROLOGICAL
ASYMMETRICAL
ASYMPTOTICAL
ATHEROMATOUS
ATTITUDINIZE
ATTORNEYSHIP
ATTRACTIVELY
ATTRIBUTABLE
AUGMENTATION
AUGMENTATIVE
AUSCULTATION
AUSPICIOUSLY
AUSTRALASIAN
AUTHENTICATE
AUTHENTICITY
AVANT-COURIER
AVARICIOUSLY
AVERRUNCATOR

B

BACCHANALIAN
BACHELORHOOD
BACHELORSHIP
BACKWARDNESS
BACTERIOLOGY
BALANCE-SHEET
BALANCE-WHEEL
BALLAD-MONGER
BARBETTE-SHIP
BATTERING-RAM
BATTLEMENTED
BEATIFICALLY
BEETLE-BROWED
BENEFACTRESS
BENEFICENTLY
BENEFICIALLY
BENEVOLENTLY
BEQUEATHABLE
BEQUEATHMENT
BESEECHINGLY
BESOTTEDNESS
BEWILDERMENT
BEWITCHINGLY
BIARTICULATE
BIBLIOGRAPHY
BIBLIOMANIAC
BIBLIOPOLIST
BICENTENNIAL
BILLINGSGATE
BIOGRAPHICAL
BLACK-CURRANT
BLACK-DRAUGHT
BLACKGUARDLY
BLACK-HEARTED
BLACK-MOUTHED
BLACK-PUDDING
BLAMABLENESS
BLANDISHMENT
BLAST-FURNACE
BLENNORRHOEA
BLISSFULNESS
BLISTER-STEEL
BLOOD-LETTING
BLOODSHEDDER
BLOOD-STAINED
BLOODTHIRSTY
BLUE-STOCKING
BOARDING-PIKE
BODY-SNATCHER
BOISTEROUSLY
BOLTING-CLOTH
BOOK-LEARNING
BOOK-SCORPION
BOOTLESSNESS
BOTTLE-HOLDER
BOW-COMPASSES
BOWLING-ALLEY
BOWLING-GREEN
BRACHYGRAPHY
BRACKISHNESS
BRANCHIOPODA
BRASS-FOUNDER
BREAST-PLOUGH
BREATHLESSLY
BREECH-LOADED
BREVIPENNATE
BRIDE-CHAMBER

BRIGADE-MAJOR
BRISTOL-BOARD
BRISTOL-BRICK
BRISTOL-PAPER
BROTHER-IN-LAW
BUCCANEERING
BUFFALO-CHIPS
BUFFLE-HEADED
BURDENSOMELY
BUREAUCRATIC
BURNING-GLASS
BURROWING-OWL
BUTTER-SCOTCH
BUTTERY-HATCH
BUZZARD-CLOCK

C

CABINET-MAKER
CACHINNATION
CADAVEROUSLY
CALABASH-TREE
CALAMITOUSLY
CALISTHENICS
CALLIGRAPHER
CALLIGRAPHIC
CALLISTHENIC
CALORESCENCE
CALUMNIATION
CALUMNIATORY
CALUMNIOUSLY
CALYCIFLORAL
CAMP-BEDSTEAD
CAMP-FOLLOWER
CANALICULATE
CANCELLARIAN
CANCELLATION
CANDLE-HOLDER
CANONIZATION
CANTABRIGIAN
CANTANKEROUS
CANTHARIDINE
CAPERCAILZIE
CAPITULATION
CAPPAGH-BROWN
CAPRICIOUSLY
CAPTIOUSNESS
CARBONACEOUS
CARDINAL-BIRD
CARELESSNESS
CARICATURIST
CARLOVINGIAN
CARPENTER-BEE
CARPET-BAGGER
CARPET-KNIGHT
CARRIAGEABLE
CARTE-BLANCHE
CARTHAGINIAN
CARTRIDGE-BOX
CASE-HARDENED
CATACHRESTIC
CATACOUSTICS
CATADIOPTRIC
CATALLACTICS
CATASTROPHIC
CATELECTRODE
CATTLE-PLAGUE
CAUSATIONISM
CAUTIOUSNESS

CEMENTITIOUS
CENSORIOUSLY
CENTENNIALLY
CENTIFOLIOUS
CENTUPLICATE
CEREMONIALLY
CEROPLASTICS
CHAIRMANSHIP
CHALCOGRAPHY
CHAMPIONSHIP
CHANCE-MEDLEY
CHAPLAINSHIP
CHAPTER-HOUSE
CHARACTERIZE
CHARLES'S-WAIN
CHARNEL-HOUSE
CHARTER-PARTY
CHARTOGRAPHY
CHASTISEMENT
CHAUVINISTIC
CHECKER-BOARD
CHEERFULNESS
CHEESEMONGER
CHEESE-PARING
CHEIROPODIST
CHEQUER-BOARD
CHERRY-BRANDY
CHERRY-LAUREL
CHERRY-PEPPER
CHIEF-JUSTICE
CHIEFTAINESS
CHILD-BEARING
CHILD-GROWING
CHILDISHNESS
CHIMERICALLY
CHIMNEY-PIECE
CHIMNEY-SHAFT
CHIMNEY-STACK
CHIMNEY-STALK
CHIMNEY-SWEEP
CHIROGRAPHER
CHIROGRAPHIC
CHIVALROUSLY
CHOLESTERINE
CHRESTOMATHY
CHRISTIANITY
CHRISTIANIZE
CHRISTMAS-BOX
CHRISTMAS-DAY
CHRISTMAS-EVE
CHRIST'S-THORN
CHROMATOLOGY
CHROMOSPHERE
CHRONOGRAPHY
CHRONOLOGIST
CHRONOMETRIC
CHRYSOPHANIC
CHURCHWARDEN
CHURLISHNESS
CHYLIFACTIVE
CIRCUITOUSLY
CIRCUMCISION
CIRCUMFLUENT
CIRCUMFUSION
CIRCUMGYRATE
CIRCUMJACENT
CIRCUMNUTATE
CIRCUMSCRIBE
CIRCUMSTANCE
CIVILIZATION

CLAIRVOYANCE
CLAIRVOYANTE
CLANNISHNESS
CLASSICALISM
CLASSIFIABLE
CLEAR-SIGHTED
CLEISTOGAMIC
CLIMATICALLY
CLINKER-BUILT
CLOTHES-HORSE
CLOUD-KISSING
CLOVEN-FOOTED
CLOVEN-HOOFED
CLOWNISHNESS
COACHMANSHIP
COALITIONIST
COAL-MEASURES
CODIFICATION
COELENTERATE
COENESTHESIS
COHABITATION
COHESIVENESS
COINCIDENTLY
COLEOPTEROUS
COLLABORATOR
COLLATERALLY
COLLECTIVELY
COLLECTIVISM
COLLECTIVIST
COLLECTORATE
COLLIGUATIVE
COLLOQUIALLY
COLOGNE-EARTH
COLONIZATION
COLOQUINTIDA
COMMEMORABLE
COMMEMORATOR
COMMENCEMENT
COMMENDATION
COMMENDATORY
COMMENSALISM
COMMENSURATE
COMMENTATION
COMMENTATIVE
COMMERCIALLY
COMMISERATOR
COMMISSARIAL
COMMISSARIAT
COMMISSIONED
COMMISSIONER
COMMODIOUSLY
COMMONWEALTH
COMMUNICABLE
COMMUNICABLY
COMMUNICATOR
COMPELLATION
COMPENSATION
COMPENSATIVE
COMPENSATORY
COMPLACENTLY
COMPLAISANCE
COMPLEMENTAL
COMPLETENESS
COMPLEXIONAL
COMPLEXIONED
COMPLICATION
COMPLICATIVE
COMPLIMENTER
COMPOSEDNESS
COMPREHENDER

COMPRESSIBLE
COMPULSIVELY
COMPUNCTIOUS
COMPURGATION
CONCENTRATED
CONCHIFEROUS
CONCHOLOGIST
CONCILIATION
CONCILIATORY
CONCLAMATION
CONCLUSIVELY
CONCOMITANCE
CONCOMITANCY
CONCORDANTLY
CONCREMATION
CONCRESCENCE
CONCRETENESS
CONCUPISCENT
CONCURRENTLY
CONDEMNATION
CONDEMNATORY
CONDENSATION
CONFABULATOR
CONFECTIONER
CONFERENTIAL
CONFESSIONAL
CONFIDENTIAL
CONFIRMATION
CONFIRMATIVE
CONFIRMATORY
CONFISCATION
CONFISCATORY
CONFORMATION
CONFOUNDEDLY
CONFUCIANISM
CONGENIALITY
CONGLOBATION
CONGLOMERATE
CONGLUTINATE
CONGRATULANT
CONGRATULATE
CONGREGATION
CONNUBIALITY
CONSCIONABLE
CONSCRIPTION
CONSECRATION
CONSENTIENCE
CONSEQUENTLY
CONSERVATION
CONSERVATISM
CONSERVATIVE
CONSERVATORY
CONSIDERABLE
CONSIDERABLY
CONSIGNATION
CONSISTENTLY
CONSISTORIAL
CONSOCIATION
CONSOLE-TABLE
CONSOLIDATOR
CONSTABULARY
CONSTIPATION
CONSTITUENCY
CONSTITUTION
CONSTITUTIVE
CONSTRICTION
CONSTRICTIVE
CONSTRINGENT
CONSTRUCTION
CONSTRUCTIVE

CONSULTATION
CONSULTATIVE
CONSUMMATELY
CONSUMMATION
CONSUMMATIVE
CONTABESCENT
CONTAGIOUSLY
CONTAMINABLE
CONTEMPLATOR
CONTEMPORARY
CONTEMPTIBLE
CONTEMPTIBLY
CONTEMPTUOUS
CONTERMINOUS
CONTESTATION
CONTIGUOUSLY
CONTINGENTLY
CONTINUATION
CONTINUOUSLY
CONTRACTEDLY
CONTRACTIBLE
CONTRADICTER
CONTRAPUNTAL
CONTRARINESS
CONTRARIWISE
CONTRIBUTION
CONTRIBUTIVE
CONTRIBUTORY
CONTRITENESS
CONTROLLABLE
CONTROVERTER
CONTUMACIOUS
CONTUMELIOUS
CONVALESCENT
CONVECTIVELY
CONVENIENTLY
CONVENTICLER
CONVENTIONAL
CONVERSANTLY
CONVERSATION
CONVEXO-PLANE
CONVEYANCING
CONVINCINGLY
CONVIVIALIST
CONVIVIALITY
CONVULSIONAL
CONVULSIVELY
CO-ORDINATELY
CO-ORDINATION
CO-ORDINATIVE
COPROPHAGOUS
COPULATIVELY
COPYING-PRESS
COQUETTISHLY
CORALLACEOUS
CO-RESPONDENT
CORN-EXCHANGE
CORN-MARIGOLD
COROLLACEOUS
CORPORALSHIP
CORPOREALISM
CORPOREALIST
CORPOREALITY
CORPSE-CANDLE
CORRADIATION
CORRECTIONAL
CORRELATABLE
CORROBORATOR
COSMOGRAPHER
COSMOGRAPHIC

COSMOLOGICAL
COSMOPLASTIC
COSMOPOLITAN
COSTERMONGER
COTYLEDONARY
COTYLEDONOUS
COUNCIL-BOARD
COUNSELLABLE
COUNTENANCER
COUNTER-AGENT
COUNTERCHARM
COUNTERCHECK
COUNTER-FORCE
COUNTER-MARCH
COUNTERPOINT
COUNTERPOISE
COUNTER-PROOF
COUNTERSCARP
COUNTER-TENOR
COUNTERWEIGH
COUNTRY-DANCE
COUNTRYWOMAN
COURAGEOUSLY
COURT-MARTIAL
COURT-PLASTER
COUSIN-GERMAN
COVETOUSNESS
COWARDLINESS
COXCOMICALLY
CRACK-BRAINED
CRANIOLOGIST
CREDIBLENESS
CREMATIONIST
CRENELLATION
CRITICIZABLE
CROSS-EXAMINE
CROSS-GRAINED
CROSS-PURPOSE
CRYPTOGAMOUS
CRYPTOGRAPHY
CUCKING-STOOL
CULPABLENESS
CUPPING-GLASS
CUPULIFEROUS
CURLING-IRONS
CURLING-TONGS
CURLING-STONE
CURRANT-JELLY
CURVIROSTRAL
CUSTARD-APPLE
CYCLOSTOMOUS
CYLINDRIFORM

D

DACTYLIOLOGY
DACTYLORHIZA
DAMNABLENESS
DANGER-SIGNAL
DEAMBULATORY
DEATH-WARRANT
DEBILITATING
DEBILITATION
DECAPITATION
DECASYLLABIC
DECENTRALIZE
DECIPHERABLE
DECIPHERMENT
DECISIVENESS

DECLINOMETER
DECOLORATION
DECOMPOSABLE
DECONSECRATE
DECREASINGLY
DECREPITNESS
DECRUSTATION
DEDICATORIAL
DEDUCIBILITY
DEER-STALKING
DEFAMATORILY
DEFINITENESS
DEFINITIONAL
DEFINITIVELY
DEFLAGRATION
DEFORCIATION
DEFORMEDNESS
DEFRAUDATION
DEGENERATELY
DEGENERATION
DEJECTEDNESS
DELIBERATELY
DELIBERATION
DELIBERATIVE
DELICATENESS
DELIGHTFULLY
DELIMITATION
DELIQUESCENT
DELITESCENCE
DELITESCENCY
DELUSIVENESS
DEMONIACALLY
DEMONOLOGIST
DEMONSTRABLE
DEMONSTRABLY
DEMONSTRATOR
DEMORALIZING
DENATURALIZE
DENDROLOGIST
DENOMINATION
DENOMINATIVE
DENOUNCEMENT
DENTICULATED
DENTIROSTRAL
DENUNCIATION
DENUNCIATORY
DENUNCIATIVE
DEONTOLOGIST
DEPARTMENTAL
DEPOPULATION
DEPRAVEDNESS
DEPRECIATION
DEPRECIATIVE
DEPRECIATORY
DEPRESSINGLY
DERIVATIONAL
DERIVATIVELY
DERMATOPHYTE
DESCENSIONAL
DESIDERATIVE
DESIRABILITY
DESOLATENESS
DESPAIRINGLY
DESPITEFULLY
DESPOLIATION
DESPONDENTLY
DESPOTICALLY
DESQUAMATION
DESQUAMATIVE
DESQUAMATORY

DESSERT-SPOON
DESTRUCTIBLE
DESULPHURIZE
DESULPHURATE
DESYNONYMIZE
DETERMINABLE
DETERMINATOR
DETERMINEDLY
DETHRONEMNET
DETONIZATION
DETRUNCATION
DEUTEROPATHY
DEUTEROSCOPY
DEVILISHNESS
DEVIL-MAY-CARE
DEVOTIONALLY
DEXTRO-GYRATE
DIABOLICALLY
DIAGRAMMATIC
DIALECTICIAN
DIALECTOLOGY
DIALOGICALLY
DIAMAGNETISM
DIAMOND-DRILL
DIAPHANOUSLY
DIATOMACEOUS
DIATONICALLY
DIBRANCHIATE
DICHROSCOPIC
DICTATORSHIP
DIDACTICALLY
DIETETICALLY
DIFFERENTIAL
DIGRESSIONAL
DIGRESSIVELY
DIJUDICATION
DILACERATION
DILAPIDATION
DILATABILITY
DILATORINESS
DILETTANTISM
DIMINISHABLE
DIMINUTIVELY
DIPHTHERITIC
DIPHTHONGIZE
DIPLOMATICAL
DIRECTORSHIP
DISADVANTAGE
DISAFFECTION
DISAGGREGATE
DISAGREEABLE
DISAGREEABLY
DISAGREEMENT
DISALLOWABLE
DISALLOWANCE
DISANNULMENT
DISAPPOINTED
DISASSOCIATE
DISASTROUSLY
DISBURSEMENT
DISCERNINGLY
DISCIPLESHIP
DISCIPLINARY
DISCOMFITURE
DISCOMMODITY
DISCOMPOSURE
DISCONSOLATE
DISCONTENTED
DISCORDANTLY
DISCOUNTABLE

DISCOURAGING
DISCOURTEOUS
DISCOVERABLE
DISCREETNESS
DISCRETIONAL
DISCRETIVELY
DISCRIMINATE
DISCURSIVELY
DISDAINFULLY
DISEASEDNESS
DISEMBARRASS
DISEMBELLISH
DISENCHANTER
DISENDOWMENT
DISESTABLISH
DISFRANCHISE
DISGORGEMENT
DISGUISEMENT
DISGUSTINGLY
DISINFECTANT
DISINFECTION
DISINGENUOUS
DISINTEGRATE
DISINTERMENT
DISLODGEMENT
DISOBEDIENCE
DISORGANIZER
DISPAUPERIZE
DISPENSATION
DISPENSATORY
DISPIRITEDLY
DISPLACEABLE
DISPLACEMENT
DISPLEASEDLY
DISPUTATIOUS
DISQUISITION
DISQUISITORY
DISREGARDFUL
DISREPUTABLE
DISREPUTABLY
DISSATISFIED
DISSEMINATOR
DISSENTERISM
DISSERTATION
DISSEVERANCE
DISSIMILARLY
DISSIMULATOR
DISSOCIATION
DISSUASIVELY
DISSYLLABISM
DISTILLATION
DISTILLATORY
DISTINCTNESS
DISTRACTEDLY
DISTRAINABLE
DISTRIBUTION
DISTRIBUTIVE
DITHEISTICAL
DIVARICATION
DIVISIBILITY
DOCTRINARIAN
DODECAHEDRAL
DODECAHEDRON
DODECANDROUS
DOGMATICALLY
DOMESTICALLY
DONKEY-ENGINE
DOUBLE-ACTING
DOUBLE-DEALER
DOUBLE-MINDED

DOUBTFULNESS
DRAGON'S-BLOOD
DRAMATICALLY
DRAUGHT-BOARD
DRAWING-BOARD
DRAWING-PAPER
DREADFULNESS
DRESSING-CASE
DRESSING-GOWN
DRESSING-ROOM
DRIVING-SHAFT
DRIVING-WHEEL
DROUGHTINESS
DUCKING-STOOL
DWARFISHNESS

E

EARNEST-MONEY
EAU DE COLOGNE
EAVESDROPPER
ECCENTRICITY
ECCLESIASTES
ECCLESIASTIC
ECCLESIOLOGY
ECLECTICALLY
ECONOMICALLY
ECSTATICALLY
ECTOPARASITE
EDUCATIONIST
EDUCTION-PIPE
EDULCORATION
EDULCORATIVE
EFFECTUATION
EFFEMINATELY
EFFERVESCENT
EFFLORESCENT
EFFUSIVENESS
EGOISTICALLY
EGYPTOLOGIST
ELECTRICALLY
ELECTROLYSIS
ELECTROLYTIC
ELECTROMETER
ELECTROMETRY
ELECTROMOTOR
ELECTROPLATE
ELECTROSCOPE
ELECTROTYPIC
ELEEMOSYNARY
ELEMENTARITY
ELLIPTICALLY
ELOCUTIONIST
EMANCIPATION
EMARGINATION
EMASCULATION
EMASCULATORY
EMBEZZLEMENT
EMBITTERMENT
EMBLAZONMENT
EMIGRATIONAL
EMOLLESCENCE
EMOTIONALISM
EMPHATICALLY
EMPRESSEMENT
EMPYREUMATIC
ENCEPHALITIS
ENCHANTINGLY
ENCLITICALLY

ENCROACHMENT
ENCUMBRANCER
ENCYCLOPEDIA
ENDOCARDITIS
ENDOPARASITE
ENDOPHYLLOUS
ENDOSMOMETER
ENDOSKELETON
ENFEEBLEMENT
ENHARMONICAL
ENTANGLEMENT
ENTERPRISING
ENTERTAINING
ENTHRONEMENT
ENTHUSIASTIC
ENTOMOLOGIST
ENTOMOSTRACA
ENTRANCEMENT
ENTREATINGLY
ENVISAGEMENT
EPENCEPHALON
EPEXEGETICAL
EPHEMERALITY
EPHEMERIDIAN
EPICUREANISM
EPICYCLOIDAL
EPIDEICTICAL
EPIDERMICALLY
EPIDEMIOLOGY
EPIGRAMMATIC
EPISCOPALIAN
EPISODICALLY
EPISTEMOLOGY
EPITHALAMIUM
EQUALIZATION
EQUANIMOUSLY
EQUATORIALLY
EQUESTRIENNE
EQUIMULTIPLE
EQUIPOLLENCE
EQUIPOLLENCY
EQUIVALENTLY
EQUIVOCATORY
ERYTHEMATOUS
ESCHATOLOGIC
ESCUTCHEONED
ESOTERICALLY
ESSENTIALITY
ESTRANGEMENT
ETHERIZATION
ETHNOGRAPHER
ETHNOLOGICAL
ETYMOLOGICAL
EUPHONIOUSLY
EVANESCENTLY
EVANGELICISM
EVIDENTIALLY
EVISCERATION
EVOLUTIONARY
EVOLUTIONIST
EXACERBATION
EXAGGERATION
EXAGGERATIVE
EXAGGERATORY
EXALBUMINOUS
EXANTHEMATIC
EXASPERATION
EXASPERATING
EXCHANGEABLE
EXCITABILITY

EXCLUSIONIST
EXCOGITATION
EXCRUCIATING
EXCURSIONIST
EXECUTORSHIP
EXERCITATION
EXHAUSTIVELY
EXHIBITIONER
EXHILARATION
EXORBITANTLY
EXOTERICALLY
EXPATRIATION
EXPERIENTIAL
EXPERIMENTAL
EXPERIMENTER
EXPLICITNESS
EXPLOITATION
EXPOSTULATOR
EXPRESSIONAL
EXSANGUINOUS
EXTEMPORIZER
EXTERMINATOR
EXTERMINABLE
EXTINGUISHER
EXTORTIONARY
EXTRAMUNDANE
EXTRANEOUSLY
EXTRAVAGANCE
EXTRAVAGANCY
EXTRAVAGANZA

F

FACTIOUSNESS
FACTITIOUSLY
FAITHFULNESS
FALLACIOUSLY
FANCIFULNESS
FARADIZATION
FARCICALNESS
FASCICULARLY
FASCICULATED
FASTIDIOUSLY
FATHERLASHER
FEARLESSNESS
FEBRIFACIENT
FELICITATION
FELICITOUSLY
FEMININENESS
FENESTRATION
FERMENTATION
FERMENTATIVE
FEVERISHNESS
FICTITIOUSLY
FISSILINGUAL
FISSIROSTRAL
FLAGELLATION
FLAGITIOUSLY
FLATTERINGLY
FLEXIBLENESS
FLITTERMOUSE
FLORICULTURE
FLUORESCENCE
FORAMINIFERA
FORBIDDINGLY
FORCIBLENESS
FORDABLENESS
FOREBODEMENT
FOREKNOWABLE

FORNICATRESS
FORTUITOUSLY
FOUNDATIONER
FRANKINCENSE
FRAUDULENTLY
FREQUENTNESS
FROLICSOMELY
FRONDESCENCE
FRONDIFEROUS
FRONTISPIECE
FRUCTESCENCE
FUGITIVENESS
FUNCTIONALLY
FURFURACEOUS
FUTILITARIAN

G

GALACTAGOGUE
GALACTOMETER
GALLIGASKINS
GALLINACEOUS
GALVANOMETRY
GALVANOSCOPE
GAMOPETALOUS
GASIFICATION
GELATINATION
GENEALOGICAL
GENICULATION
GENTILITIOUS
GENUFLECTION
GEOGRAPHICAL
GEOLOGICALLY
GEOMETRICIAN
GERONTOCRACY
GESTICULATOR
GLADIATORIAL
GLANDIFEROUS
GLAUCOMATOUS
GLOSSOGRAPHY
GLOSSOLOGIST
GLOTTOLOGIST
GLUTTONOUSLY
GLYPHOGRAPHY
GOVERNMENTAL
GOVERNORSHIP
GRACEFULNESS
GRACIOUSNESS
GRADUATESHIP
GRALLATORIAL
GRAMMATICIZE
GRATEFULNESS
GRATUITOUSLY
GREENISHNESS
GREGARIOUSLY
GRIEVOUSNESS
GROUNDLESSLY
GYMNOCARPOUS
GYMNOSOPHIST

H

HABERDASHERY
HAGIOGRAPHER
HAGIOGRAPHIC
HANDKERCHIEF
HARMONIOUSLY
HEADQUARTERS

HELIOCENTRIC
HELIOTROPISM
HENCEFORWARD
HERMENEUTICS
HERMETICALLY
HERPETOLOGIC
HESITATINGLY
HETEROGAMOUS
HETEROLOGOUS
HIBERNACULUM
HIBERNIANISM
HIEROGLYPHIC
HINDOOSTANEE
HIPPOCENTAUR
HIPPOPHAGIST
HIPPOPOTAMUS
HISTORICALLY
HISTRIONICAL
HOMOEOPATHIC
HOMOLOGATION
HOMOMORPHISM
HORIZONTALLY
HORTICULTURE
HOUSEKEEPING
HUMOROUSNESS
HYDROFLUORIC
HYDROGRAPHER
HYDROPATHIST
HYDROSTATICS
HYDROTHERMAL
HYGIENICALLY
HYMNOGRAPHER
HYPERBOLICAL
HYPNOTIZABLE
HYPOCHONDRIA
HYPOCRITICAL
HYPOSTATICAL
HYPOTHECATOR
HYPOTHETICAL
HYSTERICALLY

I

IAMBOGRAPHER
ICHTHYOLATRY
ICHTHYOPSIDA
IDENTIFIABLE
IDIOELECTRIC
IDIOSYNCRASY
IDOLATROUSLY
ILLEGIBILITY
ILLEGITIMACY
ILLEGITIMATE
ILLIBERALITY
ILLUMINATION
IMMACULATELY
IMMATURENESS
IMMEASURABLE
IMMEASURABLY
IMMEMORIALLY
IMMENSURABLE
IMMERSIONIST
IMMETHODICAL
IMMODERATELY
IMMUTABILITY
IMPARTIALITY
IMPENETRABLE
IMPENETRABLY
IMPENITENTLY

IMPERATORIAL
IMPERATIVELY
IMPERFECTION
IMPERFORABLE
IMPERISHABLE
IMPERISHABLY
IMPERSONALLY
IMPERSONATOR
IMPERTINENCE
IMPERVIOUSLY
IMPETIGINOUS
IMPONDERABLE
IMPOSTHUMATE
IMPRESSIVELY
IMPRISONMENT
IMPROPRIATOR
IMPROVIDENCE
INACCURATELY
INADEQUATELY
INADMISSIBLE
INADVERTENCE
INADVERTENCY
INAPPLICABLE
INAPPLICABLY
INAPPOSITELY
INARTICULATE
INARTIFICIAL
INAUSPICIOUS
INCALCULABLE
INCANDESCENT
INCAPACITATE
INCAUTIOUSLY
INCENDIARISM
INCIDENTALLY
INCINERATION
INCOMMODIOUS
INCOMPARABLE
INCOMPARABLY
INCOMPATIBLE
INCOMPATIBLY
INCOMPETENCE
INCOMPETENCY
INCOMPLETELY
INCONCLUSIVE
INCONSEQUENT
INCONSISTENT
INCONSOLABLE
INCONSOLABLY
INCONSTANTLY
INCORPOREITY
INCORRODIBLE
INCORRUPTION
INCREASINGLY
INCURABILITY
INDEBTEDNESS
INDECISIVELY
INDECLINABLE
INDECOROUSLY
INDEFEASIBLE
INDEFENSIBLE
INDEFINITELY
INDELIBILITY
INDEPENDENCE
INDICATIVELY
INDIFFERENCE
INDIGESTIBLE
INDIRECTNESS
INDISCREETLY
INDISCRETION
INDISPUTABLE

INDISSOLUBLE
INDOCTRINATE
INEFFACEABLE
INEFFICIENCY
INELASTICITY
INERADICABLE
INERADICABLY
INEXPEDIENCE
INEXPEDIENCY
INEXPERIENCE
INEXPERTNESS
INEXPLICABLE
INEXTRICABLE
INFECTIOUSLY
INFELICITOUS
INFILTRATION
INFINITIVELY
INFLECTIONAL
INFREQUENTLY
INFRINGEMENT
INFUNDIBULAR
INFUSIBILITY
INHABITATION
INHOSPITABLE
INNUTRITIOUS
INOSCULATION
INSALUBRIOUS
INSECURENESS
INSOLUBILITY
INSPECTORATE
INSPISSATION
INSTALLATION
INSTRUCTRESS
INSTRUMENTAL
INSUFFERABLE
INSUFFERABLY
INSUFFLATION
INSURRECTION
INTEGUMENTAL
INTELLECTION
INTELLECTIVE
INTELLECTUAL
INTELLIGENCE
INTEMPERANCE
INTERCESSION
INTERCONNECT
INTERCURRENT
INTERDICTION
INTERDICTORY
INTERDIGITAL
INTERFERENCE
INTERFEMORAL
INTERGLACIAL
INTERJECTION
INTERLINEARY
INTERLOCUTOR
INTERMEDDLER
INTERMEDIACY
INTERMEDIARY
INTERMEDIATE
INTERMINABLE
INTERMINABLY
INTERMISSION
INTERMITTENT
INTERMIXTURE
INTERMUNDANE
INTERNUNCIAL
INTEROCEANIC
INTERORBITAL
INTERPELLATE

INTERPLEADER
INTERRUPTION
INTERRUPTIVE
INTERSTITIAL
INTERTEXTURE
INTERVENTION
INTERVOCALIC
INTIMIDATION
INTOLERANTLY
INTOXICATION
INTOXICATING
INTRANSIGENT
INTRANSITIVE
INTRENCHMENT
INTRODUCTION
INTRODUCTIVE
INTROMISSION
INTUSSUSCEPT
INVALIDATION
INVEIGLEMENT
INVERTEBRATE
INVESTIGABLE
INVISIBILITY
INVOLUCELLUM
INVULNERABLE
IRASCIBILITY
IRONICALNESS
IRRATIONALLY
IRREDEEMABLE
IRREDEEMABLY
IRREFLECTIVE
IRREFRAGABLE
IRREGULARITY
IRREMEDIABLE
IRREMEDIABLY
IRREMISSIBLE
IRREPEALABLE
IRREPROVABLE
IRRESISTENCE
IRRESISTIBLE
IRRESISTIBLY
IRRESOLUTION
IRRESOLVABLE
IRRESPECTIVE
IRRESPIRABLE
IRRESPONSIVE
IRREVERENTLY
IRREVERSIBLE
IRREVERSIBLY
IRRITABILITY

J

JOHANNISBERG
JOURNALISTIC
JURISCONSULT
JURISPRUDENT
JUVENESCENCE

K

KALEIDOSCOPE
KINDERGARTEN
KLEPTOMANIAC

184

L

LACHRYMATORY
LAEMMERGEIER
LAEMMERGEYER
LANGUISHMENT
LARYNGOSCOPE
LASCIVIOUSLY
LATICIFEROUS
LAUDABLENESS
LAUREATESHIP
LEGITIMATELY
LEGITIMATION
LEIOTRICHOUS
LENTICULARLY
LEPTOCARDIAN
LEXICOGRAPHY
LEXICOLOGIST
LIBIDINOUSLY
LIBIDINOSITY
LICENTIOUSLY
LIFELESSNESS
LIGNIPERDOUS
LIKEABLENESS
LIQUEFACIENT
LIQUEFACTION
LISTLESSNESS
LITHOGRAPHER
LITHOGRAPHIC
LITHOLOGICAL
LITHOPHAGOUS
LITURGIOLOGY
LOCALIZATION
LOMENTACEOUS
LONESOMENESS
LONGITUDINAL
LOQUACIOUSLY
LUGUBRIOUSLY
LUKEWARMNESS
LUMINIFEROUS
LUMINOUSNESS

M

MACHICOLATED
MACROPTEROUS
MADEMOISELLE
MAGNETICALLY
MAGNETIZABLE
MAGNIFICENCE
MAGNILOQUENT
MAIDENLINESS
MAINTAINABLE
MAJESTICALLY
MALEVOLENTLY
MALFORMATION
MALLEABILITY
MALTREATMENT
MALVERSATION
MANIFESTABLE
MANIFESTIBLE
MANIPULATION
MANIPULATIVE
MANIPULATORY
MANSLAUGHTER
MANUFACTURER
MARLINESPIKE

MARRIAGEABLE
MARVELLOUSLY
MATERIALNESS
MATHEMATICAL
MECHANICALLY
MEDIATORSHIP
MEDITATIVELY
MEGALOSAURUS
MELODRAMATIC
MENSTRUATION
MERCHANTABLE
MERCIFULNESS
MERCURIALIZE
MERETRICIOUS
MERIDIONALLY
METEMPIRICAL
METEOROGRAPH
METHODICALLY
METROPOLITAN
MEZZORILIEVO
MICROBIOLOGY
MICROGEOLOGY
MICROPHONOUS
MICROSCOPIST
MINISTRATION
MINISTRATIVE
MIRACULOUSLY
MIRTHFULNESS
MISAPPREHEND
MISBELIEVING
MISCALCULATE
MISDEMEANANT
MISDEMEANOUR
MISDIRECTION
MISINTERPRET
MISPLACEMENT
MISPRONOUNCE
MISREPRESENT
MISSTATEMENT
MISTRANSLATE
MITRAILLEUSE
MOBILIZATION
MODIFICATION
MODIFICATORY
MOIREANTIQUE
MONASTICALLY
MONETIZATION
MONODELPHIAN
MONOGRAPHIST
MONOMANIACAL
MONOMETALLIC
MONOMORPHOUS
MONOPETALOUS
MONOPHYLLOUS
MONSEIGNEURS
MONUMENTALLY
MORPHOLOGIST
MOURNFULNESS
MUCILAGINOUS
MUCOPURULENT
MULLIGATAWNY
MULTICOSTATE
MULTIFARIOUS
MULTIFORMITY
MULTILATERAL
MULTIPLIABLE
MULTIPLICAND
MULTIPLICITY
MULTITUBULAR
MUNICIPALIZE

MYSTERIOUSLY
MYTHOGRAPHER

N

NAMELESSNESS
NARCOTICALLY
NATURALISTIC
NAVIGABILITY
NECTOCALYCES
NEEDLESSNESS
NEGLECTFULLY
NEOLOGICALLY
NEVERTHELESS
NIDIFICATION
NOCTAMBULIST
NOMENCLATURE
NOMINATIVELY
NONAGENARIAN
NONCHALANTLY
NORTHERNMOST
NOTIFICATION
NUTRITIOUSLY

O

OBDURATENESS
OBLIGATORILY
OBLIGINGNESS
OBLITERATION
OBLITERATIVE
OBSCURANTIST
OBSEQUIOUSLY
OBSOLESCENCE
OBSOLETENESS
OBSTREPEROUS
OCCIDENTALLY
OCEANOGRAPHY
OCTOGENARIAN
OCTOPETALOUS
OLEOMARGARIN
OMNIPOTENTLY
OMNIPRESENCE
OMNISCIENTLY
ONOMATOPOEIA
ONOMATOPOEIC
OPHIOPHAGOUS
OPINIONATIVE
OPPRESSIVELY
ORATORICALLY
ORGANIZATION
ORGANOGRAPHY
ORNAMENTALLY
ORNITHOMANCY
ORNITHOSCOPY
OROGRAPHICAL
ORTHOGNATHIC
ORTHOGRAPHER
ORTHOGRAPHIC
OSSIFICATION
OSTENTATIOUS
OSTEODENTINE
OSTEOGRAPHER
OSTEOMALACIA
OUTMANOEUVRE
OUTRAGEOUSLY
OVERESTIMATE

P

PAEDOBAPTIST
PALAEOBOTANY
PALAEOGRAPHY
PALAEOLITHIC
PALINGENESIS
PALPABLENESS
PANHELLENISM
PANTISOCRACY
PAPISTICALLY
PARACENTESIS
PARADISIACAL
PARAGRAPHIST
PARALIPOMENA
PARASITICIDE
PARENCHYMOUS
PARIDIGITATE
PARISYLLABLE
PAROCHIALISM
PAROCHIALIZE
PARONOMASTIC
PARSIMONIOUS
PARTICIPATOR
PARTISANSHIP
PARTIZANSHIP
PATHETICALLY
PATHOLOGICAL
PATRIARCHATE
PATRIARCHISM
PEACEFULNESS
PELLUCIDNESS
PENTAGONALLY
PERAMBULATOR
PERCEPTIVITY
PEREGRINATOR
PEREMPTORILY
PERFIDIOUSLY
PERGAMENEOUS
PERICARDITIS
PERIOSTEITIS
PERIPHERICAL
PERIVISCERAL
PERMEABILITY
PERPETRATION
PERPLEXINGLY
PERQUISITION
PERSEVERANCE
PERSISTENTLY
PERSPICACITY
PERSPIRATION
PERSPIRATORY
PERSUASIVELY
PERTINACEOUS
PERTURBATION
PERVICACIOUS
PESTILENTIAL
PETRIFACTION
PETRIFACTIVE
PETROGRAPHER
PETTIFOGGERY
PHAENOGAMOUS
PHARMACOLOGY
PHARYNGOTOMY
PHILANTHROPY
PHILHARMONIC
PHILHELLENIC
PHILISTINISM
PHILOSOPHISM

PHILOSOPHIZE
PHLEBOTOMIST
PHONETICALLY
PHOSPHORESCE
PHOTOGRAVURE
PHRASEOLOGIC
PHRENOLOGIST
PHYLOGENESIS
PHYLOGENETIC
PHYSIOCRATIC
PHYSIOGRAPHY
PHYTOGENESIS
PHYTOPHAGOUS
PISCICULTURE
PITIABLENESS
PITILESSNESS
PLACABLENESS
PLANISPHERIC
PLEASANTRIES
PLEBISCITARY
PLENIPOTENCE
PLENIPOTENCY
PLURILITERAL
PLURILOCULAR
PNEUMATOLOGY
POLLUTEDNESS
POLYANTHUSES
POLYMORPHISM
POLYPHYLLOUS
POLYSPERMOUS
POLYSYLLABLE
POLYSYNDETON
POLYTECHNICS
POPULOUSNESS
PORCELLANEOUS
PORTABLENESS
PORTENTOUSLY
POSITIVENESS
POSSESSIVELY
POWERFULNESS
PRACTICALITY
PRACTITIONER
PRECEPTORIAL
PRECIOUSNESS
PRECIPITABLE
PRECISIANISM
PRECOCIOUSLY
PRECOGNITION
PREDESTINATE
PREFERENTIAL
PRELATICALLY
PREMAXILLARY
PREOCCUPANCY
PREPONDERATE
PRESBYTERIAL
PRESBYTERIAN
PREREQUISITE
PRESCRiPTION
PRESCRIPTIVE
PRESENTATION
PRESIDENTIAL
PRESUMPTUOUS
PREVAILINGLY
PRUDEFULNESS
PRIESTLINESS
PRIMIGENIOUS
PRIMOGENITOR
PRINCIPALITY
PROBATIONARY
PROCLAMATION

PRODIGIOUSLY
PROFESSORATE
PROFOUNDNESS
PROLEGOMENON
PROLETARIATE
PROLIFICNESS
PROLONGATION
PROMULGATION
PROPAGANDISM
PROPENSENESS
PROPITIATION
PROPITIOUSLY
PROPORTIONAL
PROSCRIPTION
PROSCRIPTIVE
PROSELYTIZER
PROSOPOPOEIA
PROSPEROUSLY
PROSTITUTION
PROTESTATION
PROTHONOTARY
PROTOPLASMIC
PROTRACTEDLY
PROTUBERANCE
PROVERBIALLY
PROVIDENTIAL
PRUDENTIALLY
PSEUDONYMOUS
PSYCHOLOGIST
PSYCHROMETER
PTERODACTYLE
PUGNACIOUSLY
PULVERACEOUS
PULVERIZABLE
PURBLINDNESS
PURIFICATION
PUTREFACTION
PYROMETRICAL
PYROTECHNIST

Q

QUADRAGESMIA
QUADRANGULAR
QUADRINOMIAL
QUADRUMANOUS
QUALMISHNESS
QUANTITATIVE
QUAQUAVERSAL
QUERIMONIOUS
QUESTIONABLE
QUESTIONABLY
QUINQUENNIUM

R

RAMIFICATION
RATIFICATION
READJUSTMENT
READMITTANCE
REANNEXATION
REAPPEARANCE
REASSUMPTION
REBELLIOUSLY
RECALCITRANT
RECAPITULATE
RECENSIONIST
RECEPTACULAR

RECIPROCALLY
RECKLESSNESS
RECOMMITMENT
RECONCILABLE
RECONVEYANCE
RECORDERSHIP
RECRUDESCENT
RECUPERATION
RECUPERATIVE
RECUPERATORY
REDINTEGRATE
REDISTRIBUTE
REFLECTIVELY
REFRACTORILY
REFRESHINGLY
REFUTABILITY
REGARDLESSLY
REGENERATION
REGENERATIVE
REGENERATORY
REGISTRATION
REHABILITATE
REILLUMINATE
REIMPOSITION
REINSPECTION
REINSTALMENT
REINVESTMENT
REINVIGORATE
REJUVENATION
RELATIONSHIP
RELATIVENESS
RELENTLESSLY
RELIABLENESS
RELIGIONLESS
RELINQUISHER
REMEMBRANCER
REMINISCENCE
REMONSTRANCE
REMORSEFULLY
REMOVABILITY
REMUNERATION
REMUNERATIVE
RENEWABILITY
RENOUNCEMENT
RENUNCIATION
REPARABILITY
REPERCUSSION
REPERCUSSIVE
REPREHENSION
REPRESSIVELY
REPROACHABLE
REPROACHABLY
REPRODUCTION
REPRODUCTIVE
REPUBLICATES
REQUIESCENCE
RESIDENTIARY
RESINIFEROUS
RESISTLESSLY
RESOLUTENESS
RESOLUTIONER
RESOLVEDNESS
RESOURCELESS
RESPECTFULLY
RESPECTIVELY
RESPLENDENCE
RESPLENDENCY
RESPONDENTIA
RESPONSIVELY
RESTAURATEUR

RESTRAINABLE
RESTRAINABLY
RESURRECTION
RESUSCITABLE
RESUSCITATOR
RETICULATION
RETRACTATION
RETRENCHMENT
RETRIEVEMENT
RETROCESSION
REVENGEFULLY
REVERBERATOR
RHINOPLASTIC
RHIZOPHAGOUS
RHODODENDRON
RHODOMONTADE
RHOMBOHEDRAL
RHOMBOHEDRON
RHYTHMICALLY
RIDICULOUSLY
ROMANTICALLY
RUTHLESSNESS

S

SACERDOTALLY
SACRAMENTARY
SACRILEGIOUS
SACROSANCTLY
SALEABLENESS
SALUBRIOUSLY
SALUTARINESS
SALVATIONIST
SANGUIFEROUS
SANGUINENESS
SANGUINOLENT
SAPONIFIABLE
SAPROPHAGOUS
SARCOPHAGOUS
SARSAPARILLA
SATISFACTION
SATISFACTORY
SCANDALOUSLY
SCANDINAVIAN
SCARIFICATOR
SCARLATINOUS
SCENOGRAPHIC
SCHOOLMASTER
SCHORLACEOUS
SCLERODERMIC
SCORNFULNESS
SCOUNDRELISM
SCRIPTURALLY
SCROFULOUSLY
SCROPHULARIA
SCRUPULOSITY
SCRUPULOUSLY
SCULPTURALLY
SCURRILOUSLY
SCUTELLIFORM
SECESSIONISM
SECESSIONIST
SECRETARIATE
SECTARIANISM
SECTARIANIZE
SEDULOUSNESS
SEGMENTATION
SEIGNIORALTY
SEISMOLOGIST

SELENOGRAPHY
SEMEIOGRAPHY
SEMINIFEROUS
SEMPERVIRENT
SENATORIALLY
SENSIBLENESS
SENSIFACIENT
SEPARABILITY
SEPARATENESS
SEPTENNIALLY
SEPTUAGENARY
SEPTUAGESIMA
SEQUESTRATOR
SERAPHICALLY
SERPENTIFORM
SHAKSPEARIAN
SHAMEFACEDLY
SHAMEFULNESS
SHEEPISHNESS
SHREWISHNESS
SHUDDERINGLY
SIDEROGRAPHY
SIGNIFICATOR
SIMONIACALLY
SIMULTANEITY
SIMULTANEOUS
SLANDEROUSLY
SLAUGHTEROUS
SLIPPERINESS
SLOVENLINESS
SLUGGISHNESS
SLUTTISHNESS
SNAPPISHNESS
SNOBBISHNESS
SOCRATICALLY
SOLICITATION
SOLICITOUSLY
SOLIDIFIABLE
SOLISEQUIOUS
SOLITARINESS
SOMNAMBULATE
SOMNAMBULISM
SOMNAMBULIST
SONOROUSNESS
SOPHISTICATE
SOPORIFEROUS
SOUTHERNMOST
SPACIOUSNESS
SPECIALITIES
SPECIFICALLY
SPECTROMETER
SPECTROSCOPE
SPECTROSCOPY
SPERMATOZOON
SPHENOGRAPHY
SPHRAGISTICS
SPHYGMOGRAPH
SPIRITEDNESS
SPIRITLESSLY
SPIRITUALISM
SPIRITUALIST
SPIRITUALITY
SPIRITUALIZE
SPITEFULNESS
SPORADICALLY
SPOTLESSNESS
SPURIOUSNESS
STALWARTNESS
STANNIFEROUS
STATISTICIAN

187

STEATOPYGOUS
STENOGRAPHIC
STEPDAUGHTER
STEREOGRAPHY
STEREOPTICON
STEREOTYPIST
STERNUTATION
STERNUTATIVE
STERNUTATORY
STOCKBROKING
STRAIGHTNESS
STRAWBERRIES
STRENGTHENER
STRIDULATION
STUBBORNNESS
STUDIOUSNESS
STUPEFACIENT
STUPEFACTIVE
STUPEFACTION
STUPENDOUSLY
STYLOGRAPHIC
SUBCOMMITTEE
SUBCUTANEOUS
SUBDIVISIBLE
SUBEPIDERMAL
SUBFEUDATORY
SUBJECTIVELY
SUBJECTIVITY
SUBLINEATION
SUBMAXILLARY
SUBMISSIVELY
SUBOCCIPITAL
SUBSCRIPTION
SUBSEQUENTLY
SUBSERVIENCE
SUBSERVIENCY
SUBSTANTIATE
SUBSTANTIVAL
SUBSTITUTION
SUBSTRUCTION
SUBSTRUCTURE
SUBTERRANEAN
SUCCEDANEOUS
SUCCESSFULLY
SUCCESSIONAL
SUCCESSIVELY
SUCCINCTNESS
SUDORIFEROUS
SUFFICIENTLY
SUFFRUTICOSE
SUGGESTIVELY
SUITABLENESS
SULPHURATION
SULPHURETTED
SUPERANNUATE
SUPERCILIARY
SUPERCILIOUS
SUPEREMINENT
SUPERMUNDANE
SUPERNACULAR
SUPERNACULUM
SUPPLICATORY
SUPPRESSIBLE
SUPRAMUNDANE
SUPRAORBITAL
SURMOUNTABLE
SURPRISINGLY
SURREJOINDER
SURVEILLANCE
SURVEYORSHIP

SURVIVORSHIP
SUSCEPTIVITY
SUSPICIOUSLY
SUSTENTATION
SYCOPHANTISH
SYCOPHANTISM
SYLLABICALLY
SYMBOLICALLY
SYNANTHEROUS
SYNARTHROSIS
SYNONYMOUSLY
SYNOPTICALLY
SYSTEMATICAL

T

TABERNACULAR
TACHYGRAPHIC
TALISMANICAL
TAMELESSNESS
TANGENTIALLY
TANGIBLENESS
TASTEFULNESS
TECHNOLOGIST
TELAUTOGRAPH
TELEGRAPHIST
TELEOLOGICAL
TEMPERAMENTS
TEMPORALNESS
TENUIROSTRAL
TERCENTENARY
TEREBINTHINE
TERGIVERSATE
TERRIBLENESS
TERRIFICALLY
TETRAPTEROUS
THALLOGENOUS
THANKFULNESS
THANKSGIVING
THEATRICALLY
THEOCRATICAL
THEOREMATIST
THEOSOPHICAL
THERAPEUTICS
THERAPEUTIST
THICKSKINNED
THIEVISHNESS
THITHERWARDS
THOUGHTFULLY
THRIFTLESSLY
TICKLISHNESS
TITANIFEROUS
TOPOGRAPHIST
TORREFACTION
TORRICELLIAN
TORTUOUSNESS
TOXICOLOGIST
TRADITIONIST
TRADUCIANISM
TRAITOROUSLY
TRANQUILLIZE
TRANQUILLITY
TRANSFERABLE
TRANSFERENCE
TRANSFUSIBLE
TRANSGRESSOR
TRANSHIPMENT
TRANSITIONAL
TRANSITIVELY

TRANSITORILY
TRANSLATABLE
TRANSLUCENCY
TRANSMIGRATE
TRANSMISSION
TRANSMUTABLE
TRANSMUTABLY
TRANSPARENCE
TRANSPARENCY
TRANSPICUOUS
TRANSPLANTER
TRANSPONTINE
TRANSPORTING
TRANSPOSABLE
TRANSUDATION
TRANSUDATORY
TRANSUMPTIVE
TRANSVERSELY
TRIADELPHOUS
TRIANGULARLY
TRICENTENARY
TRICHINIASIS
TRICHOMATOSE
TRICUSPIDATE
TRIDACTYLOUS
TRIGRAMMATIC
TRIPARTITELY
TRIPHTHONGAL
TRIUMPHANTLY
TROPOLOGICAL
TRUNCHEONEER
TRUTHFULNESS
TUBERCULATED
TUBERCULOSIS
TUMULTUOUSLY
TYRANNICALLY

U

UBIQUITOUSLY
ULTRAMONTANE
UMBRAGEOUSLY
UNACCEPTABLE
UNACCUSTOMED
UNACQUAINTED
UNADULTERATE
UNANSWERABLE
UNANSWERABLY
UNAPPEALABLE
UNAPPEASABLE
UNASPIRINGLY
UNASSAILABLE
UNBECOMINGLY
UNBREATHABLE
UNCHALLENGED
UNCHANGEABLE
UNCHARITABLE
UNCHARITABLY
UNCOMMERCIAL
UNCOVENANTED
UNCTUOUSNESS
UNCULTIVATED
UNDECEIVABLE
UNDECLINABLE
UNDERCLOTHES
UNDERCURRENT
UNDERSTRATUM
UNDERWRITING
UNDESERVEDLY

UNDETERMINED
UNDISCERNING
UNDISCHARGED
UNEXPECTEDLY
UNFAITHFULLY
UNFATHOMABLY
UNFAVOURABLE
UNFAVOURABLY
UNFRANCHISED
UNFREQUENTED
UNFRUITFULLY
UNGENEROUSLY
UNGOVERNABLE
UNGOVERNABLY
UNGRACEFULLY
UNGRACIOUSLY
UNGRATEFULLY
UNHANDSOMELY
UNHESITATING
UNHISTORICAL
UNIMPORTANCE
UNIMPUGNABLE
UNINSTRUCTED
UNINTERESTED
UNITARIANISM
UNIVERSALISM
UNIVERSALIST
UNIVERSITIES
UNIVERSOLOGY
UNKINDLINESS
UNLAWFULNESS
UNLIKELIHOOD
UNLIKELINESS
UNMANAGEABLE
UNMARKETABLE
UNMERCIFULLY
UNMISTAKABLE
UNOBSERVEDLY
UNOBSTRUCTED
UNPARALLELED
UNPATRONIZED
UNPLEASANTLY
UNPLEASINGLY
UNPOETICALLY
UNPOPULARITY
UNPREJUDICED
UNPREPAREDLY
UNPRETENDING
UNPRINCIPLED
UNPRIVILEGED
UNPRODUCTIVE
UNPROFITABLE
UNPROPITIOUS
UNPROSPEROUS

UNQUENCHABLE
UNQUENCHABLY
UNQUESTIONED
UNREASONABLE
UNREASONABLY
UNRECONCILED
UNREGENERACY
UNREGISTERED
UNRESERVEDLY
UNRESTRAINED
UNRESTRICTED
UNSANCTIFIED
UNSATISFYING
UNSCRIPTURAL
UNSCRUPULOUS
UNSEARCHABLE
UNSEEMLINESS
UNSTABLENESS
UNSTEADINESS
UNSTRATIFIED
UNSUCCESSFUL
UNSUPPRESSED
UNSUSPECTING
UNSUSPICIOUS
UNSYSTEMATIC
UNTENANTABLE
UNTHINKINGLY
UNTOWARDNESS
UNTRAMMELLED
UNTRUTHFULLY
UNWIELDINESS
UNWONTEDNESS
UNWORTHINESS
UPROARIOUSLY

V

VAINGLORIOUS
VALETUDINARY
VALUABLENESS
VANQUISHABLE
VAPORIZATION
VARIABLENESS
VATICINATION
VELOCIPEDIST
VENDIBLENESS
VERIFICATION
VERNACULARLY
VERSIFICATOR
VERTICILLATE
VICTORIOUSLY
VIGOROUSNESS
VILIFICATION

VILLAINOUSLY
VINDICTIVELY
VISCOUNTSHIP
VISITATORIAL
VITALIZATION
VITREOUSNESS
VITRIFACTION
VITRIFACTURE
VITRIOLATION
VITUPERATION
VITUPERATIVE
VIVIPAROUSLY
VOCABULARIES
VOCALIZATION
VOCIFERATION
VOCIFEROUSLY
VOLUMINOUSLY
VOLUPTUARIES
VOLUPTUOUSLY

W

WAREHOUSEMAN
WATCHFULNESS
WELLINGTONIA
WHENCESOEVER
WHERETHROUGH
WHIMSICALITY
WHISPERINGLY
WHORTLEBERRY
WOMANISHNESS
WORSHIPFULLY
WRANGLERSHIP
WRATHFULNESS
WRETCHEDNESS

X

XYLOBALSAMUM

Y

YOUTHFULNESS

Z

ZINCOGRAPHIC
ZOOCHEMISTRY
ZOOPHYTOLOGY

THIRTEEN-LETTER WORDS

A

ABSORBABILITY
ACCESSIBILITY
ACCIDENTALISM
ACCIDENTALLY
ACCLIMATATION
ACCOMMODATING
ACCOMMODATION
ACCOMMODATIVE
ACCOMPANIMENT
ACCOUTREMENTS
ACETABULIFORM
ACETIFICATION
ACIDIFICATION
ACOTYLEDONOUS
ACQUISITIVELY
ACRIMONIOUSLY
ADMEASUREMENT
ADMINISTRATOR
ADMIRABLENESS
ADMISSIBILITY
ADUMBRATIVELY
ADVENTUROUSLY
ADVERTISEMENT
ADVISABLENESS
AESTHESIOLOGY
AESTHETICALLY
AFFIRMATIVELY
AFFORESTATION
AGGLOMERATION
AGGLUTINATION
AGGLUTINATIVE
AGGRAVATINGLY
AGREEABLENESS
AGRICULTURIST
ALCOHOLOMETER
ALGEBRAICALLY
ALLEGORICALLY
ALLOWABLENESS
ALTERNATIVELY
ALUMINIFEROUS
AMBASSADORIAL
AMBIDEXTERITY
AMPLIFICATION
AMPLIFICATIVE
AMPLIFICATORY
ANACHRONISTIC
ANAGRAMMATIST
ANAPHRODISIAC
ANDROPETALOUS
ANGIOSPERMOUS
ANGLO-AMERICAN
ANGLO-CATHOLIC
ANIMADVERSION
ANIMALIZATION
ANNEXATIONIST
ANTAPHRODITIC
ANTHROPOLATRY
ANTHROPOLOGIC
ANTHROPOMETRY
ANTHROPOPATHY
ANHROPOPHAGI
ANTHROPOPHAGY

ANTIARTHRITIC
ANTIASTHMATIC
ANTICHRISTIAN
ANTICORROSIVE
ANTIEPHIALTIC
ANTIEPISCOPAL
ANTILOGARITHM
ANTIMONARCHIC
ANTIMONIANISM
ANTINEPHRITIC
ANTISCORBUTIC
ANTISPASMODIC
ANTITYPICALLY
APHANIPTEROUS
APOGEOTROPISM
APOSTOLICALLY
APPELLATIVELY
APPENDICULATE
APPLICABILITY
APPORTIONMENT
APPREHENSIBLE
APPROPRIATELY
APPROPRIATION
APPROXIMATELY
APPROXIMATION
APPROXIMATIVE
ARBITRARINESS
ARBORICULTURE
ARCHAEOLOGIST
ARCHAEOPTERYX
ARCHBISHOPRIC
ARCHIDIACONAL
ARCHIMANDRITE
ARCHITECTURAL
ARGENTIFEROUS
ARGUMENTATION
ARGUMENTATIVE
ARITHMETICIAN
ARUNDINACEOUS
ASCERTAINABLE
ASCERTAINMENT
ASCRIPTITIOUS
ASSASSINATION
ASSIDUOUSNESS
ASSOCIATESHIP
ASSYRIOLOGIST
ASTHMATICALLY
ASTONISHINGLY
ATHEISTICALLY
ATROCIOUSNESS
ATTAINABILITY
ATTENTIVENESS
ATTRIBUTIVELY
AUDACIOUSNESS
AUTHENTICALLY
AUTHORITATIVE
AUTOBIOGRAPHY
AUTOCHTHONOUS
AVAILABLENESS
AXIOMATICALLY

B

BACCALAUREATE

BACKWARDATION
BALLAST-HEAVER
BALL-CARTRIDGE
BALSAMIFEROUS
BAREFACEDNESS
BEATIFICATION
BEAUTIFULNESS
BEGINNINGLESS
BELIEVABILITY
BELLES-LETTRES
BESSEMER-STEEL
BIBLIOGRAPHER
BIBLIOLOGICAL
BIBLIOTHECARY
BLACKGUARDISM
BLAMELESSNESS
BLASPHEMOUSLY
BLINDMAN'S-BUFF
BLISTER-BEETLE
BLOCK-PRINTING
BLOOD-RELATION
BLOODSHEDDING
BLOOD-SPILLING
BLOTTING-PAPER
BOARDING-HOUSE
BOMBASTICALLY
BOOKING-OFFICE
BOROGLYCERIDE
BOUNDLESSNESS
BOUNTIFULNESS
BREECH-LOADING
BREVILOQUENCE
BREVIROSTRATE
BROKEN-HEARTED
BROTHERLINESS
BUMPTIOUSNESS
BURGLARIOUSLY
BURNING-MIRROR
BURNT-OFFERING
BUTCHER'S-BROOM

C

CALCIFICATION
CALICO-PRINTER
CALLISTHENICS
CALORIFACIENT
CAMPANOLOGIST
CAMPEACHY-WOOD
CAMPHORACEOUS
CANDIDATESHIP
CAPACIOUSNESS
CARBONIFEROUS
CARBONIZATION
CARNIFICATION
CARPET-BEDDING
CARRIER-PIGEON
CARTE-DE-VISITE
CARTILAGINOUS
CASTLE-BUILDER
CATASTROPHISM
CATECHISTICAL
CATEGOREMATIC
CATEGORICALLY

CAT-O'-NINE TAILS
CAUSELESSNESS
CAUTERIZATION
CEPHALO-THORAX
CEREBRO-SPINAL
CEREMONIOUSLY
CERTIFICATION
CHALCOGRAPHER
CHALLENGEABLE
CHANCEL-SCREEN
CHANGEABILITY
CHANGEFULNESS
CHARACTERLESS
CHARTOGRAPHIC
CHEERLESSNESS
CHEIROPTEROUS
CHEVAL-DE-FRISE
CHIMNEY-CORNER
CHOPPING-KNIFE
CHOREPISCOPAL
CHREMATISTICS
CHRISTMAS-ROSE
CHRISTMAS-TREE
CHROMATOPHORE
CHRONOGRAPHER
CHRYSANTHEMUM
CHUCK-FARTHING
CHURCHMANSHIP
CHURCH-SERVICE
CHYLIFICATION
CHYMIFICATION
CICATRIZATION
CINCHONACEOUS
CINEMATOGRAPH
CINNAMON-STONE
CIRCUMAMBIENT
CIRCUMDUCTION
CIRCUMFERENCE
CIRCUMFLUENCE
CIRCUMJACENCE
CIRCUMJACENCY
CIRCUMSPECTLY
CIRCUMVALLATE
CIRCUMVENTION
CIRCUMVENTIVE
CLAMOROUSNESS
CLANDESTINELY
CLARIFICATION
CLEARING-HOUSE
CLEISTOGAMOUS
CLIMATOGRAPHY
CLINCHER-BUILT
CLOISTER-GARTH
COADJUTORSHIP
COARSE-GRAINED
CO-BELLIGERENT
COCHLEARIFORM
COESSENTIALLY
COEXTENSIVELY
COLLABORATION
COLLABORATEUR
COLLECTEDNESS
COLLOQUIALISM
COLLOQUIALIST
COMBATIVENESS
COMMANDERSHIP
COMMEMORATIVE
COMMENSURABLE
COMMENSURABLY
COMMISERATION

COMMISERATIVE
COMMUNICATIVE
COMMUTABILITY
COMMUTATIVELY
COMMUNICATION
COMPANIONABLE
COMPANIONABLY
COMPANIONLESS
COMPANIONSHIP
COMPARATIVELY
COMPASSIONATE
COMPATIBILITY
COMPENDIOUSLY
COMPLAININGLY
COMPLAISANTLY
COMPLEMENTARY
COMPLIMENTARY
COMPREHENSION
COMPREHENSIVE
CONCATENATION
CONCAVO-CONVEX
CONCEITEDNESS
CONCENTRATION
CONCENTRATIVE
CONCEPTUALISM
CONCEPTUALIST
CONCOMITANTLY
CONCRETIONARY
CONCUPISCENCE
CONDESCENDING
CONDESCENSION
CONDITIONALLY
CONDUCIVENESS
CONFABULATION
CONFABULATORY
CONFECTIONARY
CONFECTIONERY
CONFEDERATION
CONFEDERATIVE
CONFESSIONARY
CONFESSORSHIP
CONFIDINGNESS
CONFIGURATION
CONFLAGRATION
CONFRATERNITY
CONFRONTATION
CONGRATULATOR
CONJECTURABLE
CONJECTURALLY
CONJUGATIONAL
CONJUNCTIONAL
CONJUNCTIVELY
CONSANGUINITY
CONSCIENTIOUS
CONSCIOUSNESS
CONSECUTIVELY
CONSENTANEOUS
CONSEQUENTIAL
CONSERVATOIRE
CONSIDERATELY
CONSIDERATION
CONSOLIDATION
CONSPICUOUSLY
CONSPIRATRESS
CONSTABLESHIP
CONSTELLATION
CONSTERNATION
CONSTRAINABLE
CONSTRAINEDLY
CONSUMPTIVELY

CONTABESCENCE
CONTAMINATION
CONTAMINATIVE
CONTEMPLATION
CONTEMPLATIVE
CONTENTEDNESS
CONTENTIOUSLY
CONTORTIONIST
CONTRABANDISM
CONTRABANDIST
CONTRACTILITY
CONTRADICTION
CONTRADICTIVE
CONTRADICTORY
CONTRAPUNTIST
CONTRATE-WHEEL
CONTRAVENTION
CONTRIBUTABLE
CONTROVERSIAL
CONTROVERTIST
CONVALESCENCE
CONVALESCENCY
CONVENTIONARY
CONVENTIONIST
CONVERSAZIONE
CONVEXO-CONVEX
CONVOCATIONAL
CONVULSIONARY
COPARTNERSHIP
CORALLIFEROUS
COROLLIFLORAL
CORRELATIVELY
CORRESPONDENT
CORRESPONDING
CORRESPONSIVE
CORROBORATION
CORROBORATIVE
CORROBORATORY
CORRODIBILITY
CORROSIVENESS
CORRUPTIONIST
CORYMBIFEROUS
COSMOPOLITISM
COTTON-SPINNER
COTTON-THISTLE
COUNTERACTION
COUNTERACTIVE
COUNTERCHANGE
COUNTERCHARGE
COUNTERFEITER
COUNTER-MOTION
COUNTER-POISON
COUNTER-SIGNAL
COUNTER-STROKE
COUNTERWEIGHT
COURTEOUSNESS
COXCOMBICALLY
CRAFTSMANSHIP
CRANIOSCOPIST
CREDITABILITY
CREDULOUSNESS
CROSS-BREEDING
CROSS-GARTERED
CROSS-HATCHING
CROSS-QUESTION
CROTCHETINESS
CRUSTACEOLOGY
CRYPTOGRAPHER
CRYPTOGRAPHIC
CUSTOMARINESS

CYLINDRICALLY

D

DACTYLIOGLYPH
DADDY-LONG-LEGS
DAGUERREOTYPE
DANCING-MASTER
DANGEROUSNESS
DASTARDLINESS
DAUGHTER-IN-LAW
DAUNTLESSNESS
DEAD-RECKONING
DEATH-STRUGGLE
DECEITFULNESS
DECEPTIVENESS
DECOMPOSITION
DECONCENTRATE
DECORTICATION
DECREPITATION
DEFECTIVENESS
DEFENCELESSLY
DEFENSIBILITY
DEFERENTIALLY
DEFERVESCENCE
DEFERVESCENCY
DEFIBRINATION
DELICIOUSNESS
DELIQUESCENCE
DELIRIFACIENT
DELIRIOUSNESS
DEMONSTRATION
DEMONSTRATIVE
DENATIONALIZE
DENTICULATELY
DENTICULATION
DEODORIZATION
DEONTOLOGICAL
DEPHOSPHORIZE
DEPRECATINGLY
DERMATOLOGIST
DERMO-SKELETON
DESCRIPTIVELY
DESIRABLENESS
DESTRUCTIVELY
DESULTORINESS
DETERIORATION
DETERMINATELY
DETERMINATION
DETERMINATIVE
DETRIMENTALLY
DEUTEROGAMIST
DEVELOPMENTAL
DEXTEROUSNESS
DIALECTICALLY
DIALOGISTICAL
DIAMESOGAMOUS
DIAMETRICALLY
DIAPHRAGMATIC
DIATHERMANOUS
DICHLAMYDEOUS
DICHOTOMOUSLY
DICTATORIALLY
DIFFERENTIATE
DIFFUSIBILITY
DIFFUSIVENESS
DIGESTIBILITY
DIPHTHONGALLY
DIPSOMANIACAL

DISAPPEARANCE
DISCIPLINABLE
DISCOLORATION
DISCONNECTION
DISCONTINUITY
DISCONTINUOUS
DISCREDITABLE
DISCREDITABLY
DISCRETIONARY
DISCRIMINATOR
DISEMBARKMENT
DISENGAGEMENT
DISESTIMATION
DISFIGURATION
DISFIGUREMENT
DISGRACEFULLY
DISHONOURABLE
DISHONOURABLY
DISINTEGRABLE
DISINTERESTED
DISJUNCTIVELY
DISMEMBERMENT
DISNATURALIZE
DISOBEDIENTLY
DISOBLIGEMENT
DISOBLIGINGLY
DISPARAGINGLY
DISPARAGEMENT
DISPASSIONATE
DISPLANTATION
DISPOSSESSION
DISPROPORTION
DISRESPECTFUL
DISSEMINATION
DISSIMILARITY
DISSIMILATION
DISSIMILITUDE
DISSIMULATION
DISSOLUBILITY
DISSOLUTENESS
DISTASTEFULLY
DISTINCTIVELY
DISTINGUISHED
DISTRESSFULLY
DISTRESSINGLY
DISTRIBUTABLE
DISTRUSTFULLY
DIVERSIFIABLE
DOMESTICATION
DOMICILIATION
DOUBLE-DEALING
DOUBLE-HEARTED
DOUBLE-TONGUED
DRAGGLE-TAILED
DRAWING-MASTER
DRESSING-TABLE
DRILL-SERGEANT
DRINK-OFFERING
DWELLING-HOUSE
DYNAMO-MACHINE
DYSMENORRHOEA

E

EARTHLY-MINDED
ECCENTRICALLY
ECHINODERMATA
ECONOMIZATION
EDUCATIONALLY

EFFECTIVENESS
EFFERVESCENCE
EFFERVESCIBLE
EFFICACIOUSLY
EFFLORESCENCE
EGOTISTICALLY
EGPYTOLOGICAL
ELABORATENESS
ELECTRIFIABLE
ELECTROCUTION
ELECTRO-MAGNET
ELECTROMETRIC
ELECTROMOTIVE
ELECTROPHORUS
ELEPHANTIASIS
EMBARRASSMENT
EMBELLISHMENT
EMBRYOLOGICAL
EMIGRATIONIST
ENCOMIASTICAL
ENCOMPASSMENT
ENCOURAGEMENT
ENCOURAGINGLY
ENCYCLOPAEDIA
ENCYCLOPAEDIC
ENCYCLOPEDISM
ENCYCLOPEDIST
ENDURABLENESS
ENERGETICALLY
ENIGMATICALLY
ENLIGHTENMENT
ENTERTAINMENT
ENTOMOLOGICAL
ENTOMOPHAGOUS
ENTOMOPHILOUS
ENTOZOOLOGIST
EPIGRAMMATIST
EPIGRAMMATIZE
EPIPERIPHERAL
EQUESTRIANISM
EQUIDIFFERENT
EQUIDISTANTLY
EQUILIBRATION
EQUIPONDERANT
EQUIPONDERATE
EQUISETACEOUS
EQUITABLENESS
EQUIVOCALNESS
ERYSIPELATOUS
ESTABLISHMENT
ESTIMABLENESS
EUCHARISTICAL
EVANGELICALLY
EVERLASTINGLY
EXANTHEMATOUS
EXCEPTIONABLE
EXCEPTIONALLY
EXCITABLENESS
EXCLUSIVENESS
EXCOMMUNICATE
EXCORTICATION
EXCUSABLENESS
EXPANSIBILITY
EXPANSIVENESS
EXPECTORATION
EXPECTORATIVE
EXPEDITIONARY
EXPEDITIOUSLY
EXPENSIVENESS
EXPERIMENTIST

EXPOSTULATION
EXPOSTULATORY
EXPROPRIATION
EXQUISITENESS
EXSANGUINEOUS
EXTEMPORARILY
EXTENSIBILITY
EXTENSIVENESS
EXTERMINATION
EXTERMINATORY
EXTERRITORIAL
EXTRAJUDICIAL
EXTRAOFFICIAL
EXTRAORDINARY
EXTRATROPICAL
EXTRAVAGANTLY
EXTRAVASATION
EXTRINSICALLY

F

FACETIOUSNESS
FALSIFICATION
FANTASTICALLY
FARINACEOUSLY
FAULTLESSNESS
FEATHERWEIGHT
FEROCIOUSNESS
FERTILIZATION
FILIBUSTERISM
FLASHINGPOINT
FLESHCOLOURED
FLOCCILLATION
FLORICULTURAL
FOOLHARDINESS
FORAMINIFERAL
FOREKNOWLEDGE
FOREMENTIONED
FORGETFULNESS
FORMULIZATION
FORTIFICATION
FOSSILIFEROUS
FOSSILIZATION
FRACTIOUSNESS
FREQUENTATIVE
FRIGHTFULNESS
FRIVOLOUSNESS
FRUMENTACEOUS
FUNAMBULATION
FUNDAMENTALLY

G

GALVANIZATION
GALVANOPLASTY
GASTEROPODOUS
GASTROCNEMIUS
GENERALISSIMO
GENTLEMANLIKE
GEOMETRICALLY
GESTICULATION
GESTICULATORY
GLORIFICATION
GLOSSOGRAPHER
GLOSSOLOGICAL
GOODNATUREDLY
GRACELESSNESS
GRAMINIVOROUS

GRAMMATICALLY
GRANDILOQUENT
GRANDMOTHERLY
GRAPPLINGIRON
GRATICULATION
GRATIFICATION
GROSSULACEOUS
GROTESQUENESS
GUBERNATORIAL
GUILTLESSNESS
GYMNASTICALLY
GYMNOSPERMOUS

H

HAEMAGLOBULIN
HAIRSPLITTING
HALLUCINATION
HALLUCINATORY
HARBOURMASTER
HARMONIZATION
HEALTHFULNESS
HEARTBREAKING
HEARTLESSNESS
HELMINTHOLOGY
HEMIMETABOLIC
HEMISPHERICAL
HERMAPHRODISM
HERMAPHRODITE
HERMENEUTICAL
HERPETOLOGIST
HETEROCARPOUS
HETERODACTYLE
HETEROGENEITY
HETEROGENEOUS
HETEROGENESIS
HETEROMORPHIC
HETEROPLASTIC
HETEROPTEROUS
HIEROGLYPHIST
HOLOMETABOLIC
HOMOEOPATHIST
HORIZONTALITY
HORRIPILATION
HORTICULTURAL
HOUSEBREAKING
HUNDREDWEIGHT
HYDROCEPHALUS
HYDRODYNAMICS
HYDROKINETICS
HYDROMETRICAL
HYMENOPTEROUS
HYPERCRITICAL
HYPERMETROPIA
HYPOCHONDRIAC
HYPOCONDRIUM
HYPOPHOSPHITE
HYPOTHECATION
HYSTERANTHOUS

I

IATROCHEMICAL
ICHTHYOLOGIST
IDEOGRAPHICAL
IDIOMATICALLY
IDIOSYNCRATIC
IGNOMINIOUSLY

ILLEGIBLENESS
ILLUSTRIOUSLY
IMMATERIALISM
IMMATERIALISTS
IMMATERIALITSY
IMMOVABLENES
IMMUTABLENES
IMPARIPINNATE
IMPARTIBILITY
IMPASSIBILITY
IMPASSIONABLE
IMPASSIVENESS
IMPECCABILITY
IMPECUNIOSITY
IMPERFECTNESS
IMPERIOUSNESS
IMPERSONALITY
IMPERSONATION
IMPERTINENTLY
IMPERTURBABLE
IMPETUOUSNESS
IMPLACABILITY
IMPORTUNATELY
IMPOSSIBILITY
IMPRACTICABLE
IMPRACTICABLY
IMPRESSIONIST
IMPRESSIONISM
IMPROBABILITY
IMPROPRIATION
IMPROVABILITY
IMPROVIDENTLY
IMPROVISATION
IMPROVISATORY
INADVERTENTLY
INAPPRECIABLE
INAPPROPRIATE
INATTENTIVELY
INCANDESCENCE
INCARCERATION
INCOGNOSCIBLE
INCOMBUSTIBLE
INCOMPETENTLY
INCONCEIVABLE
INCONCEIVABLY
INCONDENSABLE
INCONGRUOUSLY
INCONSEQUENCE
INCONSIDERATE
INCONSISTENCE
INCONSISTENCY
INCONSPICUOUS
INCONTESTABLE
INCONTESTABLY
INCONTINENTLY
INCONVENIENCE
INCONVERTIBLE
INCONVINCIBLE
INCORPORATION
INCORPOREALLY
INCORRECTNESS
INCORRUPTIBLE
INCORRUPTIBLY
INCREDIBILITY
INCREDULOUSLY
INCURABLENESS
INDEFATIGABLE
INDEFATIGABLY
INDEPENDENTLY
INDESCRIBABLE

INDETERMINATE
INDIFFERENTLY
INDISPENSABLE
INDISPENSABLY
INDISPOSITION
INDISSOCIABLE
INDISSOLVABLE
INDIVIDUALISM
INDIVIDUALITY
INDIVIDUALIZE
INDIVIDUATION
INDUSTRIALISM
INDUSTRIOUSLY
INEFFECTIVELY
INEFFECTUALLY
INEFFICACIOUS
INEFFICIENTLY
INELIGIBILITY
INEXHAUSTIBLE
INEXHAUSTIBLY
INEXPEDIENTLY
INEXPENSIVELY
INEXPERIENCED
INEXPRESSIBLE
INEXPRESSIBLY
INFALLIBILISM
INFALLIBILIST
INFERENTIALLY
INFINITESIMAL
INFLEXIBILITY
INFLORESCENCE
INFLUENTIALLY
INFUNDIBULATE
INGENIOUSNESS
INHOSPITALITY
INJUDICIOUSLY
INOBSERVANTLY
INOFFENSIVELY
INOPPORTUNELY
INQUISITIONAL
INQUISITIVELY
INQUISITORIAL
INSATIABILITY
INSECTIVOROUS
INSENSIBILITY
INSIDIOUSNESS
INSIGNIFICANT
INSINUATINGLY
INSPECTORSHIP
INSTANTANEOUS
INSTINCTIVELY
INSTITUTIONAL
INSTRUCTIVELY
INSUBORDINATE
INSUFFICIENCY
INSUPPORTABLE
INSUPPORTABLY
INSUSCEPTIBLE
INTANGIBILITY
INTEGUMENTARY
INTELLIGENCER
INTELLIGENTLY
INTEMPERATELY
INTENSIVENESS
INTENTIONALLY
INTERCALATION
INTERCELLULAR
INTERCOLONIAL
INTERDIGITATE
INTERESTINGLY

INTERLACEMENT
INTERLINEARLY
INTERLOCUTION
INTERLOCUTORY
INTERMARRIAGE
INTERMEDIATOR
INTERMITTANCE
INTERMUSCULAR
INTERNATIONAL
INTEROSCULATE
INTERPETIOLAR
INTERPOLATION
INTERPOSITION
INTERPRETABLE
INTERRELATION
INTERROGATION
INTERROGATIVE
INTERROGATORY
INTERRUPTEDLY
INTERSIDEREAL
INTERSPERSION
INTERSTELLARY
INTERSTRATIFY
INTERTROPICAL
INTRAPARIETAL
INTRATROPICAL
INTRINSICALLY
INTROSPECTION
INTROSPECTIVE
INTRUSIVENESS
INVENTORIALLY
INVESTIGATION
INVESTIGATIVE
INVIDIOUSNESS
INVINCIBILITY
INVIOLABILITY
INVISIBLENESS
INVOLUNTARILY
IRASCIBLENESS
IRRATIONALITY
IRRECLAIMABLE
IRRECOVERABLE
IRRECOVERABLY
IRRELIGIOUSLY
IRREPRESSIBLE
IRREPRESSIBLY
IRRESPONSIBLE
IRRESPONSIBLY
IRRETRIEVABLE
IRRETRIEVABLY

J

JOLLIFICATION
JUDICIOUSNESS
JURISPRUDENCE
JUSTIFICATION
JUSTIFICATIVE
JUSTIFICATORY

K

KALEIDOSCOPIC

L

LABYRINTHODOM

LACKADAISICAL
LANGUISHINGLY
LARYNGOSCOPIC
LAUGHABLENESS
LECHEROUSNESS
LEPIDODENDRON
LEPIDOPTEROUS
LETHARGICALLY
LEUCOCYTHEMIA
LEXICOGRAPHER
LEXICOGRAPHIC
LIBRARIANSHIP
LICHENOGRAPHY
LICKERISHNESS
LIGHTSOMENESS
LIGNIFICATION
LIPOGRAMMATIC
LITHOFRACTEUR
LITHOGLYPHICS
LITIGIOUSNESS
LOATHSOMENESS
LOGARITHMICAL
LUDICROUSNESS
LUXURIOUSNESS
LYENCEPHALOUS

M

MACHICOLATION
MAGISTERIALLY
MAGNANIMOUSLY
MAGNETIZATION
MAGNIFICENTLY
MAGNILOQUENCE
MALACOSTRACAN
MALICIOUSNESS
MALLEABLENESS
MANIFESTATION
MANUFACTURING
MARSIPOBRANCH
MARTYROLOGIST
MASCULINENESS
MATERFAMILIAS
MATERIALISTIC
MATHEMATICIAN
MATRICULATION
MATRIMONIALLY
MEDIATORIALLY
MEDITERRANEAN
MEGACEPHALOUS
MELLIFLUENTLY
MELLIFLUOUSLY
MELODIOUSNESS
MELODRAMATIST
MEMBRANACEOUS
MENSURABILITY
MERCENARINESS
MERCILESSNESS
MERITORIOUSLY
MESENCEPHALON
MESOCEPHALOUS
METALLIFEROUS
METAMORPHOSIS
METAPHYSICIAN
METEMPIRICISM
METEOROLOGIST
METHODISTICAL
METONYMICALLY
MICROMETRICAL

MICROSCOPICAL
MINERALOGICAL
MINISTERIALLY
MISADVERTENCE
MISCEGENATION
MISCELLANEOUS
MISCHIEVOUSLY
MISCONCEPTION
MISERABLENESS
MISGOVERNMENT
MISMANAGEMENT
MISUNDERSTAND
MODERATORSHIP
MOHAMMEDANISM
MOHAMMEDANIZE
MOLLIFICATION
MOMENTARINESS
MOMENTOUSNESS
MONARCHICALLY
MONOCHROMATIC
MONOCOTYLEDON
MONOGRAMMATIC
MONOGRAPHICAL
MONOMETALLISM
MONOMETALLIST
MONOTHALAMOUS
MONOTREMATOUS
MONSTROUSNESS
MORPHINOMANIA
MORTIFICATION
MOUNTAINOUSLY
MULTANGULARLY
MULTICAPSULAR
MULTIPLICATOR
MULTIPRESENCE
MULTISYLLABLE
MULTITUDINOUS
MUMMIFICATION
MYSTIFICATION

N

NECESSITARIAN
NECESSITOUSLY
NEGOTIABILITY
NEIGHBOURHOOD
NICKELIFEROUS
NIGGARDLINESS
NOISELESSNESS
NONCONFORMING
NONCONFORMIST
NONCONFORMITY
NONSENSICALLY
NOTORIOUSNESS
NULLIFICATION

O

OBJECTIONABLE
OBJECTIONABLY
OBJECTIVENESS
OBLIVIOUSNESS
OBNOXIOUSNESS
OBSERVATIONAL
OBSTINATENESS
OBSTRUCTIVELY
OCCIDENTALIZE

ODONTOGLOSSUM
ODORIFEROUSLY
OFFENSIVENESS
OFFICIOUSNESS
OPERASBOUFFES
OPHIOMORPHOUS
OPHTHALMOLOGY
OPHTHALMOTOMY
OPPORTUNENESS
OPPOSITIONIST
OPPROBRIOUSLY
ORCHESTRATION
ORGANOGENESIS
ORGANOLOGICAL
ORNAMENTATION
ORNITHICHNITE
ORNITHOLOGIST
ORTHOEPICALLY
ORTHOGNATHOUS
OSTENSIBILITY
OSTREACULTURE
OUTSETTLEMENT
OVERFLOWINGLY
OVERSTATEMENT
OVERVALUATION
OVOVIVIPAROUS

P

PALAEOCRYSTIC
PALAEOGRAPHIC
PALAEONTOLOGY
PALAEOTHERIUM
PALAEOZOOLOGY
PALATABLENESS
PANDICULATION
PANEGYRICALLY
PANSPERMATISM
PANTHEISTICAL
PAPAVERACEOUS
PARABOLICALLY
PARADOXICALLY
PARAGRAPHICAL
PARALLELOGRAM
PARAPHERNALIA
PARASITICALLY
PARENTHETICAL
PARLIAMENTARY
PARTICIPATION
PARTICIPIALLY
PARTICOLOURED
PARTICULARISM
PARTICULARIST
PARTICULARITY
PARTICULARIZE
PATERFAMILIAS
PATHOGNOMONIC
PATRIMONIALLY
PATRIOTICALLY
PATRONIZINGLY
PEACEABLENESS
PEDESTRIANISM
PENDULOUSNESS
PENETRABILITY
PENETRATINGLY
PENITENTIALLY
PENNILESSNESS
PENTADELPHOUS
PENTAPETALOUS

PENTAPHYLLOUS
PENTASTICHOUS
PENURIOUSNESS
PERAMBULATION
PEREGRINATION
PERFECTIONISM
PERFECTIONIST
PERFUNCTORILY
PERICHONDRIUM
PERIPATETICAL
PERISHABILITY
PERPENDICULAR
PERSCRUTATION
PERSEVERINGLY
PERSONALITIES
PERSPECTIVELY
PERSPICACIOUS
PERSPICUOUSLY
PESTIFEROUSLY
PHANEROGAMOUS
PHARISAICALLY
PHARMACEUTICS
PHARMACEUTIST
PHARMACOPOEIA
PHENOMENALISM
PHILANTHROPIC
PHILHELLENISM
PHILOMATHICAL
PHILOSOPHICAL
PHILOSOPHIZER
PHONAUTOGRAPH
PHONOGRAPHIST
PHOSPHURETTED
PHOTOMETRICAL
PHRASEOLOGIST
PHRENOLOGICAL
PHYLACTERICAL
PHYLACTERICAL
PHYLLOPHAGOUS
PHYSIOGNOMIST
PHYSIOLOGICAL
PICTURESQUELY
PISCICULTURAL
PLAINTIVENESS
PLATITUDINOUS
PLATYCEPHALIC
PLAUSIBLENESS
PLECTOGNATHIC
PLENTEOUSNESS
PLETHORICALLY
PLURALIZATION
PNEUMATICALLY
PNEUMATOMETER
PNEUMOGASTRIC
POCOCURANTISM
POISONOUSNESS
POLLINIFEROUS
POLYCHROMATIC
POLYCOTYLEDON
POLYDACTYLISM
POLYSYNTHETIC
POLYTHALAMOUS
PONDERABILITY
PONDEROUSNESS
PORCELLANEOUS
PORPHYRACEOUS
POSSESSIONARY
POWERLESSNESS
PRACTICALNESS
PRAGMATICALLY

PRAYERFULNESS
PRECAUTIONARY
PRECENTORSHIP
PRECIPITANTLY
PRECIPITATELY
PRECIPITATION
PRECIPITOUSLY
PRECONCEPTION
PREDESTINATOR
PREDICABILITY
PREDICAMENTAL
PREDICATIVELY
PREDOMINANTLY
PREFIGURATION
PREFIGUREMENT
PREJUDICATION
PREJUDICIALLY
PRELIMINARILY
PREMATURENESS
PREMEDITATION
PREOCCUPATION
PREORDINATION
PREPARATIVELY
PREPONDERANCE
PREPOSITIONAL
PREPOSSESSING
PREPOSSESSION
PRESBYTERSHIP
PRESCIENTIFIC
PRESCRIPTIBLE
PRESIDENTSHIP
PRESSIROSTRAL
PRESUMPTIVELY
PRETENTIOUSLY
PRETERMISSION
PRETERNATURAL
PRETERPERFECT
PREVARICATION
PRIMITIVENESS
PRIMOGENITURE
PRISMATICALLY
PRIVATEERSMAN
PROBABILITIES
PROBLEMATICAL
PROCONSULSHIP
PROCRASTINATE
PROFESSORIATE
PROGNOSTICATE
PROGRESSIONAL
PROGRESSIVELY
PROLEPTICALLY
PROMISCUOUSLY
PRONOUNCEABLE
PRONOUNCEMENT
PRONUNCIATION
PROPAEDEUTICS
PROPHETICALLY
PROPORTIONATE
PROPOSITIONAL
PROPRIETORIAL
PROSPECTIVELY
PROTECTIONISM
PROTECTIONIST
PROTECTORSHIP
PROTERANDROUS
PROTEROGYNOUS
PROTESTANTISM
PROTESTANTIZE
PROVERBIALIST
PROVINCIALISM

PROVISIONALLY
PSYCHOLOGICAL
PULMONIFEROUS
PULVERIZATION
PUNCTILIOUSLY
PURITANICALLY
PUSILLANIMITY
PUSILLANIMOUS
PYRHELIOMETER
PYROTECHNICAL

Q

QUADRAGESIMAL
QUADRIFOLIATE
QUADRILATERAL
QUADRILITERAL
QUADRILOCULAR
QUADRIPARTITE
QUADRUPLICATE
QUALIFICATION
QUALIFICATIVE
QUALITATIVELY
QUERULOUSNESS
QUINCENTENARY
QUINQUAGESIMA
QUINQUANGULAR

R

RAPACIOUSNESS
RATIOCINATION
RATIOCINATIVE
RATIOCINATORY
RATIONALISTIC
READJOURNMENT
REALISTICALLY
REAPPOINTMENT
REARRANGEMENT
RECEIVABILITY
RECIPROCATION
RECOMMENDABLE
RECONCILEMENT
RECRIMINATION
RECRIMINATIVE
RECRIMINATORY
RECRUDESCENCE
RECRUDESCENCY
RECTANGULARLY
RECTIFICATION
RECTILINEALLY
REDUPLICATION
REFLEXIBILITY
REFRIGERATION
REFRIGERATIVE
REFRIGERATORY
REGISTRARSHIP
REGURGITATION
REIMBURSEMENT
REIMPORTATION
REINFORCEMENT
REINSTATEMENT
REINTERROGATE
REINVESTIGATE
REJUVENESCENT
RELIGIOUSNESS
REMISSIBILITY
REMONSTRATIVE

REMONSTRATORY
REMORSELESSLY
REPLENISHMENT
REPREHENSIBLE
REPREHENSIBLY
REPRESENTABLE
REPROACHFULLY
REPROBATENESS
REPUBLICATION
REPULSIVENESS
RESISTIBILITY
RESOLVABILITY
RESPIRABILITY
RESPIRATIONAL
RESPLENDENTLY
RESTRICTIVELY
RESUSCITATION
RETENTIVENESS
RETROGRESSION
RETROGRESSIVE
RETROSPECTION
RETROSPECTIVE
REVERBERATION
REVERBERATORY
REVERENTIALLY
REVERSIBILITY
REVOLUTIONARY
REVOLUTIONISM
REVOLUTIONIST
REVOLUTIONIZE
RHAPSODICALLY
RHIZOMORPHOUS
RHOPALOCEROUS
RIGHTEOUSNESS
RUSSOPHOBISTS

S

SACCHAROMETER
SACCHARIMETER
SACERDOTALISM
SACRAMENTALLY
SACROSANCTIFY
SAGACIOUSNESS
SALACIOUSNESS
SANCTIMONIOUS
SARCASTICALLY
SCARIFICATION
SCEPTICALNESS
SCHIZOMYCETES
SCHOLASTICISM
SCINTILLATION
SCRIPTURALISM
SCRIPTURALIST
SCULPTURESQUE
SECONDARINESS
SECRETARYSHIP
SECRETIVENESS
SEDENTARINESS
SEDIMENTATION
SEDITIOUSNESS
SEISMOGRAPHIC
SENESCHALSHIP
SENSELESSNESS
SENSITIVENESS
SENTENTIOUSLY
SENTIMENTALLY
SEPARABLENESS
SEPTISYLLABLE

SEPTUAGESIMAL
SEQUESTRATION
SESQUILATERAL
SHAMELESSNESS
SHAPELESSNESS
SIGHTLESSNESS
SIGILLOGRAPHY
SIGNIFICANTLY
SIGNIFICATION
SIGNIFICATIVE
SIGNIFICATORY
SINGULARITIES
SOLEMNIZATION
SOLICITORSHIP
SOLIDUNGULATE
SOMNAMBULATOR
SOMNILOQUENCE
SOPHISTICALLY
SOPHISTICATOR
SORROWFULNESS
SPASMODICALLY
SPECIFICATION
SPECTROSCOPIC
SPECULATIVELY
SPERMATORRHEA
SPLANCHNOLOGY
SPLENETICALLY
SPONTANEOUSLY
SPORTSMANSHIP
SPRIGHTLINESS
SQUEAMISHNESS
SQUEEZABILITY
STALACTITICAL
STALAGMITICAL
STALWORTHNESS
STAMINIFEROUS
STAPHYLORAPHY
STATESMANLIKE
STATESMANSHIP
STATISTICALLY
STEADFASTNESS
STEGANOGRAPHY
STENOGRAPHIST
STERCORACEOUS
STEREOGRAPHIC
STETHOSCOPIST
STOLONIFEROUS
STRANGULATION
STRATEGETICAL
STRATEGICALLY
STRATIGRAPHIC
STRENGTHENING
STRUCTURELESS
SUBDEACONSHIP
SUBORDINATELY
SUBORDINATION
SUBORDINATIVE
SUBPERITONEAL
SUBSTANTIALLY
SUBSTANTIVELY
SUBTILIZATION
SUCCESSIONIST
SUFFRAGANSHIP
SUFFUMIGATION
SULPHUREOUSLY
SUPERABUNDANT
SUPERADDITION
SUPERANNUATED
SUPERDOMINANT
SUPEREMINENCE

SUPERFETATION
SUPERFICIALLY
SUPERFLUITIES
SUPERFLUOUSLY
SUPERFORTRESS
SUPERLATIVELY
SUPERPOSITION
SUPERSATURATE
SUPERSENSIBLE
SUPERSTITIOUS
SUPPLANTATION
SUPPLEMENTARY
SUPPOSITIONAL
SUPRASCAPULAR
SURREPTITIOUS
SYLLOGISTICAL
SYMMETRICALLY
SYMPATHETICAL
SYMPIESOMETER
SYMPTOMATICAL
SYNCHRONOUSLY
SYNECDOCHICAL
SYNECPHONESIS
SYNTACTICALLY
SYNTHETICALLY
SYPHILIZATION

T

TALKATIVENESS
TANTALIZATION
TASTELESSNESS
TEACHABLENESS
TELEGRAPHICAL
TEMPERATENESS
TEMPESTUOUSLY
TEMPORALITIES
TEMPORIZATION
TENACIOUSNESS
TERGIVERSATOR
TERMINATIONAL
TERPSICHOREAN
TERRESTRIALLY
TERRITORIALLY
TETRASYLLABLE
THALAMIFLORAL
THANKFULNESS
THAUMATURGIST
THAUMATURGICS
THEANTHROPISM
THEATRICALITY
THEOLOGICALLY
THEORETICALLY
THERIOMORPHIC
THOUGHTLESSLY
THREATENINGLY
TINTINNABULAR
TOLERABLENESS
TOPOGRAPHICAL
TOXICOLOGICAL
TRACKLESSNESS
TRADITIONALLY
TRANQUILLIZER
TRANSATLANTIC
TRANSCENDENCE
TRANSCENDENCY
TRANSCRIPTION
TRANSCRIPTIVE
TRANSGRESSION

TRANSIENTNESS
TRANSITIONARY
TRANSLUCENTLY
TRANSMIGRATOR
TRANSMISSIBLE
TRANSMITTABLE
TRANSMITTANCE
TRANSMUTATION
TRANSPARENTLY
TRANSPIRATION
TRANSPORTABLE
TRANSPOSITION
TRANSPOSITIVE
TRANSVERSALLY
TREMULOUSNESS
TRIANGULARITY
TRIANGULATION
TRIPINNATIFID
TROUBLESOMELY
TYPOGRAPHICAL

U

UMBELLIFEROUS
UMBRACULIFORM
UNACCOMPANIED
UNACCOUNTABLE
UNAPOSTOLICAL
UNAPPRECIATED
UNASSIMILATED
UNCERTAINTIES
UNCOMFORTABLE
UNCOMFORTABLY
UNCOMPLAINING
UNCONDITIONAL
UNCONDITIONED
UNCONFORMABLE
UNCONFORMABLY
UNCONQUERABLE
UNCONQUERABLY
UNDERCLOTHING
UNDERGRADUATE
UNDERESTIMATE
UNDERSTANDING
UNDERSTRAPPER
UNDISCERNIBLE
UNDISCIPLINED
UNDISSOLVABLE
UNDISTURBEDLY
UNDIVERSIFIED
UNEMBARRASSED
UNENLIGHTENED
UNFAMILIARITY
UNFASHIONABLE
UNFASHIONABLY
UNFORTUNATELY
UNGRAMMATICAL
UNGUARDEDNESS
UNIMPASSIONED
UNIMPEACHABLE
UNIMPRESSIBLE
UNINHABITABLE
UNINSTRUCTIVE
UNINTERESTING
UNINTERMITTED
UNINTERRUPTED
UNJUSTIFIABLE
UNJUSTIFIABLY
UNMENTIONABLE

UNMINDFULNESS
UNNECESSARILY
UNNEIGHBOURLY
UNOBTRUSIVELY
UNPERCEIVABLE
UNPHILOSOPHIC
UNPRECEDENTED
UNPRESENTABLE
UNRECOMPENSED
UNREPRESENTED
UNRIGHTEOUSLY
UNSAVOURINESS
UNSERVICEABLE
UNSIGHTLINESS
UNSKILFULNESS
UNSUBSTANTIAL
UNSURPASSABLE
UNSUSCEPTIBLE
UNSYMMETRICAL
UNTHRIFTINESS
UNTRUSTWORTHY
UNWARRANTABLE
UNWARRANTABLY
UNWILLINGNESS
UNWORKMANLIKE
UNWORLDLINESS

V

VEGETARIANISM
VENERABLENESS
VENTRILOQUIAL
VENTRILOQUISM
VENTRILOQUIST
VENTRILOQUIZE
VENTRILOQUOUS
VERMICULATION
VERNACULARISM
VERSICOLOURED
VERSIFICATION
VEXATIOUSNESS
VIOLONCELLIST
VISIONARINESS
VITRIFICATION
VIVACIOUSNESS
VOLATILIZABLE
VOLUMENOMETER
VOLUNTARINESS
VORACIOUSNESS
VULCANIZATION
VULNERABILITY

W

WEARISOMENESS
WHITHERSOEVER
WHOLESOMENESS
WONDERFULNESS
WORTHLESSNESS

X

XEROPHTHALMIA
XYLOGRAPHICAL

Y

YACHTSMANSHIP
YELLOWISHNESS

Z

ZYGODACTYLOUS

FOURTEEN-LETTER WORDS

A

ABOMINABLENESS
ABSTEMIOUSNESS
ABSTRACTEDNESS
ACCEPTABLENESS
ACCOMPLISHABLE
ACCOMPLISHMENT
ACCOUNTABILITY
ACCOUNTANTSHIP
ACKNOWLEDGMENT
ADMINISTRATION
ADMINISTRATIVE
ADSCITITIOUSLY
ADVANTAGEOUSLY
ADVENTITIOUSLY
AFFECTIONATELY
AFOREMENTIONED
AGGRANDIZEMENT
AGGRESSIVENESS
ALPHABETICALLY
AMPHIBOLOGICAL
ANAGRAMMATICAL
ANTAPHRODISIAC
ANTHROPOGRAPHY
ANTIPHLOGISTIC
ANTIQUARIANISM
ANTISCRIPTURAL
ANTISYPHILITIC
ANTITHETICALLY
APHELIOTROPISM
APHORISTICALLY
APOLOGETICALLY
APOPHTHEGMATIC
APPREHENSIVELY
APPRENTICESHIP
ARBORICULTURAL
ARCHAEOLOGICAL
ARCHDEACONSHIP
ARCHIEPISCOPAL
ARITHMETICALLY
ASTROLOGICALLY
ASTRONOMICALLY
ATTAINABLENESS
ATTRACTIVENESS
AUGMENTATIVELY
AURORA BOREALIS
AUSPICIOUSNESS
AUTHENTICATION
AUTOBIOGRAPHER
AUTOBIOGRAPHIC

B

BACTERIOLOGIST
BAROMETRICALLY
BATHING-MACHINE
BEAUTIFICATION
BELIEVABLENESS
BILLIARD-MARKER
BIOGRAPHICALLY
BIRD-OF-PARADISE
BITUMINIFEROUS

BLANK-CARTRIDGE
BLITHESOMENESS
BOA-CONSTRICTOR
BOARDING-SCHOOL
BOISTEROUSNESS
BOROUGH-ENGLISH
BOULEVERSEMENT
BRACHYCEPHALIC
BRANCHIOSTEGAL
BREADFRUIT-TREE
BREATHLESSNESS
BRIGHT'S-DISEASE
BRISTOL-DIAMOND
BRITANNIA-METAL
BROBDINGNAGIAN
BRUSSELS-CARPET

C

CABINET-COUNCIL
CALAMANDER-WOOD
CALCOGRAPHICAL
CALICO-PRINTING
CAPITALIZATION
CAPRICIOUSNESS
CAPTAIN-GENERAL
CARDINAL-FLOWER
CARLINE-THISTLE
CARTRIDGE-PAPER
CASTLE-BUILDING
CASTRAMETATION
CATADIOPTRICAL
CATECHETICALLY
CATHERINE-WHEEL
CENSORIOUSNESS
CENSURABLENESS
CENTRALIZATION
CHALCOGRAPHIST
CHAMBER-COUNSEL
CHANCELLORSHIP
CHANGEABLENESS
CHARACTERISTIC
CHARGEABLENESS
CHARITABLENESS
CHICKEN-HEARTED
CHIMNEY-SWALLOW
CHOROGRAPHICAL
CIRCUITOUSNESS
CIRCUMAMBIENCY
CIRCUMAMBULATE
CIRCUMFERENTOR
CIRCUMGYRATION
CIRCUMLITTORAL
CIRCUMLOCUTION
CIRCUMLOCUTORY
CIRCUMNAVIGATE
CIRCUMNUTATION
CIRCUMSPECTION
CIRCUMSTANTIAL
CIRCUMVOLUTION
CLASSIFICATION
COESSENTIALITY
COGNOSCIBILITY
COLORADO BEETLE

COLOURABLENESS
COLOUR-SERGEANT
COMMENSURATELY
COMMENSURATION
COMMENTATORIAL
COMMISSARYSHIP
COMMODIOUSNESS
COMPOSING-STICK
COMPREHENSIBLE
COMPREHENSIBLY
CONCAVO-CONCAVE
CONCEIVABILITY
CONCENTRICALLY
CONCESSIONAIRE
CONCLUSIVENESS
CONDENSABILITY
CONDITIONALITY
CONFIDENTIALLY
CONGLOMERATION
CONGLUTINATION
CONGLUTINATIVE
CONGRATULATION
CONGRATULATORY
CONGREGATIONAL
CONSANGUINEOUS
CONSCRIPTIONAL
CONSTITUTIONAL
CONSTITUTIVELY
CONSTRUCTIONAL
CONSTRUCTIVELY
CONSUBSTANTIAL
CONSUETUDINARY
CONTAGIOUSNESS
CONTEMPTUOUSLY
CONTIGUOUSNESS
CONTINENTALIST
CONTINENTALISM
CONTINUOUSNESS
CONTRACTEDNESS
CONTRADICTABLE
CONTRADICTIOUS
CONTRAINDICATE
CONTRAPOSITION
CONTROLLERSHIP
CONTROVERTIBLE
CONTROVERTIBLY
CONTUMACIOUSLY
CONTUMELIOUSLY
CONVALESCENTLY
CONVENTIONALLY
CONVERSATIONAL
CONVERTIBILITY
CONVEXO-CONCAVE
CO-ORDINATENESS
COPPER-BOTTOMED
COPPER-FASTENED
CORNET-A-PISTONS
COROLLIFLOROUS
CORRESPONDENCE
CORRESPONDENCY
CORRUPTIBILITY
COSMOPOLITICAL
COTEMPORANEOUS
COUNSELLORSHIP
COUNTERBALANCE

COURAGEOUSNESS
CREDITABLENESS
CROSSREFERENCE
CRYSTALLIZABLE
CRYSTALLOMANCY
CUCURBITACEOUS
CURTAINLECTURE

D

DACTYLIOGLYPHY
DECEIVABLENESS
DECHRISTIANIZE
DECOLORIZATION
DECONSECRATION
DECORATIVENESS
DEFINITIVENESS
DEGENERATENESS
DELIBERATENESS
DELIGHTFULNESS
DEMOBILISATION
DEMOCRATICALLY
DEMONETIZATION
DEMORALIZATION
DENOMINATIONAL
DENOMINATIVELY
DEPLORABLENESS
DEPOLARIZATION
DEROGATORINESS
DESCENDIBILITY
DESPICABLENESS
DESPITEFULNESS
DESTRUCTIONIST
DETESTABLENESS
DIABOLICALNESS
DIAHELIOTROPIC
DICOTYLEDONOUS
DIFFUSIBLENESS
DIGESTIBLENESS
DIMINUTIVENESS
DIPHTHONGATION
DIPLOMATICALLY
DISAGGREGATION
DISAPPOINTEDLY
DISAPPOINTMENT
DISAPPROPRIATE
DISAPPROVINGLY
DISARRANGEMENT
DISCIPLINARIAN
DISCONSOLATELY
DISCONTENTEDLY
DISCONTENTMENT
DISCONTINUANCE
DISCOUNTENANCE
DISCOURAGEMENT
DISCOURAGINGLY
DISCOURTEOUSLY
DISCRETIONALLY
DISCRIMINATELY
DISCRIMINATING
DISCRIMINATION
DISCRIMINATIVE
DISCURSIVENESS
DISDAINFULNESS
DISEMBARKATION
DISEMBOGUEMENT
DISEMBOWELMENT
DISENCHANTMENT
DISENCHANTRESS

DISENCUMBRANCE
DISENGAGEDNESS
DISENTHRALMENT
DISGUSTFULNESS
DISILLUSIONIZE
DISINCLINATION
DISINCORPORATE
DISINGENUOUSLY
DISINHERITANCE
DISINTEGRATION
DISINVESTITURE
DISJOINTEDNESS
DISORDERLINESS
DISQUISITIONAL
DISRESPECTABLE
DISSERTATIONAL
DISTEMPERATURE
DISTENSIBILITY
DISTINGUISHING
DISTRACTEDNESS
DISTRIBUTIVELY
DIVERTISSEMENT
DODECASYLLABLE
DOUBLEBREASTED

E

ECCLESIASTICAL
ECCLESIOLOGIST
EDUCATIONALIST
EFFEMINATENESS
ELECTIONEERING
ELECTROBIOLOGY
ELECTRODYNAMIC
ELECTROKINETIC
ELECTROLYTICAL
ELEMENTARINESS
ELEUTHEROMANIA
EMBLEMATICALLY
EMPYREUMATICAL
ENCYCLOPAEDIST
ENHARMONICALLY
ENTERPRISINGLY
ENTHRONIZATION
ENTHUSIASTICAL
ENTOPERIPHERAL
EPIGRAMMATICAL
EQUIPONDERANCE
ETHNOGRAPHICAL
ETYMOLOGICALLY
EULOGISTICALLY
EVANGELICALISM
EVANGELIZATION
EXCOMMUNICABLE
EXCREMENTITIAL
EXCRUCIATINGLY
EXPERIMENTALLY
EXPRESSIONLESS
EXPRESSIVENESS
EXTEMPORANEOUS
EXTINGUISHABLE
EXTINGUISHMENT
EXTORTIONATELY
EXTRAPAROCHIAL
EXTRINSICALITY

F

FAINTHEARTEDLY
FALLACIOUSNESS
FANTASTICALITY
FARSIGHTEDNESS
FASTIDIOUSNESS
FAVOURABLENESS
FELLOWCOMMONER
FELLOWCREATURE
FIBROCARTILAGE
FIGURATIVENESS
FLAGITIOUSNESS
FLORICULTURIST
FORAMINIFEROUS
FOREORDINATION
FORISFAMILIATE
FORMIDABLENESS
FORTUITOUSNESS
FRATERNIZATION
FREESPOKENNESS
FRIENDLESSNESS
FRINGILLACEOUS
FROLICSOMENESS
FRUCTIFICATION

G

GASTROVASCULAR
GENEALOGICALLY
GENERALIZATION
GEOCENTRICALLY
GEOGRAPHICALLY
GOODHUMOUREDLY
GRANDILOQUENCE
GREGARIOUSNESS
GROUNDLESSNESS
GUILLOTINEMENT
GYRENCEPHALATE

H

HANDICRAFTSMEN
HARMONIOUSNESS
HELMINTHAGOGUE
HEMISPHEROIDAL
HERESIOGRAPHER
HERMAPHRODITIC
HETEROCLITICAL
HETEROMORPHOUS
HETEROPHYLLOUS
HIEROGLYPHICAL
HIPPOPOTAMUSES
HISTRIONICALLY
HONOURABLENESS
HORTICULTURIST
HYDROGRAPHICAL
HYPERAESTHESIA
HYPERBOLICALLY
HYPERCRITICISM
HYPOCRITICALLY
HYPOSTATICALLY
HYPOTHETICALLY

I

ICHNOLITHOLOGY
ICHTHYOLOGICAL
ICHTHYOPHAGOUS
ICHTHYOPHAGIST
IDENTIFICATION
IDIOPATHICALLY
ILLEGITIMATELY
ILLUSTRATIVELY
IMPARIDIGITATE
IMPASSABLENESS
IMPERVIOUSNESS
IMPLACABLENESS
IMPOVERISHMENT
IMPRESSIBILITY
IMPRESSIONABLE
IMPRESSIVENESS
IMPROVABLENESS
IMPROVISATRICE
INALIENABILITY
INAPPREHENSION
INAPPROACHABLE
INARTICULATELY
INARTIFICIALLY
INAUSPICIOUSLY
INCAPACITATION
INCAUTIOUSNESS
INCOMMENSURATE
INCOMMUNICABLE
INCOMPRESSIBLE
INCONCLUSIVELY
INCONSIDERABLE
INCONSIDERABLY
INCONSISTENTLY
INCONVENIENTLY
INCORPOREALITY
INDECIPHERABLE
INDECOMPOSABLE
INDECOROUSNESS
INDEFINITENESS
INDESTRUCTIBLE
INDESTRUCTIBLY
INDETERMINABLE
INDIFFERENTISM
INDISCREETNESS
INDISCRIMINATE
INDISPOSEDNESS
INDISTINCTNESS
INDIVISIBILITY
INDOCTRINATION
INEXPRESSIBLES
INFECTIOUSNESS
INFLEXIBLENESS
INHARMONIOUSLY
INORDINATENESS
INQUISITIONARY
INSATIABLENESS
INSEPARABILITY
INSIGNIFICANCE
INSIGNIFICANCY
INSTITUTIONARY
INSTRUMENTALLY
INSUFFICIENTLY
INSUPERABILITY
INSUPPRESSIBLE
INSURMOUNTABLE
INSURRECTIONAL
INTANGIBLENESS

INTELLECTUALLY
INTERCESSIONAL
INTERCOMMUNION
INTERCOMMUNITY
INTERDEPENDENT
INTERJECTIONAL
INTERLINEATION
INTERMAXILLARY
INTERMEDIATELY
INTERMEDIATION
INTERMIGRATION
INTERPELLATION
INTERPENETRATE
INTERPLANETARY
INTERPRETATION
INTERPRETATIVE
INTRACTABILITY
INTRANSITIVELY
INTRANSMUTABLE
INVARIABLENESS
INVINCIBLENESS
INVIOLABLENESS
IRRATIONALNESS
IRRECOGNIZABLE
IRRECONCILABLE
IRRECONCILABLY
IRREMOVABILITY
IRREPARABILITY
IRREPROACHABLE
IRREPROACHABLY
IRRESOLUTENESS
IRRESPECTIVELY

J

JURISDICTIONAL

K

KNICKERBOCKERS

L

LAMELLIROSTRAL
LAPIDIFICATION
LATITUDINARIAN
LEUCOCYTHAEMIA
LIBERTARIANISM
LIBIDINOUSNESS
LICENTIOUSNESS
LIEUTENANTSHIP
LONGITUDINALLY

M

MACADAMIZATION
MACROCEPHALOUS
MAGNILOQUENTLY
MATHEMATICALLY
MENSURABLENESS
MERETRICIOUSLY
METAPHORICALLY
METAPHYSICALLY
METEMPSYCHOSIS
METENSOMATOSIS
METEOROLOGICAL

METROPOLITICAL
METTLESOMENESS
MICROCEPHALOUS
MINERALIZATION
MINISTERIALIST
MIRACULOUSNESS
MISANTHROPICAL
MISAPPLICATION
MISCALCULATION
MISINFORMATION
MISMEASUREMENT
MULTIFARIOUSLY
MULTIPLICATION
MULTIPLACATIVE
MYSTERIOUSNESS
MYTHOLOGICALLY

N

NATURALIZATION
NEUROHYPNOTISM
NEUROHYPNOLOGY
NEUROPATHOLOGY
NEUTRALIZATION

O

OBLIGATORINESS
OBSEQUIOUSNESS
OBSTREPEROUSLY
OBSTRUCTIONIST
OPHTHALMODYNIA
OPHTHALMOSCOPE
OPHTHALMOSCOPY
OPINIONATIVELY
OPISTHOCOELOUS
OPISTHOGRAPHIC
OPPRESSIVENESS
ORNITHODELPHIA
ORNITHODELPHIC
ORNITHOLOGICAL
ORTHOGRAPHICAL
OSTENTATIOUSLY
OUTRAGEOUSNESS
OVERPOWERINGLY

P

PACHYDACTYLOUS
PACHYDERMATOUS
PALAEOGRAPHIST
PAPILIONACEOUS
PARAGRAMMATIST
PARALLELEPIPED
PARALLELOPIPED
PARAPHRASTICAL
PARENCHYMATOUS
PARSIMONIOUSLY
PASSIONATENESS
PATHOLOGICALLY
PENTADACTYLOUS
PERCEPTIBILITY
PERFECTIBILITY
PERFIDIOUSNESS
PERIPATETICISM
PERIPHRASTICAL
PERISHABLENESS

PERISSODACTYLE
PERMISSIBILITY
PERNICIOUSNESS
PERSPIRABILITY
PERSUASIVENESS
PERTINACIOUSLY
PESTILENTIALLY
PHANTASMAGORIC
PHANTASMAGORIA
PHARMACEUTICAL
PHARMACOLOGIST
PHARMACOPOLIST
PHELLOPLASTICS
PHILANTHROPIST
PHONOGRAPHICAL
PHRASEOLOGICAL
PHYSIOGNOMICAL
PHYTOGEOGRAPHY
PHYTOPATHOLOGY
PISCICULTURIST
PLECTOGNATHOUS
PLEONASTICALLY
PLEURAPOPHYSIS
PNEUMATOLOGIST
POLYSYLLABICAL
POLYTHEISTICAL
POPULARIZATION
PRACTICABILITY
PREBENDARYSHIP
PRECARIOUSNESS
PRECOCIOUSNESS
PRECONCERTEDLY
PREDESTINARIAN
PREDESTINATION
PREDETERMINATE
PREFERENTIALLY
PREPONDERATION
PREPOSTEROUSLY
PRESUMPTUOUSLY
PROCRASTINATOR
PROCURATORSHIP
PRODUCTIVENESS
PROFESSIONALLY
PROGNOSTICATOR
PROHIBITIONIST
PROLETARIANISM
PROPAEDEUTICAL
PROPITIATORILY
PROPITIOUSNESS
PROPORTIONABLE
PROPORTIONALLY
PROPRIETORSHIP
PROCENCEPHALON
PROSPEROUSNESS
PROVIDENTIALLY

Q

QUADRAGENARIAN
QUADRIDIGITATE
QUADRIGEMINOUS
QUADRISYLLABLE
QUANTIFICATION
QUANTITATIVELY
QUERIMONIOUSLY
QUINQUEPARTITE

R

RANUNCULACEOUS
REASONABLENESS
RECALCITRATION
RECAPITULATION
RECAPITULATORY
RECEIVABLENESS
RECOMMENDATION
RECOMMENDATORY
RECONCILIATION
RECONSTRUCTION
RECONNAISSANCE
RECTILINEARITY
RECURVIROSTRAL
REDINTEGRATION
REDISTRIBUTION
REFLECTIVENESS
REFRACTORINESS
REGARDLESSNESS
REGENERATENESS
REHABILITATION
REIMPRISONMENT
REINTRODUCTION
REJUVENESCENCE
RELENTLESSNESS
RELINQUISHMENT
REMINISCENTIAL
REMONETIZATION
REMORSEFULNESS
REMUNERABILITY
REORGANISATION
REPREHENSIVELY
REQUISITIONIST
RESISTIBLENESS
RESOLVABLENESS
RESPECTABILITY
RESPIRABLENESS
RESPONSIBILITY
RESPONSIVENESS
RETROGRADATION
REVENGEFULNESS
REVIVIFICATION
ROSICRUCIANISM

S

SABBATARIANISM
SACCHARIFEROUS
SACRAMENTARIAN
SACRILEGIOUSLY
SANCTIFICATION
SANGUINIVOROUS
SATISFACTORILY
SCANDALOUSNESS
SCHOLASTICALLY
SCIENTIFICALLY
SCRUPULOUSNESS
SCURRILOUSNESS
SEASONABLENESS
SECULARIZATION
SENSATIONALISM
SENSATIONALIST
SENTIMENTALISM
SENTIMENTALIST
SENTIMENTALITY
SENTIMENTALIZE
SESQUIPEDALIAN

SESQUIALTERATE
SIMPLIFICATION
SIMULTANEOUSLY
SLATTERNLINESS
SOLIDIFICATION
SOMNAMBULATION
SOMNAMBULISTIC
SOPHISTICATION
SPECIALIZATION
SPECTROSCOPIST
SPEECHLESSNESS
SPHAERISTERIUM
STATIONARINESS
STENOGRAPHICAL
STIGMATIZATION
STRATIFICATION
STUPENDOUSNESS
SUBARBORESCENT
SUBCONSCIOUSLY
SUBINFEUDATION
SUBMISSIVENESS
SUBSTANTIALITY
SUBSTANTIALIZE
SUBSTANTIATION
SUFFERABLENESS
SUPERABUNDANCE
SUPERANNUATION
SUPERCELESTIAL
SUPERCILIOUSLY
SUPEREMINENTLY
SUPEREROGATORY
SUPERFICIALITY
SUPERINCUMBENT
SUPERINTENDENT
SUPERNATURALLY
SUPERSCRIPTION
SUPERSENSITIVE
SUPERPHOSPHATE
SUPERSTRUCTURE
SUPPOSITITIOUS
SUPRAMAXILLARY
SUSCEPTIBILITY
SUSPICIOUSNESS
SYNCHRONICALLY
SYSTEMATICALLY

T

TABULARIZATION
TATTERDEMALION
TAUTOLOGICALLY
TELEOLOGICALLY
TELESCOPICALLY
TERMINOLOGICAL
TETRADACTYLOUS
THOUGHTFULNESS
THRIFTLESSNESS
TINTINNABULARY
TRADITIONALISM
TRANSCENDENTAL
TRANSITORINESS
TRANSMIGRATORY
TRANSVERBERATE
TRIDIMENSIONAL
TRIPERSONALIST
TUMULTUOUSNESS

U

ULTRAMONTANISM
ULTRAMONTANIST
UNACKNOWLEDGED
UNAPPROPRIATED
UNCONSCIONABLE
UNCONSCIONABLY
UNCONTROLLABLE
UNCONTROLLABLY
UNDECOMPOSABLE
UNDERSTATEMENT
UNDISCOVERABLE
UNFAITHFULNESS
UNFRUITFULNESS
UNGRACEFULNESS
UNGRATEFULNESS
UNINCORPORATED
UNINTELLIGIBLE
UNINTELLIGIBLY
UNINTERMITTING
UNIPERSONALIST

UNMERCIFULNESS
UNOSTENTATIOUS
UMPREMEDITATED
UNPREPOSSESSED
UNPRESUMPTUOUS
UNPROSPEROUSLY
UNQUESTIONABLE
UNQUESTIONABLY
UNRECOGNIZABLE
UNRELIABLENESS
UNRESTRAINEDLY
UNSATISFACTORY
UNSCRIPTURALLY
UNSCRUPULOUSLY
UNSOCIABLENESS
UNSUCCESSFULLY
UNSUITABLENESS
UNTRANSLATABLE

V

VALETUDINARIAN

VILLAINOUSNESS
VINDICTIVENESS
VITUPERATIVELY
VIVIPAROUSNESS
VOLATILIZATION
VULNERABLENESS

W

WONDERSTRICKEN

Z

ZINCOGRAPHICAL
ZINGIBERACEOUS
ZINZIBERACEOUS
ZOROASTRIANISM

FIFTEEN-LETTER WORDS

A

ACCLIMATIZATION
ACCOUNTABLENESS
ACQUISITIVENESS
ADDISON'S-DISEASE
ADVENTUROUSNESS
AFFRANCHISEMENT
AMPHITHEATRICAL
ANNIHILATIONIST
ANTEPENULTIMATE
ANTERO-POSTERIOR
ANTHROPOLOGICAL
ANTHROPOMORPHIC
ANTHROPOPHAGOUS
ANTI-EVANGELICAL
ANTIMONARCHICAL
ANTISABBATARIAN
ANTITRINITARIAN
APPROPRIATENESS
ARBORICULTURIST
ARCHIEPISCOPACY
ARGUMENTATIVELY
AUTHORITATIVELY

B

BIBLIOGRAPHICAL
BLEACHING-POWDER
BLOOD-GUILTINESS
BRACHYCEPHALOUS
BRANCHIOSTEGOUS
BRUSSELS-SPROUTS

C

CAMPYLOSPERMOUS
CATECHISTICALLY
CEREMONIOUSNESS
CHAMBERLAINSHIP
CHAMBER-PRACTICE
CHARGE D'AFFAIRES
CHEMICO-ELECTRIC
CHRISTADELPHIAN
CHRONOGRAMMATIC
CHRONOLOGICALLY
CIRCUMFORANEOUS
CIRCUMNAVIGABLE
CIRCUMNAVIGATOR
CIRCUMSCRIBABLE
CIRCUMSCRIPTION
CIRCUMSCRIPTIVE
CIRCUMSPECTNESS
CIRCUMSTANTIATE
CIRCUMVALLATION
COLOUR-BLINDNESS
COMBUSTIBLENESS
COMMONPLACE-BOOK
COMMUNICABILITY
COMMUNICATIVELY
COMPASSIONATELY
COMPREHENSIVELY

COMPRESSIBILITY
COMPTROLLERSHIP
CONCEIVABLENESS
CONDESCENDINGLY
CONFESSIONALIST
CONJUNCTIONALLY
CONNOISSEURSHIP
CONSCIENTIOUSLY
CONSENTANEOUSLY
CONSEQUENTIALLY
CONSIDERATENESS
CONSPICUOUSNESS
CONSUBSTANTIATE
CONTEMPLATIVELY
CONTEMPORANEITY
CONTEMPORANEOUS
CONTEMPTIBILITY
CONTENTIOUSNESS
CONTRACTIBILITY
CONTRADICTORILY
CONTRAVALLATION
CONTROVERSIALLY
CONVENTIONALISM
CONVENTIONALIST
CONVENTIONALITY
CONVENTIONALIZE
CONVERSABLENESS
CONVOLVULACEOUS
CORRELATIVENESS
CORRESPONDENTLY
CORRESPONDINGLY
CORRUPTIBLENESS
COSMOPOLITANISM
COUNTER-APPROACH
COUNTER-EVIDENCE
COUNTER-IRRITANT
COUNTER-MOVEMENT
COUNTER-PRESSURE
CROOK-SHOULDERED
CRYPTOGRAPHICAL
CRYSTALLIZATION
CRYSTALLOGRAPHY

D

DECALCIFICATION
DECARBONIZATION
DECARBURIZATION
DEFENCELESSNESS
DELIGHTSOMENESS
DEMAGNETIZATION
DEMONSTRABILITY
DEMONSTRATIVELY
DEPHLOGISTICATE
DESCRIPTIVENESS
DESTRUCTIBILITY
DESTRUCTIVENESS
DETERMINABILITY
DETERMINATENESS
DEVITRIFICATION
DIAHELIOTROPISM
DIALOGISTICALLY
DIAPHORETICALLY
DIAPHRAGMATITIS

DIFFERENTIATION
DISADVANTAGEOUS
DISCONTINUATION
DISCOUNTENANCER
DISCRETIONARILY
DISENTANGLEMENT
DISGRACEFULNESS
DISINTERESTEDLY
DISINTHRALLMENT
DISORGANIZATION
DISPASSIONATELY
DISPROPORTIONAL
DISRESPECTFULLY
DISSATISFACTION
DISSATISFACTORY
DISTASTEFULNESS
DISTINGUISHABLE
DISTINGUISHABLY
DISTRUSTFULNESS
DIVERSIFICATION
DOLICHOCEPHALIC
DOUBLE-BARRELLED
DRAUGHTSMANSHIP
DREDGING-MACHINE

E

ECCLESIASTICISM
ECHINODERMATOUS
ECLAIRCISSEMENT
EFFICACIOUSNESS
ELDER-FLOWER-WINE
ELECTRIFICATION
ELECTRO-DYNAMICS
ELECTRO-KINETICS
ELECTRO-MAGNETIC
ELECTRO-NEGATIVE
ELECTRO-POSITIVE
ELEUTHEROMANIAC
EMANCIPATIONIST
ENCOMIASTICALLY
ENFRANCHISEMENT
ENTENTE CORDIALE
ENTOMOLOGICALLY
EPIDEMIOLOGICAL
EPISCOPALIANISM
ETHEREALIZATION
EXCHANGEABILITY
EXCOMMUNICATION
EXCREMENTITIOUS
EXEMPLIFICATION
EXPERIENTIALISM
EXPERIENTIALIST
EXPERIMENTALIST
EXPERIMENTALIZE
EXPERIMENTATION
EXTERNALIZATION
EXTRAJUDICIALLY
EXTRAORDINARILY

F

FALLING-SICKNESS
FANTASTICALNESS
FORMULARIZATION
FOUNDATION-STONE
FRAGMENTARINESS

G

GENTLEMANLINESS
GOVERNOR-GENERAL

H

HENDECASYLLABLE
HERMENEUTICALLY
HETERODACTYLOUS
HISTORIOGRAPHER
HISTORIOGRAPHIC
HOMOGENEOUSNESS
HUMANITARIANISM
HYDROSTATICALLY
HYPERCRITICALLY
HYPOCHONDRIACAL

I

IDEOGRAPHICALLY
IMPRESCRIPTIBLE
IMPENETRABILITY
INACCESSIBILITY
INALIENABLENESS
INAPPLICABILITY
INAPPROPRIATELY
INATTENTIVENESS
INAUTHORITATIVE
INCOMMENSURABLE
INCOMMUNICATIVE
INCOMPATIBILITY
INCOMPREHENSIVE
INCONSIDERATELY
INCONSPICUOUSLY
INCORRIGIBILITY
INDEMNIFICATION
INDETERMINATELY
INDETERMINATION
INDIVIDUALISTIC
INDOMITABLENESS
INEFFICACIOUSLY
INEXCUSABLENESS
INEXPLICABILITY
INFLAMMABLENESS
INFUNDIBULIFORM
INJUDICIOUSNESS
INOFFENSIVENESS
INQUISITIVENESS
INQUISITORIALLY
INSCRUTABLENESS
INSEPARABLENESS
INSIGNIFICANTLY
INSTRUMENTALIST
INSTRUMENTALITY
INSTRUMENTATION
INSUBORDINATION
INSURRECTIONARY
INSURRECTIONIST
INTELLECTUALISM
INTELLECTUALIST
INTELLECTUALITY
INTELLECTUALIZE
INTELLIGIBILITY
INTEMPERATENESS
INTERCHANGEABLE

INTERCHANGEABLY
INTERCOLONIALLY
INTERCOMPARISON
INTERCONNECTION
INTERDIGITATION
INTERFOLIACEOUS
INTERJECTIONARY
INTERNATIONALLY
INTERROGATIVELY
INTOLERABLENESS
INTRACTABLENESS
INTRANSMISSIBLE
INTROSUSCEPTION
INVULNERABILITY
IRRELIGIOUSNESS
IRREPREHENSIBLE
IRRESISTIBILITY
ISOPERIMETRICAL

PHENAKISTOSCOPE
PHOSPHORESCENCE
PHRENOLOGICALLY
PHYSIOGRAPHICAL
PHYSIOLOGICALLY
PICTURESQUENESS
PLEURO-PNEUMONIA
PRACTICABLENESS
PREPOSITIONALLY
PRESTIDIGITATOR
PRETENTIOUSNESS
PRIVY-COUNCILLOR
PROCRASTINATION
PROGNOSTICATION
PROMISCUOUSNESS
PROPORTIONATELY
PROTEMPORANEOUS
PULMOBRANCHIATE

J

JURISPRUDENTIAL

Q

QUATERCENTENARY

K

KALEIDOSCOPICAL

R

REPROACHFULNESS
RETROGRESSIVELY

L

LEXICOGRAPHICAL
LOPOBRANCHIATE

S

SABBATH-BREAKING
SELF-EXAMINATION
SELF-EXPLANATORY
SENTENTIOUSNESS
SHOOTING-GALLERY
SPEAKING-TRUMPET
STRAIGHTFORWARD
STRAIT-WAISTCOAT
STRATEGETICALLY
STRATIGRAPHICAL
SUPEREXCELLENCE
SUPERFICIALNESS
SUPERNATURALISM
SUPERNATURALIST
SUPERNUMERARIES
SYMPATHETICALLY
SYMPTOMATICALLY

M

METROPOLITANATE
MICROSCOPICALLY
MISCHIEVOUSNESS
MISCONSTRUCTION
MONOCHLAMYDEOUS
MORPHOLOGICALLY

N

NATIONALIZATION
NOTWITHSTANDING

O

OPHTHALMOPLEGIA
ORNITHORHYNCHUS

T

TETRASYLLABICAL
TONOGRAPHICALLY
TRANSFIGURATION
TRANSLITERATION
TRANSMUTABILITY
TRANSPARENTNESS
TRANSPLANTATION
TRANSPOSITIONAL
TREACHEROUSNESS
TREASONABLENESS
TRIGONOMETRICAL
TROUBLESOMENESS
TRUSTWORTHINESS

P

PALAEOGRAPHICAL
PALAEONTOLOGIST
PALAEOPHYTOLOGY
PARTHENOGENESIS
PARTHENOGENETIC
PERGAMENTACEOUS
PERPENDICULARLY
PERSONIFICATION
PERSPICACIOUSLY
PERSPICUOUSNESS

U

UNCEREMONIOUSLY
UNCOMMUNICATIVE
UNCONDITIONALLY
UNCONSCIOUSNESS
UNCONSTRAINEDLY
UNDEMONSTRATIVE
UNEXCEPTIONABLE
UNGENTLEMANLIKE
UNGRAMMATICALLY
UNPARLIAMENTARY
UNPHILOSOPHICAL
UNPRONOUNCEABLE
UNRIGHTEOUSNESS
UNSOPHISTICATED

V

VICISSITUDINARY
VICISSITUDINOUS

W

WHEEL-ANIMALCULE
WOODY-NIGHTSHADE
WRITING-CHAMBERS

X

—

Y

—

Z

—

SIXTEEN-LETTER WORDS

A

ACANTHOPTERYGIAN
ACQUAINTANCESHIP
ADVANTAGEOUSNESS
ANAGRAMMATICALLY
ANGLO-CATHOLICISM
ANTHROPOMORPHISM
ANTHROPOMORPHOUS
ANTIPHRASTICALLY
APPREHENSIVENESS
ARCHAEOLOGICALLY
ARISTOCRATICALLY
AUTOBIOGRAPHICAL

B

—

C

CADUCIBRANCHIATE
CARYOPHYLLACEOUS
CHONDROPTERYGIAN
CHROMO-LITHOGRAPH
CHRONOGRAMMATIST
CHRYSELEPHANTINE
CIRCUMAMBULATION
CIRCUMNAVIGATION
CIRCUMSTANTIALLY
CLEAR-SIGHTEDNESS
CLIMATOGRAPHICAL
COMMANDER-IN-CHIEF
COMMENSURABILITY
COMMISSIONERSHIP
CONSTRUCTIVENESS
CONSUBSTANTIALLY
CONTEMPORARINESS
CONTEMPTIBLENESS
CONTEMPTUOUSNESS
CONTRADICTIOUSLY
CONTRAINDICATION
CONTUMACIOUSNESS
COSMOGRAPHICALLY
COUNTER-SIGNATURE
CROSS-EXAMINATION
CRYPTOBRANCHIATE
CRYSTALLOGRAPHER
CRYSTALLOGRAPHIC

D

DECENTRALISATION
DEMONSTRABLENESS
DENOMINATIONALLY
DIAGRAMMATICALLY
DIPHTHONGISATION
DISAGREEABLENESS
DISCONTENTEDNESS
DISCRIMINATIVELY
DISESTABLISHMENT

DISFRANCHISEMENT
DISINGENUOUSNESS
DISPROPORTIONATE
DISQUALIFICATION
DISTINGUISHINGLY
DOLICHOCEPHALISM
DOLICHOCEPHALOUS
DRINKING-FOUNTAIN

E

ECCLESIASTICALLY
ELASMOBRANCHIATE
ELECTRO-BALLISTIC
ELECTRO-BIOLOGIST
ENTHUSIASTICALLY
EPIGRAMMATICALLY
EXTEMPORANEOUSLY
EXTERRITORIALITY
EXTRAPAROCHIALLY

F

FAINTHEARTEDNESS
FALSE-HEARTEDNESS
FELLOW-COUNTRYMAN
FORISFAMILIATION

G

—

H

HERMAPHRODITICAL
HIEROGLYPHICALLY
HIGGLEDY-PIGGLEDY
HOMOEOPATHICALLY
HYDROGRAPHICALLY

I

IMMEASURABLENESS
IMPERCEPTIBILITY
IMPERISHABLENESS
IMPERTURBABILITY
IMPRACTICABILITY
INACCESSIBLENESS
INCOMBUSTIBILITY
INCOMPARABLENESS
INCOMPREHENSIBLE
INCOMPREHENSIBLY
INCONCLUSIVENESS
INCONTROVERTIBLE
INCONTROVERTIBLY
INCONVERTIBILITY
INCORRIGIBLENESS
INCORRUPTIBILITY
INDISCRIMINATELY
INEXHAUSTIBILITY

INEXPRESSIVENESS
INEXTINGUISHABLE
INEXTINGUISHABLY
INSUSCEPTIBILITY
INTELLIGIBLENESS
INTERCOMMUNICATE
INTERCONTINENTAL
INTERJECTIONALLY
INTERPENETRATION
IRRESPONSIBILITY

J
—

K
—

L
—

M

MALACOPTERYGIOUS
MALAGUETTA-PEPPER
MELODRAMATICALLY
MICROCHRONOMETER
MICROPHOTOGRAPHY
MISANTHROPICALLY
MISAPPROPRIATION
MISPRONUNCIATION
MISUNDERSTANDING
MONOCOTYLEDONOUS
MUSCULOCUTANEOUS

N

NECESSITARIANISM

O

OBSTREPEROUSNESS
ORTHOGRAPHICALLY

P

PALAEONTOLOGICAL
PARADIGMATICALLY
PARALLELEPIPEDON
PARAPHRASTICALLY
PERIPHRASTICALLY
PERISSODACTYLOUS
PERPENDICULARITY
PHARMACEUTICALLY
PHONOGRAPHICALLY
PHOTOGRAPHICALLY
PHOTO-MICROGRAPHY
POLYCOTYLEDONOUS
PRAISEWORTHINESS
PREDETERMINATION
PRE-ESTABLISHMENT

PRESTIDIGITATION
PRESUMPTUOUSNESS
PRETERPLUPERFECT

Q

QUERIMONIOUSNESS
QUESTIONABLENESS

R

REPRESENTATIONAL
REPRESENTATIVELY
RETRANSFORMATION
RETURNING-OFFICER

S

SCENOGRAPHICALLY
SELF-PRESERVATION
SHORT-SIGHTEDNESS
SIMPLE-MINDEDNESS
SIMULTANEOUSNESS
SOPHONOSTOMATOUS
SPHYGMOMANOMETER
SPIRITUALIZATION
STEREOSCOPICALLY
STEREOTYPOGRAPHY
STETHOSCOPICALLY
SUPERCILIOUSNESS
SUPPOSITITIOUSL
SUSCEPTIBILITIES

T

TELESPECTROSCOPE
THEOPHILANTHROPY
THERMOMETROGRAPH
THERMOMETRICALLY
TINTINNABULATION
TRANSCENDENTALLY
TRANSFERRIBILITY
TRANSMISSIBILITY
TRANSMUTABLENESS
TRANSMUTATIONIST
TRANSPORTABILITY
TRANSUBSTANTIATE
TRESPASS-OFFERING

U

UNCHARITABLENESS
UNCONSTITUTIONAL
UNDENOMINATIONAL
UNDISCRIMINATING
UNGOVERNABLENESS
UNPRODUCTIVENESS
UNPROFITABLENESS
UNSEASONABLENESS
UNSUBSTANTIALITY

W

WELL-PROPORTIONED

SEVENTEEN-LETTER WORDS

A

ADMINISTRATORSHIP
ANTIHYPOCHONDRIAC
AUTHORITATIVENESS

B

BEGGAR-MY-NEIGHBOUR

C

CHROMO-LITHOGRAPHY
CHRONOGRAMMATICAL
CIRCUMSTANTIALITY
COMMUNICATIVENESS
COMPREHENSIBILITY
COMPREHENSIVENESS
CONCENTRATIVENESS
CONGREGATIONALISM
CONGREGATIONALIST
CONSCIENTIOUSNESS
CONSEQUENTIALNESS
CONSTITUTIONALISM
CONSTITUTIONALIST
CONSTITUTIONALITY
CONSUBSTANTIALITY
CONSUBSTANTIATION
CONTEMPLATIVENESS
CONTEMPORANEOUSLY
CONTRADICTORINESS
CONTRADISTINCTION
CONTRADISTINCTIVE
CONVERSATIONALIST
COUNTER-ATTRACTION
COUNTER-ATTRACTIVE
COUNTER-IRRITATION
COUNTER-REVOLUTION

D

DEMONSTRATIVENESS
DENATIONALISATION
DENOMINATIONALISM
DISADVANTAGEOUSLY
DISHONOURABLENESS
DISINTERESTEDNESS
DISPROPORTIONABLE
DISPROPORTIONALLY

E

EARTHLY-MINDEDNESS
ELECTRO-METALLURGY
ELECTRO-PHYSIOLOGY
EXTRAORDINARINESS

F — G
—

H

HETEROGENEOUSNESS

I

IMPERCEPTIBLENESS
IMPRACTICABLENESS
INCOMMUNICABILITY
INCOMPRESSIBILITY
INCONCEIVABLENESS
INCONSEQUENTIALLY
INCONSIDERATENESS
INDISTINGUISHABLE
INEFFICACIOUSNESS
INSUPPORTABLENESS
INTERCOLUMNIATION
INTERCOMMUNICABLE
IRRECONCILABILITY

J
—

K
—

L

LAMELLIBRANCHIATE
LATITUDINARIANISM
LIEUTENANT-COLONEL
LIEUTENANT-GENERAL

M

MALADMINISTRATION
MARSIPOBRANCHIATE
MISINTERPRETATION
MISREPRESENTATION

N
—

O

OPISTHOBRANCHIATE

P

PALAEOICHTHYOLOGY
PARTICULARIZATION
PERENNIBRANCHIATE
PHILANTHROPICALLY

PREDESTINARIANISM

Q
—

R

REPREHENSIBLENESS

S

SELF-CONSCIOUSNESS
SELF-CONTRADICTION
SELF-CONTRADICTORY
SELF-FERTILIZATION
SELF-RIGHTEOUSNESS
SPECTROSCOPICALLY
SPLANCHNO-SKELETON
STEREOGRAPHICALLY
STEREOTYPOGRAPHER
STRAIGHTFORWARDLY

T

THEOPHILANTHROPIC
THERMO-ELECTRICITY
TRANSCENDENTALISM
TRANSCENDENTALIST
TRANSUBSTANTIATOR
TRIGONOMETRICALLY

U

UNFASHIONABLENESS
UNGENTLEMANLINESS

V

VALETUDINARIANISM

W — X
—

Y — Z

EIGHTEEN-LETTER WORDS

A
ANTI-CONSTITUTIONAL

C
CHARACTERISTICALLY
CHROMO-LITHOGRAPHER
COMPREHENSIBLENESS
CROSS-FERTILIZATION
CRYSTALLOGRAPHICAL

D
DISPROPORTIONATELY

E
ESTABLISHMENTARIAN

I
INCOMMENSURABILITY

INCOMMUNICABLENESS
INTERCOMMUNICATION
IRRECONCILABLENESS

L
LIGHTNING-CONDUCTOR

P
PARALLELOGRAMMATIC
POCKET-HANDKERCHIEF
PUBLIC-SPIRITEDNESS

T
THEOPHILANTHROPIST
TRANSUBSTANTIATION
TRAVERSING-PLATFORM

U
UNCONSTITUTIONALLY

NINETEEN-LETTER WORDS

C
CONTEMPORANEOUSNESS

D
DISADVANTAGEOUSNESS

I
INCONTROVERTIBILITY
INCOMPREHENSIBILITY
INTERSTRATIFICATION

S
STRAIGHTFORWARDNESS

TWENTY-LETTER WORD

P
PHILOPROGENITIVENESS